BEYOND DESIGN

THE SYNERGY OF APPAREL PRODUCT DEVELOPMENT

Sandra J. Keiser, Mount Mary College

Myrna B. Garner, Illinois State University

FAIRCHILD PUBLICATIONS, INC. / NEW YORK

Director of Sales and Acquisitions: Dana Meltzer-Berkowitz
Executive Editor: Olga T. Kontzias

Assistant Acquisitions Editor: Jaclyn Bergeron
Senior Development Editor: Jennifer Crane
Production Editor: Elizabeth Marotta
Art Director: Adam B. Bohannon
Production Manager: Ginger Hillman
Line Editor: Jeannine Ciliotta
Copy Editor: Candie Frankel
Interior Design: Barbara Balch
Cover Design: Adam B. Bohannon
Photo Research: Shaie Dively/Photosearch Inc.
Produced by Fair Street Productions

Library of Congress Catalog Card Number: 2007929088

ISBN: 978-1-56367-556-0

GST R 133004424

Printed in the United States of America
CH10, TP12

CONTENTS

EXTENDED CONTENTS

PREFACE

This new edition of *Beyond Design: The Synergy of Apparel Product Development* reflects the current relationship among processes in the overall apparel product development cycle, from inception of ideas to delivery of finished products. Features new to this second edition include updated visuals and information, relevant case studies, an appendix illustrating fashion art, an appendix focusing on preparation for and transition into the job market, and a glossary.

The apparel industry has been undergoing a metamorphosis in recent years, and many commonly held perceptions of the field must be amended to reflect changes in methods, content, and emphasis. The apparel business was built on the concept of fashion change; but as we move further into the 21st century, new technological developments, growing globalization of the business, and a changing consumer marketplace are making increasing demands to compress the turnaround time required to complete the product development cycle. Computer applications in the design and production of products, enhanced real-time communications, and the increasing complexity of the logistics of global trade are changing the entire face of the apparel product development business.

Organization of the Text

This book provides an overview of the processes required to bring a garment into being and provides a context for these creative and technical processes within the reality of the current business environment.

Part One provides the context for the apparel product development process. Chapter 1 describes the development process and its place in the overall product pipeline. The focus of chapter 2 is the business planning process that provides the foundational framework for decisions impacting development of apparel products. Chapter 3 approaches the consumer market through an understanding of definable target market groups.

Part Two explores concepts within the creative design process. Chapter 4 discusses how to initiate style ideas via trend forecasting. The theories of color selection and usage are the topic of chapter 5, which is enhanced with an expanded full-color insert. Chapter 6 introduces the field of textiles and the place of fabric selection in the overall design process. The focus of chapter 7 is silhouette development and the process of designing individual garment styles. This chapter concludes with a visual appendix, Apparel Design Details Illustrated, by the renowned fashion illustrator Steven Stipelman. Chapter 8 explores methods for developing and editing individual garment style suggestions to form the company's product line. An appendix, new to the second edition, provides graphic examples of presentation methods introduced within the chapter.

Part Three focuses on the processes of technical design. Chapter 9 explains how the design drawing of a style is translated into product through pattern-making and begins to define the specification forms needed for the production phases that will follow. Chapter 10 adds the findings and trims used to enhance the style and provide its unique design characteristics. The concepts of garment sizing and fit are covered in chapter 11. Chapter 12 explores the growing importance of a quality assurance program through the development of product standards, establishment of tolerances, and awareness of additional specifications. An appendix details commercial seams by class.

Part Four moves into the production planning and distribution phases of the product development process. Chapter 13 discusses the sourcing of garment components and volume production of a style, with emphasis on the increasing role of global trade. Chapter 14 is an overview of the pricing and costing of a product to provide company profit and consumer value. Chapter 15 explores the final stages of the process through marketing, production, and distribution of garment styles, including identification of newest business trends. An appendix to chapter 15 explores the job market in apparel product development. The book concludes with a comprehensive glossary.

Pedagogical Features

The text is targeted to sophomore and junior year collegiate-level students and provides enough flexibility to accommodate students with varying learning styles. The text may be used in its entirety to provide a one-semester overview of the apparel product development cycle. Alternately, it has been arranged in a manner so that it may be used in a more project-oriented mode over two semesters, where the first semester emphasizes the creative design processes and the second semester focuses on the technical design aspects of the overall cycle.

It is suggested that prerequisites include an introductory textiles course, a basic illustration course, and a garment construction course. A basic understanding of business, including accounting, is suggested as a prerequisite or follow-up to this course, while a patternmaking course could precede or follow this overview, depending on how the text is approached.

A number of pedagogical features enhance both the overview and project-oriented approaches to the course. Each chapter begins with a set of objectives and concludes with a summary, a list of key terms, discussion questions, activities, a list of references, and additional resources, if applicable. Where appropriate, case studies have been added within chapters to amplify the chapter topic. To ensure an accurate and current presentation, the authors have relied on industry contacts, many of whom provided illustrations as well as information about their practices and procedures. The text aims to prepare career-minded students of apparel design and production to enter the job market with a realistic, up-to-date understanding of the industry in which they will be employed.

ACKNOWLEDGMENTS

Writing this second edition has been a remarkable endeavor. We, the authors, are grateful to our families, friends, and colleagues who have supported us through this experience.

We are particularly indebted to the alumnae who opened doors for us and to all of the industry professionals who generously shared their time and expertise for the original book, and now for this new and expanded edition. Their efforts have contributed significantly to ensuring that the processes identified were based on accurate industry practice. These individuals represent some of the best in their field at all levels of the product development process.

We are indebted to product developers that opened their doors to us including Jones, New York, Donna Ricco, Liz Lange, Esprit, Nordstrom, Pacific Trail, Ex Officio, Eddie Bauer, Cutter & Buck, Tommy Bahama, Target Corporation, Kohl's Department Stores, Shopko, Bon-Ton Stores, Inc., Harley Davidson MotorClothes, and Lands' End. Jodi Wahlen at the Gap, Inc., and John Coffman at Jockey International provided insights into merchandise planning. Bread and Butter, Inc., a print agent in New York, and textile designer Joan Kadow were generous with their time. In Seattle, a good friend, Deborah Vandermar, opened many doors for us. Abbas Fadel, President of Excel Leather, Inc., consulted with us regarding the special requirements of designing with leather. Alumnae Michelle Wahlen, Chris Clerkin-Zenz, Patrice Henderson-Glad, Tanya Gross, and Deb Selm as well as numerous student interns have been ongoing resources for new developments in the product development process.

Further support came from Shannon O'Hara of Merchandise Testing laboratories; Mark McGovern, SCOTDIC; Kevin Loughrey, GretagMacBeth; and Ken Sandow, American & Efird, Inc. A special thanks to [TC]2 for their continuing contributions, especially Mike Fralix, Jim Lovejoy, and most recently, Kim Anderson.We also appreciate the generosity of the many businesses that provided visuals for this new edition or allowed us to photograph their facilities to use for illustrative purposes throughout the book.

We are indebted to Steven Stipelman for his illustrations in chapter 7 and its appendix. His friendship, encouragement, and artistic talents are much appreciated. We are also grateful to Grace Kunz, Iowa State University, who generously contributed her expertise to this new edition by reviewing chapter 14 on pricing and costing and for helping develop the business plan for our fictional firm, Callie Blake Collection.

A special thanks to Mount Mary College students who allowed us to publish their projects in the appendix to chapter 8. They are Marcelle Buchholz, Kate Tischer, Erica Fox, Cassandra Schmidt, and especially Jaclyn Ghazazadeh.

We are grateful to the following readers and reviewers, selected by the publisher, who provided thoughtful comments and encouragement throughout the development of the first edition of this text: Catherine Burnham, Brigham Young University; Cynthia Istook, North Carolina State University; Jo Kallal, University of Delaware; Teresa Mastrianni, Kingsborough Community College; Beth Phillips, Drexel University; and Elizabeth Rhodes, Kent State University.

And finally, a special thank-you to all our editors at Fairchild Books and Fair Street Productions.

PART ONE

PLANNING FOR SUCCESS

CHAPTER 1

THE ROLE OF PRODUCT DEVELOPMENT IN THE APPAREL SUPPLY CHAIN

"The world hates change, yet it is the only thing that has brought progress."

—— CHARLES KETTERING

OBJECTIVES

- To examine the changing dynamics of the apparel supply chain

- To understand growth strategies employed within the apparel supply chain

- To understand the impact of globalization on apparel product development, manufacturing, and distribution

- To define the product development process and differentiate it from the design process

- To identify various types of product development

- To understand how information technology systems speed up processes and enhance decision-making within the apparel supply chain

Managing Perpetual Change

New technology is creating chaos in the old industrial order and transforming how we do business. The changes that are propelling the world into the information age are reminiscent of the flurry of inventions that sparked the Industrial Revolution. During that time, technology and process innovations in the manufacture of textiles and apparel helped to define the industrial age and bring us from an era of craft production in the home to mass production in factories (Figure 1.1). Historically, the introduction of innovations such as the cotton gin and the automated loom was followed by periods of incremental change, which gave industry an opportunity to refine technological applications and adjust to the impact of the innovations.

Businesses today must position themselves to manage perpetual change—change in consumer demands and expectations, as well as changes in technology, the business climate, and the world order. In order to remain competitive, they must choose among a variety of information and telecommunication

EVOLUTION OF APPAREL MANUFACTURING

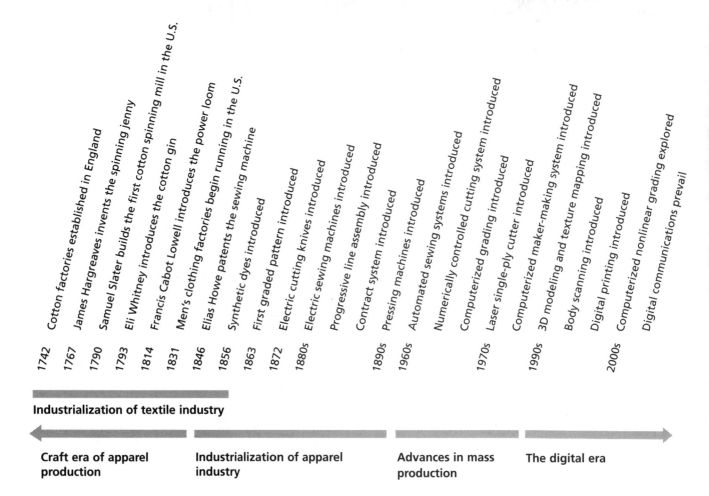

Figure 1.1. *A timeline shows the technology developments that have propelled the apparel industry from the craft era, to the mass production era, and now to the digital era.*

technologies and integrate them with emerging product technologies, knowledge of customer preferences, and the resources of a global marketplace.

Product development is the strategic, creative, technical, production, and distribution planning of goods having a perceived value for a well-defined consumer group; these goods are designed to reach the marketplace when that group is ready to buy. Apparel product developers must constantly redefine what they produce, how they produce it, and how they market and distribute it to customers, thereby translating change into opportunity. Working in a dynamic environment requires flexibility and agility.

This chapter provides a context for understanding how the apparel industry is positioning itself to adapt to change and meet the challenges of an increasingly sophisticated consumer. It sets the stage for a new business paradigm based on consumer-centric goods and services and on a new definition of production. Today's changing organizational dynamics and global partnerships are connecting human, physical, and intellectual resources in ways never before possible.

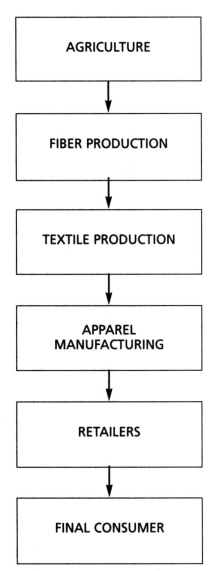

LINEAR APPAREL SUPPLY CHAIN

AGRICULTURE

FIBER PRODUCTION

TEXTILE PRODUCTION

APPAREL MANUFACTURING

RETAILERS

FINAL CONSUMER

Figure 1.2. *In a linear supply chain, the roles of each industry segment were distinct, each with its own product and customer.*

Apparel Supply Chain Overview

The **apparel supply chain** is the network of fiber, textile, and findings (trim, thread, label) suppliers; apparel product developers; manufacturers and contractors; and all the channels of apparel distribution that work together to bring apparel products to the ultimate user. This network also includes **auxiliary businesses,** such as design bureaus, software providers, sourcing agents, factors (credit agents), patternmaking services, testing labs, consultants, warehouses, shipping companies, and advertising agencies. The expertise of these businesses improves the efficiency of the entire chain.

History

Historically, we have looked at the apparel supply chain as a linear model, with each partner in the chain performing a specific task that flows in a successive order to complete the process (Figure 1.2). Within this model, textile, apparel, and retail businesses were categorized as distinct industries, each with its own customer and sphere of influence. Each company controlled the decision making and information flow for the processes it performed.

In the 1980s, the distinctions among the various levels within the apparel supply chain began to blur. Retailers, such as The Limited ventured into product development in order to bypass the profit center of wholesale brand apparel manufacturers and procure exclusive product at a more competitive price. Their early attempts were primitive by today's standards. They purchased products they liked from their branded competitors, specified changes, and then sourced them offshore with whichever supplier could produce them most cost-effectively. Caught off guard, other members of the supply chain explored processes previously not in their domain in order to remain competitive. Notably, wholesale brand manufacturers began to open their own retail stores. Although this initial exploration of roles was met with fear and mistrust, it became the impetus for today's more flexible, adaptive supply chain.

Today's Virtual Supply Chain

A new competitive environment has evolved in which members of the supply chain now function as integrated units rather than as independent businesses. The days of producing standardized products and services based on limited information and store-based transactions are gone. Today, companies must compete globally with products that are geared to niche markets defined by customer preferences and delivered through multiple distribution channels, including stores, catalogs, and the Internet. Product ranges that are broader, produced in smaller lot sizes, and made available for shorter periods of time are the norm. This requires an agile manufacturing environment that has the flexibility to respond quickly to the constantly changing preferences of the consumer. Goldman, Nagel, and Preiss define an **agile manufacturing environment** as a comprehensive response to the business challenges of profiting

APPAREL INDUSTRY VIRTUAL SUPPLY CHAIN

Auxiliary Businesses:

Agents
Factors
Testing Labs
Distribution/Warehousing
Color Labs
Forecasting Services
Design Bureaus
Patternmaking Services

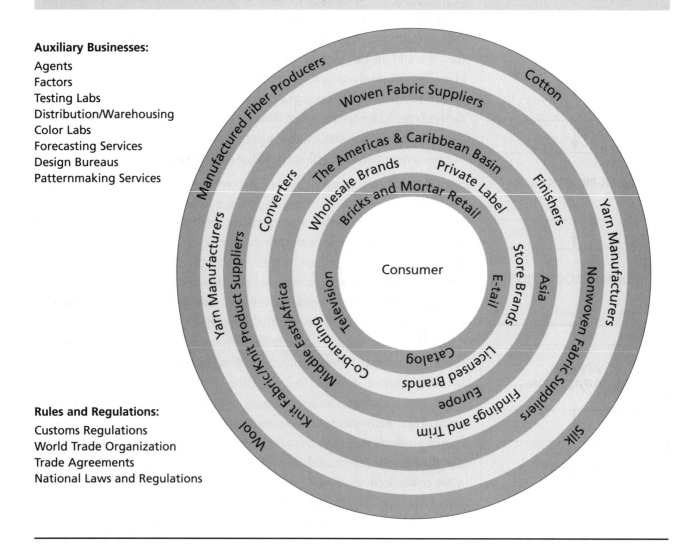

Rules and Regulations:

Customs Regulations
World Trade Organization
Trade Agreements
National Laws and Regulations

Figure 1.3. *In a virtual supply chain, many different businesses form partnerships to get the right product to the consumer. The supply chain partnerships for each product produced may vary.*

from rapidly changing, continually fragmenting, global markets for high-quality, high-performance, customer-configured goods and services (Goldman, Nagel, and Preiss 1995).

In order to compete in an agile environment, companies are restructuring to create, produce, and distribute goods and services that appeal to micro-markets of customers. Customer groups are defined and marketed to with increasing accuracy because of direct customer input. Agility demands that companies identify their core competencies—the things they do best—and partner with other specialists to establish processes that support the development and distribution of goods and services that are customer-centered. This provides them with the flexibility to make whatever the consumer wants.

Product developers must compete on a number of levels—cost, speed to market, product innovation, manufacturing expertise, and access to technology and resources. Business capabilities can be synthesized by forming alliances with other companies that already possess the required resources. A **virtual supply chain** is an interactive network of manufacturing specialists that integrate complementary resources to support a particular product effort for as long as it is economically justifiable to do so. Virtual supply chains rely on the synergy of computer networking and telecommunication technologies to deliver products at Internet speed. These tools make it possible for groups of companies, regardless of geographic location, to coordinate their core competencies into a single effort and to achieve powerful competitive advantages in the process (Goldman, Nagel, and Preiss 1995).

The virtual supply chain can be illustrated as a series of concentric circles attached at the hub (Figure 1.3). The hub represents the ultimate consumer. Each circle around the hub can turn in order to link up with the options on the circle before and after it. The combinations that can be created from this movement represent the supply chain variations that companies manage every day. Each supply chain is a virtual manufacturer, a group of partners equipped to make a particular apparel style for a particular retailer and final consumer. This unique partnership ends when the style it produces is no longer in demand, but the links of the partnership may be reconfigured to fill another need in creating other styles. Partners may be part of numerous supply chains within a given design season, depending on how many styles they have the core competencies to produce.

In Figure 1.3, the auxiliary businesses listed outside the virtual model are facilitators that support and supplement the core competencies of the businesses within each chain. They may be contracted by one of the links within the chain, or they may be fully owned subsidiaries of one of the links. To understand the evolution from a linear to a virtual supply chain, it is necessary to understand the methods of growth that have characterized the industries within the supply chain over the past 40 years.

Growth Strategies

Businesses are frequently classified as being part of either a growth industry or a mature industry. Industries for products such as hybrid cars and flat screen plasma or LCD high definition televisions can be described as **growth industries** because they produce products that have not yet saturated the marketplace. When growth industry products are introduced, the emerging technology they utilize commands a relatively high price, placing them out of reach for some consumers. As the technology comes down in price, these products have the potential to grow through increased market saturation (new customers or markets) or market penetration (increased market share in a given market).

The businesses that make up the domestic apparel supply chain are classified as mature industries. **Mature industries** produce products that are characterized by relatively stable sales from year to year and by a high level of

Figure 1.4a. *High-definition large-screen televisions are still a growth industry.*

Figure 1.4b. *Mature products such as polo shirts need to differentiate themselves to maintain market share.*

competition. Given a relatively stable population rate, the domestic apparel market is saturated with suppliers who must compete by maintaining a differential advantage (Figure 1.4a–b). **Differential advantage** refers to a competitive edge such as lower price, superior quality, or unique product features. In their book *Agile Competitors and Virtual Organizations* (1995), Goldman, Nagel and Preiss coined the term **sneakerization** to describe the process of transforming an inexpensive commodity product into a cutting edge specialty product. Keds took their dated and inexpensive tennis shoe and transformed it into a fashion product, while companies like Nike and Adidas concentrated on the athletic

Figure 1.5a. *Keds brand has utilized a "sneakerization" strategy by adding a fashion element to the traditional tennis shoe.*

Figure 1.5b. *Nike has used the same strategy but focused on performance to add value to the same product.*

shoe category, developing expensive, high-tech, function-specific products dependent on extensive research and development (Figure 1.5a–b).

The ability of a business in a mature industry to turn a profit is not measured by volume alone. Other elements to consider are market share, profit margins, capital investment, capacity utilization, and inventory levels. Given these criteria, many companies in the apparel supply chain have looked to acquisitions and mergers as a means of strengthening their competitive position. The purchase of another company is an effective means of increasing market share or competitive advantage, or both. The 1980s and 1990s witnessed numerous consolidations throughout the supply chain. Early mergers, particularly in the retail sector, were highly leveraged and frequently hostile.

The resulting companies, although larger, were often saddled with heavy debt that hampered their competitive position.

Since the year 2000, the industry has witnessed a new wave of vertical and horizontal consolidation within the pipeline. Federated Department Stores' purchase of May Co., which had just completed the purchase of Marshall Field's; Talbots' purchase of J. Jill; Adidas-Salomon AG takeover of Reebok International; and DuPont's sale of its Invista textile division to Koch Industries are examples of a few recent transactions that have changed the apparel, textile, and retail landscape. Retail, vendor, and banking executives agree that the current wave of mergers represent strategic business decisions, with the parties involved hoping to benefit from the resulting combination of core competencies.

Strategies driving mergers and acquisitions include, but are not limited to, extending the company's global presence, acquiring new brands that have potential for growth, expanding distribution channels, and capitalizing on economies of scale in management, technology, purchasing, and sourcing. It remains to be seen whether this consolidation will ultimately benefit or hurt the final consumer. The fear is that these mega-conglomerates will result in more sameness in the marketplace and that less competition will mean fewer incentives to keep prices down.

Trends often produce countertrends. A business environment characterized by mega-conglomerates often provides new opportunities for small entrepreneurial business ventures with which the final consumer can identify and interact.

Vertical Integration

Mergers and acquisitions can be used to support several different growth strategies. **Vertical integration** is a strategy that seeks to consolidate a supply chain by acquiring a company at another stage in the supply chain. A fully vertical manufacturer seeks to control the processes previously handled by specialized firms so that one conglomerate can perform all the steps of production or distribution, or both. Vertical integration rarely affects market penetration, but it can have an impact on a firm's competitive advantage in getting the right product to market at the right time and the right price.

Early vertical integration frequently involved companies within the same segment of the industry. For instance, a fiber manufacturer might develop the capability of making fabric and then converting fabric in order to control the entire scope of textile production. Today, companies are examining their core competencies and integrating other activities in the supply chain that complement their core competencies but were previously handled by other segments. Thus, retailers such as Kohl's, Target, and Nordstrom develop private label products, which are made exclusively for their stores. They have ventured into product development to complement their retail business. Specialty stores such as Abercrombie & Fitch, Chico's, and the Gap are vertically structured retailers that develop, source, and distribute their own product. Spanish retailer Zara's ability to deliver fashion-right merchandise in a matter of weeks is due to its ownership of or control of its production facilities (Case Study 1.1, Zara).

Another example of vertical integration occurs when wholesale brand product developers such as Donna Karan, Nike, and Levi Strauss & Co. open their own stores. Some manufacturer-owned stores are run as off-price outlets and others as full-price specialty stores or **signature stores**. Signature stores give these manufacturers a direct line to their ultimate consumer; **outlet stores** provide a means of controlling the distribution of excess goods (Figure 1.6a–b).

Not to be outdone, some textile manufacturers have attempted to offer **full-package manufacturing** services in which they supply both the fabric and the garment production for a product developer, either domestically or offshore. They are buying businesses and forming partnerships with apparel manufacturers in Mexico and the Caribbean Basin in order to compete with Asian full-package suppliers.

Vertical integration has the potential to shorten cycle times and reduce costs. Throughout the supply chain, each company that plays a role in production must schedule its task, charge for its services, and make a profit. By owning more of the links in the process, cycle times are reduced and some profit centers can be eliminated. All of this helps to get the right clothes to the market at the right price and the right time.

Although many companies continue to focus on a vertical growth strategy, others see vertical growth as a strategy that restricts agility. These companies are seeking to **deverticalize**, which means they want to divest themselves of the processes that other companies may perform better. This relatively new strategy is based on the belief that a more flexible organization can better adapt to rapidly changing consumer demands.

Vertical growth and deverticalization both have a place in an agile business environment. Vertical growth is appropriate when a partner cannot guarantee sufficient capacity for vital processes on a regular basis. However, the same company that pursues vertical growth within certain segments of its business may need to divest itself of other business segments that are no longer efficient or required on a regular basis. Vertical growth continues to be prevalent in developing countries that seek to increase the business they do with product developers in the United States and Europe. A vertical structure helps these companies to offer the full-package manufacturing programs that Western product developers seek and helps them to shorten production cycles.

Horizontal Integration

Mergers and acquisitions can also support growth through **horizontal integration**. This strategy prioritizes the acquisition of companies that make or sell similar products in order to expand market penetration and reduce competition; it may be used to acquire brands at the same price point or to penetrate

CASE STUDY 1.1   ZARA: A FAST FASHION SUPPLY CHAIN

Quick Response, Speed-to-Market, and Fast Fashion are some of the catch phrases used to describe a not-so-new concept. Fine-tuning the supply chain in order to produce the right product at breakneck speed has been a hot-button topic for almost twenty years. Today, the supply chain has become increasingly complicated, and attempts to speed it up have often resulted in unwanted bottlenecks. Ken Watson, Director of the London-based Industry Forum, has studied the successful Zara model and has come to some enlightening conclusions that might help with this daunting task.

No doubt, Zara has a very successful business model, but ironically, nothing is revolutionary. Through a clear focus and vision, it has streamlined the cumbersome old supply chain response time of 40 to 50 weeks down to 8 to 10 weeks, and its customers are eagerly awaiting next week's—take note, not next season's—new fashion. Zara has tapped into the power of fashion. Small and frequent shipments keep product inventories fresh and scarce—compelling customers to frequent the store in search of what's new and to buy now . . . because it will be gone tomorrow.

Under the Zara model, the retail store is the eyes and ears of the company. Instead of relying solely on electronically collected data, Zara utilizes word-of-mouth information to understand more about its customers. Empowered store managers report to headquarters what real customers are saying. Products that are not selling well are quickly pulled and hot items quickly replenished. Zara's quick turnaround on merchandise helps generate cash, which eliminates the possibility of incurring significant debt.

Zara doesn't invest in traditional advertising but does manage to get great visibility. The stores' ambience is consistent and appealing from the interior design and window displays to lighting and music.

Controlling notorious trouble spots along the supply chain is key to speed. Potential bottlenecks can be thwarted because Zara is a vertically integrated structure. Dyeing and cutting are critical processes within the supply chain. Zara is a large investor in a dye and finishing plant, allowing it to oversee the color management process—a notorious bottleneck. Although Zara uses subcontractors for sewing, it does the vast majority of cutting—a crucial process that determines fit. For quick turnaround, 60 percent of the manufacturing processes are outsourced in countries close to the Zara headquarters in Spain. Zara maintains a strong relationship with its contractors and suppliers, viewing them as part of the company.

To react successfully to consumers' demands, design decisions are delayed as long as possible. Typically, Zara commits to 50 to 60 percent of its production in advance of the season, whereas other apparel retailers commit to 80 percent. Zara practices precommitment, meaning it reserves capacity to ensure production facilities are available when needed.

Traditionally, design and development precedes fabric procurement. Zara has turned this practice upside down—Zara is fabric-driven. Designs are developed with available fabrics and trims. This eliminates waiting for the long and laborious process of fabric formation.

Poor communication is often the culprit in bottlenecks. Zara invested in information technology (IT) early on. Its in-house IT is simple and effective. Vendors and suppliers report that people are accessible and answers can be obtained quickly. Internal communication is maximized by housing the designers, patternmakers, and merchandisers, as well as everyone else involved in getting the product completed, on one floor.

Zara hires young designers and trains them to make quick decisions. Decision making is encouraged, and bad decisions are not severely punished. Designers are trained to limit the number of reviews and changes, speeding up the development process and minimizing the number of samples made.

Some say Zara's real strength is its well-developed culture, and that isn't something that can be easily knocked off. Not everyone can be Zara, nor does everyone want to be. The stages of the supply chain will not change, but to obtain quicker speeds the sequence and focus have to be flexible.

The information on Zara was collected from the Fast Fashion workshops conducted by Ken Watson, Director of the London-based Industry Forum and produced by the Industry Form and [TC]².
Written by Kim Anderson, Ph.D., writer/reporter for [TC]², and Jim Lovejoy, Director, Industry Programs, [TC]².

multiple price points. Talbots bought J. Jill to increase its penetration of the 35-and-older market of professional women. Liz Claiborne started as a better brand in the 1970s and now owns multiple brands in the mass merchandise, moderate, better, and bridge price points. Often a company will purchase a competing brand and reposition it at another price point. Liz Claiborne purchased the J. H. Collectibles brand in the late 1990s and later launched it as a moderate brand so that it would no longer compete directly with the Liz Claiborne brand at the better price point. This strategy can give new life to a brand, making it accessible to customers who previously felt that it was too expensive.

As with vertical growth, sometimes a horizontal acquisition that meets strategic goals at one point in time may later no longer suit a company's core competencies. During the 1980s and 1990s, Profitt's acquired Parisian, Boston Store, Carson Pirie Scott, Bergner's, McRae's, Younkers, Herberger's, Saks Fifth Avenue, and Saks Off Fifth and changed its name to Saks Holding Co. In 2005 it sold off the southern group of stores to Belk, Inc. In 2006 it sold the 38-store Parisian chain to Belk, Inc., and the northern group of department stores to Bon-Ton, leaving it with the Club Libby Lu tween specialty chain, Saks Fifth Avenue, and Saks Off Fifth.

Diversification

Diversification is a growth strategy in which a firm expands its product mix in order to capitalize on brand recognition, increase sales, and thus enhance efficiencies for greater profit. Diversification may be achieved through licensing or by the acquisition of related or unrelated companies. An apparel company might purchase a jewelry company or a shoe company in order to increase the company's product mix and facilitate brand extension. For example, Liz Claiborne owns and distributes Monet jewelry. Companies such as Ralph Lauren, Donna Karan, and Liz Claiborne have also successfully diversified their product offerings by licensing naming rights to accessory and fragrance companies, thus capitalizing on the widespread name and quality recognition they have earned in the apparel industry.

Figure 1.6a. *Ralph Lauren signature store in New York*

Figure 1.6b. *Polo Ralph Lauren outlet store*

Globalization

Industry growth achieved through acquisitions and mergers only partially explains the changes taking place within the apparel supply chain. Digital technology enables companies to conduct business globally. Furthermore, the economics of doing business have changed significantly because products that were once produced domestically, at considerable cost, are now being produced offshore at a lower cost.

At the present time, approximately 90 percent of apparel sold in the United States is actually produced outside of the country. Products may be

- developed here with production contracted offshore by U.S. manufacturers or retailers

- purchased directly from foreign producers or foreign sourcing agents such as Li & Fung Limited in Hong Kong

- produced in U.S.-owned/operated plants in far-flung locations, such as Invista textile plants in China and Levi jean factories in Turkey and South Africa

Many nations increased their participation in international textile and apparel trade during the twentieth century and tried to manage their competitiveness and market access through an extensive framework of bilateral trade agreements that eventually evolved into the Multi-Fiber Arrangement (MFA), administered by the General Agreements on Tariffs and Trade (GATT). The temporary GATT structure evolved into the more permanent World Trade Organization (WTO), whose primary purpose is to abolish trade restrictions. One requirement for members of the WTO was to dismantle the quota system inherent to the MFA. As a result, quotas on most apparel and textile products were eliminated by 2005.

The current economic environment and loosening of trade restrictions has encouraged U.S. and European manufacturers, product developers, and retailers to pursue offshore markets as a means of expansion. American signature stores are common in cities such as Paris, London, and Tokyo. Wal-Mart has launched stores in China, Mexico, and other emerging economies. French and Italian designers are opening boutiques in such locations as Shanghai and Beijing, China. The current marketplace is truly global (Figure 1.7a–b).

Product Development in an Agile Manufacturing Environment

Large conglomerates today may manage and develop multiple product brands but outsource all production. The same business may also outsource advertising, warehousing, distribution, and accounts payable. Is it a manufacturer or a product developer? During the era of mass production–based competition, the center for adding value lay in manufacturing. This made the terms production and manufacturing almost synonymous. We now recognize that production is of greater scope than manufacturing. These days production encompasses everything that it takes to create, produce, and distribute products. The product

Figure 1.7a. *Wal-Mart in Shenzhen, China*

Figure 1.7b. *Louis Vuitton store in Beijing, China*

development function is charged with creating apparel that has value for the consumer. Thus, the circular model of a virtual apparel supply chain helps product developers achieve the agility they need to respond to a rapidly changing world. Companies are forming ongoing alliances and partnerships with other companies whose expertise complements their own. The composition of supply chain partnerships varies by brand, fabrication, style, and price point. Woven cotton garments may be made in India with Indian cotton.

Woven sportswear may be produced in Mexico with U.S.-made fabric. Sweaters may be made in Korea with Japanese yarns. An agent in Hong Kong may manage the Korean and Indian production. In-house sourcing managers may manage the Mexican business. These are just a few examples of the supply chain scenarios being administered concurrently by a single product developer.

Within a virtual environment, when a company determines that a particular process is not a match to its core competencies, it contracts out that process. Companies subscribe to **trend services** to help them sort through fashion trends in color, fabric, and silhouette, to determine which trends are right for their brand's customer. **Design bureaus** and **patternmaking services** work in tandem with a brand's own product development team to ensure that design concepts are correctly interpreted throughout the supply chain (Figure 1.8). **Factors** are financial middlemen that finance suppliers and manufacturers and who assume responsibility for billing and accounts receivable between various members of the supply chain. **Agents** assume responsibility for linking product developers with offshore textile suppliers and apparel producers, managing the interface necessary among all partners. **Testing labs** are contracted to test fabrics, findings, and finished apparel products, making sure they meet quality standards and specifications. Outside agencies may also be used to monitor quality throughout production or to certify that an offshore manufacturer meets standards regarding working conditions and child labor laws.

In virtual manufacturing environments, trust and teamwork between supply chain partners is more important than ownership. Sometimes ownership of other links or auxiliary businesses can facilitate the strength of the partnership. For instance, Target Corporation owns AMC, a major sourcing agent. AMC serves as an agent for most of Target Corporation's contracting for offshore production. Although AMC also does sourcing for other product developers, because of its special relationship with Target Corporation, Target stores are assigned a higher priority.

Very large product developers frequently prefer the control of owning critical links within their production chain. If they find a partner that is well suited to their needs, it may be advantageous to own that link, thereby guaranteeing access for the capacity they require. Other product developers prefer the flexibility of seasonal contracts so that, as their needs change, they are free to change partners. Regardless of ownership within the chain, all links work together as interconnected partners rather than as independent businesses. They jointly assume the responsibility and the risk to produce a well-defined product.

These changes have altered the focus of the apparel supply pipeline. The implementation and management of offshore production has controlled production costs. The industry now recognizes that product development and supply chain management are the keys to survival.

Many global supply chains today are based on the ability of developing countries to supply low-cost labor; however, global supply chains of the future

Figure 1.8. *Design bureaus such as Design Works International support the work of product development teams by providing trend research, contributing design ideas, and developing textile patterns.*

may derive their competitive edge from their ability to produce customer-configured products with technology that decreases the importance of labor costs. The potential for mass customization is just beginning to be explored and will undoubtedly stimulate further change in the apparel supply chain.

The Role of Product Development

The synergy of a virtual supply chain is necessary to successfully meet and interpret the ever-changing demands of the consumer. At no juncture is this concept more important than product development. Offshore sourcing requires designers to engineer product quality. The development of standards and specifications—once the responsibility of production managers and engineers—is now the responsibility of creative and technical design teams who work with merchandisers and sourcing teams to create product that meets the needs of consumers. The process that was once called design has become more inclusive:

- It is consumer-driven.

- It eliminates steps that do not add value to the end product.

- It defines the desired product through detailed standards and specifications.

- It requires partners within a virtual supply chain to share the responsibility and risk for producing a quality product.

- It is dependent on each partner's ability to meet schedules in order to deliver a product that reaches the marketplace when consumers are ready to buy.

- It must lend itself to distribution through multiple channels (e.g., stores, Internet, and catalog).

Product Development Variations

Product development processes vary, depending on whether the products being developed are wholesale brands, private label or store brands, licensed brands, or customized. It is important to understand the product development process for each type of product (Figure 1.9a–c).

Wholesale Brands

Wholesale brands are created under a proprietary label and sold at wholesale for distribution to retailers that also carry other wholesale brands. Department stores, specialty stores, chain stores, and discount stores may all carry branded products. Assortments in these stores may consist of all wholesale brands or wholesale brands that compete with the store's own private label products. Wholesale brand product developers may also distribute their products online or through their own signature or outlet stores, but typically, these sales do not constitute the bulk of their business. Wholesale brand product developers may own their own manufacturing facilities or use contractors to produce their product. It is increasingly common for wholesale brand product developers to focus on the development, sales, and marketing of product and to rely on

Figure 1.9a. *Jockey is an example of a wholesale brand.*

Figure 1.9b. *Victoria's Secret is a store brand that is widely recognized in part due to the brand's runway shows, which are available on the Web and on television.*

Figure 1.9c. *The Jaclyn Smith brand is a private label for Kmart.*

sourcing partners for manufacturing. This allows them to respond more quickly to shifts in fashion and changing consumer preferences, while taking advantage of lower wages abroad.

Private Label and Store Brands

Private brand products are developed and merchandised for exclusive distribution by a particular retailer. Private brands sold by mass merchants and department stores typically compete with wholesale brand products also carried by the retailer. Specialty stores such as The Limited and the Gap sell only private brands. To distinguish between these two approaches, brands developed for stores that sell only private brands will be identified as **store brands**. The term **private label** will be used when discussing private brands developed to compete with wholesale brands.

Most private label product is developed by the retailer's own product development team. Kohl's product development team develops product under its *Sonoma Life+Style, Croft & Barrow,* and *Apt. 9* labels. Similarly, Target Corporation, Federated Department Stores, J. C. Penney, and Nordstrom all have extensive product development divisions. Specialty stores such as The Limited and the Gap develop all of their own store brands.

Some retailers obtain a portion of their private brand merchandise by buying exclusive merchandise from wholesale brand companies and replacing the brand label with their own private label. The terms of these arrangements may require that the branded supplier adapt the styles purchased to the sizing specifications of the private label. The product itself is usually a knockoff of product sold as part of the wholesale brand line, but customized in color or fabric to make it unique.

A few large retailers have the resources to actually buy the rights to a brand. Sears acquired Lands' End in 2002 in order to add cachet to its private brand apparel business. The acquisition was part of a strategy that would give Lands' End, primarily a catalog/Internet brand, a store presence and Sears a brand with an upscale image and clientele. Unfortunately the strategy has not lived up to its potential.

A third option for developing/distributing private brands is to enter into a licensing agreement with a product developer that gives the retailer exclusive rights to a brand for an agreed-upon length of time. The *Tony Hawk, Vera Wang,* and *Daisy Fuentes* lines for Kohl's and the *Isaac Mizrahi* and *Liz Lange* brands for Target are examples of **exclusive brands**. Many wholesale brand product developers also have agreements with mass merchandise retailers to develop exclusive product lines. Liz Claiborne produces *Villager, Stamp 10,* and *Axcess* for Kohls; *Liz & Co.* for J. C. Penney, and *First Issue* for Sears, to name but a few.

The concept of private labels has been around since the mid-1980s. Historically these labels looked like cheap knockoffs of last year's fashion trends. They received little advertising support and were merchandised in less-than-prime floor space. Today's consumers are no longer interested in low-quality knockoffs. They respond to brands that are trend-right, high-quality, and value-priced, backed by savvy marketing, celebrity spokespeople, and a hip image (Baker 2003). Private brands allow retailers to customize merchandise for their specific customer and at the same time apply higher margins and control the timing of markdowns. Conversely, if private label merchandise doesn't sell, there's no one to go to for markdown money or vendor support.

Private label brands may make up 15 to 50 percent of a mass merchant or department store's merchandise mix, with most hovering around 20 to 30 percent. Wholesale brand products make up the remaining assortment for these stores. As private label product developers become increasingly sophisticated in offering fashion-forward, high-quality products, they tend to decrease their reliance on wholesale brands. In September 2005, Saks Fifth Avenue announced it was closing its private label apparel business in line with a strategy to focus on higher-priced designer brands. By the middle of 2006, Saks had reversed this decision and was seeking ways to quickly reenter the private label market. Even at the high end of the market, consumers expect value-priced private brands to supplement their designer purchases. Categories where private label is particularly strong include casual sportswear, dressed-up casual (appropriate for casual workplaces), plus-sizes, and activewear.

Product developers of **store brands** offer a complete assortment of privately developed products under their own labels for exclusive distribution in their own stores, catalogs, or both. Companies that rely on this strategy include The Limited, the Gap, J. Jill, Chico's, and Abercrombie & Fitch. Store brands have led the way in giving private brands a distinctive image that consumers seek out. These companies tend to capitalize on their intimate knowledge of a particular market niche as opposed to mass merchants and department stores that attempt to cater to a wide range of consumer ages, lifestyles, and price points. Carrying a 100-percent exclusive assortment of merchandise helps them differentiate themselves in the marketplace, cater to their particular target customers, and control their profit margins (Wickett, Gaskill, and Damhorst 1999, 21–35). However, in a marketplace where keeping up with change is a *hip* commodity, they are vulnerable to shifts in consumer loyalty. This is particularly true with younger customers. As one generation grows out of a particular retailer's brands, there is no guarantee that the next generation will consider that same brand "cool."

Licensed Products

Licensing agreements grant a business partner exclusive rights to produce or sell products under a proprietary brand name. Licensing agreements may be entered into in order to expand a brand's product mix, to expand distribution into a global market, to capitalize on the popularity of a proprietary character, to partner with another brand in order to maximise the value of the

Figure 1.10. *Barbie apparel for young girls was previewed at a 2001 licensing show.*

combined brands, or, as discussed above, to provide exclusive product to a particular retailer.

Donna Karan distributes hosiery, lingerie, and shoes under its brand label; the product is designed and produced by companies that are expert in the development of those product categories. In return for granting the use of its label, Donna Karan receives a royalty on all units sold. Distribution of the licensed product varies, depending on which party is better suited to get the product to market.

Often companies facilitate global distribution by partnering with a company that is knowledgable about the complexities of that market's sizing, labeling, and business practices. The licensing partner may assume responsibility for distribution only or for manufacturing and distribution if the product being licensed requires modification or local sourcing to manage the price point. Once again, the brand owner receives royalties on all sales managed by the licensee.

Character licensing is another form of licensing. The images of popular characters ranging from Mickey Mouse and Winnie the Pooh to SpongeBob SquarePants and college mascot logos are all copyright-protected. Companies that own the rights to these images grant licenses to a variety of product developers to use these images on their products. Character licensing is prevalent in children's apparel, men's ties, and sports apparel (Figure 1.10).

The concept of co-brands and exclusive brands was introduced in the discussion of private brands. These arrangements are another form of licensing that has gained momentum in recent years. **Co-branded products** are the result of a partnership between a branded product developer or designer and a retailer. The branded product developer or designer designs an exclusive collection for the retailer. The design team responsible for co-branded lines is responsible for incorporating agreed-upon design parameters. The terms of the agreement may be for a single collection, as in the case of Karl Lagerfeld and Stella McCartney's collections for H & M in 2005, or for a number of years, as are Target agreements, which typically last for three years. Target Corporation has had great success with lines designed by Peter Graves (homegoods), Liz Lange (maternity), and Isaac Mizrahi (contemporary apparel).

Co-branded collections have the feel of the designer or brand but are modified to meet the needs and price point of the retailer's target customer. Nordstrom has an agreement with BCBG for a contemporary collection called "BCBG Exclusively for Nordstrom." The collection is in the spirit of the BCBG line, but it has a casual flair, is sized more generously, and is priced 25 percent below the BCBG line. These agreements may, or may not, be renewed at the end of their term.

Customized Products

Customized products made to consumer specifications were once the domain of custom tailors and professional seamstresses. However, the technology available today makes mass customization an increasingly attainable reality. **Mass customization** utilizes mass production technology and applies it to the creation of products and services for a market of one. Levi Strauss & Co. and Brooks Brothers have both purchased body scanners that enable them to capture measurement data that can then be applied to the creation of a custom-fit garment or best size prediction. Lands' End began offering its customers the opportunity to be scanned in the fall of 2000. It hopes to use scanned body measurements to better serve its customers' fitting expectations and to use collected data to continually improve sizing specifications.

A variety of product developers are giving customers limited options in the design of garments by allowing them to choose the finished length, fabric, or styling details. Companies that are exploring the possibilities of mass customization and the technology that supports it are discussed in later chapters.

A product developer must determine which variation of product development—from branded to licensed—gives it the strongest competitive advantage. It is not uncommon for a brand to evolve into a private label or store brand as the market environment changes. As product developers become more adept at positioning their product, the lines of distinction will blur.

Supply Chain Management Tools

Quick Response strategies were introduced in the early 1980s in response to the rapid growth of apparel imports that began flooding the market in the late 1960s. It was hoped that implementation of these strategies would encourage the purchase of domestically made apparel and home fashions in order to stimulate the U.S. apparel business and enhance its competitive position. **Quick Response (QR)** is defined as getting the right product to the right place at the right time and at the right price.

The QR strategy identified tools to help domestic manufacturers take advantage of their well-honed knowledge of the American lifestyle and to capitalize on their proximity to the marketplace by delivering fashion goods with short lead times—the time it takes to process an order from authorization to delivery. QR relies on the following tools:

- **Just-in-time (JIT) inventory** prioritizes getting fabrics, notions, and finished goods to their destination as they are needed, eliminating the non–value-added cost of warehousing. Suppliers are required to meet all quality specifications through thorough inspection before shipping.

- **Specification ordering** involves defining quality by setting product standards and specifications for every order placed. In the case of fabric, for example, width, length, shade variance tolerances, and acceptable levels of flaws must be identified.

- **Bar coding** technology allows all products to be preticketed before shipping. These 13-digit UPC codes, upgraded from 12 digits in 2005 to conform to international standards, carry vendor, style, color, and size information, which can be easily read by scanning devices to check in shipments, record sales, and keep track of inventories.

- **Electronic data interchange (EDI)** refers to the electronic transmission in standard formats of transactional information such as forecasts of requirements, purchase orders, shipping notices, and invoices. When QR was introduced, this exchange of information was accomplished by fax; today information is exchanged digitally.

- **Computer-aided design (CAD)** systems offer digital design and patternmaking capability, enabling the compression of the product development calendar.

- **Automatic replenishment systems** were introduced to manage inventories and eliminate stockouts. A **stockout** occurs when a particular unit is not available when a customer wants it.

While these tools were not enough to prevent most apparel manufacturing from moving to lower-wage developing countries, much of the product development function continues to be located in developed countries. However, newly developing countries aspire to become more competitive in the product development area.

The principles of QR have served as a foundation for today's new information systems that facilitate communication and processes throughout the apparel supply chain. New technology has the amazing ability to collect, archive, analyze, and transmit reliable data, in real time, in order to facilitate decision making throughout the supply chain (Tait 2005). These systems must support the needs and resources of global supply chain partners.

The globalization of the apparel business means dealing with communication issues, time zones, language barriers, technology, logistics and infrastructure complications, as well as the less predictable external forces of natural disasters, terrorism, wars, politics, and outbreaks of disease. Changes in any of these conditions may require alternative planning. With the removal of the protectionism afforded by the quota system, competition among both manufacturers and retailers is getting more intense. Both vendors (product developers and manufacturers) and retail buyers are consolidating their suppliers to those who can provide what they want, when they want it, and at the right price. Agility and flexibility are paramount.

For wholesale brand product developers and manufacturers, survival depends not only on their product, but their service. The right product relies on good design, the quality of the raw materials and manufacturing processes, and value pricing in the eyes of the intended consumer market. Equally important are speed to market, inventory management, ability to meet the retailer's delivery demands (distribution center or direct-to-store, floor-ready requirements, demand for re-orders or a continuous flow of new product), and teamwork (Tait 2005).

Similarly, retailers must differentiate themselves from their competition through unique product assortments. Survival necessitates more accurate planning to know what they need and in what assortments, an appropriate geographic and distribution channel allocation, and a pricing strategy to obtain the best possible net margin. Larger conglomerates/organizations capitalize on economies of scale, but are faced with far more complex decision making.

There are numerous software solutions in the marketplace—some developed exclusively for the apparel supply chain, and others which can be customized for any industry group. Basic functionality can be grouped into three categories. Supply chain management systems manage core transactions with suppliers and customers. Retail software encompasses forecasting, planning, point-of-sale data collection and analysis, and price optimization. Design and product development software functionality includes textile design, color management, fabric and trim procurement, apparel design, patternmaking and grading, marker making, product specification management, product

Figure 1.11. *Gerber Technology's Web PDM software allows technical design teams to customize specification packages and communicate with supply chain partners in real time.*

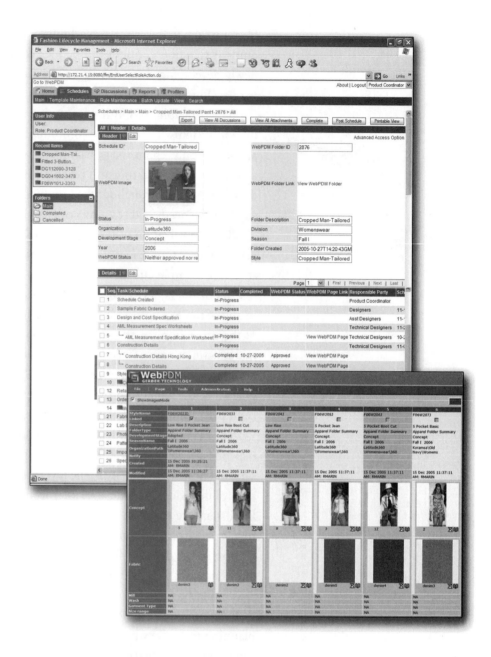

development collaboration, and product line management (Figure 1.11). Definitions for commonly used terms and acronyms are summarized in Table 1.1.

Different members of the product development team must become proficient with the functionality utilized within their area. Early functionality revolved around computerized patternmaking and grading and product data management (PDM) systems that merge graphic and word files which help to define products in a specification (spec) package that can be sent to domestic or offshore producers. Newer to the mix are product lifecycle management (PLM) tools that help to ensure that the development of each product stays on schedule. Improved digital asset management functionality in PDM/PLM tools helps to manage digital assets so that similar styles made in past seasons

Table 1.1 A SUMMARY OF CURRENT TECHNOLOGY TERMS AND ACRONYMS

SUPPLY CHAIN MANAGEMENT FUNCTIONS

Advanced Planning and Scheduling (APS)—Programs that develop constraint-based production and distribution plans based upon expected demands. These systems help produce schedules as to what, how, when, and where to produce product, keeping in mind inventory availability, plant capacity, and other business objectives.

Automated Financial Transaction Processing—System for processing payments or advances, such as between importers, global suppliers, banks, and factors.

Automated RFQ—System for soliciting bids for products or production, often including issuance of specifications/job requirements to a pool of prospective vendors, which respond with information via the system.

Collaborative Planning, Forecasting and Replenishment (CPFR)—A best-practices framework, established and empowered by a formal agreement to cooperate on strategy, tactics, and execution by resolution of exceptions. The framework was developed by the VICS committee for managing the planning and replenishment process through the confidential sharing of sales and inventory data and trends among business partners.

Continuous Replenishment Programs (CRP)—The practice of partnering with distribution channel members that changes the traditional replenishment process from distributor- –generated purchase orders, based on economic order quantities, to the replenishment of products based on actual and forecasted product demand. The use of CRP triggers the manufacturing and movement of product through the supply chain when the identical product is purchased by an end user.

Cut Order/Spread Planning—System for creating plans for fabric spreading and cutting.

Dashboard Reporting Capability—System that provides configurable, at-a-glance views of key data, usually in real -time, without the need to perform multiple steps to extract a report of this data.

Direct Shipping (DC Bypass)—Systems that enable vendors to ship goods directly to the retail store instead of to a regional distribution center. A variation on this is Cross Docking where a shipment from a vendor goes to a retail DC which sorts and ships ordered goods immediately to the stores.

Electronic Data Interchange/Autonomous System Numbers (EDI/ASN)—System for generating and transmitting industry-standard data communications, such as invoices, purchase orders, and advance shipment documentation.

Enterprise Resource Planning (ERP)—Functionality that manages core transactions with suppliers and customers, accounts payable and receivable, and payroll.

Radio Frequency Identification (RFID)—Identification tags and labels, made with silicon chips containing product data, send out an interrogation signal and receive the data back from the tag via radio frequency waves; can be used for inventory tracking, point- of- sale information, security, anti-counterfeiting, or any number of other applications. No line of sight is required to read the tags, and multiple items can be read at once. The RFID technology may replace bar codes.

RFID Support—Systems with architectural upgrades to manage RFID data and translate it to match existing SKU data.

Third-party Logistics Management—System that provides a holistic view of information from external logistics services providers, such as shippers, freight forwarders, and fulfillment houses.

Transportation Management—System to handle contracts and goods movement with multiple shippers and modes of transportation.

Vendor Scorecard—System for capturing and monitoring data about supplier performance, such as quality, on-time delivery, and social/customs compliance.

Warehouse Management—System that controls movement of goods within, entering, or exiting the DC (distribution center).

continued

Table 1.1 A SUMMARY OF CURRENT TECHNOLOGY TERMS AND ACRONYMS *continued*

Work in Progress (WIP) Tracking—System for monitoring production status, such as what percentage of an order has been cut and sewn.

DESIGN AND PRODUCT DEVELOPMENT FUNCTIONALITY

3-D Simulation—System that provides a 3-D view of styles during product development, often with manipulation of a digital human avatar to simulate garment performance in response to lifelike body movements. May also apply to consumer virtual "try-on" or dressing room applications.

Apparel Design—System for creating garment silhouettes, concepts, styles, and collections.

Color Management—System for communicating data that are related to color consistency, lab dip approvals, and testing.

Computer Aided Design (CAD)—Computer software with functionality that enables product design, 3-D modeling, and patternmaking.

Digital Asset Management (DAM)—Software of functionality that stores, organizes, and retrieves all types of digital assets into searchable files that include all relevant information associated with the asset, such as copyright information, creation date, color information, and usage restrictions (Ludolph 2000).

Fabric and Trim Procurement—System for managing textile and trim inventory for sample making or production.

Marker Making and Nest Optimization—System for creating markers and achieving best fabric utilization.

Patternmaking and Pattern Grading—System for creating garment patterns and grading them for different sizes.

Product Lifecycle Management (PLM)—System that allows product developers to track and manage continuous changes throughout the pre-season and communicate between design partners, merchandisers, material suppliers, and finished goods factories in order in order to ensure timely and accurate progress through the supply chain (Speer 2005).

Product Specification Management (PSM)—System for centralized storage of product data, such as size standards, raw materials, and costing information and design illustrations. These systems are also known as product development management systems (PDM).

Textile Design—System for designing textiles or related prints, colorways, and textures.

RETAIL FUNCTIONALITY

Customer Relationship Management (CRM)—Systems that manage customer data and the various contact points between the retailer and the consumer across various distribution channels in order to improve customer loyalty and drive profits.

E-Tail Transaction Processing and/or Fulfillment—System for managing online orders from consumers shopping on the Internet.

E-Tail Web Analytics—System for analyzing Web site activity, usually with recommendations for improvements to optimize sales in the Web channel.

Forecasting and Demand Planning—System for projecting sales for different lines of business and developing sales forecasts, merchandising proposals, and replenishment plans.

Inventory Management—System for tracking and controlling SKUs by location and volume in stores or DCs.

Merchandise Management—System for executing the sales and order plan, including assortment planning and store/cluster allocation by SKU.

Point of Sale (POS)—System for collecting, storing, or analyzing data from sales transactions.

Price Optimization—System for recommending optimal pricing scenarios and markdown plans.

Vendor Management—System for communicating with suppliers about orders, reorders, shipment problems, etc.

Visual Merchandising—System for creating store layout and/or assortment planograms, often including tools for virtual rendering of apparel amid store fixtures and lighting, for store planning, sales presentations, and virtual catalogs.

Sources: Ludolph 2000; Speer 2005; *Apparel* 2006

may be called up and used as a template for new styles. The information captured in PDM programs supplements the transaction documentation managed within supply chain management (SCM) systems.

No single computer system can provide all the information necessary to manage an apparel supply chain. Integrated computer systems are the key to transforming a company's business processes in order to meet strategic goals and objectives. The greatest efficiencies are achieved when disparate systems serving different functions within the company can communicate with each other and with other supply chain partners who require the same information but use different systems. This requires open architecture that allows for the translation of data so that it can be shared across the supply chain.

Many of today's technologies are available as web-based exchanges, sometimes labeled Collaborative Product Commerce (CPC) solutions and other times referred to as enterprise application integration (EAI). These systems provide secure global communications that can be accessed via the internet, under controlled conditions, by a community of companies that work together—no matter what computer-based tools they use, no matter where they are located geographically or within the supply chain—to collaboratively develop, build, and manage products throughout the entire lifecycle. The systems perform at three levels. They ensure data integrity; handle data transport between supply chain partners; and translate the data into a format that can be read by each supplier.

Technology investments must be tied to strategic business objectives. In today's competitive environment, removing weeks from a production calendar, thereby enabling a company to be more on trend, is far more valuable than eliminating staff. The goal should be improved sales, margins, and inventory levels that allow personnel to refocus their time on tasks that add value to the product or brand, such as better design and more accurate business analysis (Corcoran 2005, 13–14). The best technology solutions require the least customization, offer excellent training and support, have the potential to grow with the company's needs, and offer timely updates as technology grows.

Summary

A state of perpetual change is driving the apparel industry into the future. The apparel supply chain, which used to function as somewhat independent industries (fiber, textile, apparel manufacturing, and retail), is now intrinsically and strategically linked. Each company within the chain must form virtual partnerships to meet the demands of the customer. The virtual nature of these partnerships provides the flexibility that is required in the marketplace. Individual manufacturers, suppliers, or retailers will no longer dominate the market of the future. Companies that survive in the current business environment must be networked enterprises with the knowledge and capacity to integrate, collaborate, and optimize efficiencies throughout the supply chain faster and more profitably than the competition. Competition is no longer based solely on a company and its products, but rather on an integrated supply chain's ability to service its customers. Partnerships are dynamic and may be realigned as customer preferences evolve.

Product development expands the design process in a manufacturing environment where contractors produce most apparel. In today's global marketplace, the majority of apparel products sold in the United States are produced offshore. Because product developers cannot manage a contractor's shop floor from continents away, they must manage via the contractual agreement containing the specifications and standards that define the product ordered. Accurate planning, exact communication, and critical thinking are paramount to ensure a quick response time.

Although there are differences among product developers that produce wholesale brands and those that produce private brands—private label or store brand apparel—the similarities in their processes are more significant than the differences. Increasingly, they borrow successful strategies from one another in order to meet the demands of the marketplace.

In an agile manufacturing environment, product value has shifted from manufacturing toward services and information. Apparel manufacturers who survive must be proactive in the creation of new customer opportunities and be able to react quickly to unanticipated opportunities. One of the most important investments they can make is in technology that helps them stay connected to their supply chain partners.

Key Terms

agents	growth industries
agile manufacturing environment	horizontal integration
apparel supply chain	just-in-time (JIT) inventory
automatic replenishment systems	licensing agreements
auxiliary businesses	mass customization
bar coding	mature industries
co-branded products	outlet stores
computer-aided design (CAD)	patternmaking services
core competencies	private brands
design bureaus	private label
deverticalize	product development
differential advantage	Quick Response (QR)
diversification	signature stores
electronic data interchange (EDI)	sneakerization
exclusive brands	specification ordering
factors	stockout
full-package manufacturing	store brands

testing labs

trend services

vertical integration

virtual supply chain

wholesale brands

Discussion Questions

1. What are the core competencies of companies such as Ralph Lauren, Zara, Wal-Mart, and Nike?

2. What apparel product developers have successfully "sneakerized" their product line to revitalize their brand or product?

3. Identify mergers and acquisitions in recent headlines. What growth strategies do you think motivated these business decisions?

4. Discuss some of your favorite products. What differentiates them from their competition in the marketplace?

Activities

1. Go to the library and access annual reports or search for the Web sites of several major wholesale or retail product developers. Identify the brands for which they develop product.

2. Select a brand that is widely available in your shopping area. Identify several stores that carry the same brand. Compare and contrast the assortment of merchandise at each store for its fashion level, price point, and styling range.

3. Look at the country of origin on labels from a variety of items of a single brand. How many different countries of origin can you identify? Discuss how the country of origin might have an impact on the product development process relative to cost, lead time, and quality.

References

2006. Special report: Apparel's software scorecard. *Apparel 47*, no. 9 (May): 36–42.

Baker, Stacy. 2003. Private label: The state of the market. Just-style exclusive management briefings. February, www.just-style.com/briefings.

Corcoran, C. 2005. Fashion tech boosts revenue, doesn't cut costs. *Women's Wear Daily,* December 14.

Goldman, S. L., R. N. Nagel, and K. Preiss. 1995. *Agile competitors and virtual organizations.* New York: Van Nostrand Reinhold.

Ludolph, R. 2000. Creating value through supply chain management. www.techexchange.com.

Speer, Jordan K. 2005. Design development & pre-production. *Apparel,* September 1, www.apparelmag.com/articles/sept/sept05_1.shtml.

Tait, Niki. 2005. Manufacturing IT: the holistic approach. www.just-style.com.

Wickett, J. L., L. R. Gaskill, and M. L. Damhorst. 1999. Apparel retail product development: Model testing and expansion. *Clothing and Textiles Research Journal 17*, no. 1.

CHAPTER 2

BUSINESS PLANNING

"It's all about execution—execute the plan, or it will execute you."
—Brad Beal, Executive Vice President, Global Trade, Jockey International Inc.*

OBJECTIVES

- To recognize basic business functions and the importance of business planning

- To identify the position of product development processes within the corporate structure

- To identify the components of the product development process

- To identify product categories within the apparel business

- To understand the importance of brands

- To identify the factors contributing to brand identity and appreciate the variables in managing the brand portfolio

Central to the decision-making process of any apparel firm is its overall **business plan**—its aims, objectives, and strategy for the future. Emphasis on the components within the plan depends heavily on whether the basic core business of the firm is manufacturing or retailing and whether the business will be marketing itself as a wholesaler, a retailer, or a combination of the two. The intent of the business plan is to provide structure to an ongoing process that is constantly being adjusted to respond to consumer demands. The highest level of planning in a business is strategic planning. Developed by a firm's executive staff, the **strategic plan** links concepts related to the target consumer and the product line to the financial goals of the business and forms the basis for the merchandise planning, line planning, assortment planning, line development, and sourcing of materials and production that will follow.

*Appeared in *AAPN Journal*, www.AAPNetwork.net

Basic Business Functions

Although top-level management conceives the particular organizational structure and strategic plan that is best for its firm, every apparel business is built on the premise that a number of basic functions must be included within the structure of the firm. The organizational and managerial structure of a company provides a context for the many tasks and processes of the marketing, merchandising, production, finance, and operations functions that are integral to any business.

Merchandising consists of the planning, development, and presentation of the product line. Product line refers to the assortment of product categories that a business offers for sale. The merchandising area typically plans assortment and prices of product, approves styling, and schedules timing of deliveries. Current practice within apparel production firms suggests that the merchandising function is often distributed among three subtracks, identified as merchandising, creative design, and technical design.

The responsibility for making the product is traditionally called production. Activities that are part of the **production** function are approval of the technical design of the garment, developing the engineering specifications, and costing of the product. Production activities in apparel firms may include development of production patterns from the sample pattern, grading the patterns to sizes desired, developing the markers used for configuring fabric usage, cutting, sewing, finishing, and arranging for distribution. In current practice many of the functions of merchandising and production overlap; the purpose of this text is to identify and explore the synergy of these complex and diverse processes.

The finance and operations functions may appear to contribute to the product development process in less direct ways, but they are decidedly basic functions in all forms of business. The **finance** area is responsible for all of the accounting activities of the firm, including expenditures for materials used in the production of products, salaries of employees, and the overall business budget. Because accounting activities reflect all of the financial dealings of the firm, most are beyond the scope of this text. However, we must address the basic financial context and the critical costing areas required during the development stages of the product. The **operations** area typically oversees the upkeep of equipment used by employees, such as computers and building facilities, and the distribution activities required for securing materials and shipping the finished products.

Marketing determines the advertising and promotional objectives, recommends sales goals, and creates marketing programs and tools. The sales team is part of the marketing function. It is their responsibility to gather data relative to target customers as well as to sell the product.

Planning Components

Business plans are made up of different elements or components. At the top planning levels the big picture is defined and business goals are established. At each successive level of planning, more and more detail is worked out in order to meet overall business goals. Planning is the foundation of the product development process. The following types of planning are typical of product development businesses and are linked to the functional areas described above.

Strategic Planning

Strategic planning focuses on a company's business direction and financial goals. Business direction includes decisions regarding brand image, brand portfolio, product mix, price points, channels of distribution, strategic partnerships, and growth and divestment. The financial plan, as part of the strategic plan, covers the analysis of growth opportunities, planning and managing investments, and setting profit goals. A strategic plan should be dynamic; it must evolve as situations change and new information becomes available. The intent of the strategic plan is to provide structure to all other company activities. The strategic plan forms the platform for the other components of the business plan. (Refer to Figure 2.1 for an overview of planning areas.)

Developing profitable business strategies is dependent on matching products and services of the business with its target customer. This process includes an analysis of the competition. Starting with an understanding of the customer, the decision-making process for the strategic business plan focuses on profit. Without making a profit, the firm cannot continue in business. It is at the time of strategic planning that budgets are established. **Budgets** are the written plans for anticipated monetary income and expenditures of the firm. Among other things, the budget will dictate the percentages of projected sales that will be assigned to developing, producing, marketing, and distributing the goods. A budget must also cover all administrative costs and overhead.

At the second level of the overall business plan are four well-defined areas that must interact seamlessly. They are merchandise planning, creative planning, technical planning, and production planning.

Merchandise Planning

Merchandising is the process of planning, developing, and presenting product lines for identified target markets with regard to pricing, assorting, styling, and timing (Glock and Kunz 2005). It occurs at every point within the supply chain from textiles, fibers, yarns, and fabrics to findings, trims, and support materials. Wholesale brands, private brands, and licensed products are merchandised as are buying plans for catalogs, Web sites, and sales floors. The

LINE PLANNING

MARKETING PLAN	EVALUATE MERCHANDISE OFFERINGS	FORECAST MERCHANDISE OFFERINGS	PLAN MERCHANDISE BUDGETS
Position the firm Create marketing Plan advertising/ promotions	Categories Classifications Subclassifications Groups	Sales history Selling periods Product types Size ranges Price points	Sales Reductions Required merchandise Prices Initial markup Allowable costs

LINE DEVELOPMENT

BUSINESS PLAN	LINE CONCEPT		CREATIVE DESIGN
Mission Goals Merchandise mix Fashion emphasis Policies and practices Price range(s) Quality standards	Synthesize current issues/trends • economic • social • cultural • technological • demographic • lifestyle Describe fashion trends • line • detail • silhouette • color • pattern • fit	Establish line direction • color palette • styling guidelines Describe materials • fiber content • yarn type • fabric structure • finishes Identify group concepts • separates • related separates • coordinates Analyze current line • continued styles • modified styles • new designs	Develop designs • sketches • precosting • first patterns • design specifications • fit standards • materials descriptions Create design prototypes Review prototypes • styling • fit • fabric • assembly methods Revise patterns Create prototypes until designs are perfected

LINE PRESENTATION

SOURCING STRATEGY

MATERIALS

INTERNAL

Review for adoption
• line concept
• image strategy
• groups and designs
• applications to line plan
• design specs and costing
• pricing strategy
• visual merchandising

MAKE OR BUY	PROCESS	MATERIALS
Finished goods Materials Product development Production Domestic International Global Full package Cut/make/trim	Screen contractors Assign styles Place initial orders Finished goods Materials production Style assignment Manage trade regulations Evaluate vendors	Product characteristics Variety Prices Lead times Minimums Quality standards Specifications Performance standards

Figure 2.1. *Overview of product development from the manufacturer's perspective. Source: Kunz 2005, 86–87*

LINE PLANNING

PLAN MERCHANDISE ASSORTMENTS	**DETERMINE DELIVERY AND ALLOCATION**	**ANALYZE AND UPDATE MERCHANDISE PLANS**
Model stocks	Sequence delivery	Update budgets
Basic stocks	Allocate to stores	Update assortments
Automated replenishment	Arrange resupply	Update delivery plans

LINE DEVELOPMENT

LINE ADOPTION	**TECHNICAL DESIGN**
Determine styles in line	Perfect styling and fit
• wholesale finished goods	Finalize patterns
• product development	Test materials
Establish list or first prices	Test assembly methods
Assign styles/sizes/ colors to line plan	Develop style samples
Balance assortments	Develop style/quality specifications
• variety	• styling
• volume	• fit
• diversity	• materials
• allocation	• assembly methods
Produce sales/photo/ catalog samples	• labeling
	• ticketing
	Detailed costing
	Grade patterns

LINE PRESENTATION

WHOLESALE		**RETAIL**	
Line preview	Line/style release	Types	Power of appeal
• line concept	• fashion shows	• specialty	• display space
• image strategy	• wholesale markets	• department	• fixtures
• assortment strategy	• sales presentations	• mass	• lighting
• style appeal	• trunk shows	• off price	• signage
• marketing strategy	Customer service	• manufacturer's outlet	• labels
• pricing strategy		• catalog	• tickets
• visual merchandising		• television	• pricing strategy
		• Internet	• customer service
			• inventory management

GARMENT PRODUCTION

PRODUCTION PLANNING	**ASSEMBLY AND FINISHING**	**PACKAGING AND DISTRIBUTION**
Make to order/ make to stock	Production scheduling	Labeling/ticketing
Cut order planning	Work study	Packaging
Marker making	Quality control	Hanger or shelf ready
Engineering specifications	Spreading/cutting	Loading
Plant layout/startup	Sewing	Shipping
Methods development	Pressing	Quality audits
Training/ergonomics	Finishing	

discussion in this text will focus on the merchandiser role in apparel product development.

Merchandising starts with the **merchandise plan or budget**, which identifies the resources needed to meet profit, sales, and margin objectives for a specific season by company division. The merchandise plan links strategic planning to creative planning, technical planning, production planning, and sales and marketing. Merchandisers analyze historic data and consider new seasonal information to determine how to best meet profit goals within their division.

This information is further delineated through a **line or range plan**, which sets sales and margin goals for groups or lines within that division. Line planning involves evaluation of the merchandise mix, forecasting merchandise offerings to meet merchandise budgets, and planning merchandise assortments. From the line plan, goals for each group are further broken down into assortment plans. **Assortment plans** break down the line plan into components that address customer preferences—what product, how much of it, what colors, what sizes, and for what delivery. A **merchandise calendar** controls the events required to get the planned apparel products to the customer at the right time. A well-assorted product presentation ensures enough selection without overstocking. It gives focus to the design team, ensuring that their efforts are directed to the items required for the seasonal line.

The merchandising process requires that the merchandiser meet with the buyers and managers of retail accounts to understand patterns and shifts in consumer preferences. She or he fine-tunes the brand's niche in the market in comparison to the competition. Merchandisers for wholesale brands work with the sales team to determine which products are needed for each delivery, ensuring appropriate breadth (number of styles) and depth (quantity of each style) of assortment and line characteristics—e.g., new vs. ongoing trends, skirts vs. pants, knits vs. wovens. They work with the trend team and/or the creative design team to interpret trends in color, fabrication, trim, and silhouettes for their specific customer to ensure that their product line has a competitive edge. They work with technical design and production planning to ensure that the appropriate quality level is built into each garment through fabric and trim testing, construction specs, fittings, and garment testing. They use their knowledge of production to ensure that the product can be made at the desired price point and within the constraints of the merchandising calendar. The merchandising calendar manages the product life cycle: It determines the dates by which orders must be confirmed, fabrics and trims delivered, samples approved, garment testing and production completed, and garments shipped by working backward from the date the goods need to be in-store. Merchandisers also review and edit the line, monitor costs, and are part of the team that sets prices in order to meet sales, margin, and profit goals.

Some of today's product developers have set up supply chains that can take a concept to market in 8 to 10 weeks. Although many product developers still follow a 10- to 12-month calendar, shortening the cycle time helps to develop product that is trend-right and reduces risk. The key to achieving greater efficiency is to develop product to plan (Kurt Salmon Associates 2003).

Designers are forward-thinking and want to explore all of their creative ideas. Buyers are numbers-driven and make decisions based on last season's history. The merchandiser must function in both worlds, using his or her knowledge of the customer to arbitrate between the two and define the parameters of the line. He or she needs to ensure the correct level of newness while not wasting precious time developing product that won't sell.

Today's business environment presents many challenges for the apparel merchandiser:

- Increased competition between wholesale and private brands
- Increased demand for newness and innovation
- Consolidation of the retail market
- Increased demand for speed to market, high quality, and value pricing

Creative Planning

Creative planning tracks trends and interprets them for the company's target market. Trend and design professionals require keen instincts to pick up on social, political, cultural, and aesthetic trends as they affect fashion. With the merchandiser, trend specialists and designers look at the global fashion picture and anticipate what their customers will be ready to embrace in upcoming seasons. They rely on fabric shows, subscriptions to trend resources, and regular shopping trips to put together a seasonal forecast that sets the direction for the product development process and ensures that creative, technical, merchandising, and sourcing personnel are working toward the same goals (Figure 2.2).

Trend and design professionals determine the seasonal color palette and approve color standards. They determine fabric stories and may design prints or work with fabric suppliers to develop new fabrics. They typically determine style silhouettes by delivery groups. In simple terms, they select the color combinations, the textiles, and the basic design of the products that will be produced.

Technical Planning

Technical planning further defines styles by developing fit standards and materials and construction specifications. Individuals responsible for this area of planning match new styles with styles from past seasons and interpret changes. They articulate any design changes needed for sample garments or sketches to meet production requirements. Some technical design teams include in-house patternmakers; others contract this process out. They make sure that color standards are matched at each phase of production, and they oversee fabric and garment testing. They develop fabric specifications, determine

Figure 2.2. *Donna Ricco's design studio. Creative planning relies on research from a variety of sources.*

sizing grade rules, and specify construction and labeling requirements. They communicate with contractors or production staff regarding styling, fit, and construction issues.

Technical designers evaluate prototype garments and ensure that a style has been perfected before it is approved for production. The specifications and standards they develop are the foundation for building a quality garment that meets customer expectations. These tasks are complex, and their explanation forms the content of many chapters of this text.

Production Planning

Production planning links merchandising decisions with design and technical decisions. Production planners must understand the cost of materials, trims, and value-added finishes and processes; quantity and quality capacity; production and transit timelines; and tariffs and quotas in all of the countries in which they source. In apparel, trims and value-added finishes include all of the materials and processes used in garment construction beyond the basic fabric selection. The capacity of factories reflects the ability of these facilities to produce the correct product, in the ordered quantity, at the desired quality, and to transport it to its destination at the contracted time. Duties and quotas are expenses and regulations involved in garment distribution that are generated via the process of importing materials or finished products from other countries. They are highly variable and have a large impact on final production decisions.

Production planners negotiate fabric and garment costs, order prototypes, assign production contracts, inspect factories, oversee quality, and schedule production. Their goal is to make a garment at the level of quality the customer expects at the lowest possible cost.

The basic functions of the company and the extent of its business plan must be structured in a way that is consistent with the firm's customer expectations and the company's goals. In an agile environment, apparel product development requires unique synergies among firms, based on shared, cross-functional decision making that results in a seamless virtual supply chain. Although variations in the structure and process are inevitable, all the areas outlined here must be considered and all individuals responsible for these functions must work as a team to make the best possible decisions. Whatever decisions are made, all participants bear equal responsibility for both successes and failures.

The Apparel Product Development Process

In chapter 1 we defined product development as the strategic, creative, technical, production, and distribution planning of goods that have a perceived value for a well-defined user group and are designed to reach the marketplace when that group is ready to buy. Apparel product development includes all of the processes needed to take a garment from design inception to delivery to the final customer. Individuals who work within any of the functions described above understand that the contributions they make provide the most benefit when they are collaborative.

Stages of Product Development

The stages of product development have evolved as the apparel business has changed and become increasingly more competitive. The process varies depending on whether the line is to be sold at wholesale or is developed as a private label to be sold within a company's own retail channels. Although the stages can be reconfigured in numerous ways with different participants, the

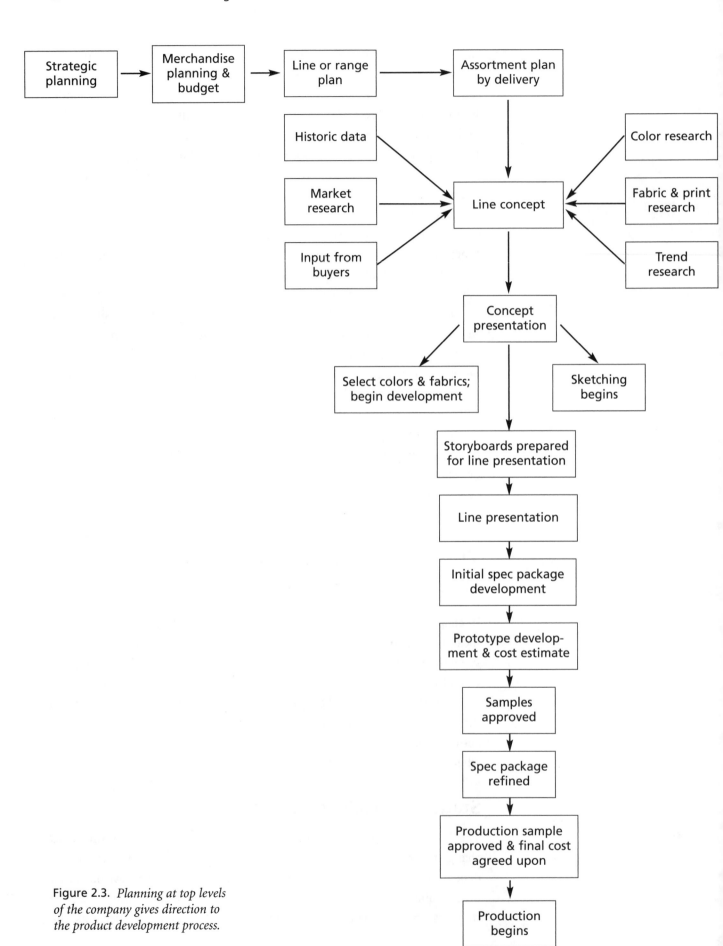

Figure 2.3. *Planning at top levels of the company gives direction to the product development process.*

elements tend to be consistent. At some point, each of the functions must occur in order for the product to be produced (Figure 2.3).

Line Concept

The design process begins with a **line concept**, which includes the mood, theme, and key elements that contribute to the identity of the line. The line concept is the result of trend research. The company's trend forecasting team collects information on concepts and styles from a variety of resources and interprets these forecasts for their specific target market. The trend forecast helps merchandisers and designers make decisions as to which styles should be carried over from past seasons and which new ideas should be developed. This edited forecast provides the focus for the rest of the product development process.

Line Development

The **line development** stage begins as the design team translates the line concepts into groups of product to be delivered throughout the selling season. Once the group concept is determined, color and fabric decisions can be made and the actual silhouette design can begin. The design team works closely with merchandisers to ensure that they are working within the parameters of the assortment plan. Design may sketch 25 to 50 percent more garments than the plan requires, and then work with merchandisers to review and edit the line before first samples are made. Styles are reviewed to determine whether they can be produced within targeted price points and on schedule, as well as for design aesthetics. Those styles that appear to be feasible are made into samples. The **prototype** sample is the first garment made from a pattern. It provides product developers with preliminary cost estimates. Prototype samples are contracted or constructed so that the feasibility of the design can be further evaluated and the styling and fit of the product can be assessed on a fit model.

Line Presentation

The **line presentation** stage consists of showing the proposed line of products to the sourcing managers and technical design staff, for selection of styles to include in the season's product line. Some firms include the sales and marketing team in this presentation. The sourcing managers will be responsible for contracting and securing the materials used in construction of the selected product styles and for contracting the actual production of the garments. The technical designers will translate each design into a specification package that details the required fit and construction expectations.

Once the line is adopted, color matching and textile and garment testing can proceed. The pattern is graded into a full range of sizes and a more detailed cost analysis is completed. Once the prototype is fully approved, a **production sample** is made. It should reflect how the product will look as it comes off a production line. Evaluation of the production sample is the final stage before the product goes into full production.

Decisions Regarding Product Mix

Product developers must understand how the product they produce will be categorized when it is imported or exported, when retail buyers consider it, and when the final consumer shops for it.

NAICS

Until recently, the government classified apparel firms in the United States as textile producers, apparel manufacturers, or retailers. The Standard Industrial Classification (SIC) code system previously used by the government and businesses to identify the primary activity of firms, had a process orientation according to K. G. Dickerson (Dickerson 1999, 288–291). Today, firms are crossing those traditional boundaries. Some firms produce a full range of products from fiber to finished goods. For example, there has been significant growth in acceptance of knit products that are developed differently from cut, make, and trim (CMT) woven products. The makers of men's wear or women's wear may now produce unisex products, adding to the confusion in classification. Also, some categories of apparel, such as active sportswear, are relatively new. Changes in the methods of doing business, along with the need for providing compatibility in record keeping with global partners, have precipitated a new method of classifying firms by the type of product they produce. The **North American Industry Classification System (NAICS)** was introduced in 1997 and revised in 2002 to reflect current industry activities. (Refer to Figure 2.4 for NAICS Codes for classification categories within the textile and apparel manufacturing business.)

Product Categories

The category of product a company produces strongly influences the decision-making process. Throughout the industry, recognized product classifications are used to identify the type of company. The majority of companies in the industry use these identifiers for their product lines. Some firms cross over and encompass several categories, while others specialize and produce only those types of product they know best. For example, dress manufacturers may concentrate on daytime wear or eveningwear.

A product category is typically defined by the use for which the product is intended. Examples include bridal wear, coordinated sportswear, activewear, and coats. Active sportswear, lingerie, and plus sizes are examples of categories that are considered ripe for further growth (Figure 2.5a–b). Both J. C. Penney and Kohl's announced new launches of private label lingerie lines in 2006. Currently recognized categories of women's wear are summarized in Table 2.1.

The men's wear industry is structured a bit differently. For example, men's suits can be found at price point categories ranging from completely custom-tailored suits in the thousands of dollars to tailored pants and jackets sold as separate pieces at mass retailers for less than $100 each. The categories have

Figure 2.4. *NAICS Codes for Textile and Apparel Manufacturing.*

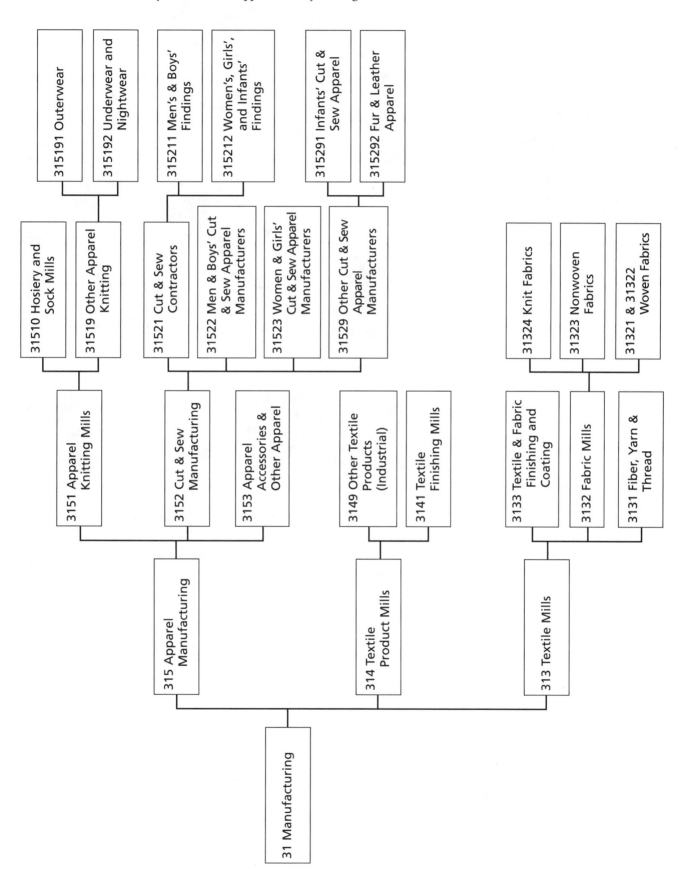

Figure 2.5a–b. *Plus sizes and activewear are two categories that analysts have projected as having potential for growth.*

evolved over the past century, as clothing needs, economic conditions, and lifestyles have changed. Current men's wear categories are summarized in Table 2.2.

The children's market had for many years moved away from adapting adult styles to creating its own fashions. However, more recent trends indicate that many manufacturers of adult clothing are again producing adult styles for children. For example, Ralph Lauren produces boy's products. Stores such as Gap and The Limited, with its Limited, Too stores, are producing lines that resemble their adult products (Figure 2.6). Because of these recent trends, the children's wear classifications tend to parallel those in the adult markets. The exception to this would be the infant's layette product area, which is a category unto itself. Children's wear categories are summarized in Table 2.3.

Table 2.1 WOMEN'S WEAR CATEGORIES

CLASSIFICATION	DESCRIPTORS
Sportswear: separates and coordinates	Separates are designed to mix and match. Coordinates are designed to be merchandised as outfits or multiples.
Knitwear and sweaters	Because of requirements of fabrication, knit products form their own category. Usually sold at retail within the sportswear category.
Active sportswear	Evolved into separate category with many specializations dedicated to specific sports. Frequently produced for both men and women. Most are separates—pants, tops, jackets. Swimwear, previously seasonal, is now sold year-round.
Coats and suits	A specialized category due to unique construction requirements. Major producers may produce men's and women's tailored goods.
Dresses	Popularity ebbs and flows with fashion trends. Tends to be more important in spring/summer than fall/winter.
Eveningwear	Includes bridal, bridesmaids, after-five and prom specializations.
Intimate apparel	Includes lingerie, foundations, robes.
Uniforms	Job and career apparel other than office attire. Often defined by job function.
Accessories	Hosiery, handbags, small leather goods, gloves, hats/millinery, jewelry.

Size Range

Typically, one of the first decisions in planning the merchandise mix of products to be offered by the company will be the size range for the classification of merchandise to be produced. For example, when differentiating between body types in women's wear, a size range is selected from misses, juniors, petites, and women's categories. Within the misses' size range there are additional considerations that relate to styling. For example, the missy category is considered more conservative in its styling than contemporary misses, which is considered more fashion-forward. Firms that produce women's wear in the misses size range may or may not produce related categories such as women's for the larger woman, petites for the smaller-stature woman 5 feet 4 inches and under, and talls for the woman over 5 feet 7inches. A full discussion of the size ranges offered in today's marketplace, including those for men and children, is included in chapter 11.

Table 2.2 MEN'S WEAR CATEGORIES

CLASSIFICATION	DESCRIPTORS
Tailored clothing	Suits, coats, sport coats, slacks. A few giant companies control most of this category. Declining in importance with changing fashion trends.
Casual wear (casual Friday)	Evolved from dressing down in business. Casual suits, contrasting coat and trousers. Sweaters, knit shirts, pants. Usually sold at retail within the sportswear category.
Men's furnishings	A catchall category that includes shirts, neckwear, underwear, socks, pajamas, scarves, gloves, hats. Includes many licensed products with designer names or logos.
Active sportswear	Growing category with many specialized products dedicated to specific sports.
Outerwear	Casual jackets, ski jackets, parkas. Moving to sportswear look with use of color and new fabrics. Often from producers of active sportswear and rainwear.
Work clothes	Uniforms, often for specific occupations. Category has expanded with popularity of jeans.
Rainwear and coats	Tailored outerwear. Category is shrinking as casual outerwear category expands.

Price Range

The next decision is establishing a price range or price point for the category. Most firms define their product type by selecting the price point or range that their intended target customer would be willing to pay for products they produce. Some companies produce product at a single price point; others produce more than one and vary the materials and construction techniques they use in order to distinguish between the price points. There is an implied relationship between cost and quality that may or may not be true; however, customers tend to have higher expectations for more expensive products (Kadolph 1998). Many manufacturers produce similar product types for several price point categories. They use different brand identification to differentiate the products. Women's wear can be found in the following price categories: couture; designer ready-to-wear, known as prêt-à-porter in France; contemporary designer; bridge; better; moderate; fast fashion or low-end contemporary; junior/tween; and mass market (formerly discount or budget). (Refer to Table 2.4 for price point categories in women's wear.) The lower-end mass market price classification makes up over half of the apparel merchandise sold in the United States,

Figure 2.6. *Stores such as J. Crew have launched children's lines, capitalizing on the popularity of their brands for adults.*

while the bridge, contemporary designer, and designer ready-to-wear price categories represent a relatively small proportion of total U.S. sales (Glock and Kunz 2005, 6). Private brand merchandise may be found in all price point categories from bridge to mass market. These products may be priced lower than the same item in that category with a wholesale label.

Season

Another critical consideration at the planning stage is the season for which the product is intended. The **season** identifies the time of the year the products will be worn or used. Season influences fabric selections, colors, and styles, reflecting the weather conditions and consumer needs for that time of year. The season identity helps to establish the delivery dates that will be required for the finished product.

Designer **ready-to-wear (prêt-à-porter)** firms show their collections during fashion weeks in New York, Paris, Milan, and London. These shows are attended primarily by the press and buyers from major designer and specialty stores, and they are covered extensively by papers such as *Women's Wear Daily* and the *New York Times* and online at sites such as www.style.com. Fashion weeks also take place in Tokyo, Barcelona, and São Paulo. Though the designers who show at these secondary markets have less name recognition, they

Table 2.3 CHILDREN'S WEAR CATEGORIES

CLASSIFICATION	DESCRIPTORS
Infant wear	Layettes including shirts, onesies, gowns. Stretch coveralls, diaper pants. Outerwear, snowsuits. Knit sweaters, booties, hats.
Toddler wear	Boy and girl sets. Shorts, pants, skirts, overalls, shirts.
Sportswear	Pants, shorts, skirts, overalls. Blouses, shirts. Jackets, sweaters. Swimwear.
Dresses	Tailored and party dresses. Jumper and blouse sets.
Outerwear	Coats, jackets, parkas, snowsuits.
Lingerie and sleepwear	Robes, pajamas, nightgowns. Slips, undershirts, panties. Hosiery.

Table 2.4 DESCRIPTION OF PRICE POINT CATEGORIES FROM MOST TO LEAST EXPENSIVE

PRICE POINT	DESCRIPTION	EXAMPLES
Couture	Made to order; consumer goes to the designer's salon to be fitted for the garment.	Chanel Couture, Dior Couture, Christian LaCroix Couture
Designer	Designer brands available off the rack in a range of sizes.	Prada, Dolce & Gabbana, Donna Karan, Ralph Lauren, Karl Lagerfeld for Chanel, Armani, Chado Ralph Rucci
Contemporary designer	A price point similar to that of bridge or a bit higher; this category includes many new designers who target a younger, fashion-savvy customer	Tracy Reese, Nanette Lepore, Catherine Malandrino, Marc by Marc Jacobs
Bridge	A price point between better and designer, with a focus on career wear and weekend wear.	Dana Buchman, Ellen Tracy, Anne Klein, Lafayette 148, Elie Tahari
Better	Products with wide market appeal, often the highest price point available in department stores.	CK Calvin Klein, Liz Claiborne, Sigrid Olson, Jones New York, Lauren
Moderate	Large, price-conscious market. Styling appeals to more mature customers.	Chaus, Sag Harbor, Norton McNaughton, Villager, J.H. Collectibles
Low-end contemporary/ fast fashion	A relatively new category that offers fast fashion at a moderate to better price point.	Zara, H & M, Kors by Michael Kors, BCBG Max Azria, T Tahari
Junior/tweens	Apparel with styling and fit geared to teenagers.	Rampage, Hot Topic, Aéropostale, American Eagle Outfitters, Old Navy, Pac Sun, Delia's
Mass merchant	A variety of brands that appeal to many different market segments, all at low affordable prices.	Metro 7, Jaclyn Smith, Isaac, Merona, George, Apt. 9

reflect fashion's growing global scope and offer fashion-forward boutiques a unique design perspective (Figure 2.7). Fall/winter lines are shown in February/March for delivery during late summer into fall; spring/summer lines are shown in September/October for delivery in February or March.

The fall/winter season is considered critical for most firms because the clothing sold for those seasons is typically more costly and difficult to produce, thus making the company's investment much higher. The spring/summer season is second in importance because, although the number of garments

Figure 2.7. *Gloria Coelho is a South American designer who shows in São Paulo, Brazil. The increasing visibility of fashion weeks in secondary markets reflects fashion's growing global scope.*

typically sold is quite high, clothing is usually of lighter-weight fabrics and simpler construction and therefore less expensive.

Haute couture refers to a small group of designers in Paris, France, who meet formal criteria set by the Chambre syndicale de la haute couture. Other nations, such as Italy, have similar criteria for their major high-fashion or couture designers. Couture garments are made from high-quality, expensive fabric and sewn with extreme attention to detail and finish, often using time-consuming hand-executed techniques. They are made to order for a specific customer. Couture collections are shown closer to the actual selling season—in January for spring/summer and in July for fall/winter—giving them added fashion mystique. The couture is an incubator for new ideas, fabrics,

Figure 2.8a–b. *Expensive designer collections don't sell in great numbers, but the name recognition they generate helps to sell bags, perfumes, and secondary lines.*

and silhouettes. Not all styles in a couture show are necessarily sold to customers, but the cachet of couture shows helps to sell perfume, bags, and secondary lines (Figure 2.8).

Product developers at lower price points may not have the resources to mount a show during the major market weeks. Retail buyers typically view these lines in the showroom or at regional markets where they can work with a sales rep to determine the assortment that is right for them. Showrooms generally begin to sell the line after fashion week and then the collection will travel to regional markets. Although the most publicized fashion weeks occur only twice a year, markets for buyers occur many times throughout the year, dependent on product category. Markets are held in a variety of locations from Chicago to Singapore, so that buyers can commit to a season as it unfolds, gauging everything from early selling, to current events and the weather.

Many women's wear firms now offer four to six seasonal collections a year, with several deliveries available within each seasonal collection. Decisions to increase the number of seasons reflect changing consumer lifestyles and buying patterns, as well as the need to spread out production on the basis of actual orders rather than projections. When there are more than two seasons, the typical offerings are fall, winter, spring, and summer. If fall and winter are combined, a firm might produce a separate holiday collection to be sold in the summer for late fall delivery. Or it might produce a resort collection to be sold right after the holidays for those customers who winter in warmer climates. Product developers that cater to the southern states often prefer to combine spring and summer and then produce an early fall or transitional fall collection, which contains deeper fall colors but lighter-weight fabrics for warm fall weather. Each of these additional seasonal offerings is designed to help manufacturers spread out their production schedule demands and keep their facilities active during slower seasons, but they are marketed under the premise that they keep the merchandise fresh in the stores throughout the year.

Firms such as Liz Claiborne have moved toward a continuous calendar for some of their product categories. Customers are given the option of new deliveries every 4 to 6 weeks, with different assortments of product available for each delivery. This type of calendar provides a more continuous flow of goods into the retail environment and also allows more flexibility for scheduling production capacity because the merchandise is not all needed at a few peak periods of the year. The industry is seeing an increasing trend toward this continuous flow of product into the market, which is having a big impact on the product development cycle.

The Product Development Cycle

All product decisions related to garment classification, size, price point, and season combine to provide a framework for the strategic plan and to facilitate the selection of the appropriate product designs for the entire production and delivery process. The length of time devoted to product development processes varies by firm and type of product. Original designs take the longest amount of time to produce. Companies that produce **knockoffs**, copies, or adaptations of products already on the market are able to shorten the amount of time needed to complete the product development process. Knockoffs may be adapted from a style previously produced by the firm, or they may be copied or adapted from another firm's design. When a product developer bases a new style on the silhouette of a style it created in a past season, they often refer to the style number of the past season silhouette as an **'as number'** to alert the technical design team that patterns, specs, and standards for a similar garment already exist.

The traditional timetable for completion of a product development cycle is 4 to 6 months. If production is sourced offshore or materials come from locales far from the production site, the lead time might be longer. Some product developers are under additional pressure to have seasonal lines ready to present to the press at fashion week. All seasonal lines must be ready to show buyers during market weeks. In this regard, private brand product developers have an advantage since their buyers are internal. The development of products destined for retail sale during the fall season usually begins in January. Products from two or more delivery dates, at different stages in the product development cycle, are generally worked on simultaneously. The implementation of newer methods of communication and computer product development technologies continues to shorten the product development calendar.

Delivery dates to the retailer are the most significant points on the apparel product development calendar. The product development team works backward from the delivery dates to establish the time required for distribution, production, sourcing, production samples, production patterns, selling, design samples, design, and trend analysis for each product line. (Refer to Table 2.5 for an example of a traditional five-season product development timeline.)

Branding

Competition for consumer dollars is fierce. Brands are a tool that product developers and retailers use to drive repeat business. A **brand** is a distinctive name or logo used to identify products or services in a way that is meant to influence consumer behavior. **Branding** is the process of planning the direction, inspiration, and energy that a brand represents in a way that immediately implies value to the customer.

Today's brands are developed to make an emotional connection with the consumer. The branding process attempts to create a positive **brand image**— a consumer's set of assumptions and feelings about products and/or services provided under the brand name. This can be achieved through packaging, advertising, store environment, promotion, customer service, word of mouth, or association with a lifestyle, celebrity, or popular cause or event (Figure 2.9). A misstep in living up to any of the attributes associated with a brand's image can cause long-term damage. Walter Landor, a pioneer of the use of branding as a strategic business tool, defines a brand as a promise that authenticates a product or service's pledge of satisfaction and quality (www.landor.com).

Building Brand Image

Building a brand's image is more challenging than ever before. Traditional forms of advertising are less effective as consumers look to the Internet rather than newspapers and magazines for their news and fashion direction. The most successful brands of the 2000s have evolved into lifestyle brands. **Lifestyle brands** go beyond their origins in a single product category to include additional apparel and accessory categories, perfumes, cosmetics, or home goods such as bed linens. In early 2007 Ralph Lauren announced that he would offer his services as a lifestyle brand consultant. Branding is critical for all types of product developers. Many consumers don't discern the differences between

Table 2.5 PRODUCT DEVELOPMENT SCHEDULE: WOMEN'S MARKET FOR FIVE SEASONS

JAN	FEB	MAR	APRIL	MAY	JUNE	JULY	AUG	SEPT	OCT	NOV	DEC
Show summer	Finalize summer	Manufacture and ship summer	Manufacture and ship summer						Trend summer	Style summer	Style summer
Style fall	Show fall	Finalize fall	Manufacture and ship fall	Manufacture and ship fall						Trend fall	Style fall
Style fall II/winter	Style fall II/winter	Show fall II/winter	Finalize fall II/winter	Manufacture and ship fall II/winter	Manufacture and ship fall II/winter						Trend fall II/winter
				Trend holiday/resort	Style holiday/resort	Style holiday/resort	Show holiday/resort	Finalize manufacture holiday/resort	Manufacture and ship holiday/resort		
Manufacture and ship spring						Trend spring	Style spring	Style spring	Show spring	Finalize spring	Manufacture and ship spring
		Europe prêt-à-porter fall							Europe prêt-à-porter spring		

Figure 2.9. *Celebrities such as Hilary Duff have capitalized on opportunities to lend their name to apparel brands.*

wholesale, licensed, and private brand products as long as the brand represents the quality level and styling aesthetic that appeal to them. To resonate with the consumer, a brand must reflect that consumer's overall image and lifestyle preferences.

Leveraging Brand Equity

Brands need to stay relevant in a dynamic market. It is the consumer's image of a brand that creates **brand equity** for its owners, making the brand a corporate asset (www.landor.com). New product categories, recent mergers and acquisitions, and changing distribution scenarios affect the market constantly. Since it is very difficult and costly to launch a new brand from scratch, businesses look for creative ways to leverage existing brand equity in order to maximize revenue streams.

Brand extensions refer to the practice of expanding a brand's reach. This can be achieved by expanding a brand's assortment—launching a women's brand into men's wear or children's wear or vice versa. Another variation of a brand extension is to launch a new product category or service under an existing brand label. Designers such as Ralph Lauren, Calvin Klein, and Donna Karan have been very successful in extending their labels into product categories such as home furnishings, jewelry, and shoes, to name a few. In many cases launching a brand into a new category is achieved through licensing with a product developer that has expertise in the category.

Brand equity can also be leveraged by launching the brand across price points. For years wholesale brands struggled with how to grow their brand while protecting their image. Department stores threatened that if the brand was distributed in discount or mass market chain stores, it would no longer have cachet at the department store level, but this practice precipitated numerous legal battles. Today the marketplace accepts that high-profile brands offer differentiated lines at a variety of price points. For example, the Web site www.levi.com offers links to Levi Signature Jeans that are sold in Target, ShopKo, Kmart, and Wal-mart, as well as moderate and better labels including Levi's Redwire, Levi's red, Levi's {Capital E}, and Levi's eco that are sold in stores such as Kohl's, Sears, J. C. Penney, Macy's, and Nordstom.

Designer brands have also found it difficult to survive on the profits from their designer lines alone. They have varied their designer price point offerings and launched labels at the bridge and better price points to maximize their brand equity. Ralph Lauren's Web site lists the following labels: Collection, Black Label, Blue Label, Lauren, Polo Jeans Co., Pink Pony, Ralph Lauren Golf, and RLX.

In other scenarios, wholesale brands have experienced market shrinkage from the growth of private labels. Some have closed their doors and sold their brand equity to megabrand conglomerates. J. H. Collectibles sold its brand name to Liz Claiborne in 1997. Liz Claiborne relaunched it as a moderate label. Others have survived by entering into licensing arrangements with retailers and becoming exclusive brands, distributed only through that retailer. Kohl's has exclusive brand licenses with Candie's and Daisy Fuentes, while Target has exclusive agreements with Isaac Mizrahi and Liz Lange, to name a few.

In a global market, brands must protect their equity internationally. Since marketing and distributing a brand in a global market is fraught with challenges, especially counterfeiting, brand owners often use licensing arrangements to protect their brand while capitalizing on the brand's value in a foreign market. Recently brands such as Polo and Sears Holdings have bought out their international distributors in Canada once those businesses proved to be lucrative.

Brand Portfolios

Forward-thinking apparel manufacturers are focused on brand expansion and management. The management of multiple brands by a single company is referred to as a company's **brand portfolio**. Product developers are hard-

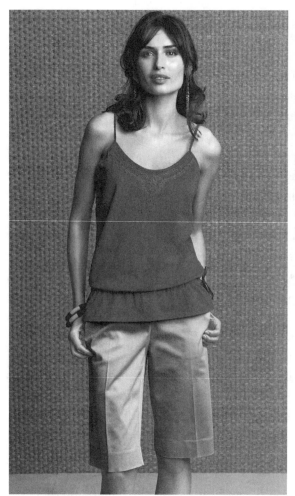

Figure 2.10a–d. *Liz Claiborne, Inc., manages a large portfolio of brands that includes* (clockwise from top left) *Axcess, an exclusive brand for Kohl's; Enyce; Juicy; and Bora Bora for men and women.*

pressed to increase volume by brand, but they can build market share by expanding brand portfolios and catering to niche lifestyles. Some brand portfolios are transparent or obvious to the final consumer; others are anonymous. Table 2.6 lists the brand portfolio of Liz Claiborne. Figure 2.10a–d illustrates just a few of those brands. Most consumers are unaware that one firm owns and manages all of those brand names. The Gap is more transparent; most consumers recognize that the company's divisions include Gap (GapBody, GapMaternity, GapKids, babyGap), Old Navy, and Banana Republic, each

Table 2.6 LIZ CLAIBORNE INC. BRAND PORTFOLIO

CLASSIC	MODERN	RELAXED	COSMETICS
Dana Buchman	Axcess	J. H. Collectibles	Bora Bora
Ellen Tracy	C&C California	Sigrid Olsen	Curve
Emma James	Claiborne		LIZ
First Issue	Concepts by Claiborne	**DENIM/STREETWEAR**	Mambo
Kate Spade	Intuitions	DKNY Jeans/DKNY Active	Realities
Liz Claiborne	Juicy Couture	Enyce	Soul
Villager	Kenzie	Lucky Brand Jeans	Spark
YZZA	Kenziegirl	Stamp 10	
	Laundry by Shelli Segal	Tint	**JEWELRY**
	Mac & Jac		Kenneth Cole New York
	Mexx	**ACTIVE**	Monet
	Tapemeasure	Liz Golf	Monet 2
		Prana	Reaction Kenneth Cole
			Trifari

Source: Liz Claiborne Inc., www.lizclaiborneinc.com/ourbrands (accessed February 11, 2007).

with their own set of in-store brands. Each store within the Gap portfolio is directed to a specific consumer segment or lifestyle.

A brand is more than product, which is seasonal and becomes outdated. It is bigger than a company, which may change ownership. A brand has a life beyond its founder or manager. A brand represents a reputation. It is a promise that is publicly conveyed to customers by the sum total of the brand name, the product, the advertising and promotion, the channels it is distributed through, and the service associated with the entire experience (Underhill 1999). Consistency and continuous improvement are imperative to a brand's continued success.

Summary

A firm that produces apparel is built on an organizational structure that includes marketing, merchandising, production, finance, and operations functions. In today's marketplace, success of a business depends on developing and following a strategic plan that provides focus for the firm. Incorporation of Quick Response methods and an understanding of the components within the apparel product development process make a company more competitive.

Each company must decide which classifications of products it will produce. It must also determine which categories of products it will sell and distribute, the size range of products it will produce, the intended price range(s) of the products, and the schedule for distribution of those products. Timing of delivery to the customer is the pivotal point in the product development process. The seasonal calendar for marketing products drives the entire business schedule.

Much of current business in the apparel industry is based on the development of branded products. Brand development, including private label and licensed goods, is central to distinguishing one product from another. Therefore, brand management decisions have become a major component of the strategic business planning process.

Key Terms

as number	line or range plan
assortment plan	line presentation
brand	marketing
brand equity	merchandise calendar
brand extensions	merchandise plan or budget
brand image	merchandising
brand portfolio	NAICS (North American Industry Classification System)
branding	
budgets	operations
business plan	production
creative planning	production planning
finance	production sample
haute couture	prototype
knockoffs	ready-to-wear (prêt-à-porter)
lifestyle brands	season
line concept	strategic plan
line development	technical planning

Discussion Questions

1. Find an article in WWD that discusses a company's strategic plan and discuss the key strategies identified.

2. Identify your favorite brands of garments. Are they wholesale brands, private labels, store brands, or licensed brands?

3. Look up the brand portfolio of several multibrand conglomerates. How does the brand portfolio strategy affect market penetration?

Activities

1. Go to the Web and find a brand that offers its total collection online. Analyze a single group as to the number of bottoms (pants and/or skirts) to tops (tops, sweaters, shirts, blouses, jackets). Further analyze the group as to the items that are new vs. ongoing, the style assortment, etc.

2. In small groups, begin the semester project, making the pre-production business decisions for a fictitious apparel company. Develop a business plan for this company by determining the following:

   a. Select specific men's, women's, or children's product categories that will be produced.

   b. Select the price point categories that will be followed.

   c. Select the size range(s) that will be produced.

   d. Develop a timeline for one seasonal line for this business, beginning with the delivery of the product line to stores and working backward to establish the time allotment for each of the functions identified in this chapter.

References

Dickerson, K. G. 1999. *Textiles and apparel in the global economy.* 3d ed. Upper Saddle River, NJ: Prentice-Hall.

Glock, R. E., and G. I. Kunz. 2005. *Apparel manufacturing: Sewn product analysis.* 4th ed. Upper Saddle River, NJ: Prentice-Hall.

Kadolph, S. J. 1998. *Quality assurance for textiles and apparel.* New York: Fairchild.

Kunz, G. I. 2005. *Merchandising: Theory, principles, and practice.* 2d ed. New York: Fairchild.

Kurt Salmon Associates. 2003. Maximizing potential: Seven habits of highly effective product development. www.kurtsalmon.com/content/main/body/industries/consumer_products>.

Liz Claiborne Inc. www.lizclaiborneinc.com (accessed September 22, 2006).

NAICS Codes and Titles. 2002. U.S. Census. www.census.gov/epcd/naics02/ (accessed July 11, 2004).

Underhill, R. W. 1999. Who's minding the brand? *Arthur Anderson Retailing Issues Letter* 11 no. 4 (July).

www.landor.com/?do=cBranding.getLexicon&g=1200

CHAPTER 3

CONSUMER MARKETS

"What we sell is the ability for a 43-year-old accountant to dress in black leather, ride through small towns and have people be afraid of him."
—Harley Davidson Executive quoted in *Results-Based Leadership*

OBJECTIVES

- To understand the evolution of markets from a production focus to a marketing focus to a consumer focus

- To discuss the data sources used to segment the market-place

- To understand the tools available for researching target markets

- To examine how product developers define their target markets

- To examine how marketers communicate with their target market

- To recognize current consumer trends in the United States and the global marketplace

---

The relationship between the consumer and the producer is central to product development. Relying solely on traditional demographic and psychographic classifications of customers is not enough in today's complex and competitive marketplace. Terrorist threats, the instability of a global economy, the impact of natural disasters and global health scares, concerns about privacy, and a general mistrust of civic, business, and media institutions have given rise to a consumer who is more pragmatic and less spontaneous than in the recent past. Never before have consumers been as finicky as they are today—changing loyalties to a brand, retailer, or fashion look in a flash (Casabona 2006, 18). Retailers and product developers must carve out a unique niche for themselves with distinctive products and services. They must continually test new products and store concepts utilizing dynamic management and creative teams to appeal to uncompromising consumers who expect them to produce and distribute exactly what they want at an affordable price. Intimate knowledge of the consumer is an essential component of this process.

Figure 3.1. *Consumers gather fashion information from Internet sources such as blogs. Fashion blogs may be more influential than advertisements among some market groups.*

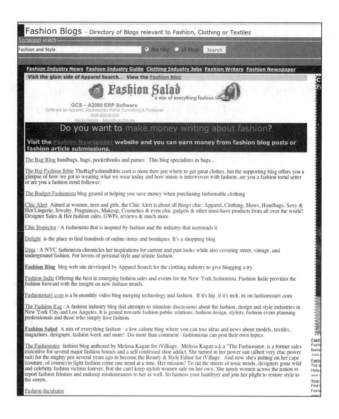

The marketplace is increasingly diversified, serving micromarkets of audiences and price points. Product developers are attempting to win customers' loyalty by giving the customer an emotional connection with their products. To do this, product developers must employ a multibrand, multichannel strategy to capture consumers wherever and whenever they shop. Developers must understand the shifts and nuances in buying patterns. Today's brands must be clearly edited and defined, resulting in exciting product with a definitive point of view.

Innovation, creativity, and service will increasingly drive the profitability of product development. Ultimately, if consumers don't feel special, they will find products other than apparel on which to spend their disposable income.

The Consumer-Producer Relationship

During the Industrial Revolution, product output was limited, and the goal of most companies was to increase production in order to keep up with demand. This time period was known as the **production era**. As manufacturers' ability to produce products in sufficient quantities to meet demand grew, the production era evolved into the sales era.

In the **sales era**, businesses manufactured and sold products without first determining consumers' wants and needs. It was up to the sales force and the advertising department to convince consumers that they needed the products that had been manufactured.

Figure 3.2. *Young people assume responsibility for their own apparel purchases at an earlier age; young men are more involved in shopping for themselves.*

The sales era was followed by the **marketing era**. During the marketing era, companies began to research consumer preferences and appeal to those preferences through advertising. Input gathered from consumers was used to enable companies to make decisions on design, price, distribution channels, and promotions. Competition to produce product grew, and supply began to exceed demand.

A wave of business mergers and acquisitions began in the late 1970s and escalated in the 2000s, creating conglomerates with the capacity to create large marketing and product research and development departments. Successful marketers learned to create demand for their product by saturating the media with advertising. The strategy worked. Calvin Klein created media frenzies (and increased sales) with his controversial advertising campaigns. Manufacturers believed that with innovative promotional campaigns they could drive sales and increase market share.

Today fashion firms continue to spend large amounts of money on advertising in order to create consumer demand; however, sales promotion can win acceptance for a fashion only to an extent. If the consumer does not want a product, no amount of advertising can change that (Frings 2002, 34). Increasingly, consumers have become immune to heavy-handed promotional campaigns. They are skeptical of advertisements and the claims made in them. Thanks to TiVo, and streaming personalized content on the Web, many groups of customers have become immune to traditional advertising. They research their purchases on the Internet and seek out the opinions of other consumers with similar taste levels to their own, which creates a "buzz" around products that are considered highly desirable (Figure 3.1).

Customers are more confident and more savvy: they consider value, function, versatility, comfort, and quality, along with fashion trends. The runways in Paris, London, Milan, and New York have increasingly less impact on the average customer's purchasing decisions. Women, traditionally the primary

Figure 3.3. *Chico's appeals to women in the 40 to 60 age range, which has been identified as an underserved market niche.*

shoppers in most family units, often balance careers with family duties. Shopping is just one more demand on their time; for many women it is no longer considered a pleasurable leisure activity. Young people assume responsibility for their own purchasing decisions at an earlier age. Men are more involved in shopping for themselves than ever before (Figure 3.2).

Merchandise at all price points is available through discount venues, giving consumers the upper hand. Everyone knows how to get the lowest price, but in certain circumstances people may be willing to pay more for better quality or more personal service or to secure the newest fashion item. The challenge to product developers and retailers is to create products and environments for which consumers are willing to pay full price.

Time-constrained consumers seek well-edited assortments that fit their lifestyles and budgets. Too many choices can be confusing. Consumers expect to find what they want with minimal time and energy, but they don't want to look like cookie-cutter clones. This is the paradox of today's marketplace. Additionally, consumers seek guaranteed satisfaction both at the point of purchase and throughout the life of the product, and they know how to use their economic clout to express their demands.

Product developers must find ways to gather information regarding consumer preferences and translate that information into product. Kurt Salmon Associates suggests that product developers get to know and respond to customers through what they call **consumer intimacy**. To develop consumer intimacy, a product developer must

- develop an individual knowledge of its consumers

- implement well-honed processes from concept to delivery

- create an environment in which consumers come first and success is measured by consumer response

- create an organizational structure in which innovation and imagination are rewarded (Kurt Salmon Associates 1998)

We are entering a **consumer era** in which producers are able to provide products tailored to consumer preferences. As consumers invest their time in teaching a particular company about their preferences, they form a partnership that ultimately provides that company with a competitive advantage. They create a synergy between the demand chain and the supply chain. The better the company becomes at providing exactly what the consumer wants, the more difficult it will be for a competitor to entice the consumer away (Pine, Peppers, and Rogers 2000, 53–74).

Consumer Analysis and Market Segmentation

If the central focus of marketing is the consumer, then it is necessary to find out as much about consumers as possible. Today's retailers and product developers are information-driven. The capture and use of consumer data will be the competitive weapon of the future, enabling businesses to focus on their core customers. Manufacturers and retailers expend a great deal of effort identifying consumers who have the potential to be regular customers. A **target market** is a well-defined customer group to which a business wants to sell.

The trend in marketing apparel is to break down markets into increasingly smaller, well-defined niche markets through **market segmentation** or **micro-marketing**. A **niche market** aims to appeal to a narrowly focused target customer. In marketing, the 80/20 principle refers to the fact that 20 percent of customers typically account for 80 percent of sales for a product. Niche markets may be defined along the lines of age, income, ethnicity, or lifestyle. Recently analysts have identified the following under-served niche markets:

- Women in the 40- to 60-year-old age range

- Fashionable plus-size clothing for women and teens

- Petite, petite-plus, and plus-tall sizes (Figure 3.3)

Figure 3.4a–b. *A brand's image is developed to appeal to the age and lifestyle of its core customer, as illustrated by these designs from American Eagle and Nautica.*

Market segmentation is made possible by sophisticated methods of collecting and analyzing consumer data. Data are typically classified as demographic, psychographic, or cohort.

Demographics

In order to reach a target market effectively, companies must learn all they can about their preferred customers. Companies find great value in demographic information. **Demographics** are statistics about a given population with respect to age, gender, marital status, family size, income, spending habits, occupation, education, religion, ethnicity, and region. The *Census of Population* is a federal government publication that presents a broad range of demographic data. These data can be broken down by zip code to enable companies to distribute and sort their products according to the demographics of particular geographic markets.

• *Age.* Many apparel products are age-specific. Customers at different ages have different criteria in relation to styling, price, fit, care, and performance. A product that appeals to a college-age student may not appeal to her mother and most certainly will not appeal to her grandmother. Most product developers define an age range for their target market before they begin to develop a product. Their trend research should focus on the lifestyles and preferences of their targeted market. When companies are planning growth strategies, they must be aware of how population projections by age will influence the goals they set (Figure 3.4a–b).

- *Gender.* Spending habits and apparel preferences also vary by gender. Men's shopping preferences and priorities are different from those of women. For example, women tend to buy more clothes than men, but men may spend more on individual items, especially business suits. Men whose wives work outside of the home tend to shop more for their own clothing.

- *Marital Status.* Single consumers tend to have a higher interest in fashion and more opportunities to experiment with fashion than married consumers. Married consumers must balance the needs and resources of their families and tend to conform to a somewhat more conservative dress code. According to the 2000 census, for the first time in history, there are more people living alone in single-person households than there are traditional families (husband, wife, and one or more children). Single-person households account for 26 percent of households (Morrow 2003, 1–3).

- *Family Size.* The size of a family affects the resources available for apparel expenditures. Newlyweds tend to spend less on apparel than single individuals because their income is needed for home-related goods. As the family expands, clothing expenditures increase; maternity wear is required and apparel must be provided for each additional child. The age range of siblings within a family may influence the exposure of the family to particular fashion trends.

- *Income.* Consumer income level shapes the apparel preferences of each consumer. Disposable income determines what brands are affordable to a particular consumer and shapes the lifestyle of that consumer, resulting in the need for particular categories of clothes.

- *Spending Habits.* As age and income levels have changed, so have spending habits. The federal government monitors consumer spending through the **Consumer Price Index (CPI)**. The CPI measures the monthly and yearly changes in the prices of selected consumer items in different product categories. Tables 3.1 and 3.2 illustrate women's apparel spending by generation as defined by age and by income.

Table 3.1 SPENDING ON WOMEN'S AND GIRLS' APPAREL BY GENERATION

GENERATION	AGE	12 MO. ENDED OCT. 31, 2004 (billions)	10 MO. ENDED OCT. 31, 2005 (billions)	% CHANGE
Millennials	10–27	$39.8	$41.7	+4.8%
Gen X	28–38	$17.1	$16.4	-4.1%
Baby Boomer	39–59	$34.3	$34.5	+0.6%
Matures	60-plus	$8.6	$9.4	+9.3%
TOTAL	**10-PLUS**	**$99.7**	**$102.0**	**+2.3%**

Generation X was the only group to spend less on women's and girls' apparel in the 12 months ended in October. The biggest increase in rate of spending on apparel for females was made by the Matures.

Source: NPD Group 2005, 15

Table 3.2 SPENDING ON WOMEN'S APPAREL BY GROUP INCOME

ANNUAL HOUSEHOLD INCOME	SPENDING 12 MONTHS (000) ENDED MAY 2003	ENDED MAY 2004	% CHANGE
$200,000 and up	$3,378,810	$3,174,489	-6.0%
$150,000–$199,999	$3,982,702	$3,558,713	-10.6%
$100,000–$149,999	$14,552, 840	$14,363 760	-1.3%
$99,000–$75,000	$14, 460,920	$13,178,060	-8.9%
Subtotal ($75,000 and up)	*$38,375,272*	*$34,275,022*	*-10.7%*
$50,000–$74,999	$19,855,110	$17,225,690	-13.2%
$25,000–$49,999	$21,967,660	$18,477,050	-15.9%
$15,000–$24,999	$6,655,854	$6,127,936	-7.9%
Under $15,000	$6,397,071	$6,555,338	+2.5%
Subtotal (Under $15,000–$74,999)	*$54,875,695*	*$48,386,014*	*-11.8%*
TOTAL	**$93,250,967**	**$82,661,036**	**-11.4%**

Source: NPD Group 2005

- *Occupation.* A consumer's occupation, be it student or an employee, generally carries informal or formal dress expectations. Student dress may be influenced by peer expectations; occupational dress is generally influenced by employer expectations. Because much of the average consumer's time is spent either in school or on the job, apparel for these roles is often the primary thrust of apparel purchases.

- *Education.* The education of an individual consumer influences occupation, income, and lifestyle, all of which have an impact on apparel preferences. Those with more education tend to consider a broader range of styling options. Education may also affect the value consumers place on function and serviceability.

- *Religion.* As our worldview becomes more global, we are increasingly aware of how religious beliefs influence apparel selections. Consumers with strong religions beliefs, no matter the faith, tend to dress more conservatively than the general population. For example, Muslim women often wear head scarves and may wear veils to mask their faces, while Sikh men wear turbans. Orthodox Jewish

CASE STUDY 3.1 EFFECTS OF ETHNICITY

Ethnic diversity and cultural pluralism is a central characteristic of the American Experience and has had a profound effect on the American character. During the past 50 years, the ethnic mix of the United States as well as other countries around the world has become increasingly varied. Multiculturalism enriches our lives as we learn the traditions and tastes of other cultures.

Hispanics are the largest and fastest-growing minority group in the United States, with a population of 42.5 million; Hispanic women spent in excess of $6 billion on apparel in 2004 (Williamson 2005, 8). Their median age is 24, versus 34 overall in the United States. They may be more heavily swayed by advertisements, especially those that feature Hispanic spokespeople (Seckler 2003, 10). According to a WSL Strategic Retail survey, they like convenient locations where they can accomplish a lot in one trip, find good bargains, and receive good customer service. Their favorite retail venues are mass merchants and super centers (*Women's Wear Daily* 2004a). Sandra Diaz,

Director of Multicultural Marketing for Sears, states: "When Hispanics account for more than 15 percent of the population within a 10-mile radius of a Sears store, we designate that store as an Hispanic site, [where we] use bilingual signs, hire bilingual associates, and offer a larger selection of small sizes, suited to a healthy portion of Hispanic customers" (Seckler 2003).

The Asian market, 11.9 million in 2004, represents 4.4 percent of the U.S. population. This market is challenging to compartmentalize because its members come from many countries, encompassing numerous cultures and languages. However, it is very attractive due to its above-average birth rates, highly educated consumers, and high income levels. It is also very concentrated in California, Illinois, New York, Hawaii, and the Washington D.C. area around Maryland, Virginia, and West Virginia. These consumers have a keen fashion sense and are interested in high-quality clothing, usually in small sizes (*Women's Wear Daily* 2004b).

Figure 3.5. *Young girls in the Tween market are highly influenced by the opinions of their friends.*

women seek out modest apparel selections in a marketplace filled with overtly sexual clothing choices.

• *Ethnicity.* Ethnicity is an important component of demographic data. Increasingly, product developers, retailers, catalogers, and e-commerce sites are recognizing that different ethnic groups want different kinds of products and services and that they respond differently to marketing stimuli.

Sources of Demographic Data

Demographic census data are available by region—city, county, state, and zip code, providing snapshots of specific populations. Regional data allow product developers and retailers to assort the merchandise they offer to a specific regional population. Whenever a chain store enters a new market, its marketing department studies census data and works with the local chamber of commerce to define the demographics of the newly targeted region. Analysis of these data provides information that guides the stocking of new stores and directs editing of weekly advertising supplements. Stores with a national or international presence must print multiple versions of their advertising supplements to reflect how they have stocked their stores in response to consumer needs and preferences in a specific geographical area. Weather and allegiance to sports teams are examples of two factors that may influence the content of regional advertising supplements.

Claritas, Inc., is a marketing firm that specializes in providing demographic estimates for whatever areas its customers define. Claritas starts with U.S. census data and analyzes these data against data from local government, consumer databases, and the U.S. Postal Service to tease out the demographic data any client needs. Demographic data used in isolation have their limitations. First, used in isolation, these data send a stereotypical message, that people who are similar statistically make decisions and live their lives similarly. Second, the information is quickly dated. Census data are collected every ten years, but complete analysis of that data is generally not available for two years after collection, thereby dating the information before it is ever published. Overall, demographic data may be too broad to help companies identify opportunities and risks in small markets and specialized product categories.

Psychographics

Demographic data do not capture the activities, interests, and opinions that differentiate populations within statistical groupings. **Psychographics** is the study of the social and psychological factors that influence consumer lifestyles. The social aspects of lifestyle include reference groups, life stage, and activities. Psychological aspects include personality, attitudes, level of class consciousness, and motivation.

- *Reference Groups.* Reference groups influence a person's thoughts or actions. They may be determined by association, by membership, by aspiration, or by disassociation. A teenager is a member of a family. He or she associates with a particular group of friends and may aspire to be part of a more popular group, while giving clear messages that he or she wants nothing to do with other less-popular groups. Reference groups have an important impact on purchasing behavior for many products and services (Figure 3.5).

- *Life Stage.* Life stage refers to the typical junctures of adult life that have an impact on decision making. Adults who marry and have families evolve from the lifestyle of a single person to one of marriage, children, empty nest, and retirement. Life stages also include the growing number of people who do not marry, do not have

Figure 3.6. *Leisure-time activities may impact apparel purchases; golf apparel is popular for both men and women.*

children, are single parents, or are divorced. At each life stage, needs, experience, household composition, and resources influence what consumers buy and how much they spend.

• *Activities.* Activities refer to how individuals spend their free time. Two-income families usually have more resources to spend on leisure-time activities than families with one income. An individual's activity preferences—be it golf, hunting, skiing, computers, or scrapbooking—have a great impact on his or her purchasing behavior (Figure 3.6). Nike launched a social networking site, Joga.com, in February 2006 so that soccer fans in 140 countries can blog, create fan communities around their favorite teams or players, organize pickup games, download videos, and rant against the encroaching commercialism of the game. It was launched to coincide with the World Cup, but was so successful it continues (Holmes 2006).

• *Personality.* Personality refers to the behavioral and emotional traits that make an individual unique. Personality traits are expressed through an individual's self-confidence, sociability, flexibility, and emotional reactions. These traits influence an individual's behavior and decision making. A self-confident person will make very different apparel selections than a shy or inhibited person.

• *Attitudes.* Attitudes refer to a person's opinions about issues, products, services, and institutions, among other things. Experience, peer group thinking, demographics, and personality all contribute to shape attitudes.

• *Class Consciousness.* Class consciousness reflects a person's desire for social status. It is seen in our choices of friends, where we choose to live, and how we spend our disposable income. In the past, membership in the upper classes was expressed through the purchase of luxury items that only the rich could afford. Today, thanks to a robust economy, a global marketplace, and technological improvements, many luxury items are within the means of a wider segment of the population. This has tended to make class distinctions less obvious.

• *Motivation.* Motivation is an internal or external stimulus that causes a person to act. Product developers and marketers must understand consumer motivations in order to be successful.

Psychographic Tools

Psychographic factors are difficult to measure because they are subjective. Data have traditionally been gathered through activity, interest, and opinion inventories completed by consumers. Today, information may be obtained from actual consumer reports or they may be "mined" by applying computer programs to data that are captured through credit applications and purchasing history. Data mining is discussed later in this chapter. Whichever approach is used to capture psychographic data, the information obtained is subject to interpretation. When interpreted, it can be a very effective way of speaking to a particular customer group.

One tool for capturing these data is the VALS™ segmentation system. Created in 1978, SRI Consulting Business Intelligence's (SRI-BI's) VALS system categorizes the U.S. adult consumer into groups based on psychological characteristics found to be correlated with purchase behavior and several key demographics. VALS is short for values and lifestyles. The VALS system defines eight consumer segments. VALS shows that consumers with the same demographics often have different motivations. A person's tendency to consume goods and services extends beyond age, income, and education. Energy, self-confidence, intellectualism, adventure, innovativeness, impulsiveness, leadership, and vanity play critical roles.

The eight VALS segments are based on two dimensions. Primary motivations shown on the horizontal axes represent the psychological drivers of consumer behavior identified as ideals, achievement, and self-expression. The vertical axes represents resources (age, education, income, health, self-confidence, and willingness to take risks)—either high resources or low. Consumer products and service companies throughout the United States have used VALS to improve product development, brand positioning, advertising effectiveness, and corporate image (VALS 2003)(Figure 3.7). Japan VALS and U.K. VALS are also available. GeoVALS estimates the percentage of the VALS types by U.S. zip code or block group.

Other psychographic marketing tools include LifeMatrix by RoperASW; Monitor MindBase offered by Yankelovich; and BehaviorGraphics, a joint venture between Simmons Research Bureau and Nielsen Media Research that uses TV-viewing behavior to predict product preferences. All of these systems use different assumptions and psychological profiles to sort consumers into categories or market segments (Paul 2003, 1).

Generational Cohort Groups

Using only demographics as a tool, we might expect that as each generation of consumers passes through the various life stages, its behavior would reflect the behavior of past generations in the same life stage. In fact, marketers and sociologists have observed that each generation passing through a life stage is characterized by its own unique set of values and behavior.

Members of a generation are linked through shared life experiences in their formative years. Their common experience with pop culture, economic conditions, world events, natural disasters, celebrities, politics, and technology creates a bond that causes them to develop and retain similar values and life skills as they pass through life. Social scientists call these members of a

Figure 3.7. *The VALS segmentation system defines eight segments of adult consumers according to their attitudes and decision-making patterns.*

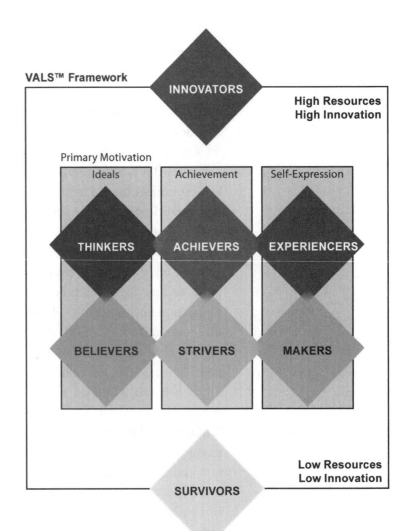

generation a **cohort group. Generational marketing** is the study of the values, motivations, and life experiences that drive generational cohorts, influencing how they spend and save their money (Smith and Clurman 1997).

In 1992, sociologists William Strauss and Neil Howe published a book that outlined the recurring dynamics of generational behavior. *Generations: The History of America's Future, 1584 to 2069,* identifies 18 generations through five centuries of American history. The book categorizes each generation as one of four recurring types of peer personalities that have followed one another in a fixed order: idealist, reactive, civic, and adaptive. Each generational cohort group experiences the phases of life (youth, adulthood, midlife, and elderhood) differently, depending on historic moments that have shaped the lives of their generation.

Four generational cohorts are the most active in today's marketplace: matures (includes both silents and GIs), boomers, generation X, and millennials. Table 3.3 indicates when members of each cohort group were born and identifies a few key shared life experiences. The newest generational cohort includes those born since 2001. Following Strauss and Howe's theory, they will be a reactive generation. Although generations are not usually named until they near adulthood, some are referring to this emerging generation as "homeland."

Yankelovich Partners Inc. was one of the first marketing firms to recognize that "the common experiences of a generation create a specific sensibility that touches each of its members in some way—that teaches its members what's funny, what's stylish, what's status, what's taboo, what works and what doesn't, what to aspire to and what to avoid." This shared generational behavior is a central tendency that differentiates one generation from other generations. In 1971, Yankelovich formalized its study of values and buying motivations with the launch of the Yankelovich Monitor, which is the longest-running and most complete continuous tracking study of American values, lifestyles, and buying motivations (Smith and Clurman 1997).

Marketers and product developers have found generational analysis to be a valuable tool, although they may use slightly different cutoff points to define a specific generation. They have learned that a product and marketing approach that reaches one generation may be ineffective with another. As a result, a store that was extremely popular with generation X may struggle with generation Y. Because generational characteristics evolve as each generation passes through different stages of life, retailers and product developers must constantly reinvent themselves to appeal to a changing customer. They

Table 3.3 GENERATIONAL COHORT GROUPS ACTIVE IN TODAY'S MARKETPLACE

GENERATION	BORN	SHARED EXPERIENCE
Matures, including GIs (Civic) and Silents (Adaptive)	1909–1945	Great Depression, World War II, Korea, Cold War; great civic organizers.
Baby Boomers (Idealist)	1946–1964	Born during postwar expansion and prosperity, unprecedented employment and educational opportunities; social activists.
Generation X (Reactive)	1965–1978	Born in the wake of tumultuous political and economic conditions; coming of age during a period of business downsizing and reengineering; many were products of broken homes; grew up with MTV and the AIDS epidemic.
Millennials or Generation Y (Civic)	1979–2000	Raised during the longest bull market in history, the first members of this generation cam of age as a new millennium began only to face a war on terrorism and a recession; more diverse than previous generations and more tolerant of diversity; schooled with technology.
Homeland	2001–	

Sources: Strauss and Howe 1992; Smith and Clurman 1997; and Generation Watch 2006

must either follow a generation from one life stage to the next or attempt to capture the attention of the next generation in the life cycle they know best.

Both strategies are risky. In order to serve multiple cohort groups with clarity, retailers are extending their store offerings—Gap launched Forth & Towne in 2005 to win back female baby boomers, who grew up in Gap jeans, but who find the Gap fit no longer accommodates their body type. In February 2007, Gap announced that it was closing all of its Forth & Towne stores. Analysts pointed out that the store never really caught on with its intended market, a group of shoppers that appears to be looking for more upscale clothing and driving the resurgence in department stores. H & M announced in June 2006 that it would launch a new chain for men and women in 2007, offering fashion and quality at higher price points, presumably to appeal to a slightly older cohort. Figure 3.8 illustrates the odds against brand loyalty after college graduation in a number of product categories. For apparel, the odds are 6 to 1 that graduates will not shop the same stores they frequented in college.

Generations move from one stage of life to another at 15- to 20-year intervals. Increasingly, marketers are realizing that even within a generational cohort, those born in the first 8 to 10 years act and respond somewhat differently from those born during the last 8 to 10 years of the cohort. They are also coming to realize that millennial marketing professionals are not effective in marketing to Xers and boomers; likewise, boomer marketing professionals seldom understand how to market to Millennials and Xers.

Millennials (or Generation Y)

The first born of the Millennials have entered early adulthood; many have graduated from college and started families of their own. The latter half of the Millennial cohort is redefining the teen years. Many of the early Millennials were raised by generous baby boomer parents, in smaller households with larger household income than in previous generations. Others were raised by Generation X parents who came of age during financially difficult times. Generally they are optimistic, civic-minded, and put off by extreme behavior. They have been characterized as having great energy and short attention spans, thriving on a fast pace and seeking constant stimulation. As a result of highly scheduled childhoods, many aspire to have a more balanced life in early adulthood. They are highly educated and have a great facility for technology. They respond to an interactive approach to marketing that respects their intelligence. They seek out authenticity and rely on the Internet and word of mouth to identify desirable products. They are turned off by marketing that they deem judgmental and bored with the use of sexuality in ads.

Millennials are more comfortable living with diversity; they prefer marketing campaigns and products that respect cross-cultural influences. Though influenced by brands, their loyalties change more rapidly than those of previous generations. Teenage Millennials have been drawn to American Eagle, Urban Outfitters, and Abercrombie & Fitch; as they enter young adulthood,

Figure 3.8. *Upon college graduation, young adults frequently change their brand loyalty.*

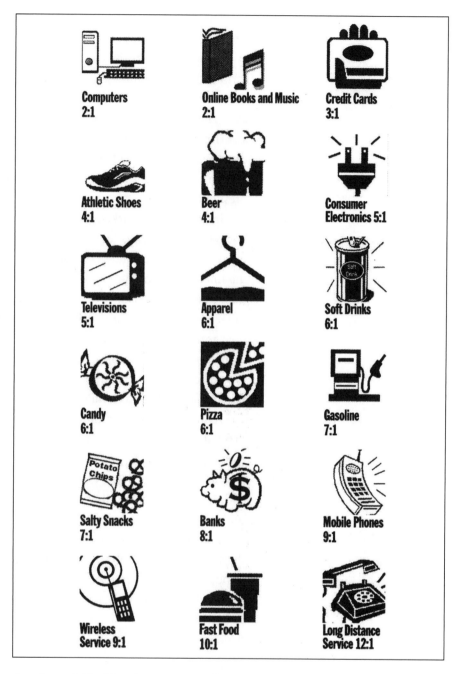

they have shifted loyalties to new stores like H & M and Forever 21, believing that these stores better understand their eclectic fashion point of view. This is a generation that seeks to be entertained nonstop. They are attracted to big productions, cutting edge technology, and either a strong sense of fantasy or an authentic view of reality. Shopping is just one more form of entertainment, whether in the mall or online. Millennials respond well to promotions that feature celebrities they consider authentic. They mimic role models on television and in the movies. Consumption-oriented, they spend more than previous generations at the early adulthood stage. A vast marketplace of products and ideas has been at their disposal throughout their formative years. Retail choice is a key issue in selling to Millennials (Schneiderman 2000, 4).

The most technologically savvy generation in history has grown up with computers and televisions in their bedrooms; they are rarely without their music; and they are in constant communication with friends and family through their cell phones. They live in a constant state of noise. As consumers, they demand personalized, customized, and individualized products and services. They are eager to codesign their jeans and download their own music assortments. Through their high school and college years they have sophisticated tastes but limited incomes. Once they enter the work force, they are extremely confident and aspirational, valuing brand names they consider prestigious.

In the junior market, product developers must limit their advertising budgets to keep prices low. These developers increase their business through niche marketing, product extensions, and visibility in the media, especially on the Internet (which is much cheaper than advertising in other media). Delia's is an example of a retailer that has successfully used niche marketing to relate to teenage or "tween" girls who love trendy apparel. Tween brands promote their product through sponsorship of events that teens follow, product placement, catalogs that mimic magazines, and interactive Web sites that offer fashion advice, free screen savers, and lifestyle chat rooms. The success of tween brands has led to successful brand extensions in home furnishings.

As Millennials enter the work force they are quick to assert their well-defined taste level in the marketplace, buying more premium products at an early age than their predecessors in earlier generations. They continue to respond to participatory experiences. In 2003 the Gap asked customers to audition to model for their ads; 200,000 people submitted photos for an online vote.

As the most recent civic generation, Millennials have already experienced the tragedy of Columbine, the terror of 9/11, and U.S. entanglement in an unpopular war. Generational theory suggests that their generation will be the one to grapple with global warming, the insolvency of Social Security, and the potential breakdown of a myriad of other civic institutions. Their engaged dialog on these issues seems to indicate that they are preparing for the task.

Generation X

Generation X has sometimes been labeled the "baby bust" generation, which refers to its being a much smaller population than that of the Boomers who preceded it or the Millennials who followed. The formative years for Generation X were characterized by divorce, a latchkey lifestyle, a rise in the numbers of homeless people, soaring national debt, holes in the ozone layer, gangs, junk bonds, corporate downsizing, and the first serious talk of a bankrupt Social Security system. For Xers, the future is uncertain. Though wary and cautious, they are savvy consumers who are more spontaneous than the generations that preceded them. Xers defy categorizing. Although common themes apply to all Xers, the ways in which they express themselves are much more diverse than those of previous generations. They are culturally, politically, sexually, racially, and socially diverse. They are the first generation to have been raised with computers and are comfortable relying on the Internet for answers. Their attitudes and values have been shaped much more by the visual image than by the written word. They are a generation that is ready to buy but skeptical of marketing. As a generation, Xers are more conservative than their boomer parents. According to Yankelovich research, they want to do a better job raising their kids than the generation before them.

Marketers are beginning to recognize the Xer market as a lost opportunity. At a stage in life where households are established and they have more discretionary income, few product developers and retailers have targeted this group. As consumers, Xers value functionality, practicality, affordability, and a sense of style, although their style sensibility is diverse and independent of fashion dictates (Seckler 2005a, 15). Too many of the stores out there are perceived as bland or catering to boomers, e.g., Ann Taylor, Banana Republic, and Eddie Bauer. Xers with families value stores like Kohl's and Target, which have the ability to edit the trends and provide one-stop shopping for this value-conscious shopper. The more fashion-conscious element of this generation seeks to express their individuality by shopping at specialty stores such as Anthropologie, BCBG, and Zara or boutiques that carry contemporary brands where they can mix and match from different sources. The bridge category is something they identify with boomers more than their own lifestyle.

Baby Boomers

In 2006 the first of the Baby Boomers began turning 60, redefining retirement and our image of seniors; others may be raising families started late in life or in a second marriage; and some are living a single lifestyle due to the fact they never married or have become divorced. Baby Boomers are a large generation; they like to believe they have changed the norm at every stage of their lives. They have been exposed to marketing and advertising all their lives, and they expect advertisements to be informative, lifestyle-oriented, and feature models their age. Highly educated, they are the first generation to challenge authority and stereotypes (Ware 1999). By 2010 this segment of consumers will represent 23 percent of the population (Kurt Salmon Associates 2004).

Currently, Boomers are enjoying midlife and planning for retirement using their buying clout to demand products that are geared to their generation. They are unlike their parents, in that age is not something to which they readily admit. Young at heart, they have redefined lifestyles at every life stage and will undoubtedly fight the aging process every step of the way (Figure 3.9). Characterized as a somewhat narcissistic generation in their youth, Boomers will be one of the youngest, healthiest, wealthiest, and best-educated groups of retirees ever (Stein 1998). Driven by an optimistic and impulsive nature, these consumers will continue to be big spenders. They are also high-demand shoppers who want extensive information, quick service, and personal gratification

Figure 3.9. *Tina Turner is an icon for baby boomers who hope to set a new standard for aging.*

from the shopping experience. Although they are an affluent and appealing target market, the diversity of their ranks is a constant challenge to product developers and marketers.

Matures

Matures have triumphed over the Great Depression. They were the first Boy Scouts and Girl Scouts, helped to win World War II, developed miracle vaccines, fueled an economic boom, and dominated the presidency from John F. Kennedy through George Bush. Matures accomplished their goals through hard work, conviction, sacrifice, and teamwork. Today's matures represent two generations, identified by sociologists as the GIs and the Silents. Although there are some big differences between these two groups in earlier life stages, they have shared the same generational experiences and in their older years act cohesively as consumers. More than half the GI men served in the armed forces. The Silents served as crucial support for GIs in their roles as fighting men and political leaders. Silents married young and had their children early. They sacrificed much in young adulthood, putting duty before pleasure. They have been rewarded well in their later years with federal programs such as Medicare and senior citizen discounts. Matures believe in conforming to shared values and that hard work is its own reward. Their belief that financial security comes through savings has made them conservative spenders. Their respect for institutions and their desire to conform translates into enduring brand loyalty. The brands they preferred 50 years ago are the same brands they buy today. Their diligence in financial planning enabled them to pay off homes, put their kids through college, and save money for retirement.

Matures have retired earlier than any previous generation and created a market for retirement centers and senior communities that reflect their preference for conformity. They wear their AARP (formerly American Association of Retired Persons) membership like a badge of honor. Marketers must avoid depicting older consumers in negative ways and categorizing them by their age. Having weathered all the rainy days they saved for over the years, they are now willing to spend the fruits of their labors (Smith and Clurman 1997).

The cohort group referred to as matures continues to grow as the first of the baby boomers turn 60. The current population of the United States is demographically older than at any point in its history. Canada, Japan, and Western Europe have similar demographics. By 2010, 43 percent of adults will be 50 and over, according to Census Bureau projections. However, it is important to remember that each new generation that enters a life stage redefines it to meet its needs and resources.

Market Research Tools

Market research may be quantitative or qualitative. **Quantitative research** involves objective methodology in which data are collected about a sample population and analyzed to generalize behavioral patterns. **Qualitative research** is more subjective and relies on methodology such as observation and case studies in which experiences are recorded as a narrative to describe observed behaviors within the context of environmental factors.

Over the years, our ability to analyze the social, psychological, and generational characteristics of consumers has increased dramatically. Market researchers rely on a variety of tools to monitor consumer habits.

Environmental Scanning

Environmental scanning involves the interpretation of political, economic, social, demographic, and psychographic forces as they affect consumers' motivation to buy. Environmental scanning may be facilitated by clipping or information-retrieval services that track a company's interest areas by providing clippings or electronic references of published news stories. Numerous free online newsletters track relevant articles in a variety of publications and provide hyperlinks to the full text. Environmental scanning will be discussed further in chapter 4.

Point-of-Sale (POS) Data

The capture of **point-of-sale (POS)** data relies on the use of software, scanners, and a universal product code (UPC) in order to capture data regarding style, size, and color. The information captured through POS can be shared with partners throughout the supply chain, using **electronic data interchange (EDI)**. EDI is the computer-to-computer exchange of information between business partners. The success of these tools depends on the accurate entry of recorded data such as pricing, receiving, transfers, sales, and returns. This is referred to as **data integrity**. These data enable product developers to analyze the performance of products down to the individual **stock keeping unit (SKU)** by store and time period. The SKUs are a means of designating individual products for inventory purposes by style, color, and size. The collection of point-of-sale data helps businesses determine which styles, sizes, and colors are selling in which store. It allows retailers and product developers to pinpoint the right products for the right time in different places by responding to variations in selling seasons due to climate variations and other factors.

Data Profiling and Data Mining

Today, the consumer data captured at the cash register, provided through credit applications, and given voluntarily on Web sites have the potential to provide a wealth of information when fully analyzed. **Data profiling** refers to the gathering, assembling, and collating of data about individuals in databases. This stored data can be **mined** to identify, segregate, categorize, and make decisions about individuals known to the decision maker only through their computerized profile (Belgum 1999). The profile patterns may be used to predict trends and define geographically based purchase behavior.

Data mining is a valuable tool in developing **automatic replenishment** programs for fashion merchandise. These programs predetermine an agreed-upon inventory level that triggers an automatic reorder of stock. Fashion-oriented products do not lend themselves to one-for-one replenishment. Inventory levels for these products can be maintained by using attribute replenishment and data warehousing. **Attribute replenishment** replaces one item with a different item that has similar characteristics in terms of purpose, silhouette, and price. A **data warehouse** contains information collected from a variety of transactions over time that can be used to determine patterns and trends.

Data mining can also be used to better allocate merchandise assortments among stores by exploring the behavioral relationships between what is selling and the consumer needs of particular stores, rather than allocating merchandise based on store clusters. **Sell-through** refers to the percentage of merchandise a retailer sells at full price. By linking store-performance measures such as sell-through data and product attributes, including color, size, fabric, construction, and price, retailers and manufacturers can customize assortments that match consumer characteristics from store to store. Accurate data capture is imperative. For example, a retail sales associate must scan a pair of black pants and a pair of khaki pants separately, not as two pairs of black pants. Data warehouses use filters to identify new trends and potential changes in the rules. This information can be used to modify merchandise plans. Data mining can also help marketers plan more effective advertising campaigns.

Engaging the Consumer

Companies have traditionally used focus groups and surveys to gather customer opinions. Today some big companies are turning to a range of video techniques to document consumer behavior. The technique a company uses must be appropriate to the consumer group studied.

Video Documentation

With young people, many companies find that the information they get through surveys and in focus groups is not all that accurate. With the technology of video and digital cameras, consumer shopping patterns can be observed and analyzed. Envirosell is a behavioral market research and consulting company that studies consumer shopping behavior using a combination of in-store video recording, observation, and customer intercept interviews. The use of video cameras must be evaluated carefully; it may be very insulting to consumers who see it as an invasion of privacy.

Focus Groups

A **focus group** is a carefully guided discussion between a skilled moderator and members of a select target market. The discussion is designed to capture a range of feelings and attitudes about a product or service. Focus groups are a form of qualitative research. Key to the success of focus groups is finding the right participants, people who are articulate and appropriately represent the target population. These groups tend to generate more reliable information with older customers as opposed to younger customers.

Anthropologie is an example of a company that uses focus groups, exit surveys, and fit sessions to better understand customer preferences. They will ask 20 to 30 customers to try on clothing for the production and design teams. These fit sessions have a tremendous positive impact on sales: "For example, more than 50% of our customers have kids. They're bending down to pick up the kids in the supermarket. They want to look hip but not flash the people behind them. We raised the rise in our jeans and added Lycra. If you know your customer, you can do that" (Edelson 2003, 1).

Surveys

Surveys involve the systematic gathering of information from respondents by communicating with them in person, over the telephone, by mail, or through the Internet. A company can collect its own data or hire an outside research firm for a specific project. The first step in developing a survey is to determine what information needs to be collected. Generally, marketers seek to learn

CASE STUDY 3.2   EX OFFICIO USES FOCUS GROUPS TO TARGET THE ADVENTURE TRAVEL CUSTOMER

Ex Officio is a company founded on the belief that thoughtfully designed, stylish travel clothing greatly enhances any travel experience. Ex Officio is committed to perfecting the balance between preparation and mobility with packable, versatile wardrobes that accommodate travel needs in a variety of settings. It has identified six activities or environments common to vacation travel:

1. Active garments with the versatility to accommodate a wide range of active pursuits.
2. Urban Exploration garments designed to accommodate city touring.
3. Nights Out garments designed to accommodate evening activities.
4. In-Transit garments designed specifically for travelers' in-transit needs.
5. Stay Warm outerwear and garments that can be layered for warmth.
6. Stay Dry breathable and waterproof outerwear for wet weather.

Garments in Ex Officio's line are loaded with features such as Airomesh-lined sleeves and torso vents, security pockets, special Action Back construction, shoulder epaulettes to secure camera straps, and the multipurpose Utility Tab to secure sunglasses or a headphone cord.

In 1999, Ex Officio participated in two market research projects to learn more about its customers. For the first project, it contracted Q2 Brand Intelligence to conduct four focus groups, three with potential Ex Officio customers and one with current Ex Officio customers. The goal of the research was to better understand the lifestyles and attitudes of adventure travelers for future brand development. Focus groups were made up of women 25 to 55 years of age who travel domestically or internationally 3 to 12 times a year for business or pleasure. Household income ranged from $85,000 to $160,000 annually.

Findings of the focus groups confirmed Ex Officio's demographic customer profile. Its core customer ranges in age from 35 to 54, with a median age of 39. Household income varies between $75,000 and $124,000, with the majority of households over $100,000. Customers tend to be married and travel three or more times per year. They prefer to shop at specialty stores for apparel.

A psychographic profile revealed "yin-yang travelers" who place importance on both activity and relaxation as part of their ideal vacation destination. They enjoy getting away to nearby locales for short excursions as well as remote global destinations where they can interact with local cultures. Their goal is to experience the environment or culture they visit. They are resourceful planners who go to great effort in order to maximize the value of their trips. The Internet is their key research tool. They travel light, packing only what's necessary with an emphasis on easy care, versatility, and comfort.

In addition to the focus groups, Ex Officio was a corporate sponsor of a research project conducted by Radar Communications and summarized in The Adventure Travel Report. This project tracked three weeks in the lives of 29 men and 31 women who were identified as frequent adventure travelers. The goal was to engage participants in an editorial and creative process to gather lifestyle and adventure travel information. This research technique gave participants the ability to express themselves in their own words and on their own time. Forty percent of the group was aged 23 to 34; the remaining 60 percent was aged 35 to 59. Participants were drawn from trendsetting areas, identified as Colorado, California, Illinois, New England, Washington state, and Texas.

Results of this survey verified the profile developed by Q2 Brand Intelligence and differentiated the preferences and needs of younger and older travelers. It revealed that younger travelers are more focused on activities and have less disposable income, whereas older travelers seek to balance activity with a desire for relaxation and have more income to pamper themselves by flying first class or staying in a luxury hotel. Both age groups seek travel off the beaten path that will provide physical and cultural challenges. Besides travel, their interests include family, career, the environment, volunteer work, and education. When packing, these travelers carry no more than is necessary. They seek out high-quality, comfortable footwear, and waterproof, breathable fabrics.

These insights will influence the future design of Ex Officio's Web site. The company may choose to align its brand image with issues important to its target customer, such as the environment. It may include Web site links that facilitate travel planning. The research will help to pinpoint target price points and validate styling details that customers value most. Above all, the information will help the company to strategize how it can best increase its business and reach new customers.

Source: Interviews with Janine Roberson, Carrie Bendeak, and Susan Glynn.

more about shopping behaviors, shopping attitudes, product attributes, and demographics. The next decision is to determine who should be studied. This is known as the **sample**. Information may be collected from current, former, or potential customers. Samples may be geared to particular demographic, psychographic, or cohort segments of a target market. Decisions regarding the information to be collected and the targeted sample will influence how the survey is completed (Case Study 3.2, Ex Officio Uses Focus Groups to Target the Adventure Travel Customer).

Online surveys are the most common form of survey used in relation to apparel products. Consumers are frequently willing to complete a short online survey regarding a purchase—especially an online purchase. However, consumer behavior is often subconscious and therefore not readily articulated in a survey.

An increasing concern with online surveys or with any online shopping experience is that product developers may also be collecting data consumers are not aware of, such as how they use the site and what they look at. This means of data collection is increasingly controversial. Legally companies are allowed to obtain data through both voluntary disclosure of information and involuntary extraction of information through clickstream data—data collected as a Web user communicates with other computers and networks over the Internet. This includes cookies—information that a Web site puts on your hard drive so it can remember something about you at a future date and can track your visits to the site, often unbeknown to you at the time.

Benefits of online data collection are that it is far less expensive than either mail or telephone surveys and results can be tabulated continuously. When information is voluntarily given online, it is less invasive than mall intercept or telephone surveys. That leaves marketers torn between the temptation to tap their customers for data and risk alienating those same customers by invading their privacy. Generation X and Y consumers who have grown up with computers are more likely to feel comfortable sharing information online. Baby boomer and mature customers may have trouble shaking the sense of invasion in requests for personal information.

One approach is to ask customers one or two questions every time there is an interaction rather than inundating them with long, time-consuming interrogations that may appear invasive. Margery Myers, spokesperson for Talbots, Inc., says that Talbots stays close to its core customer by encouraging her to talk to the company. The company's CEO personally corresponds with the best customers via e-mail. Each week, store managers send field notes to the company's headquarters summarizing interactions with consumers (Derby 2004, 21). Ellen Wessel, President of Moving Comfort in Chantilly, Virginia, gathers a handful of store owners a few times a year to interview them about what's happening in their stores. She wants to know what colors, fabrics, and styles women are requesting. At one such session it was reported that female shoppers over 50 were telling sales clerks that they didn't want to expose their flabby upper arms. As a result, the company reduced its offering of sleeveless shirts and increased production of short-sleeve styles (Lach 1999).

Another approach is to persuade customers to provide information about themselves by rewarding them with something of value. This may be a gift with purchase, free delivery, a discount, or information that allows the consumer to make a more satisfactory selection. For instance, consumers may be willing to divulge their measurements if, as a result, the company is able to assist them in selecting the correct-size garment.

Style Testing

As product developers become more astute in listening to consumer preferences, style testing has become more prevalent. **Style testing** allows retailers, consumers, or both to view early prototypes and offer their opinions. Style testing can take several forms. Some product developers call in a group of buyers from their biggest retail accounts and ask them to help edit the line. Other product developers ask for buyer input over the Internet by showing virtual garments that exist only on the computer but have not been made up into samples. They ask consumers to look at the virtual product and indicate whether they would buy it. Auburn University has developed Life/Style OnLine, a Web-based interactive data collection technique that allows online shoppers to manipulate product images to express individual tastes (Just-style.com 2001).

Yet another means of style testing is to utilize a marketing firm that collects consumer profiles of a cross section of the population. These firms will then give out samples of a product identified for testing to a select group of customers who match the product developer's customer profile. Customers selected for the style test are asked to use the product and report back on their experience.

CASE STUDY 3.3 WEAR-TESTING 101

The wake-up call "Rise and shine, porcupine" kick-started 48 hours of near nonstop activity at a Women's Quest fitness camp in October 1999. Activities included mountain bike riding in the snow, climbing a 65-foot-high pole, and bungee jumping 1,400 feet. Adidas, a major sponsor of Women's Quest, used this opportunity to wear-test its products. Among the attendees was world-class runner Paula Radcliff, an athlete who represents the Adidas brand.

A trail run gave campers the opportunity to grab Adidas gloves and ear bands to help them withstand unseasonably and unexpectedly cold weather. Gretchen Garside, a researcher at the Adidas human performance lab in Beaverton, Oregon, led the pack. Later the same morning, participants donned sweatpants and royal blue fleece pullovers before a strenuous session of mountain biking. Adidas executives took the opportunity provided by an afternoon meeting to discuss Gore-Tex sneakers and other new products in development. The popularity of trail running, especially in the Northwest, was discussed as an emerging market opportunity. The executive team was disappointed when reminded that many New York women frequently wear trail-running sneakers with skirts or dresses when they commute to and from work.

Garside talked about a $15,000 research project on running and the company's plans to do the same with other categories. Following the meeting, participants were asked to write about their fitness goals and expectations before a challenging yoga workout.

Day two was more of the same. A wake-up call at 6:30 began the day with participants back in the same Adidas uniform. A 10 o'clock hike challenged the group to elevations of 12,200 feet. Rope drills at 2:45 put the clothes to a real test.

Source: Adapted from Feitelberg 1999b, 9

Style testing may also be facilitated using laboratory stores or test stores. Some product developers open prototype stores in major shopping meccas or near their product development headquarters to test new styles. The response to new styles in these stores will determine whether or not the styles will be produced in quantity for wider distribution. Other product developers designate a few of their bigger stores as test stores where new product ideas are evaluated before they are produced for wider distribution.

Fashion product developers may use the fall transition season and the resort season to test new fashion ideas. Product developed for these seasons is produced in smaller quantities, thereby reducing the risk to test a new idea. If the concept sells through, it may be reinterpreted in a similar style for a later shipping date.

Wear-testing is a variation of style testing often used as an important research tool, particularly in the active sportswear category, for which performance is a key criterion of purchasing decisions. Adidas is a company that relies heavily on wear-testing. It then uses its advertising to capitalize on its association with athletes. The company sponsors athletes who wear its fitness apparel competitively and uses these athletes in catalog shoots. After a catalog shoot, athletes are asked to return to the company headquarters in Burlington, Vermont, to evaluate the collection item by item.

Table 3.4 THE POWER OF PERSUASION: MEDIA INFLUENCES REPORTED BY WOMEN DEPARTMENT STORE SHOPPERS

MEDIA TYPE	PERCENTAGE OF WOMEN SHOPPERS WHO SAY THIS MEDIA TYPE INFLUENCES PURCHASES	MEDIA TYPE	PERCENTAGE OF WOMEN SHOPPERS WHO SAY THIS MEDIA TYPE INFLUENCES PURCHASES
Newspaper inserts	44.4%	Coupons	30.6%
Word of mouth	39.9%	TV/Broadcast	29.8%
Direct mail	34.0%	Newspapers	26.6%
Magazines	33.3%	E-mail advertising	22.0%
In-store promotions	33.1%	Internet advertising	17.2%

Source: Bigresearch 2005, 12

Adidas also relies on employees, 70 percent of whom are recreational runners, for wear-testing. Although the feedback and visibility the company gets from athletes is a valuable piece of its research, its core customer isn't a world-class athlete. The average runner spends a longer period of time running and runs at a slower pace (Feitelberg 1999a). Fashion product developers may also ask employees to wear-test merchandise other than activewear in order to validate performance characteristics (Case Study 3.3, Wear-Testing 101).

Marketing to Consumers

With time becoming an increasingly valuable commodity, traditional forms of advertising are not as effective as they once were. Multidimensional customers are less predictable and harder to reach than ever before. The growing intrusiveness and saturation of marketing and advertising and a more independent mindset in terms of how they want to dress has caused consumers to tune out traditional forms of advertising. Consumers feel bombarded with unwanted spam, telemarketing, and pop-up ads that are an annoyance and do little to meet their needs and desires.

But strong consumer spending has blinded marketers to consumer frustration with their invasive tactics. Yankelovich President J. Walker Smith believes that marketers can reverse this trend by making marketing a source of competitive advantage. Marketers can gain competitive advantage by communicating precise and relevant messages geared toward specific individuals and providing reciprocity for their time and attention. This involves personalized marketing to a particular name and address rather than blanketing the market

(Smith 2004). According to BIGresearch's 2005 Simultaneous Media Usage Survey, women are most influenced in their apparel purchases by newspaper inserts, word of mouth, direct mail, and magazines (Table 3.4). Fashion product developers and retailers have traditionally relied on print mediums as opposed to TV/broadcast mediums to get the attention of customers. Broadcast ads were too expensive for all but the largest brands until the advent of cable TV, with its potential to reach local markets independent of national channels.

Print Advertising

Print advertising allows consumers to select the advertisements that most interest them and thus are considered less invasive. Newspaper inserts allow consumers to zero in on what's available locally and at what price. Kohl's, J. C. Penney, Wal-Mart, and Target regularly use weekly inserts. Magazine advertising appeals to the aspirational side of fashion—consumers can tear out an ad or mark a magazine in order to remind themselves to look for the exact product pictured or something similar in their price range. According to the Magazine Publishers of America, product developers and retailers see magazines as a means of communicating with a specific demographic. In an attempt to improve its fashion image, Wal-Mart began advertising in *Elle* and *Vogue* in 2005. Coupons in an ad appeal to price-conscious shoppers and sometimes draw new customers into a store.

Screen-Based Marketing

Television advertising on network programs during primetime is usually too costly for all but the largest apparel product developers, although cable channels now provide an avenue for less expensive ads in local markets. The value of television advertising as a marketing tool is increasingly called into question as consumers use new technologies to eliminate commercials. In an attempt to reengage the customer, some retailers are adding television screens to their selling space. Approaches range from the use of small 4-inch monitors placed on the shelf next to the merchandise to large plasma TVs designed and placed to raise the status quotient. They may play anything from a 30-second commercial to a 15-minute loop of a runway show.

The high-end route to enhance the selling environment is to install high-definition plasma TVs that can be connected to a computer station using wireless technology. This technology is able to deliver content that is more interesting to the consumer. Women love to see a collection in its entirety, as it appeared on the runway, and men are generally ready to relive the highlights of an important sporting event. When not limited to 30- to 60-second spots, brands can communicate with the customer on a different level (Figure 3.10) (Moin 2005, 20–21). The low-tech application of TVs is to place small ones

Figure 3.10. *The use of high-definition televisions in-store can help to sell a brand as long as the content is well chosen.*

right next to the product and play 10-, 20-, or 30-second commercials while promoting the product's price. Use of video screens must be considered carefully. With the wrong content, consumers may find them an irritation.

Product Placement

Another option to promote product on-screen is to pay to promote a product within the content of a television show or movie. Increasingly movies and television shows are boldly zooming in on brand logos to promote the products used on film. Fashion was an important aspect of *Sex in the City,* with numerous references to Manolo Blahnik shoes and the "it" bag of the moment. Audiences of *Match Point,* a Woody Allen film, recognized that the women in the film wear *7 for All Mankind* jeans, even though the brand was never mentioned. This form of promotion works best for brands with high name recognition and status.

Celebrity Exposure

Associating a brand with a celebrity gained increasing clout in the mid-1990s. When fashion magazines like *Vogue* and *Harper's Bazaar* first began using celebrities on their covers, the modeling community complained that these celebrities, who appeared in order to promote their name or cause, were taking work away from professional models. Today, magazines such as *Lucky* and *In Style* are designed around how to achieve celebrity looks for less. Many consumers are fascinated by which celebrities attend runway shows and what the celebrities wear on the red carpet at award shows. Their choices are quickly reproduced for the mass market. Brands that celebrities wear get a boost, which gives designers impetus to give away product in the hope that a celebrity will be photographed wearing it.

This has led to brands hiring celebrities to appear in ads and promote their products. Scarlett Johansson was signed by Reebok to promote its women's products in July 2006. In June 2006, H & M announced that it would dress Madonna and her dancers, back-up singers, and musicians with complete off-stage wardrobes during her "Confessions" tour. The entourage was to choose their wardrobes from H & M's 2006 collection. Madonna was contracted to appear in an advertising campaign and some items, including a Madonna tracksuit, were produced to sell in-store. Madonna's on-stage wardrobe was created by Jean Paul Gaultier (Figure 3.11).

Figure 3.11. *Madonna wore Jean Paul Gaultier designs on stage for her "Confessions" tour and H & M clothes off stage.*

CASE STUDY 3.4 CREATING BUZZ

Dave Balter is the founder of BzzAgent, a word-of-mouth marketing firm and author of *Grapevine: The New Art of Word-of-Mouth Marketing.* His firm invites consumers to sign up to become "BzzAgents." BzzAgents are profiled regarding their likes and dislikes, age, where they live, lifestyle, etc. Based on that information, the company searches its database for agents matching the demographic and psychographic profile of target customers of the product or service. The chosen BzzAgents are offered a chance to sign up for that particular buzz campaign; products range from toothbrushes to books, from apparel to cars. Volunteers receive a sample of the product and "The BzzGuide," a training manual for buzz-creating strategies. If the product is a car, volunteers might be given an opportunity to drive it for a weekend.

Strategies for creating buzz include talking about the product to friends, chatting with salespeople at retail outlets, or e-mailing friends about the product. After experiencing the product, volunteers are asked to file a report documenting their communication or "buzz" with others. BzzAgent coaches reply to each report, conveying appreciation and support for the service and providing coaching for future experiences. Although agents do get to keep the new products they promote, the network is designed to discourage volunteers from signing up just to get freebies.

Clients are intrigued by the service's authenticity—BzzAgents aren't scripted. In fact, if BzzAgents are not enamored of a product, they do not hesitate to say so. While that might deter some clients, others see it as an opportunity to redesign the product so that it does generate positive buzz.

The service is not cheap. A project that utilizes about 1,000 agents for a 12-week campaign runs about $85,000, exclusive of product samples according to an article in *Fast Company* magazine (Tischler 2004).

As celebrities have come to understand their fashion clout, several have established their own fashion brands. Some, including Sean 'Diddy' Combs *(Sean John)*, [Tina and] Beyonce Knowles *(House of Deréon)* and Gwen Stefani *(L.A.M.B.)* are involved in the design process and photographed wearing their brands; others, such as Jessica Simpson *(JS and Princy)* and Jennifer Lopez *(JLo and Sweetface)*, have signed licensing agreements and have varying degrees of responsibility for the actual design of their brands. They have both received some criticism for not wearing their own brands. According to the Cotton Incorporated's *Lifestyle Monitor*, 55 percent of young Fashion Innovators aged 16–24 stated that they look to celebrities for fashion direction (Lifestyle Monitor 2006, 2).

Word-of-Mouth Marketing—Creating Buzz

One of the most effective forms of marketing, particularly with younger customers, is word-of-mouth marketing. A natural phenomenon, word of mouth happens when consumers are happy about an experience or purchase. Today, marketers are honing their ability to organize, manage, and measure buzz, especially among younger shoppers. It works when shoppers bring along

Figure 3.12. *Bono helped to organize the ONE campaign to show how individuals can help fight poverty and AIDS in Africa. His wife is the designer of the Edun line.*

friends to the mall or find ways to incorporate their friends into online research through tools like "e-mail to a friend" or wish lists. These consumers use text messaging and write blogs; their purchasing behavior is very much influenced by what their peers think and purchase. According to Forrester Research, they respond to advertising games, instant-win games, coupons, streaming video ads, and cell phone promotions (Case Study 3.4, Creating Buzz).

Causes and Special Events

Supporting causes, sponsoring special events, and inviting prized customers to special events have all become important methods of marketing.

The sponsorship of special events has been around for a long time. Macy's celebrated its 80th year of sponsoring the annual Thanksgiving Day Parade in 2006. Sponsorship of events such as award shows, sporting events such as golf tournaments or the Olympics, and even Fashion Week are a means of communicating with a brand's target customer. Sponsorship of the right event can increase a brand's *cool factor* while also reserving rights for merchandise distribution and promotion.

A less expensive take on showing one's support for a cause is the distribution or sale of *awareness merchandise. Awareness bracelets* are typically made of silicone and demonstrate the wearer's support of a particular cause. The trend was started by Lance Armstrong after he was diagnosed with testicular cancer. He has raised over $5 million for the cancer foundation he set up by selling wristbands for a dollar each. Today wristbands in a variety of colors represent an even bigger variety of causes. A quick count on Wikipedia found that red wristbands are associated with 27 different causes. Similarly, retailers and brands have taken to selling T-shirts that promote a cause they want to be aligned with. A variety of celebrities and designers have aligned themselves with breast cancer T-shirts. Stella McCartney and Oscar de la Renta have designed these T-shirts in recent years; Glenn Close was featured as a celebrity model in the 2006 campaign. Singer Bono helped to organize a campaign to sell ONE T-shirts made by Edun and sold exclusively at Nordstrom stores. Selling for $40, the T-shirts are made from 100 percent African cotton and emblazoned with the word ONE. They promote a campaign to make poverty history and fight AIDS in Africa. Edun will donate $10 from the sale of every T-shirt sold to the Apparel Lesotho Alliance to fight AIDS (Figure 3.12).

Perhaps less lofty but no less effective, many retailers have learned that inviting their customers to special events is a good way to develop customer intimacy. Luxury retailers like Neiman Marcus, Bergdorf Goodman, and Saks Fifth Avenue host special events for their special customers. Neiman Marcus asks good customers to invite a group of friends for an event where Neiman provides food, drink, often a drawing for a generous gift certificate. It has also sponsored events in conjunction with regional museums and organizations where it provides deluxe motor coach transportation to and from the store, with beverages en route and gourmet food stations and more beverages in store for an after-hours shopping experience. Other stores such as Barney's plan their special events in conjunction with trunk shows that are open to all their customers. Smaller boutiques might invite the significant others of good customers to a special shopping night before the holidays and promise to help the men find the perfect gift. They also make trunk shows special events or plan after-hours shopping events for their clientele. Compared to the cost of advertising, these events are generally good investments.

Innovative Retail Formats

Retailers and brands continue to experiment with delivery formats. Pop-up stores and new variations on direct selling satisfy unique niches.

Pop-up stores are temporary stores opened to showcase new product or format, or to introduce a new brand or retailer to the marketplace. J. C. Penney Experience was launched in New York on March 1, 2006, and dismantled on March 26. The store showcased Penney's electronic commerce infrastructure and its new updated brands. The temporary store featured 22 Internet kiosks scattered throughout a 15,000-square-foot space where customers could order merchandise that would be sent to their homes. Adding to the virtual store ambiance were plasma screens. All purchases were made via the computer; there were no cash registers in the store. The store was launched with a glitzy invitation-only benefit to support Broadway Cares/Equity Fights Aids.

Pop-up stores are not a totally new concept. Target utilized the concept in 2002 prior to opening permanent stores in New York. Unable to find affordable space for a temporary store over the holiday selling season, Target converted a 220-foot barge into a floating store and docked it for two weeks at Manhattan's Chelsea Piers. In 2004 Target opened another pop-up store to benefit the Breast Cancer Research Foundation (BCRF). This store was located at 7 Times Square and promoted a limited edition line of pink products—everything from cashmere scarves and umbrellas to caps and flip-flops. Other stores have utilized the pop-up concept by renting kiosks in local malls during busy selling seasons in order to test the business climate for a full-fledged store.

Direct selling is another format that is experiencing a bit of a revival. Designed to bypass retailers, personal sales consultants either sell from their own homes or a space they rent temporarily, or they promote in-home parties.

Women's apparel lines such as *Doncaster, The Worth Collection, Ltd.,* and *Juliana Collezione* are all bridge lines that appeal to professional women who spend a fair amount of money on their clothes. The collections are designer-quality and are not sold in stores. Consultants receive the full line 2 to 4 times

Figure 3.13. *Brands such as Jockey and The Body Shop are reviving the concept of home parties to sell merchandise.*

a year and sell from either their homes or a suitable rented space. Like a trunk show, customers make appointments to view the line and leave their orders; production is based on sales, which eliminates markdowns. Different styles are received in different sizes so that the customer can try on at least one jacket in her own size and feel confident that the style she's ordering will fit. A number of men's wear companies sell in this same way. Several of these companies are now launching virtual stores, available to sales reps, to work with customers between trunk shows.

More recently companies have been exploring home parties as a means of putting the fun back into shopping (Figure 3.13). Clothing, jewelry, accessories, and personal care items lend themselves to the home party format. For some brands, home parties can be an effective addition to a brand's multi-channel distribution strategy; for smaller businesses, home parties may be their only channel of distribution. *Bill Blass, Jockey International, The Body Shop,* and *Aerosoles* are just a few of the brands that have launched direct sales divisions. Others such as *Soma,* Chico's lingerie brand geared to baby boomers, are considering this venue (Lee 2005, 8–9).

General Consumer Trends

Although market consultants can help businesses to identify general consumer trends, each brand must determine the tools that provide the most accurate information about its customer and the marketing strategies that attract that customer's attention. As both wholesale brands and retailers expand their distribution globally, they must also understand the nuances of the global consumer market, which is no easy task.

Time as a Commodity

Consumers see time as one of their most valuable commodities (Figure 3.14). With that in mind, the length of time they are willing to shop for a particular item is related to its price. The cost of a garment affects how long and how many stores women are willing to visit before buying clothing. When spending a lot for a garment, they shop until they find exactly what they want. When the cost is minimal, there is more of an inclination to settle in order to prevent further expenditure of time. Customers' threshold as to what they consider expensive may vary from $25 to $5,000 (Lifestyle Monitor 2004, 2).

Fashion Independence

Women increasingly understand their own personal style. With designers offering many different fashion trends in the same season—many suitable only for the runway and not real lives—women are increasingly trusting their

Figure 3.14. *Consumers see time as one of their most valuable commodities.*

own fashion instincts, choosing clothing that fits their body and their lifestyle. According to Cotton Incorporated's *Lifestyle Monitor,* 86 percent of women say they choose colors that look good on them, rather than adhering to the seasonal palette. Most women still want to look attractive, but they won't buy into trends that are not comfortable or becoming. For example, older women don't want to wear low-rise jeans. They are uncomfortable and show a portion of the body for which these women no longer have the shape.

Comfort

Increasingly, consumers in all age groups are valuing comfort over style; this trend has marginalized the impact of fashion on female consumers purchasing behavior. Many men have tended to seek comfort over fashion for some time. For young people, this trend may be a response to shifting priorities and a quest for authenticity. For others, it may be a sense of disenfranchisement because retailers do not pay attention to their needs or it may be a response to the uncomfortable place that the world has become. Relaxed dress codes and the prevalence of obesity further fuel the trend. According to Yankelovich's annual "General Lifestyle Study," about two-thirds of Millennial females, or 67 percent, placed a priority on comfort over looking their best. Seventy-seven percent of women over 60 agreed, as did 74 percent of Boomer women and 71 percent of Generation X women, ages 26–39 (Seckler 2005b, 9). Related to consumers prioritizing comfort is their tendency to buy more items rather than entire outfits. Those brands that can effectively combine comfort and style will be ahead of the curve.

Importance of Fit

One of the best ways to hook a niche customer is to understand his or her fit needs in relation to styling preferences. Eighty percent of consumers are frustrated by inconsistent fit between brands and 70 percent by inconsistent fit within the same brand (Kurt Salmon Associates 2004). Talbots increased its jeans sales significantly after it restyled the denim line with fit designed for its target customer to updated lightweight denim in classic flare and boot cuts. Cotton Inc. and Bellomy Research interviewed 1,000 men and women in the United States who spend more than $70 on denim items and found 85 percent of respondents cited fit as the crucial factor in purchase intent (Just-style.com 2005). Old Navy was cited as the most often purchased label by Millennials and Gen Xers according to a NPD Fashionworld study released in February 2005. Old Navy achieved that rank by offering apparel sizes cut more generously for consumers' expanding waistlines. Many of the company's stores offer women's sizes 16–26 (Seckler 2005c, 24).

Masstige

For years brand managers believed that a brand could not be high end and mass at the same time. Today that paradigm has changed. **Masstige** is the convergence of mass market and prestige retailing. High-income groups are mixing discount apparel with their designer duds, while lower-income groups are splurging on luxury for some pieces. Retailers that market to the middle class are treading water, trying to find their way. In general, consumers are increasingly willing to pay premium prices for products that are unique, carry status, fit well, and matter to them personally, while demanding rock-bottom prices for basic goods.

Economic statistics illustrate one side of this scenario—the percentage of households with middle-class incomes declined from 51.0 percent in 1980 to 44.9 percent in 2003, while poverty rates and the number of millionaires continue to rise (Reda 2005, 4). Mass market retailers including Wal-Mart, Target, J. C. Penney, and Kohl's are doing all they can to up the fashion quotient of the apparel they offer by offering exclusive brands that link them to designers and celebrities, leaving department stores to scramble to maintain their market share. The ironic twist to this market stratification is the desire of affluent consumers to seek out a bargain at Target or Costco or a designer outlet—the thrill of finding the ultimate bargain.

It's no longer suicide to launch a brand at multiple price points. *Karl Lagerfeld* and *Stella McCartney* lines at H & M and the *Isaac Mizrahi* line at Target have made it fashionable to offer product at both the high and low end of the market. At the same time, the consumer's desire for status and exclusivity is so great that customers will pay $350 for a pair of jeans, put their names on yearlong waiting lists to pay $6,000 for an individually stitched *Hermès* Kelly bag, and pay extra to choose the color of the pony embroidery on their shirts at polo.com. Both affluent and aspirational customers are defining luxury in their own terms. Style is becoming more individual, mixing luxury and mass merchandise in such a way that it is difficult to discern which is which (*Women's Wear Daily* 2004c). With value-priced merchants offering fashion-forward garments at very low prices, consumers can get their fashion fix without feeling guilty. And because those fashions have a very short shelf life, the longevity of the garment is not a question (Just-style.com 2005). Retailers such as J. Crew play the masstige game by leaking word that they use the same cashmere as the posh *Loro Piana* label to make their winter sweaters or the same velvet as Ermenegildo Zegna to make their blazers.

Casual Dress

Casual dress has become the norm for many businesses. This has a tremendous impact on how both men and women buy clothes. The women's suit and coordinates categories have been negatively affected, as has the men's tailored suit category. The business suit has been replaced by casual wear or uniforms for many men in the workforce. Today most women buy primarily separates that can be mixed and matched to suit the occasion. This phenomenon presents a challenge, since suits and coordinates frequently carried a higher price tag than separates. Instead of having to invest in two wardrobes—one for work and the other for leisure—women and men can more easily buy one set of clothes that works for both.

The separation between work and leisure wardrobes may have declined, but a trend that has become much more evident is the addition of an active sportswear wardrobe to the mix. This is one of the changes that has contributed to what is now referred to as "lifestyle" marketing.

Wear-Now Clothing

Eighty percent of consumers buy their clothing in season, but product developers continue to ship the bulk of their offerings prior to the season (Kurt Salmon Associates 2004, 4). As a result, consumers have learned to wait for a sale because apparel has been on the floor and is ready to be marked down by the time consumers are ready to buy and wear it. Retailers are putting spring merchandise on the floor right after the holidays in order to lure consumers with gift cards to spend on full-price product. If retailers persist in offering lines ahead of season, the prevalence of seasonal markdowns will continue. In order to sell more product at full price, product developers must improve their timing. With runway shows on the Internet, trends have an increasingly short shelf life. Introducing new product more frequently can be used to refine their assortments in terms of size, color, and details and provide new products closer to the wearing season.

Consumers now weave shopping experiences into their everyday lives. In an over-stored /over-branded environment and with the availability of shopping from home via catalogs, television, and the Internet, consumers can meet at Barnes & Noble for lunch, shop for groceries 24 hours a day, and scan e-Bay for bargains before going to bed. With apparel so readily available, most women's prime motivation for purchasing is to get a good price. Consumers use discretionary dollars to spend on fashion. With so many products vying for limited dollars, apparel manufacturers are having an increasingly difficult time competing successfully. The concept of value is different for different people and may take on different meanings for the same customers, depending on what they are purchasing. More and more customers are "cross-shoppers" who move between various types of retail venues to accommodate their needs. They shop at Wal-Mart in the morning and at Saks or Neiman Marcus on the weekend.

Summary

Consumers have high expectations for apparel products and feel frustration when these products do not meet their needs. Consumers demand unparalleled product availability, increased customization, and excellent customer service. An ongoing dialogue with consumers will be the key to growth for the apparel business.

Product developers have many tools at their disposal that enable them to collect data. Research and management of demographic, psychographic, and generational cohort data provide valuable insights into consumer preferences. Environmental scanning alerts the product developer to social, cultural, political, and economic shifts that will have an impact on the marketplace. But to truly respond to the degree of market segmentation demanded by today's consumers requires a more personal dialogue. Information can be collected and warehoused using point-of-sale data systems and mined for patterns, or dialogue can be initiated directly with the consumer. A combination of techniques will likely yield the most accurate results. This dialogue must be ongoing because consumer attitudes are constantly evolving. It is vital for companies that intend to compete in the new environment to keep the consumer at the focal point of their planning. Information learned must provide the foundation for a product development strategy.

Key Terms

attribute replenishment	masstige
automatic replenishment	micromarketing
cohort group	niche market
consumer era	point of sale (POS)
consumer intimacy	pop-up store
Consumer Price Index (CPI)	production era
data integrity	psychographics
data mining	qualitative research
data profiling	quantitative research
data warehouse	sales era
demographics	sample
electronic data interchange (EDI)	sell-through
environmental scanning	stock keeping unit (SKU)
focus group	style testing
generational marketing	surveys
market segmentation	target market
marketing era	wear-testing

Discussion Questions

1. Discuss your priorities in shopping for apparel and differentiate those priorities from those of your parents. How do your perceptions of value differ? Distinguish between the types of shopping environments and advertising messages that appeal to you and those that appeal to your parents.

2. In class, identify several brands that do an excellent job at relating to you as a consumer. Discuss the strategies and product characteristics that make each brand successful. Likewise, identify several brands, intended for your given market, that are not successful in relating to your consumer expectations.

3. Why are demographic data alone insufficient to analyze a market? Discuss examples within your own peer group where individuals with similar demographic backgrounds exhibit different shopping behavior.

4. As a consumer, what criteria do you use to determine apparel purchases?

5. How have companies solicited your consumer input in the past? What was your reaction to their questions?

6. Identify several factors that product developers don't seem to understand

about your personal product preferences. Where are they missing the mark? How might they learn this information?

7. Identify a store that is on a downward cycle in popularity. Discuss the reasons for the store's waning popularity. Identify a store that is on an upward cycle of popularity. Discuss the reasons for that store's success. Are the reasons you identify for each scenario controllable?

Activities

1. Do further research to learn more about one of the generational cohort groups active in the marketplace today. What are its shopping priorities when purchasing apparel? What types of marketing, advertising, and promotional campaigns are most effective with this cohort group? What are the functional expectations of this cohort group over the life expectancy of the garment? Compare your results with those who study the other generational cohort groups. Develop a list of attributes that you would want to build into a product line if you were designing for that market.

2. Identify an underserved niche market (e.g., tweens, maternity, petites, plus-size, school uniforms, mature markets). As a class, research that market using periodical and online resources. Prepare a set of questions to identify further information you would need to develop apparel products for this market. Invite a representative panel to class and interview them as to their apparel needs and preferences or conduct a survey to collect data. Develop design criteria based on the data you collect. Your design criteria should include preferences regarding aesthetics, fit, fabric, function, care, and price point.

3. As an individual or a class, design a store observation study to better understand consumer preferences. A few examples follow but feel free to design a study that is of interest to you. Discuss your observations and insights in class.

   • Compare the shopping experience of male and female shoppers. Jot down notes as to whether they try on clothing or not, whether they shop with someone or alone, how many displays they look at before making a decision, whether they ask questions regarding the product, and whether they make a purchase.

   • Observe customers of a particular age group in a mall. Identify which stores they shop and their shopping behaviors. Do they shop alone or with other people? Observe their interaction with sales associates. What stores do they enter? How long do they spend in a store? Observe how they take in a garment they are considering.

4. Identify a prototype store in your area. Compare the store design and merchandise carried to other stores. If a prototype store is not accessible, com-

pare a company's Web site and its local stores. Are the store image and merchandise consistent?

5. Write an anonymous description of a particular apparel need using demographic and psychographic information to describe your preferences. Demographic descriptors would include price point limits due to income and family life stage, color preferences related to ethnic heritage, and preferences related to age. Psychographic descriptors would include lifestyle preferences that influence your apparel preferences. Exchange these papers and attempt to interpret the expressed clothing need of the paper you receive in a series of 3 to 5 sketchbook designs. Share the resulting designs in class and discuss your experience in interpreting this information. Did you have enough information? If not, what further information did you need? How did this experience help you to understand the product developer's responsibility for developing customer intimacy?

References

Belgum, Karl D. 1999. *Who leads at half-time?: Three conflicting visions of internet privacy policy.* Symposium, 6 Rich. J. L. & Tech. 1, www.richmond.edu/jolt/v6i1/belgum.html.

Bigresearch. 2005. Bigresearch's simultaneous media usage survey (SIMM VII). Adapted from The WWD List, *Women's Wear Daily,* January 19, 2006.

Casabona, Liza. 2006. Factoring in consumer trends. *Women's Wear Daily,* March 20.

Derby, Meredith. 2004. Knowing your customer: Keep up with her changes. *Women's Wear Daily,* October 18.

Edelson, Sharon. 2003. The paths to growth: Know thy customer, get a niche, innovate. *Women's Wear Daily,* April 16.

Feitelberg, Rosemary. 1999a. Wear-testing athletic product. *Women's Wear Daily,* December 16.

Feitelberg, Rosemary. 1999b. Wear-Testing 101. *Women's Wear Daily,* December 16.

Frings, G. S. 2002. *Fashion from concept to consumer.* 7th ed. Upper Saddle River, NJ: Prentice-Hall.

Generation Watch. 2006. www.earthlink.net (accessed July 2, 2006)

Holmes, Stanley. 2006. Nike: It's not a shoe, it's a community. *Business Week,* July 24, www.businessweek.com/magazine/content/06_30/b3994068.htm?chan=search (accessed July 19, 2006).

Just-style.com. 2005. Fit is the hook for premium denim. www.just-style.com/article.aspx?id=92530&lk=s.

Just-style.com. 2005. The end of the road for mid-market retailers? www.just-style.com/article.aspx?id=92496&lk=s.

Just-style.com. 2001. USA: Apparel manufacturers to use online animation research. www.just-style.com/article.aspx?id=75462&lk=s.

Kurt Salmon Associates. 1998. *Consumer Outlook '98* (February). Atlanta, GA: Kurt Salmon Associates.

Kurt Salmon Associates. 2004. Retailers vs. brands: Consumer knowledge is power. www.kurtsalmon.com/content/main/body/industries/consumer_products/body.htm (accessed July 27, 2006).

Lach, Jennifer. 1999. If the sneaker fits . . . . *American Demographics*, December, www.adage.com.

Lee, Georgia. 2005. Direct sales gain as shoppers seek personal touch. *Women's Wear Daily*, October 12.

Lifestyle Monitor. 2006. Fashion's red carpet ride. *Women's Wear Daily*, March 9.

Lifestyle Monitor. 2004. Spend shift. *Women's Wear Daily*, July 22.

Moin, David. 2005. Adding plasma to in-store DNA. *Women's Wear Daily*, February 9.

Morrow, James. 2003. A place for one. *American Demographics*, November, www.findarticles.com (accessed October 1, 2006).

NPD Group. 2004. NPD fashionworld. *Women's Wear Daily*, June 30.

NPD Group. 2005. NPD fashionworld consumer data estimates. *Women's Wear Daily*, December 14.

Paul, Pamela. 2003. Sell it to the psyche. *Time Magazine*, September 15, www.acxiom.com (accessed April 1, 2007).

Pine, B. J., II, D. Peppers, and M. Rogers. 2000. Do you want to keep your customers forever? In *Markets of One*, ed. J. H. Gilmore and B. J. Pine, 53–74. Boston: Harvard Business School Publishing.

Reda, Susan. 2005. What fortune holds. *Stores*, December, www.stores.org (accessed December 5, 2005).

Schneiderman, I. P. 2000. Echo boomers: Staggering spending power. *Women's Wear Daily*, February 3.

Seckler, Valerie. 2003. Apparel missing mark with hispanics. *Women's Wear Daily*, July 30.

Seckler, Valerie. 2005a. Gen-X pinches apparel purchasing. *Women's Wear Daily*, December 14.

Seckler, Valerie. 2005b. Quest for real thing points to comfort. *Women's Wear Daily*, October 19.

Seckler, Valerie. 2005c. The squeeze on apparel's sweet spots. *Women's Wear Daily*, February 9.

Smith, J. Walker. 2004. Consumer resistance to marketing reaches all-time high, marketing productivity plummets, according to Yankelovich study. Address at American Association of Advertising Agencies conference, April 15, in Miami Beach, FL.

Smith, J. W., and A. Clurman. 1997. *Rocking the ages: The Yankelovich report on generational marketing*. New York: Harper.

Stein, M. K. 1998. *The prosperous retirement: Guide to the new reality*. Boulder: Emstco Press.

Strauss, W., and N. Howe. 1992. *Generations: The history of America's future, 1584 to 2069*. New York: William Morrow.

Tischler, Linda, 2004. What's the buzz? *Fast Company* 82:76.

VALS Program. 2003. *Understanding U.S. consumers*. Menlo Park, CA: SRI Consulting Business Intelligence. www.sric-bi.com/VALS/.

Ware, R. 1999. Over 50: Demanding and in demand. *American Demographics*, September, www.adage.com (accessed on April 1, 2007).

Williamson, Rusty. 2005. The Latin beat goes on. *Women's Wear Daily*, April 13.

Women's Wear Daily. 2004a. Hispanics' top store characteristics. April 22.

Women's Wear Daily. 2004b. Asian promise: Lost in translation. June 30.

Women's Wear Daily. 2004c. Masstige: Is it a revolution or a trend? September 1.

PART TWO

CREATIVE PLANNING

CHAPTER 4

TREND FORECASTING

"Embrace the paradoxes. For every trend you can spot, there's an equally valid countertrend at the other end of the spectrum. There is no longer one right way . . . to design a product, merchandise a line, or assort a department."

—ROBYN WATERS

OBJECTIVES

- To understand the dimensions of fashion and the life cycle of a fashion trend

- To learn to use environmental scanning to identify long- and short-term trends

- To identify resources available for trend forecasting

- To understand the importance of shopping the market

- To become familiar with color, fabric, and silhouette forecasting resources

- To understand how trends are interpreted for specific markets

- To identify the personnel responsible for trend forecasting

- To become familiar with formats for seasonal forecasts

It can be said that **fashion** is a reflection of our times, a mirror of the prevailing ideas in our society. The concept of fashion applies not only to apparel, but also to literature, automobiles, home furnishings, architecture, and food to name a few categories (Figure 4.1a–b). Fashion helps us to identify what is desirable or beautiful. In addition to its function as a form of artistic and creative expression, fashion is a response to our functional needs, a platform for new scientific applications, and the stimulus for a huge global business. Fashion has many faces, making it an elusive concept—challenging to follow, exciting to discover, and fickle should one become too attached—because fashion is ultimately about change.

The Dimensions of Fashion

Fashion has many dimensions. It exists at different levels, each of which prioritizes the artistic, functional, scientific, and business aspects of fashion somewhat differently. Fashion is also a language through which we identify our

Figure 4.1a–b. *Fashion exists not only in the world of apparel, but also in automobiles and architecture. A runway look from Donna Karan's Fall 2006 collection and the Santiago Calatrava addition to the Milwaukee Art Museum were both directional in their field of influence.*

affiliations and roles and express our attitudes about age, gender, power, and sexuality. Fashion is dynamic. It moves and morphs through a cycle of popularity that is the essence of fashion. Trend forecasters must understand the dimensions of fashion in order to interpret trends for their specific market.

Fashion Levels

The Paris couture is considered the highest level of fashion. The couture is sometimes criticized for existing in a world that is more fantasy than reality, but this no-rules environment gives birth to many directional fashion ideas. On the runway, designers show clothes that explore the limits of creativity and fantasy. The garments they sell are made to order by the best technicians, for clients who can afford prices that start at $20,000 for a suit and climb to $300,000 for an elaborate evening gown (Figure 4.2a–b). According to Sidney Toledano, president of Dior, there are about 300 core customers for couture, with most coming from the United States and the Middle East (Socha 2002, 6).

Characterized by luxurious fabrics, complex silhouettes, meticulous tailoring, exquisite beading, and unique details, couture garments are truly works of art. Designers focus on artistic and creative expression, along with a quest for publicity, rather than practicality, function, or profit motives. That being said, the publicity garnered by couture collections gives cachet to the ready-to-wear, accessories, and fragrances of the same house. These products reflect inspiration from the couture in terms of silhouette, materials, and techniques (Socha 2002, 6). The houses of Chanel, Dior, and Jean Paul Gaultier are among those that show couture lines.

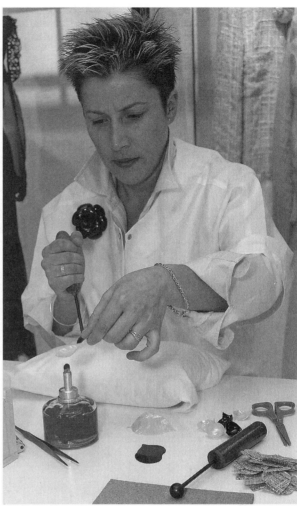

Figure 4.2a–b. *Couture garments explore the limits of creativity and are made by the best technicians in the world.* Left to right: *A couture design from Jean Paul Gaultier's 2006 collection and a couture specialist practicing her trade.*

The next level of fashion is designer ready-to-wear, sometimes known as prêt-à-porter. More profit-oriented, designer ready-to-wear styles may be produced in quantities that vary from 100 garments to several thousand. Although not as expensive as couture garments, they are beautifully designed, impeccably made, and use the finest fabrics. Designer ready-to-wear labels include *Armani, Gucci, Prada, Chanel, Donna Karan,* and many others. Trend forecasters look to designer ready-to-wear to identify the right shade of the next hot color, the newest detail or accessory, and the "of-the-moment" hemline.

Most of us make our fashion selections from mass-market, moderate, and better price points in apparel. The product developers for the labels found in mass retailers, chain stores, and department stores interpret fashion trends, taking into account the lifestyle and budget of their average target consumer. Garments designed for labels such as the *Gap, Jones New York, George ME,* and *Tony Hawk* prioritize value, practicality, and function, as well as aesthetics, for mainstream consumers in order to maximize sales and profits (Figure 4.3). Thanks to the real-time availability of news from the designer runways, important trends trickle down to these lines rapidly. Popular styles at this level of fashion may be produced in quantities of up to one million.

Figure 4.3. *George ME is an exclusive brand designed by Mark Eisen for Wal-Mart, a mass retailer.*

Street fashions originate with the consumer rather than a designer or product developer. Free spirits and innovative youth, who bristle at the cookie-cutter approach to fashion in traditional channels, express their creativity by putting together unique looks of their own. They scour flea markets, vintage stores, army surplus stores, and other eclectic but inexpensive sources for looks that define who they are and how they think. Some of the biggest trends in recent years—cargo pants, lowriders, frayed jeans, and do-rags—originated on the street with musicians, night-clubbers, and urban bohemians.

New York Times photographer Bill Cunningham has made his career chronicling fashion on the streets of New York—but street fashion can happen anywhere, not only in New York. Designers and trend forecasters track street fashions and reinterpret these trends for their own customers. Marc Jacobs identified the grunge look and made it mainstream; he reintroduced it in his Fall 2006 collection (Figure 4.4a). Leading hip-hop artists have built on the popularity of street looks and launched their own clothing lines—*Sean John* by Sean "P. Diddy" Combs, *Phat Farm* by Russell Simmons, and *Rocawear* by Jay-Z (Figure 4.4b).

Functional fashion takes advantage of scientific developments in textiles, fabric construction and finishing, and electronics to make high-tech apparel that appeals to the needs of niche markets. On July 13, 2006, Nike and Apple partnered to launch the Nike + iPod Sport Kit, which allows Nike+ ready footwear to communicate with the Apple iPod nano through a sensor in the Nike+ footwear and a receiver plugged into the nano. This system allows the runner to receive audible updates on speed, distance, and calories burned upon request throughout the run (Nike Press Release, 2006). Similarly, Levi's announced that it would launch the first jeans compatible with iPod portable music players in autumn 2006. Levi's new RedWire DLX brand features a joystick incorporated into the jean's watch pocket (just-style.com 2006) (Figure 4.5). Adidas introduced "intelligent" running shoes and "intelligent" basketball shoes in 2005. Both provide the right level of cushioning, depending on the wearer's size or movement. A magnetic sensor in the heel senses the level of compression, which is sent to a microprocessor in the shoe that understands if the cushioning level is too soft or too firm; a motor-driven cable system adapts the cushioning as needed (just-style.com 2005).

Aerodynamic fabrics can maximize an athlete's speed and are frequently introduced at high-stakes competitions such as the Olympics. Researchers and developers are exploring the use of electronic monitors that can be built into clothing in order to track a patient's vital signs. The impetus for these technologies grows out of the specific needs of niche markets; however, the resulting technologies are quickly adapted for use in other fashion markets. Knit and woven fabrics enhanced with Lycra grew out of the active sportswear market. Electronic monitors built into apparel for medical purposes might be adapted for keeping tabs on children who have a tendency to run off, or they might morph into built-in sound systems that replace headsets. The integration of technology into apparel is increasingly important to generations that are constantly "plugged in."

The Language of Fashion

As consumers of apparel, we use fashion as a means of expression. In her book *The Language of Clothes*, Alison Lurie states: "Long before I am near enough to talk to you on the street, in a meeting, or at a party, you announce your sex, age, and class to me through what you are wearing—and very possibly give me important information (or misinformation) as to your occupation, origin, personality, opinions, tastes, sexual desires, and current mood" (Lurie 1981, 3). Even the person who shows a total lack of interest in fashion is making a statement. Each time we get dressed, we are choosing the clothes that will send

Figure 4.4a–b. *Marc Jacobs and Jay-Z both take inspiration from street fashion and make it mainstream.*

a message to all those with whom we come in contact. Most of us become fairly adept at using the language of fashion to effectively articulate who we are. We celebrate the paradox of fashion that provides us with options to play a variety of roles. We know how to dress according to corporate expectations; but our colleagues may not recognize us when we're out on the town. From soccer mom to flirt, from high fashion to low fashion, today's consumer has multiple personalities.

A trend and its countertrend may both appeal to the same customer at different points in time. Product developers must understand that there are diffferent ways to satisfy the same customer. Ultimately we all try to balance our desire to fit in with our desire to stand out, and we use fashion to help us toward that end (Waters 2006, 9–20).

The Fashion Cycle

Fashion is defined by trends. A **trend** is a preference for a particular set of product characteristics within a consumer group. Trends may refer to innovations in fiber or fabric or the popularity of a particular color, silhouette, or detail. The fashion cycle helps us to follow the acceptance and rejection of fashion trends by tracking their movement, pace, and direction. The fashion cycle is represented by a bell-shaped curve that is plotted using a vertical axis that represents unit sales and a horizontal axis that represents time. As each new idea passes through the fashion cycle, it goes through a series of stages.

• At the introduction stage, new trends are recognized and worn by fashion innovators who have the means to buy designer fashions straight from the runways of Europe or who may put together innovative street looks that send fashion in a new direction.

Figure 4.5. *Levi's RedWire DLX jeans feature a side pocket for an iPod and a white control patch sewn into the watch pocket that adjusts the volume or stops and starts the music. Retractable headphones sit at the waistband.*

Introduction:	Growth:	Acceleration:	Saturation:	Decline:	Obsolescence:
Worn by fashion innovators, includes designer fashions and street fashion.	Fashion leaders pick up on trend and help to popularize.	The trend is interpreted for a mass market lifestyle and purchased by fashion followers.	The trend finds mass acceptance and looks timely to wear or buy among fashion followers.	Fashion followers still wear trend but are no longer interested in purchasing.	Looks dated to wear; no one wants to buy it.
Designer boutique and high-end specialty stores.	Fast-fashion retailers, contemporary boutiques, and specialty stores.	Moderate and better labels at department stores, mass merchants, and specialty stores.	Primarily found at moderate retailers and mass merchants.		

SALES

TIME

Figure 4.6. *The Fashion Cycle explains how fashion trends evolve through an introductory phase, to mass market saturation, and finally into obsolescence.*

Figure 4. 7a–b. *Wal-Mart is attempting to offer more fashion-forward apparel. In order to promote its new lines, Wal-Mart staged a rooftop fashion show during the Spring 2006 fashion week in New York.*

• During the growth stage, fashion leaders or early adopters purchase the fashion as it becomes more widely available at bridge and better price points.

• During the saturation stage, the fashion is at its height of popularity and is widely available to mass markets at all price points.

• During the decline and obsolescence stage, consumers may continue to wear the fashion, but they are no longer interested in purchasing additional items unless it is at greatly reduced prices. Eventually, the fashion item looks dated and is impossible to sell (Figure 4.6).

The fashion cycle is a very important tool for trend forecasters. Product developers must know when their target customer is ready to purchase. Designer signature stores, designer departments in department stores, and high-end contemporary boutiques want to offer the latest trends during the introduction phase. Bridge and better product developers as well as trend-forward mass merchants bring the price down a notch and cater to fashion leaders during the growth stage. Even discounters such as Wal-Mart are finding that they can't be complacent about the fashion level of their merchandise. Wal-Mart hosted a "Rock the Runway" show on the roof of a building in New York's Times Square during the Spring 2006 Fashion Week (Figure 4.7a–b). The event featured its fall 2006 collection and was simulcast on the ground floor of Times Square Studios, where crowds gathered to view the show. A product developer needs to anticipate when a fashion idea will reach the saturation point, since new products are planned anywhere from 3 months to one year in advance of the season.

Fashion ideas diffuse through the fashion cycle at their own pace. Innovations with short popularity spurts, called **fads**, can be disastrous to a business if the trend was projected to have a longer life cycle or a wider audience. Sometimes a trend is so easy to copy that the market is flooded in a very short time. Because the item is so widely available, consumers tire of it quickly. At other times a fashion idea is inappropriate for a wide range of customers and never catches on in those markets.

Most fashion ideas last at least through a selling season, and many continue to evolve over two or more seasons through manipulations of color, fabric, and details that give the idea new life and added longevity. Some styles are so enduring that they never go completely out of fashion. These styles are called **classics**. The Chanel-style suit, the five-pocket jean, and the slip dress are all examples of classic silhouettes.

Environmental Scanning

Technological innovation, particularly the Internet, and the globalization of fashion, have accelerated the rate of fashion change. Charting the course of fashion trends is one of the biggest challenges facing product developers at all levels of fashion. Once a trend is identified, it must be analyzed to determine its application in a particular market. After a trend has taken hold, it must be evaluated to determine whether it will be a short-lived fad, evolve into a second or third season, or have the potential to become a fashion classic. The real-time element of the Internet gives consumers the upper hand. They have immediate access to new looks once they hit the runway, and they expect to find those same looks in stores. That impatience, combined with the quest for newness and individuality that characterizes generations X and Y, has fashion forecasters scrambling to keep up with the next wave of fashion trends.

Designers, trend specialists, and merchandisers are by nature instinctive individuals who pride themselves on their ability to hone in on environmental changes and anticipate the resulting impact on fashion and lifestyles. However, it is wise for them to validate their instincts by utilizing all of the resources available in order to reduce the inherent risk in trend forecasting. It's great to recognize a trend on its upward ascent and offer merchandise that is well timed. Likewise, missing a trend or miscalculating its longevity can be costly.

Environmental scanning is the ongoing process of surveying a variety of resources for economic, political, social, technological, and cultural conditions for insights into the future. It is an important tool for long- and short-term forecasting.

Table 4.1 POPULAR FUTURISTS AND TREND FORECASTERS

Cotton Incorporated's Lifestyle Monitor conducts consumer research regarding consumer preferences in regards to apparel and shopping behavior. A column runs every Thursday in *Women's Wear Daily.*

Faith Popcorn cofounded the company Brain Reserve in 1974 and is known for her books, *The Popcorn Report* (1991), *Clicking* (1997), *Eveolution* (2000) and *Dictionary of the Future* (2001). Popcorn is a popular speaker at trade shows and professional meetings and works with a varied array of clients in her marketing consultancy. Her methodology involves scanning a continuous stream of periodicals, monitoring pop culture, shopping stores across the country and abroad, and interviewing consumers in regard to a variety of product categories.

Iconoculture is a consulting company in Minneapolis, Minnesota, that monitors pop culture and the trends transforming our lives. It is known for its quirky jargon. The company's Web site features a newsletter and "Signs of the Times" column. Company executives Vicki Abrahmson, Mary Meehan, and Larry Samuel wrote the book *The Future Ain't What it Used to Be: The 40 Cultural Trends Transforming Your Job, Your Life, Your World.* www.iconoculture.com

Pine and Gilmore are known for their books, *One to One Marketing* and *The Experience Economy.* Their predictions about the evolving consumer-driven economy are changing the way product developers market and distribute apparel. www.customization.com

Robyn Waters is the former Vice-President of Trend, Design, and Product Development at Target and author of *The Trendmaster's Guide: Get a Jump on What Your Customer Wants Next* and *The Hummer & the Mini: Navigating the Contradictions of the New Trend Landscape.* She currently runs her own consulting firm, RW Trend, that tracks the latest consumer trends and advises companies on how to stay ahead of the curve. www.rwtrend.com

TrendWatching.com calls itself an independent and opinionated trend firm that utilizes 8,000-plus trend spotters to scan the globe for emerging consumer trends and business ideas. They report on their findings in free trend briefings. The company was founded by Renier Evers and is located in Amsterdam, The Netherlands.

Watts Wacker is the founder of First Matter, a company known for its ability to identify cultural and business trends through the use of observational research. He has authored or coauthored numerous books including *The 500-Year Delta: What Happens After What Comes Next* (1997), *The Visionary's Handbook* (2001), and *The Deviant's Advantage* (2004). www.firstmatter.com

Yankelovich Monitor is a consulting company that specializes in the analysis of consumers, with an expertise on generational behaviors. www.yankelovich.com

Zandl Group is a boutique agency that specializes in what's next for business, the culture, and consumers. www.zandlgroup.com

Long-Term Forecasting

Long-term forecasting is the process of analyzing and evaluating trends that are identified by continuous scanning of a variety of sources for information. It is frequently the realm of futurists who chart movements of change and identify potential obstacles. They link breakthroughs in science, technology, and medicine to the likely course of demographic trends, and then they examine the impact those changes may have on the economy, political system, environment, and culture. Long-term forecasting seeks to identify

• major shifts in domestic and international demographics

• changes in industry and market structures

Figure 4.8a. *Ground Zero in New York City continues to symbolize the uncertainty of global current events.*

- changes in consumer interests, values, and motivation
- breakthroughs in technology and science
- changes in the domestic or global economic picture
- shifts in political, cultural, or economic alliances between countries (Brannon 2005, 143)

Long-term forecasting is integral to both strategic planning and trend forecasting. For example, the rapid impact of technology is a long-term trend that has contributed to a shift toward business casual dress over the course of the past decade. As more business is conducted via the telephone and the Internet, there is less person-to-person interaction during the course of a business day. If there is little face-to-face contact with clients, there is less need for formal business attire.

A number of marketing consultants specialize in long-term trend forecasting. They are frequent keynote speakers at trade shows and professional meetings, alerting the industry to shifting demographics and psychographics that will affect what the consumer wants. These consultants may be hired by individual companies to assess how changing patterns will influence a company's business and offer strategies that tailor the trends they see to the company's particular niche (Table 4.1).

Short-Term Forecasting

Short-term forecasting analyzes current events and pop culture to identify new trends that can be communicated to the customer through seasonal color, fabric, and silhouette stories to give fashion a fresh look each season. A new movie, a new musical group, or a popular television show can all inspire new fashion trends.

Environmental Scanning Influences

Environmental scanning relies on an analysis of news in a variety of categories, each with its own impact on fashion. These influences affect trends in color, fabric, and silhouette each season.

Current Events

Global current events have a major impact on fashion. The events of 9/11, the terrorist attacks since that time in Europe, and the war with Iraq have made global citizens around the world feel less safe and may in part be the impetus for a return to more modest apparel. The attack on the World Trade Center towers occurred at the start of New York's spring runway shows. More than 80 shows were canceled, and activity on Seventh Avenue came to a stop. Suddenly, fashions that made political statements about war required a new sensitivity. For the next few months any accessory or item of clothing that declared one's patriotism was comforting, and attendees at the twice-post-

Figure 4.8b. *India's Bollywood is modeled after Hollywood as an influence on the pop culture scene in India and beyond.*

Figure 4.8c. *High fuel costs have not only resulted in more cautious consumer spending but have also affected the cost of producing apparel.*

poned Emmy Awards opted for short cocktail dresses over ostentatious long gowns. By 2003, Americans were ready to view the world more positively. Fashion obliged with a return to a more colorful palette that lasted several years. As the war dragged on and tensions in the Middle East escalated in 2006, designers reverted to a predominately neutral palette. Over the long term, the events of September 11, 2001, affected the economy, caused consumers to reevaluate their values, and stimulated dialogue within the industry as to the relevance of runway shows (Figure 4.8a).

The opening of trade relations with China has inspired some designers to study traditional Chinese silhouettes and fabrics for inspiration. A country or culture that is in the news regularly can influence fashion trends regardless of why it is in the news. India's silk trade, the culture's rich heritage of colorful embroidery and beading, and the cinematic influence of Bollywood have made it a regular source of inspiration for designers all over the world (Figure 4.8b).

Domestic and global economic conditions have a major impact on consumer confidence and willingness to spend. When the economy is up, fashion may be more extravagant; when it is down, consumers are more conservative in their preferences. The spike in global oil prices put a fiscal scare into many consumers (Figure 4.8c).

The Arts

The arts have a major impact on fashion. Designers and fashion forecasters make it a point of being the first to see a major art opening or historic costume exhibition. Color forecasters may respond to the mere announcement of a major art exhibition. An exhibit of paintings by Monet, van Gogh, Matisse, or Klimt is sure to influence both seasonal color palettes and textile patterns (Figure 4.9a). The Balenciaga exhibit in Paris at the Musée de la Mode et du Textiles brought about a major silhouette change in 2006 (Figure 4.9b).

Figure 4.9a. *Carolina Herrera was inspired by a Gustav Klimt exhibit for her Spring 2006 collection.*

Figure 4.9b. *Museum exhibiitons that focus on a specific designer label or an individual designer's body of work often influence current fashion trends. An exhibition of Paul Poiret designs during the summer of 2007 at the Metropolitan Museum of Art impacted apparel silhouettes as well as color palette and design details.*

The performing arts can also have an impact on fashion. An exciting world-class ballerina can create a broad-based interest in the ballet and inspire a seasonal palette of soft pinks, the use of tulle, and ballet flats.

Popular culture also plays a major role in creating fashion trends. The impact of popular new musical groups is readily apparent in the youth market. Television shows such as *Sex and the City, Desperate Housewives,* and *Project Runway* have had a recognizable influence on popular fashion (Figure 4.9d). Movies such as *The Devil Wears Prada,* based on the fashion industry, *Portrait of a Geisha,* and *Marie Antoinette* are also likely sources for fashion trends. Not only are the arts important, but we anticipate the award ceremonies where we recognize the best in movies, television, and music just to see our favorite celebrities dressed in gowns from the best designers (Figure 4.9c). In general, many young people are more apt to follow celebrity magazines than they are fashion magazines for their fashion news.

Sports

Popular sports frequently influence fashion. In New York, Ralph Lauren organizes his Madison Avenue store across from the Rhinelander Mansion by specific sports. In any given season, sections might be devoted to golf, boating, hiking, or scuba diving. His spectator sportswear lines frequently take their seasonal inspiration from a popular consumer sport. The celebrity of sports stars such as golfer Tiger Woods or ice skater Sasha Cohen enhances the influence of sports on apparel and can be a major marketing tool when these stars lend their

Figure 4.9d. *The popularity of shows such as* Project Runway *have helped mainstream audiences better understand the design process.*

Figure 4.9c. *The gowns worn by celebrities at award show functions have had a strong impact on the prom market in recent years.*

names to an apparel label. Today the stars of sports such as surfing, soccer, skateboarding, and snowboarding are also influencing fashion. Skinny jeans may have grown out of a need for skateboarders to do their moves without fabric flapping in the wind. Skateboarder Tony Hawk entered into a licensing agreement with Kohl's in 2006. Technology developed for the Olympics eventually finds its way into commercial apparel (Figure 4.10a–b).

Science and Technology

Science and technology affect many aspects of fashion, from the colors we can achieve on different mediums to the fabrications available, to how garments function, to how we care for and dispose of garments. We can now grow cotton in colors. We can digitally print fabrics, which will eventually enable consumers to choose the pattern they want on a garment. New fibers and modifications of existing fibers are constantly being introduced. Such innovations can make garments easier to care for and more flexible to use. Technology has already influenced garment silhouettes, as we build in pockets for pagers, cell phones, and handheld computers. The next generation of electronic devices will include many that can be built into the garment. Variations on home dry cleaning methods are already on the market. Future apparel may include information chips with encoded care and recycling instructions.

Figure 4.11. *Resources developed for trend forecasters and product developers must project trends 18 to 24 months in advance of a season. These projections are refined as the season gets closer.*

Figure 4.10a. *Nike developed the Sphere suit for runners in the Athens Olympics.*

Figure 4.10b. *Nike is able to apply much of the specialized research it does for events such as the Olympics to its mainstream activewear lines.*

Environmental Scanning Resources

Merchandisers, trend managers, and designers must have an instinctive sense about how environmental factors will affect their target audience. They must scan news resources such as *Time, BusinessWeek,* and the cable news networks, as well as fashion resources such as *Vogue, InStyle,* and *Harper's Bazaar.* Relying only on fashion magazines directed toward the consumer can be dangerous. Once a trend appears in a magazine, consumers expect to find examples of the trend in-store. However, magazine websites frequently post fashion information before it appears in the magazine. Conde Nast's www.style.com and www.elle.com are excellent resources.

Resources developed for forecasters and product developers project trends up to two years into the future, giving the product developer time to interpret the information and develop product (Figure 4.11). Some media sources are more influential than others. Scanning a few cutting-edge sources in major spheres of influence can give product developers the information they need to recognize impending long- and short-term trends (Table 4.2).

Media-scanning services will customize searches for a particular company in the form of clippings or Internet references. Media scans can be designed to gather information about a company's target customer, track editorial references about a company's brand portfolio, or track cultural shifts that may shape the next fashion trend.

Table 4.2 SOURCES FOR MEDIA SCANNING

GENERAL NEWS

Televised news on NBC, CBS, ABC, Fox, PBS, CNN, and MSNBC

News weeklies such as *Newsweek, Time,* and *U.S. News and World Report*

National newspapers such as *The New York Times, The Washington Post,* and *USA Today*

CONSUMER TRENDS

American Demographics, Advertising Age

www.trendwatching.com, www.firstmatter.com, www.iconoculture.com, www.trendsresearch.com

NEWS WITH A SLANT

Business news—*Business Week, The Wall Street Journal, Fortune, Forbes*

Cultural news publications covering the fine arts, the performing arts and the popular culture scene—*Architectural Digest, Veranda, Art and Antiques, Ornament, American Art Review, Vanity Fair, New Yorker*

Technology news—*Yahoo Internet Life, Wired, American Scientific*

International views—*The International Herald Tribune, The Economist*

APPAREL/FASHION NEWS

Apparel supply chain—*Apparel, Women's Wear Daily (WWD),* just-style.com

Fashion trends—*International Textiles, Women's Wear Daily (WWD), Collezioni Donna, French Vogue, Collezioni Trends, View, WeAr, dressing, Viewpoint, Gap Press, Fashion Trends Forecast*

Specific markets—*Earnshaw's Review, DNR, Accessories, Kidswear, Sportswear, Sport & Street, La Piel*

WEB SITES

www.style.com
www.wgsn.edu
www.just-style.com
www.infomat.com/trends
www.elle.com
www.instyle.com
www.dailycandy.com

Fashion newsletters and forecasting services can be a product developer's eyes and ears. They can save the trend forecasting or product development team a lot of time by validating their observations and alerting them to emerging trends. These services specialize in environmental scanning and conduct their own media scans; they shop the fashion meccas of the world and observe street fashions; and they attend fabric shows and cover the runway collections. Their analysis of market trends is typically more thorough than what the average product developer could do independently. Forecasting services typically offer fashion direction on color, fabric, silhouettes, and details. They provide photographic references to runway shows and street fashions. They alert product developers to trendy new stores and labels, and they offer calendars of upcoming events. Product developers try to identify resources that are relevant for their product and customer. Many services are now online, which enables them to disseminate information quickly.

Figure 4.12a–b. *Saint-Tropez, France, is a popular trend forecasting destination for resort clothes.*

Shopping the Market

The trends identified through environmental scanning must be verified and then interpreted for a product developer's target customer. Product developers and trend forecasters make it a practice to shop key markets for their category to watch new trends. Timing is a critical element of fashion. The right fashion, introduced too soon, quickly turns into a loss; however, carrying a silhouette or color beyond its fashion cycle is equally costly. Impending change is confirmed when fashion forecasters see the first signs of it in the marketplace. This happens first in the fashion centers of the world. Trend forecasters rely on shopping the market to get a sense of how consumers are likely to respond to the stimuli to which they are exposed and to ensure a certain amount of consistency in how trends are interpreted.

In order to interpret the information gathered during shopping, trend forecasters are expected to shop their own stores and those of the competition. They are adept at noticing what is sold from one week to the next. They engage sales associates in conversation to collect their insights. Because trend forecasters have one eye on the future, it is mandatory that they have the other on the present to give their forecasts context. Any time trend forecasters shop, be it for work or themselves, they are watching for trends and consumer response.

Determining Where to Shop

Product developers must determine which shopping venues will yield the most valuable information for their specific market, product category, price point, and fashion calendar. If they develop outerwear, they might shop

Figure 4.13a–b. *Flea markets and vintage stores offer unique finds for apparel product developers.*

Toronto; for resort, they may hit Saint-Tropez. New York, Los Angeles, Paris, Milan, Barcelona, and Antwerp are other common shopping destinations (Figure 4.12).

They may have a budget that enables them to purchase garments for inspiration. Some private label product developers work derivatively; they have large shopping budgets with which to buy samples that will become the basis for styles in their new seasonal line. Designers for wholesale brands or private labels brands that have their own design team generally sketch the ideas they see, using those ideas as departure points for their own designs. They tend to purchase garments only when a material or construction is so unusual that they require it for reference.

Shopping guides are available to help novice trend forecasters locate major shopping areas. New, innovative haunts are featured in *Women's Wear Daily, Vogue, Harper's Bazaar, InStyle,* and *Lucky,* to name a few publications. Trend forecasters working for forecasting services can also provide great tips as to where the most innovative shopping areas are.

Shopping the market is serious business. Days are long, as designers and merchandisers must cover a lot of ground in a short amount of time. They shop the areas that are relevant to the line they are developing, not according to what appeals to them personally. They try to take in relevant museum exhibitions that might affect trends. They may shop vintage stores and flea markets to find unique details and trims that can be incorporated into a line. (Figure 4.13a– b)

Shopping Domestically

Some trend forecasters confine their shopping research to domestic locales, such as New York City, Los Angeles, and Chicago. New York City offers the

Figure 4.14a–b. *The Prada flagship store in the SoHo district in New York and Calypso, a contemporary resource on Madison Avenue, offer directional clues for seasonal trends.*

largest assortment of fashion in the United States. Other good regional shopping locales include Atlanta, San Francisco, and Dallas. Los Angeles has long been on the cutting edge for casual wear, and is also considered important for men's wear. With the present focus on celebrities as fashion role models, Los Angeles takes on added importance as a shopping resource.

Any fashion professional who is responsible for shopping the market must keep a file of hot new shopping locales, as these sections of the cities tend to change frequently. Fifth Avenue in New York was once the domain of upscale fashion merchants. Today, it is dominated by prototype chain stores such as the Gap, Banana Republic, and Levi's. Madison Avenue continues to be home to many high-end signature stores. It is also interspersed with bridge label signature stores and a few chain stores such as Victoria's Secret. Soho is the center for retailers of young, trendy fashions and cutting-edge signature stores (Figure 4.14a–b). As rents in Soho soar, trendy new designers are opening businesses in Nolita (north of Little Italy) and in the meat-packing district.

Shopping Internationally

Many American product developers shop in Europe, Tokyo, Hong Kong, and Canada to find inspiration. International designers are known for their innovation and creativity, while American designers are often characterized as more marketable and mainstream. By shopping Europe, domestic product developers avoid knocking off one another and bring back ideas that may not be widely distributed in the United States. Product developers reinterpret these ideas to fit the American market.

It is valuable for trend forecasters to shop signature stores in the city in which the designer is based. These stores tend to have the most complete selection. If a product developer is strongly influenced by a particular designer, the developer may want to visit that designer's signature store in each major city in which he or she shops, knowing that the merchandise will vary from store to store.

Trend teams do not all shop in the same places. Junior product developers may shop the avant garde markets of London, Paris, and Amsterdam. Bridge designers may be more influenced by designer ready-to-wear in London, Paris, and Milan. Accessory designers will look to innovative designers such as Gucci, Prada, and Dolce & Gabbana. Cutting-edge shopping areas change constantly. Trend forecasters must plan their trips carefully in order to cover the most relevant markets for a particular season.

Although the pace of fashion change continues to escalate, fashion remains an evolutionary process. Next season's hot new trend tends to develop out of the season that precedes it. Trend forecasters cannot become so visionary that they lose perspective as to what their customer is ready for. But they also cannot be so staid that they miss the next wave.

The remainder of this chapter looks at how each element of fashion—color, fabrication, and silhouette—is conceived for a given season.

Color

Color is one of the first stimuli a customer responds to when shopping. This makes accurate forecasting of tomorrow's trend-setting colors a key to survival in the world of fashion. Color can make clothes purchased a few years ago look outdated. This is not to say that consumers will automatically buy a new color that they do not like or that is not becoming. Younger generations are most open to wearing any color that is trendy; older customers tend to limit the colors they purchase to those they believe look good on them. Thus, color forecasts need to be interpreted for different consumer groups and specific market categories.

The decision about a seasonal color palette is one of the first to be made in the product development process. The seasonal color story will be the basis for solids, prints, and yarn-dyed fabrics in a variety of fibers, across all styles in the line. Product developers review a variety of sources before making color decisions.

The Color Forecasting Process

The process of color forecasting begins two to two and a half years in advance of a selling season. It is based on environmental scanning, which identifies the nonfashion events that influence fashion trends and lifestyle themes

Table 4.3 IMPORTANT COLOR INFLUENCES, 1850S TO THE PRESENT

INFLUENCE	YEAR OR DECADE	PALETTE
Development of aniline dyes	1850s	Popularity of purple
The Great Depression	1930s	Drab brown, "The Taupe Age"
Elsa Schiaparelli	1930s	"Shocking pink"
World War II	1940s	Heavy grays, somber teals, somber reds
Op art	1960s	Black and white
Tutankhamen's tomb (museum exhibit)	1960s	Egyptian colors like turquoise and gold
Andy Warhol	1960s	Avocado green and harvest gold
Pompidou Center (architecture)	1970s	Bold primary and secondary colors
The Great Gatsby (movie)	1974	Pinks and whites
The Reagan Administration	1980s	Red
Miami Vice (TV show)	1980s	Pastels for men and women
Tour of Georgia O'Keefe paintings	mid-1980s	Southwest colors
Stock market crash	1987	Popularity of black at its height
Fall of the Iron Curtain	1990	Deep Baltic blues and reds
The environment—ozone layers	1990s	Green
Matisse exhibit, MOMA	1994	Bright primary and secondary colors
Election year	1996	Historically good for brights
Evita (movie)	1996	"Evita" red
New Millennium	2000	Sci-fi, space-age colors
Unrest in Eastern Europe	2000	Bohemian colors
Terrorists attack World Trade Center	2001	Somber neutral colors
Additional terrorist attacks averted	2003	Color and embellishment return to fashion
The war in Iraq lingers on	2006	A return to neutral colors

(Table 4.3). For instance, will a new president and first lady affect style at the White House? How does a renewed interest in environmental issues influence consumer color preferences? What impact will new demographics have as baby boomers begin to retire and a new generational cohort emerges? How does the constant threat of terrorism influence color?

Color Associations

The Color Marketing Group, the International Colour Authority (ICA), and the Color Association of the United States (CAUS) are the largest color organizations. Members of these groups are color specialists representing some of the biggest companies in the world. These organizations provide forums for their members to come together to discuss the various issues of color, network with other industry professionals, exchange information, become familiar with new technology, and forecast color directions. Working in committees, they forecast one to three years in advance for a variety of industries, including fashion, transportation, architecture, communications and graphics, toys, and textiles. Their color palettes project the course that colors are likely to take—warmer or cooler, lighter or darker, clearer or grayer—and the relative importance of a hue.

Textile Consortiums

Consortiums of textile manufacturers, such as the Cotton Council, the Wool Bureau, and the Manmade Fiber Producers, refine early color forecasts for their own markets. Each of these organizations develops a seasonal color story that is geared to the end-use categories of the markets it supplies. The predictions come to life as textile manufacturers present their seasonal lines at global fabric fairs that occur about one year before a consumer season (Figure 4.15).

Color Forecasters

Color forecasting specialists such as D3 Doneger Design Directions, Huepoint, and The Color Box offer subscription color services for a fee. These services generally release their forecasts 18 months prior to a season. This is about six months after organizations such as the Color Marketing Group and CAUS

Figure 4.15. *Attendees at an Italian fabric show make notes on color.*

have made their predictions. This extra time gives these services a chance to refine the earliest color forecasts and break them down into predictions for various markets and price points. A subscription generally includes four to six forecasts a year geared to the men's, women's, or children's market. Each forecast is made up of five to nine color palettes mounted with a visual that suggests a unifying theme. The colors are generally shown as small bundles of yarn or embroidery floss, which are referred to as **poms**.

Some subscriptions include duplicate poms for the subscriber to use as it develops its own seasonal palette. The duplicate poms may also be used at color presentations and at individual consultations in which the general forecast is analyzed for specific application to a product developer's business. Written material that is included with each palette suggests how to create color harmonies and identifies the markets for which each palette is most appropriate. Product developers who subscribe to these services may also schedule private consultations to further interpret the color projections for their market.

This consensus-building process is, in a sense, a self-fulfilling prophecy whereby each level of color forecasting builds on the one before it so that the color message consumers see is somewhat unified across all markets, brands, and price points. Like fashion, color forecasting is an evolutionary process. Color morphs from season to season, with each seasonal palette taking direction from the season that preceded it and giving a hint of what is to come in seasons that follow. Table 4.4 lists a number of color forecasting sources.

Color forecaster Alison Webb believes that color cycles can be tracked using a bell curve similar to the one used to measure fashion cycles. Colors are introduced, increase in popularity, their use becomes saturated, and then they become obsolete, typically over a three-year period. Color forecasters know when a color story first developed and how it has evolved through the market. They ask a series of questions. Was the color in the market last season? How saturated was it? Was the story based on primary clear colors or offbeat, unusual ones? How should the color story be developed for the next season? Color themes help the customer understand the importance of new colors. Color forecasters achieve a visual rhythm of where colors have been and where they are going as they work their way through the bell curve. In most cases, the designer, bridge, and better markets accept new colors first. A new color story may not surface in the mass market until a year later. That is why color cycles often span three years. However, a number of mass-market companies take pride in featuring new fashion colors very quickly, especially if they serve a young market that is tuned in to fashion but is on a limited budget (Webb 1994, 203–206).

Some color forecasters have linked a predilection for certain colors to historic cycles defined by developing technology and the mood of the time. Tom Porter and others believe that the use of bright, strong, primary colors signals high points in the development of a culture. The power of these strong colors is related to an expanded capacity to manipulate color because of new

Table 4.4 COLOR FORECASTING RESOURCES

Color Association of the United
  States (CAUS)
343 Lexington Avenue
New York, NY 10016

The Color Box
29 West 38th Street, 9th floor
New York, NY 10018
212-921-1399
Color forecasting.

Color Marketing Group
4001 North Ninth Street, Suite 102
Arlington, VA 22203

Color Portfolio
201 East 17th Street
New York, NY 10003

Committee for Colors & Trends
60 Madison Avenue, Suite 1209
New York, New York 10010
www.colour-trends.com

Concepts in Colour
2 West 32nd Street, Suite 301
New York, NY 10001
212-967-5688

The Cottonworks Fabric Library
Cotton Incorporated
488 Madison Avenue
New York, NY 10022
212-413-8300
www.cottoninc.com

D3 Doneger Design Direction
463 Seventh Avenue, 3rd floor
New York, NY 10018
212-560-3720
www.doneger.com

Design Options
112 West Ninth Street, Suite 1026
Los Angeles, CA 90015
213-622-9094
*Color projections, fabric, and retail
  shopping.*

Eiseman Center for Color
  Information and Training
Leatrice Eiseman, Director
8555 Ferncliff Avenue
Bainbride Island, WA 98110
206-842-4456

ESPtrendlab (Ellen Sideri
  Partnership Inc.)
12 West 37th Street
New York, New York 10018
212-629-9200

The Fashion Service
1412 Broadway, Suite 11410
New York, NY 10018
212-704-0035

Francoise de la Renta Color Room
  at The Fashion Institute of
  Technology
Seventh Avenue at 27th Street
New York, NY 10001
212-217-7999

Here & There
104 West 40th Street
New York, NY 10018
212-354-9014
Fashion forecasting and reporting.

Huepoint
39 West 37th Street, 18th floor
New York, NY 10018-6217
212-921-2025

International Association of Color
  Consultants
73 Pennsylvania Avenue
San Diego, CA 92103

International Colour Authority
23 Bloomsbury Square
London WCIA2PJ England
www.internationalcolourauthority.com
*Provides access to thousands of color
  samples and inspiration for color
  harmonies.*

Norma Morris Design Products
110 West 40th Street, Suite 306
New York, NY 10018
212-730-0758

Pantone Inc.
590 Commerce Blvd.
Carlstadt, NJ 07072
201-935-5500
www.pantone.com
*Color forecasting and color
  specification system.*

Peclers Paris
23, rue du Mail
75002 Paris
www.peclersparis.com
*Color, style, promotion, and
  communication consulting.*

Promostyl USA
80 West 40th Street
New York, NY 10018
212-921-7930
www.promostyl.com
Color and fashion forecasting.

SCOTDIC Colours
498 7th Avenue, 10th floor
New York NY 10018
212-643-9583
www.scotdic.com
Color specification system.

Trend Union
604 East 11th Street
New York, NY 10009
212-420-7623
Color and fashion forecasting.

Figure 4.16. *Designers shop domestic and international fabric shows to identify fabric trends.*

technology (Porter 1994). During economic downturns and extended times of war or similar duress, we see colors offerings become more sober, muted, or muddied.

Fabric

The task of researching seasonal fabrics goes on simultaneously with color research and determination of a color story. Many services that provide color forecasts also offer fabric forecasts. These sources alert the product developer to new technology, fibers, blends, and finishes by providing descriptions, swatches, and sketches of possible applications. They also confirm how color palettes and color harmonies are being combined with textile fibers, fabrics, and textures to create a seasonal look. Designers may rely on these sources and on magazine sources for preliminary research so that they recognize new materials in the marketplace. *Women's Wear Daily, International Textiles,* and *Bobbin* are but a few of the periodicals that product developers rely on for information on fabric trends.

Fabric Shows

Fabric is a medium that must be touched and draped in order to be appreciated. Toward that end, a number of domestic and international fabric and yarn shows are held each year to give product developers an overview of what's available. These shows provide an opportunity for yarn and fabric vendors to introduce their seasonal lines. Fabric show vendors frequently have prototype garments made to help sell their newest offerings. These garments can jog a product developer into thinking about new and offbeat ways to use a traditional fabric.

The shows also feature an area in which trend forecasters can share their seasonal predictions Seminars and speakers are offered throughout the run of the show to alert product developers to trends and new technology. By attending such fabric fairs, designers and product developers can confirm developing trends, identify new resources, and order sample fabric yardage. Sample yardage can be used for creative experimentation before committing to production yardage. It is important for designers and product developers to attend these shows so that they keep abreast of what is new.

The International Fashion and Fabric Exhibition is held at New York's Jacob Javits Center in October and April. Premiere Vision, in Paris, is perhaps the biggest, most important fabric show in the world. There is growing interest in Asian fabric exhibits because of their proximity to significant production sources (Figure 4.16). A number of other national and international shows appeal to regional markets or specialize in particular kinds of fibers and fabrics. Product developers must determine which fabric shows best match the needs of their category in terms of product type and price point. Table 4.5 lists of some of the most popular fabric shows.

Fabric Libraries

Fabric associations often assemble representative samples of fabrics for a given season that can be reviewed in their fabric libraries. Using the library can save a designer or product developer the time it would take to visit a number of vendor showrooms in order to identify in advance which sources have the fabric they are seeking.

Fabric Purchasing

Most of the buying that takes place at large fabric and fiber shows is for sample quantities. Larger commitments are made after the product developer has had time to experiment with the fabric and determine how important it will be to the seasonal line. Product developers prefer to postpone their final commitment to fabrics until the last possible moment in order to minimize risk.

Fabrics are not always ordered as they are shown. Once a product developer commits to a fabric, the developer may work with the vendor to adapt the fabric by modifying its weight, color, or pattern scale.

With the widespread use of offshore sourcing, many of the samples purchased at fabric shows are shared with offshore sourcing agents who attempt to have the fabric duplicated at a lower cost. This has contributed to the compression of the fashion cycle because low-cost product developers are able to knock off high-price fabrics, sometimes in the same season the fabrics are introduced.

Table 4.5 SELECTED FIBER AND FABRIC SHOWS

Direction (Formerly Inprints)—The major textile print show in America; held in New York three times a year, in January, April and August.

Ideabiella—High-quality Italian textiles shown in Milan in February and September. Sharing the same dates and venue are Ideacomo, Moda In, Prato Expo, and Shirt Avenue.

International Yarns, Fibers, Fabrics, & Accessories Exhibition—Held in October in Singapore.

Interstoff Asia—Asia's leading international event for fashion fabrics; held in Hong Kong in October and March.

Los Angeles International Textile Show—The nation's largest textile show; held in April and October.

Material World—This show is sponsored by the American Apparel and Footwear Association. Exhibitors include machinery and equipment suppliers, fabric/findings vendors, sourcing experts, and information technology providers. The exhibition takes place in New York in September and in Miami in May.

Organic Fiber Show—An opportunity to see and source the latest in apparel, bed and bath products, accessories, and fabric and textiles made from organic fiber; held in Chicago in May.

Pitti Immagine Filati—An Italian yarn fair in Florence held twice a year in July and January/February.

Premiere Vision New York—A capsule version of Premiere Vision that takes place in New York in January and July.

Premiere Vision—Better to couture European fabric suppliers show in Paris in February and September. Simultaneously Mon'Amont, Indigo, and Expofil are set up at the same venue.

Printsource New York—A textile and design concepts show that features prints, embroideries, knit swatches, silhouettes, yarn dyes, trend forecasting, vintage swatches, and vintage couture. The show takes place in New York in January, April, and August.

For exact dates of annual fabric shows, check www.infomat.com/calendar

Printed Fabrics

Product developers in certain categories rely on printed fabrics to make their line unique. Children's apparel, dresses, and lingerie are examples of categories that rely heavily on prints. Prints can be acquired in one of several ways. Some product developers select prints from a fabric supplier's seasonal line. Other product developers rely on their own creative design team to develop prints in-house. Prints developed in-house are then sourced out to a textile finisher, who prints the pattern on the fabric of its choice. Yet other product developers purchase prints from print studios. Purchased prints may be developed on the computer or rendered by hand.

Inprints and Print Source are print shows that take place in New York. Like fabric shows, these shows give print designers a venue for showing their work and give product developers who depend on prints an opportunity to shop a variety of print designers from all over the world. Prints can also be purchased from print agents, who have showrooms that are open year- round

Figure 4.17. *Print agents represent a group of textile artists in a single showroom, making it easier for product developers to shop for prints and relieving textile artists of the sales function.*

(Figure 4.17). Print agents may design their own prints as well as represent individual domestic and international print designers for a sales commission. The cost of a single print may range from $400 to $500.

Because prints are so expensive, many product developers who rely heavily on prints employ their own graphic designers to develop exclusive prints for their lines. In some private label firms, the creative design staff is mainly responsible for print development; the trend department comes up with silhouettes; and technical design interprets those two elements into the final garment.

Once a print is purchased, it is the property of the product developer and can be re-colored, or rescaled, or have motifs extracted to develop coordinating prints. As purchased, a fabric painting rarely matches the color story a product developer has chosen for its seasonal line. The product developer may have artists on staff or it may ask the textile finisher who will print the fabric to re-color the print to match its color standards. Likewise, a large print may need to be rescaled for the children's market. Motifs from print paintings can be applied to knit or woven fabrics, or used as the foundation for embroidery, beading, or other special effects. Prints are always archived for future use. Product developers responsible for categories at different price points may initially use a print at their higher price point and then use it the next season on a less expensive fabric in a slightly different color combination at their lower price point.

Trim Studios

In addition to print studios, there are trim studios that specialize in generating ideas for interesting trims and details such as embroideries, pin tucking, lace insertion, and so forth. Their swatches are offered as inspiration and generally are not available in yardage. It is up to the product developer to find a sourcing partner that can duplicate the technique. Trim swatches are generally

Figure 4.18. *Trim studios specialize in generating ideas for interesting trims and details.*

priced about the same as prints. Often these swatches offer multiple ideas. These resources are especially important in seasons when trims and embellishment details predominate (Figure 4.18).

Silhouette

In modern fashion, silhouettes appear to be the element that changes least from season to season. A **silhouette** is the term used to describe the outline or shape of a garment. Today's customers are happy with the array of silhouettes available in tops, pants, skirts, jackets, dresses, and outerwear. Although fabric and color may change substantially from season to season, silhouettes usually vary in proportion and details. Periodically, there is a major shift from fitted silhouettes to less constructed ones.

Silhouette inspiration comes from a variety of sources and is an ongoing process. Trend services often suggest changes in silhouettes and details. Some generate fashion sketches that incorporate a variety of ideas into single garments. These sketches may be over-designed or missing necessary seams and darts for fit; this forces subscribers to reinterpret the ideas for their given market, rather than use them exactly as they were drawn, which in turn eliminates the possibility that multiple subscribers will come out with lines that look very much the same.

Other trend services take photographs of looks spotted on the streets in major fashion centers. As more and more fashion ideas trickle up from the streets rather than down from the runways, clothes worn in Saint-Tropez, Paris, London, New York, Los Angeles, and other trend-setting locales can be very inspirational. Shopping the market is perhaps the best source of silhouette inspiration.

Seasonal Trend Forecasts

Each seasonal collection offered by a product developer is the result of trend research focused on the target market it has defined for itself. Product developers may offer anywhere from two to six seasonal collections per year, depending on the impact of fashion trends in a particular product category and price point. Women's wear companies are more sensitive to the whims of fashion and may produce four to six lines per year. Men's wear companies present two to four lines a year, and children's wear firms typically present three to four seasonal collections.

For wholesale brand product developers, seasonal presentations correspond to the wholesale markets in which their lines are presented for sale to retailers. Store brand and private label product developers work on slightly different calendars because the presentation of their lines is internal, but in general their product development seasons parallel those of branded product developers.

Figure 4.19. *David Hacker, Trend Director for J. C. Penney, making a trend presentation to the product development team.*

Within each seasonal collection, product developers design groups of garments based on a specific theme. Each theme is linked to a color and fabric story, and has a particular fashion direction. Delivery of each group is typically scheduled at intervals throughout the selling season to provide the consumer with a continuous flow of fresh merchandise options.

Responsibility for Trend Forecasting

The responsibility for trend forecasting varies from company to company, depending on its organizational structure. A company's approach to trend forecasting is often related to whether it is a wholesale brand or private label product developer.

Many large product developers have trend departments that are responsible for pinpointing the initial trends of the seaon for their company. The advantage of a trend department is that the various divisions within the company will work from the same forecast, thereby giving a unified look to the sales floor. Merchandisers are also key players in determining trend direction. They often come from a buying background and are skilled at anticipating what the customer is ready for. Finally, it is the designer who uses his or her ability to translate the trends identified into saleable garments in the right colors, fabrics, and silhouettes. In the end, it is the collective vision of these three groups that determines a given brand's direction (Figure 4.19).

In companies that develop wholesale brands, where products must be clearly differentiated from the competition, the design team and the merchandiser generally work in tandem to develop the seasonal trend forecast. Together they review subscriptions to design resources, shop and interpret the market, attend trade shows, and meet with suppliers to determine the design direction that is right for their company. Large private label product developers often have a trend department because of the need to coordinate the research for multiple brands within a portfolio. Merchandisers and designers then fine-tune the direction from that point. Figure 4.20 illustrates a fashion forecast flowchart.

Forecast Formats

The members of the product development team responsible for trend forecasting use a variety of formats to share their seasonal research. The degree of formality in the presentation depends on how widely within the organization the information will be presented.

Designers for wholesale brands spend less time on formalizing their trend forecasts because they are responsible for both the research and creation of the line. They tend to work directly from informal collections of swatches and tear sheets to select the actual colors, fabrics, and prints they will use for each item or group in the line.

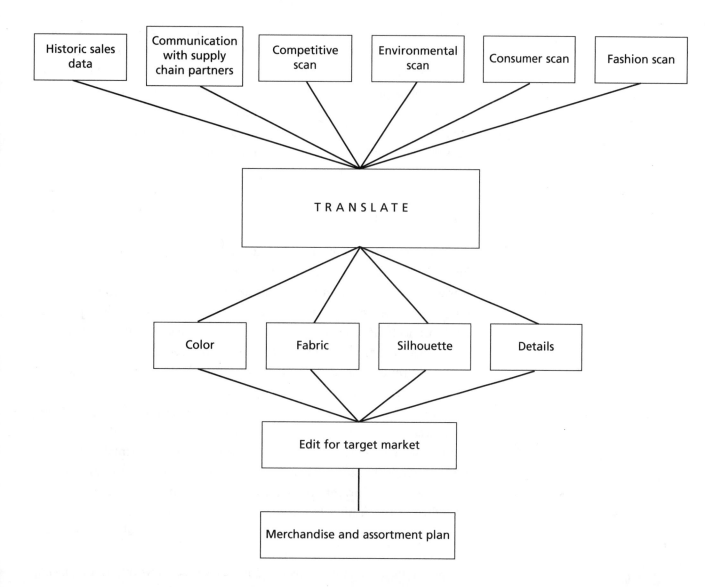

Figure 4.20. *Fashion Forecast Flowchart.*

Trend teams for private brands must prepare more formal presentations because their forecasts are applied to multiple categories across the men's, women's, and children's divisions. In these organizations, a few key members of the team are responsible for interpreting market trends for the entire organization. Their presentations must clearly define appropriate trends for each division and category that develops product. They generally present their ideas to both the product development team (merchandisers, creative and technical designers) and the buying staff of their organization. By inviting the buyers' input early in the product development process, there is more ownership of the resulting line across company functions. Ultimately, product developers of store brand and private label lines still sell the line they develop to the buying team. Introducing buyers to new seasonal trends at the same time that the product development team is starting to put the line together ensures that buyers are better prepared to commit to quantities when the line is finalized. Early collaboration makes this process go more smoothly.

In these organizations, trend forecasters frequently develop a seasonal trend book that highlights important trends in color, fabric, silhouette, and details for each category and division served. The information in the seasonal trend book is presented formally in the form of a multimedia presentation. Each team receives its own trend book, development samples are hung around the room, storyboards are displayed, and a PowerPoint presentation summarizes the most important trends for the season.

Summary

Fashion is a reflection of our times. It is a means of expression that reflects how we respond to everything happening within our own lives and in the world around us. Fashion is available at different levels. The couture represents the highest level of fashion, but most consumers make their personal fashion selections from the vast assortments available at the mass-market level, where practicality and function are prioritized in order to maximize sales and profits. Fashion is influenced not only by high fashion but also by developments in functional apparel and street fashion. Fashion trends evolve in cycles, with fads lasting for a very short time and fashion classics lasting for many seasons.

Product developers at all levels of fashion use environmental scanning to identify trends that will have an impact on consumer lifestyles and marketplace conditions. Current events, the arts, sports, and science and technology all influence the fashion trends for a particular season. Fashion forecasters must be well-read regarding current events and up to date about new developments on the social and cultural scene.

Shopping the market helps trend forecasters see how trends are playing out in fashion centers around the world. Major trends may start anywhere in the world. Sometimes they begin locally and their influence spreads; other times a trend seems to catch on simultaneously in many big cities across the globe. Trend forecasters must be aware of the development and movement of these trends.

Trend forecasting begins with research on color. Early color forecasts are available up to two years before a fashion season, with subsequent reports offering refined projections for particular market groups. Color projections help to drive fabric developments. Fabrication trends revolve around popular fibers, texture interest, woven patterns, and prints. Color and fabric developments drive silhouette changes. In Western society, popular silhouettes remain fairly consistent from season to season, but proportions and details change to reflect new fashion themes.

Trend forecasting is an integral part of the product development process. Forecasting services provide trend reports four to six times a year. Major shopping trips and visits to fabric fairs are usually scheduled twice a year, but the research process itself is ongoing. Product developers and trend forecasters are always on the lookout for a clue to the next trend.

Each product developer must decide which member of the product development team is responsible for trend research and which resources are most appropriate for the company's target market. Designers are generally responsible for their own trend forecasting at branded product developers. Merchandisers or special trend teams may be responsible for trend forecasting at private brand product developers. The process begins by collecting tear sheets, color chips, and fabric swatches that reflect an important theme. By the end of the trend forecasting process, the trend team has determined overall themes and the related color stories, fabrics, and silhouettes that will make up each group offered.

Key Terms

classics

environmental scanning

fads

fashion

long-term forecasting

poms

short-term forecasting

silhouette

trend

Discussion Questions

1. In class, look at some photos from the most recent couture or designer collections. Which elements in each design might go on to influence mainstream fashion?

2. Identify a current fashion that is likely to be short short-lived. Identify a current fashion that appears to be a fashion classic. How do they differ?

3. Identify several current events in the political, global, and cultural arena. What impact might they have on fashion?

4. What colors are currently popular in various consumer markets? Try to distinguish color preferences at several different price points and in several specialty markets.

5. How has Burberry used its signature plaid in new and innovative ways to revitalize the popularity of the label?

Activities

1. Using the Internet and recent periodicals, identify several trends recently promoted by futurists. Brainstorm as to how these trends will influence fashion. Design students should take one prediction and design a series of garments inspired by that prediction in their sketchbooks.

2. Using Pantone chips, paint chips from the hardware store, yarn, embroidery floss, or swatches of fabric, develop a seasonal color story of 6 to 8 colors that relate to a seasonal theme from a color forecaster's perspective. Present your color story on a board that includes a mood picture, color samples, and color names. Be sure to title your board to communicate a theme.

   Variation—Look at a color projection from a color service or an Internet resource. Interpret that color story for an existing product developer such as the Gap, H & M, or Esprit. Develop a color story for a coordinated group or a group of separates for that label.

3. Using swatches from your school's fabric library, develop a fabric story of 3 to 5 fabrics for a coordinated sportswear group. Identify your product category and price point. Make sure that your fabric story offers enough choice in colorization, solids versus patterns, and fabric types to make all of the garments that are typically included in a group. Mount your fabrics and give your fabric story a name.

4. As a class, select a product developer and develop a storyboard for an upcoming season. Research trends by shopping the market and using whatever resources are available to you. Begin by collecting tear sheets, color chips, and fabric swatches that you believe will be influential. Present your forecast as a series of boards or in a PowerPoint presentation.

References

Brannon, E. L. 2005. *Fashion forecasting*. New York: Fairchild.

Just-style.com. 2006. US: Denim favourite Levi's to launch iPod jeans. www: just-style.com.

Just-style.com. 2005. Germany: Adidas introduces 'intelligent' basketball shoe. www.just-style.com/new.

Lurie, A. 1981. *The language of clothes*. New York: Vintage Books.

Nike Press Release. 2006. *Nike and Apple launch Nike + iPod sport kit*, www.nike.com/nikebiz/news/pressrelease (accessed July 15, 2006).

Porter, T. 1994. Color in the looking glass. In *Color Forecasting*, ed. H. Linton, 1–9. New York: Van Nostrand Reinhold.

Socha, Miles. 2002. The Paris couture: A crop of fresh faces suggests new vitality. *Women's Wear Daily,* July 8.

Waters, Robyn. 2006. *The Hummer and the Mini: Navigating the contradictions of the new trend landscape*. New York: Penguin Group.

Webb, A. L. 1994. Timing is everything. In *Color Forecasting*, ed. H. Linton, 203–206. New York: Van Nostrand Reinhold.

CHAPTER 5

COLOR MANAGEMENT

"Only those who love color are admitted to its beauty and immanent presence. It affords utility to all but unveils its deeper mysteries only to its devotees."

—JOHANNES ITTEN

OBJECTIVES

- To review the physics of color science
- To review the impact of color decisions throughout the supply chain
- To define terminology used in color management
- To outline the process for visual and digital color approval
- To identify the variables that affect color management
- To analyze the impact of technology on color measurement

Each season, product developers select a color palette that represents the exact shades of the colors they intend to use in that season's line. The selection of a seasonal color palette is the first step in the color management function. **Color management** is the process of controlling the outcome of a color, from the initial concept (a chip, swatch, yarn, or sample) to the final production output in a way that is acceptable to the consumer.

The process starts with a color concept determined by either the trend or design department. The color concept is matched to a color standard from a color specification system which identifies the colors that can be achieved on the various fabrics required for the group. **Color specifications systems** identify the range of color that can be produced on a given material, such as paper, cotton, wool, polyester, or silk and the dye formula to obtain that color. Dyers and finishers must not only dye a sample that matches the color standard; they must also ensure that production yardage can be produced consistent with the approved sample. Quality assurance determines the color fastness requirements. Colors need to hold up during consumer use and care—that is to say, the color must not bleed, fade, or change under normal conditions of use and care. Swimwear needs to maintain its color in chlorine; active sportswear cannot discolor from perspiration.

Color management is a very complicated process that can make or break the success of a garment. Even after a careful color approval process, some color variation may still result. This can be due to uncontrollable variations in the fiber, dyes, and/or environmental conditions during the dying process. These variations must be managed through color sorting. Color consistency is imperative because the final customer is mobile and may buy one piece in-store and another online; or he or she may buy several pieces at a store near home and add to that ensemble from a store shopped on vacation or on a business trip.

Color matching is not the only challenge. The same garment made into a fabric offered in several **colorways** can shrink differently during processing or pressing. It may also respond under the needle differently. In addition, the color within a group of related pieces must read as a match under retail lights, in daylight, and under home lighting.

With all of the variables that affect color matching, those responsible for color management must have a good understanding of color science. This chapter provides a review of color science, examines the decision-making process for determining a seasonal color palette, and explains the color management function.

Color Science

In order to truly understand color management, color specialists must understand the variables that are involved in color perception. From a scientific perspective, **color** is the visual perception of certain wavelengths of light by the retina of the eye. Light consists of a spectrum of electromagnetic waves of energy, including television and radio waves, X rays, ultraviolet light, and infrared light. The electromagnetic spectrum is measured in meters, but the visible light waves that allow us to see color are so short, they require a smaller measurement. A **nanometer**, equal to one millionth of a millimeter, is the unit of measurement used to measure light waves. The human eye perceives wavelengths in a range from 400 nanometers (which we see as deep blue) to about 700 nanometers (which we see as deep red) as color. Within this limited range we are capable of distinguishing about 10 million variations of color, but not all of those colors can be reproduced with available dyes or inks. The range of color that can be perceived by the eye cannot be achieved on all available materials (Figure 5.1).

Color and Light

Visual color is a function of light. Color cannot be seen in the absence of light; we see no color in the dark. White light is perceived when all wavelengths of the visible spectrum are present in equal amounts; however, true white light is rare. Natural and incandescent lights have yellow undertones; indirect sunlight and fluorescent light have blue undertones. Sunlight is our source of natural light and has become the primary standard by which colors are measured. However, our daily activities take place under a variety of light sources: outdoor activities under sunlight, business activities under fluorescent lights, and activities at home under incandescent lights.

This variety of lighting environments presents a challenge for those responsible for color matching. Different fabrics (and their components, e.g., zippers, thread) dyed the same color must match under a variety of light sources. Many a shopper has been frustrated after taking a garment into a store to match an accessory or companion piece only to find that a product that appeared to be a perfect match under the store's fluorescent lighting looks very different under natural sunlight.

Color constancy refers to a color that is perceived to be the same regardless of the light source. The phenomenon of a single color sample reading as a slightly different color under different light sources is called color inconstancy, or flair. **Color inconstancy** is related to the color hue rather than the color recipe (Figure 5.2) One analysis of 2,300 colors in a textile palette that covered a wide gamut found that 10 to 20 percent of the colors when applied to textile products had a very high color inconstancy going from daylight (D65) to incandescent light. The shades with the highest color inconstancy between daylight and incandescent light are the red-oranges and bright blues, particularly those of medium depth. (Agarwal 2003, 1–4).

Metamerism is the perceived change in color between a pair of samples—two samples that are considered a match under one light source and not a match under another (Figure 5.3). They have different spectral reflectance curves under different illuminants. This is a problem for product developers that use different fabrics and fibers in garments intended to coordinate or match—a cotton T-shirt designed to be worn with a cotton/polyester blend used in a pair of shorts or pants. They may match in the store but not in natural daylight. Metamerism can often be controlled by using similar colorants in the color standard and the sample or in the various fabrics being matched to the color standard (Agarwal 2003, 1–4).

To understand how we perceive color, we must study color as light and as **pigment**, the substance that imparts color to another substance. Color is perceived when light strikes a surface that contains pigment. The pigments in objects cause some wavelengths to be absorbed and others to be reflected, thus giving the surface its color. The different combinations of reflected wavelengths are the basis for all observed colors.

Color Attributes

Albert Munsell (1858–1918) devoted his life to studying color and developed the Munsell Color System to describe and identify color and color relationships.

It continues to be the most widely used color system today. Munsell introduced a color vocabulary that describes the various aspects of color and how they interact (Figure 5.4).

Hue

Colors are distinguished from one another by their hue. A **hue** is the attribute of a color by which we distinguish one color family from another. There is a natural order of hues that follows the sequence of hues seen in a rainbow. That order goes from red to orange to yellow, then green, blue, and purple. Purple does not appear in the rainbow, but it completes the human perception of the hue families. Hue families can be arranged in this order to form a color circle. Within the color circle, one can mix adjacent colors to obtain a continuous variation from one color family to the next. For example, red and yellow may be mixed to obtain all the hues from red through orange to yellow. In the Munsell system, there are ten basic hue families: five major and five minor. Red, yellow, green, blue, and purple are the major families. Halfway between each of these are the five minor hue families of orange, green-yellow, blue-green, purple-blue, and red-purple. These ten hue families are further subdivided into ten more hue steps for a total of 100 hue families. Even finer distinctions can be made between similar hues through the use of decimals. Colors that have a hue are called **chromatic colors**. Black, white, and gray are neutral or **achromatic**, having no hue.

It is important to recognize that the terms *hue* and *color* are not synonymous. Hue has only one attribute, whereas color has three: hue, value, and chroma.

Value

Value is the quality by which we distinguish light colors from dark colors. A light color may be referred to as a **tint**. Painters achieve tints by mixing color with white paint or water; a commercial printer achieves a tint by leaving more space between dots; and a scientist perceives a tint when a color is mixed with white light. Tints are sometimes called pastels; examples include pink and peach. A **shade** refers to a color mixed with black to decrease the value and darken the hue. Navy blue and forest green are examples of shades.

How we perceive a color's lightness or darkness depends on the percentage of light that is reflected from the colored surface. The lightest color is white; it reflects much of the light that strikes it. The darkest color is absolute black, which reflects no light. Gray is seen when some of the light is absorbed and some of the light is reflected. The value scale applies to chromatic as well as neutral colors. All colors that have the same Munsell value, regardless of their hue, reflect the same amount of light.

The lightness or darkness of any given hue can be measured according to a gray scale. The Munsell gray scale is divided into ten value steps, with pure

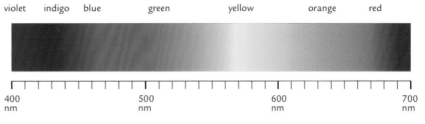

violet   indigo   blue   green   yellow   orange   red

| 400 nm | 500 nm | 600 nm | 700 nm |

Visible Light

Figure 5.1a–b. *The human eye perceives wavelengths in a range from 400 nanometers to about 700 nanometers as color. Within this limited range, we are capable of distinguishing about 10 million variations of color.*

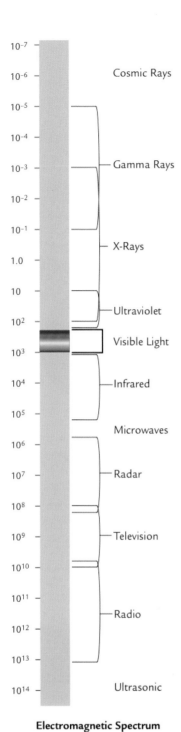

10^{-7}	
10^{-6}	Cosmic Rays
10^{-5}	
10^{-4}	
10^{-3}	Gamma Rays
10^{-2}	
10^{-1}	
1.0	X-Rays
10	
10^{2}	Ultraviolet
	Visible Light
10^{3}	
10^{4}	Infrared
10^{5}	
10^{6}	Microwaves
10^{7}	Radar
10^{8}	
10^{9}	Television
10^{10}	
10^{11}	Radio
10^{12}	
10^{13}	
10^{14}	Ultrasonic

Electromagnetic Spectrum

Figure 5.2. *The same green textile is very color inconstant under different white light sources—tungsten homelight (L), cool white fluorescent office light (M), and exterior daylight (R).*

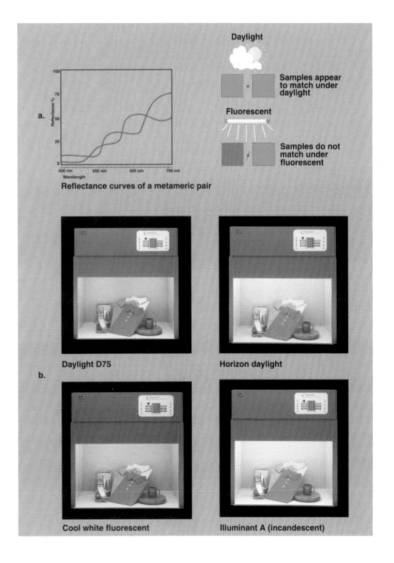

Figure 5.3. *Two metameric reds match in daylight but do not match in fluorescent light because they reflect different wavelengths, as shown in their spectrophometric curves (a). In cool white fluorescent light, reds and yellows appear vivid, but blues appear gray or greenish (b) when compared to their appearance in daylight.*

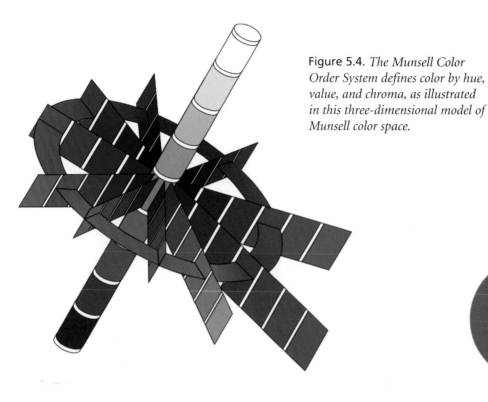

Figure 5.4. *The Munsell Color Order System defines color by hue, value, and chroma, as illustrated in this three-dimensional model of Munsell color space.*

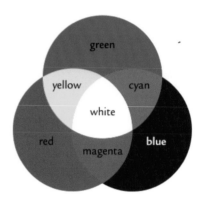

Figure 5.6. *The additive color mixing system explains how colored light is mixed using red, green, and blue or blue-violet as the primaries. When all three of the additive primaries are mixed, we see white.*

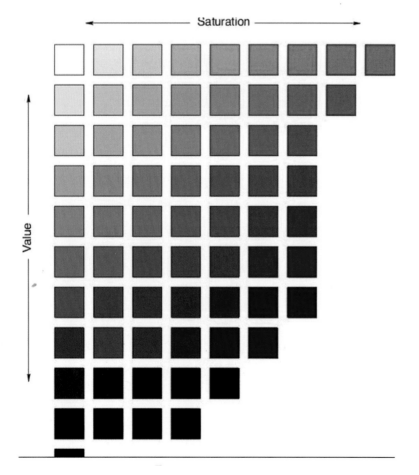

Figure 5.5. *The many shades of pink can be described by the standardized method developed by the Inter-Society Color Council of the National Institute of Standards and Technology.*

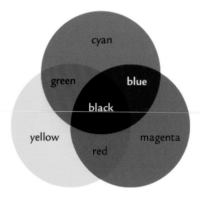

Figure 5.7. *The subtractive color mixing system explains how pigments are mixed using yellow, cyan, and magenta as primaries. When all three of the subtractive primaries are mixed, we see black.*

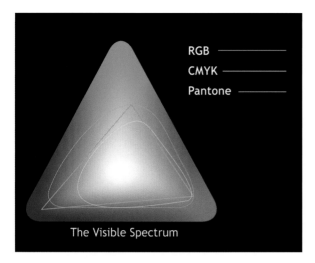

Figure 5.8. *This color gamut comparison chart plots the visible color spectrum and the gamut of color that can be achieved on the computer monitor, using CMYK colors and using Pantone RGB colors. Achieving all of the colors possible with RGB color is not necessarily possible with the CMYK inks used with most monitors.*

Figure 5.9. *A colorist selects a color with just the right attributes for a particular season.*

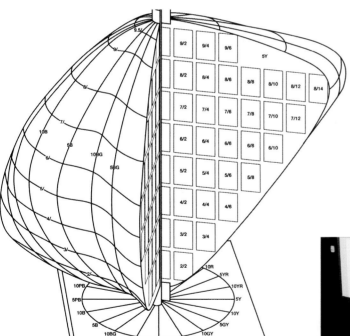

Figure 5.10. *The Munsell color solid is shaped like an amoeba. An intense yellow requires more steps on the chroma scale to go from full saturation to gray than a dark purple does.*

Figure 5.11. *The SCOTDIC color-matching system is based on the Munsell Color System and offers color-matching products for cotton, polyester, and wool.*

Figure 5.12a–b. *Accurate color management depends on inputting measurable color standards so that they can be translated digitally for accurate color output.*

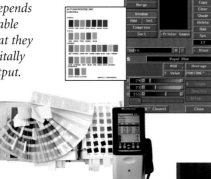

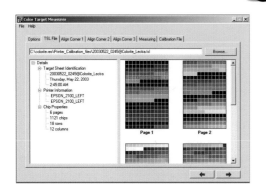

Figure 5.13. *Digital color visualization technology now allows color managers to approve lab dips on the computer screen, thus maintaining color integrity throughout the supply chain.*

Figure 5.14. *A chromaticity diagram is a two-dimensional graph on which a color's hue and chroma may be plotted. A third dimension, luminance, may be charted but is independent of hue and chroma, since the coordinates of neutral colors vary depending on the illuminant. The location of a point on the chromaticity diagram indicates its color.*

black at zero and pure white at ten. However, the human eye cannot easily distinguish among more than five to seven gray tones. The differentiation is more difficult at the lightest and darkest ends of the value scale.

Chroma

Chroma refers to a color's saturation, or degree of departure from the neutral of the same value. It is determined by the amount of pigment in a color. Hues at 100 percent intensity are fully saturated with pigment; when there is no pigment present, a gray of equal value to the color is left. Figure 5.5 illustrates the difference between value and chroma for one color. In the value direction the color goes from light to dark and in the chroma direction the color goes from gray to fully saturated color.

Color Temperature

Though color temperature is not considered a true attribute of color, there seems to be a universal human perception that hues appear to be either warm or cool. **Color temperature** is used to describe a color's apparent warmth or coolness in relation to another color. Yellow, orange, and red are traditionally known as warm colors, whereas green, blue, and violet are considered cool colors. Intermediate colors such as red-violet and yellow-green are considered temperate colors, but they can migrate toward the warm or cool temperatures depending on the proportion of colors mixed and the context of a color within a color grouping. Designers often use the perception of warm and cool colors in their color names to help their customers visualize a particular color. For example, the name *sea green* evokes the image of a cool blue-green color. Designers must be aware of how warm and cool colors relate to customer skin tone and hair color. Customers are generally advised to select apparel in colors that correspond to their warm or cool skin tone (Long and Luke 2001).

Creating and Mixing Colors

Professionals who work with color must understand how color is mixed to create the infinite variety of color that it is possible to achieve with current technology. This understanding is complicated because the hues from which all colors can be created depend on the medium or substance that is being mixed. **Primary colors** are the minimum number of hues that can be mixed to make the greatest number of other colors. When two primary colors are mixed together, they form **secondary (intermediate) colors**. Our concept of primary colors has expanded as the technology used to create color has grown. Today, three sets of primary colors and two color mixing systems are recognized. The two color mixing systems differ in how primary colors are defined, how color is mixed, and the range of colors it is possible to achieve.

Additive System

The **additive color mixing system** explains how colored light is mixed. It is used in theater lighting, on television screens, and on computer monitors. When using the additive mixing system to mix colored light, red, green, and blue or blue-violet are the primaries; yellow, magenta, and cyan are the secondaries. When all three of the additive primaries are mixed, we see white. The light wheel illustrates the primary and secondary colors in the additive mixing system (Figure 5.6). The greatest range of color can be produced using the additive mixing system.

Subtractive System

The **subtractive color mixing system** describes how pigments are mixed. Paints, inks, dyes, and other color media all absorb certain wavelengths of light, which enable an object to absorb some light waves and reflect back others. The more pigments that are blended, the more light is absorbed and the less light is reflected, thus the label subtractive color mixing system. The **simple subtractive color mixing system** explains how thin films of color are mixed; the **complex subtractive color mixing system** explains how thick films of color are mixed.

Printing inks, drawing inks, watercolor paints, and color photography film are all color media that rely on thin films of color that can be layered one on top of another to create colors. Scientifically, cyan, magenta, and yellow are considered the subtractive primaries; green, violet, and orange are the subtractive secondaries. These primaries produce the greatest range of colors, and when combined in equal amounts, mix to form a truer black. The process wheel illustrates the relationship of colors using yellow, cyan, and magenta as the subtractive primaries (Figure 5.7).

Theoretically, it should follow that painters would use the same subtractive primaries, since they work with pigments to create color. Because most paints form thick films, mixtures of yellow, cyan, and magenta result in secondaries that are too gray. Artists using thick paint as a medium find that two sets of red, blue, and yellow paints—a warm set and a cool set—provide the greatest variety of colors. These colors are sometimes referred to as the complex subtractive primaries (Long and Luke 2001).

Further complicating the subtractive model is the fact that it is a relative rather than an absolute mixing system. Equal amounts of two primaries do not necessarily produce a perceived secondary color. Pigment proportions generally need to be adjusted in order to achieve a perceived, balanced mix. Colorists and color systems frequently augment the number of subtractive primary colors they use with additional colors to extend the range of colors that can be mixed. For example, computer printer technology generally uses cyan, magenta, yellow, and black (CMYK) to obtain a truer black than the black that would be achieved from mixing cyan, magenta, and yellow.

Combining Color Mixing Systems

Unfortunately, it is not possible to create every color in the spectrum with either the additive or subtractive mixing systems. While both systems are capable of reproducing a subset of all visible color, there are colors that can only be reproduced with additive color and not with subtractive color, and vice versa. Similarly the medium, whether it is paint, digital imaging equipment, television, plastic, fabric, printed matter, or photography, affects the possible number of chroma steps. Chroma defines the color range attainable in any particular medium. The entire range of colors that can be achieved in a medium or material is referred to as its color **gamut** (Long and Luke 2001). Color systems are rarely used in isolation.

The textile artist designs prints using a computer monitor and additive color mixing. When those prints are applied to fabric, subtractive color is used to mix the dyes or pigments. Understanding the basis for the additive and subtractive color systems explains why computer software programs frequently provide two scales for mixing color using either RGB (red, green, blue) levers or CMY (cyan, magenta, yellow) levers. Different variations of color can be achieved by each. Using RGB levers produces a larger gamut of color that is clearer and brighter, especially in the orange, green, and purple ranges. The RGB gamut is similar to the gamut that can be achieved with fabric dyes. Using CMYK levers typically results in a closer match to printer colors because printers rely on cyan, magenta, and yellow as their primaries with the addition of black as a key color. (The black that is generated by mixing the subtractive primaries is muddy, therefore, color printing uses pure black ink in addition to the subtractive primaries.) Professional printers, whose customers often require a gamut beyond what can be achieved with CMYK, sometimes use a system of adding spot colors—inks that when mixed with CMYK inks expand the CMYK gamut. The drawback of using spot colors is that the ink source needs to be changed (and cleaned) each time an out-of-gamut color needs to be printed. The spot colors required vary depending on the desired print color.

The Pantone Hexachrome Color System provides an alternative to the use of spot colors. It is a six-color high-quality printing process that reproduces more accurate continuous-tone colors. It uses purer CMYK inks plus Pantone Hexachrome Orange and Pantone Hexachrome Green inks to extend the gamut of printers when compared to four-color process printing. Use of Hexachrome inks and Hexachrome separation software provides a gamut that meets or exceeds the gamut of RGB, meaning that designs created on-screen can be reproduced in print. In fact, the Hexachrome system can reproduce almost 90 percent of the Pantone Matching System colors (www.pantone.com) (Figure 5.8).

Seasonal Color Palettes

Color is one of the first aspects of a garment to get the customer's attention. If customers are not attracted enough to the color to be drawn to the rack, they may not explore other aspects of the garment, such as fabric and silhouette. Therefore, the choice of a seasonal color palette is critical to meeting profit objectives. Chapter 4 discusses how color trends are researched and highlights some of the resources that provide color direction at various stages of color development.

Each size and color in which a style is offered represents a stock keeping unit (SKU). The more SKUs there are to manage, the more complex color management and its impact on sourcing and buying decisions become. The fabrics and notions used with each style must also be color matched. Product developers strive to offer enough choices to stimulate a broad base of customer interest without offering so many choices that the customer becomes confused. They must also consider how their color assortment affects manufacturing. Offering too many colors may make each lot size too small to allow it to be produced economically.

The colors selected for a group generally share a common attribute or relationship so that they coordinate with each other. A color story based on several colors of the same hue is said to be **monochromatic**. Colors with a similar value or chroma often work well together. Another way to relate colors is to choose them in relation to their position on the color wheel. A color story based on colors positioned next to each other on the color wheel is said to be **analogous**; a color story based on colors opposite one another on the color wheel is **complementary**. A color's temperature can also be considered when combining colors (Figure 5.9).

Certain colors, such as navy, gray, and black, reappear in seasonal color stories year after year. Companies that specialize in cutting-edge fashion may vary the shades of navy or gray they use from season to season, thus relating the new color to a new fashion theme. Other product developers believe that their customers prefer practicality and promise that their navy and gray will match from season to season.

When a product developer offers merchandise from several categories or divisions in the same store or adjoining areas, the color stories must relate. Banana Republic, which features men's and women's wear in its stores, offers related colors for both divisions. These companies must also ensure that each item in a seasonal line matches other items of the same color.

Although all the colors in a seasonal color palette are not used in a single group, they should be sufficiently coordinated so that when multiple groups are merchandised on sales floors together, they look related. They should also be sufficiently varied so that buyers will be inclined to select more than one group each season. Product developers that produce lines for men, women, and children typically try to relate the color palettes among the categories.

Relating Color Palettes to Target Markets

In today's marketplace, color direction must be interpreted for each apparel category and customer group. Color trends are not necessarily the same for all segments of the market. A well-defined color palette should take into consideration the target market's age and life stage, fashion level, coloring, ethnic diversity, geography and climate, and the garment's function.

Age and Life Stage

Target customer groups have unique preferences when it comes to color. Young adults are most apt to respond to the extremes of color trends, be it the all-black palette of the Goth trend or bright, attention-getting colors in combinations that shock the eye. Their preferences are driven by a need for change, a desire to be on the cutting edge, and pressure to relate to their peers. They are less constricted by dress codes and often see clothing purchases in terms of a single-season life span rather than several years.

As consumers enter the full-time workforce or begin families, their color preferences frequently become more practical. They develop an awareness of the colors that enhance their personal coloring and the confidence to wear colors that are the most becoming rather than blindly following fashion trends. They begin to conform to unwritten dress codes that reflect their multiple life roles. They shop for clothes with the intention of wearing them for more than one season.

As customers mature, their skin and hair color begin to change, thus influencing the colors that are the most becoming on them. Older women may reject neutrals such as black, gray, and navy for more becoming middle tones that make them look and feel younger.

Fashion Level

Each fashion level interprets color trends somewhat differently. Couture and designer markets are typically the first to introduce a new color trend. That trend may take a bit longer to catch on in bridge, better, and moderate markets. Owing to the real-time availability of fashion information, it rarely takes more than a single season for a new color to be available at all price points. However, product developers at different fashion levels may interpret that color differently. A blue and green palette for designer and bridge lines may feature very inky dark shades, while better and moderate markets may offer those colors with a stronger chroma.

Within any given market there are customers who are more fashion-forward and others who are more conservative. A seasonal color palette should accommodate these preferences by including some fashion-forward colors and some mass-consumption colors.

Skin Tone

Groups within a seasonal line should offer a balance of warm and cool colors to provide compatibility with skin tones. Warm-toned skin has yellow undertones and frequently looks best against colors with warm undertones. Cool-toned skin has blue-pink undertones and looks best against colors with cool undertones. However, most colors can be adjusted through manipulation of value and chroma to look becoming on all complexions. Yellow and orange hues in their pure state are difficult for most people to wear. When they are in fashion, a product developer should never plan to sell items in those colors in huge numbers. Turquoise, on the other hand, is one of the most universally pleasing colors on most people. For a season in which neutral colors predominate, accent colors should be provided that compliment both warm and cool skin tones. Warm or cool undertones to basic skin tones may be found within all ethnicities.

Ethnicity

The United States' rich history of ethnic diversity has had a profound effect on the American character. Multiculturalism enriches our lives as we learn the traditions and tastes of other cultures. Increasingly, product developers, retailers, catalogers, and e-commerce sites are recognizing and marketing to the preferences of ethnic populations and using their rich cultural heritage as inspiration for the products they design. For example, J. C. Penney has conducted research that revealed that Hispanic-American and African-American women prefer bright colors to pastels. They also favor heavily embellished styles. Ethnicity is an important consideration in color preferences as well. Ethnic and cultural heritage affects personal coloring and the emotional response to color, which may be related to religious and cultural symbolism.

Geographic Location

Color stories should be appropriate to the geographic markets where they are distributed, taking into consideration both weather patterns and regional preferences. The southern part of the United States has warm winters that require seasonless clothes that can be worn year-round, whereas the Midwest has distinct weather patterns for each of the four seasons, ranging from very warm to very cold. In a global marketplace, seasonal considerations can extend the life cycle of a garment because seasons are reversed above and below the equator.

End Use

Each category of apparel (swimwear, active sportswear, dresses, outerwear) interprets color somewhat differently. Swimwear typically utilizes brighter color palettes, even in seasons where neutrals predominate. The children's wear market also tends to stay with more colorful palettes regardless of season, while neutrals generally dominate the men's wear market throughout the year.

Managing the Color Story

As color groups are broken out, each is developed around a specific theme. At all levels of color forecasting, colors are named according to the theme that inspired them, thereby evoking a visual image. A coral red might be called *geranium* in a floral line for women and *watermelon* in a fruit-themed line for children. These color names are a marketing tool that can be used in the showroom and in writing copy for catalogs, Web sites, and print advertising.

Decisions regarding the size (breadth or depth of selections) of the lines to be offered are typically made early in the product development process by upper management or the merchandising staff. Multibrand product developers may manage seasonal color palettes of up to 400 different colors.

The Color Management Process

Product developers have well-defined procedures for assuring color consistency across all products. The first step in the color approval process is to match the color concept to a color standard. The color concept may come from something purchased at a flea market or a high-tech item purchased on a trend shopping trip. It may be a hank of yarn or a piece of fabric, plastic, or paper. Wherever the color concept comes from, it must be standardized to a reproducible color. **Color standards** are color samples by which fabrications and notions can be matched to ensure color consistency. Color standards facilitate color management throughout the global supply chain.

Because a seasonal line uses many fabrics and related notions that may be sourced or produced anywhere in the world, color standards allow each partner in the supply chain to match the component it is producing to the same standard. Selecting seasonal color standards directly from a commercial color specification system that is linked to dye recipes helps to ensure color consistency across the line.

Color Specification Systems

Color specification systems offer color standards for the accurate communication of color. Physical standards may be available on several different materials or **substrates** and organized in libraries. Different libraries may be marketed to specific industries in order to represent the gamut of color achievable using available technology. Color standards for textiles and apparel are available on cotton, polyester, wool, and silk, although not every specification system offers all four substrates.

The range of colors offered on each substrate is indicative of the gamut of color that can be achieved on that medium. Polyester and silk substrates provide a glossy color standard, whereas cotton and wool substrates result in a matte version of the color. Cotton is the preferred substrate for textile color specification systems because color dyed on cotton can be matched, almost without exception, to other fabric types if the appropriate dye class is used. Colors that can be achieved on polyester and silk cannot always be achieved on cotton (Park and Park 2005).

Each color specification system uses its own method of notation to help users identify the increments of color by hue, value, and chroma. Today's standards must also translate physical colors into data that allow the colors to be replicated digitally and that relates to dye recipes appropriate for a variety of fibers.

Color Notation Systems

Color systems rely on visual representations of color that show how colors relate to one another in respect to their attributes of hue, value, and chroma. These visual sequential arrangements are sometimes referred to as **color solids**. Each color in a color solid can be identified using the color system's numerical notation system, which identifies the specific color in color space. The resulting notation system facilitates the visual identification, matching, and reproduction of colors.

The Munsell system notates color according to the attributes of hue (H), value (V), and chroma (C), which are notated H V/C, each expressed using code numbers that allow users to specify specific colors. The visual of Munsell's color system is organized in the general shape of a sphere. Pure hues are located at the equator of the sphere, number five on the value scale. The vertical trunk represents gradations of value and the horizontal slices represent gradations in chroma or intensity for each hue.

The Munsell color solid does not take the shape of a perfect sphere because not all hue families contain the same number of colors (Figure 5.10). Light colors, such as intense yellow, have a large number of steps on the chroma scale between the fully saturated color and gray. The purest purple is a dark color, which takes fewer steps on the chroma scale between the fully saturated color and gray. The differences in the range of chroma and value for each hue determine the outer shape of the Munsell color solid. Thus, the sphere looks more like an amoeba because the human eye is able to distinguish only so many color variations. The color solid allows for the variations in human perception of color. The National Institute of Standards and Technology (NIST) has adopted the Munsell system as the standard for communicating color.

Commercial Color Identification Systems

There are two commonly used, commercially managed code-identified color libraries in apparel product development. The Standard Color of Textile Dictionaire Internationale de la Couleur (SCOTDIC) Textile Color System applies the Munsell Color System to fabric. The SCOTDIC system currently represents, depending on substrate, 54 hue families, each in a full value and chroma range. The SCOTDIC value scale is shown in 16 steps of 5 percent increments, starting at 15 percent in the dark range and ending at 90 percent in the light range. The chroma range represents saturation of a color. The SCOTDIC table for chroma offers 16 steps in which the contrast distance is always the same independent of hue and value. The maximum number of steps of chroma using the same contrast distance is different for each hue, value, and substrate. The SCOTDIC system offers colors on three substrates—polyester (2,468 colors), cotton (2,300 colors), and wool (1,100 colors). The colors do not change from season to season, making it a permanent color resource (Figure 5.11). New colors are added as technology makes them possible to achieve (SCOTDIC 2007).

The Pantone Matching System has developed its own color notation system, which uses a six-digit numerical code to define a color's position in color space. The first pair of numbers represents value, the second pair represents hue, and the third pair represents chroma. The Pantone value scale specifies ten value levels, which are labeled with the numbers 10 to 19, representing the lightest to darkest values. The hue circle is divided into 64 sectors from yellow (01) to green-yellow (64). The chroma or saturation scale also has 64 steps from neutral gray (00) to maximum color saturation (64). Pantone offers a number of different color libraries suitable for the color gamut of different mediums. The Pantone Textile Color System for textiles is offered on a cotton substrate and includes 1,932 colors (Pantone 2006).

The use of these color systems allows for the specification of color to be transmitted with accuracy via phone, fax, or the Internet. Product developers do not necessarily rely on a single system. They may rely on standards from several color libraries to achieve the color range they need for a specific season.

Color Approval Process

Once seasonal color standards are selected, a master list is developed that identifies colors by brand, color name, delivery, and the color code that correlates to the color system used. The supply chain partner responsible for sourcing fabrics and notions (product developer, agent, or manufacturer) specifies that the fabric(s) or notion(s) that are selected must match the product developer's color standard.

Visual Color Approval

Manufacturing partners may either order 4-inch by 4-inch color standards from the designated color specification library for matching or they may rely on the spectral reflectance formula to interpret the colors if they have the software and equipment to interpret, view, and utilize these data. Spectral data must be accompanied by color tolerances, illuminant specifications, and measurement protocol.

Physical standards need to be carefully stored to protect them from dust and light; they should be touched as little as possible. Even with proper handling, swatches cut from the same cloth will not be identical after they arrive at the mills and are exposed to different handling and different temperature and humidity conditions. It is preferable to provide a measurement of the spectral reflectance of this standard and treat the physical sample as only an example that represents the standard.

Digital measurements may also be subject to irregularity. Changes in temperature, humidity, presentation of the cloth, and calibration of the spectrophotometer can cause variations in readings. Viewing conditions can, however, be controlled. Certified color partners must understand these nuances and have the most up-to-date equipment if color approvals are to be made digitally. Another advantage of digital standards is that they may be archived permanently so that they can be used in subsequent seasons if a customer wants to repeat a color.

Sourcing partners are generally given two weeks to dye a sample of the actual fabric or finding specified to match the color standard as closely as possible. If the color process is a manual one, these samples, called **lab dips**, must be submitted to the product developer for evaluation on color evaluation forms, completed by the contracted manufacturer, mill, agent, or dye house. The evaluation form includes the following information:

- Submission status (first, second, third, or fourth submission)

- Color standard (number and name)

- Vendor (mill, dye house or print facility, country, and agent)

- Garment description (collection, garment number, group, season, and delivery date)

- Fabrication (fiber content)

Separate lap dips are submitted for each fabric and color specified. If a fabric is being produced at duplicate mills, each mill is required to submit its own lab dips. Too often the first set of lab dips is not approved and a second, third, or even fourth set is required. With each set of physical lab dips, time and money are lost. Physical samples must be shipped back and forth with further instructions. Companies that have adopted digital color approval processes have developed clear tolerances, expressed in reflectance data, as to when a color can be approved or not. Suppliers don't send a physical sample for approval until they are within the appropriate tolerance range. Improved measuring equipment has made these data so accurate that many product developers are certifying their color partners to approve colors at the dye house. Others are setting up regional color labs where a final physical sample can be approved. Colors that need to be dyed on several different fabrics can be presumed to match if the reflectance data are the same.

Once the garment goes into production, the quality assurance department monitors production yardage to be sure that it is consistent with the approved lab dip. Dyeing a sample in a color lab and dyeing production yardage in the dye house can yield somewhat different results. According to David Simmonds of Ciba Textile Services, quality assurance should also be diligent to ensure the color is created and applied using the best available technology in order to minimize environmental impact from the coloration process. There is already an industry standard called Oekotex which is designed to ensure that garments do not contain unacceptable levels of things like heavy metals and free formaldehyde at the point of sale (Azoulay 2005a).

In general, tolerances for matching color standards for separates may be looser than those for coordinates. Some companies are known for repeating neutrals or colors basic to their line from season to season so that customers can grow their wardrobes and be assured that what they bought last year will coordinate with new items. These product developers are especially diligent about making sure that colors are within tolerance. Product developers at higher price points may adhere to stricter tolerances than mass merchant product developers. Sometimes colors are approved, even though they are out of tolerance, just because time has run out and orders may be cancelled if stores don't receive their full shipment of colors on time.

Visual color reports are written using directional language. For instance, "lighter" means to move the color toward white and "darker" means to move it toward black. "Brighter" suggests adding more hue and "duller" suggests moving toward neutral gray. If the hue itself is off, comments suggest adding more or less blue, green, yellow, or red. Comments are not made in terms of percentages because the amount of colorant it takes to shift a color varies dramatically; depending on the color and fiber content. A company such as Marks & Spencer in the United Kingdom visually checked 20,000 plus submissions per year against its specified color standards before it converted to digital color approvals (Ross).

Even after careful color approvals, the shade of a color may still vary within a roll or from lot to lot. Variation can be a result of the maturity of natural fibers; differences in the sizing applied to the fabric; the water source, temperature or humidity, inconsistent bleaching; variations in the composition of synthetic fibers; different levels of absorbency due to variation in the mercerization process; or differences in the pressure, temperature, or chemical concentrations of dyes (Mehta 1992, 174–175). These variations may result in the need for **shade sorting**, which refers to grouping shades together for distribution to specific customers or regions. Shade sorting of finished goods is a function of quality management.

Digital Color Approval

Many product developers now recognize that too much of the product development calendar has been spent on approval processes after the actual designing is done. When design decisions have to be made too early in order to accommodate the production process, they tend to be less accurate in anticipating consumer preferences. Color approvals have long been identified as a process that can add weeks to the production calendar.

Color system suppliers have now successfully translated color reflectance data into systems that help textile manufacturers, colorant suppliers, product developers, and retailers to "standardize" the up-until-now nonstandard art of color (Downes, 1–4). These objective numbers have allowed specialists to come up with equations that deal with different substrates and dyes; instruments that handle varying materials; and techniques that offset the variables in the dyeing process. Digital color communication takes weeks off the product development calendar and allows designers to make critical decisions closer to the actual selling season. Throughout the supply chain colors are more apt to be right the first time, saving both time and money. The elimination of the need to air ship lab dips between product developer and vendor yields further cost savings (Speer 2006).

Today companies can specify color by numbers and set clear and measurable pass/fail limits for color approval, allowing certified suppliers to make decisions and to manage exceptions. The steps to digital color communication include the following:

- A product developer selects a color standard and measures it on a spectrophotometer (a color measuring instrument).

- Color matching software identifies the closest color standard from whatever digital color libraries are available or specified.

- The color standard then appears as a digital image on the computer monitor, which has been calibrated for color accuracy.

- The standard is electronically sent to the supplier, where the digital color sample is translated to the appropriate dye formula for the fiber/component being produced, and trial color samples are produced and measured on a spectrophotometer.

- The supplier may be certified to approve the sample if it falls within accepted pass criteria or it may electronically send back a digital sample of the best possible color match to the product developer, where it can be compared to the standard on the calibrated monitor. If the match is not accepted, more color matching is requested. The supplier sends additional digital samples until the product developer approves the color match (Mulligan 2005).

- Color standards can be digitally archived for quality assurance and future use (Figure 5.12a–b).

Final color approvals are usually achieved in less than half the time of a traditional color matching process. Product developers have the opportunity to assess the color visually through the virtual color sample while making pass/fail decisions based on colorimetric data. The technology that supports digital color communication includes the following:

- Monitors that are able to repeat color with precision, day after day

- Calibration that is device-independent so that accurate conversion from computer-based color data to colorimetric data is permitted using virtually any brand monitor

- Systems that allow operators to create, edit, and visually compare colors on screen

- Software that automatically translates the correct on-screen color to the correct colorimetric data

- Systems that can accept measurements by a spectrophotometer and instantly transform the data into visual color on the screen for evaluation or adjustment

- Software that translates virtual color standards into dye recipes appropriate for the fabric used and that meet quality criteria

- Seamless linkages between color matching software, color quality control, and color-measuring instruments (Mulligan 2005)

Datacolor's Colorite ImageMaster technology allows companies to display photographic quality images on calibrated screens and to modify them as required. The system allows simulation of color effects on various substrates and textures, and allows colors to be copied from physical swatches and applied to new substrates (Figure 5.13). Screen colors can be accurately converted to synthetic reflectance data which dyers can input into their instrumental match prediction systems and obtain dye recipes. All monitors using this system are calibrated every 8 hours using the Minolta Color Analyzer CA100 (Ross).

Prints and Yarn-Dyed Fabrics

Prints and yarn-dyed fabrics must be submitted as one full repeat of pattern in the form of a **strike-off** (actual color placement on fabric) or a computer-aided design (CAD) copy with a color key of all colors that appear within the print. Color approvals must be performed for each color used. Still on the horizon is technology that will allow digital color approvals on a print with 12 to 15 different colors in it.

Color Measurement

Whether product developers rely on visual or digital color approval, they must have a basic understanding of the instrumentation used to measure color objectively and how that data can be used for color management. The American Association of Textile Chemists and Colorists (AATCC) publishes standards for the visual and instrumental measurement of color. These standards establish procedures and conditions for measuring color for the purpose of achieving a color match. A perceived color match is related to the light source, the detection system (eye or instrument), the colorant's power of absorption, and the nature of the substrate. When matching colors, the equipment, lighting, and viewing conditions under which color is measured must be parallel. The Concept 2 Consumer Interest Group was launched in 2001 as a subset of the AATCC. A subcommittee of that group is in the process of developing a guidebook that will help retailers and mass marketers clearly specify their color management practices. Because application of these standards is typically covered in textile curriculums, the discussion that follows provides only an overview.

Instruments

Two types of instruments are available for the measurements of color: colorimeters and spectrophotometers. **Colorimeters** use filters in combination with a light source and detector to emulate the three-color response functions of the eye (Gretag Macbeth 1998). Colorimeters provide data only for a single illuminant and therefore cannot pick up metamerism. They are best used for shade sorting where the concern is matching shades within shipped lots. They are less effective for use in the color approval process. A new portable colorimeter from Pantone allows designers to capture accurate color inspiration on shopping trips and cross-match it to the closest Pantone Textile Color.

Spectrophotometers compare the amount of light used to illuminate an object with the amount of light that is reflected back from that object. A ratio is calculated at each wavelength in the visible spectrum in order to measure color accurately (Gretag Macbeth 1998). Keith Hoover of Target Corporation elaborates: "Imagine the spectrum of the rainbow; when you pass a white light over the colors along every wavelength of that spectrum, the spectrophotometer measures how much light is reflected back at each point along the spectrum. When you plot those values on a graph, you get the reflectance curve—which becomes like the fingerprint of a color. That is the way you characterize a color in numbers. The way you characterize a light source in numbers is in terms of how much energy it emits at every wavelength across the spectrum, which is called the spectral power distribution (SPD) (Azoulay 2005b).

Spectrophotometers are the preferred instrument for color identification, detection of metamerism, and color formulation. They can provide color measurements that can be compared when the color is viewed under multiple light sources. Spectral data can be converted into RGB language for monitor display, into CYMK or Hexachrome language for printers, and to recipes for various dyes.

Although spectrophotometers are designed to measure samples both accurately and repeatedly, they are not perfect measuring devices. Their performance is dependent upon factors that can be controlled by the system operator. The spectrophotometer should be operated in a temperature-controlled, clean environment. If possible, the power should be left on at all times. The instrument needs to be recalibrated regularly; the schedule may vary from every 2 to 4 hours to once a week, depending on the level of accuracy needed, the instrument itself, and the conditions of the lab. Dyes and pigments change color as temperature changes.

Samples should be measured at a constant temperature and humidity, which should be specified for all color partners. Spectrophotometers come equipped with a range of viewing **apertures** or view opening areas. It is preferable to use the largest viewing area possible in order to minimize the influence of uneven dying. Samples measured with small viewing apertures should be measured in several locations on the same piece of fabric. The results should then be averaged to ensure accurate measurement information.

Illuminants

Generally, lab dips are measured under at least two light sources, commonly known as **illuminants**. One illuminant simulates store light so that the product developer can be sure that the components and resulting garments match in the store. The second illuminant simulates daylight so that an acceptable match is perceived once the garments leave the store. Evaluating lab dips under two light sources reduces problems of metamerism.

Viewing Geometry

Viewing geometry refers to the placement of a sample relative to the light source and measuring lens in a spectrophotometer. The most common geometries used today are diffuse/8 and 45/0. Either type of spectrophotometer is suitable for measuring textile materials as long as the correct techniques are used. However, because of the differences between the readings produced on these types of instruments, data cannot be transferred between the two systems (Butts 2000, 1–10).

Color Measurement Procedures

Measurement technique as well as measurement conditions and equipment must be standardized for results to be reliable. Measurements should be taken several times and should be based on the largest viewing area available using the specified equipment.

Color measuring equipment requires opaque samples in order to gather accurate reflectance data. If the material is not opaque, light will pass through the sample and reflect off the backing material or sample holder. Samples are generally folded in order to achieve sufficient opacity for an accurate measurement. Two to four layers are sufficient for most knitted and woven materials. Very sheer fabrics are sometimes backed with a white ceramic tile.

It is common practice to rotate the sample and reposition it for four or more measurements to compensate for fabric construction, directionality of yarns, and uneven dying. Color specialists may experiment with the number of readings necessary to obtain reliable information using their standard equipment. Because different materials are submitted in somewhat different formats—from yarn to knitted sleeves to fabric swatches—an appropriate measurement technique should be developed for each. Loose fiber and yarn samples pose the most problems for measurement replication.

Interpretation of Color Measurement Data

Instrumental color measurements and subsequent pass/fail decisions are calculated from colorimetric data generated by a spectrophotometer and companion software. It is not necessary to understand how values are calculated to successfully interpret the data. The Commission Internationale de l'Eclairage (CIE) has established a three-dimensional coordinate system of color known as the *chromaticity diagram* on which all visible colors can be plotted. "Chromaticity diagrams are based on an understanding of how the human eye sees color and how color has been dimensionalized with the Munsell and other systems" (Kadolph 1998, 308). **Chromaticity coordinates** refer to the light reflected by the surface of the object when it is illuminated by a standardized light source. The CIE system can be cross-referenced to the Munsell or Pantone Color Systems so that light measurements can be translated to subtractive pigment data using either CMYK primaries or RGB primaries.

The CIELAB system is a variation of CIE that adapts chromaticity values for subtractive primary color mixing. The L* measures the lightness coordinate, the a* the red/green coordinate, and the b* the yellow/blue coordinate. CIE L*C*h* is an alternative method of measuring color differences in the same location in color space. Many CIE system users prefer the L*C*h* method of specifying color, since the concept of hue and chroma agrees more closely with the visual experience. In the L*C*h* system, L* measures the lightness coordinate, C* the chroma coordinate, and h* the hue angle expressed in degrees (Figure 5.14).

Instrumental shade sorting is important in a virtual supply chain, as it allows for a common language between the product developer and the textile and notion suppliers in a timely way. This language is useful in specifying acceptable tolerances in comparison to the standard and helps to assess responsibility when errors are made. It is also the basis for developing computer software and hardware that will be more accurate in reflecting specified color across all platforms. These concerns are becoming ever more important as consumers opt to purchase goods from catalogs and the Internet.

Factors Affecting Color Management

Given the existence of color identification systems, we might assume that color management is a fairly exact science. Unfortunately, many variables affect color communication and how we perceive color, thereby complicating color management.

The challenge in color management is to arrive at the same color on a variety of garment components within a single product and on related products in a group. The components for each product may be manufactured in different locations, and each component varies in surface texture, luster, nap, and chemical composition.

Fabric

Although colors are identified by numbers that represent their hue, value, and chroma, the same color may appear different visually when applied to different materials. Fabrics of different fiber contents take up color differently and therefore require different dye formulas to achieve the same color.

The surface appearance of a fabric, created by texture—shiny or matte, reflective or diffusive—can add depth to a color's appearance. For instance, pile fabrics absorb light, thus giving the color more depth. Shiny fabrics reflect light, thus making the color appear lighter. In addition, colorants may change a fabric's reflective properties. On a single garment, different fabrics, thread, buttons, and zippers may all be required to match. Although each dyer has the same standard and identification number for matching color, different fabrics and components can end up looking very different. Even when a single colored batch of yarn is used to create fabrics of different weaves, the resulting fabrics may appear to be different colors (Welling 1999, 136–140).

Human Vision

Many things may influence how we see color. The observed color of a surface depends on the type of light, the direction of the light source, the direction of viewing, the background, and the adaptation of the eyes of the observer. Some individuals have better color perception than others. Several tests measure color perception, including the Ishihara Color Blindness Test, the HVC Color Aptitude Test, and the Farnsworth-Munsell 100 Hue Test. About 1 man in 20 and 1 woman in 50 has defective color vision, commonly called color blindness.

Even among people who are not color-blind, aptitude for judging colors varies. This capability varies even among experts as a result of normal variation in the human eye. Furthermore, color perception can be compromised by fatigue, illness, and memory loss. We can only remember specific colors for a period of 2 to 3 seconds. Color perception is also diminished by age. Because of all these variables, visual color evaluation will always be subjective. Color differences perceived by the human eye are difficult to quantify and communicate. To communicate to a supply chain partner that something is too dark or too warm does not tell the partner to what degree it needs to make an adjustment (Gretag Macbeth 1998). In spite of these limitations, the human observer will generally be the final judge when there is a question as to whether a color is within an acceptable range of the standard.

Color Calibration

Adding to the complexity of color management is the fact that color is viewed from a variety of different sources. For example, designers frequently create colors on a CAD system, in which screen colors are produced through additive mixing, whereas printer colors use subtractive mixing.

The complexity of matching screen colors and printer colors is further complicated when color graphic files are exchanged via a network. Each recipient of the file may have a different computer configuration with hardware from different vendors. Even identical equipment may produce different colors depending on ink levels, usage levels, and user settings. Increasingly, vendors whose products are integral to color matching are forging partnerships to offer devices or software that simplify the process of calibrating equipment in order to produce color consistency.

Devices used in the measurement of color, such as light boxes and spectrophotometers, are dependent on the conditions present during color measurement. Only when the devices have been calibrated and profiled is it possible to get an accurate measurement of color.

Summary

Color management begins at the moment the seasonal color palette is determined and continues until the product reaches the store. The goal of color management is to have every item in the seasonal line match the identified color standards and for garments within the line to coordinate with each other.

An understanding of color science is imperative for efficient color management. Color is the visual perception of certain wavelengths of light by the retina of the eye. Color cannot be seen in the absence of light. Pigment is the substance that imparts color to another substance. Color is perceived when light strikes a surface that contains pigment.

The Munsell Color System is commonly used to describe and identify color and color relationships. It describes the three aspects of color, which are hue, value, and chroma. The additive color mixing system explains how colored light is mixed. This color mixing system explains how color is achieved on television screens and computer monitors. The subtractive color mixing system describes how pigments are mixed. The simple subtractive color mixing system explains how thin films of color are mixed, and the complex subtractive color mixing system explains how thick films of color are mixed.

Seasonal color palettes are the colors selected for a given season by a product development division. This palette should be broad enough to appeal to a diverse range of customers, but not so large that it is unwieldy to manage and costly to produce. Color palettes may vary depending on the age, life stage, ethnicity, geographic location, and fashion level of the target customer, and on the end use of the product.

The seasonal color palette is matched to color standards. Each supplier must match components to those standards by submitting lab dips for approval. Pantone and SCOTDIC are two commonly used color libraries that offer color standards on a variety of substrates.

Product developers are increasingly relying on digital color measurement in order to speed up the process of color approval. Software is available to link the readings of spectrophotometers to the computer so that on-screen colors match physical samples and can be exchanged digitally among supply chain partners. This takes weeks off the product development calendar.

Even the most conscientious color management effort will result in a product that varies from the standard within a limited range. Depending on how perceptible this deviation is, it may need to be managed by sending lots grouped according to color to stores in certain parts of the country. A good eye for color is a valuable tool in the product development process.

Key Terms

achromatic

additive color mixing system

analogous

aperture

chroma

chromatic colors

chromaticity coordinates

color

color constancy

colorimeter

color inconstancy, or flair

color management

color solids

color specification systems

color standards

color temperature

colorways

complementary

complex subtractive color
   mixing system

gamut

hue

illuminants

lab dips

metamerism

monochromatic

nanometer

pigment

primary colors

secondary (intermediate) colors

shade

shade sorting

simple subtractive color
   mixing system

spectrophotometer

strike-off

substrates

subtractive color mixing system

tint

value

viewing geometry

Discussion Questions

1. Discuss how the seasonal colors for the current season vary between discount, moderate, and better stores in your area. How do the colors found in the marketplace relate to seasonal color forecasts that you have used?

2. What factors may cause materials that were matched to the same standard to appear as different colors?

3. How can metamerism be avoided?

4. Why is shade sorting sometimes necessary, even after diligent color matching?

Activities

1. Match the color of garments or fabric swatches you have brought to class to Pantone or SCOTDIC color chips. Do you and your classmates agree on which color chip matches the closest? Do the same for all of the colors in a print.

2. Try to find an example of metamerism—two garments that match under one illuminant but not under another.

3. Test your color sensitivity by taking the Farnsworth-Munsell 100 Hue Test.

4. Shop a store such as the Gap, The Limited, Old Navy, or American Eagle whose product consists of store brands. Identify the colors they have chosen for their seasonal color palette. If they stock both women's and men's apparel, contrast the color palette of each division. Ask store personnel when the various groups on the floor were shipped. Analyze that product developer's seasonal color palette to determine how it relates to their target customer.

5. Select a color story from a color trend forecast resource at your school. Mix those colors on your computer screen and save them as a color palette. Adjust your printer codes to match the screen colors.

References

Agarwal, Niraj. 2003. A note on color inconstancy. www.techexchange.com (accessed July 30, 2006).

Azoulay, Julia Fein. 2005a. The devil in the details: The challenge of color. www.AATCC.org (accessed July 30, 2006).

Azoulay, Julia Fein. 2005b. Color, light, and getting it right. www.ewarna.com/public_0405_Getting_It_Right.html (accessed July 27, 2006).

Butts, K. 2000. Color measurement. www.techexchange.com/thelibrary/colormeasurement.html (accessed August 2, 2005)

Downes, Terry. A total approach to color management. www.techexchange.com/thelibrary/ColorManagement.html (accessed August 2, 2005).

Gretag Macbeth. 1998. *Fundamentals of color and appearance.* New Windsor, NY: Gretag Macbeth.

Kadolph, S. 1998. *Quality assurance for textiles and apparel.* New York: Fairchild.

Long, J., and J. T. Luke. 2001. *The new Munsell student color set.* New York: Fairchild.

Mehta, P. 1992. *An introduction to quality control for the apparel industry.* Milwaukee: ASQC Quality Press.

Mulligan, Shawn. 2005. How to ensure effective color in today's manufacturing processes (and why it's more important than ever today. www.techexchange.-com/thelibrary/howtoensure.html (accessed August 2, 2005).

Pantone. 2006. www.pantone.com.

Park, J., and K. Park. 2005. Pick a shade—any shade? *International Dyer,* May, www.ewarna.com (accessed July 27, 2006).

Ross, Teri. Color creation, communication and control at Marks & Spencer. www.techexchange.com/the library/color (accessed August 2, 2005).

SCOTDIC. 2007. www.scotdic.co.uk/E06.html/ (accessed April 26, 2007).

Speer, Jordan K. 2006. Concept-to-spec roundtable report: The speed of color. *Apparel*, January 1, www.apparelmag.com (accessed January 16, 2006).

Welling, H. 1999. Color blind? Rethink your color processes! *Apparel Industry Magazine*, September.

Additional Color Resources

A to Z Color Consulting. www.atozcolor.com/color.html. Introduction to color theory, monitor calibration and color management.

Color Association. www.colorassociation.com/site. Web site for The Color Association of the United States (CAUS).

Color Marketing Group. www.colormarketing.org. Web site for the Color Marketing Group.

Color Matters. www.colormatters.com. Web site of J. L. Morton, professor of color and color consultant.

Color Pro. www.colorpro.com. Good source for information on color technology.

Color Vision. www.handprint.com/HP/WCL/wcolor.html. Useful information on color science and color theory.

Colour Group, The (Great Britain). www.city.ac.uk/colourgroup/. The Colour Group's Web site provides access to useful color diagrams and other links.

Commission Internationale de l'Eclairage [International Commission on Illumination]. www.cie.co.at/cie/home.html. This Web site provides access to *CIE News,* the quarterly news bulletin, as well as to technical reports, standards, and conference proceedings.

Concept2Consumer. www.aatcc.org/igroups/c2c.htm. Concept2Consumer is a committee of the American Association of Textile Chemists and Colorists that is dedicated to the concerns of Product Development for textiles, apparel, and home furnishings.

Datacolor. www.datacolor.com Datacolor is a leader in intelligent color management providing color matching software, on-screen color simulation software, shade sorting software, spectrophotometer calibration software, and more.

EFG's Color Reference Library. www.efg2.com/Lab/Library/index.html. Resource for books on color and a variety of color links.

EWarna. www.ewarna.com.

Gretag Macbeth. www.gretagmacbeth.com. Information on Gretag Macbeth color management products and classes.

Inter-Society Color Council. www.ISCC.org. Access to online quiz on common color myths.

Munsell. www.gretagmacbeth.com/index/products/products_color-standards.html. Information on the Munsell Color System.

Pantone Color Institute. www.pantone.com. Information about Pantone color products and articles about color management.

Physics Hypertextbook, The. www.hypertextbook.com/physics/waves/color/index.-shtml. Color science resource.

Rochester Institute of Technology. www.CIS.rit.edu. This is the only school that offers a Ph.D. in color research.

Techexchange. www.techexchange.com/thelibrary.html. Good source for articles on color management.

CHAPTER 6

FABRICATION

"Touch is the first test of a designer's desire to know a fabric better.
Next comes the urge to unfurl the bolt and drape a path of fabric across
the body, noting how it flows, crumples, and catches light."

—LAURA JACOBS*

OBJECTIVES

- To understand the differences among various fabric classifications

- To understand variations in the fabric selection process among different types of product developers

- To review the aesthetic, performance, and serviceability characteristics of fabrics

- To be aware of new technologies affecting fabric choices

- To understand the important features of prints, including how they are sourced, designed, and produced

- To be aware of copyright laws as they apply to fabric design

- To understand the responsibilities involved in managing fabric decisions

In an age when fashion silhouettes evolve slowly from season to season, it is fabric that frequently can set a line apart and propel a customer to buy. New developments in fabric are a driving force in fashion. Product developers can gain competitive advantage by offering garments with special characteristics, improving performance, eliminating the need for ironing, or improving colorfastness. Companies such as Nike maintain their own fabric libraries so that designers have an accessible reference to fabrics available from their vendors. The Nike library includes over 8,000 approved fabrics and ribs for its active sportswear lines. The Lands' End product development team develops edge statements as they plan for each new season. These statements include fabrication strategies that will make their products stand out in the marketplace. Strategic fabric decisions positively influence the customer's decision to buy.

*Skrebneski and Jacobs 1995, 72

Figure 6.1. *This coordinated group of styles illustrates how fabrics are used to merchandise a line so that items within the line can be worn together and the line looks appealing on the sales floor.*

Creating a Fabric Story

Fabrication is the process of selecting fabrics for a seasonal line, groups within a line, and each style within a group. The fabrics chosen for a particular season or group are frequently referred to as a **fabric story** (Figure 6.1). Each group and corresponding fabric story is designated for a particular delivery date. The fabric story selected must lend itself to seasonal fashion silhouettes, the brand's price point, the production calendar, production capacity considerations, the garment category, the climate where the customer base is located, and consumer expectations for aesthetics and functionality. The design of each style must include a clear description of the intended fabric. A specific fabric must be agreed upon by the product developer and the contractor, including its price and the performance characteristics it must meet. Fabrication decisions must take into account

- the aesthetic and functional needs of the target market

- the relationship between cost and value

- whether the fabric provides the product with an appropriate level of exclusivity

- whether the fabric/pattern is copyright-free

- whether the fabric can be delivered according to the needs of the production calendar

These tasks may differ considerably, depending on whether the product developer is a wholesale brand, store brand, or private label.

Fabric Classifications

Figure 6.2a. A collection of prints that would merchandise well on a sales floor but that were not necessarily designed to be worn together.

Figure 6.2b. A collection of yarn-dyed woolen fabrics that could be used together in a collection.

Product developers may buy fabrics from a textile mill's seasonal line or they may work with the mill to customize the fabric they want. Fabrics can be merchandised as collections—coordinated groups of fabrics that have been developed around a common theme. An Asian-inspired collection might include fabrics with gingko leaves, fans, and chrysanthemums used in patterns on the same base fabric. Collections are frequently used in item lines such as dresses because the related patterns merchandise well together on the floor but are not necessarily so closely related as to be worn together (Figure 6.2a–b).

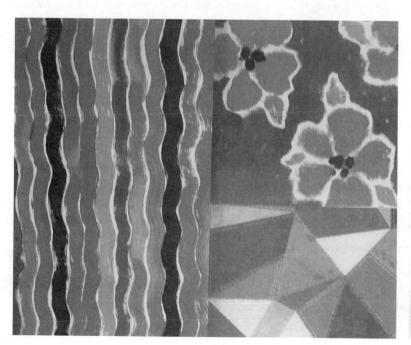

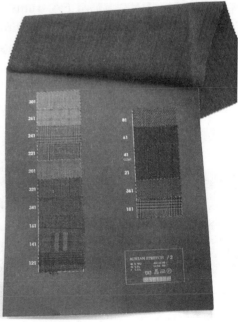

Figure 6.3. *The denim used for the pants on this model is an example of a bottom-weight fabric; the shirting fabric is considered a top-weight fabric.*

Bottom-Weight and Top-Weight Fabrics

Fabrics are frequently referred to as either bottom-weight or top-weight. **Bottom-weight fabrics** are suitable for skirts, pants, and jackets and typically weigh 4.0 to 7.0 ounces per square yard. **Top-weight fabrics** weigh less than 4.0 ounces per square yard and may also be referred to as *dress-weight* fabrics; they are used for blouses and dresses. Fabrics that weigh over 7.0 ounces per square yard are considered heavy-weight and are used for coats and some jackets. Typically, a coordinated group requires a balance of both bottom-weight and top-weight fabrics. Single category groups such as dresses or jeans may be developed around a single fabric type and weight in a coordinated colorway or pattern selection (Figure 6.3).

Basics versus Novelty Fabrics

Fabrics are further differentiated as either basic goods or novelty goods. **Basic goods** are the core fabrications of a group. These are traditional marketable fabrics that provide the foundation for a group. Seasonal basic goods do not vary much from year to year; rather, new colors, patterns, and finishes, or the addition of a special fiber such as Lycra, serve to keep them fresh. Because basic goods are typically ordered in greater quantities and used season after season, they tend to be more economical. Less money is spent on their development, and they can be produced in longer runs.

Novelty goods are unusual prints, patterns, wovens, or knits that make a group unique. Because novelty goods are typically more costly than basic goods, they are used for only a few items in the group to give it a fashion edge.

Fabric Selection

Members of the product development team responsible for fabric selection must be knowledgeable about textiles and tuned in to the current fashion environment. Their basic knowledge of textiles is continually expanded as team members are exposed to new fibers, finishes, and processes. Very large product development staffs may have fabric specialists for wovens and knits. Not all fabrication people are well versed in the technology of knits. Knit specialists must have a strong background in yarns and gauges, as well as the stitches and patterns possible in various knit processes. They must also know about the capabilities of the different sourcing regions for knits. The actual selection of specific fabrics varies by product developer.

Fabric for Wholesale Brand Product Lines

Wholesale brand product developers typically attend fabric shows and establish relationships directly with fabric suppliers. It is through these relationships that colors are defined and quality specifications are established. If their facility includes sample making, they start by buying **sample yardage**, the fabric needed for design exploration. Once a fabric is selected for the line, the product developer commits to **production yardage**, which is the amount of fabric needed to fulfill orders.

When buying a basic fabric, product developers will order a specific fabric quality and either select a color from a color card or have it dyed to their color standards. There are generally minimum yardage requirements to have a fabric custom dyed. A novelty fabric may also be developed in customized colors, or the basic goods may be developed to match the novelty fabric chosen for the group.

Wholesale brand product developers usually make fabric decisions before they design specific silhouettes. This approach is possible because designers have a sense of what the silhouettes will be from their trend research. Making the fabric decisions early is necessary in order to provide adequate turnaround time. It also results in more successful designs, since the inspiration comes from the fabric. Designing a silhouette before selecting the fabric often results in a design that does not work because the fabric may not be exactly what the designer imagined, therefore compromising the design.

Turnaround time in the textile industry refers to the lead time required for making, dyeing, and finishing the fabric in order to meet the delivery date determined by the production schedule. Initial orders are placed for minimum yardage requirements based on early sales projections. Once garment sales are finalized, the initial commitment will be revised. There is a constant tension between the product developer, who wants to leave the contract open-ended until the last possible minute so as not to underorder or overorder, and the fabric vendor, who requires a firm commitment in order to complete fabric production on time.

If wholesale brand product developers use domestic production, they may take ownership of the fabric they specify for production. If they are sourcing production of a particular style offshore, they may identify the vendor and specifications for the fabric they have chosen and require their production partner(s) to take ownership of the fabric. Requiring the contractor to take ownership of the fabric reduces the cycle time, reduces the initial investment required to begin production, simplifies customs clearance, and may reduce the tariff paid. When multiple contractors are producing the same style, the product developer may choose to take ownership of the fabric to ensure consistency, or the developer's offshore agent may assume responsibility for consistency among contractors.

Fabric for Private Label Product Lines

Private label product developers may work in a fashion similar to wholesale brand product developers. However, if they are derivative in their design approach, they may simply indicate a fabric type and require that their sourcing partners identify fabric options. This is especially true of retail product developers whose primary products are basic rather than fashion goods. For these product developers, the silhouette may be determined in the form of a purchased development sample, and a fabric type is then designated to match the target customer's preferences. These product developers put together a **specification package** that includes a design sheet with a picture of a development sample, a sketch of the product desired, and a fabrication request that indicates a range of acceptable fabrics. The agent or contractor then sources out a fabric that falls within that range and can be produced for the best value. The choice of fabric may be determined by what a supplier has in stock or what can be obtained in the least amount of time. Because derivative product developers work on a longer cycle time than do branded product developers, it is possible for them to make fabric and silhouette decisions simultaneously.

Fabric for Store Brand Product Lines

Store brand product developers may follow the procedures used by wholesale brand or private label product developers. The procedures they follow are determined by

- the sophistication of their product development team
- the price point of the garments they produce
- whether their design approach is derivative or original
- where the majority of their production is sourced

In general, product developers of commodity products at lower or moderate price points tend to be less involved in the initial fabric selection but fully engaged in approving the final choice. More expensive and fashion-forward product developers are more apt to be fully engaged in the fabrication process.

The Language of Fabrics

Fabrics "speak" to designers using their own special language. The fiber content, weight, surface interest (texture, luster, and pattern), drape, and hand communicate to the designer whether the fabric is suitable for a particular style, season, or customer. The character of the fabric dictates the limits of styling. However, designers are constantly redefining the limits of fabric choices and the rules for their end use. For example, fabrics infused with Lycra make it possible to create pants and skirts without front darts. Giorgio Armani led the way in tailoring featherweight woolens, a fabric once considered unsuitable for tailored garments.

Fiber

The fiber content of a fabric automatically communicates to the product developer a set of characteristics regarding serviceability. **Serviceability** is typically measured by properties that affect aesthetics, durability, comfort, appearance retention, and care (Kadolph 1998, 27). Although the serviceability characteristics of a fabric do not necessarily predict the serviceability of a garment, there is a strong relationship between the two. Fabric quality correlates to garment quality (Brown and Rice 2001, 183, 205).

Fibers are classified as either natural or manufactured and tend to be subject to fashion cycles similar to the cycles of silhouettes. Consumer preferences regarding the aesthetic and performance characteristics of textiles vary, depending on life stage, lifestyle, values, and income. Current textile technology can also affect the popularity of a particular fiber.

A textiles curriculum typically includes a comparative analysis of fiber performance characteristics. A fiber's aesthetic properties include luster, drape, texture, and hand. Durability is measured by factors that include abrasion resistance, tenacity, and elasticity. Comfort is related to absorbency, thermal retention, density, resilience, and elasticity. Appearance retention properties include resilience, dimensional stability, shrinkage resistance, and elasticity. A fiber's care requirements are determined by the way fibers react to water, chemicals, and heat in ironing and drying. (Note that this discussion is a review of fiber properties that can be found in any basic textile science text.) These characteristics must be matched to the garment's function and the intended consumer's preferences. Creative and technical designers *must* have a strong background in textile science; it is imperative that they keep current with new developments in textile technology.

Weight

Fabric weight is generally measured in ounces or grams per square or linear yard or meter. When comparing the weights of different fabrics, it is necessary to make sure that the weight figures are calculated on the same basis.

Fabric weight must be compatible with the season for which the garment will be sold, functional for the environment in which it will be worn, and suitable for the style of the garment. In the United States, lifestyles have evolved so that there is less need for heavy, warm fabrics. Heated cars and indoor shopping malls limit the time we spend outdoors in the cold. Textile technology has done much to develop fabrics that provide the look of heavy fabrics without the weight. Examples include Polarfleece textile fabric and acrylic sweaters that look like wool. Many fabrics for professional attire are promoted for their "seasonless" versatility. These fabrics are suitable for offices that are temperature-neutral—air-conditioned in the summer and heated in the winter. Such fabrics have appeal in areas that do not experience a very cold winter.

Fabric weight may have implications for garment construction. For example, lightweight fabrics may require a lining to make them opaque when worn, thus adding expense to the cost of the garment. Heavy or stiff fabrics do not lend themselves to added fullness.

Surface Interest

Surface interest includes the color(s), texture, luster, and pattern of a fabric. Color can be achieved through fiber dyeing, yarn dyeing, piece dyeing, garment dyeing, or any one of the many print methods. Implicit with each method of applying color is the timing when the color is applied. The later in the production cycle that the color is applied, the longer the color decision and assortment can be postponed. This gives the product developer more time to gather orders and determine production quantities. Each method of dying has its own set of advantages and disadvantages, which are related to fiber, desired color and affect, function, and end use. All of these factors must be considered when choosing the method of color application.

Texture can be achieved through the use of a novelty fiber or yarn, the choice of a particular knit stitch or weave, or the application of finishing processes such as felting, embossing, brushing, or sueding. Luster refers to the amount of light a fabric reflects. A fabric's luster is determined by the luster inherent in the fibers used, whether the fiber is used in filament or staple form, the yarn size, the amount of yarn twist, the weave or knit used to make the fabric, and the application of finishes such as glazing or waxing.

Pattern can be created through fabric construction or finishes, or it can be applied as a print. Examples of patterns that are produced through fabric construction include stripes, jacquards, intarsia knits, and lace. Finishing processes that produce patterns include embossing and flocking.

Patterns can also be created through printing. **Printing** is the application of a design or pattern to fabric, using dyes or pigments applied in limited areas. The design of prints and methods for applying the color or chemical to fabrics are discussed in greater detail in the next section.

The pattern that is selected must suit the fabric on which it is printed, the silhouette for which it is being used, and the customer's design aesthetic and figure proportions. The pattern scale must suit the size range in which it will be used. A large pattern may not be appropriate for a body-hugging garment with lots of seams because large-scale patterns lose their impact when a single motif becomes indistinguishable, as happens when the surface is divided by seams.

Patterns must be scaled to the wearer's body. Very large prints on small women tend to look out of proportion; huge prints on very large women may draw attention to their size. These effects are accentuated when the pattern is widely spaced; allover prints with low contrast tend to minimize the effects of scale.

Motifs are recurring design elements that, when used in repetition, create patterns. The background on which motifs are placed is referred to as the **ground**. One or more different motifs may be used in a single pattern. Some common categories of motifs are florals, geometrics, and conversationals. The cyclic popularity of certain print categories is central to fashion.

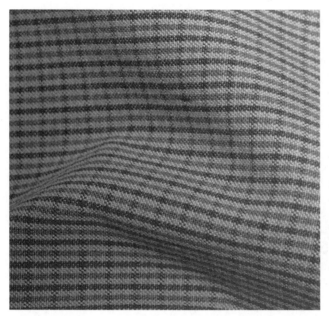

Figure 6.4a–b. *The pattern on yarn-dyed fabrics is achieved in the weaving process by using yarns of different colors to achieve checks, plaids, and other patterns such as stripes.*

Motif placement must be carefully planned. Large, widely spaced can call attention to figure extremes or fall conspicuously on the bust, crotch, or derriere, accentuating these areas. Random placement of large motifs can look off-center. Engineering these kinds of motifs to avoid clumsy placement is expensive in the time it takes to spread the fabric and the waste involved in positioning the pieces. Increased use of digital printing in the future may simplify these considerations and allow for prints to be scaled to the size of the garment and placed to enhance matching and therefore maximize the aesthetic impact of the print.

Directional patterns require additional care in matching and placement because the designs have a distinct top and bottom or right and left. These considerations may negatively affect fabric utilization.

Pattern can also be achieved through the use of dyed yarn. **Yarn-dyed fabrics** utilize yarns that have been dyed previous to weaving; patterns are achieved by using several colors of yarn strategically placed in the weaving process. Plaids, stripes, brocades, chambrays, and seersuckers are all made in this way (Figure 6.4a–b).

Hand and Drape

Fabric **hand** refers to the tactile qualities of a fabric as they are affected by fiber content, yarn, fabric construction, and finishing. Related to a fabric's hand is fabric drape. **Drape** refers to how a fabric hangs (falls, clings, flows) and bends (pleats or gathers). A fabric's hand and drape determine how it can be styled and the silhouette achieved from that styling. Tailoring and pleating require fabrics that can hold sharp edges. Gathers look very different in a soft rayon challis than they do in a crisp taffeta or stiff organza.

Table 6.1 FAVORITE FABRICS TO WEAR

Cotton	58%	Silk	6%	Other	2%
Denim	9%	Linen	3%	Wool	1%
Don't know	8%	Polyester	2%	Spandex	1%
Cotton blend	7%	Rayon	2%		

Source: Cotton Incorporated's Lifestyle Monitor 2006a, 2006b

Evolving Textile Technology

While consumers continue to rank natural fibers as their favorites to wear, new technology is changing our expectations of both natural and manmade fibers. Data published by Cotton Incorporated's Lifestyle Monitor indicates that 58 percent of women surveyed stated a preference for cotton and 66.3 percent said they were willing to pay more for natural fibers such as cotton (Cotton Incorporated's Lifestyle Monitor 2006a, 2) (Table 6.1). At the same time, one out of two women told Cotton Incorporated's Lifestyle Monitor that they had purchased apparel with a performance feature. Women indicated that they seek out apparel with performance features to run errands, to exercise, and to be comfortable around the house (Cotton Incorporated's Lifestyle Monitor 2006b). The textile industry in the United States, Europe, and Japan is using textile technology to compete with producers in nations where operating costs are lower and consumers are responding to these innovations.

Textiles integrate science, style, function, and imagination. New technology may originate in the research and development labs of textile manufacturers or from suppliers, universities, and partners within the supply chain. Many new developments come about as a response to performance and safety needs in the active sports and protective services arenas but are then recognized for their potential as higher-value fashion fabrics. Runners want pants and tops with muscle compression properties that provide a fit snug enough to hold working muscles in place; those same fabrics hold appeal for the general consumer who desires support of softer fatty tissue in order to look more fit. Similarly, swimmers want spandex that is resistant to chlorine, a characteristic equally appealing to the average swimsuit consumer. Other developments are inspired by consumers who report their functional dissatisfaction with everyday apparel and their desire for newness to retailers who pass the information back through the pipeline.

The product developments that result from new technology don't always look high-tech, but may function at a higher level. Designers such as Karl Lagerfeld, Miuccia Prada, and Hussein Chalayan embrace high-tech and handmade techniques equally as a means to creating something that hasn't been

Figure 6.5. *Miuccia Prada is known for using cutting-edge textile technology to express her fashion vision.*

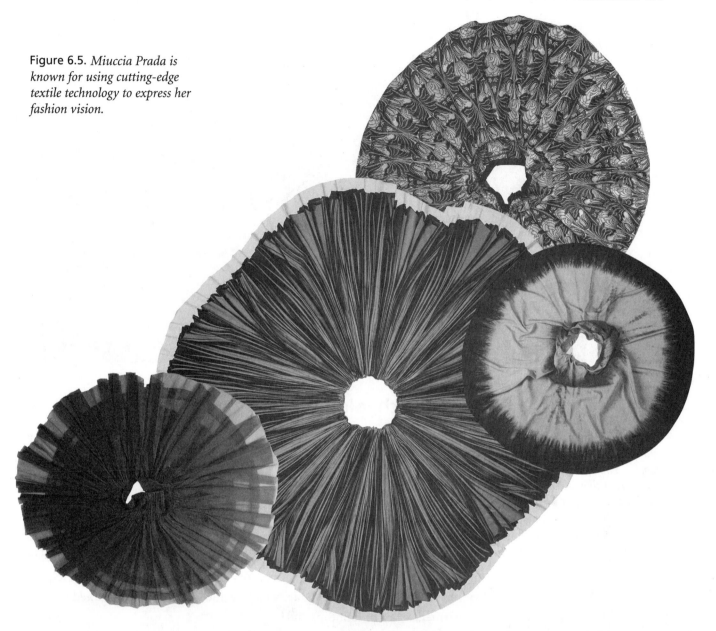

seen before. Technology can be used to renew low-tech/high-craft techniques such as embroidery, knitting, felting, needle punch, specialty dyeing, and the laser-cutting of leather into lacy patterns (Corcoran and Socha 2004, 12). Miuccia Prada says, "Technology is at the basis of my whole work in all its different applications. It can mean avant-garde, [as demonstrated by] our strong attitude toward revolutionary materials, . . .but it can also mean jumping into the past [and] revitalizing the old-time manual techniques" (Corcoran and Socha 2004, 12) (Figure 6.5).

Product developers seek out textiles that possess a range of enhanced aesthetic and performance qualities. Their ongoing dialogue with fiber companies helps both to better understand how current technology can best be applied to meet consumer preferences. New developments in textiles will result from the convergence of developments in four key areas: information technology, biotechnology, nano-scale manufacturing techniques, and new materials drawn from sustainable resources.

Figure 6.6. *Nanotechnology has many applications for performance fabrics. The model wears an outfit made from chlorine-resistant spandex. The fabric in the background is a cotton, polyester, and Lycra spandex blend that is chlorine-resistant and has a higher tear strength.*

Knit Technology

Typical of the trend and countertrend dynamic of fashion, at the same time that we are seeing a resurgence in the popularity of hand knitting, there are technological developments in seamless knitting. Seamless knitting minimizes or eliminates some or all of the labor-intensive processes of cutting and sewing, shaving time off the production cycle as well as cost. It minimizes yarn consumption, yields higher productivity, and results in garments with no bulky or irritating stitches and seams. Seamless knitting has primarily been used in the hosiery and lingerie category. Seamless knitting machines require retrofitting for each style made; therefore, the technique is best suited to basic garments such as knit tops and T-shirts.

Smart Textiles and Nanotechnology

Historically, textile solutions to achieve functional goals have been static—they were effective solutions in a homogenous environment where the user's needs and environmental conditions were consistent but less effective in environments where conditions changed constantly. New technologies provide dynamic functionality in clothing and textiles (Dunne et al. 2005). Textiles that interact with electrical current, light energy, or thermal energy; change physical properties through an external signal from the user or an internal or environmental stimulus; or change properties through the use of elements embedded into the textile or applied as a coating to the textile are referred to as **smart textiles** (Mills 2005). Although very few wearable smart textile products have been successfully commercialized, years of research and development appear to be on the cusp of paying off. The field of smart textiles represents a synergy between the design of the textile and the design of the garment.

Many of today's new textile developments are a result of **nanotechnology**, "the manipulation of atoms and molecules on the nano level with hyperfine technology in order to alter the properties of a given material" (Fitzpatrick 2004). A nano is equivalent to the width of three or four atoms; nanotechnology usually refers to the region of 1–100 nanometers—the range in which electrons display special behavior. A nanometer is one billionth of a meter. Included in this category are fiber enhancements of both natural and manmade fiber; technology that is embedded into fabrics; and new finishes.

New and Modified Fibers

Some applications of nanotechnology rely on biotechnology to modify or enhance fabrics. Kurabo Industries developed a fiber that is blended with the stem of the shell ginger plant from Japan, giving the resulting fabric a unique aroma as well as antibacterial properties (Fitzpatrick 2004). CloverTex, LLC, is transforming coconut shells into high-performance yarns. "Cocona, activated carbon derived from coconut shells, is combined with polyester during the extrusion process to produce yarn. Polyester embedded with Cocona produces a multifunctional fabric with excellent wicking properties, the capability to trap and remove odor molecules, and the ability to protect the wearer from harmful UV rays. Cocona polyester is now being combined with cotton" (Anderson 2006, 3–6). Cocona-infused fabrics are being targeted to the sport, intimate, and hosiery markets. NanoHorizons has begun to sell a line of metallic nanoparticles that are compatible with standard polymer manufacturing. The particles of silver, gold, and other metals kill bacteria and odor-causing microbes and can be incorporated into shoes, athletic equipment, and hosiery (Figure 6.6).

Fiber enhancements include the development of new manmade fibers and the modification of existing natural or manmade fibers to better meet consumer preferences. Invista has introduced a family of Lycra products. New Lycra variations include Super White Lycra, Black Lycra, and XFit Lycra. Super White Lycra makes intimate apparel more durable and prevents the yellowing that occurs from normal washing and wearing. Black Lycra provides similar improvements to durability and provides a deeper color. Black Lycra was designed for the intimate apparel market but was found to have crossover appeal in the eveningwear market. XFit Lycra was created for the premium denim market and gives denim four-way stretch. It hit the market just as skinny jeans became a trend (Tucker 2006, 10) (Figure 6.7).

Dow has introduced XLA fiber, a lastow rather than a spandex, meant to be blended with natural fibers such as cashmere to improve a garment's ability to hold its shape after cleaning without taking away from the hand and feel. XLA is already being used with linen, denim, and men's and women's shirtings (Tucker 2006, 10).

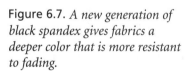

Figure 6.7. *A new generation of black spandex gives fabrics a deeper color that is more resistant to fading.*

Coolmax technology was launched by Invista. It is a polyester variation designed to move moisture away from the body, enhancing moisture management and comfort. Since Coolmax is a permanent fiber modification, these characteristics hold up to regular laundering. A new fiber that has resulted from nanotechnology is Lyocel, a product of Lenzing AG, which is sold under the Tencel label. It combines the advantages of many different fibers—including the fineness of silk, the strength of polyester, the easy-care qualities of acrylic, the coolness of linen, and the softness of cotton.

Micro Encapsulation

Micro encapsulation applies or embeds particles filled with an active ingredient to a fabric or garment. Movement activates the encapsulated particles, producing a slow release of the ingredient. Active ingredients include moisturizers, vitamins, medicines, therepeutic smells, and insect repellant, all in forms that can be absorbed through the skin. Researchers are exploring the areas of skin whitening and dieting for future applications. These forms of micro-encapsulation have a finite life—after the substance has been absorbed into the skin, the benefit stops.

Micro encapsulation can also be used to create garments with built-in temperature control systems using **phase change materials (PCMs)**, substances that store, release, and absorb heat as they oscillate between solid and liquid form. Based on technology originally developed for the U.S. space program, phase change materials are now finding applications in textiles for apparel. Fiber, fabric, and foam with built-in PCMs store the warmth the body creates and then release it back to the body, as it needs it. This dynamic process is ideally suited for activities where the level of physical activity of the body and the outside temperature is constantly changing.

Fabrics that are sensitive to UV rays and/or temperature can be manipulated to change color through the use of thermochromic, photochromic, or electrochromic dyes and inks. Most applications so far have been for fashion or novelty purposes. Sinterama introduced a glow-in-the-dark yarn in 2003 with luminescent properties triggered by exposure to light. The yarn is made from a polyester polymer and is aptly named *Ghost.* Color-change garments offer potential in protective clothing for outdoor workers, rescue teams, and the military. In fact, the U.S. and U.K. military are working with phase change materials to produce chameleon-like camouflage fabrics that use prismatic phase change to reflect light at the same wavelength of that which is striking it (Mills 2005, November 16). Another fabric, *Flash Line,* encapsulates tiny metallic glass spheres that reflect light to create optional patterns (Watkins 2005, 016–019).

Finishes

Nanotechnology has brought about major improvements in finishes that can be applied to cotton, polyester, silk, or wool. Because the chemicals are applied as a film only a few nanometers thick, they achieve unsurpassed durability without sacrificing the natural hand and breathability of the fabric. Finishes available today make fabrics stain-, wrinkle-, static-, and water-resistant. Many of the finishes withstand 50 or more home washings without significant loss of function. Some withstand dry cleaning, and others do not. Fabric softeners may also inhibit performance, so it is important when developing products with these new finishes to educate salespeople and develop clear labeling in order to inform the consumer. Nano-Tex, one of the leaders in nanotechnology, has developed a fabric it calls Nano-Touch, which has the feel and touch of cotton with the performance of a synthetic fiber. The fabric is achieved through the attachment of a cottonlike wrap around a synthetic core (www.nano-tex.com).

Electronic-Integrated Textiles

Wearable electronics are the highest-profile product segment within smart textiles. For some time, garments have been available with pockets and bags that carry technology. The next step is to incorporate electronic devices into the textile itself. The integration of electronic and textile technology confronts the designer with several challenges. A big question is whether the cost and the life cycle of the electronic function and the garment for which the textile is used can be reconciled. Consumers are not willing to pay for duplicate technology every time they purchase a new garment. Second, up until recently electronic components could be heavy and stiff. Garment-integrated technology requires better distribution of any weight and/or bulk, so that the resulting textile maintains its drape and comfort characteristics. Third, integrating electronic technology into garments requires a new approach to garment engineering. Traditional garment-making methods involve cutting the textile into pattern shapes, but circuitry built into a textile cannot be cut. Laundering and care requirements must also be considered (Dunne et al. 2005).

For these reasons and more, many prototype electronic garments have been designed for medical monitoring for which a patient does not need to wear the garment constantly; for resarch and development purposes to record data about movement so industrial designers can design products that function better; and for the protection of police officers, firefighters, and the military. But creative product developers who think out of the box see consumer applications on the horizon.

Researchers at MIT are perfecting **e-broidery**, which uses yarns and threads with electrical properties to "quilt" electronic circuitry into a garment. Their goal is to provide wearable computer functionality in clothing that is comfortable, durable, and convenient (Post et al. 2000, 840–860). Researchers have identified several textiles and yarns suitable for fabric circuitry. Numerically controlled embroidery using conductive thread defines circuits, component connection pads, and sensing surfaces. The commercial embroidery process builds on current textile technology that allows precise control of

the design, layout, and stitch patterns of the circuitry through the use of CAD processes (Figure 6.8a–b).

The MIT team is working on a washable jacket or vest with computer functionality. The small computing elements are distributed throughout the jacket and connected by a stitched network. "Electronic nodes provide sensing functionality to respond to wireless messages within its physical locale; some storage for a distributed, redundant database; and a computing element capable of executing small mobile applications" (Post et al. 2000). Think of the potential for travel overseas or on business; it could replace the need to carry a laptop. In the future the team would like to integrate different components into one digital system that works across several items of clothing. The most expensive components could be engineered into shoes and outer garments which are worn regularly, and the least expensive components into shirts, trousers, skirts, and underwear.

At present the cost of such garments may limit their commercial viability to garments that are worn frequently and to uses where health and safety are an issue, e.g., coats and jackets for children or Alzheimer's patients who are prone to running off or getting lost. As this technology becomes less dependent on batteries and more interconnected to circuitry in other garments, the applications will grow. Consider these options, which are currently under development:

- Tiny embedded chips in garments so that if you see an outfit that you covet on a friend or passerby, you can access the chip with your cell phone and find out where the product is sold and how much it costs.

- Garments with circuitry that allows you to control the temperature of your outerwear garments, hats, and gloves.

- Flexible color screens built into clothing allowing a variety of designs and images to be projected on the clothing.

- Garments that change color electronically to match and coordinate with the other garments being worn with it.

Figure 6.8a–b. *The aging suit was developed by Ford in order to better understand the issues an aging population might experience getting in and out of a vehicle. The musical jacket turns an ordinary denim jacket into a wearable musical instrument. It includes a fabric keypad on one side, a MIDI synthesizer on the other side, and speakers behind speaker grills in the pockets; the result is achieved using electronic embroidery technology.*

The Impact of "Green"

Sustainable and fair trade textiles are gaining ground as we grapple with global warming and limited natural resources. Apparel made from these textiles is referred to as *eco fashion* and *ethical fashion*, reflecting consumers' heightened concerns about apparel manufacturing that damages the environment or violates human rights. Manufacturers sensitive to these concerns promote initiatives that convey a sense of corporate responsibility. Environmental concerns revolve around the use of chemicals that can be harmful to workers or leach into the water supply and the use of petroleum products to make manmade fibers. Sustainable textiles are those that can be grown without the use of chemicals—pesticides and fertilizers. Fair trade–certified cotton guarantees higher prices for cotton producers so that workers can be paid fairly. The following fibers are examples of sustainable, organic, or recycled fibers:

- Organic cotton that is grown from seeds that are not genetically altered and grown and harvested without pesticides. Most organic cotton farms are in Texas, California, and Turkey.

- Natural colored cotton that can be cultivated in color, eliminating dyes that may be harmful to the environment. To date cotton seeds come in variations of red, green, and brown.

- Hemp is a fiber that does not require herbicides, pesticides, or crop rotation.

- Bamboo is a hollow fiber (which increases its moisture-absorbing and -releasing properties); it has a very soft texture and natural antibacterial properties. Bamboo fiber breathes and blends well with other fibers.

- SeaCell is a cellulose fiber containing seaweed. It provides wellness effects to the wearer.

- Soysilk fiber is manufactured by extracting protein from leftover soybean oil or tofu production and adding a biological enzyme to make a spinning solution. It is marketed as "vegetable cashmere" due to its soft hand, luster, loft, and drape. Its porous structure and grooves on the fiber surface give it excellent wet permeability and warmth retention.

- Vegan silk relies on a method where the silkworms are allowed to escape rather than killed in their cocoons. The thread breaks before it is unrolled, resulting in a silk fabric that offers a unique look and feel (Montgomery 2004, 32).

- Ingeo is Cargill Dow's brand name for the first manmade fiber derived from 100 percent annually renewable resources. It uses natural raw material such as corn, rice, potatoes, grass, or straw, which is converted into plant sugars and fermented before being transformed into a high-performance polymer called polyactide from which filament yarns are extruded. Purists suggest that Ingeo fiber is not organic because it relies on genetically engineered crops—crops that have been mutated with a bacteria gene to resist bugs without the need for pesticides. Genetically engineered crops have a much higher yield per acre (Elias 2006, 4D).

- Fabrics such as Malden Mill's Polartec textile fabric and Teijin's EcoCircle fiber-to-fiber recycling system utilize recycled plastic bottles and recycled polyester fabric.

A growing number of brands including *Edun,* a line launched by Bono and his wife Ali Hewson, and Nike, Timberland, Patagonia, and Nordstrom

Figure 6.9. Edun *apparel is manufactured in Africa, South America, and India in fair trade factories; they use organic cotton whenever possible.*

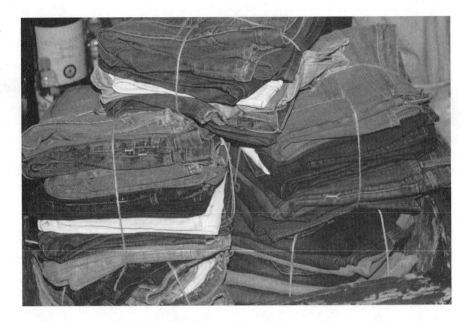

have incorporated earth-conscious fibers into their merchandise. Retail sales of organic cotton have doubled from $245 million in 2001 to $583 million in 2005 (Gunther 2006) (Figure 6.9).

Nike launched an organic cotton collection in fall 2002 but carried it only for a few seasons due to supply delays. Today its focus is on sourcing blended cotton—47 percent of its cotton garments include at least 5 percent organic cotton. Nike's goal is for all cotton materials they produce to contain a minimum of 5 percent organic cotton by 2010. Nike has also implemented a Restricted Substance List and plans to remove or replace toxic chemicals, including those that are not legislated as illegal. In addition, Nike has established waste management centers in several countries and is committed to reduce the combined CO_2 emissions from owned facilities. Its shoeboxes are made with 100-percent recycled materials, and it sponsors a program called Reuse-A-Shoe that collects worn-out shoes of any brand and transforms them into a material called Nike Grind, which is used to make sports surfaces (Ethical Insight Team at Maplecroft 2004, 9–10) (Figure 6.10a–b).

Patagonia converted its cotton consumption to organic in 1996. The company is committed to building products and working with processes that cause the least damage to the environment. It carefully evaluates raw materials, invests in innovative technologies, monitors its waste, and uses a portion of sales to promote conservation. Its Common Threads garment recycling program collects worn-out polyester garments to make new polyester, which results in an energy savings of 76 percent and a CO_2 emissions reduction of 71 percent, versus creating that fiber from new raw material. Patagonia is an active member of The Conservation Alliance, a group of businesses that work together on environmental initiatives (www.patagonia.com).

Other designers are creating new clothes out of old clothes. Companies such as Alabama Chanin (formerly Project Alabama), Deborah Lindquist,

Figure 6.10a–b. *Loomstate is one of a growing number of brands that uses only organic cotton. Anna Cohen uses primarily sustainable fibers; she chose bamboo for this halter top due to its luxurious texture and beautiful drape.*

Claudette, and Koi all redesign castoff clothing for a portion of their lines. Retailers appreciate the one-of-a-kind nature of these products.

Fair trade efforts put people and the environment before profit. Efforts revolve around making sure that workers are paid a living wage and that they are not exposed to dangerous chemicals in the process of their work. The United Nations industrial development organization collaborated with its marketing and development branch to launch a fair trade program in Ethiopia in July 2006. Taytu is an Ethiopian luxury accessories label; profits from these high-end accessories go to the collective of Ethiopian companies behind the label. Taytu guarantees employees fair pay and safe working conditions. The effort is a response to Ethiopian manufacturers' frustration in not being able to compete with mass producers. The United Nations hired Western designers to consult on the line so that the products would be saleable in the luxury market (Long 2006).

As product developers become increasingly aware of the cost of using a textile or finish that is later found to be detrimental to health, safety, or the environment, and consumers use their purchasing clout to indicate that these issues are important to them, there is more being done to promote the concept of safe stewardship in the area of textiles and finishes. Chemical companies around the world have been developing and implementing Responsible Care initiatives (www.responsiblecare.org). These initiatives have been endorsed by major trade associations; some have made adherence to these standards a condition of membership. They require open communication of activities, incidents, and achievements throughout the supply chain. The existence of a Responsible Care program is a good indicator of a supplier's integrity and commitment to best practices in regard to safety, health, and the environment. They improve the trust and confidence in chemicals used in textile finishing up and down the supply chain (Cowie and Eacott 2003, 55).

Prints

Prints are a critical element for many segments of the apparel industry in developing their seasonal line. Categories that rely heavily on prints for brand differentiation include children's, dress, and lingerie markets.

Print Sources

Product developers have several options for obtaining prints. The prints may be

- selected from a textile mill or converter's seasonal line and ordered as shown

- selected from a mill or converter's seasonal line and modified to match a product developer's seasonal color story

- purchased as fabric paintings from a design studio and applied to a fabric of the product developer's choice

- designed in-house by the product developer

In the past, textile mills and converters offered a large number of open-line patterns for product developers to choose from. These patterns were either developed by the mill's in-house designers or purchased from print studios. With the costs of screens and print runs escalating, many converters have significantly reduced their open-line offerings. This defers the cost of sample development and shifts the responsibility for print design to the product developers, who will acquire only the prints they intend to use and recolor them to match their seasonal color story. Consequently, print studios in business today primarily service product developers rather than mills and converters.

Purchasing Prints

Prints can be purchased from a freelance textile designer, from a print studio, from a print representative (usually referred to as a *rep*), or from a print library. Prints may be viewed by visiting a showroom, a library, attending a

Figure 6.11a–c. *Print studios employ teams of artists who work in-house to develop textile patterns. A print agent represents various artists, providing one-stop print fabric shopping for product developers.*

print show, or inviting freelance textile designers to come in and present their collections. Frequently, textile designers specialize in prints for a particular type of fabric or in designs for a specific market. The average print generally sells for $400 to $500, but yarn dyes can sell for as little as $100 and embroideries or trim ideas for as much as $1,500. Related prints may be priced as a group. Purchased prints may be computer-generated or painted designs on paper or silk. Once a print is purchased, product developers may modify it in any way they desire. They own the print and the copyright to its use. If a product developer does not have an in-house staff to recolor or modify the print, the print studio or another outside contractor may be hired to make those changes at an additional charge. Computer print technology allows product

Figure 6.12a. *This polyester and Lycra spandex camouflage warp knit is an example of the innovative fabric developments that can be found at the Material Connexion textile consultancy and research center; fabrics showcased there are geared to architects, interior designers, and now fashion designers.*

Figure 6.12b. *The Design Library is located 60 miles north of Manhattan and houses a collection of more than five million samples dating from the 1750s to the late twentieth century.*

developers to explore more colorways and scale options and has greatly reduced the time required to make these changes to prints. Generally, product developers who purchase prints budget a seasonal dollar amount per division and category.

Print studios employ teams of artists who work in-house to develop textile patterns, which are then made available to textile and product development clients through reps positioned globally. In the United States, most print designers contract directly with a product developer or they work independently and distribute their designs through print reps or at print shows (Figure 6.11a–c). Some print designers will work with a product developer to customize designs specifically for them.

Design libraries house historic fabric swatches that may be borrowed or purchased as source materials for the development of new fabrics. The Fashion Institute of Technology has an extensive textile library where members can borrow samples. Samples that are used for the development of a fabric are taken out of circulation for a specified period of time.

The Design Library is located in a turn-of-the-century textile bleaching factory in Wappingers Falls, New York, an artists' community 60 miles north of Manhattan. The library houses more than five million samples dating from the 1750s to the late 20th century. Its clients include high-end designers to mass market retailers, interior designers to trend forecasters. Most samples can be purchased; however, the most priceless pieces can only be rented (*WWD* 2006, 7)

A relatively new source for apparel fabrics is *Material Connexion,* a consultancy and research center for designers. This library has been a resource to architects and industrial designers; recently it has made an effort to collect textiles with appeal to apparel designers (Figure 6.12a–b).

In-House Design

Today, many product developers take a proactive role in designing their own prints. In many private label or store brand firms, the primary responsibility of the creative design team is to develop prints for a given season. This means that team members must have a strong fine arts or graphic arts background as well as excellent computer-aided design (CAD) skills. If product developers do not have talented artists to develop their own prints, they may opt to purchase prints and then customize them to their own color and scale needs. Staff members who make print selections may look for prints with multiple components that they can separate into several artistic elements, thereby yielding several prints from a single print purchase. Care must be taken not to violate copyright when doing derivative prints. Although garment styles are rarely copyrighted, fabric prints need to be treated as copyrighted material.

Designing Prints

Prints may be developed through traditional art media or directly on the computer. Art media may include dyes, gouache, watercolor, acrylic, markers, or pastels, to name a few. If a pattern is designed on the computer, the designer may use off-the-shelf software such as Adobe Illustrator or Photoshop, or industry-specific software such as Lectra's Kaledo, NedGraphics, or Monarch's Pointcarré. No matter how the pattern is developed, it may be scanned into the computer for manipulation of color and scale once it is complete. The same pattern appears very different, depending on the layout used. **Layout** refers to the placement of one motif relative to another, taking into consideration direction, coverage, and arrangement of adjacent motifs.

Direction

Mirroring, flipping, or rotating can change a motif's direction. The direction of a motif layout is generally described in one of the following ways:

- *One-way layouts*—all motifs are placed facing the same direction.

- *Two-way layouts*—motifs are alternated in up-and-down or left-and-right directions in the same pattern.

- *Four-way layouts*—motifs are alternated in up-and-down and left-and-right directions in the same pattern.

- *Scattered allover layouts*—motifs are placed at a variety of angles, giving the appearance of a haphazard placement.

Another aspect of layout is coverage. When the motifs of a design are placed closely together, the coverage is described as tight. If the motifs are separated by lots of ground between motifs, the coverage is called open (Fisher and Wolfthal 1987, 55–59).

Repeats

An important aspect of print design is putting the pattern into **repeat**. Putting a pattern into repeat refers to the process of adapting the pattern to the printing tools of the industry so it will print continuously along the length and width of the fabric. The size of the repeat depends on the size of the printing equipment. The circumference of a printer's roller will determine the vertical repeat, and the width of the cylinder will determine the horizontal repeat. The screens used in flatbed printing also come in standard sizes. Many mills prefer to take on the responsibility of the repeat, so that the repeat is scaled to match their equipment. Other considerations when developing the repeat include color limitations, sequence of rollers, engraving techniques, and potential printing problems. Putting patterns into repeat has been greatly simplified by the use of computer applications.

Arrangement

Arrangement refers to how the motifs are positioned to form a pattern. Pattern arrangements are often categorized as follows:

- **Set layouts** follow an invisible grid, with the motifs arranged in a definite geometric pattern. Set layouts are often described by the amount of drop in the repeat of the pattern. A half-drop pattern describes a layout in which the first row of the print is followed by a second row placed at alternate intervals and positioned half a repeat below the first. Computer programs have built-in functions that allow the designer to explore full-, half-, and quarter-drop repeats.

- **Random layouts** appear to be scattered haphazardly.

- **Geometric layouts** are printed designs that imitate stripes, plaids, and weaves. These pattern layouts are not to be confused with yarn-dyed stripes and plaids.

- **Border prints** are patterns that are arranged along one selvage of the fabric. Borders may be placed on a solid fabric or incorporated into a print fabric.

- **Engineered prints** are designed with the end use in mind so that the length of each pattern repeat relates to the shape that will be cut from it. Knit polo shirts or silk scarves are good examples of engineered patterns (Fisher and Wolfthal 1987).

The methods for applying chemicals to fabrics are discussed in greater detail in the next section.

Printing Methods

Once a print is designed, customized, and checked for originality, arrangements must be made for it to be printed. The printing method chosen is based on the yardage required, the fiber content of the fabric, and the dye or pigment formula required to achieve the range of colors specified. Printing processes vary in cost effectiveness, depending on the amount of yardage required. Different fibers require different dyes to be absorbed into the fabric or pigments to adhere to a fabric's surface. Not all dyes produce the same range of color. The color range achieved by varying the attributes of hue, value, and chroma may be limited with some dye classifications. Color-fastness characteristics also differ by dye classification. Synthetic dyes have better stability and are more consistent for matching colors than the results achieved with natural dyes.

As stated earlier, printing is the application of colorant in definite, repeated patterns to fabric. The four most prevalent methods of mechanized printing used today are screen printing, roller printing, heat-transfer printing, and digital printing. Each method can be used to create one or more print types, including direct, discharge, resist, and pigment prints.

Direct Printing

In **direct printing** the design is printed directly onto a white cloth or a previously dyed fabric. This is the most frequently used form of printing. Direct prints that are made with pigments are distinguished from dye printing because the pigment lies on top of the fabric rather than being absorbed into the fabric. Pigment prints are very economical to produce, but may stiffen and thicken the fabric where the pigment is applied.

Discharge Printing

Discharge printing is a variation of direct printing in which a chemical is applied to a dyed piece of fabric to remove the color in certain areas, thus leaving a lighter color. Discharge prints can be made with roller and screen methods but are not widely used because production costs are high.

Figure 6.13. *Screen printing may be used on textile yardage or finished garments.*

Resist Printing

Resist printing involves a two-step procedure in which a design pattern is printed on a white or dyed fabric with a chemical or wax that will prevent the dyes from penetrating the fabric. When the fabric is dyed, the color is absorbed only where there is no resist. Batik printing is an example of this process. This method is primarily limited to hand printing.

Screen Printing

Screen printing applies dye or pigment through a fine synthetic screen that has some areas blocked off, thus creating a pattern. A different screen must be created to apply each color. Once the color is applied, the print paste is cured. Hand screen printing is used primarily by textile artists; it is too time-consuming to use commercially, except for very small runs or special end uses like flags and banners.

Automatic or flatbed screen printing can be used for fabrics or applied to finished garments such as T-shirts and sweatshirts. The fabric or garment moves along under a series of screen printing frames (Figure 6.13). All operations are fully automatic. Rotary screen printing utilizes nickel alloy screens that are formed into cylinders. Dyestuff inside each cylinder is pressed out onto the fabric through the holes of the screen. This method is used on 70 to 75 percent of all U.S. piece goods printing. Rotary screen printing is most effective on fabrics made entirely or mostly of cotton. The speed and efficiency of this method make it suitable for long and short yardage runs. It yields clean, bright colors and excellent color definition; however, extremely fine-line designs are not possible.

Engraved Roller Printing

Engraved roller printing utilizes a steel cylinder that has an outer layer of copper, into which a design is etched. Each color in the print requires a separate engraved copper roller. The cost of etching the rollers makes this method suitable for large runs of 10,000 yards or more or classic patterns. This method works well for fine-line patterns as well as half-tone effects. The size of the pattern repeat is limited to a maximum of 16 inches for apparel and 22 inches for home furnishings. Pattern changeovers can cause long production delays (Khatua 2001).

Heat-Transfer Printing

Heat-transfer printing, also called **thermal transfer printing**, is a technique in which disperse dyes are first printed on special transfer paper, which is then placed on the fabric and passed through a heat-transfer printing machine at about 400 degrees Fahrenheit. The temperature and pressure cause the dye to transfer onto the fabric. This technique produces bright, sharp, fine-line designs but is limited to fabrics with a minimum of 50 percent thermoplastic fiber. It can be applied to cut garment parts and small completed garments, allowing for rapid pattern changeover. An example of a heat-transfer application is seen in the printing of moderately priced polyester ties. The process is used in larger-scale applications on synthetic fibers to produce print yardage. It is very durable and especially resistant to sunlight. This method can be used to create a variety of three-dimensional, foil, and other special effects. Early applications revolved around T-shirts. In March 2006 designer Giles Deacon sent knit and woven dresses down the runway featuring heat-transfer metallic holograms (Figure 6.14).

Digital Printing

Digital printing applies patterns on fabric using computer printer technology. Patterns created and stored in the computer can be selected, scaled, and printed directly onto fabric. At present, this method is used primarily to produce sample yardage and very small runs. While screen printing has a cost advantage for large-scale production, digital printing methods hold promise for short-run production and mass customization. Digital printing is not without its challenges, the foremost being color reproduction (Figure 6.15).

Standards for Print Quality

A high-quality print, regardless of printing method, should be clear and focused, free from blurring and smudging. A print's **registration** refers to the precise alignment of colors within the pattern. A print that is out of registration may have white areas between colors in the design or places where colors overlap. Patterns containing numerous colors and details are generally more costly to produce because of the time it takes to register each application of color. Patterns should be printed onto the fabric on the straight-of-grain. A pattern that is printed off-grain forces the cutter to decide whether to follow the grain or the pattern in cutting. If a pattern is applied only slightly off-grain, following the pattern will make the garment appear to be straight even though

Figure 6.14. *Giles Deacon used heat-transfer printing to press metallic holograms onto his knits and wovens for his fall 2006 collection.*

Figure 6.15`. *Digital printing holds great promise for short-run production and mass customization.*

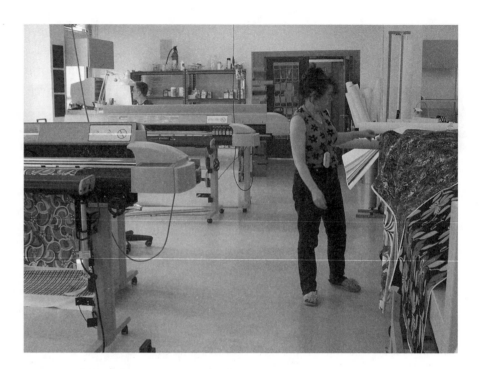

it may not hang perfectly straight. Fabrics that are printed drastically off-grain should be returned to the mill and should not be used (Brown and Rice 2001).

Prints can also be developed using one of a number of specialty processes. Table 6.2 defines some of these options.

Making and Protecting Fabric Selections

There is a constant tension in the product development goal of creating a product that reflects current trends while somehow differentiating the brand. This differentiation is frequently achieved through the fabric selection process. Product developers attempt to put together fabric stories that reflect fashion color tendencies, but they differentiate their shade through identification of their own unique color standard. Inclusion of novelty fabrics in the line is another method of differentiation. The development or purchase of exclusive prints is yet another way to create uniqueness.

Making Fabric Selections

The quest for brand differentiation requires that product developers review as many fabric lines as possible that are related to their product category. Fabric salespeople can be good barometers of market trends. By establishing a relationship with many fabric vendors, product developers keep their options open. However, partnerships are important in an agile marketplace. Management may encourage product developers to work with certain textile firms because of long-standing relationships that have developed over the years based on price agreements, consistent quality, and timely delivery. Likewise, certain textile firms may be off-limits because of poor credit ratings or an unsatisfactory performance in the past.

The product developer bases fabric decisions on price, aesthetics, fashion, and function. Fabrics for a particular line generally fall within a price range relative to sourcing costs in order to yield a finished product at an acceptable price point. In general, lower-priced fabrics can be made into more complex styles, while higher-priced goods should be used in simple silhouettes that require less yardage and construction.

It is important for product developers to know what is offered both above and below their typical price point. More expensive fabrics may be usable in a single novelty garment or as a secondary fabric requiring minimal yardage. Such usage can give the line a competitive fashion edge. Wide sampling alerts product developers to their competitors' approaches and helps to reinforce trend directions identified in their own research. Generally, product developers want to locate fabrics similar to those their higher-priced competitors are using and avoid fabrics being used by lower-priced competitors.

Table 6.2 SPECIALTY PRINTING METHODS

Blotch prints A print in which the background color is created by printing rather than dyeing. The ground and pattern design colors are printed onto a white cloth. One of the problems with blotch prints is that large background color areas of the print are not covered with the full depth of color.

Warp prints Printing the warp yarns of a fabric before weaving. The fabric is woven with a solid color filling, usually white. The result is a soft, shadowed, blurred design. These prints are found on high-quality, costly fabrics because the process requires careful, meticulous labor.

Flock prints Tiny particles of fiber are made to adhere to a fabric surface in conformance to a particular design. Rayon and nylon fibers are typically used for the flocking. The ability of flocked fibers to withstand dry cleaning and laundering depends on the adhesive. Adhesives with excellent fastness to cleaning processes are needed.

Burn-out prints This technique can be used only on fabrics made with blended yarns. The fabric is printed in a pattern with a chemical that will destroy one of the fibers in the blended yarn and leave the other undamaged.

Duplex prints Fabrics in which both sides of the fabric are printed in order to imitate more costly, woven, yarn-dyed design effects such as stripes, checks, and plaids. These are rarely used because of the high cost.

Engineered prints Prints that have two or more distinct designs, each located in separate areas of the fabric and each designed to become a specific part of a garment. Engineered prints include fabrics whose with designs that are especially planned to permit making a garment in a particular stylized effect. An example is a border print.

Source: Adapted from Khatua 2001.

When product developers find a unique fabric that meets their selection criteria for the season, they should sample and commit to it early, because new or unique fabrics are usually available in limited quantities. It is important to test new fabrics under the sewing machine needle. They frequently require special handling to meet existing quality standards. When microfibers were first introduced, seams were frequently puckered. Special adjustments in needle, thread, and tension were required for garments to pass quality audits. Fabrics with small amounts of Lycra added require seams with sufficient stretch so that stitches do not break.

When product developers commit to a fabric purchase, they generally request that their purchase be linked to some degree of exclusivity. In the case of a basic fabric, perhaps all that can be promised is that the color assortment is exclusive to the product developer. In the case of a novelty fabric, the purchase may be dependent on a commitment from the vendor that the same fabric will not be sold to a competitor. Exclusivity agreements are commonly subject to minimum yardage requirements, thus giving large product developers more clout in this area than very small product developers who are purchasing less yardage (Case Study 6.1, Leather: A Specialty Fabrication).

Online Fabric Sourcing

While fabric fairs are an important means of keeping up with the market, sourcing fabrics requires ongoing research beyond seasonal fabric shows. Increasingly, online systems assist product developers to research and reserve fabrics. Fastextile.com was launched by fiber manufacturer Invista and softwear maker Freeborders Inc. in 2004. The service is a search engine that allows manufacturers to locate fabrics they want to sample. A designer can request a 1 x 1 rib knit fabric with 2 percent nylon to be sent via FedEx and then complete the purchase offline. Fastextile.com grew out of Invista's online fabric library of fabrics containing Invista fibers; the online service does not require that fabrics be made of Invista fibers. The service allows members to set up private areas for the exchange of information. The service is free to apparel manufacturers and retailers; fabric manufacturers pay to be on the service (Corcoran 2004, 6–7).

Online fabric resources are not intended to replace in-person meetings or touching and sampling the fabrics, but it makes the process more efficient and has the potential to reduce lead times, increase innovation, decrease the need for travel, and cut costs.

Protecting Fabric Selections

A **copyright** refers to the set of exclusive legal rights granted to authors or owners of published or unpublished literary, scientific, and artistic works that are fixed in a tangible form. This includes the right to reproduce, distribute,

CASE STUDY 6.1 LEATHER: A SPECIALTY FABRICATION

Leather is a unique fabrication that requires extensive knowledge for consistent, high-quality results. Product developers who specialize in leather apparel are challenged to push the limits of leather as a fabrication by exploring new finishes, silhouettes, and construction. Product developers who design in leather during peak fashion cycles only are well-advised to build part-nerships with leather experts in order to get satisfactory results.

Kerley Biochemical is in a unique position to provide leather expertise to product developers throughout all stages of product development. Its Leather Technologies, Inc., division produces chemicals for leather processing, supplying tanneries all over the world. With 2 locations in

Italy and 17 locations in the United States, its research and development facilities can produce tanned leather samples on demand. Leather Technologies owns tanning operations in Saudia Arabia and Egypt but will recommend tanneries anywhere in the world for a particular job. The firm offers personal consulting services to all customers, helping them to select the right type of skin, tanning process, finish, design, and garment construction. In addition, it has facilities where experts can evaluate goods that do not meet quality standards; in most cases, they can resolve the problem with additional processing so that the garments are salable.

Source: Interview with Abbas Fadel, President, Leather Technologies, Inc., July 2003.

---

perform, or display the work and the right to create derivative works. Intellectual property copyright law goes back to 1769. More recently, passage of the Copyright Act of 1976, which became effective on January 1, 1978, brought the entire field of copyright law under federal control.

The duration of copyright protection changed as a result of the Sonny Bono Copyright Term Extension Act of 1998. Under the provisions of the new law, works created on or after January 1, 1978, are protected as long as the author is alive, plus an additional 70 years after the author's death. In the case of a joint work, the term lasts for 70 years after the last surviving author's death.

Copyright protection varies for works created or published before 1978. Copyrights have expired on all U.S. works registered or published prior to 1923. This means that such works have entered into the public domain. A work in the public domain can be copied freely by anyone.

Works published between 1923 and 1963 were granted copyrights for 28 years and could be renewed. If the copyright owner did not renew the term, the copyright expired and the work entered the public domain. If the owner applied for renewal, these works have a 95-year copyright term. For works published between 1964 and 1977, copyright renewal is automatic. These works also have a 95-year copyright term.

The scope of copyright protection is very broad and includes sketches, paintings, and photographs that might be used in textile design, as well as knit textures that are original and not in the public domain. When a work qualifies for copyright protection, protection extends only to the particular manner of expression of the work; it does not extend to the underlying themes or concepts. Artists are free to consult the same source that was used for a copyrighted piece of art for their own original creations.

Copyright protection attaches automatically to an original work of art from the moment it is first fixed in tangible form. Although no action is required to obtain copyright protection, the copyright can be lost if appropriate steps are not taken to preserve it. A copyright can be preserved by putting a copyright notice on all copies that are distributed to anyone for any purpose. A proper copyright notice consists of the copyright symbol (a letter C inside a circle) or the word "copyright," the year of first distribution, and the name of the copyright owner.

The introduction of CAD technology has complicated the issue of copyright protection for textile designs. The apparel and textile industries are well known for their close reproductions of hot fashion trends. References from history, nature, ethnic culture, music, or the arts may provide many rich resources for creative imagery. Computer scanners readily convert such visual images into a digital format. The visual data can then be moved from one form to another for further image manipulation. Although use of the scanner by a skilled designer can lead to innovative results, care must be taken to ensure that the final product is a complete transformation from the original scanned image (Polvinen 1995).

Designers can protect themselves by keeping records of how they design, including the resources used and changes made. If designers use older images that are in the public domain, liability is limited. The best policy is always to use your own creativity to interpret a theme and to document your design efforts and originality.

Managing Fabric Decisions

Fabrication decisions are shaped by aesthetic and performance characteristics. Once choices are made, fabric costs, fabric testing, and production scheduling must be managed.

The production of a garment from cutting to construction to finishing is referred to as cut, make, and trim. The cut, make, and trim cost of a garment includes the materials, direct labor, and factory overhead required to make that garment. Fabric costs may make up 35 to 50 percent of the cut, make, and trim cost of a domestically produced garment and 50 to 70 percent of the cut, make, and trim cost of a garment sourced offshore. Managing fabric costs is critical to making a product at the appropriate price point. The cut, make, and trim cost does not include shipping, tariffs, corporate overhead, selling costs, or profits that must be included in costing in order to determine wholesale price. Costing and pricing are covered in more detail in chapter 14.

A product developer's approach to fabric decisions varies greatly and often depends on whether it is a branded, retail-direct, or private label product developer. It generally saves both time and money to source a fabric in the same region where the garment will be produced. When planning production schedules, lead time must be built in for fabric production and shipping, usually by boat, to the contractor for production.

In an agile manufacturing environment, large product developers generally require their sourcing partners to purchase the fabric for production orders and include that cost in their pricing. In this environment, it is up to the textile supplier, the sourcing agent, or the production contractor to have the fabric tested to ensure that it meets brand standards and specifications and matches color standards. Product developers generally provide quality assurance manuals in which they specify the fabric tests required for each garment category. They also specify the supply chain partner designated to perform all required fabric testing. Fabric testing results are returned to the product developer for approval. Production yardage should not be shipped and cut orders cannot be approved until fabric approvals are complete.

Summary

The fabrication process is a critical step in apparel product development. Fabric contributes to a garment's aesthetics, function, and serviceability. It gives a garment a fashion context, and it helps to make a product developer's line exclusive. Fabric decisions play an important role in the customer's perception of value.

Fabrics are generally classified as either bottom-weight or top-weight, which refers to their suitability for skirts, pants, and jackets or shirts, blouses, and dresses. Basic goods are generally the core fabrications of a group. Novelty goods provide a fashion edge and help to differentiate the line. Some companies have separate product development divisions for knits and wovens, since the design process and sourcing partners for these fabrics are dissimilar.

Product developers may select the exact fabrics they will use in a line or they may ask that their sourcing partners to seek suitable fabrications. Branded and store brand product developers generally are more involved in the fabric selection process; private label product developers may be less specific in their fabric specifications.

The fabrics chosen for a seasonal line speak to the designer through their fiber content, weight, surface interest, and drape. These fabric characteristics influence how the designer will use the fabrics in garment silhouettes. It is important for product developers to stay current with new textile technologies that enhance aesthetics and function. Utilizing high-performance fabrics helps to maintain profit margins and gives product developers a competitive edge. Consumers perceive fabric enhancements as adding value and newness to their apparel purchases.

The use of prints helps to differentiate one product developer's line from another. Prints may be purchased or designed in-house. When working with prints, one must understand the relationship of the print motif to the ground, as explored through layout, repeat, and arrangement. Many printing methods can be used to apply prints to a fabric. The printing method chosen will be determined by the fiber content of the fabric, the desired colors, the price point of the fabric, and the yardage required.

Once a fabric selection is made, every effort should be made to ensure its exclusivity so that competitors do not use the same fabric. When developing exclusive fabrics in-house, designers must be knowledgeable about copyright law and how it applies to textile design. Once fabrics have been selected, they must be tested to ensure that they meet quality standards. Fabric testing is usually initiated by the manufacturing contractor using the testing lab specified by the product developer. Lab results must be approved by the product developer before production yardage can be shipped and cut orders can be approved.

Key Terms

arrangement
basic goods
border prints
bottom-weight fabrics
copyright
digital printing
direct printing
discharge printing
drape
dress-weight
e-broidery
engineered prints
engraved roller printing
fabric story
fabrication
geometric layouts
ground
hand
heat transfer *or* thermal transfer printing
layout

micro encapsulation
motifs
nanotechnology
novelty goods
phase change materials (PCMs)
printing
production yardage
random layouts
registration
repeat
resist printing
sample yardage
screen printing
serviceability
set layouts
smart textiles
specification package
surface interest
top-weight fabrics
turnaround time
yarn-dyed fabrics

Discussion Questions

1. What print themes have you observed in apparel stores this season? Is there any correlation between the prints being used in men's wear, children's wear, and women's wear?

2. Research textile periodicals and the Internet for new fabric and fiber developments. In what categories might these developments influence fashion?

3. Why do product developers expect their sourcing partners to take ownership of the textiles specified for apparel products?

Activities

1. Select a length of fabric from those provided in class. Analyze how the fabric's fiber content, weight, surface design, and drape will influence silhouette design. In your sketchbook, sketch a series of silhouettes inspired by the fabric you have analyzed.

2. Select an existing brand and analyze the fabrics used in the line. Develop a fabric story for that brand for an upcoming season. Present your fabric story on a board that includes a picture that suggests a theme and a swatch of each fabric with color chips to indicate color range. Use labels to identify each fabric by fiber content and name each color. Be sure to include a representative range of fabrics suitable for tops and bottoms and an appropriate balance of basic and novelty fabrics for that brand's particular market.

3. Select a piece of artwork that was published before 1923. Use it to develop a textile print in the form of a painting or computerized image. Now, select a piece of artwork that was published after 1978. Use it as a departure point for a textile design, being cognizant of copyright protection. Critique the resulting designs in class. Has the inspirational image been modified sufficiently that it does not infringe on the copyright protection of the original piece?

4. If you have access to a computer program that will put a design into repeat, take a single motif and explore how varying the arrangement, repeat, and layout gives you many different patterns. Print three of your favorite results and present them to the class.

References

Anderson, Kim. 2006. Innovate or disintegrate. [TC]² Bi-Weekly Technology Communicator, August 9 [e-mail newsletter].

Brown, P., and J. Rice. 2001. *Ready-to-wear apparel analysis.* 3d ed. Upper Saddle River, NJ: Prentice-Hall.

Corcoran, Cate T. 2004. Industry heavyweights launch Internet sourcing service. *Women's Wear Daily,* July 19.

Corcoran, Cate T., and Miles Socha. 2004. If we can build it, will they wear it? *Women's Wear Daily,* April 14.

Cotton Incorporated's Lifestyle Monitor. 2006a. Knit wits: Sweaters make smart style sense this season. *Women's Wear Daily,* September 7.

Cotton Incorporated's Lifestyle Monitor. 2006b. Performing arts. *Women's Wear Daily,* August 31.

Cowie, Peter, and Chris Eacott. 2003. Safeguarding the brand. *Fashion Business International,* February-March.

Dunne, Lucy E., Susan Ashdown, and Barry Smyth. 2005. Expanding garment functionality through embedded electronic textiles. *Journal of Textile and Apparel, Technology and Management* 4, no. 3 (Spring), www.tx.ncsu.edu/jtatm/volume4-issue3/vo4_issue3_abstracts.htm.

Elias, Paul. 2006. Clothes, fabrics made of corn not so corny now. *Milwaukee Journal Sentinel,* July 17.

Ethical Insight team at Maplecroft. 2004. Company report review: Nike corporate responsibility report 2004. www.maplecroft.com/pdf/nike2004.pdf.

Fisher, R., and D. Wolfthal. 1987. *Textile print design.* New York: Fairchild.

Fitzpatrick, Michael. 2004. Japan leads the field in nanotech textiles. www.just-style.com/article.aspx?id=923365&lk=s.

Gunther, Marc. 2006. Organic for everyone, the Wal-Mart Way. *Fortune,* July 31, money.cnn.com/2006/07/25/news/companies/pluggedin_gunther_cotton.fortune/index.htm.

Kadolph, S. J. 1998. *Quality assurance for textiles and apparel.* New York: Fairchild.

Khatua, Sandeep. 2001. Printing. Presentation given to Kohl's product development team by MTL Laboratories, April.

Long, Carola. 2006. Fashion comes in a bag. Times Online, July 12, www.timesonline.co.uk.

Mills, Bill. 2005. Smart and interactive apparel textiles. www.just-style.com/briefings/ [subscription].

Montgomery, Delia. 2004. Sustainable fibers make progress. *In Business,* September/October.

Nano-Tex. www.nano-tex.com.

Patagonia. www.patagonia.com.

Polvinen, E. 1995. The ethics of scanned imagery for textile designs. Presentation at Conference on Instructional Technologies 1995 Meeting in New York.

Post, E.R., M. Orth, P. R. Russo, and N. Gershenfeld. 2000. E-broidery: Design and fabrication of textile-based computing. *IBM Systems Journal,* 39:3&4.

Skrebneski, Victor, and Laura Jacobs. 1995. *The art of haute couture.* New York: Abbeville Press, Inc.

Tucker, Ross. 2006. Stretching products to meet needs. *Women's Wear Daily,* June 6.

Watkins, Philippa. 2005. Fibres & fabrics. *Textile View,* Summer.

Women's Wear Daily. 2006. Going to the library. *Women's Wear Daily,* January 31.

CHAPTER 7

GARMENT STYLING

"I wish I had invented blue jeans. They have expression, modesty, sex appeal, simplicity—all I hope for in my clothes."

—YVES SAINT LAURENT

OBJECTIVES

- To explore various methods of recording design ideas and experimenting with styling options

- To understand how to use design elements in combination with design principles to create an aesthetically pleasing garment

- To recognize the various classifications of garments for men, women, and children

- To understand the style variables for each silhouette classification

- To understand how design details add interest to garment styling

- To anticipate how design details affect garment cost and production scheduling

The fashion dynamic is characterized by perpetual change. A dizzying array of new colors, fabrics, and silhouettes cycle in and out of style each season at such a pace that no single product developer can expect to interpret all the new ideas on the fashion front. Instead, product developers seek to identify the core themes that come out of runway collections or percolate up from the streets and then determine which of those ideas will translate into items that their target customer will buy. Ultimately, consumers explore these offerings and rely on their personal fashion tastes and instincts to determine what they will buy and wear.

Today's consumers build their wardrobes by adding new items each season that update the basics they already have. As society becomes more casual, fashion has become increasingly item-driven. In an item-driven environment, customers tend to buy more single garments than coordinated ensembles.

This places enormous pressure on product developers, who must understand how to manipulate seasonal silhouettes to suit the needs of their consumers. Successful silhouettes must

- match the aesthetic preferences of the target customer

- be able to be produced within a targeted price point

- relate to the consumer's individual taste and lifestyle

Because consumer preferences do not change drastically from season to season, silhouettes tend to evolve with one style morphing into another.

This chapter discusses how to translate design research into silhouette ideas that are appropriate for a specific market. It also explains how to use design elements and principles to create harmonious and saleable garments, and how style variables of each garment category can be manipulated in order to change a silhouette.

Methods for Developing Design Ideas

The design process parallels the research process. The ultimate goal is to meet the needs of the target customer. Research is done through the scanning of forecasting resources and by shopping trend-setting markets. Just as the researcher tests hypotheses, the designer explores and manipulates silhouettes. Ultimately, the best silhouettes are included in the seasonal line and put to the test in the marketplace.

Each product developer has his or her own methodology for translating design research into a collection of silhouettes that make up the seasonal line. Methods range from a derivative approach, in which product samples are purchased and then interpreted in the product developer's own colorways and fabrications, to innovative approaches, in which design inspiration is collected from primary sources and then interpreted in totally original ways. Most approaches to product development fall somewhere between these two extremes and utilize a variety of techniques to document design ideas. Product developers may use one or more of the following techniques:

- Studying primary resources such as historic or cultural artifacts

- Buying actual garments for their silhouette, fit, fabrication or detailing

- Collecting **swipes**, or tear sheets, from magazines and the Internet

- Sketching design ideas observed while doing market research

The ability of the designer to communicate creative ideas effectively is pivotal to the success of a brand. The designer must convey not only the appearance of the garment, but also the mood and energy of the garment.

Figure 7.1. *Museum exhibits and access to museum archives serve as rich sources of inspiration. Shown here are the sleeve and side bodice of a Fortuny dress from the collection of the Musée Galliera in Paris.*

Studying Primary Resources

Studying primary resource material frequently results in the most original design ideas. High-end designers may get new ideas from traveling to exotic locales. Designers may maintain memberships to costume collections where they can study the work of a particular period or designer. The Metropolitan Museum of Art's Costume Institute and the Fashion Institute of Technology (FIT) offer such memberships. Costume exhibitions featuring the works of great artists, historic costumes, or cultural artifacts are another source of primary research (Figure 7.1).

Figure 7.2a–b. *Designer Trina Turk studies tear sheets for an upcoming line. The story of John Aquino's concept development day by day.*

Purchased Garments

Many product developers have budgets for purchasing garments. Those who work derivatively have the largest budgets because their lines are developed directly from the samples they buy. Branded product developers tend to have smaller budgets, which they use to buy samples when they want to interpret a particular fabric, fit, detail, or construction technique that they cannot capture through sketching. Very small product developers may have no budget for purchasing garments and are left to interpret trends in other ways.

Printed Sources and the Internet

Today, new fashion looks direct from the runways in Europe, Asia, or the United States are conveyed almost instantaneously via mass communication. Many sources that were once available only in print are now available via the Internet, making them available in real time. Some sources offer access to images without charge and others through subscriptions. Product developers are able to access a wide array of images of designer fashions or street looks and study the trends they see in order to interpret them for mass markets. Product developers use these sources to create **concept boards**, a collection of images, sketches, and swatches that express the design direction they are exploring for a particular group (Figure 7.2a–b).

Sketches

Designers use sketching to help them record and explore design ideas (Figure 7.3). Many designers carry a small sketchbook (3 in. × 5 in. or 5 in. × 7 in.) with them whenever they shop, making note of unique ideas, details, or proportions. Where possible, they may try on garments to get a feel for how they relate to the body. The privacy of a dressing room allows the designer to use a tape measure to define key measurements that are integral to achieving a unique proportion, or to study the construction of a garment. After leaving the store, designers may sketch an entire garment to document a silhouette change, or they may concentrate on a unique fashion-forward detail, later integrating the detail into their own silhouette rather than copying a design completely. These quick sketches are often referred to as thumbnail sketches.

Figure 7.3. *Sketches for a spring 2007 Garfield and Marks line.*

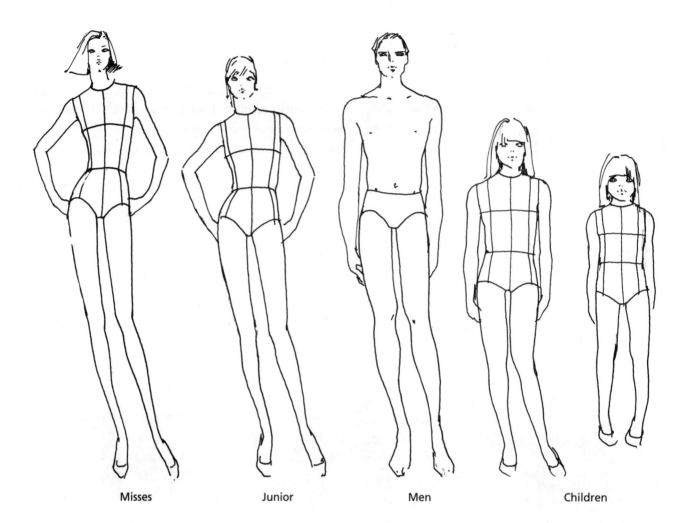

Misses   Junior   Men   Children

Figure 7.4. *Croquis bodies for misses, junior, men, and children.*

Silhouette ideas are best developed as **croquis sketches** in a sketchbook. *Croquis* is the French word for *sketch*. A realistic representation of the female figure is about eight heads high. In contrast, fashion croquis figures are elongated, drawn anywhere from nine to twelve heads high. A skilled artist can quickly sketch a croquis figure freehand, but many excellent designers have not developed that confidence. To ensure that their focus is on the design of the garment, not the proportions of the figure, they may rely on an **underdrawing** or **lay figure**—a well-proportioned pose which can be slid under a page and used as a template to help control proportions and the location of garment details (Figure 7.4). When using an underdrawing, the design idea is drawn first and then the head, arms, and legs are added. There is no need to draw in facial features or hair. Some designers sketch over an underdrawing without adding the body itself. These sketches are called floats. The most commonly used croquis poses are full frontal or three-quarter views. A larger croquis figure may be reduced on a copy machine and used as an underlay for thumbnail sketches. As designers select the ideas they are going to develop and present, they will also need to sketch the back of the design.

Some designers prefer to develop their ideas as **flats**, two-dimensional drawings of garments that represent how the garment looks when spread out on a flat surface, rather than how the garment appears on the body. These drawings may be sketched by hand or drawn on the computer. This method lends itself to products such as T-shirts, polo shirts, sweaters, blouses, and shirts—garments that have few shaping devices and lay flat readily. Hand-drawn flats may be somewhat stylized, showing a little more garment movement.

Most designers prefer to sketch by hand, but digital tablets are available that enable the designer to sketch directly into the computer. If the silhouette is sketched on paper, color and fabric rendering may be added by hand or the sketch may be scanned and then filled on the computer.

Design Elements and Principles

The design of a garment requires the selection and interpretation of color, fabric, styling, and fit. When these elements work together, the garment enhances the appearance of the wearer, thereby enticing him or her to make a purchase. When these components are haphazardly combined, the resulting design is disappointing. In the remainder of this chapter, we discuss how to use the elements and principles of design as tools to create appealing garments. We discuss the major garment categories and identify how basic silhouettes can be differentiated and manipulated. This information, used in combination with the techniques already described, provides the foundation for silhouette development.

Design is the organization of design elements, using design principles, to create products that are considered aesthetically pleasing to the observer. Professionals who work with the design elements and principles in a creative, original way are referred to as designers; those who adapt the ideas of others are sometimes called **stylists**. The design process for any product—be it automobiles or apparel, furniture or kitchen appliances—relies on an understanding of design elements and principles.

Design Elements

The **design elements** are the building blocks of design. These elements—line, color, texture, pattern, silhouette, and shape—are intrinsic to every product, including apparel.

Line

Line determines the silhouette of the garment and the shapes formed within the garment. Internal garment lines may be created through the use of garment seams and edges; fabric patterns and textures; and details such as tucks, pleats, darts, gathers, and linear trims. Lines have several aspects that determine their character. These include length, boldness, thickness, and direction (Figure 7.5).

THE APPEARANCES OR ASPECTS OF LINE

ASPECT	VARIATION	APPEARANCE	PHYSICAL EFFECTS	PSYCHOLOGICAL EFFECTS
Path	Straight		Emphasizes angularity Counters rotundity	Stiff, direct, precise Dignified, tense, masculine
	Curve	arc	Emphasizes body curves Counters thinness	Dynamic, feminine, active, youthful, unrestrained
	Jagged		Emphasizes angularity	Abrupt, nervous, jerky
	Wavy		Emphasizes roundness	Feminine, soft, flowing
Thickness	Thick		Adds weight	Forceful, aggressive
	Thin		Minimizes weight	Delicate, dainty, calm
Continuity	Continuous		Emphasizes bulges Smooth	Consistent, sure, firm
	Broken		Emphasizes irregularities	Less certain, staccato
	Dotted		Spotty, varied	Interrupted, playful
Edge/ Sharpness	Sharp		Emphasizes smooth or bumpy area	Definite, precise, assertive
	Fuzzy		Gently increases size	Soft, uncertain
Edge contour	Smooth		Emphasizes a smooth or textured surface	Suave, simple, sure
	Shaped		Varies with shape	Complex, involved, busy
Consistency	Solid/Closed		Advances boldly	Sure, smooth, strong
	Porous		Advances little, recedes little	Open, delicate, less certain
Length	Long		Emphasizes direction	Depends on the area
	Short		Breaks up space	Abrupt, staccato

Figure 7.5. *The quality and direction of lines used in garments have a physical and psychological impact on how we perceive the wearer.*

The impact of line is further defined by how frequently it is repeated, its placement, and whether it is used symmetrically or asymmetrically. The use of line can create optical illusions on the body. Use of vertical lines tends to elongate the figure, making it appear slimmer, whereas use of horizontal lines tends to shorten the figure, making it look wider. The optical illusions that line can create work best when the other design elements are used to enhance the impact.

Color

The importance of the element of color is explored in chapter 5. Because color speaks to individuals on so many levels, it is recognized as one of the first things that attracts a customer to a garment. How color is utilized in an ensemble can create figure illusions. As discussed in chapter 5, color hues are frequently classified as either warm or cool. Warm colors—red, yellow, and orange—tend to draw in the viewer and make an area appear larger. Cool colors—blue, green, and violet—tend to recede and make an area appear smaller. Ensembles that are made up of a single color or shades of that color tend to be slimming because they create the illusion of height. Darker colors that absorb light tend to be more slimming than lighter colors. Bright colors tend to call attention to the figure and give the illusion of bulk, whereas light colors tend to flatter the face.

Texture

Texture is the term used to describe the surface or hand of a fabric and can be attributed to a combination of the fabric's characteristics—fiber, yarn, construction, weight, and finish. A fabric's hand affects how it drapes. The texture of a fabric affects how we perceive color. Shiny surfaces reflect light, emphasizing the color and making the figure look larger. Pile surfaces absorb light, giving the color more variation. Pile surfaces also have more loft or thickness, thus making the figure look larger. Stiff fabrics stand away from the body; as a result, the garment silhouette may need some reference to the body to communicate its shape. Drapey fabrics tend to cling to the body, identifying its natural curves. Each fabric a designer chooses to work with should be explored, using a dress form to determine its natural attributes. Fabrics and their textures speak to the designer. They are used to best advantage when allowed to do what they do naturally.

Pattern

Some fabrics also have pattern. Patterns can be created by the texture of the fabric; they can be constructed into the fabric through weaving, knitting, or felting; or they can be applied to the fabric through printing, embossing, and other specialty techniques such as dévoré or laser cutting. The popularity of specific patterns is subject to fashion cycles. In a manner similar to line, color, and texture, patterns can help to create figure illusions. In general, the pattern should be scaled to the wearer. As noted in chapter 6, the placement of large motifs may need to be engineered on the body to avoid calling attention to certain body parts. Large patterns are generally best used in garment silhouettes where there is extra fabric and the pattern can drape in folds over the body. They should not be cut up by lots of seams and details. Smaller patterns are more appropriate for close-fitting garments.

Silhouette

The garment **silhouette** is the outer shape of a garment. The size and shape of the silhouette is the first thing we see when a garment is on the body. Silhouettes are sometimes described by letters such as A, H, T, V, or Y, in which

Figure 7.6. *Garment silhouettes may be described in terms of their geometric shape or a historic period.*

the silhouette follows the shape of the letter. Silhouettes may also be described as specific shapes (trapezoid, tent, hourglass, pear, or or bell) or identified from periods in history (Empire or flapper) (Figure 7.6). It is not always possible to see a silhouette clearly when a garment is on a hanger. When a garment is hanging, we tend to notice the color and fabric first. The silhouette comes to life when the garment is viewed on the body.

Because garment silhouettes need to be comfortable and functional in order to accommodate the lifestyle needs of consumers, they tend to evolve more slowly. The mass market is likely to reject silhouettes that are considered extreme. Designers must understand the underlying ideas in a given fashion season. They must also understand patternmaking and construction in order to translate those ideas into garment silhouettes. Understanding the various classifications of garment silhouettes and how they vary is basic to the design process.

Trapeze   Empire   Hourglass   Flapper or tubular

Figure 7.7. *Seams and details within garments create shapes that affect the rhythm and harmony of the garment.*

Shape

The silhouette is frequently sectioned off into smaller *shapes* within the garment using seam lines, details, and garment edges (Figure 7.7). These shapes

- add styling interest to the silhouette
- help to achieve fit
- allow for the combination of two or more fabrics
- allow the designer to create optical illusions through line
- create proportions within the silhouette or ensemble
- create symmetrical or asymmetrical balance

The use of shape is an important tool for achieving harmony within the garment. Garments that are sold as coordinates should be evaluated so that the shapes are related between garments.

Figure 7.8a–b. *A garment of classic unequal proportions and a garment of equal proportions.*

Design Principles

The design process revolves around determining how to combine the design elements we have just reviewed into a pleasing whole. Those decisions are guided by an understanding of **design principles**. Design principles include proportion, balance, emphasis or focal point, rhythm, and harmony or unity.

Proportion

Proportion is the relationship or scale of all of the garment's or ensemble's parts to each other and to the body as a whole. Horizontal lines such as yoke and waistline seams or jacket and top edges divide a garment or ensemble into sections. The ancient Greeks judged proportions by the rule of the golden mean. They believed that ratios of 2:3, 3:5, and 5:8 were the most pleasing to the eye. Most garment proportions commonly worn today follow this standard, as shown in Figure 7.8a, but examples of equal proportions also exist, as shown in Figure 7.8b.

Figure 7.9a–b. *A garment with symmetrical balance and a garment with asymmetrical balance.*

Balance

Balance is defined as a sense of stability or equilibrium. It is determined by dividing a silhouette vertically down the middle. A **symmetrical** garment (Figure 7.9a) appears to be the same on both sides. A symmetrically balanced garment can be easily changed with accessories and can be readily mixed and matched with other symmetrical garments in the wardrobe.

An **asymmetrical** garment (Figure 7.9b) is different on each side. Asymmetry may be achieved by an off-center closing or a pocket detail on only one side of the garment. Asymmetrical garments must be carefully thought through during the patternmaking and cutting processes. Garments designed to be worn with them must be similarly balanced or neutral with no visible center point.

Emphasis or Focal Point

A garment's **emphasis** or **focal point** is the first place on the garment to which the eye is drawn. It may be created through a convergence of lines, a combination of colors, or a detail. If several elements of the design are competing for the viewer's attention, the garment may be overdesigned. The designer should evaluate whether the second focal point would best be used in another design.

Rhythm

From the focal point, the eye should move naturally through the entire garment. **Rhythm** is the organized movement of the eye through the related elements of a garment. Rhythm can be achieved by strong silhouette lines; through the use of color, line, or shape; and through the use of repetition, radiation, and gradation.

Harmony or Unity

Successful placement of a focal point that suggests rhythm is key to achieving **harmony** or **unity** in a design. Harmony means that all of the design elements work together in a garment to produce a pleasing aesthetic appearance and to give a feeling of unity to the design.

Every so often there is a cycle in fashion, typically when a large demographic group is just reaching adulthood, which is characterized by an antifashion movement. Antifashion movements purposely tend to break the rules of design in order to call attention to a certain look. Knowing when to follow the rules and when to break or push the rules is another challenge to the product developer.

Understanding the Dynamics of Fashion Change

As stated in chapter 4, trends frequently move along a continuum, fluctuating from one fashion extreme to another. Before you begin interpreting a trend, it is helpful to think about where the dynamics that shape fashion are moving at a particular point in time. It is the existence of these multiple dynamics, each at a different point in the continuum, that makes fashion interesting. At one point, black is the "it" color and silhouettes hug the body; in another season black may be the color of the moment, but silhouettes are architectural and voluminous. One season embellishment is in and another it is out. Understanding the dynamic elements of fashion in any given season helps the designer to develop silhouettes that look right to the eye. Are skirts long or short; are colors neutral or bright, pale or dark; are knits fine-gauge or bulky? Figure 7.10 illustrates just a few of the dynamics of fashion change.

Once you recognize the dynamics of fashion, you must interpret them for your particular customer. In today's fashion culture, for almost every trend, there is a countertrend. What's right for one customer will not work for another. The next section shows how garment silhouettes can be manipulated and changed in order to vary the design.

DIMENSIONS OF FASHION

PALE ◄————————————————► DARK	VALUE	
GRAY ◄————————————————► BRIGHT	SATURATION	
NEUTRAL ◄————————————————► COLOR	HUES	
SHORT ◄————————————————► LONG	HEMLINES	
BODY-HUGGING ◄————————————————► ARCHITECTURAL / VOLUMINOUS	SILHOUETTES	
CURVY ◄————————————————► STRAIGHT	SILHOUETTES	
MINIMAL ◄————————————————► HEAVILY EMBELLISHED	EMBELLISHMENT	
PRIMITIVE / HAND-CRAFTED ◄————————————————► LUXURIOUS	EMBELLISHMENT	
FLAT ◄————————————————► NUBBY	TEXTURE	
DULL ◄————————————————► SHINY	TEXTURE	
FINE-GAUGE ◄————————————————► BULKY	KNITS	
SOLIDS ◄————————————————► PATTERN	PATTERN	
SMALL ◄————————————————► LARGE	PATTERN	
REALISTIC ◄————————————————► ABSTRACT	PATTERN	

Figure 7.10. *This chart illustrates a number of dimensions that define seasonal fashion.*

Garment Variations by Category

In Western dress there are basic classifications of garments typically worn by men, women, and children. Within each garment classification, there are certain elements that vary from season to season according to fashion trends and the specific needs of various target markets. Style variables are characteristics of the garment that contribute to its shape, fit, and identity. These may include length, degree of fit, how it hangs from the body, fullness or flare, cut of armscye, and neckline style. When the garment fits close to the body, shaping devices are necessary. **Shaping devices** are seams, darts, gathers, and pleats that help to shape the garment around the curves of the body (Figure 7.11). The use of fabrics made with fibers such as Lycra also helps to shape garments.

For product development purposes, garments for men, women, and children are often broadly classified as tops or bottoms. Included within each broad classification are subcategories of garments worn by each consumer group. Most product developers have at least two sets of specification forms, one set up for the measurements and operations involved in making tops, and another for bottoms. Product developers may have a different set of forms for every category of garment they develop.

Tops

The categories for tops are similar for men, women, and children, but silhouettes vary more dramatically for women than they do for men and children. The term *tops* has two meanings. In the broader meaning, all tops must have a front and back bodice; some also have sleeves. Tops include tops (in its narrower meaning, described below) and T-shirts, sweaters, shirts and blouses, vests, indoor and outdoor jackets, and coats. Jackets and coats are considered tops because they must fit the body torso. Dresses for women and girls are classified as tops rather than bottoms because they are developed from torso slopers.

Tops and T-Shirts

Tops are casual garments worn on the torso of the body. They include T-shirts, tank tops, and halters. They are frequently, but not always, made of knit fabric. They are differentiated from sweaters by their cut and construction methods. **Cut and sew construction** means that the garment pieces are cut from yardage

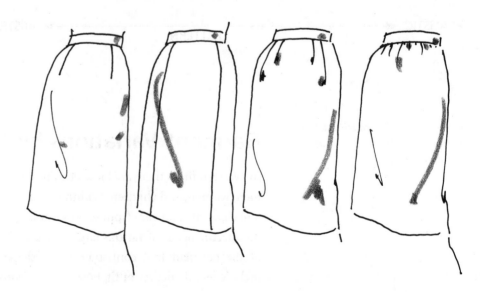

Figure 7.11. *A simple skirt may be shaped at the waist using darts, seams, release pleats, or gathers to vary the silhouette.*

Table 7.1 TOPS AND T-SHIRTS

STYLE VARIABLE	DESCRIPTION
Fit and shape	Varies from body-conforming fit achieved with stretch fabric, seaming, or darts to dartless and oversized.
Hang from body	Hangs from the shoulders or from above the bust.
Length	Varies from fitted just under the bust to cropped to waist length to hip length to tunic or dress length.
Sleeves	Vary from long or short to cap-sleeved or sleeveless to bandeau style with no armhole.
Armscye	Varies from traditional armhole to extended shoulder to raglan to kimono.
Neckline	Includes a full range of necklines from jewel to bateau to V-neck and others.

rather than knit to shape. Ribbings, when used, are sewn on with a seam rather than linked. Silhouette styling varies from tight-fitting tube tops to oversized T-shirts.

T-shirts are perhaps the simplest classification of tops. This is a garment classification with few style variables. A T-shirt consists of a front and a back bodice and sleeves. T-shirts are dartless and characterized by a ribbed band around the neck. T-shirts typically are made of cotton knits. The silhouette can be adapted by using silk, polyester, or rayon knits or woven fabrics for T-shirts that can be worn under suits instead of blouses. The addition of Lycra to any of the preceding fabrications gives the T-shirt a more body-conscious fit without the use of shaping devices. The T-shirt silhouette can be elongated for wearing as a swimwear cover-up, dress, or nightshirt. Style variables in tops and T-shirts are presented in Table 7.1 and Appendix Figure 7A.1.

Sweaters

Sweaters are knitted garments worn on the upper part of the body that incorporate some degree of full-fashion construction. **Full-fashion construction** means that some part of the sweater has been knit to shape. At a minimum, sweater lengths are linked together so that the ribbing can be attached through linking as opposed to serging. In other sweaters, shaping for the armscye (the term pattern makers use to refer to the armhole) and neckline are also knit to shape. Sweaters can be categorized as **pullovers** (sweaters that are pulled on over the head) or **cardigans** (sweaters that have a front opening). Sweaters are traditionally thought of as garments that provide warmth, but the advent of **sweater sets** or **twin sets** has popularized sleeveless knit shells that can be worn with or without the cardigan sweater with which they are paired. Sweaters typically have a front and back bodice—the front may be one piece,

Table 7.2 SWEATERS

STYLE VARIABLE	DESCRIPTION
Fit and shape	Varies from body-conforming (spandex in yarn, shaped at side seam, knit-in darts) to oversized.
Hang from body	Typically hangs from the shoulders, but off-the-shoulder or strapless styles may hang from above the bust.
Pullover or cardigan	May be designed to be pulled over the head or to open down the front.
Length	Varies from cropped at waist to elongated tunic or dress.
Sleeves	Vary from long or short sleeves to cap-sleeved or sleeveless.
Armscye	Varies from traditional armhole to extended shoulder to raglan to dropped armhole to kimono.
Neckline	Includes a full range of necklines from turtleneck or mock turtle to cowl, jewel, and bateau or V-neck.

or two pieces in the case of a cardigan—and sleeves. Sleeves are typical but not mandatory as are other accessory parts. Style variables in sweaters are presented in Table 7.2 and Appendix Figure 7A.2.

Shirts and Blouses

Shirts and blouses are garments for the upper body. They are generally made from woven fabrics. Shirts are worn by men, women, and children and feature a shirt sleeve and collar band or collar. Blouses are similar garments worn only by women and girls. They tend to be more loose-fitting and offer greater styling variation in the neck, collar, and sleeves. Style variables in shirts and blouses are presented in Table 7.3 and Appendix Figure 7A.3.

Jackets and Vests

A **jacket** is a short coat worn by men or women for indoor use, often associated with professional dress. (Jackets intended for outdoor wear are discussed in the next category.) A **vest** is a sleeveless version of a jacket with somewhat simplified construction. Jackets are more complicated than other tops. They may be boxy without shaping devices or very fitted through the use of seams and darts. Very tailored jackets incorporate construction techniques that include taping of seams and roll lines, interfacing throughout the jacket front that is either fused or pad stitched, interfaced hems, and shoulder pads. This construction helps jackets to maintain their silhouette for extended periods of time. It also tends to make them more expensive to produce and often requires them to be dry-cleaned in order to maintain their shape.

Jacket backs may be one-piece or two-piece; a two-piece back allows for shaping in the center back seam. Jacket fronts may be one-piece if minimal fit is desired, or they may incorporate a princess seam that starts from the shoulder or the armscye if a close fit through the bust is desired. A common jacket body variation is to use a back, a front, and a side panel. In this silhouette there is no side seam. The side panel starts at the armhole on the front and back and extends down to the hem. This allows for some fit through the bust and waist, but the shaping seams are less distracting. Darts can be used on the jacket front or back to further shape the garment (Figure 7.12). Jacket sleeves may be one-piece or two-piece. Two-piece sleeves are common when the sleeve hem includes a vent, although vents can be included in a one-piece sleeve if the underarm seam is moved slightly to the back of the sleeve.

Vests do not require as complicated an inner construction as jackets to maintain their shape. In some environments, they can be a viable and less expensive alternative to the jacket for professional dress. In men's wear, the vest is often sold as a third piece with a suit. Three-piece vested suits go in and out of style for men. Women's wear occasionally offers this same option. Style variables in jackets and vests are presented in Table 7.4 and Appendix Figure 7A.4.

Table 7.3 SHIRTS AND BLOUSES

STYLE VARIABLE	DESCRIPTION
Fit and shape	Varies from straight and oversized to semifitted with darts, a side-front seam, or princess seams.
Hang from body	From the shoulder, a dropped shoulder, or a yoke.
Closure	Traditionally opens down the center front. Blouses may be pulled over the head with a front or back keyhole opening or button down the back, across one shoulder, or asymmetrically down the front.
Length	Varies from the high hip level if meant to be worn out, 6 to 8 inches below the waist when tucked in, or to the thigh for an oversized look.
Sleeves	Generally feature a minimal cap and an extended shoulder seam. Blouses may be sleeveless or with sleeves. Sleeves vary from set-in to shirt sleeves to raglan to kimono.
Armscye	Most shirts feature a dropped armhole and extended shoulder that allows the sleeve to be sewn in prior to the side seam joining. Armholes on blouses match the sleeve type.
Neckline	Round necks with band, shirt, or convertible collars. Blouses may be designed with a full range of necklines and collars.

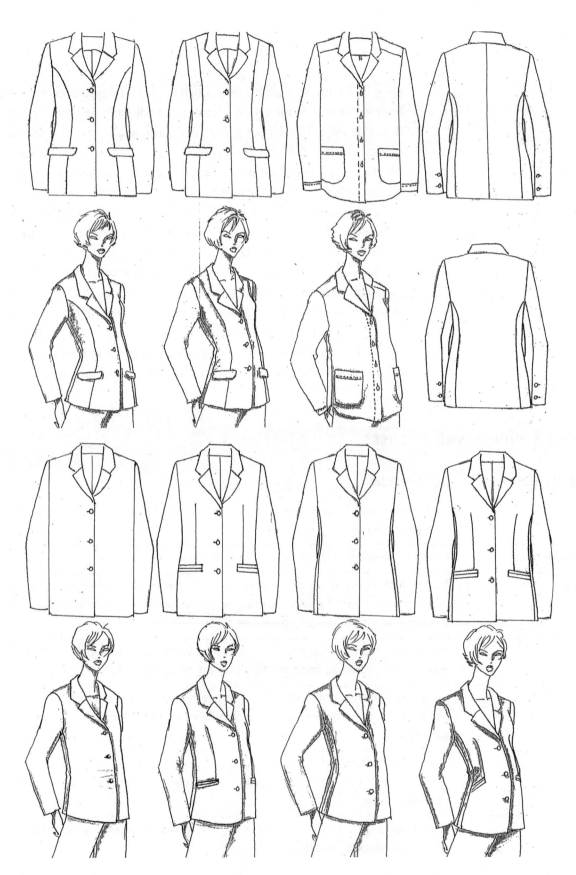

Figure 7.12. *The shaping devices used in a jacket determine its fit and affect its styling.*

Table 7.4 JACKETS AND VESTS

STYLE VARIABLE	DESCRIPTION
Fit and shape	Varies from boxy silhouettes with no shaping devices to a fit achieved through center back and side seams, darts, princess seams, and/or side panels.
Hang from body	Generally hangs from the shoulder, although the location of the shoulder seam may vary.
Length	Varies from cropped to knee-length to floor-length evening jackets.
Front opening	Single-breasted or double double-breasted, and symmetrical or asymmetrical.
Sleeves	Traditionally long, but three-quarter length or short-sleeve versions are available. Long sleeves may be one-piece, two-piece, or one-piece with the seam toward the back where a vent could be located. Vests are sleeveless.
Armscye	At the shoulder or extended from the shoulder. Raglan, saddle, and kimono sleeves are options.
Neckline	Jacket necklines may be round, V-neck, square, or sweetheart. Jackets may be collarless, but traditional jackets and jackets for men are characterized by collars. Vests are typically collarless.

Outerwear Jackets and Coats

Outerwear jackets and coats are tailored garments that are worn by men, women, and children for warmth and protection from the elements. Outerwear jackets are shorter versions of coats and may feature sportier styling. Outerwear jackets and coats have a more generous fit than innerwear jackets so that they can be worn over other clothing, including indoor jackets. Style variables in jackets and coats are presented in Table 7.5 and Appendix Figure 7A.5.

Dresses

Dresses are one- or two-piece garments for women or girls that fall from the shoulder or high bust and continue to surround the torso of the body, ending anywhere from the mid-thigh to the floor. For the purposes of this discussion, dresses are categorized as tops because they hang from the body on the shoulder or above the bust and share other characteristics of tops. However, dresses must also accommodate the hip area, and they may be designed as two pieces, consisting of a separate top and bottom. Dresses typically are developed from bodice and skirt pattern blocks that are seamed together or from a torso pattern block that combines the bodice and skirt without a waistline seam (Figure 7.13). Two-piece dresses utilize either a bodice or a torso sloper for the top and a skirt sloper for the bottom. Style and silhouette variables in dresses are presented in Table 7.6 and Appendix Figure 7A.6.

Table 7.5 OUTERWEAR JACKETS AND COATS

STYLE VARIABLE	DESCRIPTION
Fit and shape	Varies from boxy silhouettes with no shaping devices to a fit achieved through center back and side seams, darts, princess seams, and/or side panels.
Hang from body	Hangs from the shoulder, although the location of the shoulder seam may vary.
Length	Varies from cropped to knee-length to floor-length.
Front opening	Single-breasted or double-breasted, symmetrical or asymmetrical.
Sleeves	Long or three-quarter length sleeves; sleeves on jackets may be removable. Sleeves may be one-piece or two-piece.
Armscye	May be at the shoulder or extended from the shoulder. Raglan, saddle, and kimono sleeves are options.
Neckline	Generally round or V-neck in order to cover the neckline worn underneath and protect the wearer from the elements. Jackets and coats typically have collars.

Table 7.6 DRESSES

STYLE VARIABLE	DESCRIPTION
Fit or shape	Like other tops, dresses may be dartless with little shape or they may be fitted with darts, seams, yokes, and/or fullness. The fit above and below the waist may be blended seamlessly or may contrast, utilizing one shaping device above the waist and another below the waist.
Hang from body	Generally hang from the shoulder, although the location of the shoulder seam may vary. Dresses may also hang from the high bust. Two-piece dresses include skirts that hang from the waist.
Length	Varies from mid-thigh length to floor length.
Sleeves	Short or long sleeves, cap sleeves, or no sleeves. Strapless dresses that hang from the high bust typically have no armhole and no sleeve.
Armscye	May be at the shoulder, cut in toward the neck, or extended from the shoulder. Raglan, saddle, and kimono sleeve lines are options.
Neckline	Full range of neckline shapes. Dress necklines frequently have both front and back interest.

Bottoms

Bottoms are garments that surround the lower body. Bottoms for men include pants and shorts. Bottoms for women include pants, shorts, and skirts. Bottoms for children vary by age and gender but include pants, shorts, and skirts (for girls).

Skirts

A **skirt** is a garment associated with the female gender in Western culture. It hangs from the body at or near the waist and covers the hips and upper legs but is not bifurcated to go around each leg separately as do pants. The basic pattern block for a skirt is a straight skirt with two to four darts in the front and back, and a waistband. From a basic skirt block many other skirt silhouettes can be designed (Figure 7.14a–b). Culottes are sometimes classified as skirts because they are developed from a skirt block, even though they are bifurcated. The common design variables in skirts are presented in Table 7.7 and Appendix Figure 7A.7.

Figure 7.13. *A princess seam dress silhouette may be varied by changing the sleeve, neckline, or collar, adding flare, changing the closure, or adding detailing such as pockets.*

Table 7.7 SKIRTS

STYLE VARIABLE	DESCRIPTION
Length	Micro-mini length to floor-length.
Fit or shape	The body curve between the waist and hip is generally fit by darts, pleats, fullness, or flare. Darts can be eliminated in the front for flat figures; this works best in fabrics with Lycra.
Fullness	Gathers or pleats at the waist control some amount of extra fabric, which is released somewhere below the waist.
Flare	A fit that is flat at the waistline and full at the hem.
Waist location	Skirts may hang from the waist, or slightly higher on the rib cage, or fall from the high hip.

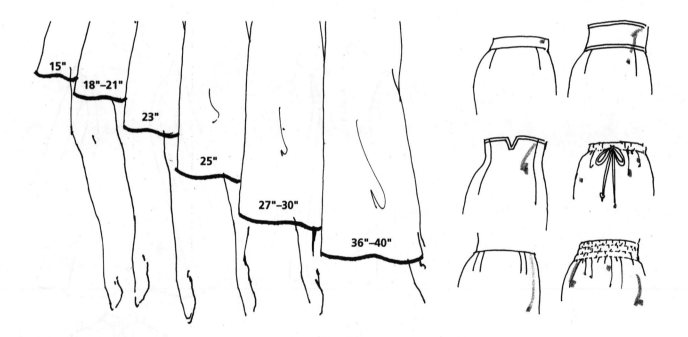

Figure 7.14a–b. *Skirts may be varied by changing the length or the waistline treatment.*

Pants

Pants are bifurcated garments worn by men, women, and children. Once considered strictly sportswear for women and children, pants today are a fashion staple for casual wear, professional dress, and evening wear. Although the preferences for design details used on men's, women's, and children's pants categories vary according to gender and age, the style variables are fairly consistent. However, women's and children's pant silhouettes typically feature a wider range of variation than men's pants. Women's pants legs vary from skintight leggings to wide, elephant leg pants or pant skirts, whereas men's pant legs tend to vary from a narrow five-pocket jean to a full-cut trouser leg. Style variables in pants are presented in Table 7.8 and Appendix Figure 7A.8.

Table 7.8 PANTS

STYLE VARIABLE	DESCRIPTION
Waist	May hang from the waist, or slightly higher on the rib cage or fall from the hip or high hip.
Length	Ranges from very short shorts (mostly worn by women and children) to Bermuda shorts, Capri pants, and long pants.
Pant leg width	May vary from body-conforming, as in leggings, to wide evening pants for women. Added width may extend all the way up the leg, as in pajama pants, or taper from the thigh or knee, as in flares or bell-bottoms. Men's pant legs tend to vary less in width from a boot-cut jean to a full-cut trouser to a drawstring casual pant.
Fit	May be shaped to fit the waist, hips, and buttocks using darts, pleats, or gathers. Darts can be eliminated in the front for flat figures; this works best in fabrics with Lycra.

Garment Details

Garment details provide a means of changing classic silhouettes from season to season. They embellish garment silhouettes and provide a visual link to a fashion theme. Details include component parts, decorative effects, and trims. **Component parts** are elements of a garment that are not part of its basic structure, but add aesthetic interest or provide functionality. Examples include collars, cuffs, pockets, and belts. **Decorative effects** are embellishments that are added to the fabric of the garment, such as smocking, quilting, tucking, appliqué, and embroidery. These embellishments may be added at the fabric yardage stage or strategically applied to a cut piece. **Trims** are details added to the garment, such as buttons, braids, and lace.

Details can be added to garments for aesthetics or functionality. Examples of decorative details include a tucked front on a blouse, a ruffle on the hem of a skirt or dress, or a monogram on a blouse. Functional details include pockets, buttons, and hoods. Details should enhance the aesthetics of the garment or add function without making the garment too expensive for its target market.

Designers and product developers should keep files of interesting details because the popularity of details and decorative techniques is cyclic in the world of fashion. For instance, the minimalism of the mid-1990s was followed by a very embellished bohemian look in 2000–2005. It is important for product developers to have good working relationships with a variety of trim vendors so that when a new trim or detail becomes important, they readily know where to source it. In the early 1980s, Norma Kamali popularized the use of snap tape

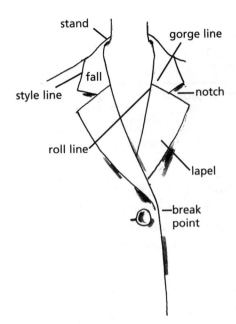

Figure 7.15. *A diagram of parts of a tailored collar.*

on sweatshirt knits made into casual wear garments other than sweatshirts. Designers who knew where to source snap tape had a head start on competitors in translating this popular trend. Findings and trim are discussed in chapter 10. The remainder of this chapter discusses component parts and closures as they relate to the design process.

Component Parts

Component parts are so much a part of the garment that they often are not thought of as details. A good designer is attuned to picking up on the subtle changes in proportion, shape, and placement of component parts.

Necklines and Collars

The neckline of a garment frames the neck and provides an opening for the head. It may be finished simply with a facing, ribbed band, or bias binding, or it may be further embellished with a collar. Necklines may be round, square, scooped, sweetheart, or V-shaped. Neckline variations are illustrated in Appendix Figure 7A.9.

    Collars are component parts that surround the neck and are attached permanently or temporarily to the neckline of the garment. Detachable collars may make garments easier to clean, but detachable details are a problem for merchants. They are easily stolen or lost, thus compromising the value of the garment. Collars are integral details for many garments—particularly shirts, blouses, jackets, and coats—and are frequently the focal point of a garment.

    A designer must understand collar terminology in order to design a successful collar. A collar **stand** is the part of the collar that fits close to the neck. The collar **fall** is the part of the collar that turns over the stand or garment. The collar **roll line** is the line where the collar fall turns over the stand. The collar **style line** is the shape of the outer edge of the collar. Additional terminology applies to tailored collars. The collar **lapels** are part of the garment front and are designed to attach to the collar and turn back over the garment. The **breakline** is the line on which the lapels turn back. The **break point** is the point along the front edge of the garment at which the lapel begins to roll back. The **gorge line** is where the collar and the lapel are joined. The **notch** is the triangular shape between the lapel and the collar, formed where the gorge line ends (Figure 7.15). With that terminology in mind, consider the four factors that determine a collar's shape:

1. The placement of the garment neckline in relation to the base of the neck

2. The shape of the neckline seam in relation to the length and shape of the neck seam on the collar

3. The shape and depth of the fall of the collar

4. Whether the collar has a revere or lapel, and the size and shape of that revere or lapel.

Flat collars have neckline curves that are the same shape as the neckline of the garment. This allows them to lie flat on the garment with no roll or stand onto the neck. Examples of flat collars include Peter Pan collars, Bertha collars, and sailor collars. They are popular on children's clothes because children have short necks. They create a youthful feel on adult garments.

Partial roll collars have neckline curves that are straighter than the neckline of the garment but not perfectly straight. This creates a stand at the back of the collar but allows the collar to lie flat on the garment as it comes around to the front. Convertible collars, Chelsea collars, tailored collars, and shawl collars are examples of partial roll collars.

Stand collars have neckline edges that are straight in relation to the neckline curve of the garment. This straight edge causes the collar to encircle the neck. Turtleneck collars, shirt collars, and tie collars are examples. Straight collars that are cut on the bias tend to hug the neck and are more easily manipulated in collars that tie. Learn to analyze the grain of collars as well as their shape when researching these details.

Gathered ruffled collars have a longer neck seam on the collar than the neckline and must be gathered or pleated in order to fit the neckline seam. *Circular ruffle collars* have a neck seam the same length as the neckline seam but a neck curve that is greater than the neckline seam, causing the style line of the collar to fall into soft folds. *Cowl collars,* as opposed to cowl necklines, are a variation of the turtleneck. They are frequently used on a neckline that is placed away from the base of the neck. Extra length is left in the fall of the collar so that it bunches over the stand. Collar variations are illustrated in Appendix Figure 7A.10.

Tailored collars are more complex than other collars and require more careful shaping during construction. They may be used on jackets, coats, and dresses. A well-designed collar can be the focal point of a tailored garment. This is an important detail for designers to explore. Study the relationship between the revere and the collar at the gorge line and the angle they form at the notch. Tailored collars can be changed dramatically by raising or lowering the break point. This may affect how a jacket is merchandised because a high break point may eliminate the need for wearing a shell or blouse under the jacket. A suit jacket that closes enough to eliminate the need of a blouse is known as a dressmaker suit. A low break point can be very slimming because it creates a long V line in the front, but it may be difficult to control gapping at the neck when the garment is worn, particularly on full-figured consumers. Figure 7.16 illustrates a few tailored collar variations.

Shawl collars are similar to tailored collars except that they do not have a gorge line. Shawl collars are drafted as an extension of the bodice front. They make a nice foil for decorative techniques or decorative edges. Shawl collars can be varied in width by lowering or raising the break point or by shaping the collar style line. Diagonal fabric designs or weaves do not translate well into shawl collar designs and should be avoided in this style.

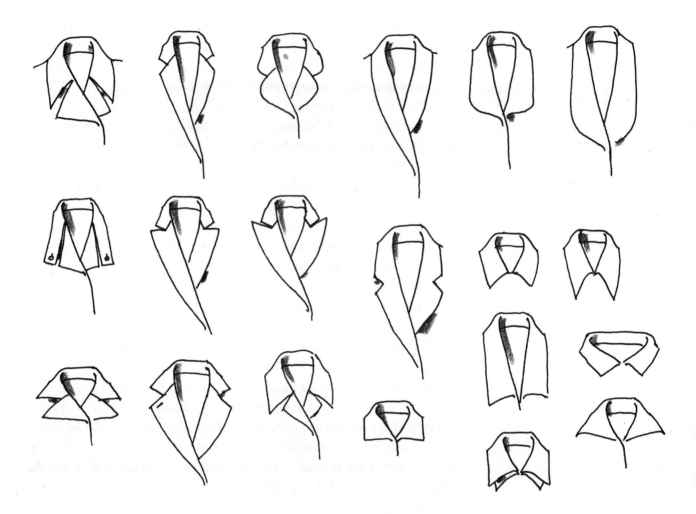

Figure 7.16. *Tailored collars may be varied by manipulating the collar and lapel length or width, changing the collar shape, changing the location of the break point, or changing the notch or gorge line.*

Sleeves and Cuffs

Although sleeves are a structural part of the garment rather than a component part, style variations for sleeves are discussed here. Sleeves are designed to fit the armscye or armhole. The armscye may be cut in a halter style, in which case a sleeve is not appropriate. Or, the armscye may be designed in its natural location on the body, in which case a set-in sleeve is appropriate. The shoulder line may be extended or the armscye may be lowered, in which case a looser-fitting sleeve is appropriate. A raglan sleeve extends the sleeve line into the neckline as does a saddle sleeve. Kimono and dolman sleeves are cut in one piece with the garment body. Common sleeve variations are illustrated in Appendix Figure 7A.11.

The bottom of the sleeve may be hemmed, finished with a vent, or attached to a cuff. Hems may be blind hemmed, machine rolled, topstitched, or finished with a facing or ruffle. Vents are frequently found on tailored jackets at better price points. A sleeve vent is located slightly back from the normal location of an underarm seam. Vents are usually found in two-piece sleeves, or the underarm seam on a one-piece sleeve may be moved to the back in order to accommodate a vent. Designers are aware of the numerous ways to construct vents and will specify the method that suits their quality level, price

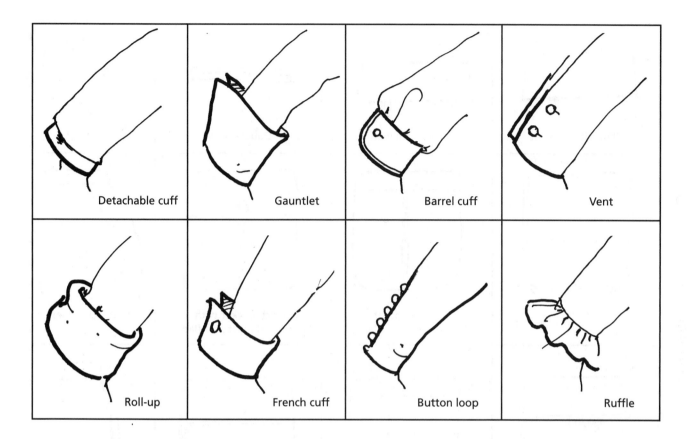

Detachable cuff	Gauntlet	Barrel cuff	Vent
Roll-up	French cuff	Button loop	Ruffle

Figure 7.17. *Examples of different types of sleeve bottoms.*

point, and fabric. Sleeve bottoms may also be finished with a cuff, which may be applied to a straight or gathered sleeve edge. Figure 7.17 illustrates various ways to finish a sleeve bottom.

Pockets

Pockets consist of extra fabric attached to the inside or outside of a garment to form a pouch with a top or side opening. Pockets play both decorative and functional roles in garment design. Pockets may be classified as inside or outside pockets. On **outside pockets**, the pouch or bag of the pocket is visible from the outside of the garment. On **inside pockets**, the pouch falls inside the garment with only an opening visible from the outside. The pocket opening is traditionally large enough to fit a hand—5½ to 6½ inches across the opening for adult women. This measurement may be smaller for a decorative effect. Some pockets are intended to be nonfunctional; they are designed as such to cut costs or prevent distortion of the garment's fit. Pockets may be used symmetrically, in pairs, or asymmetrically. Figure 7.18 illustrates various pocket styles.

Outside pockets are also known as **patch pockets**. They can be designed in many shapes and sizes to harmonize with the silhouette, details, and feeling of a garment. Patch pockets work best in fabrics that are not too soft and that hold their shape; when made of fabrics that have a great deal of drape or stretch these pockets may sag. Patch pockets tend to add bulk, which should

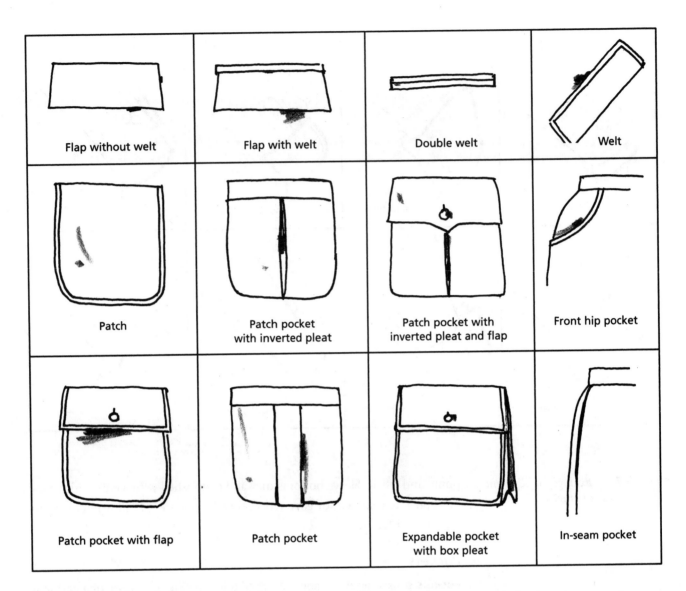

Flap without welt	Flap with welt	Double welt	Welt
Patch	Patch pocket with inverted pleat	Patch pocket with inverted pleat and flap	Front hip pocket
Patch pocket with flap	Patch pocket	Expandable pocket with box pleat	In-seam pocket

Figure 7.18. *Pockets are both a decorative and a functional garment component that can differentiate a garment silhouette.*

be considered when determining placement on the body and appropriateness for a particular fabric or figure type. A patch pocket may be embellished with pleats, tucks, topstitching, or buttons, and it may be combined with a flap. Patch pockets may also be made three-dimensional by incorporating a pleat of fabric in the perimeter of the pocket; this accommodates carrying of larger objects. Patch pockets are typically topstitched onto the garment; however, a technique for machine sewing them on invisibly is sometimes used in higher-priced garments. No matter how the pocket is attached, it should be reinforced at the pocket opening.

Inside pockets include slash pockets, pockets hidden in a seam, and front hip pockets used on jeans. **Slash pockets** are frequently used on tailored garments. They include double welt or bound pockets, welt pockets, and flap pockets. The pocket opening is slashed into the garment body and finished with a flap or welt, with the pocket pouch hidden inside the garment. The designer may vary the position of the slash by cutting horizontally, vertically, diagonally, or on a curve into the fabric. These pockets are typically basted closed for pressing; the basting must be removed when the garment is purchased to access the pocket. To ensure product quality and consistency, most product developers require contractors that bid on garments with slash pockets to have automated pocket-making equipment.

Double welt pockets consist of two welts, one sewn to the top edge of the slash and the other sewn to the bottom edge of the slash. They resemble bound buttonholes and are sometimes referred to as *bound* pockets. Welts are typically ³/16 to ¼ inch wide. Bound pockets are accessed in an opening between the two welts.

Welt pockets have a single welt, typically ¼ inch to 1½ inches wide, that is attached to the bottom edge of the slash and flips up over the pocket to cover the opening. This pocket is accessed from the top of the welt. Narrow welt pockets are sometimes used on the back of men's or women's pants. Wider welts are frequently found on tailored jackets, coat dresses, and coats.

Flap pockets consist of a flap that is sewn to the top edge of the slash and that falls over the pocket opening. The pocket flap must be lifted to provide access to the pocket. Flap pockets may be combined with upper or lower pocket welts. Sometimes flaps are attached to a garment to give the look of an inside pocket even though there is no inside pouch. This technique saves costs by making the garment simpler to produce. It may also be desirable when the garment fabric cannot support a functional pocket.

In-seam pockets are designed into an existing seam of the garment. They are most frequently found in garment side seams or princess seams, but they may also be found in yoke or waist seams. These pockets provide function without disrupting the lines of the garment. The edge may be topstitched for a crisper line or to blend with the detailing on the rest of the garment. There should be a self-fabric extension on the garment back for vertical in-seam pockets, and on the garment yoke or bodice for horizontal in-seam pockets, so that if the pocket opens, the fabric of the pocket pouch is not visible. It is important that garments with in-seam pockets be designed with enough ease so that the pocket does not pull open when not in use.

Front hip pockets are typically used on jeans and pants. They feature a style line that is cut into the garment front at the hip and faced to form the opening. Many variations can be achieved with this pocket style. They are frequently topstitched.

Belts

If a garment requires a belt, it is best to sell the belt with the garment so that the consumer is purchasing a complete ensemble. Some garments, such as jeans, are designed with belt loops but are typically worn without belts. Therefore a belt need not be sold with those garments. Belts can be made of the same fabric as the garment or may be purchased from a belt supplier to coordinate with the garment. Belts that are sold with a garment are generally made of synthetic materials rather than leather in order to keep costs down.

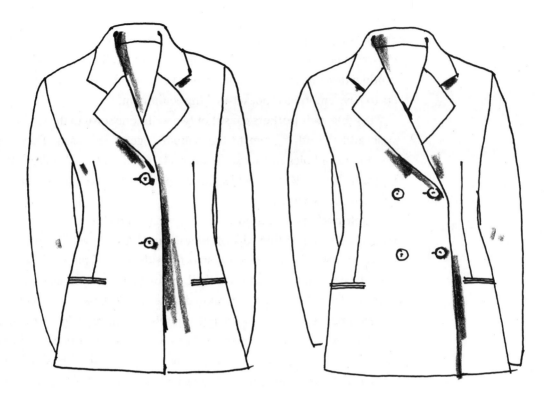

Figure 7.19. *This illustration shows the same jacket silhouette with a single-breasted and a double-breasted closure.*

Closures

Closures are an important part of any design. There must be a way to get a garment on and off the body. Sometimes there is sufficient stretch in the garment fabric, making a closure unnecessary. Examples include swimwear and T-shirts. However, most garments require some sort of closure. Closures for tops are typically at the center front or center back, but they may also be located along a shoulder or side seam. Closures on bottoms may be located at the center front, center back, or side seam. Closures include various types of zippers, button closures, tie closures, hooks and eyes, Velcro hook and loop fasteners, and snaps, all of which are discussed in chapter 10. Our focus here is to review how to plan and sketch closures in the design process.

Zipper closures are simple because the zipper is usually inserted into a seam. To indicate a zipper, place a cross mark at the bottom of the zipper and indicate stitching lines for a centered or lapped zipper. Invisible zippers require no stitching lines.

To indicate a lapped front or back closure, you must first visualize the center front or center back line with a light guideline. As you look at the garment, women's closures lap left over right and men's garments lap right over left. Determine the size of your button and draw the outer edge of the garment ¾ to 1 button diameter away from the center, making sure that the lap is in the proper direction. Once the lap is established, the neckline can be completed and the center front guideline can be erased.

On double-breasted jackets the center front line divides the placement of the two rows of buttons. Determine the center front guideline and the direction of lap and place the buttons. Then complete the outer edge, allowing ¼ to

½ inch beyond the edge of the buttons. Join the neckline to the outer edge and erase the center front guideline. Figure 7.19 illustrates how to establish accurate lapped closure lines. Figure 7.20 illustrates additional closure variations.

Planning and Sourcing for Garment Details

Designers have a variety of options when planning details. Some prefer to use ready-made trims that may or may not have to be color-matched. Others work with studios that sell prototypes of trims and decorative effects that may be copied and adapted to the product developer's line. Still others have graphic artists who design exclusive trims for in-house use.

The cost of trims and decorative effects can vary greatly depending on where the garment is sourced. Any form of handwork is too costly for U.S. production, but may be affordable in a low-wage country such as China or India. Trim houses may specialize in decorative effects that require special machinery. The use of these services and the ordering of trims must be planned within the production schedule. This planning should include any additional time necessary to obtain approval of color matching and production samples, as well as extra time for shipping. Decisions about all details must be made early enough in the process to ensure availability of these items as needed in the garment production schedule.

Figure 7.20. *Garment closures can be differentiated in a variety of ways, including choice of fasteners, topstitching, a framed or bias edge, and edge shaping.*

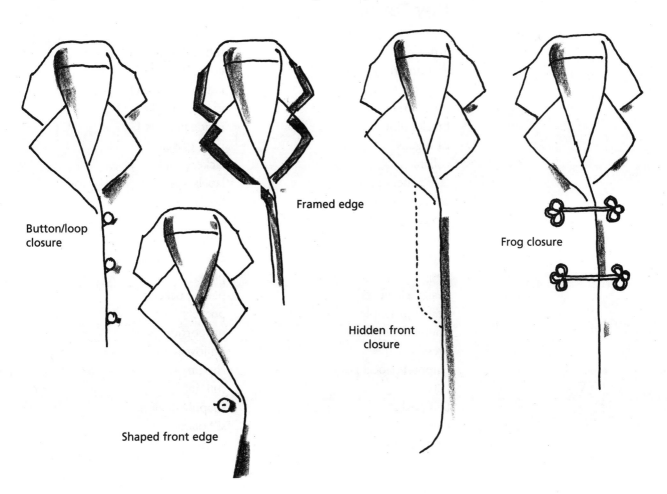

Button/loop closure

Shaped front edge

Framed edge

Hidden front closure

Frog closure

Summary

Garment design is a process that utilizes the design elements of line, color, texture, pattern, silhouette, and shape to create a garment. Understanding the principles of design can help the product developer evaluate the success of an individual garment. By identifying the proportion, balance, focal point, rhythm, and harmony, the designer can determine whether the elements combine to make an aesthetically pleasing whole.

Designers explore garment ideas through the use of croquis sketches. These quick sketches allow them to record silhouettes and details that they see when doing their research. A single sketch recording an idea seen while shopping or in a periodical may evolve into 10 to 20 different sketchbook interpretations. From those ideas, the strongest design may be chosen for an item line, or several garments may become the basis for a themed group.

Garment silhouettes worn today are relatively standard, evolving slowly from season to season. Understanding the style variables present in different garment classifications can help a designer be more creative. Once a silhouette is determined, garments can be further embellished with details, including collars, sleeves, cuffs, pockets, trims, and closures.

Key Terms

armscye
asymmetrical
balance
breakline
break point
cardigans
collars
component parts
concept boards
croquis sketches
cut and sew construction
decorative effects
design
design elements
design principles
double welt pockets
dresses
emphasis (focal point)
fall
flap pockets
flats
front hip pockets

full-fashion construction
gorge line
harmony (unity)
in-seam pockets
inside pockets
item-driven
jacket
lapels
lay figure
line
notch
outside pockets
pants
patch pockets
pockets
proportion
pullovers
rhythm
roll line
shaping devices
silhouette
skirts

slash pockets

stand

style line

stylists

sweater sets (twin sets)

swipes

symmetrical

texture

tops

trims

underdrawing (lay figure)

vest

welt pockets

Discussion Questions

1. After reviewing fashion periodicals and shopping your local market, discuss the fashion direction that you see pants taking. In the women's market, are pants or skirts more important for the season you are studying?

2. What role do skirt lengths play in the current fashion season? Can you relate the prevalent length to fashion cycles or current events? Do you notice a difference in length offerings at different price points or for different markets?

3. Bring examples of garments with symmetrical and asymmetrical balance to class. Discuss your experience in wearing those garments. Do you wear some garments more often than others? Are some garments easier to wear than others? How long have you had each garment in your wardrobe?

4. Brainstorm for additional examples of fashion dimensions that continually change in order to keep fashion current and fresh.

Activities

1. Go out shopping for jackets. In your croquis book, sketch all of the variations you see being used to fit jacket bodies. Look for different combinations with or without a center back seam; with or without side seams, side panels, and princess seams; and with or without darts. Try on some of the jackets to evaluate the resulting fit. Take your tape measure to identify some key measurements for side panel width and its relationship to two-piece sleeve seaming.

2. Study fashion periodicals and shop your local mall for jackets with tailored collars. Try on a few jackets with tailored collars and identify the various parts. In your croquis book, sketch as many interesting variations as you can find, annotating with key measurements to sensitize your eye to proportions. Continue your sketches using catalogs and fashion periodicals. Use this sketchbook as a reference whenever you are designing garments with tailored collars. Continue adding to it as you come across additional interesting variations.

3. Select a trim, such as buttons, zippers, or ruffles. Experiment with using that trim as a design element in garments. Express your ideas in a series of croquis drawings.

4. Go shopping and study garments that utilize embroidery, appliqué, or beading. Design a garment that features one of these trims. Then develop the repeat of the trim and specify the stitches and components to be used.

5. Design your own logo for the back of a jeans pocket. Select the color of stitching and the type of stitch used.

6. Identify a dress silhouette that you like through shopping or in a fashion periodical. Sketch the dress you identify and then do a series of 20 croquis sketches that maintain the basic silhouette but vary the details, balance, and proportions. Share your work with the class.

7. Select a runway garment that you find in a magazine or on the Internet. Do a series of design sketches interpreting the runway design for a particular customer and price point. Then do a second series of sketches interpreting that same design for another market.

Additional Resources

Boyes, Janet. 1998. *Essential fashion design.* London: BT Batsford Ltd.

Gehlhar, Mary. 2005. *Fashion designer survival guide.* Chicago: Dearborn Trade Publishing.

Jenkyn Jones, Sue. 2002. *Fashion design.* New York: Watson-Guptill Publications.

Sorger, Richard, and Jenny Udale. 2006. *The fundamentals of fashion design.* Switzerland: AVA Publishing.

Tatham, Caroline, and Julian Seaman. 2003. *Fashion design drawing course.* Hauppauge, NY: Barron's Educational Series, Inc.

Tain, Linda. 2003. *Portfolio presentation for fashion designers.* New York: Fairchild Publications.

www.elle.com. Online version of *Elle.*

www.fashion.about.com. An online fashion newsletter.

www.fashiontrendsetter.com. An online fashion forecasting and trend reporting resource.

www.glamourmagazine.com. Online version of *Glamour.*

www.instyle.com. Online version of *InStyle.*

www.millenialfashion.com. Trend service that offers free access to "Fashion Trends and Tips."

www.style.com. Online home of *Vogue* and *W* magazines featuring access to trend reports and runway shows.

www.wgsn-edu.com. An Internet fashion forecasting service based in Great Britain that makes its services available to students.

APPENDIX:
Apparel Design Details Illustrated

Figure 7A.1 KNIT TOPS

Sweatshirt   Halter   Polo shirt

T-shirt   Tank top   Tube top

Figure 7A.2 SWEATERS

Cardigan

Pullover

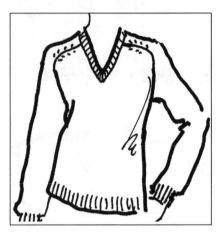

V-neck

Turtleneck

Mock turtleneck

Sweater vest

Twin set

Sweater jacket

Figure 7A.3 SHIRTS AND BLOUSES

Shirt

Blouse

Camp shirt

Tuxedo shirt

Western cut

Peasant blouse

Safari shirt

Surplice wrap

Tie

Shell

Camisole

Tunic

Jabot

Figure 7A.4 JACKETS

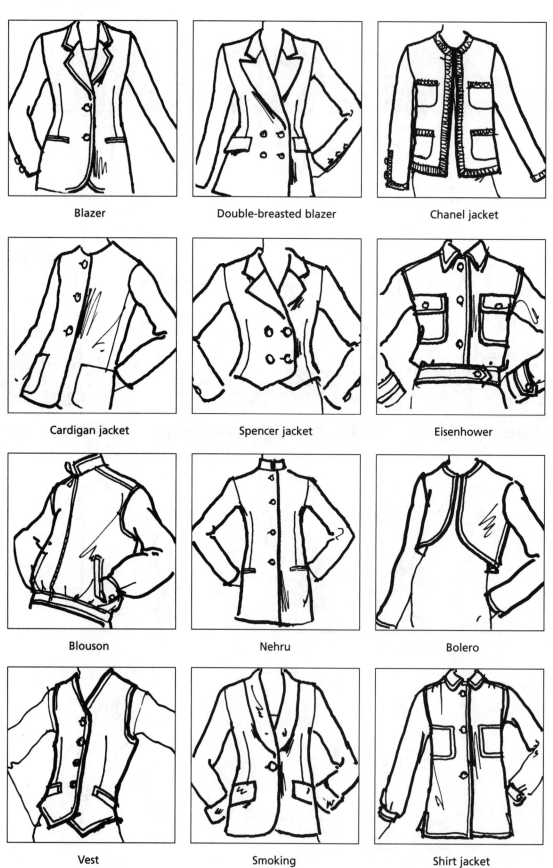

Blazer

Double-breasted blazer

Chanel jacket

Cardigan jacket

Spencer jacket

Eisenhower

Blouson

Nehru

Bolero

Vest

Smoking

Shirt jacket

Figure 7A.5 COATS

Swagger

Wrap

Trench coat

Clutch coat

Duffle jacket

Poncho

Cape

Reefer

Parka

Peacoat

Balmacaan

Chesterfield

Duster

Princess/Fit & flare

Figure 7A.6 DRESS SILHOUETTES

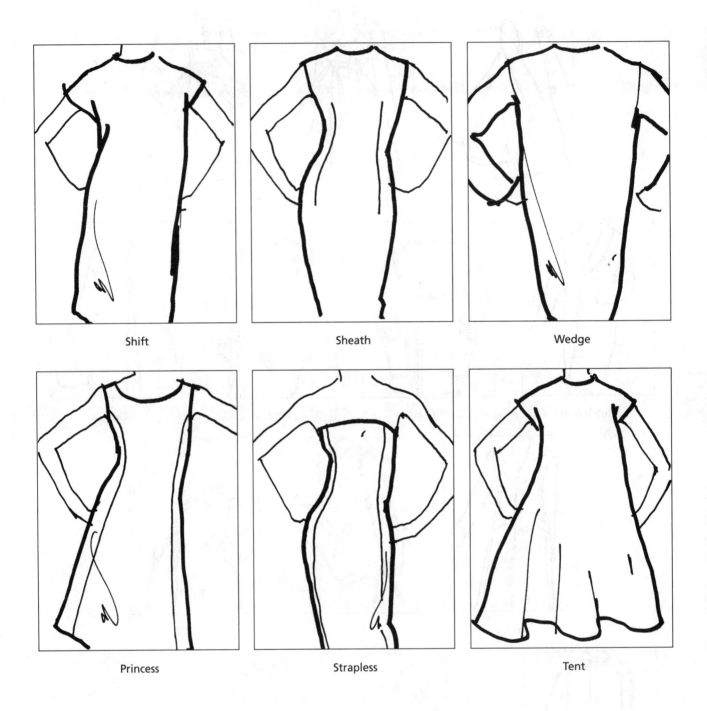

Shift   Sheath   Wedge

Princess   Strapless   Tent

Dropped waist

Jumper

T-shirt dress

Shirtwaist

Empire

Shirt dress

Coat dress

Figure 7A.7 SKIRTS

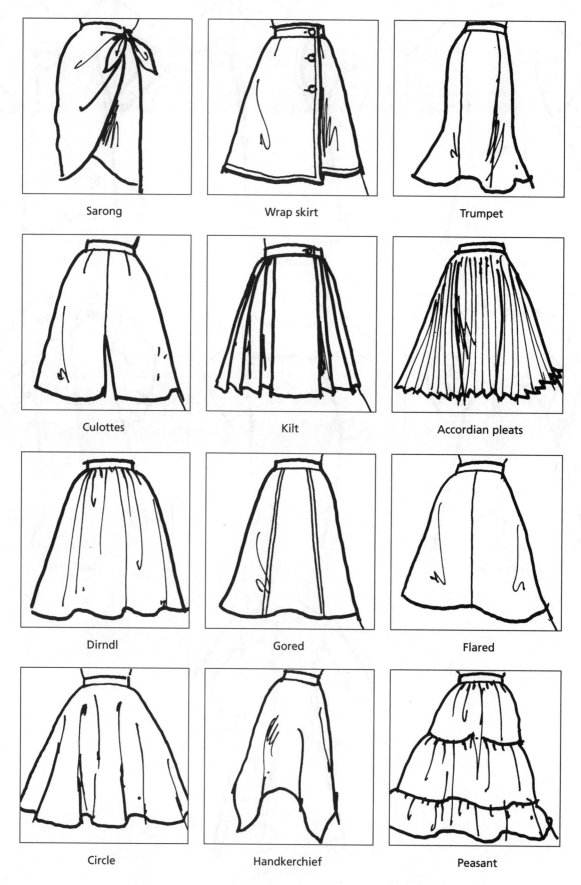

Sarong

Wrap skirt

Trumpet

Culottes

Kilt

Accordian pleats

Dirndl

Gored

Flared

Circle

Handkerchief

Peasant

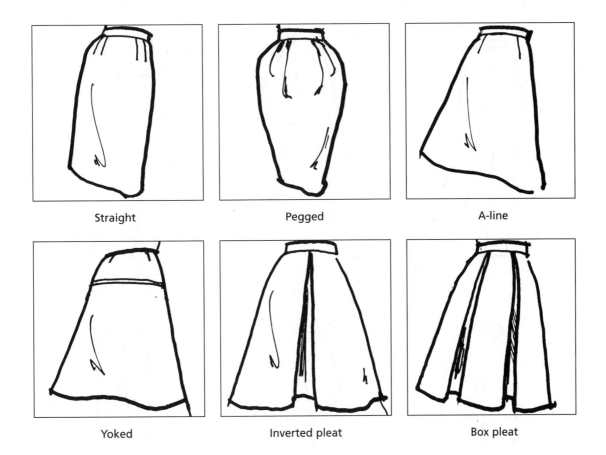

Straight

Pegged

A-line

Yoked

Inverted pleat

Box pleat

Figure 7A.8 PANTS

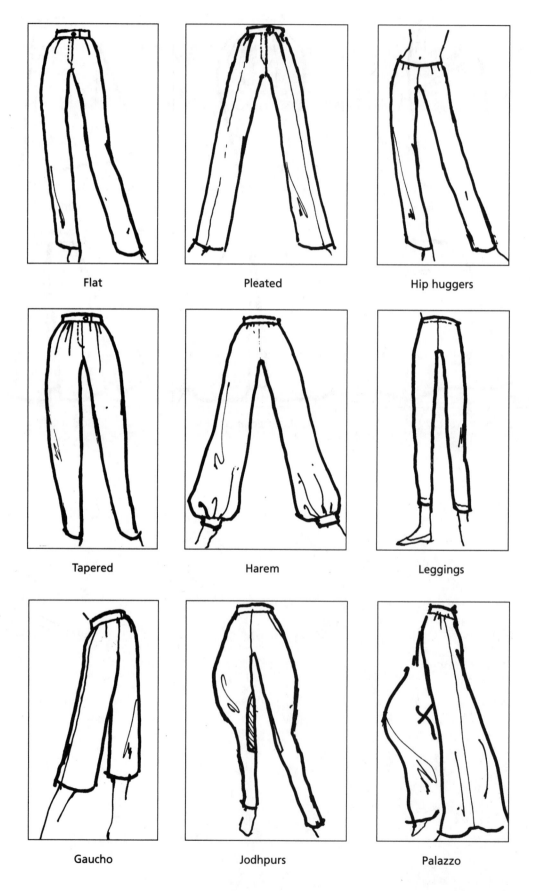

Flat	Pleated	Hip huggers
Tapered	Harem	Leggings
Gaucho	Jodhpurs	Palazzo

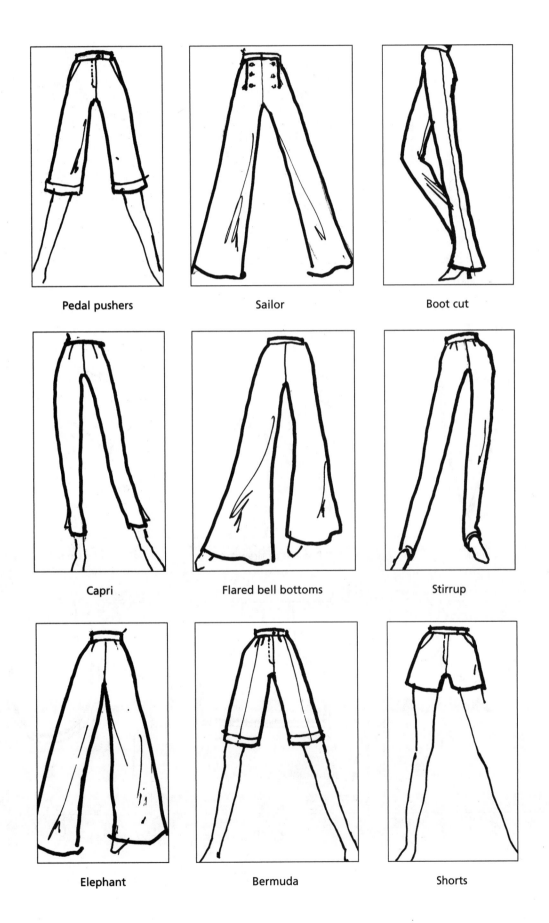

Pedal pushers

Sailor

Boot cut

Capri

Flared bell bottoms

Stirrup

Elephant

Bermuda

Shorts

Figure 7A.9 NECKLINES

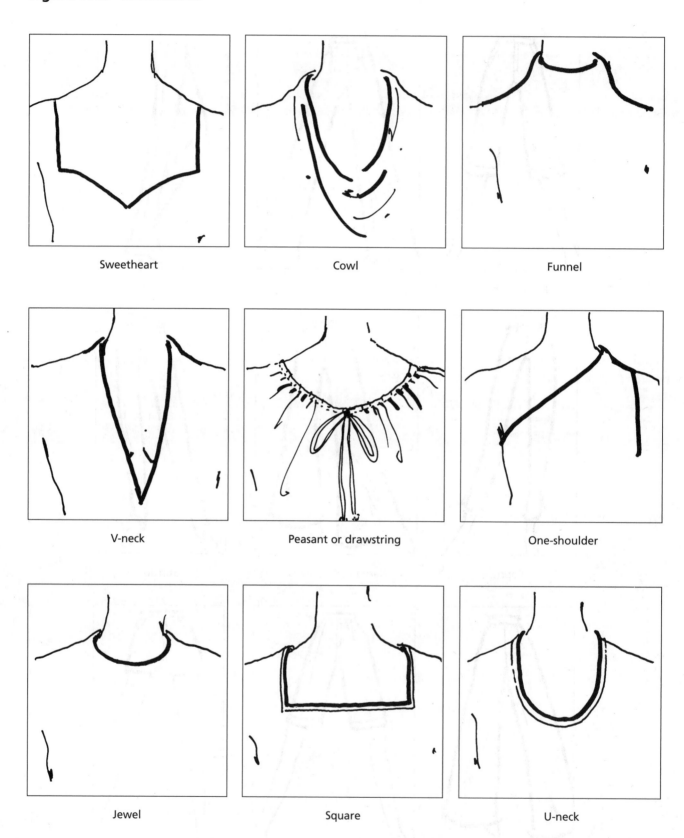

Sweetheart	Cowl	Funnel
V-neck	Peasant or drawstring	One-shoulder
Jewel	Square	U-neck

V-neck

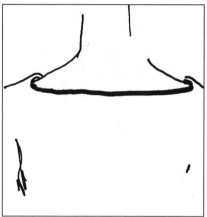

Bateau

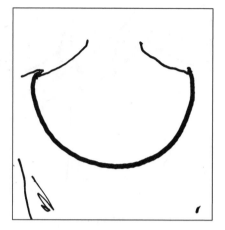

Scoop

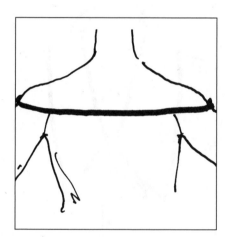

Off-the-shoulder

Figure 7A.10 COLLARS

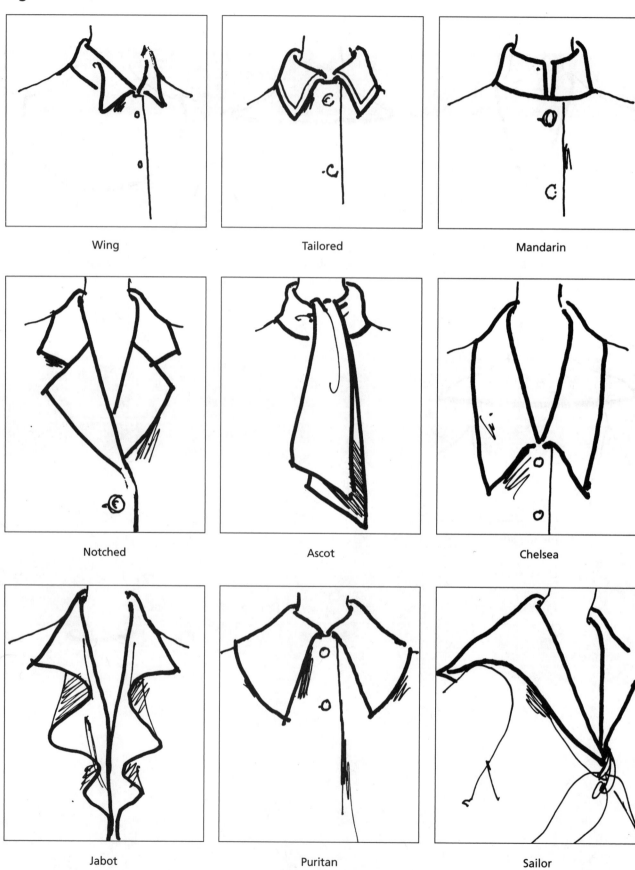

Wing

Tailored

Mandarin

Notched

Ascot

Chelsea

Jabot

Puritan

Sailor

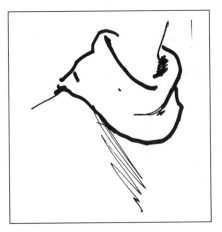

Cowl

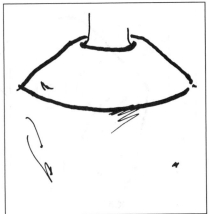

Bertha

Tie

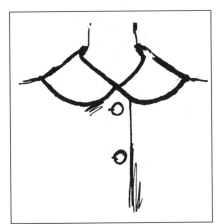

Peter Pan

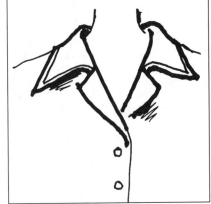

Convertible open

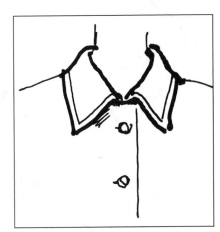

Convertible closed

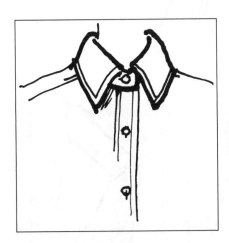

Shirt

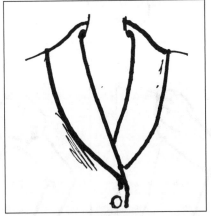

Shawl

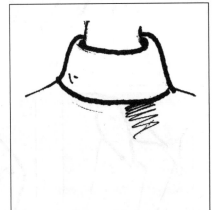

Turtleneck

Figure 7A.11 SLEEVES

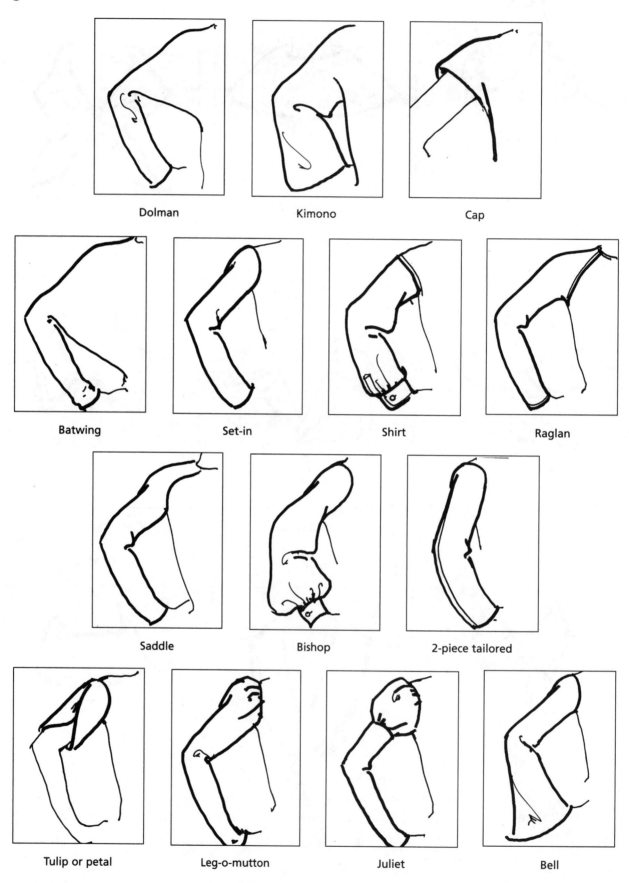

Dolman

Kimono

Cap

Batwing

Set-in

Shirt

Raglan

Saddle

Bishop

2-piece tailored

Tulip or petal

Leg-o-mutton

Juliet

Bell

CHAPTER 8

LINE DEVELOPMENT

"Contemporary designers strive to integrate the basic elements of style in a way that demarcates a signature aesthetic. . . . Each new season's styles must differ from last year's range but still retain elements that express across time a continually evolving designer identity."

—SALLY WELLER

OBJECTIVES

- To understand how the line plan and trend forecast are interpreted into designs for focused groups with specific delivery dates

- To understand the limitations of legal protection for the design of apparel

- To understand the difference between item lines and group lines

- To understand the parameters of line development

- To understand how a line assortment is balanced for production

- To explore the means used to communicate design ideas at various stages of the line development process

It is one thing to understand how to design a garment; it is quite another to understand how to design a group of garments that can be merchandised together. In a culture of fashion individualism, designers and merchandisers must work together to synthesize the merchandise budget, assortment plan, and fashion forecast into product for a selling season that may be up to one year out. A good merchandiser provides an environment that nurtures the designer's creativity and provides the controls for effective line development. Lack of merchandising leads to incongruous styling, lines that are too expensive, and lines that are poorly timed.

Approaches to Line Planning

Each garment designed is part of a group that will be merchandised together on a selling floor, online, or in a catalog (Figure 8.1). Styles within each group must satisfy a range of preferences for the brand's target customer—from the

Figure 8.1. *A designer must consider how the group he or she is designing will be merchandised on the selling floor.*

most conservative to the most fashion-forward. Garments must remain true to the customer's brand expectations in terms of styling, fit, quality, and price. Each delivery should focus on buy-now, wear-now items that encourage sell-through at full price.

A seasonal **line** of apparel consists of the overall collection of garments that will be offered for sale by a division or firm at a given time. As discussed in chapter 2, the merchandise plan determines sales and profit goals by division and/or category. The line or range plan identifies how many styles by category, and/or how many coordinated groups it will take in each delivery during the season to meet those goals. The assortment plan refines this further by determining the makeup of each delivery—the number of styles in each group and the percentage of those styles that need to be designed as basic items, key items, or fashion items (Case Study 8.1, Callie Blake Collection).

The assortment plan spells out expectations as to the variety, volume, and distribution of the line, as well as decisions regarding the balance of the line. These decisions are sometimes referred to as defining the breadth and depth of the product line. A well-conceived assortment plan helps designers to focus their efforts on the items that are most likely to make it through the line review process. Each group of styles should express a clear point of view, focusing on a theme that is relevant to the targeted customer and that reflects

CASE STUDY 8.1 BUSINESS PLAN FOR CALLIE BLAKE COLLECTION
by Grace I. Kunz

Callie Blake is a manufacturer of better career apparel primarily directed toward the U.S. specialty store market. The collection includes two divisions: misses suits and plus size coordinates. Misses suits has two categories, traditional tailored and career. Career tailored suits are more fashion-forward than traditional tailored suits. Career tops are coordinated with both tailored and career suits. Plus size coordinates focus on career and dressy casual wear. Categories of plus size coordinates include tops, bottoms, and sweaters.

As with many U.S. manufacturers, Callie Blake sources about 20 percent of its products, mostly its tops, in the California market. The rest is sourced in Eastern Europe in countries well known for better- tailored apparel, including Bulgaria, Poland, and Romania.

Callie Blake uses the language of merchandise mix, category, class, and group to break down its assortments. Model stocks (number of styles times number of sizes times number of colors) are used to control assortments. Number of stock keeping units (SKUs) is an indicator of assortment variety.

Product development and production costs are evaluated in relation to the planned retail and wholesale prices. Average retail selling price for a Callie Blake suit is $280; average wholesale price is $112. Specialty retailers commonly take percent markup on retail. Average retail selling price for plus size coordinates (a top or a bottom) is $85. The average wholesale price is $34. Because of foreign sourcing of the majority of the collection, prices will not increase next year.

EXAMPLES OF CLASS AND GROUP MODEL STOCK PLANS—MISSES, FALL 2007

	MODEL STOCK	SKUs PER GROUP
Tailored Jackets		
Princess jackets	(1 style, 8 sizes, 2 colors)	16
Blazers	(2 styles, 12 sizes, 3 colors)	72
Cardigans	(2 styles, 12 sizes, 2 colors)	48
Career Skirts		
Straight	(1 style, 12 sizes, 4 colors)	48
Wrap	(2 styles, 12 sizes, 3 colors)	72
Culotte	(1 style, 8 sizes, 2 colors)	16
A-line	(1 style, 12 sizes, 4 colors)	48

Grace I. Kunz is Associate Professor Emeritus, Iowa State University.

customer constraints, such as price point limitations and quality, fit, and care expectations. Accurate communication and teamwork between merchandiser and designers will result in a line that is marketable and supports the goals of the brand.

There are different approaches to assortment planning. Companies that rely heavily on basics for the bulk of their sales will have the most specific assortment plans. They are able to use historic seasonal data to determine what their customer expects of them. Companies like Jockey International and

Figure 8.2. *A design sketch by Luella Bartley.*

Lands' End design similar silhouettes from season to season. Their competitive edge may come from identifying the right colors, adopting the most up-to-date fabric technology, or maintaining the highest possible quality standards.

Product developers whose edge is achieved by being on top of fashion trends are subject to more risk. In these companies, merchandisers and designers may work more collaboratively, using a series of line reviews throughout the design process and requesting input from sales, marketing, and/or key retail buyers. Fashion-forward product developers are constantly seeking ways to shorten the line development calendar. They attempt to minimize risk by finalizing assortment specifics at the last possible moment. They may commit to a minimum fabric order early on, identifying the colors and/or patterns needed. This allows the fabric vendor to proceed with color approvals and strike-offs—a full repeat of a pattern printed in the approved colors on the specified fabric for approval. The exact yardage required of each color and/or pattern is specified at a later date. They may do the same in terms of manufacturing capacity.

Development of new style groups or silhouettes for a product line is achieved through one of three methods or a combination of these methods.

Original Designs

The first of these development methods is the creation of original styles through sketching or draping. The most common method in use throughout the industry today is sketching designs using either hand or computer drawing techniques (Figure 8.2). Draping is usually reserved for higher price point products that will be custom-fitted or for garments that reflect more fluid silhouettes, such as evening wear.

Style Modification

Styles from previous collections that sold well may be included in the new line with modifications made in details of styling, color, or fabrication. These recurring styles are referred to as **bodies,** defined as silhouettes for which perfected patterns have already been fitted and graded. By changing a sleeve, a neckline, a hemline, or a closure, a previously produced silhouette can be adapted for the new season. Carryover bodies or styles are very cost-efficient because they cut down considerably on overall development time and, personnel efforts, and costs (Figure 8.3).

Knockoffs

Knockoffs are garments that are adapted or modified from products designed by other firms. They may be made from pictures of products or from copying an actual product, which has been purchased off the rack. In the United States, knocking off fashion silhouettes is more or less legal. The fashion industry has historically operated with no prohibition against copying. The fashion cycle is based on the introduction of an idea which is increasingly sought after by consumers and copied or interpreted by other product developers. The practice of "borrowing" the designs of others has been justified as a way of paying homage to their good ideas. A runway look that is widely copied generally garners lots of press and greater sales (Lanman 2006).

At one time many low- and moderate-priced retail product developers designed their entire line by purchasing samples of garments designed by others and adapting them to their company's price point, aesthetic, and fit specifications. In today's global marketplace, many product developers who once relied on a *derivative* design process are rethinking that business strategy. Increasingly, product developers like Kohl's are setting up their own design departments and developing their own silhouettes. However, the practice of *borrowing* the ideas of others continues to be prevalent and is not limited to low price points; runway designers have been known to "adapt" successful ideas from their peers.

While some retail product developers are implementing a less derivative approach to design, new chains such as Zara and H & M have been credited with developing the concept of fast fashion—the ability to take an idea seen on designer runways and interpret the look for their own stores in as little as 2 to 6 weeks. These knockoffs copy the styling and proportions of the runway

Figure 8.3. *These tank tops can be classified as a basic body, a silhouette that is repeated season after season in different colors and patterns.*

garment while adding their own interpretation in terms of color and fabrication. According to Lauren Weber, a number of factors make fast fashion possible:

- The availability of runway photos almost immediately after shows take place and before the designer garments are available for purchase

- Designers and manufacturers at all price points subscribing to the same trend and color forecasting services

- Multiple designers sourcing their manufacturing with the same factories

- More sophisticated technology that allows the knockoffs to be developed faster (Weber 2004)

Runway garments and the low-price knockoffs that mimic them differ in both quality and fit, but where designers sell several hundred of their ready-to-wear garments for thousands of dollars each, the knockoff may sell tens of thousands for under $100.

The magazine *Marie Claire* includes a feature devoted to fashion knockoffs called "Splurge vs. Steal" where it pictures designer runway garments next to a cheaper knockoff. Magazines such *Lucky* and *In Style*, and TV shows like *The Look for Less*, are based on a similar premise. Shoppers are eager to re-create looks from the runway or the red carpet at a price they can afford. To a certain extent, it is this ability to enter into the world of the rich and famous that energizes fashion and keeps it alive for the mass market.

One way that designers who have runway shows are addressing this issue is by launching their own *diffusion lines*, lower-priced lines adapted from their signature line. Alexander McQueen launched a diffusion line in Fall 2006 and Badgley Mischka in Spring 2007 (Figure 8.4). Another strategy is to enter into co-branding or exclusive brand agreements with a retailer. Karl Lagerfeld, Stella McCartney, and Viktor & Rolf have all designed collections for H & M. These agreements are variations of licensing.

Legal Protection for the Design of Apparel

The premise of fashion is that basic elements are constantly mixed and morphed into new combinations that reflect the times. David Bollier and Laurie Racine explain:

With great speed and flexibility, fashion constantly expresses shifting cultural moods, social demographics and personal identities with new apparel designs and accessories. This remarkable and turbulent

Figure 8.4. *The Badgley Mischka diffusion line was launched in Spring 2007.*

drama is, in turn, seamlessly integrated into a complicated market apparatus of global production, marketing and distribution. It is no accident that fashion permits and even celebrates the appropriation and modification of other people's creative designs; these practices are an indispensable part of the process (Bollier and Racine, 2005, 6).

One of the arguments for intellectual property protection is that it is necessary to stimulate creativity by providing incentives for creators to control access to their works and collect payment for them. Interestingly, in spite of the lack of intellectual property protection for fashion, fashion companies at every price point continue to make money; designers continue to be a hot commodity;

and creativity thrives (Cox and Jenkins 2005, 5). One of the issues in protecting apparel designs is how to ascertain ownership of any design when fashion itself is so derivative. Did Coco Chanel really invent the *little black dress?* (Case Study 8.2, Control of Creativity? Fashion's Secret).

Intellectual property laws include copyright protection, trademark and trade dress protection, and patents. Patents have the least application to fashion; they protect new and useful processes, machines, products, and compositions. The ornamental aspects of fashion are generally not novel enough to be distinguishable from previous types of clothing, and ornamental patent protection is issued only when the design is not dictated by the function of the product. It is difficult to separate apparel design from its function. Therefore, most U.S. courts have ruled that apparel designs do not meet the requirements for patent (Cox and Jenkins, 2005 10). Securing a patent is relatively expensive and time-consuming; given the brief life cycle of an apparel design, patents are not a viable option for pursuing design protection.

Copyright Protection

In the United States, **copyright law** provides legal protection for authors of *nonuseful,* original compositions, including literary, dramatic, artistic, and musical works. Copyright protection is denied to clothing on the grounds that garment designs are intrinsically useful articles. Copyrights can be obtained for two-dimensional fabric designs, unique combinations of knit stitches, patterns on lace, original sketches, and on occasion the unique design of ornamental trims such as buttons and buckles. Some accessories may be copyrightable if they have a nonutilitarian purpose. In the United States, the copyright for work done while employed by a product developer is owned by the employer, not the employee, unless specific language to the contrary is written into a contract. Freelance designers must address ownership within the terms of their contract.

United States courts have been guided by the principle that although copyright protection "might benefit certain designers, it could create monopolies in the fashion industry that would stifle the creativity of future designers, hinder competition and drive up prices for consumer goods. The less affluent would not be able to afford the range of fashions they currently enjoy" (Cox and Jenkins 2005, 6). The Council of Fashion Designers of America (CFDA) thinks differently. It has been lobbying Congress to support a bill that would offer copyright-like protection to clothing designs, giving designers the exclusive right to make, import, distribute, and sell clothes based on their designs for a period of three years (Lanman 2006). Other proposals suggest that 1-year protection is more reasonable. Narciso Rodriguez met with a group of senators in July 2005 to promote the CFDA copyright proposal. During the meeting, he held up one of his dresses priced at $1,500; several hundred were sold, contributing to sales of $400,000. He then showed them a Macy's advertisement

CASE STUDY 8.2 CONTROL OF CREATIVITY? FASHION'S SECRET*

AMHERST, MASS., AND DURHAM, N.C.—Why do fashion, film, and music—the sultans of cool in our culture, . . . take such radically different approaches to the control of creativity?

The music and film industries continue to battle over the need to expand copyright protection, and to limit sharing and reuse of prior work. The fashion industry, driven by similar market interests, employs a modus operandi that accepts rather than rejects derivation and appropriation as creative tools.

. . .[T]he fashion industry long has accepted that creativity is too large and fugitive an essence to be owned outright as property. Fashion is a massive industry that thrives in a competitive global environment despite minimal legal protections for its creative design. While many people dismiss fashion as trivial and ephemeral, its economic importance and cultural influence are enormous. US apparel sales alone were $180 billion a few years ago, supporting an estimated 80,000 garment factories, and fashion is a major force in music, entertainment, and other creative sectors.

It is precisely because fashion pervades so many aspects of our lives that we fail to appreciate the "social ecology" that supports it—the open sharing, unauthorized innovations, and creative appropriations. To be sure, the fashion industry aggressively protects its brand names and logos, utilizing trademarks and licensing agreements. In most cases, however, the actual creative design of garments is not owned by anyone. The couturier dress worn by a Hollywood starlet on the red carpet can be knocked off immediately and legally appear days later on department store racks.

The fashion world understands that creativity is a collaborative and community affair. It's far too big, robust, and evolving for any one player to "own" as a legal entitlement. Long lineages of couturiers from Balenciaga to Ungaro, Chanel to Lagerfeld, and Gucci to Tom Ford have shown that designers necessarily must learn, adopt, and adapt from those who have blazed previous trails.

If one were to deconstruct their work, an evolutionary chain of distinct themes, references, design nuances, and outright appropriations could be discerned.

Occasionally someone may protest a "rip-off" and get murmurs of sympathy. And the counterfeiting of brand-name products is rightly condemned as theft. However, in general, creative derivation is an accepted premise of fashion. . . .

Is it possible that the fashion industry, long patronized as a realm of the ephemeral and insubstantial, is the real bellwether for future ideas of "ownership" of creative content? Through fashion we have a ringside seat on the ecology of creativity in a world of networked communication. Ideas arise, evolve through collaboration, gain currency through exposure, mutate in new directions and diffuse through imitation. The constant borrowing, repurposing, and transformation of prior work are as integral to creativity in music and film as they are to fashion.

Creativity can endure only so much private control before it careens into a downward spiral of sterile involution. If it is to be fresh, passionate, and transformative, creativity must have the room to breathe and grow, "unfettered and alive." The legendary designer Coco Chanel understood this reality. She once said, "Fashion is not something that exists in dresses only; fashion is something in the air. It's the wind that blows in the new fashion; you feel it coming, you smell it . . . in the sky, in the street; fashion has to do with ideas, the way we live, what is happening."

The fashion world recognizes that creativity cannot be bridled and controlled and that obsessive quests to do so will only diminish its vitality. Other content industries would do well to heed this wisdom.

*Adapted from David Bollier and Laurie Racine, *The Christian Science Monitor,* September 9, 2003, www.csmonitor.com. Copyright 2007 The Christian Science Monitor. All rights reserved. David Bollier and Laurie Racine are senior fellows at the Norman Lear Center at the University of Southern California Annenberg School for Communication.

featuring a nearly identical dress priced at $199 that generated sales of $8 million (Zargani 2005, Wilson 2006).

On March 1, 1989, the United States agreed to the Berne Convention for the Protection of Literary and Artistic works, which includes rules similar to what the CFDA is proposing. Under full international rule compliance, the creative works of fashion designers are protected by copyright for a limited term; however, the United States complies with only the minimum requirements of the Berne Convention provisions. Therefore, Europeon designs are subject to the same lack of protection that American designs get in the United States; European countries protect U.S. designs in the same way they protect the copyrights of their own nationals. As a result, some European designers choose not to distribute their goods in the United States.

French law offers even greater protection than the Berne Convention. The current French copyright system has its origins in the Copyright Act of 1793, which classified fashion as applied art. Accordingly, fashion, especially haute couture, is considered an art form rather than functional clothing. Saint Laurent was fined $11,000 in 1985 for copying a toreador jacket from designer Jacques Esterel. Similarly, in 1994 Polo/Ralph Lauren was fined $383,000 by a French court for copying Saint Laurent's tuxedo dress (Magdo 2000). Some fashion authorities assert that Paris is the center of fashion, in part, due to the copyright protection provided for the fashion industry. But these examples beg the question: How do courts discern who came up with an idea first? And do we want to saddle an already overburdened legal system with these questions?

Trademark and Trade Dress

At present, trademark and trade dress law is the best legal strategy for designers to challenge knockoffs of their work. A **trademark** is any word, name, symbol, device, or combination thereof that is adopted and used by a manufacturer or merchant to identify goods and distinguish them from those manufactured and sold by others. *Nike* and its "swoosh" logo are both examples of trademarks, as is the Levi Strauss stitching pattern on the back pocket of jeans; similarly, the name *Chanel* and the logo of the interlocking Cs are protected.

The public recognizes trademarks and expects a certain caliber of product to be associated with the mark. Trademark law protects the designer from unauthorized use of the registered mark, but does not protect the actual garment (or accessory) design. **Trade dress** is a broader term that covers the totality of elements in which a product or service is packaged and presented. Trade dress can include the shape and appearance of a product or its packaging, the cover of a book or magazine, or the unique layout and appearance of a business establishment.

Many counterfeit goods originate in China. China's accession to full WTO status requires that Chinese companies adhere to WTO guidelines when it comes to counterfeit and piracy control. The legal framework in China is for the most part complete; China is now a signatory to all relevant international conventions, treaties, and protocols. Laws pertaining to trademarks, designs, copyright, and patents are comprehensive. Border customs and inland public- enforcement officials have the power to seize offending goods (Bartman 2003, 9). To take advantage of these laws, a company's trademarks must be registered (Case Study 8.3, Trademark, Copyright, and Patent Costs, with Figure 8.6).

In spite of China's promise to crack down on fake goods, it has been difficult to stop a counterfeiting industry that generates billions of dollars and provides much-needed jobs, particularly for the rural poor. A recent lawsuit by Prada, Chanel, Burberry Group, LVMH Moët Hennessy Louis Vuitton SA, and PPR SA's Gucci was successful in closing down Beijing Xiushui Haosen Clothing Market Company; unfortunately, the next day it was operating in a new building on the same block. Experts suggest that up to 90 percent of all protected intellectual property sold in China is actually counterfeit (Fitzpatrick 2006).

Some of that product is shipped to the United States and Europe (Figure 8.5). It used to be sold blatantly on street corners throughout Manhattan. Today the goods are invisible, but still widely available. Vendors on Canal Street in Chinatown claim that they have no fake bags to sell, but then follow promising-looking customers to the sidewalk, where they offer to take the customer to the bags. The goods are sold from the basements and back rooms of storefronts that advertise manicures and pedicures or other services (Holt 2004). These same counterfeit goods are sold at *purse parties* all across the United States. Some of these goods use deceivingly similar trademarks to the trademark of the product they are counterfeiting; others blatantly use the protected trademark. Some are actually authentic goods that were rejected for quality reasons but not destroyed.

Increasingly, designers are opening signature stores in cities like Shanghai in order to better protect their brand equity. It is important for designers to develop a personal code of ethics that they incorporate into their design process (Case Study 8.4, What Makes a Fake?, with Figure 8.7).

Organizing the Line

Not so long ago, designers spent a lot of time developing ideas that never made it into the line. Today product development teams are more focused. Merchandisers and designers work together to determine the scope and creative concepts for the line so that time is not wasted on designs that will never be produced. The actual number of garments in a seasonal line varies greatly depending on the size of the business, the season, the product line, the breadth of distribution, and the economic climate. Each design reviewed is evaluated carefully based on the needs of the business. Those that do not

Figure 8.5. *A shipment of counterfeit North Face jackets.*

meet the criteria established by the product development team are weeded out. The staff settles on an assortment of product ideas that meets all the established criteria, which are then sent forward for technical design. Lines are developed either as items or as a group.

Item Line Development

In general, lines created around goods that are intended to be sold alone, one piece at a time, are considered **item lines**. Dresses, suits, coats, jeans, T-shirts, and swimwear are examples of categories that are frequently developed as item lines. Sportswear garments, designed as items as opposed to coordinated groups, are sometimes referred to as **separates**.

Separates lines frequently include a limited number of styles developed in a wide array of colors. Brands such as Lands' End and J. Crew are known for their separates lines. Their color palette is coordinated across a variety of categories so that the goods can be appealingly merchandised in the brand's stores, catalogs, and Web sites, but these product developers understand that their customers are not seeking outfits that match. Separates customers are just as likely to buy multiple items of the same style in different colors as they are to buy pieces that they intend to wear together. It is not uncommon for a single T-shirt, sweatshirt, or polo shirt style to be offered in 5 to 10 different colors. These assortments have a longer shelf life, since they are not designed for their fashion edge. They are more apt to be replenished rather than replaced

CASE STUDY 8.3 TRADEMARK, COPYRIGHT, AND PATENT COSTS

New York—WWD created a fictitious handbag with several trademark designs so attorneys could put a price tag on protecting the intellectual property.

Conservative estimates of the total cost to protect every element that might potentially qualify (such as the WWD trademark, W trademark, fabric copyright, design patent on bag shape, utility patent on clasp, etc.) put the grand total at $10,200. But if problems arise, or if the process is complicated by a legal hurdle, that figure could rise as high as $19,500. Regarding worldwide trademark registration, the price tag could reach $3 million.

Surprisingly, WWD found that several of the design elements would be difficult to protect under current laws. It's also important to note that there are two factors in determining the cost of protecting an item. There's the cost of registration with government organizations, as well as the legal fees associated with getting help to file those registrations.

Legal fees vary from firm to firm. Some industry sources estimate that in New York and Los Angeles, attorney fees range from $600 to $700 an hour. That rate differs according to the size of the law firm, the services offered, and its specific fee structure.

Overall Look of Bag/W shape: Design Patent
Cost: $2,000 to $5,000
Design patents apply to the overall shape and look of an item. Patents are difficult to obtain and take much more time and money than copyright or trademark applications. It is possible that the "W" shape of this bag could be protected by a

Figure 8.6. *This bag illustrates a number of design elements that qualify for trademark protection.*

design patent, but unlikely, according to trademark lawyers. Design patents cover the ornamental features of something that is otherwise a utilitarian item. Both kinds of patent protection are difficult to get because the item must be proven to be completely unique compared with anything that has come before it.

TYPICAL FEE SCHEDULE
Trademark
Filing fee: $375 per trademark, per class of goods on paper, $325 if filed electronically (additional fees are attached to any documents filed after registration, as well).
Search fee: Preliminary, $150 to $300.
Search fee: Full, $400 to $500, double for expedited searches.

Copyright
Filing fee: $30 to the U.S. Copyright Office.

Design Patent
Filing fee: $200
Search fee: $100
Examination fee: $130

Utility Patent
Filing fee: $300
Search fee: $500
Examination fee: $200

Source: Casabone and Tucker 2006, 12–13

CASE STUDY 8.4 WHAT MAKES A FAKE?

New York—Brand owners are shifting their attention from pursuing street-level peddlers of counterfeit goods to training police officers and Customs officials around the globe on how to spot fakes before they enter the market.

. . . [It] may be as simple a matter as pointing out that their products are only manufactured in one or two countries. [Other] brands are adding special design elements to identify their products as legitimate. While creating exact replicas of these features is not impossible for counterfeiters, spending the necessary time and money to do so is unlikely. Here are a few of the telltale signs for which [one] company trains police and Customs officials to be on the lookout. . . .

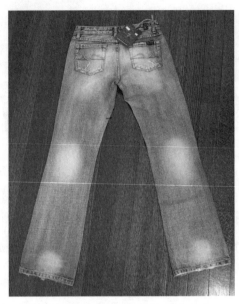

Figure 8.7. *A pair of counterfeit 7 for All Mankind jeans.*

Interior Tags

The . . . interior tag . . . reads "Made in China." Seven jeans are manufactured in the U.S. For Customs officials, isolating potential Seven counterfeits up front can be straightforward: anything imported is not genuine. Additionally, the order of the tags is wrong. The tag with the size, style, cut and country of origin on the front and the care instructions on the back is on top of the tag showing the stylized Seven trademark . . . . in genuine Seven jeans. The font is also different on the logos and text.

Exterior Tags

The hangtag logo and fonts are off on . . . the exterior tags of a pair of counterfeit jeans and a genuine pair. . . . [Also] . . . the twine is too thick and of low quality. . . . The tag on these jeans is glossy, thick card stock; [h]angtags on genuine Seven . . . jeans are made of a thinner paper with a matte finish. . . . In addition, the tags sewn onto the garment have a logo that is not accurate, and lower-quality stitching and fabric are visible.

Construction

A number of loose threads are visible on the interior of the seams—a clear sight that this is not a genuine Seven product. The rivets are missing off the back pockets and the stitching used to attach the pocket does not follow the unique pattern used on Seven jeans. Seven always uses YKK zippers—no YKK logo is visible on this zipper tab.

Source: Casabona 2006

by new merchandise and do not need to be marked down until the end of the season. Typically, product developers of separates lines use fit, proportions, styling, color assortment, and/or quality to achieve a competitive edge.

Item lines in categories such as dresses, swimwear, and coats are developed somewhat differently. Multiple small groups of three to six dresses might be designed for each delivery. Each dress group is designed using one to three related fabrics (Figure 8.8). A solid fabric might be offered in two or three colors; a challis or georgette might be used in two or three related prints.

Figure 8.8. *Donna Ricco works with a customer to get input on fabric selection for a group line of dresses.*

Although most customers purchase one dress at a time, the product developer must offer a retailer groups of dresses that will hang well together and offer the final consumer some degree of choice.

If the product developer's distribution is large enough that it frequently sells to multiple retailers in the same mall, it needs to be able to sell different styles/prints to each vendor. Using a related fabric for several styles also helps these product developers to meet minimum yardage requirements (Figure 8.9). Similarly, a single swimwear fabric may be offered in three or four different styles that appeal to different customers—for example, a tankini, a bikini, and a halter-style suit. Firms that focus on only one classification of product may find themselves vulnerable to the vagaries of fashion. Categories such as swimwear and dresses are seasonal—both doing much more business in spring-summer than in the fall.

Item lines are particularly appropriate for markets such as juniors, where disposable income is limited and fashion interest is high. Product developers may concentrate on adapting street fashion looks at the lowest price point possible. These lines are not especially focused on quality because this consumer's taste changes from season to season.

By specializing in a particular classification of product, item manufacturers can take advantage of economies of scale—ordering large amounts of fabric at the best price—and of specialized construction expertise. Item lines frequently start out making a single product category and broaden their product base as the company grows. For example, outerwear product developers might extend their item line business by offering similar products for men, women, and children.

Figure 8.9. *A group line of dresses is often developed around a coordinated group of fabrics.*

Coordinated Group Line Development

Coordinated group lines consist of items organized around fabric groups and intended to be purchased and worn together. A coordinated group line might consist of 15 to 30 or more pieces—skirts, pants, jackets, tops, blouses, and sweaters—that consumers can combine in a way that pleases their personal fashion sensibility. A large group might include wide leg and narrow leg pants (if both are in style); a cropped pant; skirts in several different silhouettes and lengths; several jackets in different proportions; and tops, blouses, and sweaters. The balance within the group depends on target customers' preferences and current fashion trends, but usually includes more tops than bottoms, since blouses and sweaters can be layered with jackets and coats. The concept of coordinates provides consumers with confidence that their look is pulled together and fashionable, while giving them the option of selecting among garments that compliment their personal needs.

The fabrics used in a coordinated group line are meant to be mixed and matched so that the customer can purchase a jacket with either a matched or coordinating skirt or pant (Figure 8.10). The colors within the fabric story are approved to match all the other fabrics included in the same group. The complete coordinated group may be available only through the brand's signature store. Individual stores will buy the line to match their target customer's preferences. Stores in warmer climates won't buy the heavy coats, jackets, and sweaters. Instead, they will choose multiseason fabrications in seasonal colors. Stores in rural areas may not buy the high fashion items; their assortments may focus on the least expensive items and most basic styles. If several anchor department stores, located in the same mall, carry the brand, the group must be large enough that it can be merchandised differently for each store.

New coordinated groups are typically delivered every 4 to 6 weeks; fast fashion suppliers, such as Zara, pride themselves on introducing new items every two weeks. Early fall collections revolve around seasonless fabrics. As the season progresses and the weather gets cooler, fabric groups will include heavier-weight wools, leather, and specialty fibers. Collections meant for holiday selling may include some dressier fabrications. Items within the group are not replenished; rather the remaining pieces are marked down and cleared out as new deliveries arrive. This is meant to encourage consumers to make their purchases at full price while their size and styling preferences are still available. In general, coordinates are on the selling floor for 6 to 10 weeks and are sold at full price for 4 to 6 weeks.

Figure 8.10. *A coordinated group of fabrics ties a group line together.*

Coordinated groups are designed around a theme that may be expressed through a distinctive color palette, a unique fabric, or repeated use of an interesting detail. The theme helps to attract the consumer to the collection. An advantage of group lines is that if one style within the group does not sell well, the style can be dropped and the yardage that was committed to it can be diverted to production of another style that is selling better than expected.

This approach has been more challenging in recent years due to the popularity of separates, the tendency for more casual professional dress, and the consumer's quest for individuality. As a response, some coordinates designers are incorporating a broader range of fabrics into a single group and mixing traditional suit pieces with more casual weekend pieces in their groupings. Other coordinates designers are doing more small capsule groups. Whatever their approach, knowledge of customer preferences is key. The current fashion environment, where more fashion choices co-exist in any given season, makes design decisions more challenging, with each decision carrying more financial risk.

Parameters of Line Development

Whether a brand is known for separates or coordinated groups, product is developed according to what is known about the preferences of the target customer. Parameters of line developent include an understanding of the price points the customer is willing to pay, styling in terms of aesthetics and fashion level, and timing. Once the line is designed, decisions must be made as to how to balance production orders to match orders and sales projections.

Pricing

A brand's price point is part of its identity. The price point is one of several factors that determines where a product will be sold, the brands it competes with, the range of fabrics that can be used, and who can afford to shop for it. Consumers tend to assume that price is also indicative of quality—this may or may not be true.

Price also affects the volume that will be produced of each style. At very high price points, hundreds of an individual style may be produced; at very low price points, hundreds of thousands may be produced. Garments that are priced very low are generally not heavily advertised and may not be marked down until they are clearanced out. Customers recognize that these garments are priced to include the lowest possible margin week in and week out. High-priced garments achieve some of their cachet through advertising, which adds significantly to their cost. Because so few are made, higher margins must be built in to the price of each piece. They are not as widely distributed because part of their value lies in their limited distribution.

A brand's price position affects the materials that can be used. Often the difference between a high-priced designer fashion and a low-priced knockoff is in the materials. The impact of price on fashion level is more difficult to categorize. H & M customers may be just as interested in fashion as their counterparts at designer signature stores, but, they most certainly will express their fashion sensibility in ways that reflect their different lifestyles and budgets. Price also affects quality expectations. Frequently customers who buy inexpensive, trendy merchandise don't expect that merchandise to last for more than a season. Customers who pay more for their apparel frequently expect it to last longer.

Most seasonal lines include a few loss lead items, styles that may be developed from a past season, that can be produced inexpensively, and that are value priced. The bulk of the line should be priced at the brand's sweet spot—a price point that the customer has come to expect and can afford. A few items may be very special; they may be priced higher due to a unique feature that will appeal to the brand's most fashion-forward customers. That feature may be use of a high-tech fabric or a hand-crafted design detail. These items can be important to a brand's image even though they typically don't sell at high volumes.

Fashion Level

Just as designers must understand their brand's price point parameters, brands also are associated with a fashion level appropriate to a particular customer. Customers return to a brand when they are successful in finding apparel that matches their fashion point of view—styles that are fashion-appropriate, age-appropriate, and role-appropriate. Brand designers must understand their customer's styling and fit preferences and should not stray too far from those expectations. Part of knowing a customer's styling preferences is understanding how closely they follow fashion trends. Both bridge customers and high-end contemporary customers are tuned in to fashion; bridge customers, however, interpret trends a bit more conservatively, seek more role-appropriate apparel, and may not be able to wear the extremes of fashion. High-end contemporary brands are sold at a price point similar to bridge, but their customer may be younger at heart, have a more toned figure, and be more playful in interpreting fashion.

No matter what the fashion point of view, most brands include both basic and fashion goods in their line; it is the balance between these two categories that varies from brand to brand. Fashion goods change frequently. A fast fashion store such as Zara brings in new merchandise every 2 weeks, allowing it to respond to the subtle changes in fashion palettes, silhouettes, and details. Basic products are those products for which there is little demand for style change. A brand such as Lands' End might introduce a basic product for fall/winter and offer that same product for a 26-week selling period. Its customer values quality over style change. The styling of basics typically changes little from one

Figure 8.11. *A pyramid assortment plan anticipates that the bulk of seasonal sales will come from basic merchandise and that the lowest percentage of seasonal sales will come from fashion items.*

FASHION ITEMS

KEY ITEMS FOR SEASON

BASIC MERCHANDISE

season to the next, allowing for carryover styles. *Carryover styles* are very cost-effective, since the pattern and fit only need to be developed once. However, subtle adjustments in the final fit may need to be made due to differences in fabric hand or shrinkage.

Some brands rely on their fashion styles to produce most of their volume, and other brands rely on their basics for volume. One model for assortment planning is the pyramid plan (Figure 8.11). The lowest and broadest level of the pyramid is made up of basic styles that carry little risk and can be ordered in large quantities and assortments. The middle level of the pyramid carries more risk. It is made up of key items that reflect how the product developer interprets current fashion trends for the core customer. These *key items* are critical to maintaining the product developer's core customer. The point of the pyramid consists of fashion-forward items that help to create an image and expose the customer to new trends. These items are not produced in great quantities. A pyramid plan works for basics product developers; the planning model for fast fashion product developers would be very different. A brand must never lose sight of what its customer expects.

Timing Considerations

A merchandise budget and the resulting line plan must consider seasonal timing as it pertains to product category. Timing considerations may vary by product category. Fall is generally the biggest season for coordinates product developers; spring is typically the bigger season for dress product developers. Timing considerations also take into account weather and seasonal shopping habits. Transitional groups may be produced in smaller volume, since they are generally worn during that brief period in which summer morphs into fall; the fall palette is appropriate but temperatures may still be warm. Resort may also be a low-volume season, since only a portion of a brand's customer base may have a lifestyle that affords warm weather vacations. Many customers may not yet be ready to purchase spring/summer apparel, since they are not ready to wear it. Although these seasons may be low-volume, they can be some of the most interesting in terms of fashion direction. Their smaller size allows the designer to perfect his or her fashion concept. They may be more experimental so that they can be used as a barometer in editing the high-volume groups to follow.

Collections delivered just before Thanksgiving are typically produced in larger volume to accommodate the holiday selling period. These collections must include items suitable for gift giving (appropriate price point and easy to fit). They may also include a greater number of dressier items appropriate for holiday entertaining. Children's wear product developers may count on the back-to-school season for heavier volume than at other times of year. Merchandise budgets are developed accordingly; they anticipate doing more business at certain times of the year and less business at other times, depending on the product category.

Balancing the Line

Balancing the assortment plan and resulting product line determines the volume that will be made of each SKU. Understanding the factors that a merchandiser considers will help the designer to know where to focus his or her efforts. A line is considered balanced when it includes a range of garments that satisfies the preferences of the target customer. Merchandisers consider a number of factors when balancing the line: the assortment variety, volume, and distribution.

Assortment Variety

Each product produced embodies several assortment factors—a style, a size, and a color—and is accounted for as a **stock keeping unit (SKU)**. A designer may design a single garment, but if that garment is made in seven sizes and three colors, it results in 21 SKUs for which fabric and trim must be ordered, manufacturing capacity reserved, specs developed, quality monitored, and the related decisions involved with sales and marketing made. Decisions must be made regarding how many styles, in how many colors, and in what size range.

Figure 8.12. *Item lines rely on a few styles in multiple colors.*

Size is perhaps the easiest decision. If a brand has a good fit and an appropriate size range, developers generally don't change it. Most styles are made in a full range of sizes. An exception might be for a high-fashion style that would not be flattering in a large size and may only be carried by top tier retailers. Some brands derive their petite and large size lines directly from their missy line. In these cases, they select the styles they believe will translate into another size category, and develop the style in another complete size range. This is not the best way of developing petite or large size lines, but the practice is prevalent.

Color decisions may be somewhat more complicated. There are different ways to view color assortments. It may be a means of selling a group in a different way to two retailers that anchor the same mall. Having a sufficient range of colors often helps sell a basic garment or key item. A cashmere sweater in the season's must-have color may help to drive sales. Offering only neutrals or colors that a consumer already has in his or her wardrobe fails to inspire interest. In general, colors should have a reason for being in the mix—one color appeals to cool skin tones and another to warm tones. One color appeals to the more conservative target customer and the other to the fashion-forward. This knowledge will be further refined as the assortment volume and distribution are planned. A more fashion-forward cropped jacket may only be made in the fashion-forward color. The conservative blazer may be best in a neutral color or a color familiar from the past season. Not every style needs to be made in a full range of colors; a style made in the wrong colors can fail to meet projections.

Item lines will frequently develop their assortments based on a few styles in multiple colors (Figure 8.12). Coordinates' lines develop their assortments based on numerous styles in very limited colors. Too few styles will frustrate the customer who can't find what he or she wants. Too many choices can cause a consumer to put off making any decision.

Assortment Volume

Assortment volume takes into account demand for certain styles, sizes, and colors. A product developer does not sell equal numbers of each style. In a coordinates group, a jacket may pair well with several skirts or pants, so more jackets may be sold than any one style of coordinating skirts or pants.

At one time most brands assumed that they would sell fewer small and large sizes and more of the sizes in the middle. For every dozen garments, the size distribution looked something like this:

1 size 6 + 2 size 8s + 3 size 10s + 3 size 12s + 2 size 14s + 1 size 16

Today many brands offer a wider range of sizes starting as low as 0 or 2. Designer brands might sell more of the smaller sizes and may not even produce garments beyond size 12. Mass market brands are finding they need to plan their volume according to historic data on their specific customer. In general, they are selling more large sizes than they have in the past. The formula that works for one brand most likely will not work for another. Stores frequently require different size assortments for stores in different parts of the country. A designer must be aware of the target customer's size range and style preferences. (See chapter 11 for more on sizing.)

Similarly, a seasonal color palette typically includes a mix of colors and neutrals. A trendy new color may be included in the palette to send a message to the customer that the brand is on trend; however, the merchandising team may know up front that their customer will not buy the new color in great volume. Assortment plans must anticipate the volume a particular style will do by color. In children's wear it may be easy. Most girls' favorite color is pink or purple. In women's wear, the decisions are much more difficult. In spite of color forecasts, customers sometimes surprise the marketplace with their long-term affection for a particular color. For example, pink defied color forecasts by its longevity between 2002 and 2007. Conversely, colors such as yellow and orange will generally not sell in high volume, even when they are "in fashion," because they are not flattering on everyone. Neutrals like black will sell well in some markets and not in others. Again, success is dependent on knowing the customer.

Assortment Distribution

Assortment distribution takes into account where each item will be sold. Signature stores and Web sites may offer the entire line. Other stores will carry only a portion of the line. Retail stores are sometimes categorized into A, B, and C levels. Stores may be categorized by volume or by fashion level; product will be shipped to them accordingly. Stores in large urban areas are likely to carry the most fashion-forward items. Stores in more rural areas will base their assortments on the more conservative, classic items. Some very large retailers may demand exclusive distribution for the groups they carry.

Communicating Design Concepts

The line is reviewed several times during its development. Generally, the initial concept for groups in each delivery are reviewed; at this time fabric and color direction are approved. Once the concept is approved, silhouette development begins. As each group is designed, it is presented to the merchandisers and vice-presidents of product development for line review. Once silhouettes have been approved, they go to technical design, where technical flats are developed. A sampling of presentation art is included in the chapter 8 appendix.

Concept Boards

With the scope of the line identified, the design team must present ideas that will meet the criteria of the assortment plan. Designers often start by developing **concept boards** that illustrate the theme for the line. Concept boards vary in their complexity; they may be developed on the computer or collaged using cut and paste methods that combine color chips, fabrics samples, and trend research in the form of tear sheets, digital images, or sketches from shopping trips. The process of deciding which images to include on the board helps the designer to focus his or her ideas. Concept boards should convey the key colors, fabrics, silhouettes, and details that the designer has identified as themes for each group in the line. They may be presented to merchandisers, vice-presidents, and buyers, so they must communicate clearly your vision of the line to come. Once the concept board is presented and approved, designing can begin in earnest.

Line Review

As the group coalesces, it is once again presented for line review. At this time, all the silhouettes in each group are presented, including their color asortment and fabrication. The stakeholders who are part of line review will make decisions as to which styles will go into production. The line review presentation may take a variety of forms. In some companies the line is presented as polished story boards that describe the concept, the colors and materials, and the silhouettes. Other companies utilize storyboards that are divided into grids. Each fabric in the line is mounted and followed by the styles that are being considered for that fabric choice.

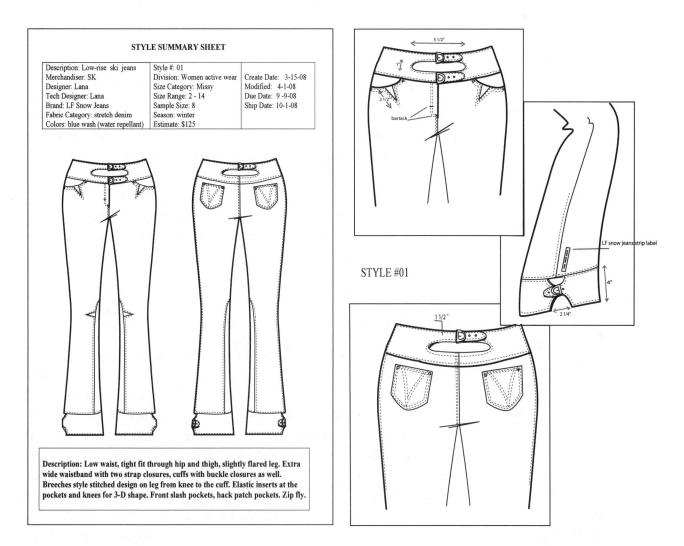

STYLE SUMMARY SHEET

Description: Low-rise ski jeans	Style #: 01	Create Date: 3-15-08
Merchandiser: SK	Division: Women active wear	Modified: 4-1-08
Designer: Lana	Size Category: Missy	Due Date: 9-9-08
Tech Designer: Lana	Size Range: 2 - 14	Ship Date: 10-1-08
Brand: LF Snow Jeans	Sample Size: 8	
Fabric Category: stretch denim	Season: winter	
Colors: blue wash (water repellant)	Estimate: $125	

Description: Low waist, tight fit through hip and thigh, slightly flared leg. Extra wide waistband with two strap closures, cuffs with buckle closures as well. Breeches style stitched design on leg from knee to the cuff. Elastic inserts at the pockets and knees for 3-D shape. Front slash pockets, back patch pockets. Zip fly.

STYLE #01

Figure 8.13. *Technical flats define the proportions, details, and construction required for production purposes. Callouts magnify construction details.*

Flats

Once a design has been reviewed and accepted into the line, the technical design department will develop what's called a spec flat or a technical flat. Technical flats are generally developed on the computer so they can be included in the spec package which will be communicated to supply chain partners digitally. **Technical flats** define the proportions, details, and construction required for production purposes. They may include measurements and sewing notations. Complex details are sometimes enlarged in a separate **callout** that magnifies an area in a way that a patternmaker or sewer understands exactly what is expected (Figure 8.13).

The ability to develop accurate flats quickly is an imperative skill for technical designers. Industry preference suggests finished flats use a bolder pen stroke for the silhouette outline, a medium pen stroke for interior construction lines, and a fine pen stroke for details. Topstitching should be drawn as broken lines.

Using a computer to develop flats can save a great deal of time. Silhouettes can be developed and stored in the computer so that the next time a similar silhouette is being developed, it is not necessary to start from scratch. Each flat should be developed over a template so that garments in the same category are the same size and garments in different categories are proportionate to one another. Each flat should be developed in layers, with the basic silhouette on one layer, component parts on another, and topstitching details on another. This will make it easier to modify an existing flat into a new style. Detail files may also be kept in the computer and combined with basic silhouettes in a host of variations. Digital flats do not require expensive industry-specific software; many companies use Adobe Illustrator to develop their flats. An advantage of industry-specific software packages is that they may include files of commonly used styling details, along with basic silhouettes that can facilitate the overall design process.

Summary

Only after the business plan has been established, the style trends have been explored, and the fabrics identified, does line development commence. With a potential line plan in mind, designers can focus their efforts on developing a range of styles that will meet all of the requirements of the business while providing appropriate, up-to-date choices for the customer. Lines may be developed as item lines or coordinated group lines. The design process varies depending on the type of line, the garment category, the price point, and the season. A production quantity must be determined for each stock keeping unit within the line. The line is reviewed at several times during line development, typically once the group concepts, colors, and fabrics have been determined and again after the silhouettes have been developed. Styles can be edited out of the group at any time if sales projections change, if it appears as though the silhouette cannot be manufactured on schedule, or if sales of that item fail to materialize.

Line concepts are presented as boards complete with fabric swatches and color chips. Once the line concept is approved, fabric development can commence as garment silhouettes are being developed. The finished line is presented in a line review. Each group may be presented on story boards or on a grid that includes each style in the line and the colors and fabric(s) it will be made in. Once the line is reviewed, approved styles are passed on to technical design where a technical flat is developed to indicate garment construction.

Key Terms

bodies	copyright law
callout	item line
concept board	knockoffs
coordinated group line	line

separates
stock keeping unit (SKU)
technical flats

trade dress
trademark

Discussion Questions

1. Identify some of your favorite brands. Are they organized as item lines or coordinated group lines?

2. Discuss the variety required for a group line targeted to young adults just entering the job market versus a group line targeted to professionals who are well established in their careers.

3. What are some of the reasons for eliminating potential garment styles from a line, other than their aesthetic value?

Activities

1. Visit an area mall. Shop a store that focuses on item lines. Identify several styles and how they are assorted by size and color. Then shop a store or department where the focus is on coordinated group lines. Study one group and identify the number of styles, fabrics, colors and sizes in which this line is available.

2. Using the business plan developed in Case Study 8.1, complete the following tasks:

   - Develop color and fabric selections for the season.

   - Develop the preliminary line plan for your selected product category, including decisions about the number of styles to include and an estimate of the number of preliminary sketches that will be needed to arrive at a final line plan.

   - Develop an array of croquis sketches for a line of coordinated sportswear or a well-defined item line. (Plan for enough extras to explore your styling ideas and to provide good variety for selection of the final line.)

   - Develop a completed storyboard presentation for the line, adding flats for each final selection; include technical flats where needed.

References

Bartman, Nick. 2003. How to fight fakes in China. *Business International,* February-March, 9–13.

Bollier, D., and L. Racine. 2005. Ready to share: Creativity in fashion and digital culture. Conference paper presented January 29. www.learcenter.org/html/publications (accessed September 8, 2006).

Casabona, Liza. 2006. What makes a fake. *Women's Wear Daily,* May 25.

Casabona, Liza, and Ross Tucker. 2006. Fighting knockoffs by protecting a brand. *Women's Wear Daily,* February 1.

Cox, C. , and J. Jenkins. 2005. Between the seams, a fertile commons: An overview of the relationship between fashion and intellectual property. Conference paper presented January 29. www.learcenter.org/html/publications (accessed September 9, 2006).

Fitzpatrick, Michael. 2006. Clamping down on Chinese copycats. www.just-style.com (accessed January 25, 2006).

Holt, Emily. 2004. Crackdowns aside, counterfeits galore. *Women's Wear Daily Weekend,* September 11–12.

Lanman, Henry. 2006. Jurisprudence: Copycatfight. www.slate.com (accessed March 14, 2006).

Magdo, Christine. 2000. Protecting works of fashion from design piracy. www.leda.law.harvard.edu. (accessed September 8, 2006).

Weber, Lauren. 2004. Better technology means faster fashion knockoffs. *Newsday,* September 25. www.newsday.com (accessed September 24, 2004).

Weller, Sally. 2003. Fashion's influence on garment mass production knowledge, commodities and the capture of value. Ph.D thesis, Centre for Strategic Economic Studies, Victoria University, Melbourne Australia, p. 91.

Wilson, Eric. 2006. O.K, knockoffs, this is war. *New York Times,* March 30. www.nytimes.com/2006/03/30/fashion (accessed September 30, 2006).

Zargani, Luisa. 2005. France, Italy focusing on copyrights, counterfeits. *Women's Wear Daily,* September 14.

Additional Resources

Boyes, Janet. 1998. *Essential fashion design.* London: B. T. Batsford Ltd.

Denny, Melanie, and Nancy Riegelman. 2003. *If informed fashion: Illustrations and flats.* Los Angeles, CA: Denny & Riegelman Publications.

Jones, Sue Jenkyn. 2002. *Fashion design.* New York: Watson-Guptill Publications.

Riegelman, Nancy. 2006. *9 heads: A guide to drawing fashion.* Los Angeles, CA: 9 Heads Media.

Riegelman, Nancy. 2006. *Colors for modern fashion: Drawing fashion with colored markers.* Los Angeles, CA: 9 Heads Media.

Seaman, Julian. 2001. *Foundation in fashion design and illustration.* London: B. T. Batsford, Ltd.

Sorger, Richad, and Jenny Udale. 2006. *The fundamentals of fashion design.* Switzerland: AVA Publishing SA.

Sultan, Barbara. 2003. *Computer-aided flat sketching for the fashion industry.* Los Angeles, CA: Da-max.

Sultan, Barbara. 1998. *Applied flat sketching for the fashion industry.* Los Angeles, CA: Da-max.

Sultan, Barbara. 1995. *Flat sketching for the fashion industry.* 9th ed. Los Angeles, CA: Da-max.

Tain, Linda. 2003. *Portfolio presentation for fashion designers.* 2nd ed. New York: Fairchild.

Tatham, Caroline, and Julian Seaman. 2003. *Fashion design drawing course.* Hauppauge, NY: Barron's Educational Series, Inc.

APPENDIX: Design Process Visuals

Concept board, illustrations, and filled flats for a young contemporary collection, courtesy of Jackie Ghazazadeh, Mount Mary College.

Concept board, color and fabric story, and illustrations for contemporary collection, courtesy of Marcie Buchholz, Mount Mary College.

Illustration and photo of sample garment for contemporary collection, courtesy of Erica Fox, Mount Mary College.

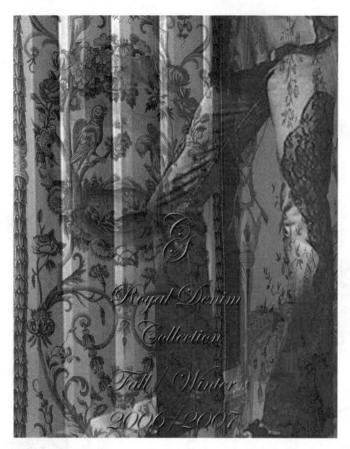

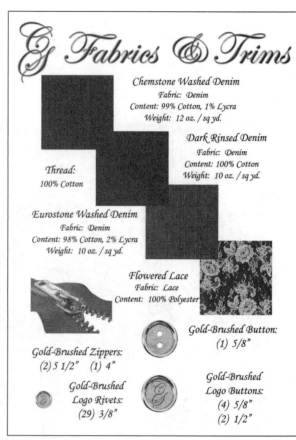

Concept board, fabric and trim specifications, and style summary sheet with flat, courtesy of Cassandra Schmidt Baumann, Mount Mary College.

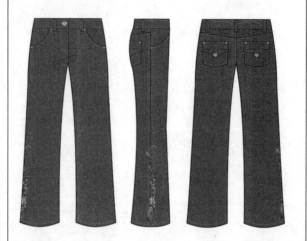

Style Number: 15690	Color: Eurostone Washed
Description: Boot-cut pants	Size Category: Misses'
Division: Womens' Coordinates	Size Range: 2-18
Designer: Cassandra Schmidt	Sample Size: 8

Description:
Low waist, slim fit through hips, boot-cut at hem. Contoured waistband, fly and button closure. Back yoke, back patch pockets with button closure, front pockets. Embroidered floral design on on right side leg, back waistband, and back pockets.

PART THREE

TECHNICAL DESIGN

CHAPTER 9

TRANSLATING CONCEPT TO PRODUCT

"The production of a pattern is an intermediate step, a technical guide through an established protocol. It contains information on how to set about the work. . . . The pattern invites us not to look but to do." —DIRK LAUWAERT*

OBJECTIVES

- To learn the role of patternmaking processes within product development

- To understand the role of standards and specifications in product development

- To identify the stages and components of the specification package

- To understand the importance of communication skills among partners in the supply chain

Previous chapters focus on methods of establishing a line's design direction from trend analysis through color management, fabrication, styling concepts, and sketching. The next step is for style ideas to be developed for production. Two interwoven processes occur at this time: the first is patternmaking; the second is the development of the specification package. The patternmaking process typically proceeds through development of a sample size pattern, which is followed by the creation of a sample garment that is checked for fit and adjustments to the style. Simultaneously, the specification package is begun. This spec package contains the pages of graphic and written information needed for producing the garments. It is at this stage that a style number for each design is assigned, fabric and component identification information developed, and costs of producing the style are projected. Once these decisions are made, the process moves to the technical design staff for preparation and approval of the production patterns and development of fit and construction specifications. The resulting specification package will become the foundation for communications with all partners throughout the product development process (Case Study 9.1, The Product Manager's Role at Moksha Worldwide).

*Lauwaert 2005, 42

Patternmaking

Patternmaking represents a critical step in the supply chain. **Patternmaking** is the interpretation of a garment concept, from either a sketch or another existing product, into a paper representation or model for use in production of a finished garment style. How this step will be accomplished is an important part of the product development process. Patternmaking capabilities for the projected product style must match the original garment concept, yet also meet the expectations of the target customer in relation to fashion, fit, price, and turnaround time. *Turnaround time* refers to the time frame required for completion of a garment from inception to delivery.

Methods of Pattern Development

Patternmaking methods have evolved over centuries into a set of highly technical skills. Patterns for new garments may be completed in numerous ways utilizing either two-dimensional (2D) or three-dimensional (3D) methods. The most used methods of patternmaking are 2D and include "flat, drafting and reverse engineering" (Anderson 2005). Historically, draping was the first method of patternmaking to be developed and is 3D. Product developers may use one method or utilize a combination of methods that is most appropriate for the specific product.

Flat-Pattern

Figure 9.1a. *The five-piece basic sloper used for flat-pattern development. Seam allowances are added to the pattern blocks as new styles are developed.*

The most widely used method of developing patterns in today's manufacturing environment is the flat-pattern method. **Flat-pattern** development involves making styling changes to a basic two-dimensional pattern. One

FIVE-PIECE SLOPER FOR PRODUCT DEVELOPMENT

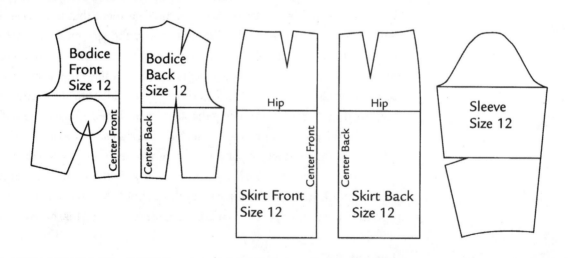

CASE STUDY 9.1 THE PRODUCT MANAGER'S ROLE
AT MOKSHA WORLDWIDE by Kelly Poorman

Moksha Worldwide is a small company in the Chicagoland area that specializes in manufacturing children's sports sleepwear and playwear. There are several daily responsibilities I juggle within my job description as a product manager for this company. We typically work a year in advance, which means that now [August 2006] I am beginning development for Fall 2007.

A typical season begins when the graphic design department develops a style that I will review and confirm as to whether the product is salable as illustrated. In mid-September, I begin costing with the overseas vendors to negotiate costs on each style. At that time I will also be sending out the CADs for licensing approval. CADs, the term we use for our specification package, is the illustrated art that goes to the vendor with specifics of silhouette, size ranges, body and trim content and color, season, screen/embroidery size and color, etc.

I am responsible for submitting all styles to our licensing contacts for the league the style pertains to, which could be for MLB (major league baseball), NFL (National Football League), or a college and university. Costs and licensing approvals will come in around the beginning of October. Once licensing has approved the style, I request the vendor to make samples of the style for fitting, fabric, and color approval.

While licensing is in the approval process, I will be negotiating back and forth with the vendors on cost, ordering salesman samples, and approving fabrics and colors for those samples.

When the sample arrives, I am in charge of measuring the garment to confirm it meets spec and fits on the body form. After completing that part of the process, I verify that the colors of the art and fabric are what design has illustrated on the CADs.

The product will officially go on sale to retailers around January 2 [2007]. The selling period is usually a 2-month time frame. As the orders come in, I am in charge of getting the official production CADs to the vendor overseas for making the goods.

Orders are expected to ship from Asia around the end of July, but of course there are special cases when a retailer requests some products earlier. For cotton-based garments, we typically work with a 4-month lead time between placed orders and shipped product [meaning shipped from Asia, not in-store date]. For example, if product is ordered on March 23, we will tell the retailer that it will ship from Asia on July 25 and be in the store September 2. However, flame-resistant (FR) garments need to have a longer lead time because of the testing requirements that are necessary. For those garments, we will tell the retailer to allow a $4\frac{1}{2}$- to 5-month lead time between placed orders and shipped product. Therefore, if FR product is ordered on March 23, we tell the retailer that it will ship from Asia on August 11 with an in-store date of September 29.

Kelly Poorman is a product manager for Moksha Worldwide, Glencoe, Illinois.

approach is to use a **sloper**, a five-piece pattern of previously developed and perfected basic body **blocks**. The basic sloper is created in a cut and fit that have proved successful with the company's target market in the past. The original pattern is kept intact; it has fitting ease and may or may not include seam allowances. It can be copied and manipulated to produce patterns for new garment styles. Figure 9.1a shows an example of a basic sloper.

Figure 9.1b. *Patternmaking by the flat-pattern method.*

Another approach to flat-pattern patternmaking is to select a previously perfected final pattern, or **body**, from the company archives that is similar in style to the proposed design and to modify it to achieve the new style. That proven body might have been originally developed by flat-pattern, drafting, or draping methods, but at this stage the pattern is treated as a new sloper for achieving the new style. Many companies refer to these past season style bodies by their pattern style number. Using proven basic body blocks and styles significantly cuts development time and costs.

Either way, the basic patterns can be stored on a computer and modified to create a new style, or the modifications can be made by manipulating a flat paper copy of the original style blocks to achieve the new final pattern. (Figure 9.1b shows an example of patternmaking by the flat-pattern method).

The first pattern version of a new style is usually made up in fabric as a first sample. Adjustments are then made in the sample's styling and fit. Only when the desired fit and look are achieved is a production pattern developed. The revised pattern may be cut in a heavy manila-colored tagboard to be used as the production pattern (see Figure 9.2a). It is marked with grain lines and other essential locations needed to facilitate its use during grading and marker making processes. Many of these flat-pattern steps are now performed on computer-aided design (CAD) systems developed expressly for flat-pattern manipulation. If computerized patternmaking is used, patterns may be stored and manipulated for grading and marker making directly on the system. Many computerized patternmaking systems are now available, including those from Gerber, Assyst-Bulmer, and Lectra. Figure 9.2b shows a computer patternmaking system in use.

Pattern Drafting

Another method of patternmaking is **pattern drafting**. This process begins from scratch for each garment style. First, body measurements are taken. Then style lines and ease (extra measurement allowances for movement and for appearance) are added, resulting in a two-dimensional paper pattern for the design. This process can be done by hand or directly on a computer using either an engineering software package such as AutoCad or a dedicated pattern-drafting computer software program. Pattern drafting is more commonly used by higher-priced, fashion-forward producers and offshore contractors, as it is a more time-consuming and therefore more costly method than standard flat pattern methods.

Reverse Engineering

Reverse engineering is the third method of 2D patternmaking. The pattern is made by either transferring the measurements of another garment to paper or taking apart an existing garment and actually tracing or digitizing the outline of each piece to achieve new pattern pieces. When a garment is copied in this way it is often called a knockoff. This method may be very cost-effective for production of basic garments, as it saves the development of the individual pattern blocks. In the United States copyright rules typically do not apply to copying the silhouette or style lines of another garment, but the issue of design ownership can become a problem in cases of trademark infringement or fabric design.

Draping

Draping is the method of patternmaking in which a fabric, either the intended fabric or another less expensive type such as muslin, is draped or shaped around a body form to create a three-dimensional garment prototype (Figure 9.3a). Once the fabric pattern for a style is established, the shaped fabric is flattened

Figure 9.2a. *Traditional tagboard pattern storage in a technical design room.*

Figure 9.2b. *Preparation of patterns by a computer patternmaking system.*

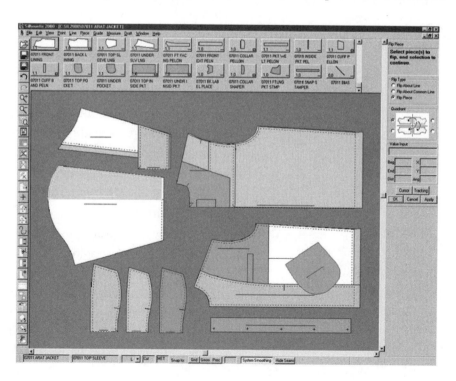

Figure 9.3a. *Draping the back bodice of a garment directly on a dress form.*

Figure 9.3b. *Jennifer Lopez appears in a draped gown.*

out and its outline is transferred to paper or digitized into the computer to create a first pattern of two-dimensional pattern blocks. This method is typically used for garments at higher price points, especially garments with unique silhouettes, such as women's formal wear, or garments made from unusual fabrications (Figure 9.3b).

New Technologies

The cutting edge in pattern development is the evolving technology of draping styles directly on the computer. A 3D garment may be designed through illustration directly on the screen and the resulting style sketch literally unwrapped from the computerized figure and laid flat to form the 2D outline for pattern pieces. This method seems to be working in upholstery applications and accessories such as purses and shoes; garment applications have remained a bit elusive due to the less predictable nature of the range of body movements and variations in textile properties such as fluidity of motion and thickness (Figure 9.4).

Perhaps the most promising new patternmaking technology is the application of body scan technology. New scanning methods enable retrieval of three-dimensional body measurements from an individual consumer and may be directly applied to pattern development in flat pattern, using hand or computerized techniques, to produce a customized product. Also, 3D scanning data is being combined to develop sloper sizes that provide better-fitting garments without the need for repeated samples to achieve final fit.

Patternmaking Needs

The pattern determines the silhouette; its complexity affects both price and fit. Patternmaking needs vary, depending on whether a product developer is working in a design-driven or a manufacturing-driven environment.

Design-Driven Product Development

In a design-driven firm, the integrity of the design is considered more important than production efficiencies. Some companies are willing to deal with more complex patterns and construction in order to remain on the cutting edge of fashion. Fabrics they use tend to be less standard, **markers** (the layout of pattern pieces on the fabric) will vary in efficiency, and specialized sewing capabilities may be required. Design-driven companies typically produce smaller quantities of each style in order to suggest uniqueness.

Generally, offshore contractors are more willing to work with unusual construction processes than are domestic plants, which rely more heavily on automated equipment. When patternmaking and construction needs vary from season to season, a larger pool of contractors may be needed. Additional contractors may have the specialized production skills that are not needed on a consistent basis. These factors will significantly affect the final price of the garment. Given these variables, it is often advantageous for design-driven companies to make their patterns in-house or to use a patternmaking service in order to achieve accuracy and consistency in fit.

Figure 9.4. *The OptiTex patternmaking system provides 2D into 3D virtual modeling capability.*

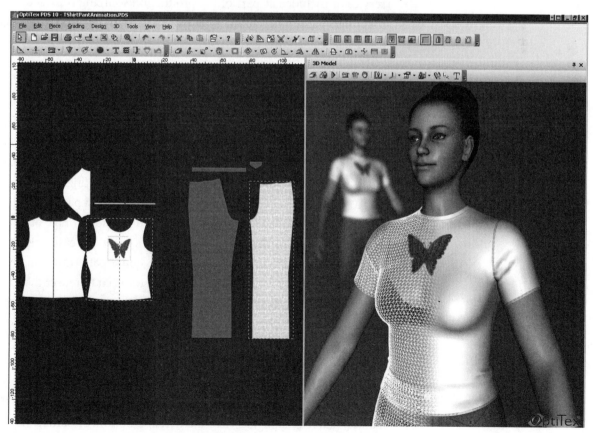

Manufacturing-Driven Product Development

Manufacturing-driven companies take their inspiration from the same styling trends as do design-driven companies, but they "commoditize" a style, by lowering the level of detail, uniqueness, or fit, or by simplifying construction techniques in order to maximize production efficiencies. These modifications enable them to make massive quantities of the product in multiple plants at different locations. They use automated equipment wherever possible or source in locations where hand labor is less expensive to keep down costs. Manufacturing-driven companies engineer all styles so that they can be made as efficiently and economically as possible. These companies must always be prepared for sales to surpass projections, requiring that they find additional production capacity very quickly. Pattern rooms in manufacturing-driven companies are sensitized to making the pattern easy to sew in order to produce many finished garments at the lowest possible price in a timely manner.

Sourcing Patternmaking

Where patterns are made has a great impact on the technical design and quality assurance processes and the role of product developers. Each product developer must decide whether to make patterns in-house or to outsource the process. Patternmaking may be outsourced with a separate patternmaking service or included as part of the production sourcing contract. A contractor that offers pattern development as part of its sourcing services is referred to as a full-package contractor.

In-House Patternmaking

There are many advantages to having an **in-house patternmaking** department within a firm. The most obvious advantage has to do with fit. In-house pattern makers rely on their years of experience with a particular target market to make adjustments that accommodate their customers' expectations. Their proximity to the market allows for frequent fittings on a live model.

Most in-house departments rely on computerized patternmaking systems. These systems facilitate greater accuracy and provide storage of patterns from previous seasons so that a style that fit last season can easily be retrieved and used as the foundation for a new style. In-house patternmaking departments often utilize dress forms that have been customized to reflect their target market's body measurements. Companies that have their own patternmaking departments typically rely on them for their grading activities as well.

Patternmaking Services

Small start-up companies may not have the resources to hire their own pattern makers. They also may be too small for full-service contractors. For these companies, patternmaking services are a viable option. A patternmaking service will generally use a computerized patternmaking system, giving the product developer the accuracy and efficiency of computerized patterns without having to invest in a system.

Patternmaking services tend to be located regionally so that any needed corrections can be made in a timely and efficient manner. They are familiar with domestic body shapes and can use measurements and patternmaking techniques that accommodate them. Patternmaking services usually maintain files of previous work so that they can retrieve files for future styling needs.

Full-Service Contractors

Full-service contractors assume all the responsibility for patternmaking, allowing product developers to concentrate on their own core competencies. Many retail private label product developers have expertise in styling, merchandising, and distribution of products, but they are happy to outsource the patternmaking process. Full-service contractors are more often an option when product development is based on a purchased sample that is to be knocked off. The product developer can send the contractor a sample garment, a mechanical drawing of the desired modified garment, and measurement specifications. The contractor will interpret that information into a completed pattern and make a sample garment. Full-service contractors are not the best choice for companies that produce primarily original design work and do not have a sample to send.

By having contractors make the patterns, product developers are sacrificing the consistency of fit and some construction details that they would achieve with an in-house patternmaking department. Contractors have their own ways of doing things. Their basis for new patterns will be limited to the previous work they have done for the product developer. If they are knocking off a sample garment, the fit they achieve will be influenced as much by the sample garment as by the measurement specifications they are sent. This could result in less consistency of fit across the brand, especially if several contractors are involved in producing the product line.

Full-package contractors are common in Asia. To better compete with these contractors, Central and South American as well as Caribbean Basin manufacturers are attempting to develop their full-service patternmaking capacity. There was a dramatic increase in imports from Mexico as a result of the North American Free Trade Agreement (NAFTA), which created a very favorable business climate for Mexico in the late 1990s. Legislation passed by Congress gave the Caribbean Basin parity with Mexico in trade relations with the United States. These regions became good options for product sourcing because of their proximity to the United States. However, before contractors in these regions could be considered full-service providers, they had to improve their patternmaking capabilities. By the mid-2000s, China and other Asian locations usurped some of the emerging Mexican market in part due to their ability to provide full-package service.

Additional Considerations

Pattern makers trained in different parts of the world may use different methods. For example, Asian pattern makers rely more heavily on drafting than their American counterparts. This means that each garment may be started from scratch rather than being built on fit achieved from style blocks or bodies that have proved successful in past seasons. Pattern makers in different parts of the world also have different perceptions of the body and body proportions, and their patternmaking reflects these differences. For example, French and Italian consumers expect less wearing ease than American customers.

Another drawback to the use of offshore pattern makers is the time required to check samples. When a pattern is complete and a sample made, it must be sent back to the product developer for approval. Fit notes are generally written for each fit session. The technical designer will refer to these notes and add specific instructions before the sample garment is sent back for adjustment. The product development process may allow time for two or three fittings before a style is approved for production. Further fittings could throw off the schedule and delay delivery dates. However, approving a garment for production before the fit is fully corrected may adversely affect sales and frustrate the ultimate consumer. In this era of fast fashion turnaround, getting correct fit as early in the process as possible heavily affects not only the original sourcing decision for that product, but future overall business success.

Another dimension that may add to problems when using offshore contractors is their lack of familiarity with English versus metric measurements. Domestic product developers may face a significant challenge in communicating with an offshore pattern maker unless they can extrapolate metric measurements from specifications originally given in inches. Remember that the rest of the world uses metric measurements, so communication is critical not only in pattern sizing and fit, but in all measurement-related sourcing decisions.

These are only a few of the problem areas to be negotiated in providing successful garments for the target market. Product development staff need to know the patternmaking process well enough to articulate to sourcing partners how to correct problems related to styling and fit. They need the ability not only to be good problem solvers and communicators but to act while working against the clock. Too often, when time runs out, a poor fit is approved in order to stay on schedule. Fit problems are like a bad gene; a pattern that gets passed through the system because there is no time left to fix it multiplies, reappearing later as the basis for additional styles.

When multiple full-service contractors are asked to sample the same style, each of them is putting effort into making a first pattern and securing fabrics that accommodate for shrinkage and color stability. This results in considerable duplication of effort.

No matter who assumes responsibility for patternmaking, the pattern and resulting fit must satisfy the designer, merchandiser, sourcing manager, and quality assurance team, and it must be able to be mass-produced. Each member of this team views the garment from a different perspective, but they must work together to achieve a product that will meet the needs of the target market.

Standards

The firm's strategic business plan sets the stage for development of specific standards. By establishing the target customer, product category, distribution mix, and branding strategy, the strategic plan provides the foundation for the standards that define the business. **Standards** can be described as characteristics used as the basis of judgments made about products. They provide parameters for such things as quality requirements and materials expectations for all products produced by the business. Specific standards on apparel product fabrics, findings, fit, and quality are discussed in chapters 6 and 10–12.

In general, standards are established to reflect the two major goals of any business:

1. To enable the company to make a profit

2. To meet target customers' expectations

Standards are utilized within the product development cycle to provide the framework for decision making in the development of product specifications. Everyone involved in a company needs to understand the firm's specific standards for product sizing and fit, the intrinsic quality standards that provide the baseline for consistency of product, and the performance standards for materials and finished products. Standards focus the efforts of employees and prevent spending valuable resources on concepts that are not feasible for that firm.

Some standards are decided on within the firm, such as styling requirements, construction methods, and measurements that will be used for the sample product. Other standards are imposed by agencies outside the firm. Examples of enforced standards are the Federal Trade Commission (FTC) requirements to include specific care and fiber identification labels in each garment, and the Consumer Product Safety Commission (CPSC) flammability standards for children's sleepwear. The United States has a limited number of mandated standards. Most standards are voluntarily adhered to by individual businesses. Some of these voluntary standards have become so commonly applied that they are assumed by many people to be required. An example of such an assumed standard is placing a size label in a garment. A size label may be a company standard, but it is not mandated.

If the company elects to do business outside the United States, other standards related to product development must be addressed as a condition of doing business with foreign markets. An example of such a standard is the requirement by the European Union that metric measurements be used in sizing garments produced for distribution in its member nations.

Specifications

Specifications (**specs**) are graphic representations and written descriptions of styling, materials, dimensions, production procedures, and finishing instructions for a garment style. The specs communicate desired visual and physical outcomes and the methods of production required in order to meet product standards. They make provisions for control of products throughout the production process. The specifications for each style contain complete product descriptions and expectations. They provide a basis for communication with everyone involved in the product development chain, including creative design, technical design, production, merchandising, and marketing departments that will develop, produce, promote, and sell the products, and suppliers and vendors that will provide materials and distribution.

Product developers must write and notate specs in a way that is understood by sourcing partners. They must avoid the use of slang, easily misunderstood terms, or terms that suffer during translation to other languages. A combination of graphic and written instructions should be utilized wherever possible. Specifications are not only used throughout the firm for communication purposes, but they also form the basis for contracts with contractors and vendors for materials, production, and establishment of criteria for maintaining quality standards. The importance of accurate communications provided by written and graphic specifications cannot be overemphasized in today's global environment, where so many individuals, languages, and cultures are involved in the development process for each product.

The trend is toward computerization of written specifications so that everyone in the operation, whether on-site or at another location, will have access to identical information on the status of a style or an order. In the manufacturing environment, immediate access to all computerized current information is referred to as working in real-time. Real-time computer systems record each operation within the written specifications as it occurs, providing instant access to information on every project within the system to everyone involved. A real-time system enables those in product development, marketing, and merchandising to monitor the progress and status of any individual style within the system. Specifications in the system are used for communication between buyers and sellers; between manufacturers and contractors; between management and production; and among designers, pattern makers, and sample makers.

Information Included

Specification packages generally include a technical flat, closeup drawings of detail areas, and written information such as a physical description of all needed materials and trims; vendor identification; construction methods, which may include identification of stitches and seams to be used; minimum performance standards, including tolerances; and test methods used to confirm the performance of materials. Materials are precisely described, including the exact colors, fiber content, yarn count, weight, width, and finishes applied to the fabrics. Every component part must be accurately identified. The specifications may go so far as to identify a specific supplier. Sometimes product developers of branded goods locate the fabric supplier and specify who should be used. At other times, a sample is provided by the product developer, and the agent or contractor is expected to source the fabric and have samples approved before committing to a specific supplier. When a fabric sample is provided, product developers expect it to be matched by fiber, weight, texture, and color for every garment style that comes off the production line from that contractor.

When the information provided is somewhat generic and contains only the very basic necessary facts, the specifications are considered **open specs**. Open specs allow for flexibility on the part of the producer or contractor. When the information provided is very detailed and specific, it requires the use of an exact material and predetermines the exact supplier. In these cases the specifications are considered **closed specs**. Closed specs can significantly increase the end cost of products because they severely limit flexibility in the use of materials and methods of production, but conversely, they ensure the consistency of final products.

Tolerances are the variation from identified criteria that will be allowed during production. Tolerances establish the standard used to determine which products will be accepted for sale as first-quality products, and which will be rejected. Products that do not fit within the tolerances are designated as **seconds** or **irregulars**, and are rejected. The most commonly expressed tolerances are the variations in measurements of the finished garments. The acceptable tolerance amount is communicated as a part of the product measurement charts and expressed in fractions of an inch, plus or minus. When setting tolerances, the acceptable measurement range for one size must not extend into the spec for the next size larger or smaller than the original measurements.

The smaller the variation allowed in the specification, the "tighter" the spec is said to be. Rigid tolerances, which provide little allowance for variation, can be critical for the function of some products and can provide consistency between like products. However, tight specs also require precision in construction and will increase production costs. When "looser" specs are written, the products coming off of the production line may vary considerably; deciding what constitutes an acceptable variation that can still be considered first-quality becomes a problem. The greatest issues regarding specification tolerances come when the criteria are applied in the manufacturing environment. The problem becomes one of balancing the design concept, acceptable product outcomes, and the costs that consumers will be willing to pay for the finished product. Demanding conformance to some criteria may increase the time required to secure the product or generate a final cost beyond what the consumer is willing to pay, requiring product developers to make compromises.

Specification packages vary considerably from firm to firm, depending on the product being produced, the price point goal, the suppliers, and whether the production will be done in-house or contracted out to domestic or offshore contractors. Most large product development programs have books of standards and specification requirements that they provide to their sourcing partners. These books identify procedures, forms, approval schedules, and responsibilities required of sourcing partners. They may also include the product developer's requirements for standard testing procedures for fabrics and findings; required sources for trims, hangers, and labels; label requirements; methods for taking garment measurements; and any other items deemed important for maintaining quality standards.

When specifications are well written and applied throughout the supply chain, the resulting products will be as envisioned in the design process and all participants will be satisfied. When specifications are not communicated well, there is no guarantee that the final product will even closely resemble the concept the designer envisioned. The written specifications also become legal and financial bargaining tools when issues arise between the firms that order product and the contractors that produce them.

Specification Development

Firms use specs for communicating with everyone in the product development process. Therefore, they must require all those who come in contact with specs to understand these visual tools and their language. Specs are presented in written and graphic formats; they are developed in stages; and they can vary from simple to complex depending on the product, the firm's mission, and the underlying standards adopted by the business. Specification development may be described as occurring in three general phases.

Phase 1a: Design Specs

The first phase of spec development is based on the line plan summary and the initial prototype garments for specific styles. These forms are developed for each style being considered for adoption. The specifications developed at this stage reflect the graphic description, listing of materials, and preliminary cost estimates for making the first sample of a style. This stage may be identified as **design specs**, *prototype specs, preliminary specs,* or *preadoption specs.*

The focus at this stage is on the development of the design itself and decisions about first samples of the style.

At a minimum, the design specs include a **style summary sheet** with a drawing of the front and back of the style, and a **preliminary cost sheet** with product cost estimates.

A drawing of the garment style is developed specifically for inclusion in the spec package. This drawing could be in a croquis format, but a technical flat is more typical. The front and back views of the style are included. General style information is provided, including a style number, which is assigned to identify that specific garment, followed by very basic fabric information, a brief item description, identity of the selling season, date for design approval, size range, and planned colors. Figure 9.5 is an example of a style summary sheet.

The brief identifying descriptions of the style stated on these preliminary forms are typically repeated on other forms in the garment's overall spec package to ensure that everyone who is working on some phase of the process is working on the same product. Computerized spec packages automatically duplicate the basic information from the style summary sheet onto subsequent sheets in the overall spec package for that style, cutting down on costly duplication of effort.

Phase 1b: Costing

A **preliminary cost sheet** is usually completed at the same time as the first sample. This cost sheet provides an introductory record of the style and is used to establish the cost of materials to produce the first sample and estimates of labor and other costs incurred in production and distribution of this product. It also aids in estimating the wholesale price of the garment and the potential value of the product at retail. **Wholesale price** is the amount charged by a wholesale product developer or manufacturer when the garment is sold to the retailer or distributor. This rough estimate is only useful in determining whether a garment is suitable for remaining within the line or for comparison with estimates provided by potential contractors in their bids. More detailed costing will occur later in the process. Figure 9.6 is an example of a preliminary cost sheet.

The components of a preliminary cost sheet include information about the style. First, the general style information is repeated from the original style summary sheet. The second area of information is the fabric identification, including price and quantity of yardage estimates for an individual garment. The third area of information is a listing of trimmings, called **findings** by most producers, with their quantity and cost estimates. Linings and interlinings are included in the fabric descriptions by some developers or in the findings section by others, depending on their preferences, but should be included on this sheet.

The fourth area of information included on the preliminary cost sheet is

Figure 9.5. *The specification package begins with the style summary sheet.*

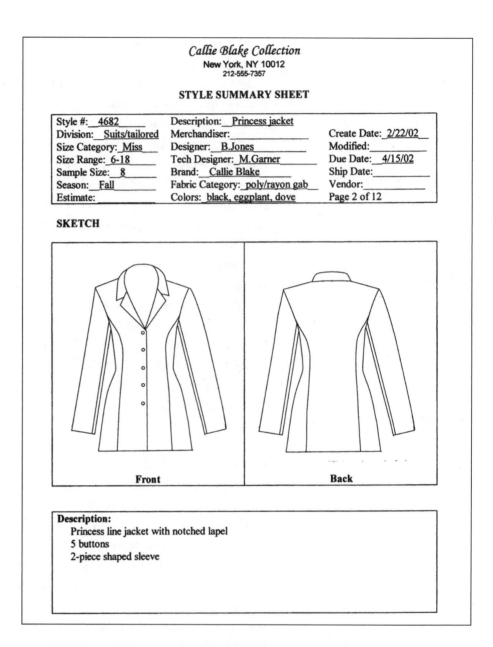

an estimate of labor costs for producing the garment. This information is more detailed for in-house production and domestic contractors; offshore contractors do not typically provide a labor breakdown. Sometimes other cost estimates are included, such as cost of shipping, quotas, insurance, and customs clearance, but these vary by type of producer and the accounting system used by the firm. At this stage the labor costs are just estimates; however, they ultimately will be used to provide a rationale for accepting or rejecting contractors' bids. Product developers must understand the components included in contractor bids; they must be sure when comparing bids that each bid reflects all of the components and services required to complete the garment. For example, forgetting to include costs of additional shipping and import duties associated with an Asian contractor's bid over that of a domestic contractor could prove a very costly error.

Figure 9.6. *First cost estimates are calculated on the preliminary cost sheet.*

Callie Blake Collection
New York, NY 10012
212-555-7357
Preliminary Cost Sheet

Style #: 4652   Description: Princess Suit
Division: Suits/Career   Merchandiser: Create Date: 2/20/02
Size Category: Miss   Designer: S. Smith   Modified:
Size Range: 6-18   Tech Designer: M. Garner   Due Date: 4/15/02
Sample Size: 8   Brand: Callie Blake   Ship Date:
Season: Fall   Fabric Category: Poly/Rayon Gab   Vendor:
Estimate: Colors: Black, Eggplant, Dove   Page 1 of 12

Materials   **Sketch**

	Yards	Price	Cost
Shell 60"	3.3	4.92	16.24
Lining 45"	1.9	1.96	3.72
Interfacing	1.29	1.11	1.43

Sub-Total Materials 21.39

Findings and Trims

	Qty	Price	Cost
Buttons	5	2.16/gr	.075
Zipper			
Pads 1/2"	1 pr.	.58	.58
Trims			
Labels Co. & Care	2	.18	.36
Thread	1	.86	.86

Sub-Total Findings & Trim 1.88
TOTAL MATERIALS 23.27

Fabric Swatch

Labor

	Cost
Cutting	2.25
Marking	2.02
Grading	1.50
Labor	22.30
Packaging	.25
Shipping	6.92
Import fees	10.50

Materials + **TOTAL LABOR** 44.72 = **TOTAL COST OF GOODS** 67.99
+ **GROSS MARGIN** 68.00 = **WHOLESALE PRICE** $136

For these early cost sheets, the total wholesale selling price for the style is estimated by adding the materials and labor sections to form a cost- of- goods estimate, followed by a markup estimate. The markup is added to cover all of the other operating costs of the business plus a desired profit (see chapter 14 on costing and pricing for further explanation of this concept). Once the costing components have been completed, a sketch of the garment is typically attached to this sheet along with a small swatch of the desired shell (main body) fabric. As with all the components of the spec package, the preliminary cost sheet may be done by hand or completed using a computer software package designed for the development and communication of specifications.

Phase 2: Technical Specs

The second phase of spec development occurs after a style has been adopted

Callie Blake Collection
New York, NY 10012
212-555-7357
Materials Specifications

Style #:   4682   Description: Princess Suit

Division: suits/career   Merchandiser: Create date: 2/20/02

Size Category: miss   Designer: S.Smith   Modified:

Size Range: 6-18   Tech Designer: M. Garner   Due Date: 4/15/02

Sample Size: 8   Brand: Callie Blake   Ship Date:

Season: fall   Fabric Category: Poly/Rayon Gab   Vendor:

Estimate $136   Colors: black, eggplant, dove   Page 6 of 12

C	Description	Vendor/ Item #	Use	Material	Width/ Size	Unit	Qty	Loss Factor	Adj. Qty.
F	Poly/Rayon Gab	Millikin 9762	Shell	Poly/Rayon 70/30	62"	yd	3.3	1%	3.33
F	Lining	Windsor 4302	Lining	Polyester lining	59"	yd	1.96	.5%	1.97
F	Interfacing	Avery 9703	Fusible/ Interfacing	Polyester	48"	yd	1.29	.5%	1.35
T	Partial dome/ shank buttons	Fastener 4020-43		Resin	24L	ea	6	2%	6.12
T	Shoulder pads	Hollingswood F 1-2		Form	9 x 5	pair	1	2%	1.02
T	Thread	American 1033-DTM			90/10 cotton/poly	ea	1	2%	1.02
T	Label-woven stock	Avery 4660 label			100% nylon	ea	1	2%	1.02
O	Hanger - clear	Global 3600-2A	Packing	Plastic	16"	ea	1	2%	1.02
O	Plastic bag	American 116-3067	Packing	Plastic	21x5x00	ft	1	2%	4.08

Figure 9.7. *Specifications writing continues with a listing of all materials needed for the sample garment on the component spec sheet labeled* Materials Specifications.

and requires decisions as to how the garment will be produced. These specs might be called, variously, **technical specs**, *style specifications*, or the *design spec package*. Technical specs reflect detailed information regarding materials, including identification of specific fabrics, findings, and trims and their quality requirements; fit standards and tolerances; and identification of preferred construction methods. The focus at this stage is on the development of first production patterns and sales samples.

This phase includes all the information needed for the style to be readied for production. The first steps of this phase are the completion of a component chart and a pattern chart. The **component spec sheet**, sometimes labeled Materials Specifications, is a listing of all of the fabrics, findings, and trims that will be needed to complete construction of the garment. The main functions of this form are to identify all the materials needed to construct the sample garment and to ensure that all the needed components will be available in the appropriate colors and quantities when production begins. The component spec sheet indicates details such as the fiber size and color of thread, the length of zippers, the size and color of buttons, and the width and characteristics of the shell fabrics. Figure 9.7 is an example of a component spec sheet.

The **pattern chart** spec form is a listing of all of the pattern pieces that make up the set needed to make the style. This form includes a drawing of each pattern piece's shape and the name of each pattern piece, along with the actual count of each piece required for one garment. The diagrams of the linings and interlinings may be color coded to distinguish them from the main shell pieces. **Interlinings** include those materials commonly referred to as interfacings by people outside the business. Some of these spec sheets require sewing guides for unusual construction procedures or for achieving specific or uncommon appearance. Some companies include a marker diagram for individual sample garments, especially if the contractor will be making up the fabric layout by hand or using its own pattern blocks. Those full-service contractors that have computerized marker-making capability may no longer need a marker layout as a part of this spec package. Figure 9.8 is an example of a pattern chart spec sheet with its technical flat drawing to aid in recognition of the necessary pattern pieces.

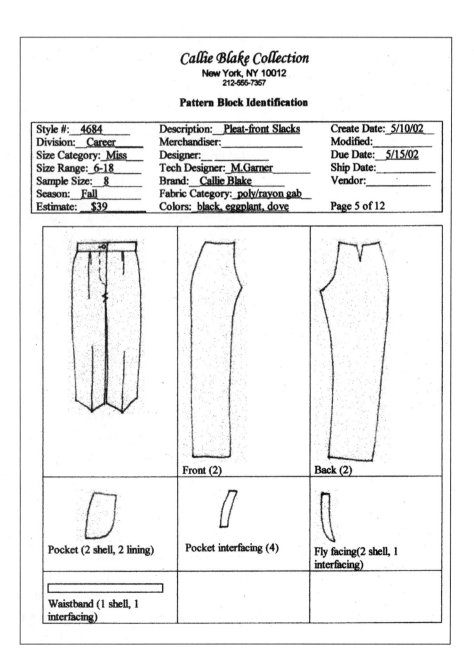

Figure 9.8. *Diagrams of all pattern pieces needed to make a sample garment appear on the pattern chart spec sheet labeled* Pattern Block Identification.

Table 9.1 SAMPLE SIZES USED FOR PRODUCT DEVELOPMENT

PRODUCT CATEGORY	APPROPRIATE SAMPLE SIZE
Newborn	6 months or 3/6
Infant	18 months
Toddler	3T
Girls	5 or XS, and 10 or L
Boys	5 or XS, and 12 or L
Misses	8, 10,or medium
Women's	18W or 20W
Men's tops	40 or medium
Men's bottoms	34W X 32L

The **size chart** containing garment measurement specs for all the sizes that are planned for that style is another essential component of the spec package. Size charts are based on the measurements of the sample size garments, usually an 8 or a 10 for misses clothing, and full application of the company's grade rule table for establishing increments between sizes. Table 9.1 lists sample sizes used in garment development. (Refer to chapter 11 for more information on sizing and grade rule tables). The charts will be different from one garment style to the next because the fit and styling ease amounts vary between styles and contractors. In addition to the basic measurements of the major body markers on the garments, many other specific detail measurements need to be communicated in these charts. Examples of items that might need to be included are the length of the elastic in a waistband; the length of a skirt's side slit; the width of the hem; and the placement of pockets, buttons, and trim.

The goal is to be as precise and clear as possible in communicating requirements. Tolerances are usually located within this portion of the specification package. These charts may also need to be translated into metric measurements, especially for products that are contracted to production facilities outside of the country. Figure 9.9 shows an example of a measurement spec sheet with finished garment dimensions for each size.

The form and length of the remaining Phase 2 specs will depend on the firm, its established standards, and the complexity of the product itself. This portion of the specification package is usually completed after prototype sample approvals and forms the basis for production specs, which are the next phase. The details and language of the notations on these forms must be clear because they will be used to give instructions to those who construct the

Figure 9.9. *A measurement specification sheet is used to chart major measurements needed for producing garments of different sizes. Note the first column in the table; it lists the tolerances allowed for variations within one size.*

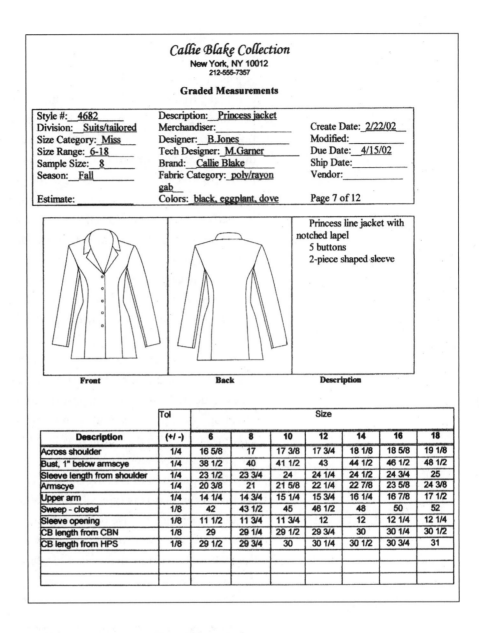

Callie Blake Collection
New York, NY 10012
212-555-7357

Graded Measurements

Style #: __4682__

Division: __Suits/tailored__

Size Category: __Miss__

Size Range: __6-18__

Sample Size: __8__

Season: __Fall__

Estimate: _____

Description: __Princess jacket__

Merchandiser: _____

Designer: __B.Jones__

Tech Designer: __M.Garner__

Brand: __Callie Blake__

Fabric Category: __poly/rayon gab__

Colors: __black, eggplant, dove__

Create Date: __2/22/02__

Modified: _____

Due Date: __4/15/02__

Ship Date: _____

Vendor: _____

Page 7 of 12

Princess line jacket with notched lapel
5 buttons
2-piece shaped sleeve

Front Back Description

Description	Tol (+/-)	Size 6	8	10	12	14	16	18
Across shoulder	1/4	16 5/8	17	17 3/8	17 3/4	18 1/8	18 5/8	19 1/8
Bust, 1" below armscye	1/4	38 1/2	40	41 1/2	43	44 1/2	46 1/2	48 1/2
Sleeve length from shoulder	1/4	23 1/2	23 3/4	24	24 1/4	24 1/2	24 3/4	25
Armscye	1/4	20 3/8	21	21 5/8	22 1/4	22 7/8	23 5/8	24 3/8
Upper arm	1/4	14 1/4	14 3/4	15 1/4	15 3/4	16 1/4	16 7/8	17 1/2
Sweep - closed	1/8	42	43 1/2	45	46 1/2	48	50	52
Sleeve opening	1/8	11 1/2	11 3/4	11 3/4	12	12	12 1/4	12 1/4
CB length from CBN	1/8	29	29 1/4	29 1/2	29 3/4	30	30 1/4	30 1/2
CB length from HPS	1/8	29 1/2	29 3/4	30	30 1/4	30 1/2	30 3/4	31

production garments, including necessary finishing procedures (such as pressing directions), criteria for any unusual styling details, labeling requirements, and directions for packing and shipping. Depending on the business, these sheets may even identify stitch and seam requirements and equipment needs for production. When appropriately developed, specifications give the production and distribution staffs all the critical directions needed to complete and deliver the intended product.

Phase 3: Production Specs

The final stage of specification development is accomplished during production planning as information is provided for producing quantities of a product, rather than individual prototype garments. All previous activities lead to this third phase of specification development, identified as **production specs** or **engineering specs**.

In today's apparel environment, the emphasis is on developing as much of this specification information as early in the product development process as is feasible so that the data can be used in securing appropriate production contracts. In some businesses, several of the items identified here may have been completed earlier in the technical design or style spec phase of specification package development. When product development staff shift these production spec decisions to full-package contractors, the potential for deviation from original intent increases and the time needed for development and approval of production samples is greater than when these decisions are defined earlier in the process. However, when some of the construction details and equipment requirement details are left to the contractors' discretion, the availability of potential construction sourcing sites increases. The practice of who completes detailed production specs varies, but they must be completed at some point for production to commence.

The production staff provides precise information for completion of the specification package that accompanies the style into production, and it reworks preliminary cost estimates to reflect actual costs. This task requires development of an **operations list** that identifies each step of construction that will be performed during production of the garment, including the identification of the stitches and seams involved in completing the operations. Labor costs for each operation may be added to the spec package at this time if the production is being done in-house. See chapter 12 for more information.

When production is being done by outside contractors, the breakdown of operations and costs is typically proprietary to the contractor, and the product developer may receive only a summary of this information. Nevertheless, more exact fabric and materials requirements and their costs are needed at this stage to determine materials allocation, establish overall production costs, and award production contracts.

Types of Spec Sheet Forms

The types of forms used in spec packages vary with the product and the firm; examples in this chapter are considered basic. Table 9.2 contains a listing of potential specification sheets that may be developed for inclusion in a total computerized spec package for a new style. It is a rather comprehensive list that provides awareness of the overall complexity of specification development. Note that some of the suggested forms have automatic retrieval of often-used information from other databases to which a product developer may or may not have access. Also, documentation for this software package refers to three specification development phases: prototype, costing sample, and production, indicating that users may change the titles of their packages and the forms to suit the language of the firm. This text has elected to use design specs, technical specs, and production or engineering specs to reflect the three phases of specifications development.

Table 9.2 POTENTIAL SPECIFICATION PACKAGE FORMS

FORM TITLE	CONTENT OF FORM
Style summary	Introductory information for duplication on other forms. Serves as cover sheet for spec package for each style.
Assembly diagram	Text and graphic areas for product assembly information.
Design specifications	Text and graphic areas for fabric and trim information.
Cost sheet	Text and graphics for materials and labor costing information, including cost per item and total cost computed; labor cost from a general sewing data package. It is connected to design specification.
Pattern sheet	Basic header information. Inventory of all pattern pieces for a style. Text field for additional pattern information: style names, pattern piece names, quantities, piece message, marking/spreading restrictions, and material groups.
Cutting ticket	Cutting and spreading information for the cutting room.
Cutting instruction	Specific information about markers, quantities, and sizes to be cut. Used to plan markers in the cutting room.
Measurement specifications	Finished dimensions and measurements locations for each individual size in range.
Incremental measurement	Grading increments between sizes for all areas of measurement in sizes in a range.
Calculated measurements	Sample size measurements. Other size measurements are calculated from data on incremental measurement form.
Packaging and shipping	Packaging, shipping, and handling information.
Free-form pages	Extra forms that can accommodate information from other graphic formats such as markers and pattern pieces.
Checklist	Records of important dates in product cycle. Completion dates: planned, revised, and actual.
Send-out sheet	Text format for cutting and sewing information for outside contractors.
Sample initiation	Large graphic and text fields for first sample information.
Piece reference	Multiple image areas for pattern pieces and their names; or trim items, fabric swatches, button cards, swatch cards, etc.
Material usage	Multiple image areas for pattern pieces and their names, plus area of piece, number of pieces in final product, and variances such as waste allowance.
Material specifications	Sketch area and information on materials. It is connected to materials database for retrieval of needed data.

continued

Table 9.2 POTENTIAL SPECIFICATION PACKAGE FORMS continued

FORM TITLE	CONTENT OF FORM
Cost specifications	Sketch area and information on materials and costing. It is connected to other databases for automatic retrieval of data used repeatedly in other style spec packages.
Detailed operations list	Text format for detailed labor operations.
Cutting specifications	Multiple image areas for individual pattern pieces and text. Provides autimatic fill-in for other sizes after entering sample size.
Revisions status sheet	Chronological log of activities on individual style. It is automatically updated as modified or edited.

Source: Microdynamics Integrated Systems 1993, 13–15.

Many computer firms now specialize in product spec sheet packages as part of their integrated product development software systems. Gerber's AccuMark facilitates patternmaking, grading, and marker making functions, which integrate with their spec packages managed through PDM, as well as their automated spreading and cutting systems. Lectra has launched its Mikalis tools, which are dedicated to apparel specifications. Mikalis produces technical specifications and can draw on work from past collections to eliminate redoing repetitive tasks. One of its features is that "specifications can then be sent electronically to external partners through a secure web interface" (Tait 2004, 64). Assyst-Bulmer has focused on marker making and cutting; its largest customer base is in China.

Summary

Translating a style concept into a marketable product involves many tasks. There are two major interwoven processes that occur at this stage: the first is patternmaking; the second is the development of the specification package.

The patternmaking process focuses on development of the pattern for a style sample, followed by the creation of a sample garment. The sample is checked and the original pattern is adjusted until a final production pattern is developed.

Simultaneously, the specification package is begun. The spec package contains the pages of graphic and text information that provide instructions for producing a style. The development of specifications can be divided into three phases: design specs, technical specs, and production or engineering specs. Each style is assigned a number, fabric and component identification information is determined, and costs of production are projected. The process then moves to the technical design staff for preparation and approval of the production patterns and the development of sizing and construction details. Production specifications determine the costs for producing quantities of a garment style and identify the construction methods and equipment needs. The resulting specification package will become the foundation for communications with all partners throughout the production process.

Computerization of the specification process improves the speed and accuracy of the product development process. Many companies use commercially available, industry-specific software for their specification packages. This software may be adapted to meet the specific needs of the product developer. Gerber, Lectra, and Assyst-Bulmer all offer such programs.

Key Terms

blocks	pattern chart
body	pattern drafting
closed specs	patternmaking
component spec sheet	preliminary cost sheet
cost sheet	production (engineering) specs
design specs	reverse engineering
draping	seconds or irregulars
findings	size chart
flat-pattern	sloper
full service contractor	specifications (specs)
in-house patternmaking	standards
interlinings	style summary sheet
markers	technical specs
open specs	tolerances
operations list	wholesale price

Discussion Questions

1. Compare the merits of using

   a. in-house staff versus contractors for pattern development

   b. open or closed specifications for component materials

   c. tight and loose specifications for tolerances

2. What products might be better served by draping rather than flat-pattern methods?

3. What is the importance of standards and specifications in the product development process?

Activities

1. Using forms found in this chapter, prepare a style summary sheet and a preliminary cost sheet for one of the garments designed as an activity in chapter 8.

2. Using forms found in this chapter, prepare a component summary sheet and a size measurement chart, with tolerances, for the garment in Activity 1.

Note: Technical flats should be completed at this time to complement the flats and croquis sketches prepared in previous assignments.

References

Anderson, K. 2005. *Patternmaking: Past and present.* www.techexchange.com (accessed July 25, 2006).

Lauwaert, Dirk. 2005. The consciousness of a seam. *Patterns.* Antwerp: Ludion.

Microdynamics Integrated Systems. 1993. *PDM product data management: User's manual.* Dallas, TX: Microdynamics Integrated Systems [now Gerber Garment Technologies].

Tait, N. 2004. Great days in Miami Beach. *Fashion Business International.* June-July, 63–67.

Additional Resources

Armstrong, H. J. 2006. *Patternmaking for fashion design.* 4th ed. New York: HarperCollins.

Brown, P., and J. Rice. 2001. *Ready-to-wear apparel analysis.* 3d ed. Upper Saddle River, NJ: Prentice-Hall.

Bryant, M. W., and D. Demers. 2006. *The spec manual.* 2d ed. New York: Fairchild.

Diamond, J., and E. Diamond. 2002. *The world of fashion.* 3d ed. New York: Fairchild.

Glock, R. E., and G. I. Kunz. 2005. *Apparel manufacturing: Sewn product analysis.* 4th ed. Upper Saddle River, NJ: Prentice-Hall.

Kadolph, S. J. 1998. *Quality assurance for textiles and apparel.* New York: Fairchild.

Tate, S. L. 2004. *Inside fashion design.* 5th ed. New York: Addison Wesley Longman.

CHAPTER 10

FINDINGS AND TRIM

"It has been said that haute couture lives in Paris because Paris itself is home to incomparable ribbon and button makers—a conjuring of crown jewels."

—LAURA JACOBS*

OBJECTIVES

- To understand the role of findings and trim in the product development process

- To explore the vocabulary of findings and trim

- To understand the appropriate uses of a variety of findings and trim categories

---

As the color, fabrication, silhouette, and basic styling of garments are determined, functional and decorative additions must be chosen to complete each garment. All these additional material components of the garments, beyond the shell or body fabrics, are classified as findings and trim. Although sometimes referred to as sundries or notions by some segments of the marketplace, the apparel industry now prefers to refer to these component materials as findings and trim.

Product developers are always seeking new forms of findings and trim to use as embellishment and to enhance the desirability of their designs. The Bobbin Show in Orlando, Florida, the Trimmings Expo in New York, and numerous individual distributors provide help to designers seeking inspiration. Also, specialized trim houses make it their business to offer novelty trims and provide for the actual application of trims to another firm's garments.

Findings and trims are called upon to perform either functional or decorative roles, but some may do both. Functional findings and trims are those that are an integral part of the garment structure and its use. An example of a functional finding is an interlining. Decorative trims are used to enhance the aesthetic appeal of the style, but they are not necessary to the functioning of the garment. An example of a decorative trim is an appliqué. Products such as buttons and zippers may fulfill both decorative and functional roles.

Findings and trim must be compatible with the outer shell fabrics during wear and maintenance. The performance standards for them should be based on the use, care, and construction of outer shell fabrics for the style.

*Skrebneski and Jacobs 1995, 111

Although these components may at first seem to play a relatively minor role in the overall design of a garment, if the wrong finding or trim is selected or if one of them fails when in use, the consumer will deem the entire garment useless. Therefore, great care must be taken in their selection and application.

Findings

The category of component materials called **findings** includes support materials, closures, thread, elastics, and labels. Thread may be the most universal of these components because it is essential to every stitch and seam in every garment; it will be discussed here and again in chapter 12 in relation to stitches and seams.

Support Materials

Garment components that fall into the category of **support materials** include interlinings, linings, and other support devices. In the industry, the term interlining has come to represent what most home sewers refer to as interfacing. During wear, these parts of a garment style are not seen, but they definitely affect the overall aesthetic appearance of the style. Their basic function is to enhance and preserve the shape of the garment. Most garments contain at least one of these components in order to foster shape retention and durability. The presence of these support materials is considered a sign of quality. However, consumers typically do not make purchasing decisions based on these components. Rather, they make their decision based on the effect these components have on the overall look and performance of the product. Because support materials influence the serviceability of the end product, they must be compatible with the garment shell in terms of dimensional stability, including shrinkage, elongation, and elasticity; appearance retention, such as abrasion resistance and colorfastness; comfort; and care requirements (Case Study 10.1, Guidelines for Meeting Quality Standards).

Interlining

Interlining, or **interfacing**, is an extra layer of supporting fabric used in almost all structured garments. This fabric supplies body, shape, and reinforcement to areas of the garment. Without it, most garments will become shapeless during wear. Interfacing is typically hidden from view between the garment and a facing made of the shell fabric. Areas commonly interfaced include collars, cuffs, button and buttonhole areas, pocket openings, and waistbands. In general, better-tailored coats and jackets include more interfacing than do simple blouses and unstructured jackets. Complex tailored garments may incorporate several types of interfacings in a single style (Figure 10.1).

Interlinings are available in a variety of weights, constructions, and fiber

---

CASE STUDY 10.1 GUIDELINES FOR MEETING QUALITY STANDARDS

Product developers provide their suppliers with written guidelines of standards they require to ensure a consistent level of quality in finished garments. This fictitious example of quality standards for components is based on the technical design manual used by Shopko.

Callie Blake Collection
954 East 38th Street
New York, NY 10012
212-555-7357

COMPONENT SPECIFICATIONS

Lining Requirements

Linings used must be dyed to match main color of garment unless otherwise specified.

Lining must meet requirements of the shell fabric regarding shrinkage, colorfastness, and crocking.

Lining weight must be heavy enough to conceal interior construction; transparent lining is not acceptable.

Lining must have no raw edges; all edges must be clean-finished or serged.

Lining must be finished so it does not show below or beyond the shell fabric.

Skirt, pant, and coat lining must be swing-tacked to hem of shell fabric to prevent visibility during movement.

Patch pocket lining must be 1/8 inch smaller than pocket to avoid rolling to surface.

Lining must be secured in such a way as to avoid being caught in any closure during normal use of garment.

Skirt and pant lining must be cut slightly smaller than the shell fabric to prevent bunching.

Tailored jacket lining must have a jump hem in bottom and sleeve hems.

Tailored jacket and coat linings must have a center back pleat to allow for movement.

Interfacing Requirements

Interfacing must be compatible with the shell fabric and meet requirements of the shell fabric regarding shrinkage, colorfastness, and crocking.

Interfacing weight must be of the same or lighter weight than the shell fabric and provide the intended stability to the garment silhouette.

Woven interfacings must be cut on the same grain as facings.

Garment parts must be fed through the fusing machine lengthwise for fabrics with texture such as crinkle, seersucker, crepe, and fine-wale corduroy.

Interfacings must not show through to the right side of the garment.

Fusible interfacings must not cause puckering or strike-through of adhesive after laundering.

In addition to standard shell fabric testing, fusible interfacing must be tested for thermal shrinkage, bond strength, and hand.

Interfacing Color Standards

Shell Color	Acceptable Interfacing Color
White	White
Pastels	White or Natural
Mid-tones	Gray
Darks	Black

---

contents. The general rule regarding their selection is that they be of similar or lighter weight than the outer shell fabric. Interlining fabrics range from extremely lightweight (about 0.4 ounces per square yard) to very heavy (about 4 ounces per square yard) (Brown and Rice 2001, 228). Some interlinings are quite crisp and are used in structured or tailored garments, whereas others are soft and are used in more drapable, unstructured garments.

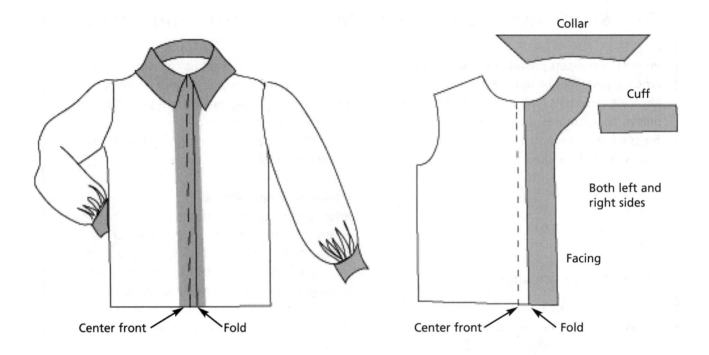

Collar

Cuff

Both left and
right sides

Facing

Center front   Fold

Center front   Fold

Figure 10.1. *Shaded areas to be supported by interfacing.*

Interlinings are available in woven, knitted, or nonwoven fabrics. Each has distinct advantages and disadvantages. Woven interlinings tend to be strong and do not stretch, but they must be cut on the grain. Also, they tend to be more costly than other types of interlining fabrics. Knit interlinings tend to stretch and are softer in shape and drape, but they do not ravel and they cost less than woven interlinings. Combination structures, such as weft insertion knits, provide the stability of woven types and still maintain the other advantages of knits. Nonwoven fiberweb interlinings are the most common type in use today. They lend good stability, do not have a grain, and are the least costly type. However, they are not very drapable and they tend to pill in use. **Pilling** is the formation of fiber balls on the surface of a fabric.

Interlinings have another characteristic, in addition to construction, that must be considered. Is it fusible or is it a sew-in? The most common type is fused onto the back of the shell fabric via a thermoplastic adhesive. Great care must be taken to ensure that these adhesives do not show through (called **strike-through**) to the surface of the garment during pressing, making the garment very unattractive or potentially unwearable. Sew-in interfacings may be stitched to a facing before the facing is applied or inserted directly to the underside of a garment as seams are constructed. Although this method of application may take more care and potentially be more costly, it eliminates some of the problems inherent in the fusibles. Sew-in interfacings are especially important to the shaping and body of quality tailored garments.

Another form of interlining is an extra layer of fabric between the shell and the lining that is used strictly for warmth or stability. It is typically selected for its insulation value and is sometimes used in cold-weather clothing such as coats and jackets. It is completely hidden from view. Thinsulate is an example of interlining used in ski pants, ski jackets, and ski gloves. Polyester fleece is a low-cost interlining for use in quilted fabrics and is valued for its easy care in children's winterwear. Down and lambs' wool interlinings have the best insulation value, but they are significantly higher in cost and, therefore, are traditionally used only in higher-quality garments.

Lining

Lining is a lightweight fabric that is sewn into a garment to give a finished appearance to the garment's interior. Lining enhances the appearance of the inside of the garment, but it also serves some functional purposes, including making the garment more comfortable to the touch and helping the wearer slide in and out of the garment with ease. Linings may also contribute support and shape retention, provide opacity to sheer fabrics, or provide additional warmth. In general, linings are perceived as adding quality to a garment (Figure 10.2).

A lining may be complete, as in a coat or jacket, or it may be partial. Partial linings are commonly used in summer suits and sports jackets to make them cooler to wear and in skirts to aid in shape retention. Pants may be fully or partially lined to provide opacity or shape retention, or both. When partial linings are used, the seams left exposed on the inside of the garment must be more completely finished than in fully lined garments in order to maintain quality level.

Linings are typically constructed separately from the garment and are then sewn into the outer garment. There is a variation called **underlining**, in which the outer shell fabric and the lining are layered together before the garment is constructed. This variation of lining is used to stabilize shell fabrics or to make the shell fabric opaque. It may also hide seam allowances from showing on the surface in sheer fabrics and lace garments such as wedding gowns. Fabrics used for underlinings are generally different than those used for linings. They are typically not as slippery.

The color of a lining may enhance or detract from the overall marketability of a garment. Sometimes it is critical to have the lining dyed to match the shell fabric so as to enhance the color image of the overall garment. If this is done, product developers must allow time in the production schedule for the color matching process, and consider the additional costs involved in securing linings dyed to match.

The fiber content and the weave structure of lining fabrics heavily influence the use and the cost of this component. Nylon and polyester are used extensively as durable, lightweight linings. But they can be clammy and allow buildup of static electricity. Many newer fabrics in this category have **wicking** capability, which is the ability of the fabric to transfer moisture away from the surface of the body. Wicking makes the fabric much more comfortable to wear. Acetate is used extensively for lining coats and jackets; it is quite inexpensive,

Figure 10.2. *Lining enhances the appearance of the inside of the garment.*

but it does not wear well. Fume fading (color change from exposure to the atmosphere) and color changes from perspiration are common problems with some linings, especially those made of acetate. Bemberg rayon lining is preferred for its softness next to the skin, but use of less expensive and readily available polyester and acetate now greatly exceed the use of rayon as a lining fabric. Silk is used in status garments, but the cost is prohibitive for general use.

The weave structure of a lining may have almost as much impact on the durability of lining fabrics as the fiber content. In general, twill weave linings wear the best and have the greatest dimensional stability. Satin linings are used often in coats, especially fur coats, because they slip on and off over other clothing with great ease. However, satin weaves tend to snag easily and may not wear well over time.

Support Devices

Additional components that fall into the support devices category include shoulder pads, sleeve headers, collar stays, boning, and seam tapes.

Shoulder pads are shaping devices used in the shoulder area of tailored jackets and coats, and sometimes in dresses and blouses when fashion trends require them to achieve a desired look. They are made of either a single layer of molded foam or multiple layers of cotton or wool wadding or polyester fiberfill. They should be graduated in depth toward the edges so that they do not create a ridge on the outer garment. When these pads are exposed on the inside of the garment, they are often covered in a piece of the shell fabric or of the lining fabric to make them less conspicuous. If the lining hides the shoulder pad, no covering is required.

Foam pads are the least expensive, while those made of layers of wadding or fiberfill can be more costly. Shoulder pads of common sizes and depths, such as ¼- or ½-inch depth, are typically purchased in bulk quantities and covered as they are needed in the construction of specific garment styles.

Sleeve headers are folded narrow strips of bias cut lamb's wool, tailor's canvas, or fiberfill sewn into the sleeve cap of tailored coats and jackets to create a soft roll in the cap of the sleeve. Without this header, the armscye seam can collapse and wrinkle. The header is a signature detail of fine-tailored garments. Occasionally designers utilize a strip of fabric such as organza or netting as a sleeve header in blouse and dress sleeves to maintain the puff of the sleeve cap, as in a wedding dress.

Collar stays are thin strips of plastic inserted into the points of collars on dress shirts to prevent the collar from curling up or wrinkling. These stays may be permanently sewn into a collar or they may be removable; removable stays are placed in channels specifically sewn into the collar to enable their insertion. **Boning** is used in the bodice of some garments, such as bras, corsets, or strapless dresses, to ensure that the shape of the garment is maintained. Boning can be made of steel, plastic, or polyester rigilene. Boning is an intrinsic component of bustiers.

Seam tapes are used in a variety of applications. They are narrow (less than an 1 inch in width) woven strips of fabric, similar to ribbon. One example of their use is sewing a length of seam tape into a shoulder seam on a knit top in order to stabilize the shoulder seam. Another use is placing a tape on the interior of a jacket front to establish the roll line of a lapel.

Occasionally **bra cups** are added to garments such as swimsuits and strapless evening gowns to provide shape and support to the bustline. These cups are usually made of fiberfill or foam and must be constructed to withstand the care procedures of the outer garment without lumping.

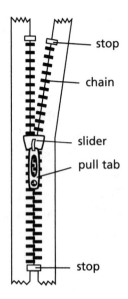

Figure 10.3. *Identification of component parts of a zipper.*

Closures

Closures are fastenings that may contribute to the aesthetic appeal of a garment, in addition to their functional use of allowing access to the garment and adjusting the fit of the garment to the body. Some closures have a traditional use, such as molded plastic zippers on skiwear, four-hole buttons on men's shirts, and rubber buttons on rugby shirts. Others are selected for their aesthetic contributions to a style, such as decorative buttons. In general, closures are subjected to more horizontal stress during wear than vertical stress. This factor should influence how they are selected and where they are placed on individual garments, including the location of buttons and the direction (whether horizontal or vertical) of buttonholes.

Faulty closure materials or their improper application during construction can cause problems after production has been completed. This can result in considerable financial loss to a firm. Therefore, these products need to be selected early in the design process and must be tested thoroughly to prevent potential failures.

Because of the huge quantities of most orders in the apparel business, closures are often purchased by the **gross**. This measure consists of 12 dozen or 144 individual pieces. Smaller quantities are typically reserved only for more exclusive, high-priced garments, or for trial sample garments. Great care must be taken in ordering closures such as decorative buttons or specialty closures so that little or no stock is left over at the end of the production run. Excess stock of special trims can become a financial burden.

Zippers

Zippers are continuous closures developed for use in garments. They are somewhat stiff and best used in flat areas rather than over folds or gathers. Zippers tend to be used in place of buttons on more fitted garments such as dresses, skirts, or pants. There are thousands of styles, sizes, and colors of zippers, so great attention must be given to the selection of the appropriate one for each garment style. Some people believe that no one element of a garment can cause as much grief for a product developer as a zipper that fails. Appropriate materials must be selected so that the zipper tape is compatible in weight and care requirements with the outer shell, the color must come close to matching the shell fabric, and the zipper must remain operational during the life of the garment. Figure 10.3 illustrates the component parts of a zipper.

The cost of the zipper is higher than the cost of a seam sewn of the same length, so the length of the zipper should be as short as possible yet still provide access into the garment. The most common lengths of zippers in adult clothing are 7 inches in women's skirts and slacks, 9 inches in men's slacks, and 22 inches in dresses, although they may be made in any custom length. Zippers come in a range of colors, but unique colors may need to be dyed to match.

Product developers must gauge their needs carefully. Sometimes a single garment such as a jacket may require a slightly longer or shorter zipper as sizes grade up and down. Changing the length proportions of a garment in fittings could also change the length of the zipper required for the closure. These factors must be considered and planned for in the development of the garment.

Common application methods for zippers include slot or centered application, lapped, invisible, fly front, and exposed. The slot or centered application is appropriate in jackets with separating zippers, or skirts, pants or dresses with center back zippers. The lapped application is appropriate for side seam or center back applications; invisible zippers are used in back or side applications in women's wear where top stitching would detract from the design. Exposed zipper applications are sometimes used in sportswear; fly fronts are typically used in skirt and pant fronts. Figure 10.4 illustrates common zipper applications.

Invisible zippers are a specialty item in that they are used only on seams where a zipper would interfere with the aesthetic look of the seam. Because they are bulkier and more costly than other types of zippers, they are typically used only in higher-priced lines or eveningwear.

Zipper chains or teeth are made of metal, plastic, or nylon. In general, the plastic teeth zippers are most comfortable in cold weather and lend themselves to decorative uses. Zippers with metal teeth are very sturdy, making them a good choice for jeans and other work-related garments; however, they may rust. Nylon coil continuous chain zippers are the most flexible, may be dyed to match the color of the garment, and may be used in a wide variety of lightweight to medium-weight garments. However, they are the most susceptible to failure, especially in garments with a snug fit.

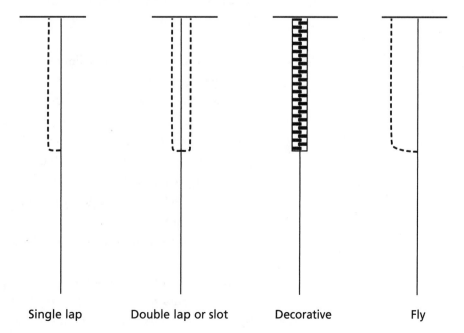

Figure 10.4. *Zipper application methods.*

Single lap   Double lap or slot   Decorative   Fly

Buttons

Buttons are usually both functional and decorative because most of them are visible on a garment. A few are only functional, such as the hidden button on the inner fly extension of a pair of slacks, or only decorative, such as the buttons on the cuffs of a tailored jacket. To be functional, buttons require the presence of a buttonhole.

Buttons are available in a wealth of materials. The most common types of buttons are either molded of plastic (nylon) or stamped out of a sheet of plastic (polyester) (Brown and Rice 2001 218). These may be dyed to match almost any color, but appropriate lead time must be included in the product development calendar if they must be custom-dyed. Other materials traditionally used for buttons include metal, wood, animal horn, rubber, or shell. These natural materials are more costly and represent only a small portion of all buttons being used today.

Some buttons are covered in the same fabric as the shell garment, but these are usually used when the color is difficult to duplicate or when they need to visibly blend into the garment. Covered buttons must be made to order by the contractor who constructs the garments.

Buttons are attached with holes, called **eyes**, or a shank. Buttons with holes are considered less formal and are made with two or four holes that are used for sewing them to the garment. Those with **shanks** have a loop extension on the back that is used to attach the button to the garment. This leaves the surface of the button free to be more decorative. Holed buttons tend to lie flatter on the surface, although they may be attached to the garment with a thread shank so that they will not pucker the surface of the garment when they are buttoned. Traditionally, four-hole buttons are used on men's shirts, although there is no other real reason for this practice. Though decorative, shank buttons tend to protrude from the surface of the garment and can be uncomfortable if used on the back of a garment where one might sit or lean up against them.

Button size is measured in **lignes**, which are equal to 1/40 of an inch or 40 lignes per inch of diameter. Therefore a 20-ligne button would be ½ inch in diameter (Figure 10.5). Button sizes should be selected to be aesthetically pleasing, and they should be in proportion to the size of the garment. Exceptions may be made for some garments, such as toddlers' clothing. Small children are unable to manipulate buttons that are too small, and small buttons could become a choking hazard should they be dislodged. Elderly consumers who lack manual dexterity may be unable to use buttons smaller than ½ inch in diameter. In these cases, buttons might be selected for decorative impact, but the functional closure on the garment might be a hook and loop fastener.

In addition to buttons, some alternative closures that might be considered part of the button category are loops, frogs, and toggles. **Loops** are tubes of fabric or thread used instead of buttonholes for securing buttons during wear.

Figure 10.5. *Common styles of buttons are those with holes and those with a shank. Button sizes are measured in lignes.*

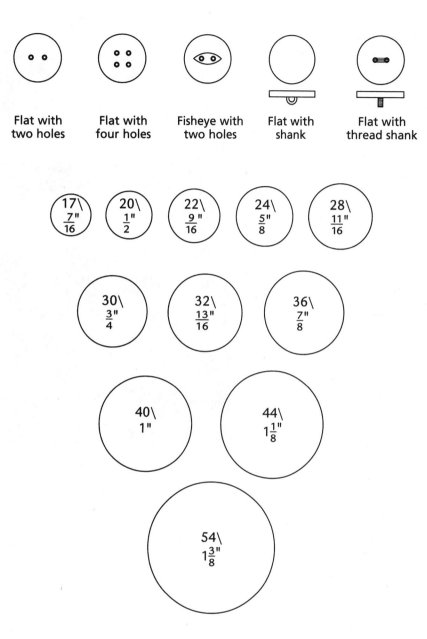

Frogs are decorative coiled cording used to replace traditional buttons and buttonholes. A **toggle** is a pair of cord loops secured by a rod that replaces the more traditional button (Figure 10.6).

In the United States, garments for women and girls traditionally lap right over left, from the wearer's point of view; garments for men and boys lap left over right. In sportswear a more unisex approach may be taken, and garments for both men and women may lap left over right. Designers try to place buttons and buttonholes on the straight grain of the fabric to ensure durability and crisp finishing. They space them an equal distance apart. Another consideration in the placement of buttons on the front of women's garments is the location of the crown of the bust. A button placed at a height parallel to or just above the crown of the bust will prevent gapping in the front of the garment during wear. If placing a surface button in that location is distracting to

Figure 10.6. *Novelty closures include toggles and frogs made of cording.*

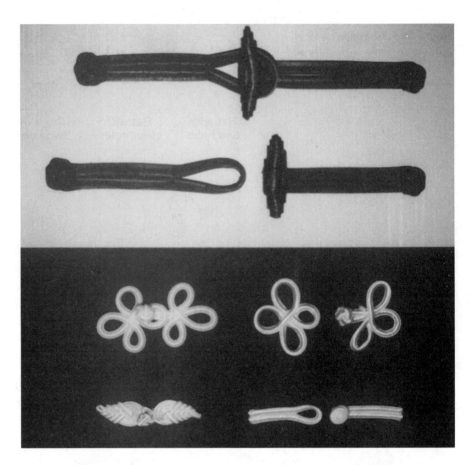

the overall design of the garment, a hidden button (sometimes called a modesty button) can be placed underneath at this location to prevent the top from gapping open and exposing lingerie or skin. The use of a modesty button is one of the hallmarks of a better-quality blouse.

Buttonholes

Buttonholes tend to be functional in their construction. They need to be secure and evenly placed. Also, they must be long enough for the button to slip through and remain in place, without being so long that buttons easily come unbuttoned during wear. The general rule for determining the length of a buttonhole is to measure the diameter of the button plus the button's thickness. A ball button requires a buttonhole that is equal to one-half the circumference of the button. Buttonholes should be reinforced with interfacing to ensure their durability and shape retention.

Horizontal buttonholes tend to stay buttoned better during wear than do vertical buttonholes. Therefore, most buttonholes are horizontal. Three exceptions to this are buttonholes placed on the narrow placket (a fabric strip) on the front of a dress shirt or blouse, where vertical buttonholes are more visually pleasing; buttonholes on knitted tops, where the fabric would ripple if horizontal buttonholes were used; and buttonholes on hidden closures.

Buttons and buttonholes are placed on extensions called **overlaps** and **underlaps**. These extensions need to reach beyond the center front line into

Figure 10.7. *The location of buttonholes and buttons affects both aesthetic and functional aspects of a style.*

Figure 10.8. *Major types of buttonholes include stitched buttonholes, either straight or keyhole; bound buttonholes made of fabric strips; and slot buttonholes, which are openings in seams.*

BUTTONS ON CENTER FRONT

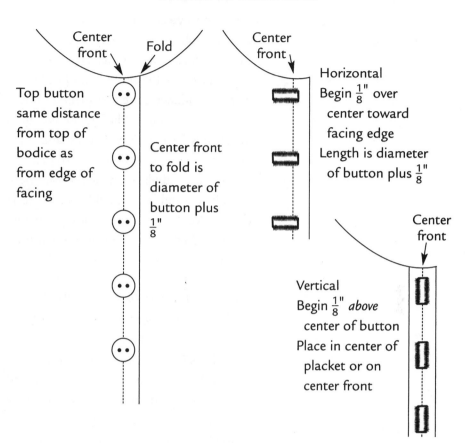

Center front

Fold

Top button same distance from top of bodice as from edge of facing

Center front to fold is diameter of button plus $\frac{1}{8}$"

Center front

Horizontal
Begin $\frac{1}{8}$" over center toward facing edge
Length is diameter of button plus $\frac{1}{8}$"

Center front

Vertical
Begin $\frac{1}{8}$" *above* center of button
Place in center of placket or on center front

Straight machine-made

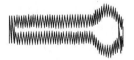

Machine keyhole

Fishtail keyhole

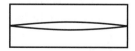

Bound (self-fabric)

the garment by at least the radius of the button plus ¼ to ½ inch, depending on the size of the button. During wear, the buttons should ride on the center of the garment, except in a double-breasted garment (Figure 10.7). The top button should be equidistant from the top and the side of the overlap.

Buttonhole construction tends to be driven by tradition. For example, straight machine buttonholes are the most commonly used style or shape on shirts and blouses. They are always used for vertical buttonholes. The keyhole-shaped buttonhole is often used on coats for men and women because the circle hole at the end of the buttonhole provides room for the shank of the sturdier buttons used on these garments. Keyhole buttonhole machines may be set to include a piece of fine cording under the zigzag stitching in order to produce a three-dimensional visual effect and improve durability. The end opposite the keyhole may be finished with a bar tack or with a long fishtail; buttonholes with a bar tack are considered of higher quality. Bound buttonholes are constructed by the same method as double-welt pockets. They are used on women's higher-priced jackets and dresses and on leather goods, but they are rarely used on men's clothing. Occasionally, a buttonhole is placed in a seam such as on a coat yoke seam or where a band is attached down the front of a dress. This application is almost invisible and is a design feature of the garment (Figure 10.8).

Hooks and Eyes

Hook-and-eye closures consist of two parts—a type of hook and a receptacle for the hook. Hooks and eyes tend to hold up well under strain, so they are used in places where other closures, such as snaps, might give way during wear. The eye of the closure may be of the same material as the hook, typically metal. On higher-priced garments, a thread eye, made by hand, may replace the metal eye. Some of the larger hook-and-eye systems used on skirt and pant waistbands have adjustable eyes; and many of these systems used on men's slacks are mechanically attached so that they are almost completely hidden. In one specialty application of hook-and-eye closures, used on fur coats, the entire hook-and-eye assembly is covered in gimp thread so that no metal is visible. Occasionally, hook-and-eye tape is used where a series of hooks and eyes are needed to complete the closure, as on the back closure of some brassieres.

Hook and Loop Tape Fastener

A relative newcomer to the closures field is the **hook and loop tape fastener** best known by the brand name Velcro. This product consists of two separate tapes that stick when pressed together. They can be pulled apart when force is exerted. It is a convenient closure for specific uses such as in children's wear, where it can speed up the dressing process, and for people who have problems with finger dexterity and cannot use more traditional buttons, snaps, or hook-and-eye closures. This closure is available in a wide variety of sizes, shapes (e.g., small squares and precut rounds), and degree of grip for use in an array of applications. The stronger forms tend to be a bit bulky. One common use today is for attaching shoulder pads in misses' blouses; this makes the pads easily removable.

Snaps

Snaps are fasteners or closures that fall into two categories. One type is sewn onto the garment; the other type is mechanically attached. Sew-on snaps are used on lightweight to medium-weight garments to secure areas that do not encounter much stress, such as the corner of the top of the overlap on a dress or blouse. They can also be used to attach temporary components such as detachable collars and cuffs. They are made up of two parts, a ball and a socket, that lock when pressed together. Typically the ball portion is placed on the top side and the socket on the bottom layer of the snap application. Occasionally, snaps are covered in a lining fabric or other matching lightweight fabric to hide them from view. Covered snaps are used only on high-priced garments. Sew-on snaps are available in sizes 4/0 (small) to size 4 (large). Most snaps are metal, although small, clear plastic ones are available for use on lightweight blouses. Plastic is not as durable as metal and can melt if ironed.

Mechanically attached snaps are used on medium- to heavy-weight casual garments. Secured to the garment by machine, they are used in areas that must withstand repeated snapping and unsnapping. They make ideal closures for jeans, western wear, and infant and toddler pants' inseams. For optimal wear on infant and toddler wear, it is recommended that snap closures be able to sustain 15 pounds of pull before they open. This will keep the garment closed during wear but be relatively easy for an adult to manipulate when dressing and undressing the child.

Snap tape may be used to apply a series of snaps. It is a strip of fabric, often twill tape, with mechanically attached snaps. Snap tape is easier to apply than rows of individual snaps, but the twill tape has a propensity to shrink, it is available in only a few colors, and the preset distance between snaps may not be compatible with the size of the garment. Nevertheless, it is often found in infant and toddler pants.

Belts

Belts hold garments together or in place at the waist and provide a decorative finish to some garment styles. They may be tied, buckled, or held together by another form of closure. Self-belts are those that are made of the shell fabric of the garment. Other materials may be used, such as contrasting fabrics, leather, metal, or vinyl. The cost of self-belts tends to be lower than that of other materials. Those that are stitched cost more than those that are glued together, but stitched belts have better durability. The three main shapes of belts are straight, contoured, and tie (Figure 10.9). The importance of belts and the selection of materials used to construct them tends to follow fashion trends.

Rather than developing their own coordinated belts to match each style, some manufacturers purchase premade belts to accompany their garments as a means of increasing the overall appeal of the finished garment to the consumer. These add-on belts tend to be of lower quality than those constructed specifically for an individual style.

Figure 10.9. *Belt styling categories include straight, tie, string, and contoured.*

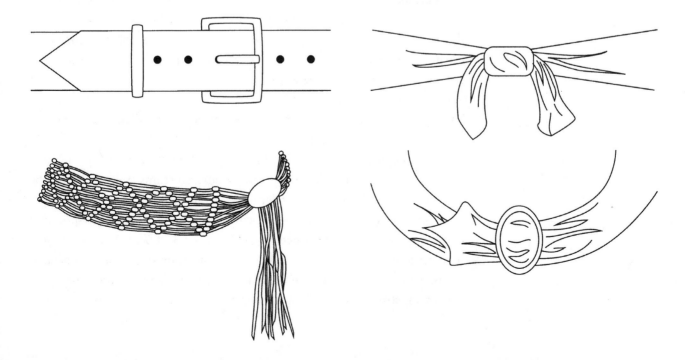

Table 10.1 THREAD SIZE SELECTION BY FABRIC WEIGHT

FABRIC WEIGHT	FABRIC WEIGHT OUNCES/SQUARE YARD	THREAD TEX SIZE	APPLICATION
Extra-light	2–4 ounces	T-18, T-21, T-24	Sheer blouses, T-shirts
Light	4–5 ounces	T-24, T-27, T-30	Dress shirts, dresses, knit tops
Medium	6–8 ounces	T-30, T-35, T-40	Chino pants, fleece sweatshirts
Medium-heavy	8–10 ounces	T-50, T-60, T-70	Lightweight demins, coveralls
Heavy	10–14 ounces	T-80, T-90, T-105	Heavy denims, parkas
Extra-heavy	Over 14 ounces	T-120, T-135	Heavy stretch denims

Source: American and Efird, Inc. 1997

Thread

Thread is a strong, slender form of yarn used for stitching in garments. It must be selected with great care so that it is compatible with the shell. Thread can have a strong impact on the quality of the finished product and on the durability of the product during wear. Thread is selected not only for its color, but also for its size, strength, elasticity, colorfastness, and ability to form stitches during the construction process. Factory sewing methods can precipitate thread breakage, skipped stitches, melting of thermoplastic fiber threads, and puckered seams. Selection of appropriate threads can help prevent these problems. Table 10.1 provides guidelines for thread size according to fabric weight.

Threads are available in a variety of fiber types and combinations. Among the most common is cotton, which is weaker than synthetics but performs well during sewing. The major problem with cotton thread is potential shrinkage during garment maintenance. Mercerized cotton thread has been treated with sodium hydroxide to increase its strength and luster, improve its ability to absorb dyes, and improve its dimensional stability. Polyester and nylon lend enormous strength to threads and can be made in very fine diameters. However, threads made of these substances may not be resistant to the heat created by high-speed construction and could actually melt or stretch during stitching, then relax after cooling down and cause puckered seams. Silk thread can be very beautiful and dyed in a wonderful color range, but it is very expensive.

The majority of threads used in commercial construction are spun and corespun threads. **Spun thread** is made of staple fibers that are twisted together to form the thread. It may be made of cotton or synthetic fibers and is strong and elastic. **Corespun thread** is built with a spun nylon or polyester core that is strong and elastic. It is then wrapped with cotton or another staple fiber that is resistant to the heat created during sewing and comfortable to the touch during wear. It is used extensively in garments made of woven fabrics; however it is one of the more expensive forms of thread. **Monofilament thread** is made of a single strand of fiber and is very strong, inexpensive, and transparent in color, so it does not need matching, but it is also stiff and slippery and the ends are annoying and scratchy when worn. This thread is typically used only in lower-priced garments or hems. **Multifilament thread** is made of several filaments twisted together, and if texturized on the surface, it will not slip. This type of thread has greater elasticity than some other types, making it especially useful in constructing knit garments.

Thread that is color-matched to the shell fabric is a sign of quality in a garment, but this step raises the overall cost of garments because the thread color must be changed for every fabric color that comes through the production line. Although the color of thread used on the interior seams may be of somewhat different color, the color of thread used in visible stitching should be carefully matched to the fabric. The exception, of course, is decorative stitching, which may be purposefully done in contrasting colors.

Thread is purchased by fiber content, diameter (size), color, and type of put-up. The diameter of the thread is selected for its compatibility with the fabrics selected for garment construction; the size is usually cited by the *tex* system used for yarns. The tex is based on metric measurements; the larger the number, the larger the diameter of the thread. **Put-up** refers to the type of spool or cone that the thread is on. If small quantities are needed, spools are used; but if greater quantities of a color are required, they may be ordered in cops or cones. Cones are the most commonly used put-up form in factory settings, while spools are used more often in haute couture construction and the making of sample garments.

Elastics

Elastics are a specific category of fabric that is defined by the ability to repeatedly stretch and return to its original size. As long as the product can do both, it is useful; but if it fails to perform either the stretch or the recovery function, it is not only defective but also can render an entire garment unwearable.

Elastics are used to shape garments and hold them close to the body. Elastics may be completely covered when they are inserted into casings formed by garment fabric; they may be a complete garment component, such as a bra strap or panty waistband; or they may be a facing that finishes the edge of a garment, such as on a swimsuit or jogging shorts. Elastic thread may be stitched directly onto the garment surface in rows, thus creating an area of shirring that conforms to the contour of the body.

The type of elastic used depends on the styling requirements of the garment. The amount of stretch required, the way it will be used, the compatibility of its weight to the shell fabric, its flexibility and holding power, and its hand are all considerations for elastic selection. Elastic is made of either rubber or spandex fibers covered with polyester, cotton, or another fiber to make it more comfortable and aesthetically pleasing. Fiber content and care instructions must be compatible with the shell. In general, rubber is less expensive, whereas the synthetic spandex is stronger and lasts longer. Chlorine bleach can degrade rubber elastics. The structure of elastic may be woven, knitted, or braided. Braided elastic stretches very well, but is bulky and should only be used in a casing. Woven elastic is the most costly and tends to be heavy, but it is very stable and is the best selection where firm control is needed. Knitted elastic is soft, lighter in weight, and less expensive. Both woven and knitted elastics may be sewn directly into a garment. The width of an elastic should be determined by the look desired in the style, while taking into account that the wider the elastic, the higher is its cost.

Labels

Labels are printed or woven attachments to garments that provide written information for the consumer. The government requires some labeling information and specifies where labels must be located, but most decisions about labels are at the discretion of the product developer. Because what the labels say cannot be determined until other materials are selected and tested, the testing of fabrics should be done as early as possible in the product development process to provide lead time for preparation of appropriate labels.

Materials for Labels

When selecting the fabric to use in a label, the product developer must consider compatibility with the garment shell as well as the label fabric's durability and ease of attachment to the garment. Another consideration is whether the cost of the preferred label is within the overall budget. Purchasing label stock and handling the printing is the most flexible method of preparation of labels for a firm. Preprinted labels may be secured from a label supplier. Printed labels are the least expensive. They can be coated to improve print durability; but this treatment stiffens the fabric, and, if the label becomes uncomfortable during wear, the customer may remove it and lose needed information. Nonwoven labels, called **paper labels** in the industry, are printed and frequently used on casual and lower-priced clothing.

Woven labels are the most costly and require the longest lead time, but they are also the most durable and create a high-quality impression. Woven labels are available in plain or jacquard weave and in widths of ¼ inch to several inches.

Government Requirements

The government requires some categories of information on labels, including the generic fiber content, producer's identification (either brand name or regis-

Figure 10.10. *Methods of attaching labels to garments.*

Flat-stitch all around

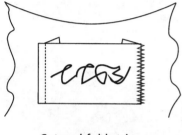

Cut and fold strip
Stitch ends with straight
or zigzag stitch

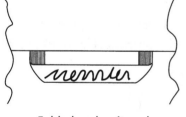

Folded ends mitered
and sewn into seam

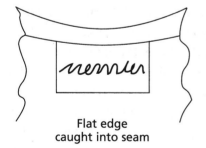

Flat edge
caught into seam

tration number), and country of origin. The Federal Trade Commission (FTC) also regulates the location of that information on the garment. The other major FTC requirement in labeling is that the care instructions for the garment, either in specific wording or approved care symbols, be permanently attached to the garment. (This information is described in detail in chapter 12.)

Brand Labels

Brand labels are usually large, colorful, and affixed in a prominent location. They help the consumer quickly identify the product. Size labels are also often prepared to help customers easily find their choice. Larger temporary labels, referred to as hangtags, are especially helpful in self-service environments. These hangtags, along with tickets, are used to communicate useful information about style number, size, season, color, and price. Tickets and hangtags are useful at the point of sale but are removed after purchase. The information they contain may be presented in bar codes suitable for scanning, in simple readable form, or in a combination of both. If the garment is being produced in a union shop or factory, provision will be made for inclusion of a union-made label.

Label Styles

There are several styles of labels. The most common styles are variations of **flat labels**. These labels are simply strips of narrow fabric. The most common use of these labels is identification of the brand on a variety of products. One style of flat label is finished on two edges and heat-sealed on the other two edges. It may be sewn into the garment either on the unfinished ends or on all four edges. Another flat label variation is cut on two ends and folded under to prevent raveling before being sewn into the garment on the folded ends. A third type of flat label is an iron-on or fused label. Manufacturers who produce private-label goods for several retailers and have to place the labels into the garment at the last minute often use these fused labels; they are frequently found on lower-priced garments.

A **folded loop label** is a longer flat label with ends folded diagonally to the underside to leave extensions that can be sewn into the seam at the neckline. This is a common method for attaching brand labels to a shirt or blouse without leaving a visible stitching line on the garment surface.

Another style is a flat or **folded label**, which is a flat piece folded in half. This style is sewn directly into a seam or attached to the edge of another label. It is usually printed and is often nonwoven; it provides a flexible method for inclusion of a variety of additional information, both required and voluntary (Figure 10.10).

A newer form of labeling apparel is printing label information directly on the shell fabric via heat transfer. This form of labeling eliminates the need for a sewn-in label and is most frequently found on knit shirts, undergarments, and socks. When properly applied, this permanent print label will

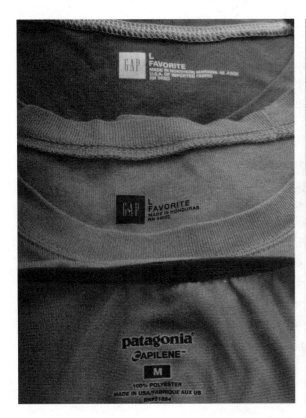

Figure 10.11a. *Labels may be printed directly on garments.*

Figure 10.11b. *Machine used for printing labels directly on socks.*

satisfy some of the government's permanent labeling requirements and remain visible throughout the useful life of the garment (Figure 10.11a–b).

Trims

Trims may be classified as decorative materials or surface treatments that embellish a garment and add distinctiveness to a style. When trims are selected for a style, several broad design factors must be considered: The cost of the trim must be within the overall price guidelines established for the garment. The trim should be the same quality as the shell fabric so that neither the trim nor the shell overwhelms the other. Acquisition of the selected trim should not delay production. Care instructions for the trim should be compatible with those for the shell fabric. And finally, the design of the trim, including its color, shape, and scale, should be compatible with the overall silhouette of the style and contribute to the desirability of the garment.

Some designers consider trim to include components of the garment such as pockets, cuffs, collars, and buttons. These components are addressed elsewhere in this text. The trims discussed here are decorative details added to the basic garment silhouette. Categories of trim include linear trims, such as decorative edgings and seams; narrow fabrics trims, such as ribbons, passementerie, and laces; surface embellishments, such as embroidery, appliqués, and screen printing; and decorative edgings, such as ruffles and bindings.

Linear Trims

Linear trims form lines on the surface or edges of the garment. **Decorative edgings and seams** are forms of linear trims. They are developed during the basic construction process and are among the least expensive forms of trim. This category includes seam variations, such as welt seams and slot seams; surface stitching, such as topstitching, hem stitching, fagoting, and pin tucks; and seam edgings, such as cording, piping, overlock stitching, picot edging, and lettuce edging. Many of these decorative edgings and seams require special machines for their execution. Rather than investing in additional machines that will be used infrequently, product developers may elect to send garment components to a trim house that specializes in completing these novelty applications.

Topstitching and **edge-stitching** are done on the outside of the garment and are ornamental in purpose. The only difference between them is the distance they appear from the edge. They may be done as a single row of stitching or as several parallel rows. **Hemstitching** is done by removing parallel threads in the shell fabric and securing groups of the remaining threads together to form a decorative ladder. **Fagoting** appears very similar to hemstitching at first glance, but it is made by connecting two folded edges of shell fabric together via decorative stitching.

Piping and **cording** entail the insertion of a folded strip of self-fabric or contrasting fabric into the seam. The major difference between them is that piping does not require cording to plump up the edge.

Some of these types of decorative stitching have more traditional applications, such as pin tucks on the bodice front of a blouse or lettuce edging as a substitute for a folded hem on lingerie. Many of the other trims in this category come and go with the whims of fashion.

Narrow Fabric Trims

A second form of linear trims is **narrow fabric trims**. This is a broad category that includes ribbons, passementerie, and laces. Flat varieties of these narrow trims are used for straight lines, whereas braids and gathered laces can be used in straight or curved applications. Linear trim varieties are sold on cards and come in widths ranging from ⅛ inch to 4 inches.

Ribbon

Ribbon is a narrow woven fabric with finished edges. It is available in widths of ⅛ inch to several inches. Ribbons, similar to other fabrics, vary significantly in quality. Colors may bleed onto the garment, and heavily sized (stiffened or starched) ribbons may not hold their shape during wear. It is recommended that ribbons sewn onto a garment be preshrunk. The ribbons discussed here should not be confused with craft ribbon, which is cut from wider fabric. Craft ribbon will fray at the edges and should not be used on garments.

Common types of ribbon include satin ribbon, with a shiny, smooth surface; grosgrain ribbon, with a ribbed surface and crisp appearance; velvet ribbon, with a pile surface; novelty ribbon, with a pattern woven into it; picot-edge ribbon, with tiny loops woven on the edges; and **ruching**, which is a pleated ribbon.

Passementerie

Passementerie is an umbrella term that includes a broad range of braids and cords in straight, curved, fringe, or tassel forms. The braids and cords are made by twining sets of threads into a pattern to form narrow strips of braid or thick strings of cording that are heavier than ribbon. Several types are commonly used in apparel:

- *Soutache*—a narrow flexible braid used to form scrolling patterns on a fabric surface

- *Middy braid*—wider than soutache and traditionally used on sailor collars

- *Gimp braid*—more decorative and heavier than soutache or middy braid; made of cord

- *Rickrack*—a woven zigzag trim available in several widths

- *Fold-over braid*—knit or woven trim with a built-in crease to allow encasing a garment edge, such as on a boiled wool jacket

Cording is heavier than thread and stronger and more compact than yarn. It can be curved and twisted into many design variations. Three prime examples of the use of cording as a garment trim are frogs, lacings, and tie belts.

Lace

Lace is an openwork trim or fabric that is made into intricate designs by the intertwining of many threads. Lace can be light and airy or heavily textured. Lace is most frequently used in lingerie and bridal wear. Today, most laces are machine-made, but lace has a long and illustrious history as a handicraft. The cost of handmade laces is prohibitive for all but the most costly garments. The cost of the machine-made laces depends on the quality of the threads and the complexity of the design. The three main categories of lace are identified by the machines that are used to make them:

1. **Leavers machines** produce the higher-cost laces that involve considerable complexity and open work.

2. **Raschel knit machines** produce lower-cost knit laces in a variety of weights.

3. **Schiffli embroidery machines** produce eyelet and Venetian laces.

Although eyelet is not a true lace, it is commonly treated as one. Eyelet is made of cotton lawn with holes punched in it; embroidery work is done on

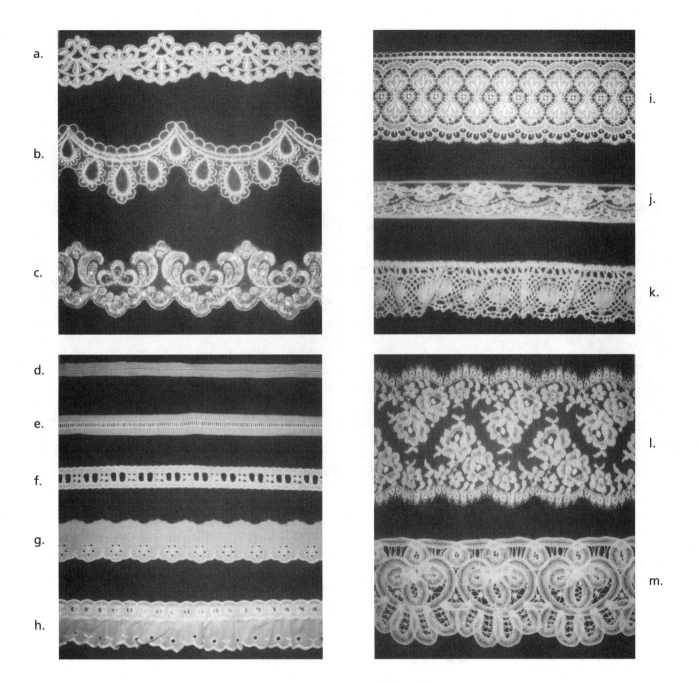

Figure 10.12. *Examples of a variety of laces, identified by style: (a), (b), (c), and (l) are galloon; (h), (i), (k) and (m) are edging; (d), (e), (f) and (j) are insertion, while (f) is a beading. Laces are also identified by type: (b), (c) and (l) are Venetian; (m) is a Battenburg; (d) through (h) are forms of eyelet; (k) is a Cluny knit; (i) and (j) are Raschel knits; and (a) is a Chantilly.*

the surface around the holes. Machine-made Venetian laces are characterized by the appearance of lacy embroidery on a fine tulle netting background surface. Battenburg lace is made of loops of narrow, flexible tape secured in place by threads.

Figures 10.12 and 10.13 show the styles and types of lace and garments featuring lace. Lace can be identified by its style:

- *Edging*—any flat or gathered lace with one scalloped edge and one straight edge

- *Insertion*—any flat lace with two straight edges that enable it to be inset between two pieces of fabric, making a continuous surface

Figure 10.13a. *Belted dress utilizing lace medallions as trim.*

Figure 10.13b. *Youthful maternity dress made of lace.*

- *Galloon*—any flat lace with two scalloped edges

- *Beading*—any flat lace with eyelets positioned for threading ribbon into it

- *Medallion*—any separate lace motif that can be applied to another fabric or to a shaped opening

Surface Embellishments

Surface embellishments are additions to a garment whose sole purpose is to add decorative appeal. This category includes appliqués, embroidery, and screen printing.

Appliqués

Appliqués are surface decorations formed by thread, fabric, or nonfabric materials such as grommets, sequins, and beads. Fabric appliqués are produced by fusing cut pieces of fabric to a backing to stabilize them and then applying the pieces to the garment with machine stitching such as satin stitches. Other appliqués are made as separate emblems or shapes, such as badges or insignia, and are then sewn to the garment surface. The inside of the shell shows only the stitching used to attach the appliqué to the garment.

Some nonfabric forms of appliqué include sequins and beading. Sequins are disks of reflective material that are sewn onto a fabric surface individually or in threaded strings. Beading may also be done individually, in strings, or stitched onto separate pieces of fabric backing and then stitched to the surface of the finished garment. The costs of applying sequins and beading by hand can heavily affect the overall cost of a garment. Gluing them onto the garment may control costs, but this method significantly lowers the quality level. Beading is often used on bridal wear; it cycles in and out of fashion as an embellishment in many categories of apparel (Figure 10.14).

Embroidery

Embroidery is trim formed by making thread patterns on the surface of the garment. As in the case of sequins or beading, the costs of embroidery vary significantly depending on whether the design is done by hand or by machine (Figure 10.15a–b). The type of threads that are used (preferably lustrous and colorfast ones) and the complexity of the design (number of colors involved) affect costs. Another cost factor is whether the design is individualized or

Figure 10.14. *Oscar de la Renta jacket featuring beading as its trim.*

Figure 10.15a. *Embroidered trim contributes aesthetically to Halle Berry's gown for the Academy Awards.*

Figure 10.15b. *People for Peace jeans feature denim embellished with embroidery.*

mass-produced. The availability of intricate embroidery designs produced by computer-controlled Schiffli machines has popularized this form of trim in recent years. In recent collections, four embroidery choices have been notably popular:

- *Monograms*—usually satin-stitched in the form of initials

- *Floral*—motifs of flowers and/or leaves worked in thread, and sometimes further enhanced by the addition of beads, gems or sequins

- *Cutwork*—produced by making holes in fabric and surrounding the holes with embroidery (similar to eyelet, but with larger motifs)

- *Trapunto*—done by padding a stitched pattern on the garment surface to produce a three-dimensional design

Screen Printing

The application of a printed design to an area of a garment rather than to the whole garment is another form of surface embellishment. This decoration may be applied via screen printing or heat-transfer printing as described in

Figure 10.16a. *Comparison of construction for ruffles and flounces.*

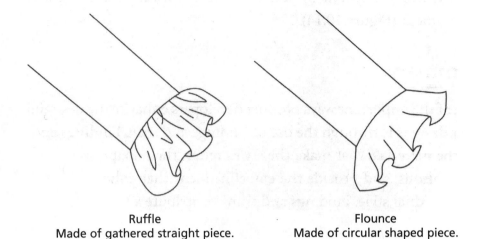

Ruffle
Made of gathered straight piece.

Flounce
Made of circular shaped piece.

chapter 6. The cost for this kind of printing varies, depending on complexity and the amount of individualization required. As with all trims, the use of appropriate colors and dyes to ensure colorfastness is a critical factor with this form of embellishment. Furthermore, screen-printed motifs must be carefully placed on a garment in order to avoid inappropriate accenting of some areas, such as the crotch, the crown of the bust, or the stomach. Indiscriminate placement makes the garment look more like a costume than appropriate daily dress.

Decorative Details

Some decorative trims defy classification. These details of style design include ruffles, flounces, and smocking. Each of these details involves manipulation of the shell fabric in some way beyond the basic structure of the garment.

Ruffles

Ruffles are strips of self-fabric or contrasting fabrics that are gathered to add considerable fullness and then attached to the garment to enhance an area such as the bottom of the hem or the edge of a sleeve (Figure 10.16a–b). If ruffles are built into stair-step layers to further increase the fullness, they are referred to as *tiers*.

Flounces

Flounces are used in a similar manner to ruffles, but are constructed from circular cuts of fabric rather than strips (Figure 10.16a, c). A more specific application of a ruffle or flounce is a cascade of fabric down the front of a blouse. This is called a **jabot**. Flounces are often more expensive to construct than ruffles because of the amount of fabric required to produce them and the curved nature of their construction.

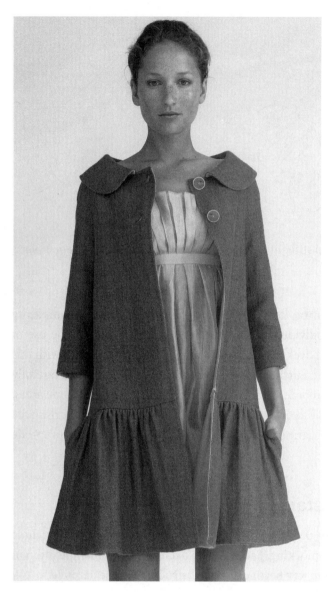

Figure 10.16b. *A ruffle trims the bottom of a coat.*

Figure 10.16c. *Tiers of flounces form the skirt of this dress.*

Smocking

Smocking is a technique in which a section of fabric is pulled into a smaller area by making many tiny parallel tucks and securing them into place with decorative embroidery. It is a traditional trim on the neckline yoke of children's wear (Figure 10.17). It may be achieved by hand or machine. As with other trims, if it is done by hand, the cost of the garment will increase significantly.

Summary

One of the important ways product developers enhance the desirability of their designs is through the use of findings and trim. Findings and trims are the materials that help the styles retain their shape, that meet customer expectations, and that provide the embellishment that enhances the look of an indi-

Figure 10.17. *Smocking is traditionally used on the yoke of children's dresses.*

vidual style. Findings and trims contribute a wide range of attributes to finished garments, from improving their functional characteristics to providing unique and distinctive aesthetic decoration.

Findings are a category of component materials that include support materials, closures, threads, elastics, and labels. Closures include zippers, buttons, hooks and eyes, snap tape, and Velcro hook and loop tape.

Trim is a comprehensive category that includes structural decorations that are built into the garment or attached to the surface. Examples of structural decoration include cording and pin tucks. Examples of applied trims include lace sewn on an edge or a monogram embroidered on the surface.

The choice of appropriate findings and trims is critical. If the wrong one is selected, or if one of these components fails when in use, the entire garment may be rendered unwearable. Therefore, great care must be taken in the selection and use of these materials.

Key Terms

appliqué	edge-stitching
belts	elastic
boning	embroidery
bra cups	eyes
buttons	fagoting
closures	findings
collar stays	flat label
cording	flounces
corespun thread	folded label
decorative edging and seams	folded loop label

frog

gross

hemstitchng

hook-and-eye closures

hook and loop tape

interfacing

interlining

jabot

labels

lace

Leavers machine

lignes

lining

loops

monofilament thread

multifilament thread

narrow fabric trim

overlap

paper labels

passementerie

pilling

piping

put-up

Raschel knit machine

ribbon

ruching

ruffles

Schiffli embroidery machine

seam tapes

shank

shoulder pads

sleeve headers

smocking

snap

snap tape

spun thread

strike-through

support materials

thread

toggle

topstitching

trims

underlap

underlining

wicking

zipper

Discussion Questions

1. What criteria are used to select interlinings?

2. What criteria are used to select trims?

3. Which findings and trims would be required to complete the entire line of garments you designed as an activity in chapter 8?

Activities

1. Select examples of all findings and trims needed for the line designed in chapter 8.

2. Select three sets of possible alternatives for the findings and trims needed for the garment developed for your cost sheet in chapter 8. Base your selections solely on costs ranging from budget to expensive.

3. Make your final choices of findings and trims for your line and defend these choices to your design group, based on the business plan set up in chapter 2.

    or

4. Design a three-piece group that utilizes embroidery or appliqué as a trim. Design your trim motif and spec the appropriate materials, e.g., threads.

    or

5. Research a culture related to your heritage. Develop an embroidery motif based on your research and put it into a repeat scaled for a garment. Apply the embroidery motif you designed to several garments.

References

American and Efird, Inc. 1997. Thread selection chart. www.amefird.com/-fabric_weights_thread_size_chart.htm (accessed September 10, 2006).

Brown, P., and J. Rice. 2001. *Ready-to-wear apparel analysis.* 3d ed. Upper Saddle River, NJ: Prentice-Hall.

Skrebneski, Victor, and Laura Jacobs. 1995. *The art of haute couture.* New York: Abbeville Press, Inc.

Additional Resources

Diamond, J., and E. Diamond. 2002. *The world of fashion.* 3d ed. New York: Fairchild.

Friggs, G. S. 1996. *Fashion from concept to consumer.* 5th ed. Upper Saddle River, NJ: Prentice-Hall.

Glock, R. E., and G. I. Kunz. 2000. *Apparel manufacturing: Sewn product analysis.* 3d ed. Upper Saddle River, NJ: Prentice-Hall.

CHAPTER 11

SIZING AND FIT

"Sizing data have consistently shown that the average woman in America is a size 14."

—SUSAN REDA, *STORES*

OBJECTIVES

- To define sizing as interpreted in today's market
- To examine the history of voluntary sizing standards
- To identify the size categories of women's, men's, and children's apparel
- To define fit and its components
- To understand the role of dress forms and fit models
- To understand the use of grading

Garments must be designed and produced to fit the target customer. Manufacturers tend to believe that if the line they produce is selling, there is no problem with fit. Yet they have a responsibility to provide a degree of consistency of sizing across styles and product offerings, to meet customer expectations, and to communicate brand identity to the potential customer. This consistency is achieved through the use of a sizing system. Apparel product developers are responsible for determining their firm's sizing system as a reflection of the needs of their target customers.

Sizing

Sizing refers to the assignment of individuals of a particular body type into categories that reflect the body measurements of those in that size group. Sizing issues are common to all categories of clothing, including men's and children's, but are more fully documented in women's ready-to-wear. Women's sizing issues appear more complex because of changing fashion, arbitrary sizing nomenclature, and evolving body types.

One of the major sources of some of the sizing problems in the apparel industry is the diversity of the U.S. population. Because of the presence of many different ethnic groups, the U.S. population of close to 300 million people poses a more complex sizing issue than any other consumer market in the world. Homogeneous ethnic populations are much easier to supply. For example, in Japan less than a dozen sizes of women's apparel are typically needed. In the United States, by comparison, women's clothing is developed and sold in categories for misses, juniors, petites, women's, women's petite, and maternity, with about eight to ten sizes in each category. In addition to the issue of diversity, the typical American figure is still evolving because of intermarriage and lifestyle changes, including eating habits and general fitness. Product developers and buyers must be knowledgeable about the target population of the geographic area to which they market if they are to produce apparel that will fit their target customers.

History of Women's Apparel Sizing

In the past, sizing charts were developed to reflect groupings of young women and mature women. Numbers were assigned that reflected the age or girth of the women within these groupings. Early in the 20th century, firms that were producing garments for catalog sale needed to have some consistency in the measurements of their products so that consumers could purchase garments without trying them on. This need precipitated some of the first American sizing charts. The original charts became inadequate as more and more garments were produced for an increasingly diverse population of customers. Although some attempts were made to standardize sizing in the United States, the Federal Trade Commission and the Bureau of Standards of the Department of Commerce (DOC) could only recommend measurements that were in common use in the business. Remember, there are no mandatory sizing standards in the United States. Available tables serve only as voluntary guidelines for product development and as starting points for each firm to size its styles for its own target consumers.

First Sizing Systems

The first full sizing system in the United States consisted of a set of size charts based on anthropometric data collected by the military in 1941. The data comprised body measurements of women in the U.S. Army at that time. The measurement data were analyzed by O'Brien and Shelton, and the results were published by the Department of Commerce (DOC) in 1948 (Standard Table of Body Measurements, 1994). The original database was geared toward younger white women and contained a low representation of women over 55 years of age.

Recognizing the inadequacy of the original charts, largely caused by lack of ethnic diversity and age group representation, the DOC revisited the original database and updated the sizing charts for women. The resulting revised standard was published by the National Institute of Standards and Technology (NIST) as Voluntary Product Standard PS 42-70 in 1971.

This revision also proved to be of limited usefulness because limitations in the original database continued to have an impact on the final charts. The government finally revoked the standard and turned the charts over to what was the American Society for Testing and Materials (now ASTM International); ASTM assigned the task of updating and monitoring the voluntary apparel sizing standards to Committee D13.55, a subcommittee of the larger textiles committee that develops and refines voluntary standards in many areas of textile and apparel testing and materials for the United States. Over the years, the original military numbers have been reworked and adapted several times. In 1994, ASTM published a revision of the misses size range as voluntary standard D5585-94. This revision was based on information collected from manufacturers, retailers, and the U.S. military and was believed to reflect measurements actually in use in the industry.

Updates

The only new contributions of actual body measurement data during ensuing years were added in the late 1980s. A group of academics from the University of Arizona at Tucson directed a study that measured a large sample of women over age 55. Although this study was heralded as a way of improving fit for the female population, some found that its results only added to the problem. The variations between the mature and general populations tended to occur only in the location and distribution of weight and shape. The study discerned no need for a separate size range because it found that mature women's measurements tended to parallel those of younger populations in most areas of the body. However, the results did reflect the need for fitting changes for mature consumers to accommodate

- vertical slippage due to lost muscle tone and compression of the vertebrae

- thickening of the waist

- a tendency of the head and shoulders to roll forward, causing a broadening of the back and a shortening of the front bodice areas

In 2001 ASTM released another update, D5585-94R01 Standard Table of Body Measurements for Adult Female Misses Figure Type, Sizes 2–20 (Table 11.1). To appreciate the complexity of the voluntary sizing charts that are available, note that for each of the ten sizes in the chart, 39 girth, vertical, length, and width locations are identified and measurements given. In the last decade, ASTM has updated size ranges for petites and womens sizes, and in 2006 it added a maternity table of sizes to their available voluntary standards. A variety of updated tables for men and children have also been released.

The end result of all of these past efforts to standardize the sizing charts is that individual companies wishing to use the ASTM voluntary sizing charts do so, but they are free to adapt them to their own needs. While some companies follow the ASTM International body measurement charts, many consumers, manufacturers, and retailers agree that the voluntary sizing standards in use today do not represent women's body measurements.

New Body Measurement Data

SizeUSA was an anthropometric research study developed by [TC]², industry participants, and the Department of Commerce. The purpose of the study was to gather actual body measurement data on U.S. consumers using a 3D measurement system and a body scanner and to feed that data into measurement extraction software (Case Study 11.1, The [TC]² Body Scanner; Figure 11.1). Data collection was completed in September 2003. Jim Lovejoy, SizeUSA Director, reported that measurement data were gathered on over 10,000 participants: 63 percent women and 37 percent men. The ethnicity of the participants was 51 percent white, 18 percent black, 16 percent Hispanic, and 15 percent Asian and other; they came from the east, west, and middle of the country (www.sizeusa.com). Table 11.2 shows comparisons of basic SizeUSA and ASTM International average size findings.

Janice Wang claims that the "root cause of many ill-fitting garments is the industry misconception that the hourglass figure is the dominant body shape today" (Speer 2006, 40). The SizeUSA data showed that the hourglass is the least dominant shape even though the industry has persistently based its grade rules on that shape. In her work with the SizeUSA data, Cynthia. L. Istook actually defined nine body shapes and honed in on four dominant types:

- *Rectangle shape*—bust and hips are basically the same circumference; the waist is less than 9 inches smaller than the bust. This shape represents 46.12 percent of those scanned.

- *Spoon shape*—hips are larger than the bust by 2 inches or more; the waist is less than 9.25 inches smaller than the bust. This shape represents 20.92 percent of the sample.

- *Inverted triangle*—bust is larger than the hips by 3.6 inches or more; the waist is less than 9 inches smaller than the bust. This shape represents 13.83 percent of those scanned.

- *Hourglass*—bust and hips are basically same circumference; the waist is smaller than the bust by 9 inches or more. This shape made up 8.4 percent of the sample.

Other shapes were 10.72 percent of the scanned participants and varied in shape descriptions (Speer 2006, 40).

Additional general findings from SizeUSA are: (1) 58 percent of the women surveyed thought they were somewhat to quite a bit overweight; (2) we get larger as we get older, especially through the waist and hip area; and (3) only 10 to 20 percent of most groups fit the ASTM standard size tables,

Table 11.1 STANDARD TABLE OF BODY MEASUREMENTS FOR ADULT FEMALES MISSES FIGURE TYPE, SIZES 2–20

Girth Measurements in inches.

Size	2	4	6	8	10	12	14	16	18	20
Bust	32	33	34	35	36	$37\frac{1}{2}$	39	$40\frac{1}{2}$	$42\frac{1}{2}$	$44\frac{1}{2}$
Waist	24	25	26	27	28	$29\frac{1}{2}$	31	$32\frac{1}{2}$	$34\frac{1}{2}$	$36\frac{1}{2}$
High hip	$31\frac{1}{2}$	$32\frac{1}{2}$	$33\frac{1}{2}$	$34\frac{1}{2}$	$35\frac{1}{2}$	37	$38\frac{1}{2}$	40	42	44
Hip	$34\frac{1}{2}$	$35\frac{1}{2}$	$36\frac{1}{2}$	$37\frac{1}{2}$	$38\frac{1}{2}$	40	$41\frac{1}{2}$	43	45	47
Mid-neck	13	$13\frac{1}{4}$	$13\frac{1}{2}$	$13\frac{3}{4}$	14	$14\frac{3}{8}$	$14\frac{3}{4}$	$15\frac{1}{8}$	$15\frac{5}{8}$	$16\frac{1}{8}$
Neck base	$13\frac{1}{2}$	$13\frac{3}{4}$	14	$14\frac{1}{4}$	$14\frac{1}{2}$	$14\frac{7}{8}$	$15\frac{1}{4}$	$15\frac{5}{8}$	$16\frac{1}{8}$	$16\frac{5}{8}$
Armscye	$14\frac{1}{4}$	$14\frac{5}{8}$	15	$15\frac{3}{8}$	$15\frac{3}{4}$	$16\frac{3}{8}$	17	$17\frac{5}{8}$	$18\frac{3}{8}$	$19\frac{1}{8}$
Upper arm	10	$10\frac{1}{4}$	$10\frac{1}{2}$	$10\frac{3}{4}$	11	$11\frac{1}{8}$	$11\frac{3}{4}$	$12\frac{1}{8}$	$12\frac{3}{4}$	$13\frac{3}{8}$
Elbow	$9\frac{3}{8}$	$9\frac{1}{2}$	$9\frac{5}{8}$	$9\frac{3}{4}$	$9\frac{7}{8}$	$10\frac{1}{8}$	$10\frac{3}{8}$	$10\frac{5}{8}$	11	$11\frac{1}{8}$
Wrist	$5\frac{5}{8}$	$5\frac{3}{4}$	$5\frac{7}{8}$	6	$6\frac{1}{8}$	$6\frac{1}{4}$	$6\frac{3}{8}$	$6\frac{1}{2}$	$6\frac{5}{8}$	$6\frac{3}{4}$
Thigh, max	$19\frac{1}{2}$	$20\frac{1}{4}$	21	$21\frac{3}{4}$	$22\frac{1}{4}$	$23\frac{1}{2}$	$24\frac{1}{2}$	$25\frac{1}{2}$	$26\frac{3}{4}$	28
Thigh, mid	$18\frac{1}{4}$	$18\frac{3}{4}$	$19\frac{1}{4}$	$19\frac{3}{4}$	$20\frac{1}{4}$	21	$21\frac{1}{4}$	$22\frac{1}{2}$	$23\frac{1}{2}$	$24\frac{1}{2}$
Knee	13	$13\frac{3}{8}$	$13\frac{3}{4}$	$14\frac{1}{8}$	$14\frac{1}{2}$	15	$15\frac{1}{2}$	16	$16\frac{1}{2}$	17
Calf	$12\frac{1}{2}$	$12\frac{7}{8}$	$13\frac{1}{4}$	$13\frac{5}{8}$	14	$14\frac{1}{2}$	15	$15\frac{1}{2}$	16	$16\frac{1}{2}$
Ankle	$8\frac{3}{8}$	$8\frac{5}{8}$	$8\frac{7}{8}$	$9\frac{1}{8}$	$9\frac{3}{8}$	$9\frac{5}{8}$	$9\frac{7}{8}$	$10\frac{1}{8}$	$10\frac{3}{8}$	$10\frac{5}{8}$
Vertical trunk	56	$57\frac{1}{2}$	59	$60\frac{1}{2}$	62	$63\frac{1}{2}$	65	$66\frac{1}{2}$	68	$69\frac{1}{2}$
Total crotch	25	$25\frac{3}{4}$	$26\frac{1}{2}$	$27\frac{1}{4}$	28	$28\frac{3}{4}$	$29\frac{1}{2}$	$30\frac{1}{4}$	31	$31\frac{3}{4}$

(Continued on page 353)

Table 11.1 STANDARD TABLE OF BODY MEASUREMENTS FOR ADULT FEMALES MISSES FIGURE TYPE, SIZES 2–20

Vertical Measurements in inches.

Size	2	4	6	8	10	12	14	16	18	20
Stature	$63\frac{1}{2}$	64	$64\frac{1}{2}$	65	$65\frac{1}{2}$	66	$66\frac{1}{2}$	67	$67\frac{1}{2}$	68
Cervical height	$54\frac{1}{2}$	55	$55\frac{1}{2}$	56	$56\frac{1}{2}$	57	$57\frac{1}{2}$	58	$58\frac{1}{2}$	59
Waist height	$39\frac{1}{4}$	$39\frac{1}{2}$	$39\frac{3}{4}$	40	$40\frac{1}{4}$	$40\frac{1}{2}$	$40\frac{3}{4}$	41	$41\frac{1}{4}$	$41\frac{1}{2}$
High hip height	$35\frac{1}{4}$	$35\frac{1}{2}$	$35\frac{3}{4}$	36	$36\frac{1}{4}$	$36\frac{1}{2}$	$36\frac{3}{4}$	37	$37\frac{1}{4}$	$37\frac{1}{2}$
Hip height	$31\frac{1}{4}$	$31\frac{1}{2}$	$31\frac{3}{4}$	32	$32\frac{1}{4}$	$32\frac{1}{2}$	$32\frac{3}{4}$	33	$33\frac{1}{4}$	$33\frac{1}{2}$
Crotch height	$29\frac{1}{4}$	$29\frac{1}{2}$	$29\frac{1}{2}$	$29\frac{1}{2}$	$29\frac{1}{2}$	$29\frac{1}{2}$	$29\frac{1}{2}$	$29\frac{1}{2}$	$29\frac{1}{2}$	$29\frac{1}{2}$
Knee height	$17\frac{5}{8}$	$17\frac{3}{4}$	$17\frac{7}{8}$	18	$18\frac{1}{8}$	$18\frac{1}{4}$	$18\frac{3}{8}$	$18\frac{1}{2}$	$18\frac{5}{8}$	$18\frac{3}{4}$
Ankle height	$2\frac{3}{4}$	$2\frac{3}{4}$	$2\frac{3}{4}$	$2\frac{3}{4}$	$2\frac{3}{4}$	$2\frac{3}{4}$	$2\frac{3}{4}$	$2\frac{3}{4}$	$2\frac{3}{4}$	$2\frac{3}{4}$
Waist length (front)	$13\frac{1}{2}$	$13\frac{3}{4}$	14	$14\frac{1}{4}$	$14\frac{1}{2}$	$14\frac{3}{4}$	15	$15\frac{1}{4}$	$15\frac{1}{2}$	$15\frac{3}{4}$
Waist length (back) (on Curve)	$15\frac{1}{2}$	$15\frac{3}{4}$	16	$16\frac{1}{4}$	$16\frac{1}{2}$	$16\frac{3}{4}$	17	$17\frac{1}{4}$	$17\frac{1}{2}$	$17\frac{3}{4}$
True rise	$9\frac{3}{4}$	10	$10\frac{1}{4}$	$10\frac{1}{2}$	$10\frac{3}{4}$	11	$11\frac{1}{4}$	$11\frac{1}{2}$	$11\frac{3}{4}$	12

Width and Length Measurements in inches.

Size	2	4	6	8	10	12	14	16	18	20
Across shoulder	$14\frac{3}{8}$	$14\frac{5}{8}$	$14\frac{7}{8}$	$15\frac{1}{8}$	$15\frac{3}{8}$	$15\frac{3}{4}$	$16\frac{1}{8}$	$16\frac{1}{2}$	17	$17\frac{1}{2}$
Cross-back width	$13\frac{7}{8}$	$14\frac{1}{8}$	$14\frac{3}{8}$	$14\frac{5}{8}$	$14\frac{7}{8}$	$15\frac{1}{4}$	$15\frac{5}{8}$	16	$16\frac{1}{2}$	17
Cross-chest width	$12\frac{7}{8}$	$13\frac{1}{8}$	$13\frac{3}{8}$	$13\frac{5}{8}$	$13\frac{7}{8}$	$14\frac{1}{4}$	$14\frac{5}{8}$	15	$15\frac{1}{2}$	16
Shoulder length	$4\frac{15}{16}$	5	$5\frac{1}{16}$	$5\frac{1}{8}$	$5\frac{3}{16}$	$5\frac{5}{16}$	$5\frac{7}{16}$	$5\frac{9}{16}$	$5\frac{3}{4}$	$5\frac{15}{16}$
Shoulder slope (degrees)	23	23	23	23	23	23	23	23	23	23
Arm length shoulder to wrist	$22\frac{15}{16}$	$23\frac{1}{8}$	$23\frac{5}{16}$	$23\frac{1}{2}$	$23\frac{11}{16}$	$23\frac{7}{8}$	$24\frac{1}{16}$	$24\frac{1}{4}$	$24\frac{7}{16}$	$24\frac{5}{8}$
Arm length shoulder to elbow	$13\frac{1}{4}$	$13\frac{3}{8}$	$13\frac{1}{2}$	$13\frac{5}{8}$	$13\frac{3}{4}$	$13\frac{7}{8}$	14	$14\frac{1}{8}$	$14\frac{1}{4}$	$14\frac{3}{8}$
Arm length center back neck to wrist	$30\frac{1}{8}$	$30\frac{7}{16}$	$30\frac{3}{4}$	$31\frac{1}{16}$	$31\frac{3}{8}$	$31\frac{3}{4}$	$32\frac{1}{8}$	$32\frac{1}{2}$	$32\frac{15}{16}$	$33\frac{3}{8}$
Bust point to bust point	7	$7\frac{1}{4}$	$7\frac{1}{2}$	$7\frac{3}{4}$	8	$8\frac{1}{4}$	$8\frac{1}{2}$	$8\frac{3}{4}$	9	$9\frac{1}{4}$
Neck to bust point	$9\frac{1}{4}$	$9\frac{1}{2}$	$9\frac{3}{4}$	10	$10\frac{1}{4}$	$10\frac{5}{8}$	11	$11\frac{3}{8}$	$11\frac{7}{8}$	$12\frac{3}{8}$
Scye depth	$7\frac{1}{8}$	$7\frac{1}{4}$	$7\frac{3}{8}$	$7\frac{1}{2}$	$7\frac{5}{8}$	$7\frac{3}{4}$	$7\frac{7}{8}$	8	$8\frac{1}{8}$	$8\frac{1}{4}$

CASE STUDY 11.1 THE [TC]² BODY SCANNER

Anyone who has ever been frustrated by trying to determine which size shirt, jeans, or other clothing item will fit best or has spent a lot of time going through the alteration process will benefit from a new technology developed by [TC]². This technology is a three-dimensional body measurement system that includes a white light–based scanner and proprietary measurement extraction software. The scanner captures hundreds of thousands of data points of an individual's image, and the software automatically extracts dozens of measurements. This measurement information can be electronically compared to garment specifications and other data in order to recommend the size an individual should purchase or use as a basis for made-to-measure clothing. This technology has tremendous implications for consumers shopping throughout all distribution channels, including bricks-and-mortar, catalog, and online. [TC]²'s scanning process is quick, fun, and generates extremely accurate measurements.

Numerous apparel CAD (computer aided design) packages have made-to-measure or pattern-alteration functions that can be used in concert with the scanner-based measurements to create a custom pattern for the customer. The measurements are formatted specifically for the target apparel CAD package so that the input of the data to the system and the output of the made-to-measure pattern, either to a fabric cutter or to a plotter, occur automatically. Additionally, the possibility exists for the customer to view the fit and appearance of both made-to-measure and standard-sized garments as a computer simulation (virtual try-on). The garment is draped on the consumer's three-dimensional scanned image, and he or she can see how the garment looks and fits before the purchase is made.

Source: Textile and Clothing Technology Corporation 2001

primarily because they are closer to a pear shape than an hourglass (*Modern Uniforms*, 2004).

J. C. Penney has already applied the findings of the SizeUSA study to product styles. It previously used the hourglass figure type but has adjusted grade rules to reflect the more dominant shapes of its customers. Mike Hannaford, Penney's manager of technical design, reports that changes have already been made to the company's private label collections. "Patterns were cut fuller and the differential between the waist and hips was adjusted to be more in line with current proportions" (Reda 2006).

Women's Sizing

Women's clothing is sized for adult women and is assigned numbers that reflect the relationship of height, bust, waist, hip, and torso length measurements.

Figure 11.1. *Before stepping into [TC]²'s scanner, a woman dons shorts and a top that won't distort her figure.*

The difference from one size to the next in a range is called the **grade**. Before the ASTM standards were developed, a 2-inch grade was used between all sizes. The 2-inch grade "rule" reflects the difference in girth of the bust, waist, and hip measurements as they increase from size to size. Today many manufacturers use a 1-inch grade difference between smaller sizes, a 1½-inch grade difference between sizes 10 and 12, and 2-inch grade difference between sizes larger than 12. In addition to the girth measurements, manufacturers must decide whether the proportional increase is consistent all over. For example, do height and length increase along with circumference? Are changes only to the circumference? Or is a combination of these measurements most appropriate for a company's target customer? As the findings of the SizeUSA study are applied, there is potential for continuing and significant changes in industry grading and grade rule applications.

Product developers must choose a sample size as a starting point for sizing garments. The **sample size** represents the body measurements from which the full size range is developed. It is common for the manufacturer to use a midsize as the sample size within the range. This necessitates grading down to the smallest size and up to largest size, and results in a more accurate grade

Table 11.2 COMPARISONS OF ASTM AND SIZEUSA BODY MEASUREMENTS

WOMEN	Bust	Waist	Hips	Height	Weight
ASTM Sample Size 8	35	27	37.5	5'5"*	NA
ASTM "Average" Size 14	39	31	41.5	5'6 1/2"	NA
SizeUSA "Average"	40.7	34.3	43	5'3.9"	
"Median"				5'4"	148
MEN	Chest	Waist	Hips	Height	Weight
ASTM Sample Size 40	40	34	40	5'10 1/4"	NA
ASTM "Median" Size 42	42	36	42	5'10 11/16"	NA
SizeUSA "Average"	42.6	36.9	41.6	5'9"	185

*Note that Sample styles for women are sometimes done for a model figure of over 5'9".

than if the grading were done in only one direction. A misses size 8 or 10 is commonly designated the sample size. Although a midsize sample designation yields a more accurate grade, some manufacturers select a slightly smaller sample size than their dominant customer sizes because sample size garments are frequently the ones available for advertising shoots and special promotions. Refer to Table 9.1 in chapter 9 for a listing of typically used sample sizes.

Because manufacturers make their size designations independent of one another, the variations from one company to the next can be extreme, meaning that the measurements of the actual garments labeled as being a particular size vary considerably from one company to the next. Some manufacturers have contributed to the sizing confusion by increasing the body measurements of their size designations so that the size numbers actually fit women of larger dimensions. This migration to larger measurements in a labeled size is commonly referred to as vanity sizing. We are defining **vanity sizing** as placing a smaller size label on a larger size garment. Hence, a woman of size 12 proportions can wear a size 10.

Although the ASTM International standard for misses is still in use, most apparel manufacturers have adjusted their sizes to reflect their own niche customers. "As a result, no two brands fit exactly the same. A woman can wear a size 4 in Banana Republic clothes, a size 6 in Ellen Tracy, and a size 10 in Ann Taylor" (Reda 2006). Viewed from the consumer perspective, this inconsistency in products has produced a phenomenon called **size migration**, which means that one woman typically fits into a range of three or more sizes, depending on the manufacturer and cut of the garment.

CASE STUDY 11.2 THE RIGHT FIT FROM INTELLIFIT

New technology is bringing the potential for clothing that actually fits the consumer closer to reality. Intellifit has adapted imaging technology, created to detect weapons in airports, to its body scanning booth, which bounces radio waves off your skin and can size you up in about ten 10 seconds, recording about 200,000 data points on your body. Unlike the light technology used in the [TC]² 3D light scanner, which requires that you wear a body-fitting garment and step into a dark booth to be scanned, there is no need to disrobe. The Intellifit scanner reads your body shape through your street clothing when you step into a clear plastic booth. The booth itself is rather large and lends itself to mall locations when used for data collection at retail sites.

Manufacturers and retailers are finding the Intellifit scanning booth a solution for many of their sizing problems. Intellifit's core products are customized markers, the leasing of the scanning booths, and developing a final product for firms who use its services in the form of a database of their individual customers' measurement points, and new measurement specs and grade rules for use in developing new product styles unique to that firm.

Some of the firms that have utilized the Intellifit scanning system include David's Bridal, Macy's, Lane Bryant, Lands' End, and Levi's. David's Bridal has used the results to revise its pattern size tables and grade rules for new product lines. Macy's is using the technology to improve the fit of some of its private label brands. Levi's utilized the system in some of its stores in major U.S. cities to predict best-fitting sizes of existing products; it had an accuracy of 92 percent in one test of 150 customers. More recently, Levi's used the scanner in conjunction with its Signature brand line of mass market jeans at Wal-Mart.

Sources: Corcoran 2005; Weathers 2006

Consumers have been confused by these inconsistencies and are putting pressure on manufacturers to improve their sizing systems. This pressure is expected to increase as nonstore purchases, such as catalog and Internet sales, continue to grow. Many retailers and product developers are including body measurement charts in their catalogs and on their Web sites so customers can make informed selections. Industry sources are encouraging the use of actual body measurement data on the size chart designations from individual firms. Rather than requiring a sizing standard that must conform to specific body measurements, they are suggesting that manufacturers may call a size any number they wish as long as they communicate the actual body measurements that the garment is designed to fit on the hangtag, label, Web site, or catalog. Chico's is a company that has successfully devised its own unique sizing system by designating sizes as 0 through 3, and then explained this system with a measurement chart in its stores, in its catalogs, and on its Web site (www.chicos.com).

Figure 11.2. *An Intellifit scanning booth in a Levi's store in New York.*

A relative newcomer to the sizing wars is Intellifit. This company uses a different form of 3D scanner to measure consumers than the one used in the SizeUSA study (Case Study 11.2, The Right Fit from Intellifit; Figure 11.2). The Intellifit approach has also been a bit different in that the company is going to a firm that produces and sells apparel and collecting scanned data of customers and applying the results directly to that firm's grade rule tables. David's Bridal used the Intellifit system to measure 5,000 of its customers and converted the resulting data into new fit specs and grade rule for its products (Just-style.com 2006a).

Even with all the variations in sizing applications that are found in the marketplace, some generalizations regarding the groups or categories of product sizing may be made. The names of the major size categories of women's apparel currently in use include misses, petites, talls, women's plus, women's petites, and juniors (Figure 11.3 reflects five of these). A newly recognized sizing category that has gained importance is maternity.

Misses

Misses' sizes are designed to fit adult females of average build. Records indicate that a body from 5'5" to 5'6" was considered an average height when this category was established. The ASTM voluntary standard for misses identifies sizes in this category range from 2 to 20, even numbers only. Many retail stores

Figure 11.3. *Comparison of silhouettes for women's size categories.*

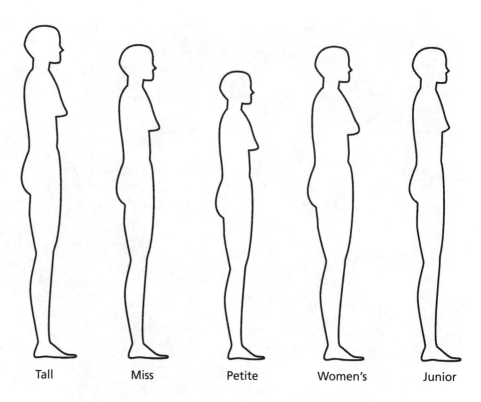

Tall   Miss   Petite   Women's   Junior

typically stock only sizes 6 to 16 in their misses merchandise mix. Many industry sources indicate that over half of the U.S. female population would wear a size larger than size 14 if the ASTM body measurements were routinely applied, and the SizeUSA study confirms that proposition. This fact has great implications for product developers, who must decide on the size range of the products they are providing to the target market.

Petites

Petites are designed for shorter women—5 feet 4 inches and under—who are of average build. Unfortunately, there is considerable disagreement about whether shorter means short height only or whether the scale is smaller all over. The most recent ASTM petite size range is published for even sizes from 2P to 20P and reflects girth measurements similar to those for misses sizes, but scaled down allover in height. Retailers typically stock sizes 4P to 14P in petites. Once again, producers have been increasing the girth of the garments while leaving the size numbers the same, thereby leaving the truly small woman without options and opening a larger target customer base for those sizes at the upper range.

Before availability of SizeUSA measurement data on the petite population, the only sources of data for this size range were medical and insurance records, the military and "guesstimates" of individual manufacturers. We now know that the average female in the United States is 5 feet 3.9 inches tall and weighs 157 (median 143) pounds, which puts her at the larger end of the industry's petite size category; yet most apparel in the marketplace is provided for the misses size catergory. (See Figure 11.4 for size distribution.) This information suggests that the petite market may be open for significant additional development. A few manufacturers have discovered an emerging market for more of the larger petite sizes, such as 16P and 18P, and potential for the Women's Petite range (see below).

Talls

A few manufacturers include **talls** in their product mix. These products are sold along with the misses sizes, especially in bottoms categories (skirts and pants) and are designed for women who are of average girth but above average in height (up to 6 feet 1 inch). Recognizing the changing shape of the U.S. population, the Gap recently introduced tall and petite size offerings to its Web site (Just-style.com 2006b) (Case Study 11.3, Petite and Tall Consumer Markets).

Women's Plus

Women's plus sizes are for the adult woman of average to above-average height but who is fuller and more mature, especially in torso girth, and typically weighs more than the misses category figure. The ASTM International Standard D6960-04 voluntary standard chart for this range was revised in 2004 to include sizes 14W to 32W. The old standard began by overlapping the girth in sizes 16 through 20 but assumed women were of greater overall height, estimated initially at 5 feet 6 inches and over. This category now commonly begins with a 14W or 16W for a woman of average height and a more developed, rounded contour. The typical range produced or stocked at retail is 16W to 24W, but additional sizes are becoming more readily available. For

Figure 11.4. *Distribution of ready-to-wear apparel sizes in the United States.*

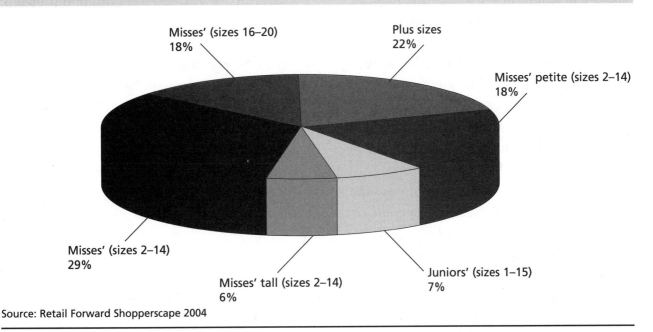

SIZES TYPICALLY WORN BY THE AMERICAN WOMAN

Misses' (sizes 16–20)
18%

Plus sizes
22%

Misses' petite (sizes 2–14)
18%

Misses' (sizes 2–14)
29%

Misses' tall (sizes 2–14)
6%

Juniors' (sizes 1–15)
7%

Source: Retail Forward Shopperscape 2004

CASE STUDY 11.3 PETITE AND TALL CONSUMER MARKETS

Consumer products are mass-produced for the average individual, so for a long time women who are taller or smaller than average have had a problem when shopping for clothes. Since the early 1980s, their situation has improved. Today, petite clothing can be found in department stores, specialty stores, and mail-order catalogs. However, the availability of clothing for tall women is still limited, and the needs of those who wear petite sizes are still not as well satisfied as the needs of the average-size woman.

One study of 177 petite- and 144 tall-sized women sought to explore the fitting problems encountered by these consumer groups. The petite-sized group was defined as women approximately 4'8" to 5'4" tall who wear sizes 2P to 16P. Petite women were identified as having a fully developed figure, similar to misses but shorter, with diminutive overall proportions. The tall-sized group was defined as women whose height exceeds the average height of the misses category, 5'7", along with having longer-than-average arms and legs.

The findings of this study suggest that clothing offerings in the petite- and tall-sized categories should be changed to increase the level of satisfaction among these consumer groups. In the study, petite and tall consumers expressed high levels of dissatisfaction with most apparel that is currently available. Size, variety in available style selection, product assortment, number and quality of stores, comfort, attractiveness, construction quality, and fabric quality were the most frequently reported problems.

Based on the results of the study, the authors offer the following suggestions to apparel manufacturers and retailers, with the dual goals of improving satisfaction among these customers and increasing practitioners' profit:

- Labeling of petite- and tall-sized clothing should be improved to help consumers select the correct size of clothing. Specifically, body dimensions need to be disclosed on the label.
- Petite- and tall-sized clothing should be offered in more varied assortments and provide selections for varied occasions, especially in sportswear, career suiting, and evening wear categories.
- More apparel products in sizes larger than 14 for petite and smaller than 8 for tall women need to be produced.
- Petite- and tall-sized clothing should be produced in various price ranges.
- The number and quality of stores that carry petite- and tall-sized clothing should be increased, as well as the inventory level.
- Mail-order companies need to focus on geographic areas with limited shopping options.
- Apparel manufacturers and retailers ought to conduct research to gain further insight into the needs of their customer base.

Source: Yoo, Khan, and Rutherford-Black 1999, 219–235

example, Talbots begins its women's plus range with a size 12W, which provides for more room in the waist area than a misses size 12.

Women's Petites

In the past, a range for shorter-than-average women of full figure was produced and distributed as half sizes. The category was greatly misunderstood, especially by consumers, and has been replaced by a designation called **women's petites**. This category is designed to reflect a shorter figure of larger girth, generally with a fuller torso and shorter sleeves and hemlines, in comparison to the misses category. When available, these sizes are usually found in 12WP to 20WP. With an aging population and the findings of the SizeUSA study, this women's petite range is poised for significant growth as a market sector.

Juniors

Junior sizes fit a woman of about 5 feet 6 inches with a shorter torso and longer limbs, and less mature body development than the misses category. The category is labeled with odd numbers from 1 to 19 in newest revision of ASTM standard D6829-02, although many retailers currently limit the range they stock to sizes 5 or 7 to 13. There appears to be some stereotyping of styling in this category, reflecting a bias toward younger customers and making it difficult for mature women of this figure type to find appropriately styled clothing.

Maternity

Expectant mothers buying maternity clothing have different sizing needs as their body dimensions change during pregnancy. A new size grouping, **maternity**, has evolved within the industry and is now represented by ASTM7197-06 Standard Table of Body Measurement for Misses Maternity Sizes Two to Twenty-Two (2–22) (ASTM 2003). The increased visibility of this market and consumer desire for fashionable wear specifically designed for pregnant women precipitated the development of the new range of sizes in this product category.

Other Merchandise Categories for Women

Throughout the women's size categories, manufacturers have attempted to control their stock keeping units (SKUs) by combining some sizes. This is particularly true in the sportswear product classifications and in the separates and coordinate categories where knit fabrics are common. In these categories, products may be sized as small (S), medium (M), large (L), and extra-large (XL). These sizes are typically based on the chest measurement, reflecting the misses sizes from 6 or 8 through 16 or 18. When combining these sizes into four groups, the combination size must of necessity cover the larger body to be represented in that size. Some suppliers also produce petites in the combined ranges, but they typically elect to begin with a more diminutive size, labeled petite, before the small, medium, and large sizes. Some producers have also grouped women's sportswear into fewer sizes. The designations used in women's sportswear are 1X, 2X, and 3X and parallel the combining of the women's range into three size groups for sizes 14W through 24W. Another possible use of combination sizes reflected in the marketplace is the combining of junior and misses sizes, such as 7/8, 9/10, and 11/12, to accommodate varying torso lengths.

Sizing for some kinds of women's apparel, such as nightwear, lingerie, and other products categorized as **intimate wear**, are identified by other means. For example, bras are sized with a two-part designation that has evolved from a French system. The size is a number representing an under-bust measurement plus 5 to 6 inches, depending on the manufacturer. The second part of the size designation is a letter representing the cup size, usually ranging from an AA or A to a D or DD. Measuring over the fullest part of the bust and finding the difference between that measurement and the under-bust measurement identifies the cup designation. The average cup is 2 inches larger than the bra size and is labeled a B. The AA is ½ inch larger than the under-bust measurement, the A is 1 inch larger, the C is 3 inches larger, the D is 4 inches larger, and the DD is 5 inches larger.

Panties are most commonly sold in sizes 5, 6, and 7, which parallel the hip measurements of the misses size range. The larger women's sizes of panties are typically sold in sizes 8 through 11. Pantyhose are most often found in average, tall, and queen, based on height and weight.

Women's categories of ready-to-wear sizing have been characterized by some confusion from the beginning. Some of this lack of consistency may be attributed to the fact that women's apparel styling is in a constant state of flux due to fashion trends. In addition, women's alterations have traditionally not been a part of the original price of the garment; as long as the product is selling, the manufacturer has little motivation to be precise in the fit. The female customer must either pay for alterations or shop until she finds something that does fit her. As lifestyles of consumers continue to change and demands on time become more rigorous, this laissez-faire approach to sizing may require some rethinking on the part of the producers.

Men's Sizing

Men's sizes include clothing designed for the fully developed adult man. The category includes the major classifications of men's clothing, sportswear, and furnishings. Men's apparel is most often sold in numbered sizes that represent body measurements, although some products are identified by figure type.

Men's wear sizing, designed for the average male, tends to be more consistent than sizing of women's wear because men's styles do not fluctuate as much as women's. In addition, men do not always shop for themselves. Because someone else may be making the purchases, there is greater dependence on the sizing labels. Also, because alterations are traditionally included in the price of men's garments, manufacturers have found it to be a wise business practice to be more accurate in the original measurements. Although consistent size measurement had been effective for many years, since the 1990s these product categories have been marked by many instances of vanity sizing, especially in men's casual pants, and the reduced availability of tapered woven shirts that hug the torso.

Suits, Jackets, and Coats

Men's suits, jackets, and coats are labeled first with the chest girth measurement followed with height classifications such as short, regular, tall or long, and extra-tall. The majority of men wear a 38 to 44 size, based on 2-inch increments, but some manufacturers expand their range to include sizes from 32 to 50. Most products are produced only in even sizes, but a few uneven sizes are included by some producers, especially in smaller sizes. The size is expressed as a number for the chest girth followed by a letter representing the height, such as 36S or 38R.

Suits include both a jacket and slacks. The styling of the jacket will affect the size of the slacks that come with it. A **drop** of 7 to 10 inches—the difference in the circumference between the chest and waist measurement—is common depending on the cut of the suit. Continental styling tends to reflect a more tapered style with up to a 10-inch drop to the waist, while traditional styling tends to reflect a more rectangular body cut, with the more typical 7-inch drop. Both styles tend to reflect slim styling through the slacks. Athletic cuts in suits tend to be more tapered from chest to waist, but also tend to include more ease in the leg thigh area to accommodate a more fully developed muscle structure.

Pants

Pants sizes are based on two basic measurements. The waist girth is the most common and is usually stocked by the retailer in even sizes from 28 to 40, in 2-inch increments. A few retailers also stock pants in 1-inch increments in the smaller sizes. The second number in pants sizing represents the **inseam** measurement, which typically ranges from 29 to 34 inches. This inseam measurement is taken on the inside of the leg from the crotch seam to the bottom of the hem of the pants. Dress slacks are usually sold with hems unfinished; they are then custom-tailored to length upon purchase. Although it is not generally publicized, manufacturers typically use a third measurement when sizing pants. Called the rise, it is the measurement from the top of the inner leg seam at the crotch to the top of the waist. Within the business, the rise is most often identified as short or regular and corresponds to the variation in torso length of the target customer. However, some catalogs use the terms regular and long to describe the distinction between their two categories of rise. As a basis of comparison, men's jeans tend to have a low rise, while slacks for the average to tall male usually provide a regular or tall rise.

Furnishings

Men's furnishings include other items of clothing such as shirts, ties, underwear, sleepwear, and accessories. Dress shirts are sized on a two-number system that is based on the neck size and the sleeve length. The neck circumference is identified first, by half-inch increments. A number representing the length of the sleeve, measured from the center back to the wrist bone, follows this. The average men's dress shirt size is a 15½/34, which indicates a 15½-inch neck circumference and a 34-inch sleeve length. Sport shirts are usually sized S, M, L, and XL. This system enables the producer to provide more style options in fewer sizes and keep the total SKUs (stock keeping units) under control.

Most other men's products, such as sweaters, underwear, and pajamas, are sized by chest measurement and labeled S, M, L, and XL. Belts are typically sold by waist measurement.

Due to the voluntary nature of sizing systems and the introduction of vanity sizing into the men's market, consumers need to consult any sizing tables provided for an individual firm's product offerings.

Young Men's

Young men's sizes are designed for younger men whose builds have not reached full maturity. Sizes are labeled with the same number or letter designations as the parallel men's products. The difference is that the garments are proportionately smaller. Their relationship to men's sizes is comparable to that of junior sizes to misses sizes in the women's market.

Children's Sizing

Sizing for children's apparel was originally based on age groups. However, consumers who purchase children's wear should never base size selection on the child's chronological age. Because there is so much variation in the growth patterns of children, the size of children's clothing should be based on the height and weight of the child.

Infants

Infants' apparel is styled for babies from birth to approximately 18 months of age or whenever the child begins to walk. Infant wear may be labeled 0–3 months, 6 months, 9 months, 12 months, and sometimes 18 months, but it is designed to represent the height and weight of the babies, not their age. Lettered sizing is sometimes used and is labeled XS or NB for newborns, S, M, L, and XL. The industry has encouraged the use of height and weight charts on hangtags for products in this category.

Toddlers

Toddlers' apparel is styled and sized for children who are walking but not yet toilet-trained. This means that there must be more room in the crotch area to accommodate diapers. There may be other aspects to the clothing that accommodate changing diapers, as well. The sizes in this category are 2T, 3T, and 4T, which correspond to the height and weight of children at this stage of development.

Children's

By the time children are out of diapers, they are ready for **children's** sizes, which are sized unisex from 2 to 6 or 7. These sizes also are categorized by height and weight, increasing proportionately. The size labels S, M, L, and XL may be substituted for the parallel number in this category. Typically, products in this group are styled and marketed for preschool-age children.

Girls

Girls' sizes are designed to fit girls of approximately 7 to 11 years of age, although parents are once again advised to consider the height, weight, and development of the individual child. Many retailers carry only sizes 7 to 14 for an average body weight for the corresponding height, although some provide for other body-build categories such as slim and plus for those of smaller or larger-than-average builds, respectively.

Boys

Boys' sizes are designed for boys approximately 7 to 17 years old with developing bodies. They are usually placed in the children's category for both manufacturing and government classification purposes, although the styling in this category becomes more adult as the sizes progress upward. The full range is labeled 2 to 24, but most retailers carry only even-numbered sizes from 8 to 20. The ASTM standard correlates sizes in this range to height, weight, chest, and waist measurements. There are a few manufacturers that go beyond the regular build to include slim and husky categories for those boys who are of slight or heavier build for their heights.

Metrics and Sizing

The United States is currently the only country in the world that does not use the metric system. Therefore, when product developers do business with suppliers and contractors in other countries, it becomes critical to recognize that conversions to metric measurements may be necessary in order to guarantee communication about the intended size and shape of products. Many countries refuse to accept products that are not graded according to the metric system, and garments produced here for export may require metric labels. This requirement of metric measurements may become even more of an issue in the not-too-distant future as international trade increases and the system for determining tariffs for textile products is calculated using metric measurements.

The International Organization for Standardization (ISO) has developed its own set of standards regarding size of garments; ISO 3635-1981 (Size Designation of Clothes, Definition and Body Measurement Procedures) and ISO 8559 (Garment Construction and Anthropometric Surveys—Body Dimensions) spell out the requirements that are becoming the standard for the rest of the world. If a firm from the United States is planning to sell products in the European Union, those garments need to be labeled in their sizing format.

Garment Fit

The biggest complaint from consumers about apparel products is that the customer cannot find something that fits. According to Kathleen Fasanella (Fasanella 1998, 106), the fundamental problems underlying the complaints are an outdated median-size measuring standard, inconsistent grading, and a lack of understanding of comfort. Manufacturers who focus on products that consistently fit their target market find they have greater consumer satisfaction and greater overall sales. The reader is reminded that sizing is based on body measurements, whereas fit is based on garment measurements.

As we look at the basic tenets of what constitutes good fit, we see that there are some fundamental guidelines to help us assess whether a garment fits, but even then we are confused by fabric innovations and properties of the materials used in new style construction. The issue is further complicated by individual preferences and the influences of what constitutes fashion rightness at any given time.

Simply stated, **fit** implies the conformance of the garments to the shape and size of the individuals who wear them. The five elements of fit, identified by Erwin, Kinchen, and Peters, are grain, set, line, balance, and ease (Erwin, Kinchen, and Peters 1979). These five elements, while interrelated, describe different aspects of fit.

Grain

Grain reflects the direction of the threads in the fabric used in a garment. The lengthwise grain in most garments should run parallel to the height of the body at center front and center back, while the crosswise grain should run perpendicular to the lengthwise threads. When the garment is **on-grain**, with lengthwise and crosswise threads meeting at exactly 90 degrees, it will hang evenly and appear symmetrical; when **off-grain**, the garment may twist or hang crooked. The exception to the basic on-grain concept is in bias-cut garments that are cut with the threads running at 45-degree angles to the floor. Bias garments tend to stretch out as they hang and will be very uneven if they are not cut carefully to true **bias** (45 degrees). Bias is the property that provides the unique softness and fluidity of many draped garments.

Set

Set reflects a smooth fit with no unwanted wrinkles. If wrinkles appear in the garment, it typically means that the garment is too small or too large in the area where the fabric pulls or sags. A savvy pattern maker can identify problems in fit by observing the direction of the wrinkles. These fitting problems can then be corrected while the garment is in the sample stage, before it goes into production.

In general, diagonal wrinkles tend to point to areas where a garment is too snug. For example, if a bustline is too tight, wrinkles tend to form in the side seams and point to the crown of the bust; if the crotch line of a pair of pants is too snug in the hip or rise, wrinkles will form across the lap or in the back thigh area and point toward the crotch. A horizontal wrinkle across the high shoulder indicates the back neck area is too short.

If a garment is too large or the shape is too long, horizontal or vertical wrinkles or folds tend to appear. For example, if a coat is too wide through the shoulder, vertical folds tend to appear across the back or into the armscye.

Line

Line refers to the manner in which the structural lines of garment conform to the lines of the body. An example of this criterion is that side seams should hang straight on the body and perpendicular to the floor. Center front and center back seams should also be straight and perpendicular to the floor. Curved lines in garments should follow the contour of the body.

Balance

Balance occurs when the right and left sides of the body appear to be even when viewed from the front, back, and side. Although poor posture is often the culprit in this area, bad balance can be caused by errors in patternmaking or by inaccurate construction techniques.

Most people are not perfectly symmetrical, right and left, but the eye can be easily fooled into the appearance of symmetry by appropriate design and accurate construction. Asymmetry can become a real issue when customizing garments for individual consumers with physical differences, but today computer patternmaking tools provide solutions for coping much more easily with these issues.

Ease

The last of the fit elements is the most complex because it involves all parts of the garment in different ways. **Ease** is the amount of difference between the body measurements of the intended wearer and the measurements of the finished garment. Garments must have ease added to the base body measurements so that they can be worn. Ease allowances vary according to the intended look of the garment. For dresses, tops, jackets, and coats, the ease allowance is usually determined by the bust measurement. For skirts and pants, ease is usually determined by the measurement of the hips. It is important for product developers to recognize that the sizing charts discussed earlier in this chapter reflect body measurements, whereas product measurements must include all forms of ease. The amount of ease required to make any garment wearable is classified into two categories: functional ease and design ease (Figure 11.5).

Functional Ease

Functional ease, or wearing ease, is the amount added to body measurements to compensate for body movement. Functional ease is required in order for the garment to actually be worn. Manufacturers typically provide wearing ease of approximately 2.5 inches in the bust, 1 inch in the waist, and 2 inches in the hip. Pattern companies that produce for the home sewing market typically allow a minimum wearing ease of 2 inches, 1 inch, and 1½ inches for the bust, waist, and hip, respectively.

Functional ease requirements in general are significantly less for knit fabrics than for wovens. The traditional rules of ease are also in a state of flux because of the introduction of spandex into many fabrics, such as in denim used for jeans and knit fabrics used for T-shirt tops. Spandex content provides fabrics with elasticity, enabling a much tighter fit with less functional ease than is required of a regular woven fabric.

Functional ease also varies with the garment type and intended use of the garment itself. For example, swimsuits must be snug so that they do not stretch out when the wearer uses them to actually swim. Uniforms often need to provide more functional ease for greater body movement or extension during wear.

Design Ease

The second type of ease is **design ease**. It reflects the amount added to the combined body and functional ease measurements to make the garment produce the look desired by the designer. Although design ease is not technically required for the garment to be worn, it is typically needed in varying amounts to complete the intended look of the garment. The amount of design ease used at any given time varies significantly depending on the individual garment style and the fashion of the time. In the 1980s and 1990s looser garments were fashionable, such as oversized sweaters and T-shirts; in the 2000s these styles have less design ease and conform more closely to the body.

Forms and Fit Models

Styling and fit are evaluated throughout the product development cycle. It is wise to make any changes needed in the overall fit before the garment goes

SUGGESTED EASE ALLOWANCES FOR MISSES' GARMENTS

BODY MEASUREMENTS	+	WEARING EASE	+	DESIGN EASE	=	FASHION SILHOUETTE

The following chart reflects guidelines for achieving basic garment silhouettes by adding wearing and design ease to body measurements. These guidelines are suggested for designing garments made of woven or stable knit fabrics. They are not applicable to garments made of stretchable knit fabric or for wovens that contain a significant amount of spandes. The measurements for Tops, Jackets, and Coats reflect the ease allowances needed for the bust. the measurements for Skirts and Pants reflect the allowances for the hip. The rest of the garment should be graded to coincide with these measurements.

DESCRIPTION	Close-fitting	Fitted	Semifitted	Loose-fitting	Very loose-fitting
SILHOUETTES					
Dresses, blouses, shirts, tops	0"–2 7/8"	3"–4"	4 1/8"–5"	5 1/8"–8"	Over 8"
Jackets	not applicable	3 3/4"–4 1/4"	4 3/8"–5 3/4"	5 7/8"–10"	Over 10"
Coats	not applicable	5 1/4"–6 3/4"	6 7/8"–8"	8 1/8"–12"	Over 12"
Skirts, pants	0"–1 7/8"	2"–3"	3 1/8"–4"	4 1/8"–6"	Over 6"

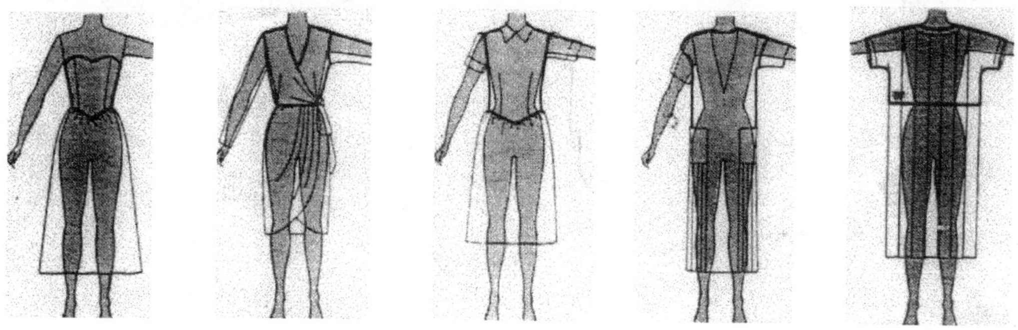

Adapted from "Understand Ease Allowances"; Butterick Company, Inc. 1992.

Figure 11.5. *Suggested ease allowances for misses' garments.*

into full production. To determine if the styling and fit are truly developing as desired, sample garments are produced and placed on **dress forms** to evaluate the grain, set, line, and balance. Dress forms are partial body shapes placed on a stand to use in patternmaking and fitting activities. Several companies provide dress forms for the industry. Many of you saw them in use in the Project Runway TV series. One of the better-known dress form firms is Wolfe. This company is able to provide a myriad of body shapes varying from torsos on a

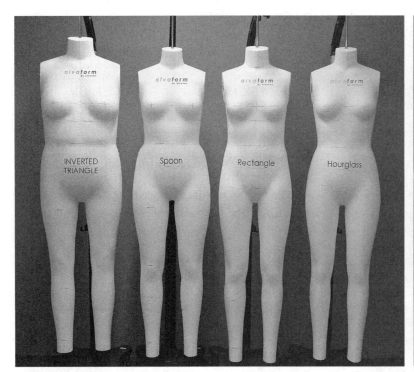

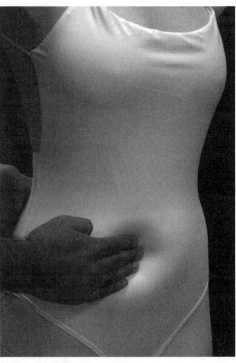

Figure 11.6a. *New inverted triangle, spoon, and rectangle dress form shapes supplement AlvaProducts' traditional hourglass form.*

Figure 11.6b *TUKATECH's new Soft Body Form can be squeezed just like the human body.*

stand to bodies with legs, and in a variety of size measurements for men, women, and children. They are used by many designers in the industry. Companies frequently update their forms to represent the body types and sizes of the customers they are currently attempting to please (Figure 11.6a–b).

To establish the appropriate ease, sample garments are often tried on fit models. **Fit models** are individuals who have been selected to represent the age and build of the target customer and who conform to the measurements of the intended master size of the original design (Figure 11.7). Fit models are able to move around in the garment and help establish if the garment is providing the level of comfort and movement that will be required of it after it is sold to the consumer.

Grading

Garment styling and fit are established based on one size in a range, typically designated as the master or sample size. As previously mentioned, the most common sample size in women's clothing is a misses 8 or 10. Each new style of garment introduced by the product developer requires that a master pattern be developed in the sample size and that each of the style's master pattern blocks be established. These pattern blocks are then scaled up for the larger sizes and down for the smaller sizes that are being considered for production. This process of scaling the master size of a garment to the range of sizes to be produced is called **grading**. The basic concept in the application of grading techniques is that the difference between the sizes of the garment pieces should evolve from the body measurements taken from a sizing chart. The potential for error in the grading process is great, but techniques have been developed to achieve satisfactory results. It is anticipated that the SizeUSA data will continue to provide information for improvements in the grading of garments to fit real people rather than relying strictly on linear grade rules.

The amounts that are added (or subtracted) from each measurement as it changes from one size to the next are sometimes referred to as **grade rules**. Most companies have developed a set of grade rules that they routinely apply to the new styles they develop. The sets of measurements that reflect the increments between sizes for each of the grade rules are referred to as **grade rule tables** (Figure 11.8).

Any one of several methods can be used for grading. It may be done by hand drafting, in which case each piece is drawn out by hand. However, in today's business environment, grading is usually done either with a grading machine or by employing a computer grading system. Figure 11.9 shows an example of pattern grading being done by a computer.

Figure 11.7. *Oscar de la Renta works with his design team to establish the fit of a garment on a live fit model.*

Callie Blake Collection
New York, NY 10012
212-555-7357

Grade Rule Specifications

Style #: 4682
Division: Suits/tailored
Size Category: Miss
Size Range: 6-18
Sample Size: 8
Season: Fall
Estimate:

Description: Princess jacket
Merchandiser:
Designer: B.Jones
Tech Designer: M.Garner
Brand: Callie Blake
Fabric Category: poly/rayon gab
Colors: black, eggplant, dove

Create Date: 2/22/02
Modified:
Due Date: 4/15/02
Ship Date:
Vendor:
Page 8 of 12

Front | Back | Description

Princess line jacket with notched lapel
5 buttons
2-piece shaped sleeve

Description	Sample	Size						
	8	6	8	10	12	14	16	18
Across shoulder	17	- 3/8	0	3/8	3/8	3/8	1/2	1/2
Bust, 1" below armscye	40	-1 1/2	0	1 1/2	1 1/2	1 1/2	2	2
Sleeve length from shoulder	23 3/4	- 1/4	0	1/4	1/4	1/4	1/4	1/4
Armscye	21	- 5/8	0	5/8	5/8	5/8	3/4	3/4
Upperarm	14 3/4	- 1/2	0	1/2	1/2	1/2	5/8	5/8
Sweep - closed	43 1/2	-1 1/2	0	1 1/2	1 1/2	1 1/2	2	2
Sleeve opening	11 3/4	- 1/4	0	0	1/4	0	1/4	0
CB length from CBN	29 1/4	- 1/4	0	1/4	1/4	1/4	1/4	1/4
CB length from HPS	29 3/4	- 1/4	0	1/4	1/4	1/4	1/4	1/4

Figure 11.8. *Grade rule specifications form used for establishing the difference between the sample product measurements and each of the other larger or smaller sizes.*

Circumference Grading

Grading rules are developed to accommodate size variations in girth, length, and width. Circumference grade indicates how much the garments are to increase in girth from one size to the next. It is important that the growth be distributed somewhat evenly around the body rather than being added in one place. These measurements are often the most changed from one size to another size, as individuals tend to reflect more differences in girth than in height.

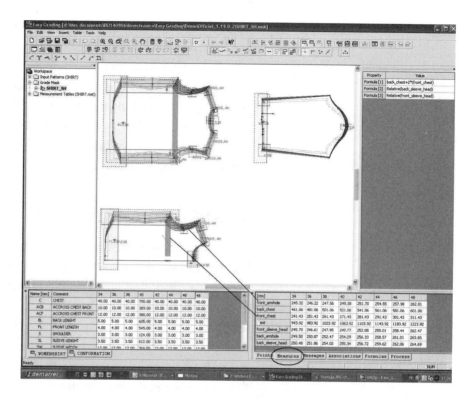

Figure 11.9. *Pattern grading using Lectra software.*

Length Grading

Length grade refers to the measurement to be added to the length of garment pieces as sizes progress from one size to the next. Most of these measurements are related to height. Length must be added in proportion to the body's natural growth. The typical amount of ¼ inch in length per grade in the bodice should be distributed evenly by applying ⅛ inch above and ⅛ inch below the bust level. This increase must be applied to each piece that is involved in the grade.

Width Grading

Width grading refers to the amount of measurement added to a cross-body area, such as from shoulder point to shoulder point. A grade rule table is very helpful for determining these increments because they tend to be quite small in comparison to other measurements.

Uneven Grading

Uneven grading or nonlinear grading is achieved when it is determined that the target customer is shaped somewhat differently than the standards in sizing charts. In these cases, the waist or hips may increase at a different rate than the bust as the design is graded to different sizes, producing a different shape of the finished garment to fit consumers who may be thicker through the hips and thighs or in the waist. The variations can be almost endless when combined with changes between styles and intended ease allotments.

One of the more pervasive issues with grading has been the perception that bodies grow similarly in all directions, and that as garment sizes got bigger, the consumer was also getting taller. Many producers are finding that this perception is untrue, since people may vary in weight throughout their lifespan, but their height remains about the same. In fact, many mature women actually lose height as they age. Even if they maintain the same weight, it has to go somewhere and this usually produces larger girth in the torso; hence a larger size, but not a longer garment. For these reasons it is anticipated that as computerized grading is universally used, we will see significantly more uneven or nonlinear grading begin to appear in garment size and grade rule tables and in commercially available garments.

Mass Customization

Mass-produced apparel was not designed to accommodate uneven grades, but the recent advent of body scanning and computerized alteration programs now make mass customization a possibility. **Mass customization** is the application of mass-production techniques to the production of a single customer–configured garment. One way to achieve a customized product in a manufacturing environment is through application of body scanning technology. This method takes measurements of the customer electronically and transfers those measurements directly into a computer database or into pattern alteration software. The manufacturer then alters one garment in the production run for the individual customer.

Brooks Brothers has been using a light scanner in its New York store for about four years, measuring customers for custom-fitted jackets, suits, slacks, and shirts. Once a customer is scanned and selects the style he prefers from the photos and fabric samples available in the store, the garment is constructed in a nearby factory and delivered to the customer's door in about two weeks.

Another application of scanning technology is the ability to facilitate a consumer's selection of specific ready-made garments without having to take armloads of garments into a fitting room. The fitting process is done virtually by comparing the measurements provided by the manufacturer of a specific garment with the scanned measurements of the consumer, thus eliminating the need to try on those garments that are recognized in advance as not fitting that body shape. The ability to use a card containing an individual's scanned measurement data has great future potential for use by those who prefer to shop online or by catalog or who simply don't want to select sizes by time-consuming trial and error.

Summary

Producers of apparel take considerable care to ascertain the size and fit of products for their intended consumer market, but they are handicapped by a lack of current concrete data on actual body measurements. The sizing charts and body measurement information needed to produce garments for men, women, and children in the United States may be extensive, but they remain a problem. Most companies use a set of sizing measurements they have developed from a combination of the voluntary standard sizing charts published by ASTM International and estimates they have about their own target customers. The results of this evolution in sizing are numbering systems for apparel that vary widely from company to company and from product to product.

A sample garment, usually in a size 8 or 10 for misses products, is made of each style being developed. The sample is carefully fitted, on a form or a fit model, to ensure that it will provide a comfortable product. Once fit is established and applied to the pattern, the pattern can be graded to the desired range of sizes based on the grade rule table.

Product developers typically select a body measurement table that most closely represents their target customers. Then they develop a grade rule table that reflects the increments between the sizes for the garment styles they are going to produce.

The potential for easing many of the issues consumers have with fit may be helped by the completion of the SizeUSA study. This study utilized computer scanning methods to measure a large sample of Americans and provides a new database of actual body measurements that can be used to build more realistic grade rule tables and develop better-fitting apparel products.

Key Terms

balance	mass customization
bias	maternity
boys'	men's furnishings
children's	men's wear
design ease	misses'
dress forms	off-grain
drop	on-grain
ease	petites
fit	rise
fit model	sample size
functional ease	set
girls'	size migration
grade	sizing
grade rules	talls
grade rule tables	toddlers'
grading	uneven grading
grain	vanity sizing
infants'	women's petites
inseam	women's plus
intimate wear	women's wear
junior	young men's
line	

Discussion Questions

1. What differences exist between the size categories for body types in women's wear and what might these differences mean to garment styling?

2. What is fit and how is it achieved?

3. How much do you think the body scanner will be used in the apparel industry?

4. Do you think the body scanner will make a difference in sizing in the industry in the next decade?

5. Do you think that nonlinear or uneven grading will be used more in the future?

Activities

1. Establish the measurements for a sample garment. This measurement chart may be for the garment used in the chapters 8 and 9 activities or for a garment assigned to the class by the instructor. Remember to add functional ease and design ease where needed.

2. Develop a sizing spec sheet in a range of four sizes for the sample garment in Activity 1. Use the sample specification sheet in this chapter or chapter 9 to develop your own garment's sizing spec sheet, selecting critical measurements from that chart and adding those you think might be important to the design you are using. (It is suggested that you use a 2-inch grade for this first sizing exercise.)

References

ASTM. 2003. New standard sizes for maternity apparel. *Standardization News,* December. www.astm.org/SNEWS/DECEMBER_2003/maternity_dec03.html (accessed Auguest 26, 2006).

ASTM. 2005. D5585-95R01, standard table of body measurements for female misses figure type, sizes 2–20. *ASTM Book of Standards* 07, no. 02. www.normas.com/ASTM/CONTENTS/Vol.07.02.html (accessed August 28, 2006).

Butterick Company. 1992. *Understand ease allowances.* Manhattan, KS: Butterick Company.

Corcoran, C. T. 2005. Fit to be tried. *Women's Wear Daily,* June 15, Section II WWDEXECTEC.

Erwin, M., L. Kinchen, and K. Peters. 1979. *Clothing for moderns.* 6th ed. Englewood Cliffs, NJ: Prentice-Hall.

Fasanella, K. 1998. The myth of consumer apathy. *Bobbin,* August.

ISO 3635-1981, size designation of clothes, definition and body measurement procedures. Available from American National Standards Institute, 11 West 42nd Street, New York, NY 10036.

ISO 8559, garment construction and anthropometic surveys—body dimensions. Available from American National Standards Institute, 11 West 42nd Street, New York, NY 10036.

Just-style.com. 2006a. Bringing the right fit to the masses. www.just-style.com (accessed March 1, 2006).

Just-style.com. 2006b. US: Gap.com launches petite, tall women's ranges. www.just-style.com (accessed January 18, 2006).

Modern Uniforms. 2004. Research firm tackles tough apparel sizing issues. *Modern Uniforms,* October 1. www.modernuniformsmag.com/mag/research_firm_tackles/index.html (accessed August 26, 2006).

Reda, S. 2006. Sizing up sizing. *Stores,* January. www.stores.org/archives/cover.asp (accessed January 11, 2006).

Seckler, V. 2005. A plus-size embrace, *Women's Wear Daily,* March 9.

Speer, J. K. 2006. Time's up for the hourglass. *Apparel,* January. www.apparelmag.com (accessed February 15, 2006).

Tamburrino, N. 1992. Sized to sell. *Bobbin,* June.

Textile and Clothing Technology Corporation. 2001. [TC]^2's body scanner. Available at www.tc2.com.

Weathers, N. R. 2006. Bringing the right fit to the masses. Bromsgrove, Worcs, UK: Aroq Ltd. Available at www.just-style.com (accessed March 1, 2006).

Retail Forward Shopperscape. 2004. In "A plus-size embrace" by V. Seckler, *Women's Wear Daily,* March 9, 2005.

Yoo, S., S. Khan, and C. Rutherford-Black. 1999. Petite- and tall-sized consumer segmentation: Comparison of fashion involvement, pre-purchase clothing satisfaction and clothing needs. *Journal of Fashion Marketing and Management* 3, no. 3.

Additional Resources

Abend, J. 1993. More makers taking the plus size plunge. *Bobbin,* August.

Ashdown, S. 1998. An investigation of the structure of sizing systems. *International Journal of Clothing Science and Technology* 10, no. 5.

Bobbin. 1993. Body shapes no hoax. *Bobbin,* August.

Brown, P., and J. Rice. 2001. *Ready-to-wear apparel analysis.* 3d ed. Upper Saddle River, NJ: Prentice-Hall.

Devarajan, P., and C. L. Istook. 2004. Validation of 'female figure identification technique (FFIT) for Apparel' software. *Journal of Textile and Apparel, Technology and Management* 4, no. 1 (Summer). www.tx.ncsu.edu/jtatm (accessed August 25, 2006).

Glock, R. E., and G. I. Kunz. 2005. *Apparel manufacturing: Sewn product analysis.* 4th ed. Upper Saddle River, NJ: Prentice-Hall.

Goldsberry, E., S. Shim, and N. Reich. 1996. Women 55 years and older: Part I. current body measurements as contrasted to the PS42-70 data. *Clothing and Textiles Research Journal* 14, no. 2.

Loker, S., S. Ashdown, and K. Shoenfelder. 2005. Size-specific analysis of body scan data to improve apparel fit. *Journal of Textile and Apparel, Technology and Management* 4, no. 3 (Spring). www.tx.ncsu.edu/jtatm (accessed August 25, 2006).

O'Brien, R., and W. C. Shelton. 1941. *Women's measurements for garment and pattern construction.* U.S. Department of Agriculture Miscellaneous Publication no. 454. Washington, DC: U.S. Government Printing Office.

Palmer, P., and M. Alto. 1998. *Fit for real people.* Portland, OR: Palmer/Pletsch.

Simmons, K., C. L. Istook, and P. Devarajan. 2004. Female figure identification technique (FFIT) for apparel; Part 1: Describing female shapes. *Journal of Textile and Apparel, Technology and Management* 4, no. 1 (Summer). www.tx.ncsu.edu/jtatm (accessed August 25, 2006).

CHAPTER 12

QUALITY ASSURANCE

"I believe that quality level is determined primarily by the actual design of the product itself, not by quality control in the production process."
—Hideo Sugiura, Chairperson (retired), Honda Motor Company

OBJECTIVES

- To define the concept of quality

- To understand the role of quality in the product development process

- To relate the concepts of quality in a firm's standards to written quality specifications for products

- To know the government and voluntary requirements for product labeling and safety standards in apparel products

- To understand the basics of stitch, seam, and edge finish requirements for production of quality products

- To become familiar with an array of criteria used to evaluate quality of products before, during, and after assembly

---

Quality must be built into a product from its conception; it cannot be added at the end of the construction process. During the 20th century the concept of quality in apparel production in the United States evolved through several stages. Shortly after World War I, quality focused on inspection. The quality inspector was a gatekeeper whose focus was judging garments that came off the assembly line. Garments that were acceptable passed, and those that were unacceptable were rejected. By midcentury, manufacturers began to recognize the need for preventing defects rather than reacting to defects that already existed. Following the principles of W. Edwards Deming and Joseph M. Juran, manufacturers refined quality management into a precise science. Today, companies on the cutting edge see quality as an integral part of their management philosophy.

A Product Development Perspective on Quality

To achieve a consistent quality product, companies rely on **quality assurance**, a commitment to quality that permeates the entire business and requires a proactive, participatory management style. Every employee is involved in trying to achieve error prevention. Quality is integral to the processes of product development, production, sales, and marketing, where everyone works as a team with management to achieve goals. Making it right the first time is seen as less expensive than deciding what to do with seconds (garments with defects).

It is apparent that quality production need not cost more and that it often costs less. The reality is that lack of quality is more expensive. Not ordering fabrics by specification, willingness to accept a percentage of seconds, lack of inventory, and unclear language in garment specifications or technical drawings all add up to unnecessary costs (Figure 12.1).

Quality assurance is based on defect prevention rather than detection. It is market-driven because quality is what the customer says it is. Quality assurance involves conformity to standards and specifications that meet or exceed customer quality expectations. This applies to internal customers within the product development supply chain and external or final consumers. The customer at each price level perceives quality differently. Product developers must understand their customers' quality expectations as manifested in a quality-to-cost ratio. This ratio may be explained as how much consumers are willing to pay in order to have quality, measured against what they will give up in order to have a lower price. Consumers tend to believe there is a positive relationship between price and quality, whereby high price may lend an aura of quality to a garment. This is an extrinsic cue that is quite subjective. When consumers cannot see a difference in two similar garments, they may rely on price in deciding which garment is of higher quality. However, price does not necessarily reflect quality. High-quality goods can be found at low prices and low-quality goods can be found at high prices. It is up to the product development team to develop a strategy that balances the price and quality expectations of customers with the needs of the business.

Product quality has two dimensions. The physical features of a product involve what the product actually is; the performance features of a product involve what the product does (Solinger 1988). Apparel quality is related to the physical features of design, materials, construction, and finishing. These are part of the physical construction of the product. The quality performance of the product may be aesthetic, which is quite subjective and covered in previous chapters, or it may be functional. Functional performance relates to the utility and durability of a product. Utility can be explained as the product's usefulness and can be measured by fit, comfort, and care requirements. The

Figure12.1. *Producing quality garments includes obvious costs and many less visible costs.*

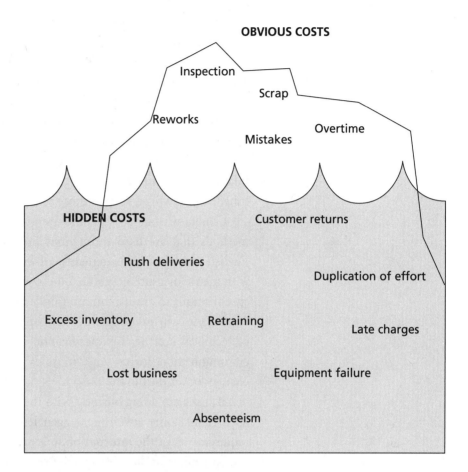

QUALITY COST ICEBERG

OBVIOUS COSTS

Inspection

Scrap

Reworks

Overtime

Mistakes

HIDDEN COSTS | Customer returns

Rush deliveries

Duplication of effort

Excess inventory | Retraining

Late charges

Lost business | Equipment failure

Absenteeism

durability of the product is the product's ability to retain its appearance after purchase; it can be measured by testing for things such as resistance to shrinkage and seam strength.

The role of quality assurance in the overall product development cycle is present in many areas of the process. Areas requiring particular attention to quality include fabric testing, specification writing, testing of sample garments, factory inspections, and sampling of stock deliveries.

Quality Standards

Standards for fabrics and findings, or **raw material standards**, are used to communicate with suppliers during the planning stages of product development. Standards help to define components that will be used in the production of the finished garments.

Garment standards include diagnostic tools to measure the quality of a product. Included in these standards are defect guides to be used throughout the production process. Defects can be classified as major or minor. Major defects are not acceptable in the finished product; examples include a garment that has sleeves put in backward or one that has a broken zipper or stains. Defects considered minor are those that do not affect the end use but that should be corrected in future products. Examples would be hanging threads or a hook and eye missing from above a zipper.

Quality standards originate in the strategic business plan for the firm. They are related to defining the end use of the product and describing what the product is designed to do. Standards may be mandatory or voluntary. There are just a few mandatory standards for apparel sold in the United States, such as those from the Consumer Product Safety Commission (CPSC) that require conformance to specific criteria for flammability in fabrics used for infants' and children's sleepwear. Many standards are voluntary and are established within a firm, such as those relating to size, fit, and aesthetics.

Company standards should establish the language and measurement methods that are used throughout the company. Most U.S. firms use the English system of measurements. However, if contractors are more familiar with metric measurements, then these must be incorporated into the garment specifications to ensure common understanding of the goals. Decisions need to be made early in the product development process regarding consistent use of technical sketches on specification forms, formats that will be used for communication forms, and routines for maintaining records as styling changes occur during the season.

If firms are doing business with the European Union (EU) or producing apparel for some government agencies, they may need to conform to the requirements of the **International Organization for Standardization (ISO)**. This organization has developed a series of voluntary standards that, if met and followed, enable certification of a business. When a firm is certified, products coming from its factories are recognized as acceptable or as having met certain criteria. The ISO has very specific requirements regarding such areas as management of deliveries, labeling of products, and sizing standards. These standards are somewhat different from those required for doing business within the United States. In some cases they are more stringent, so firms that intend to compete internationally should know international requirements before they start product development.

Quality Specifications

Quality specifications evolve from the company's standards, but they focus more narrowly on directions for production and evaluation procedures that ensure the product will do what the firm said it would do. Specifications are an integral part of the product development process. It is essential that firms find a balance between specifications that are too flexible and those that are too stringent.

Specification Libraries

As the seasons pass and new products evolve, **specification libraries** can be built within the firm. These libraries are especially effective if they are computerized. Accessibility to previously developed style, pattern, and measurement specifications that can be recalled and reused within specification packages for new styles is proving to be a real time-saver and a money saver for many firms. Several commercial computer software packages have been developed specifically for this purpose, including Gerber's PDM for product data management and Lectra's Mikalis tools for specification development, including a library function for drawing on past work. The product development team may also utilize a database of information on suppliers, product components, and regulations that govern production and acceptance of the end product.

Voluntary Testing Methods

Voluntary testing methods are used to assess garment specifications. Tests may be performed on the raw materials in order to ensure their adherence to quality standards before a commitment to production yardage is made. Other tests must be run on sample garments to determine how construction and finishing affect the ability of the garment to function. Testing methods usually come from one of two major organizations. The American Association of Textile Chemists and Colorists (AATCC) focuses on the development of testing methods related to fabric coloration, dyes, finishes, and laundry methods. In general, if the testing procedure involves any application, use, or measurement of moisture or other liquids, the test method was probably devised and described by AATCC because most of its tests utilize wet or chemical testing methods.

ASTM International (formerly known as the American Society for Testing and Materials) is an organization that focuses on testing product performance. Most of its specifications and testing methods involve dry methods of testing. Therefore, if the characteristic is being tested by application of stress or pressure, such as elongation or strength, or if it is to be measured or counted in a dry environment, then the test method is often one from ASTM (Case Study 12.1, Quality Assurance Standards: Basic Testing Requirements for Fabrics, Findings, and Trims, with Figure 12.2a–b).

Sizing Specifications

Sizing concepts are addressed in chapter 11. The measurements for an individual style are based on a combination of body measurements, functional ease required for body movement, and styling ease to achieve the desired look for the product.

CASE STUDY 12.1 QUALITY ASSURANCE STANDARDS: BASIC TESTING REQUIREMENTS FOR FABRICS, FINDINGS, AND TRIMS*

Callie Blake Collection
New York, NY 10012
212-555-7357

This table is a part of the Callie Blake Collection company specification manual. It lists the quality assurance tests commonly requested by retailers and manufacturers for merchandise to be sold in the U.S. marketplace.

TEST TYPE	TEST METHOD RECOMMENDED	COMMENTS ON REQUIREMENTS
Flammability	ASTM D1230 or Title 16 CFR, Part 1610	Required by U.S. government. This is a minimal standard.
Children's sleepwear flammability	Title 16CFR, Parts 1615 and 1616	More stringent than above. Required by U.S. government for children's sleepwear. Excludes diapers and underwear.
Fiber content	AATCC 20 and 20A	Required for permanent label on apparel by U.S. government.
Dimensional stability (shrinkage)	AATCC 135	Excessive shrinkage results in consumer dissatisfaction.
Durable press or wrinkle-free	AATCC 145	A rather subjective test, but of use to determine whether the finish meets expectations after washing.
Skewing	AATCC 179	Used mostly on knits. Identifies issues of garments twisting when washed, when it is too late to correct.
Colorfastness to laundering	AATCC 61	Color fading and staining during laundering is unacceptable.
Colorfastness to water	AATCC 107	Sometimes called static wetting; color staining or migration when left wet for periods of time.
Colorfastness to non-chlorine bleach	AATCC 172	Used to determine whether non—chlorine bleach will affect colors during washing. Labeling must be adjusted if color affected.
Colorfastness to chlorine bleach	AATCC 188	If fabric is affected by chlorine bleach only, warning on label to read: "Only non-chlorine bleach if needed." If sensitive to both bleach types, label to read: "Do not bleach."
Crocking	AATCC 8	Color rubs off onto other surfaces due to poor dye penetration.

CASE STUDY 12.1 QUALITY ASSURANCE STANDARDS *continued*

TEST TYPE	TEST METHOD RECOMMENDED	COMMENTS ON REQUIREMENTS
Colorfastness to light	AATCC 16	Colors fade or change when exposed to light for periods of time. Time varies dependent on product end use.
Colorfastness to perspiration	AATCC 15	Perspiration causes staining or color change. Useful to test linings.
Thread count	ASTM D3775; ASTM D3887	Yarn count; reported separately for warp and filling. Critical in verifying fabric quality.
Fabric weight	ASTM D3776; ASTM D3887	Designated in terms such as "ounces per square yard" or "grams per square meter." Critical in verifying fabric shipped is same as fabric ordered.
Pilling	ASTM D3512	Small balls of fiber appear on surface, caused by rubbing or abrasion. Long-staple fiber and higher-twist yarns pill less.
Water repellency Water resistance Waterproof	AATCC 22 AATCC 35 AATCC 127	Good, Better, Best: in order, from light showers to full immersion in water. Do not confuse first two with being waterproof.

*Listed tests are for fabrics used in apparel; findings and trims are tested for many of the same criteria to determine compatibility with shell fabrics. Additional tests required for safety of children's wear (Birnbaum 2005, 110–132).

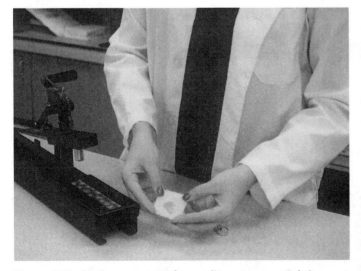 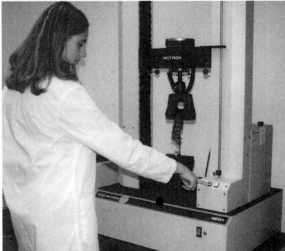

Figure 12.2a–b. Common tests for quality assurance. Fabrics are tested for crocking with a crockmeter and for strength with an Instron tester.

CASE STUDY 12.2 QUALITY ASSURANCE STANDARDS: HOW TO MEASURE APPAREL

The following measurement standards are recommended for use in checking sample garment measurements against the measurement specification sheet for an individual style.

- Give all measurements in inches.
- Record measurements to the nearest 1/8 inch.
- Use a flexible vinyl or soft tape measure (not metal).
- Measure with the garment smoothed flat on a table.
- Do not allow any portion of the garment to drape over the edge of the surface.
- Measure extended neck openings, cuffs, skirt sweeps, waistbands, and leg openings as follows:
    - Woven fabrics—extend garment fully, without distorting stitches.
    - Knit fabrics—extend garment to its maximum stretch.

- If a measurement is stated as "along curve" or "at edge" that is shaped, the tape measure should be "walked" around the curve (held and pivoted at intervals maintaining the exact shape to perform the measurement), or held on its narrow edge to follow the edge accurately.
- A point of measure using the term *high point shoulder (HPS)* must be laid flat so side seams are even. High point is determined to be the point at the shoulder and neck intersection where the natural fold of the garment falls.
- Circumference measurements:
    - Woven garments—require *full circumference* measurements.
    - Fine knits or sweater knit garments—require flat measurement of *half circumference.*

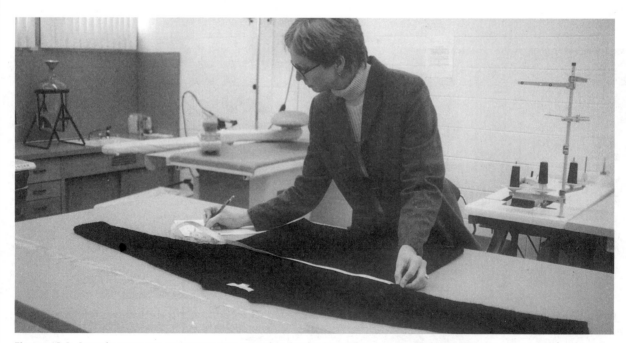

Figure 12.3. Sample garment measurements must be checked against the spec sheet before the garment goes into full production.

Garment measurements must be clearly communicated on the specification sheets that are used for patternmaking and sampling. Critical measurements that are different from usual, such as for a new style, may be communicated via technical sketches with locations and measurements carefully notated within the spec sheet drawing. During quality audits of production samples, key points of measure are evaluated to ensure that the garments are conforming to the original concept. Examples of key points to include in measurements of garment tops are collar circumference or minimum neck stretch (in knits); bust or chest circumference; armhole, sleeve opening, and sleeve length; and center back length. Key points to measure on garment bottoms include waist, hip, front and back rise, functional zipper opening, and pant inseam or center back skirt length. Finished garments that do not fall within the measurement tolerances established on the style's size specification sheet are deemed unacceptable (Case Study 12.2, Quality Assurance Standards: How to Measure Apparel, with Figure 12.3).

Labeling Standards

Within the United States, the Federal Trade Commission (FTC) establishes mandatory labeling requirements that affect an apparel firm's product development activities. (Details regarding these federal requirements may be found on the FTC Web site; refer to Additional Resources at the end of this chapter.) Other labels that are found on manufactured apparel are voluntary.

Mandatory Labeling Requirements

Mandatory labeling requirements apply to four areas: fiber content, manufacturers' identification, country of origin, and care. They are administered by the FTC.

Fiber Content

One of the major label rulings is the **Textile Fiber Products Identification Act (TFPIA)**. This act requires that garment labels disclose three things: the fiber content, the identification of the manufacturer or importer, and the country of origin. Because the fiber content affects many of the characteristics of the finished product, this law focuses on identifying the generic name(s) of the fiber(s) contained in the garment. In general, the generic names of the fibers are listed, along with the percentage of their content, in descending order. Anything over 5 percent of the total weight is listed by generic fiber name and percentage on the label, while fibers that constitute fewer than 5 percent of the total weight may be listed as "other." The exception is wool; it must be identified, even if it is less than 5 percent of the total weight. The FTC permits there be a 3 percent allowance of tolerance in these figures, but the total must equal 100 percent.

Although fiber content is identified by generic name, trade names may be used on the label along with the generic identification. An example of this might be the use of "Dacron polyester," which is a combination of the Dacron trade name owned by Invista with the generic name of that fiber.

Fiber content of trims does not have to be identified if the trim covers less than 15 percent of the surface of the garment, but the label has to include the phrase "exclusive of decoration." According to government information, linings and interlinings have to be identified only if they are incorporated for warmth.

Manufacturer Identification

The manufacturer's identification must be stated on the fiber identification label. The FTC registers an identification number or brand name for each manufacturer. Either the brand name or the number may be used on the label. The number used on the label states: "RNxxxx" (in which numbers replace the x's) or, if it is an older wool producer, "WPLxxxx" (in which numbers replace the x's). Further information regarding identification numbers can be found on the FTC Web site. When contractors are used, labeling requirements can get very confusing because some labels list the producer while others use the brand identifier.

Country of Origin

All products sold in the United States are required to name, on the fiber content label, the identity of the country where the product was produced. The country of origin is not necessarily a valid clue to the quality of the product, because no consistent evidence is available regarding measurable quality related to country of origin. According to recent changes in the law, country of origin is determined by where the garment was "substantially transformed." This is a U.S. Customs and Border Protection (CBP) term used to clarify the ruling for all imported goods.

The country of origin is straightforward when a garment is developed and produced in one location. However, identifying the country of origin can become very confusing when several locations are involved. Some examples of correct identification of country of origin include "Made in USA of imported fabric" or "Made in (name of country), finished in USA." Otherwise the label is to read "Made in (name of country)." Those products that are produced under Chapter 98/Item 807 import regulations are labeled "Made in (name of country) of U.S. materials." Chapter 98/Item 807 consists of a set of rules for U.S. tariffs regarding the value added to apparel that is assembled in Caribbean nations. They are commonly referred to in business as "807" regulations.

Country of origin becomes a critical issue when garments are imported. If tariffs are imposed on imported garments as they come into the United States, those tariffs will be calculated based upon the location where they were produced. Those items produced in countries that have free trade agreements

Figure 12.4. *Care symbols for use on garment labels provide instructions for commercial and home laundering and dry cleaning of apparel products.*

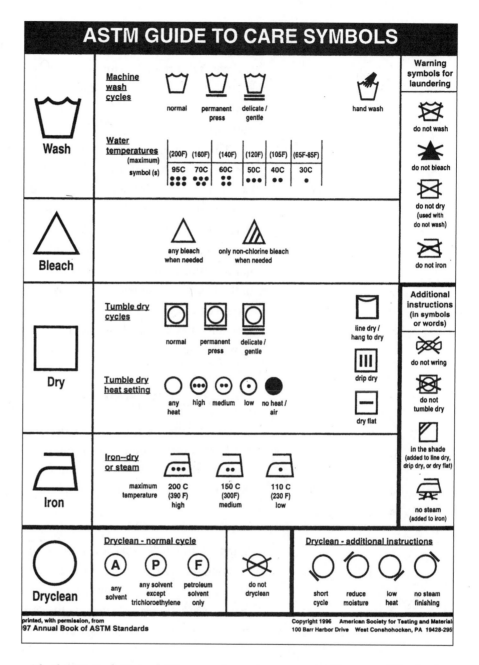

with the United States will enter through customs with no tariffs, further increasing the importance of establishing country of origin.

Care

The **Care Labeling Rule** requires apparel to carry a permanently affixed label with instructions on regular care. This rule is also regulated by the FTC and applies to all garments with two exceptions. Exceptions are garments that can use any care method and garments on which the label would interfere with use, such as hosiery. The care label may be stated in words or it may utilize a system of care symbols to use in place of words. The guide to care symbols is copyrighted by ASTM International as D5489—Standard Guide for Permanent Care Labels on Consumer Textile Products (Figure 12.4). If words are used, the FTC has an approved listing for most conditions. These written care label requirements may also be obtained from ASTM International. Because of the complexity of these labeling instructions, product developers are encouraged to consult the latest *Annual Book of ASTM Standards* for a complete set of care symbols and acceptable wording for apparel care labels appropriate to their own specific products.

The EU uses its own variant of a care symbol system for apparel, which is quite similar to that from ASTM International. A major difference between care labeling requirements for Europe and the United States is that water temperature for laundering is required on European labels. Since washing machines sold in the United States do not have water temperature designations other than hot, warm, or cold, there is no label requirement for water temperature designations. However, if products are being produced for sale in the EU, or in countries that follow EU regulations, it would be wise to check the specific regulations regarding labeling products for care and sizing labeling standards. Some of the EU regulations are also part of ISO certification standards and may be obtained directly from the ISO.

Voluntary Labeling

Voluntary labeling for product developers includes labels related to trademark, warranties and certification, union manufacture, and size designation. Many of these labels are in common use. However, because the government does not require them, their use is considered voluntary.

Trademarks

Using a company's own trademark is voluntary and considered a good marketing tool, but using someone else's trademark is considered illegal. Garments carrying look-alike trademarks are considered counterfeit goods. When such products are discovered entering the country by U.S. customs, they are seized, and the owner is fined or prosecuted for trademark infringement.

Warranties and Certification

All products have an **implied warranty** that they will do what they are designed to do. For instance, a raincoat should repel water and snow boots should keep feet warm. If a warranty is **written** and appears on a label or hangtag claiming some characteristic, it becomes legally binding. For example, if a label states that a garment will not shrink more than 2 percent or if a garment is guaranteed not to fade, then those statements are a binding contract between the producer and the consumer. If this product shrinks more than 2 percent or fades, the producer is responsible. It should be noted that shrinkage of 4 to 5 percent can change a garment one full size.

Most voluntary labeling on the product and hangtags is intended to be more of a marketing tool than a legitimate quality claim. For example, the use of the cotton seal from Cotton, Inc., only claims that the product is made of cotton. It does not indicate the quality of that cotton. The same is true of Woolmark's wool seal. Monsanto's "Wear-dated for 1 year" tag does not clearly explain what "wear-dated" actually means in terms of quality standards, but it does give the consumer some confidence in the serviceability of the product.

Union Labels

Union labels that appear in many clothing products are voluntary labels and are not required to be there. These, too, are used more as marketing tools than as any real indication of quality. The most common of these in the United States is the **UNITE-HERE!** tag, which represents the combined Union of Needletrades, Industrial, and Textile Employees and the Hotel Employees and Restaurant Employees International Union. This label simply means that union members produced the garment.

Size Designations

The U.S. government does not require that the size of a garment appear on any apparel product sold in the United States. Although inclusion of a size designation on the label or hangtag is voluntary, it is an almost universal practice. Companies that do business with the EU are required to use European sizing charts and to state in metric units any measurements included on apparel.

Safety Regulations

Most safety regulations for garments are applicable to children's clothing. There are three major areas of regulations: flammability, drawstrings, and small objects.

Flammability

The CPSC, a division of the FTC, has regulations for children's apparel. The **Flammable Fabrics Act** affects mostly infant and children's sleepwear in sizes 0 to 6X and 7 to 14. This act requires the use of fabric finishes to retard or prevent the spread of flames. In 1996 it was amended to permit the sale of tight-fitting children's sleepwear and sleepwear for infants aged 9 months and younger, even if the garments in question did not meet minimum flame resistance requirements that had previously been applied. However, garments that do not meet flammability requirements must contain a permanently attached, visible label at center back, written in all capital letters in sans serif font and surrounded by a border, reading "wear snug-fitting not flame resistant". Because of these changes, it is recommended that producers who work with these products contact the CPSC for current interpretations of rulings regarding sleepwear.

The Flammable Fabrics Act also covers apparel items for adults that have been identified as dangerously flammable. Included in this category are sheer rayon or silk scarves, longhair sweaters, some fleece garments, and terrycloth robes. Because these fabrics burn easily, compliance with flammability standards is required.

Drawstrings and Small Parts

Regulations from the CPSC include guidelines for drawstrings on children's outerwear. These regulations are a response to concerns about the risks of children strangling or choking. For example, drawstrings at the neck, waist, or bottom of jackets or sweatshirts should be sewn in and extend no more than 3 inches when the garment is fully extended. The agency suggests substitution of snaps, buttons, hook and loop tape (Velcro), or elastic as alternatives to drawstrings.

The CPCS also has laws regulating the use of small parts that could be choking hazards for children younger than 3 years of age. These rules apply to snaps and buttons, so the size, pull strength, and sharpness of trim items are regulated. A specific example: Safety pins cannot be used to attach bows or flowers to garments for infants or children.

Preproduction Activities Related to Fabric, Findings, and Trim

Quality issues that must be addressed during preproduction include fabric testing and setting the specs for the fabrics, findings, and trims. Some wear-testing of products is done, but the majority of testing is related to the components of the products, especially the fabrics. Retailers are concerned with colorfastness to the light and atmosphere in their stores; consumers are more concerned with shrinkage and crocking (dyes rubbing off) after they take the garments home. Participants in product development are concerned with preventing visible flaws in garment materials and construction techniques.

A typical way of testing fabrics is to request a one-yard to two-yard sample of the fabric being considered and then run appropriate standard tests on that fabric. These tests may be conducted in-house or contracted to an outside laboratory. Once it is determined that the fabric meets the minimum requirements for the garment, the spec is written to purchase that exact fabric or to purchase a fabric that looks and feels like the original sample and also meets the performance criteria of the same standard tests that were used on the sample. Standard ASTM International and AATCC testing procedures are readily available from those organizations and recognized throughout the industry as appropriate standards for quality testing (see Case Study 12.1).

Tests are run to determine characteristics such as crocking and wrinkle resistance, colorfastness, and, if appropriate, weather resistance. The type of product determines the tests needed. For example, running gear needs to wick moisture (pull moisture away from the skin) and raincoats need to shed water. There are standard testing procedures to determine whether a fabric sample meets either of these characteristics. Color requirements may include color matching of coordinate fabrics made of different fibers and yarns and color shade sorting between similar fabrics that need to match. Further information about color matching is found in chapter 5. Fabrics with stretch require testing for properties such as elongation and recovery to determine if they will maintain their shape during use.

Specs need to be written to establish the suitability of shell fabrics and to identify compatible findings and trims for each garment style (refer to chapter 10 for more information on findings and trim). An interlining that has different care requirements from the shell fabric and causes a garment to appear rippled after it is washed is unacceptable; if the specifications had provided for similar shrinkage characteristics for both components, there would have been no such problem. All components, including interlinings and trims, must have compatible care and appearance retention characteristics with the selected shell fabric. Also, color matching of trims cannot be left to chance.

Thread is one of the findings that must meet stringent criteria to prevent seam failures in finished products. In addition to typical shrinkage and colorfastness testing, thread may need to be evaluated for strength, elongation, and in some cases abrasion resistance. For example, threads used to construct jeans that will be surface treated by sanding or acid washes must be resistant to abrasion.

The current trend to facilitate faster turnaround time of product from idea to delivery has led companies to accept certification of suppliers. Certification of suppliers means that the supplier does the testing and the product development company accepts the supplier's results and does not conduct the tests itself. Such certification is built on trust, but it also may require contracts between the supplier and contractor that spell out liability responsibilities if the end results do not match the agreed-upon precertification requirements.

Specifications for Stitches, Seams, and Edge Finishes

Determining the degree of detail to include in the specs for stitch, seam, and edge finishes varies considerably from firm to firm and product to product. Some apparel firms leave decisions regarding these areas up to the engineering staff or the contractor. Other firms spell out these specifications to the last detail to ensure that the finished products conform to the original concept for that garment's construction. Detailed construction specs aid in establishing criteria for acceptable quality and determining acceptability of finished products. This approach also makes it possible for garments to be consistent when more than one contractor is used to produce a style.

Stitches

Because stitches are what hold garments together, they have a critical impact on the overall quality of the finished product. Understanding the types of stitches that are commonly used in commercial apparel construction and identifying the type of machine, threads, and needles that are required to produce those stitches may be of considerable benefit to anyone involved in the product development process, but especially to those who are responsible for the garment's quality.

Stitches are configurations of thread that form stitching and seams. The majority of stitches are made on a **lockstitch machine**, which requires both a needle thread and a bobbin thread, or a **chain-stitch machine**, which interlocks several threads supplied from cones and eliminates the need for frequent bobbin changes. For many years the U.S. government had a standard, identified as U.S. Federal Standard No. 751a—Stitches, Seams, and Stitchings, which provided schematic drawings of the conformation of each stitch type and a definition of each. In 1997, the ASTM revised that federal standard, removing it from the auspices of the government to a consensus civilian standard. The newest designation of this document is ASTM International D6193-97 (Reapproved 2004)—Standard Practice for Seams and Stitches. This document is widely used throughout the industry for specifying stitch types.

Commercial stitches are divided into six classes based on complexity, configuration, and the type of machine that is required to form the stitching. A three-digit number identifies each **stitch class**. The first number identifies the class and the other digits identify a specific stitch type within that class. Each of these classes has distinct advantages and disadvantages; therefore, stitch selection for garment construction depends on their proposed use. Figure 12.5 illustrates the following class categories:

- *100 stitch class*—single-thread chain stitches. While inexpensive, these stitches unravel too easily for use in quality apparel. They may be used in hems and for attaching buttons.

- *200 stitch class*—hand stitches and a few machine imitations. Extremely expensive if done by hand, the machine version requires special machinery and is of very limited use.

- *300 stitch class*—lockstitches. These stitches are flat, nonbulky, and strong, but they are nonextendible. They produce a reversible row of stitching. Bobbins require frequent changing, which slows production. This is the most widely used stitch class in the apparel industry.

100-CLASS STITCHES

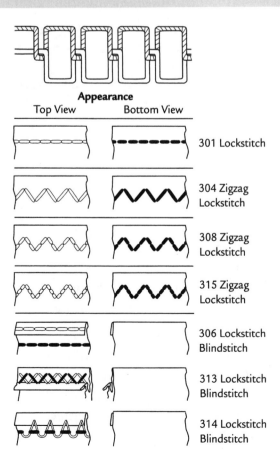

Appearance

Top View	Bottom View	
		101 Single-Thread Chainstitch
		103 Single-Thread Blindstitch
		104 Saddle Stitch
		104 Modified Saddle Stitch

200-CLASS STITCHES

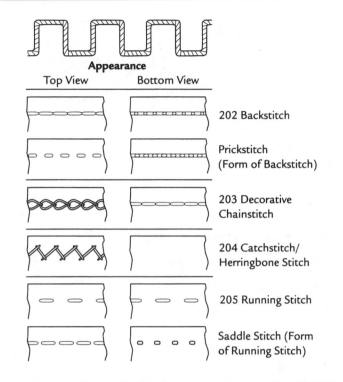

Appearance

Top View	Bottom View	
		202 Backstitch
		Prickstitch (Form of Backstitch)
		203 Decorative Chainstitch
		204 Catchstitch/ Herringbone Stitch
		205 Running Stitch
		Saddle Stitch (Form of Running Stitch)

300-CLASS STITCHES

Appearance

Top View	Bottom View	
		301 Lockstitch
		304 Zigzag Lockstitch
		308 Zigzag Lockstitch
		315 Zigzag Lockstitch
		306 Lockstitch Blindstitch
		313 Lockstitch Blindstitch
		314 Lockstitch Blindstitch

400-CLASS STITCHES

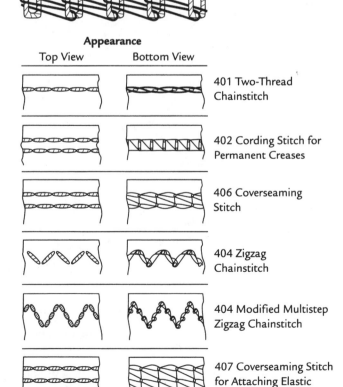

Appearance

Top View	Bottom View	
		401 Two-Thread Chainstitch
		402 Cording Stitch for Permanent Creases
		406 Coverseaming Stitch
		404 Zigzag Chainstitch
		404 Modified Multistep Zigzag Chainstitch
		407 Coverseaming Stitch for Attaching Elastic

500-CLASS STITCHES

600-CLASS STITCHES

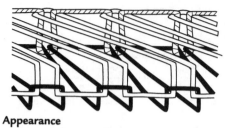

Appearance

Top View		Bottom View	Stitch Type	Application
	1 Thread	Ndl. Thd.	501	Break-open Seaming (easily unraveled) Note: no purl
	2 Threads	Ndl. Thd.	502	Seaming Bags, etc. Note: no purl
	2 Threads	Ndl.Thd.	503	Serging Blindhemming Break-open Seaming Note: purl on edge
	3 Threads		504	Seaming Knit Goods, etc. Serging Note: purl on edge
	3 Threads	Ndl.Thd.	505	Serging Break-open Seaming Note: Double purl
	4 Threads	Ndl. Thd.	512	Seaming Switch Mock Saftey (simulated saftey stitch) Note: purl on edge
	4 Threads	Ndl. Thd.	514	Seaming Switch (produces strong seams on wovens or knits) Note: same as 512 but with long upper looper
	4 Threads		515 (401 & 503)	Safety Stitch Seaming
	5 Threads		516 (401 & 504)	Safety Stitch Seaming

600-CLASS STITCHES

Appearance

Top View	Bottom View
602 Coverstitch	
605 Coverstitch	
607 Flat Seaming Stitch	

Figures 12.5. *Six categories of stitches used in commercial garment construction, showing view from the top and underside.*

- *400 stitch class*—multithread chain stitches, interlooped. The labor cost is less than for stitch class 300, but these stitches use more thread. Stitches are more extendible than the 300 stitch class, but bulkier. This class provides the main competition to the 300 stitch class series.

- *500 stitch class*—overedge stitches, interlooped. These stitches are strong, durable, and extendible; however, seam grin is a problem. (When the thread tension allows the threads to show between the two sides of seamed fabric, instead of holding the sides together tightly, the threads look like a row of teeth crossing the space between the sides; the term seam grin derives from this image.) This class stitches a seam, trims, and finishes the edge simultaneously. Hence, these stitches can be used only on edges. This class is most widely used in knitwear and leg seams on jeans.

- *600 stitch class*—cover stitches, interlooped. These stitches are extendible but strong. Several threads show on face and back. They are used to join abutted or overlapped edges.

Safety stitches contain two parallel rows of stitches that produce a very secure seam. They are formed by a row of overedge stitches and a row of either multithread chain stitches or lockstitches and found in the 500 stitch class.

In general, shorter stitches produce more durable seams. However, there is a point of no return at which, if stitches become too packed together, puckering and seam distortion can occur. A stitch length of 10 to 12 stitches per inch (SPI) is considered average, although the weight of the fabric and the purpose of the finished stitching should be taken into consideration. Typical stitch lengths recommended by thread manufacturers for commercially produced woven and knit garments are:

Blindstitching hems, 3–5 SPI

Casual blouses and tops, 10–14 SPI

Childrenswear, 8–10 SPI

Jeans, 7–8 SPI

Dress shirts, 14–20 SPI with finer threads to prevent puckering

Trousers and slacks, 10–12 SPI

Knit shirts, 10–12 SPI

Infantwear, 10–12 SPI

Stretch knits with Lycra or spandex, 14–18 SPI

Swimwear, 12–16 SPI

Underwear, 12–14 SPI (American & Efird, Inc. 1997c)

Signs of quality in stitching include even stitches with no ruptures, neat and straight stitches, and removal of excessive visible thread ends. Poor stitch quality results in defects (Figure 12.6).

The amount of thread used to construct a garment has to be estimated in advance, especially when the thread has to be dyed to match the fabric. To facilitate calculation of estimated thread usage, see Table 12.1.

Seams

Stitching that holds together pieces of fabric forms **seams**. The extension between the row of stitching and the edges of the fabric is called the **seam**

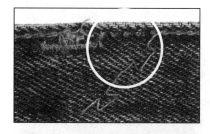

Figure 12.6a–c. *Common seam quality defects. Unraveling is caused by a broken or skipped stitch. Restitched seams reflect a "splice" in the stitch line where a thread broke or ran out during construction. A ropy hem is caused by poor operator handling or too much pressure on the presser foot.*

Table 12.1 ESTIMATED THREAD CONSUMPTION*

PRODUCT SEWN	TOTAL YDS/GARMENT	GARMENTS/6000-YD CONE
Men's slacks	225	27
Men's jeans	200	30
Dress shirt	131	46
T-shirt	63	95
Fleece sweatshirt	280	21
Women's lined coat	246	24
Dress	141	43
Women's jeans	250	24
Panties	62	97
Girl's swimsuit	65	92

*Based on typical garment construction and including a 25% waste factor
Source: American & Efird, Inc. 1977b

allowance. Although home sewing patterns consistently provide ⅝-inch seam allowances, commercial construction most often utilizes a ½-inch seam allowance on straight seams and a ¼-inch seam allowance on curves. At the highest price points, women's tailored garments and those at the haute couture level sometimes provide a full 1-inch seam allowance on major vertical seams to facilitate alterations. Also, the back crotch seam of men's tailored trousers often provides up to a 1½-inch seam allowance near the waistline to provide fabric for alterations. In general, wide seam allowances are a mark of quality but they increase costs and can create excessive bulk.

Garments often contain several different seam types depending on the seam location, the intended end use of the garment, styling factors, and the equipment available for production. Costs increase if special machines or attachments are required and when the seam structure is more complex.

The ASTM International D6193-97 (Reapproved 2004)—Standard Practice for Seams and Stitches outlines four classes of seams. They are written into specifications by using two uppercase letters that identify the seam class, followed by a lowercase letter or letters that identify the seam type (Figure 12.7). The seam designation is preceded by the stitch class and type number and may be followed by a number that clarifies the number of independently sewn rows of stitching required to form the seam. Figure 12.8 and Appendix 12.1 illustrate the following major seam classes:

301 SSae-2
(Stitch type) (Seam type)

Figure 12.7. *Notation format for identifying stitches and seams on specification sheets.*

- **Superimposed seams (SS)**—the most-used seam class, formed by stacking plies of fabric on top of one another and stitching them together near the edge. There are 54 variations.

- **Lapped seams (LS)**—formed by overlapping the seam allowances of two or more plies of fabric and sewing them together. With 102 variations, this is the largest seam class.

- **Bound seams (BS)**—made by encasing the raw edges of a seam with fabric strips.

- **Flat seams (FS)**—join fabric plies by butting the raw edges together and securing them with a 600-class cover stitch or a zigzag stitch. There are only 6 variations.

The other ASTM International classes in this standard are **ornamental stitching (OS)** and **edge finishes (EF)**. They bridge the gap between stitch types and true seams. They include embroidery forms and edge finishes. The appendix for this chapter contains cross-section views of all recognized ASTM International seam variations.

Superimposed Seams

The most used seam class is the superimposed seam group. The cut edges of the fabric layers are stacked on top of one another to form a **booked seam** ready for stitching. The most common seam is the 301SSa, used for major structural seams. The 301 designation is the stitch type, and the SSa is the seam type. When this seam is pressed open on the inside of the garment, it is said to be butterflied or busted. This pressing reduces bulk and makes the seam almost invisible on the face side of the garment. Some plain seams are never pressed open, including the armscye seam and the crotch seam near the leg inseams, and those identified as enclosed seams.

The second most common seam type found within the SS class is the **enclosed seam**. These seams are completed in two stages. The process hides the edges of the seams on the inside of the garment by folding the edges between other layers of fabric. Examples of this category are the outer edges of necklines, collars, and cuffs. Quality in these seams is achieved by eliminating bulk in areas where these seams are placed. To accomplish this, the seam allowances are often layered, referred to as **graded** or blended, by trimming out the excess seam allowances to different lengths. The danger is in trimming them too close to the stitching line. This can cause fraying.

Lapped Seams

The lapped seam class contains the most variations; however, many of them have very specialized uses. Placing one layer over the other and stitching, leaving the exposed edges, forms the LSa, the simplest form of this class. This version can be used for sewing nonravel materials, such as felt and leather, and for shaping nonwoven interlining applications. The more commonly used

SUPERIMPOSED

SSa (1.01)
Most common seam. Usually finished on cut edge with serging, or pressed open (busted).

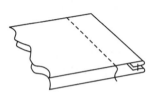

SSae (1.06.03)
Commonly known as a French Seam. Done in 2 steps: first an SSa and then folded to inside and top-stitched. Seen on edges of collars.

SSh (4.04.01)
A 2-step seam. Very narrow SSa is pressed open and restitched with a cover stitch. Seen on sweatshirts.

LAPPED

LSd (5.31.01)
A folded edge placed on top of another layer. Seen on patch-pocket edges.

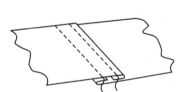

LSc (2.04.06)
Commonly known as a flat fell seam. Done in one step with a double-needle machine. Seen on seams of jeans.

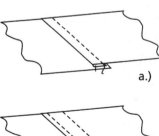
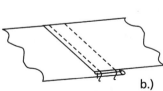

a.)

b.)

LSq (2.02.03)
a.) Known as a welt seam.
b.) Known as a fake flat fell. Done in 2 steps: first an SSa followed by folding to one side and 2 rows of topstitching. Seen on jean side seams.

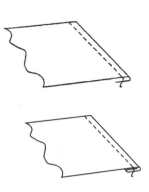

EDGE FINISH

EFa (6.02.01)
Single turned hem used on knits.

EFb (6.03.01)
Turned twice and stitched close to edge. Known as a shirt-tail hem.

EFc (6.06.01)
Method used to provide blind hem on garments such as T-shirts. When unfolded it is barely visible on right side.

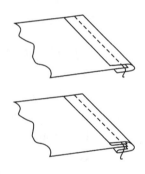

BOUND SEAM

BSa (3.01.01)
Used to attach foldover braids.

BSc (3.05.01)
Used to attach double fold bias tape to an edge.

Figure 12.8. *Most commonly used commercial seam types; the ASTM notation is followed by the ISO notation in parenthesis.*

versions of this seam class are those in which the raw edges are folded under. This forms a bulkier seam that can be used only on fairly straight edges, but one that is very strong, durable, and cannot ravel. The flat-felled seam (LSas) or mock flat-fell (LSbm) are commonly found on jeans.

Bound Seams

Bound seams are listed as a seam but are not used to form the structural seams of a garment. They are used to finish the raw edges of seams such as at necklines, armholes, hems, and seam allowances. A common binding used for bound seams is bias tape. Bias tape would form a BSc seam. With increased use of serging to finish seam edges with thread and the growing use of knit fabrics that do not ravel, the regular use of bound seams has decreased. However, high-priced designer garments and garments made of bulky, loosely woven wool fabrics still utilize bound seams to provide neat seam finishes and prevent raveling of cut edges.

Flat Seams

Flat seams look the same on both sides. The stitches cover the raw edges and are visible on the face and back. They are economical because they have no seam allowances, but they leave little room for error in construction and consume a significant amount of thread compared to other seam types. Flat seams appear most often in knit garments such as underwear and raglan-sleeve sweatshirts.

Edge Finishes

Edge finishes prevent raveling of woven fabrics and also keep the edges of lightweight to medium-weight knit fabrics from curling. There are three subcategories of edge finishes. The first is in the category system for seams because it appears on seam edges. The other two types of edge finishes are hems and facings. Consumers often think of garments with neatly finished edges as being of a higher quality than those with untreated edges. However, the process of finishing the edge may cause distortion and create more of a problem than if it were left unfinished. Some edge finishes create unwanted bulk, whereas others require the finish to prevent losing the entire seam allowance to raveling. Today, most producers of low- to moderate-priced garments finish the raw edges of seams together or booked, usually with a 500-class stitch type known as serging because it is a cost-effective way of creating the illusion of quality. Producers of high-quality apparel may finish the seam allowance of major seams separately and bust the seam allowance open (separate the edges with an iron) to produce a smooth seam that can be altered, even though this may cost twice as much as other edge finishing methods.

Hems may be the most common form of edge finish. Hems on higher-quality garments tend to be wider than those on lower-quality garments. Because wider hems require more fabric, they are more costly. Most single-fold hems are 1 to 2 inches in width. Double-fold hems tend to be narrower.

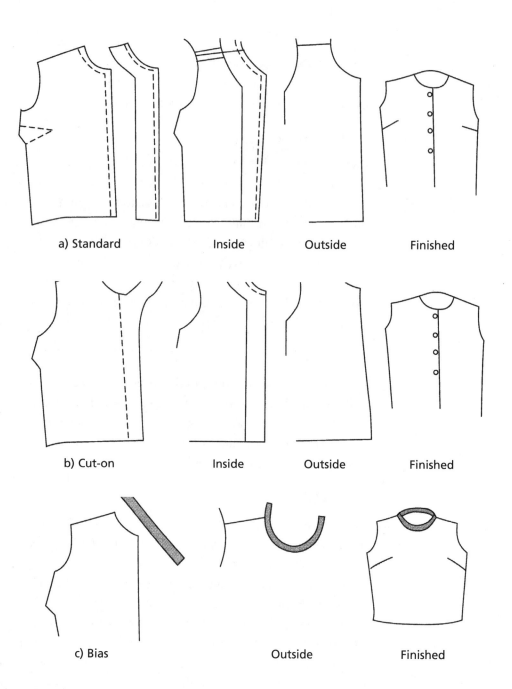

a) Standard   Inside   Outside   Finished

b) Cut-on   Inside   Outside   Finished

c) Bias   Outside   Finished

Figure 12.9. *Methods of finishing garment edges other than hems, include facings, cut-on facings, and bias strip.*

In general, wider hems tend to hang more smoothly and are more readily altered to conform to fashion changes. Selection of appropriate hem width also depends on the sweep or flare of the garment and on the weight of the fabrics. Hem finishes on full skirts tend to be narrower than those on slimmer styles due to the bulk created when the curved edge is turned up.

Facings are a form of edge finish. They are usually visible only on the inside of a garment and are expected to remain tucked into the underside of the garment. If cut too small, they may work themselves to the outside when worn. If improperly cut or pressed, they may roll to the outside at the sewn edge. These occurrences would be signs of poor quality. Facings are shaped to conform to the shape of the garment edge. They may be extensions of the main style block, a separate shaped piece, or a bias strip (Figure 12.9).

Assembly

Garment specifications list every operation used to make a garment in sequential order. They specify these operations down to the size and color of thread to be used for each seam and the machine type suggested to accomplish the desired end result. Companies vary in the degree of detail they require, but those that produce in quantity or use many contractors find that being as specific as possible contributes to the overall quality and consistency of product (Figure 12.10).

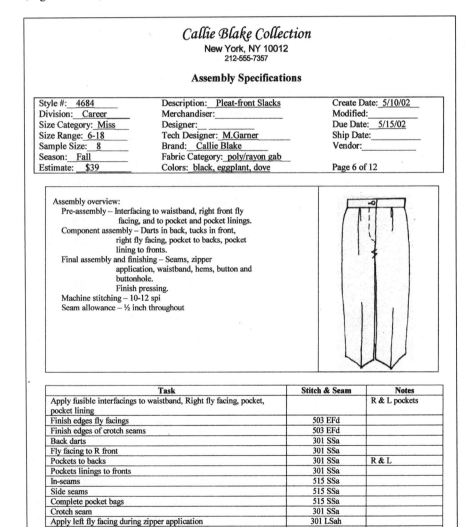

Callie Blake Collection
New York, NY 10012
212-555-7357

Assembly Specifications

Style #: 4684	Description: Pleat-front Slacks	Create Date: 5/10/02
Division: Career	Merchandiser:	Modified:
Size Category: Miss	Designer:	Due Date: 5/15/02
Size Range: 6-18	Tech Designer: M.Garner	Ship Date:
Sample Size: 8	Brand: Callie Blake	Vendor:
Season: Fall	Fabric Category: poly/rayon gab	
Estimate: $39	Colors: black, eggplant, dove	Page 6 of 12

Assembly overview:
Pre-assembly – Interfacing to waistband, right front fly facing, and to pocket and pocket linings.
Component assembly – Darts in back, tucks in front, right fly facing, pocket to backs, pocket lining to fronts.
Final assembly and finishing – Seams, zipper application, waistband, hems, button and buttonhole.
Finish pressing.
Machine stitching – 10-12 spi
Seam allowance – ½ inch throughout

Task	Stitch & Seam	Notes
Apply fusible interfacings to waistband, Right fly facing, pocket, pocket lining		R & L pockets
Finish edges fly facings	503 EFd	
Finish edges of crotch seams	503 EFd	
Back darts	301 SSa	
Fly facing to R front	301 SSa	
Pockets to backs	301 SSa	R & L
Pockets linings to fronts	301 SSa	
In-seams	515 SSa	
Side seams	515 SSa	
Complete pocket bags	515 SSa	
Crotch seam	301 SSa	
Apply left fly facing during zipper application	301 LSah	
Apply right front fly	301 SSa	
Complete zipper with J-stitch to R front	301 SSak	
Apply waistband, inserting front tucks	301 SSa	
Finish waistband, inserting labels at CB	301BSo	
Buttonhole	404	Bar tack both ends
Button applied	101	
Hem	EFa306	1 ½ inch finished
Finish pressing		Set leg creases

Figure 12.10. *Stitch and seam notations are indicated on a garment assembly spec form.*

Quality requirements may be stated as general standards for all products produced by the company. These requirements reflect characteristics that cannot be determined until a garment is assembled. Some examples of statements that might appear in the overall quality standards or specifications for a company's garments include the following:

- Fit must be evaluated and approved prior to production.

- Styles must allow ease for comfort in moving and sitting.

- Garments must be free of wrinkles that are not part of the design.

- Vertical seams must be perpendicular to the floor.

- Hems must be parallel to the floor.

- Interlining, interfacing, and lining must be compatible with the shell fabric in weight, color and care requirements.

- Linings must not hang below the outer hem or lower edge or cause distortion of the shell.

Tolerances

When written specifications are developed from the overall standards, product developers must understand that tolerances need to be clearly spelled out to reflect what will be accepted during the construction process. The difference between the allowable minimum and maximum on a process or finished measurement is the **tolerance**. If a finished garment falls between those specs, it will be acceptable; but if it goes under or beyond the tolerance, it will be rejected. An example of an unrealistic tolerance would be demanding 12 stitches per inch on a seam. With variations in machinery, fabric, and operator behavior, this is too tight a specification. A more realistic tolerance level would be stating the number of stitches per inch as "12 +/- 2 spi" (which is requesting a tolerance of 2 stitches per inch over or under the desired 12 stitches per inch, or 10 to 14 stitches per inch). This tolerance would be acceptable and more easily produced. Other specifications require exact levels, called **minimums**, for acceptance. An example would be requiring five buttons on the front of a blouse; any smaller number of buttons would be unacceptable for the product.

Each company develops its own standards for tolerances for each type of product it produces and uses them when spelling out the written specifications for each new style. In general, torso girth measurements can vary +/− ¼ inch to +/− ½ inch, depending on the size and style. A few measurements, such as the sweep of a skirt, may vary up to +/− ¾ inch. Shorter or smaller detailing seams usually move down to a +/− ⅛-inch variation. An example of this lower variation requirement might be the length of the shoulder seam or the width of a pocket. Tight tolerances of +/− ¹⁄₁₆ inch are reserved for critical details such as the length of collar points or buttonholes. The smaller the tolerances, the more precise the machine operators must be during construction.

The type of product will also affect the amount of tolerance permitted. For example, a pair of sweatpants made of fleece may have more flexible or looser tolerances than a brassiere which has many small parts and cannot withstand much variation before the overall structure of the garment is impaired.

Construction Criteria

In general, finished garments are subjected to visual inspections to determine if they comply with the written specifications. When inspection takes place on the manufacturing floor where corrections may still be made in a flawed product, it is called in-process inspection. If the inspection takes place after the product is finished, it is called end inspection. In general, more waste occurs in environments where end inspection is employed because it may be too late to correct flaws if they are found after the garment is completed. To ensure acceptable levels of quality in a finished garment, criteria must be established before the garments are produced and communicated to the contractor or production facilities. Knowing what will be deemed acceptable before the run is initiated helps eliminate wasted effort and materials. Various construction details that must be spelled out as quality requirements include the following:

- There should be no stitching errors such as skipped stitches or uneven seams.
- There should be no uneven collar points or pocket placements.
- Thread should be secure with no loose ends.
- There should be no noticeable repairs.
- Fabric patterns should match at seams where specified.
- There should be no oil, ink, or soil marks.
- Closures must be securely attached and as specified as to type, color, and application.
- Garments must be pressed and free of scorch or burn marks.

Product developers often keep a detailed notebook of all of the construction criteria they use on a regular basis for developing new style specification packages for the company. This notebook is a valuable reference tool for communicating with vendors and contractors (Case Study 12.3, The Impact of Thread on Product Quality).

Dealing with Flawed Products

It is common practice to inspect garments either when they come off the production line or when they arrive at the purchasing firm's distribution center. The purpose is to check for compliance to the written specifications spelled

CASE STUDY 12.3 THE IMPACT OF THREAD ON PRODUCT QUALITY
by Kenneth L. Sandow

Many companies find that by specifying key trim items that go into their products, they can better assure the total quality of the finished product. Thread makes up only a small fraction of the cost of the finished product, approximately 1 to 3 percent of wholesale cost, but it shares 50 percent of the responsibility for the quality of finished seams. Thread can affect seam quality in a variety of ways:

- Restitched seams due to thread breakage or skipped stitches.
- Restitched seams due to cut or broken stitches after laundering.
- Poor stitch appearance.
- Poor colorfastness through fading or transfer of color.
- Seam puckering and/or needle cutting.
- Seam failures or open seams.

Many designers spend a lot of time and energy trying to select the right zipper, button, snap, label, and even interlining to make their products look stylish and attractive. However, they also have to remember their products have to stand up to the rigors of the manufacturing and finishing processes and still meet the performance demands of the consumer. Proper thread selection is a key element in the success of this process.

Remember: there is no perfect thread for all applications; however, there is a perfect thread for a specific application. In order to select the right thread for a specific application, there are three elements to consider: fiber type, thread construction, and thread size.

Most experts who are involved in the selection of thread make their thread decisions based on one or all of the following characteristics:

- Sewability (manufacturing or sewing efficiencies)
- Seam performance (seam strength, seam durability, elasticity, etc.)
- Seam appearance (color, colorfastness, stitch appearance, puckering, etc.)
- Availability (is the product available to meet my needs)
- Cost (cost includes both the price and the hidden costs associated with quality)

American & Efird, Inc., has an excellent Web site with thread selection tables to assist in making the proper thread choice. Visit the Web site at www.amerfir.com/technical_information.htm.

Kenneth L. Sandow is Vice President of Global Retail Solutions, American & Efird, Inc.

out at the time contracts were awarded. If the quantity of garments is small or the garments are very high cost, 100 percent inspection is not unusual. At this time, garments that are found not to be of first quality (meet specs) are repaired to join the first-quality products, sent back to the contractor as unacceptable, or disposed of as irregulars.

If the order is very large, a random sample of garments is pulled from the shipment and thoroughly examined. If these sample garments meet specs, the entire lot is passed on for distribution; but if flaws are found in the sample garments, the decision becomes more complex. The firm may inspect all of the garments in the lot that contained defective garments and separate out the flawed pieces; or it may simply reject the entire lot as unacceptable and return it to the vendor or contractor.

Even when the criteria are spelled out in advance and all precautions are taken, the human error factor may run about 6 percent. So while perfection is desired, the reality is that a few flawed products may be included in shipments. The role of establishing tolerances and minimums is to permit some variation to occur in the product and still be within acceptable parameters, thereby reducing the costs of waste that would occur from demanding perfection. While there is always the potential of some flawed merchandise arriving at the distribution center or being directly drop-shipped to individual retail stores, having well-written specifications for contractors strengthens the potential for receiving a higher percentage of first-quality goods and may even provide a means for refusal of payment or for return of defective goods. If the spec package is not clear, the contractor has every expectation of receiving payment for goods, even if they are later deemed defective in the eyes of the firm or the consumer. Of further concern is the reality that returning defective garments to a contractor may not be an option with imported goods, and the firm will have to absorb the cost of defective merchandise. All these factors contribute to the rationale for providing well-written spec packages that boost the potential of receiving first-quality garments from manufacturers and contractors.

Summary

Setting the standards for quality at the beginning of the product development process facilitates production of quality products. Product developers must understand many areas of garment production in order to communicate quality requirements for each style to others in the production cycle. The details required for achieving quality in a style are communicated through complete and accurate specification sheets.

Areas of particular concern for assuring the quality of garments include mandatory and voluntary labeling and safety regulations for apparel; preproduction activities related to testing of fabrics, findings, and trim; identification of stitches, seams, and edge finishes to be used in the construction of the garment; and company requirements for assembly standards for the product.

Although perfection might be admirable, the cost of achieving such a lofty goal is high. It is up to the product development team to develop a strategy that balances the price and quality expectations of customers with the needs of the business.

Key Terms

booked seam

bound seams (BS)

busted seam

Care Labeling Rule

certification of suppliers

chain-stitch machine

edge finishes (EF)

enclosed seam

facings

Flammable Fabrics Act

flat seams (FS)

garment standards

graded seams

hems

implied warranty

International Organization for
    Standardization (ISO)

lapped seams (LS)

lockstitch machine

minimums

ornamental stitching (OS)

quality assurance

raw material standards

seam allowance

seams

specification libraries

stitch class

stitches

superimposed seams (SS)

Textile Products Fiber Identification
    Act (TFPIA)

tolerance

UNITE–HERE!

written warranty

Discussion Questions

1. How is quality defined in apparel products?

2. When high quality in a product conflicts with the amount of money that a business can spend on that product, how can this dilemma be resolved?

3. Which garments in your wardrobe provide examples of the stitches and seam classes listed in the chapter?

4. What is the importance of a well-written spec package when evaluating the quality of finished garments?

Activities

Make a reference notebook, on index cards, of a selection of at least 20 of the major stitches and seams that represent all of the classes identified in this chapter.

• Work in groups with other students.

• Use discarded clothes from your wardrobe or those you purchase from a thrift shop or garage sales. (A pair of jeans, a men's dress shirt, and one other garment such as lingerie or a T-shirt should provide almost all of the needed examples.)

• Cut an example representing each stitch and seam.

• Place examples on index cards that also contain critical identifying facts about that stitch or seam and a sketch of how it appears in the ASTM International standard.

References

American & Efird, Inc. 1997a. Technical bulletin: Common seam quality defects. www.amefird.com/seam_quality.htm (accessed September 9, 2006).

American & Efird, Inc. 1997b. Technical bulletin: Estimating thread consumption. www.amefird.com/estimating_consumption.htm (accessed September 9, 2006).

American & Efird, Inc. 1997c. Technical bulletin: Selecting the right SPI. www.amefird.com/spi.htm (accessed September 10, 2006).

ASTM International. 2004. Designation D6193-97 (reapproved 2004) standard practice for stitches and seams. ASTM International. www.astm.org (accessed September 9, 2006).

Birnbaum, D. 2005. *Birnbaum's global guide to material sourcing.* New York: Fashiondex, Inc.

Solinger, J. 1998. *Apparel manufacturing handbook.* 2d ed. Columbia, SC: Bobbin Media Corp.

Additional Resources

ASTM International. 2005. *Annual book of ASTM standards.* Vol. 07.02 Textiles. West Conshohocken, PA: ASTM International. www.astm.org.

Brown, P., and J. Rice. 2001. *Ready-to-wear apparel analysis.* 3d ed. Upper Saddle River, NJ: Prentice-Hall.

Crosby, P. B. 1979. *Quality is free.* New York: McGraw-Hill.

Federal Trade Commisssion. www.ftc.gov/bcp/rn/index.shtml. Information about federal requirements for labeling and manufacturer's identification numbers.

Glock, R. E., and G. I. Kunz. 2005. *Apparel manufacturing: Sewn product analysis.* 4th ed. Upper Saddle River, NJ: Prentice-Hall.

International Organization for Standardization. www.iso.ch/cate/cat.html.

Juran, J. M., ed. 1974. *Quality control handbook.* 3d ed. New York: McGraw-Hill.

Kadolph, S. J. 1998. *Quality assurance for textiles and apparel.* New York: Fairchild.

Mehta, P. 1992. *An introduction to quality control for the apparel industry.* Milwaukee: ASQC Quality Press.

Rules and regulations under the textile fiber products identification act (Revised January 1, 2000). Code of Federal Regulations, Title 16—Commercial Practices, Volume 1, Ch. I—Federal Trade Commission, Part 303. Washington, DC: U.S. Government Printing Office.

Smith, G. 1995. *Statistical process control and quality improvement.* Englewood Cliffs, NJ: Prentice-Hall.

U.S. Consumer Product Safety Commission. www.cpsc.gov/businfo/sleepstay.html.

APPENDIX:
Index of Commercial Seams by Class

Seam Class SS (Superimposed Seam)

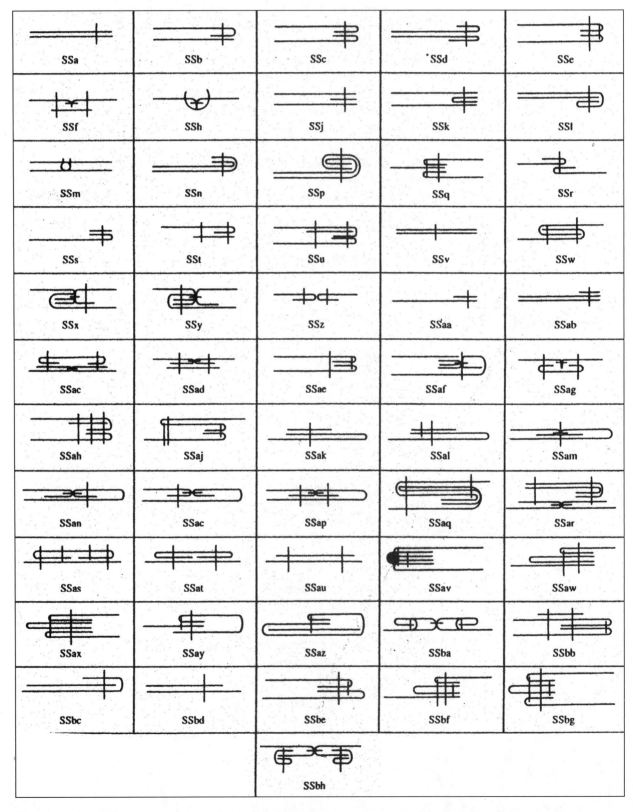

Seam Class LS (Lapped Seam)

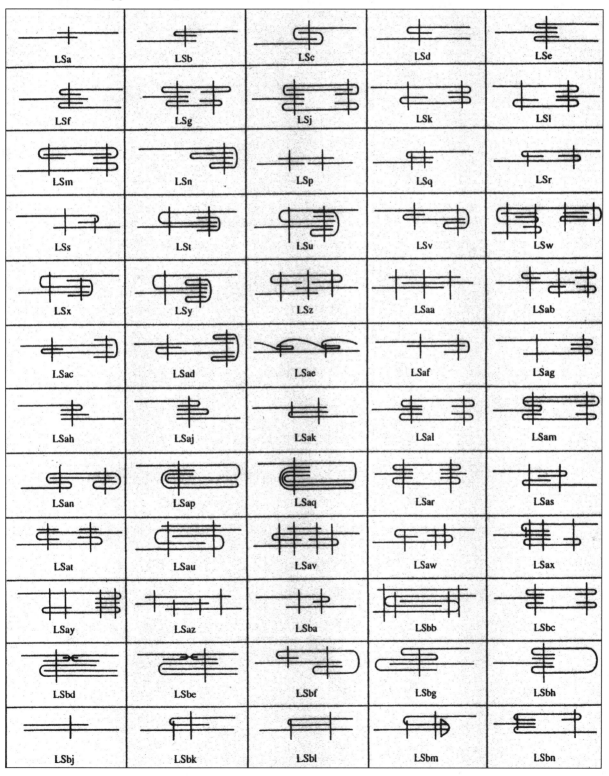

Seam Class LS (Lapped Seam) (continued)

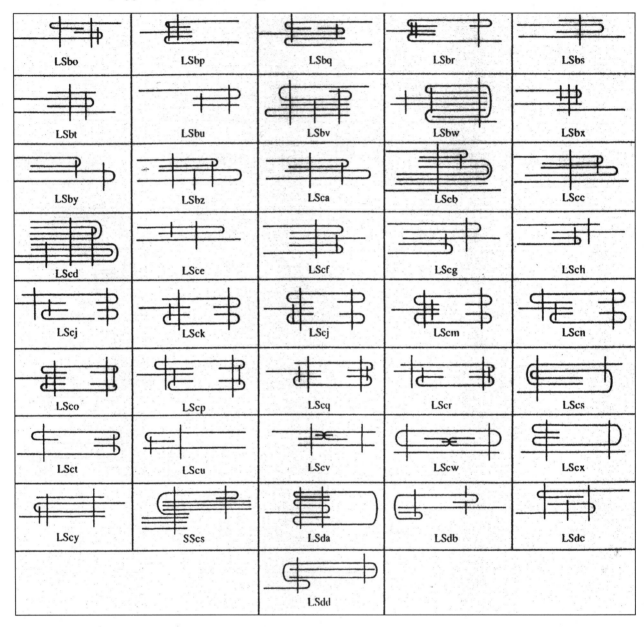

Seam Class BS (Bound)

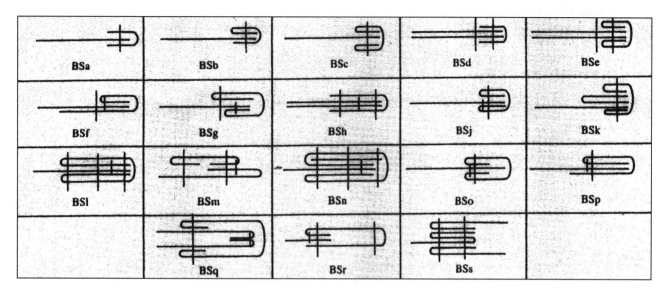

Seam Class FS (Flat)

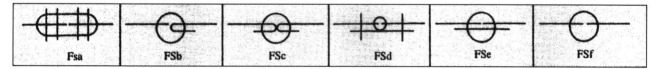

Seam Class OS (Ornamental)

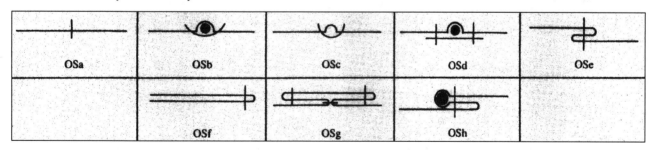

Seam Class EF (Edge Finishes)

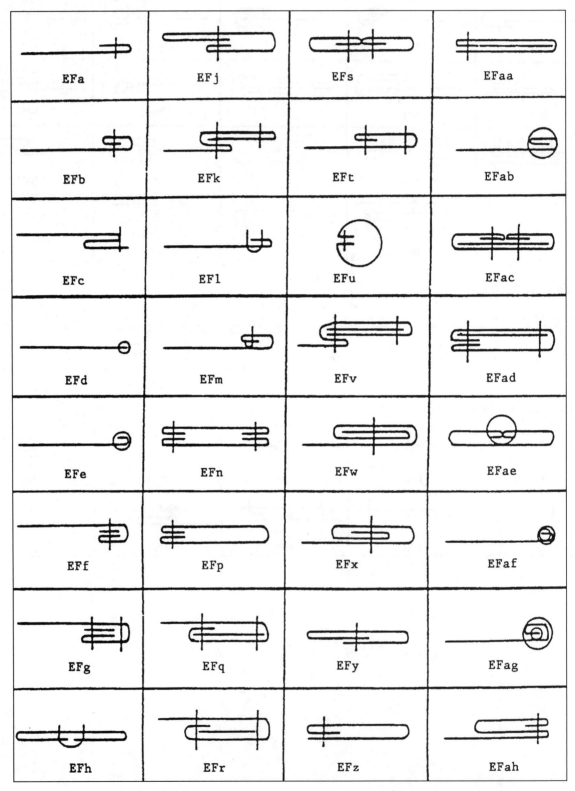

PART FOUR

PRODUCTION PLANNING AND DISTRIBUTION

CHAPTER 13

THE ROLE OF SOURCING

"Today, 90 percent of all apparel sold in the United States is imported.
That number rises to . . . an astounding 98.5 percent of the U.S. footwear market."
—KEVIN BURKE, PRESIDENT AND CEO, AAFA (AUGUST 11, 2006)

OBJECTIVES

- To understand how sourcing decisions affect the product development process, particularly in terms of the production calendar and price point

- To understand the options in determining an appropriate sourcing mix

- To be aware of how global trade agreements influence sourcing decisions

- To learn how to evaluate potential sourcing partners

- To understand how sourcing decisions influence a product's price

---

Today's consumer expects apparel manufacturers and retailers to offer a wide array of apparel products that provide both style and quality at a good value. Product developers and retailers need to meet these demands while remaining profitable. The textile and apparel industries have become a part of an integrated global production system that utilizes worldwide resources to create value for the consumer. Apparel product developers can procure almost anything their customers want if they know how and where to source it.

The scope and complexity of sourcing decisions make it imperative that sourcing personnel work cross-functionally. As soon as the merchandising plan is finalized, the sourcing team can begin to line up seasonal production capacity. In branded companies, sourcing personnel are present at initial concept meetings to determine the capabilities needed for seasonal production. Decisions as to whether the line will focus on wovens or knits, fine-gauge or bulky sweaters, or blouses, shirts, or tops all affect the selection of sourcing partners to be utilized in a given season. If the team utilizes fabrics found at

Figure 13.1a. *Textile factory worker in Heifei, China.*

Figure 13.1b. *Textile trade fair in Asia.*

trade fairs or through domestic reps, sourcing the fabric selection is less involved. But if the fabrics sampled are too expensive for the target customer, members of the sourcing team will see whether the samples can be reproduced more reasonably offshore. Sourcing personnel provide a wealth of knowledge in terms of what can and cannot be done at a given price point. They possess the ability to suggest design or construction trade-offs that may be helpful in expressing a trend in a less expensive way.

Manufacture means "to make," but many American apparel manufacturers no longer actually make apparel. As discussed in chapter 1, they are virtual manufacturers who develop the concepts for products, determine the components, and make the decisions as to how and where the products will be produced and distributed. **Sourcing** is the practice of procuring materials and production elsewhere, usually in plants owned by others and, most frequently today, located in other countries. Companies refer to the combination of resources they utilize for production as their **sourcing mix**.

The overall role of sourcing in today's product development environment has changed appreciably in the last decade. Perhaps the most telling statistic is the increase in the quantity of merchandise sourced in other countries. In the last few years, the percentage of apparel sold in the United States that is imported has increased from 60 percent to 90 percent (Figure 13.1a–b). This change significantly affects the role of all product developers.

Sourcing Options

Successful sourcing must be dynamic—with a network of sourcing partners that provides a complex balance of capacity, flexibility, value, and efficiency. All partners in the sourcing mix must be able to manage continual change in a global environment. A sourcing mix typically includes several different types of domestic and offshore sourcing options in order to meet these changing needs.

Sourcing Domestically

Some product developers choose to include domestically owned manufacturing facilities in their sourcing mix. By owning their own plants, product developers can respond quickly to shifts in market demand. In-house manufacturing requires shorter lead times and can accommodate short runs. In-house plants are generally equipped with cutting-edge technology and utilize a highly skilled work force. The product developer maintains control of quality, costs, scheduling, support functions, and working conditions. Unfortunately, it is increasingly difficult to remain price-competitive while relying exclusively on domestically owned facilities (Figure 13.2). Thus, company-owned production facilities generally account for a diminishing portion of a product developer's production capacity, with the balance contracted elsewhere. This mix provides the balance and flexibility necessary to meet seasonal and fashion fluctuations.

Domestic contracting relies on the use of manufacturing facilities located in the same country as the product developer, but not owned by the product developer. Similar to the situation in domestically owned manufacturing facilities, use of domestic contracting facilitates Quick Response. It is easier and faster to develop partnerships with domestic suppliers and contractors who understand the domestic marketplace and who have implemented Quick Response technology.

Including domestic contractors as part of the sourcing mix may allow a product developer to increase the order size for styles that sell beyond expectations, something that may not be feasible when using offshore sourcing.

Figure 13.2. *Domestic production in the United States has been declining.*

Another advantage is the ease of communication that results when partners speak the same language and work in a similar time zone. Also, quality inspections or certification visits are less costly. There is generally a shared paradigm in terms of manufacturing methodology and quality and delivery expectations. The risks involved with quotas, clearing customs, and shipping are eliminated. Care must be taken that the contract shop is well run and complies with workers' rights. Ultimately, it is the product developer's reputation that is at stake.

Los Angeles is the leader in U.S. apparel production employment, followed by New York City. The following areas contribute less than 15 percent each to employment in apparel manufacturing in the United States today:

• Miami, Dade County, Florida

• El Paso County, Texas

• San Francisco County, California

• Orange County, California

• Hudson County, New Jersey

• Bristol County, Massachusetts

• Chicago, Cook County, Illinois

• Dallas County, Texas (Bonacich and Appelbaum 2000)

The number of production workers employed in textiles and apparel manufacturing in the United States has dropped significantly in the past 50 years, largely due to the influx of imported products. The U.S. Department of Labor reported that in 1950 there were 1.26 million employed in textile production and 1.20 million in apparel production in the United States. By 2002, those employment figures were down to 0.43 million textile workers and 0.52 million apparel workers. This was a drop of 64 percent in textiles and 56.6 percent in apparel employees (U.S. International Trade Commission 2004, 4). Since 2002 those figures have continued to decline even though more products are being produced, indicating the infusion of advanced technology to replace workers. The apparel sector appears to have lost more employment than the textile sector until very recent years. The products are simply being sourced elsewhere.

Offshore Sourcing

Offshore sourcing has become the predominant model for acquisition of capacity for apparel production throughout much of the developing and developed world. Most of the over 200 nations in the world have some form of apparel production, and many of them offer unique qualifications in the form of lower costs, expertise, or availability of materials and labor. It is of interest that the United States imports from almost all nations except from the countries the U.S. government has placed embargos against, such as all products from Myanmar (formerly Burma).

Where Goods Are Sourced

Countries making the biggest contributions to global textile and apparel trade have also shifted in recent years. While many consumers consider Europe, especially France and Italy, to be the source of considerable quantities of imported apparel products, the contributions of the EU tend to be more in the area of design trends and higher-priced goods, or woolen tailored goods from eastern Europe (Figure 13.3). Imports from Europe make up only a small percentage of the overall U.S. market. By far the largest supplier to the U.S. apparel market today is China, and some nations that were not even on the radar a decade ago have gained significant market share. Vietnam is an example. Table 13.1 lists the biggest contributors of textiles and apparel products to the U.S. market.

Rationale for Offshore Sourcing

Because the apparel industry is so labor-intense, it is one of the first industries that developing countries promote. **Labor-intense** industries require many workers to complete each product made, therefore putting many people to work in locations with otherwise high unemployment. The labor intensity of the apparel industry also contributes to the fact that it is somewhat low-paying. The apparel industry has looked to offshore manufacturing for a variety of reasons, but the most obvious is the cost savings. Workers earning $7 to $15 per hour would add significantly to the price of garments, thereby placing them out of reach of many consumers. In our present over-stored environment, there is a great deal of pressure on manufacturers and product developers to offer the best possible product for the lowest price.

The average hourly wage for apparel workers in the United States, including benefits, was $10.61 in 2005 (U.S. Department of Labor 2006). In China,

Figure 13.3. *New line of Chanel prêt-à a- porter being shown at fashion show in Paris.*

the wage for comparable work was $0.88, and in Indonesia it was $0.27 (U.S. International Trade Commission 2004). While labor costs alone should not be the basis for sourcing decisions, the impact that these low-wage countries can have on providing apparel value is obvious.

Although it has been difficult for many Americans to see jobs diverted to low-wage countries, manufacturers who have attempted to keep a manufacturing base in the United States have found it increasingly challenging to find skilled workers willing to work at the going wage rate. Most of the industry remaining in the United States produces basic goods for which technology has been able to decrease the labor intensity of the product. Most fashion goods, however, are developed in the United States and sourced offshore.

Table 13.1 TOP APPAREL-PRODUCING NATIONS RANKED BY U.S. IMPORTS FOR THE 12 MONTHS ENDING MAY 31, 2006

RANK	COUNTRY	SME* EQUIVALENTS	% CHANGE FROM PREVIOUS YEAR	PRIMARY CONTRIBUTIONS
1	China	5.6 billion	+38%	Full package suppliers, factory capacity
2	Mexico	1.6 billion	-13%	Largest producer of jeans shipped to U.S., man-made fibers
3	Bangladesh	1.2 billion	+18%	Cotton goods, underwear and men's and boy's knit shirts
4	Honduras	1.17 billion	-6%	Cotton apparel
5	Indonesia	880 million	+18%	Cotton apparel; struggles with infrastructure
6	Vietnam	873 million	+10%	Cotton apparel
7	India	837 million	+21%	Assorted apparel products
8	Cambodia	786 million	+19%	Man-made fiber apparel and cotton apparel
9	El Salvador	760 million	-14%	Cotton products
10	Dominican Republic	655 million	-16%	Cotton and man-made fiber apparel
11	Hong Kong	629 million	-3%	Assorted apparel products
12	Pakistan	610 million	+12%	Cotton apparel up; man-made fiber apparel down

*SME (square meter equivalents) measurement method for determining quantity

Source: U.S. Commerce Department and Central Intelligence Agency as reported in Gustke and Clark 2006

As the apparel industry becomes increasingly globalized, the textile industry is also becoming more regionalized. Apparel product developers seek to source fabrics near the region where their products will be made in order to minimize shipping time and costs. The textile industry differs from the apparel industry in that it is a low-labor, capital-intensive industry. For that reason, textile yardage can still be produced in developed countries at a profit. However, as more countries develop full-package apparel programs, they seek to develop their own domestic textile industry. These conditions have created a business environment in which more and more U.S. textile suppliers have succumbed to pressure from offshore producers.

Offshore contractors are willing and eager to vie for American business. Contractors in developing countries offer substantial price advantages. But once a contract is signed, relationships with offshore contractors require a lot

GARMENT INDUSTRY COST CHART

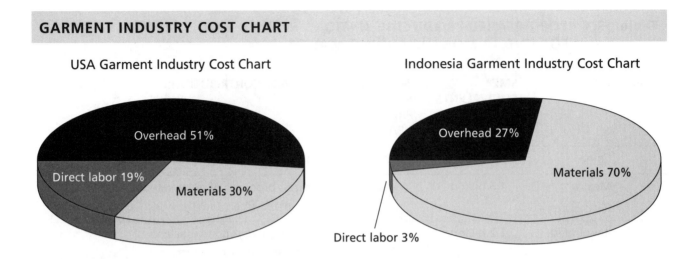

USA Garment Industry Cost Chart

Overhead 51%

Direct labor 19%

Materials 30%

Indonesia Garment Industry Cost Chart

Overhead 27%

Materials 70%

Direct labor 3%

Figure 13.4. *The decision between domestic and offshore manufacturing makes a big difference in how the costs of fabric, manufacturing, and overhead affect the total cost of the garment.*

of work. Overseas contractors do not necessarily understand American design concepts, figure types, consumer expectations, or quality standards. When comparing the cost of doing business offshore with the costs for in-house production facilities or domestic contractors, product developers must also consider many other factors besides low labor costs in their overall decision (Figure 13.4).

Use of contractors enables product developers to maintain control over design and fabric procurement, but they lose some control over quality, scheduling, and shipping. There is less security over product designs, specifications, and manufacturing or technical information. Product developers must develop very detailed specifications for contractors and require compliance to rules regarding workers' rights. However, using contractors, either domestic or offshore, provides significant flexibility compared to in-house domestic production.

Sourcing Alternatives

There are other potential options for sourcing products beside using domestic production or going directly to foreign producers. These other avenues provide viable alternatives to acquisition of production capacity.

Domestically Owned Offshore Facilities

Offshore production facilities owned by the product developer are another way of taking advantage of less expensive labor sources abroad. These arrangements increase a company's control of production processes and scheduling. However, they carry a fair amount of risk and responsibility. Initial investment costs are high in obtaining a building, bringing in machines and technology, and staffing the facility. A change in a country's political climate can put the company at risk and rapidly alter favorable tax breaks. Finding employees willing to relocate and run an offshore facility may be difficult. Relying on local management brings its own set of risks. Owning a plant locks a company into a fixed asset. If market conditions change, it may be more difficult to develop the flexibility needed to shift categories or convert production. Opening offshore plants in free trade zones avoids some of these risks. **Free trade zones** allow for the duty-free movement of equipment and supplies between plants and promise added security.

Joint Ventures

A slightly less risky alternative to owning offshore production facilities is a joint venture. A **joint venture** is a shared ownership of a facility with a business based in another country. Because the offshore owners understand the culture and are familiar with the legalities governing that business, capacity can be guaranteed and more control is maintained than with nonowned contractors; yet some of the risks of ownership can be avoided. The initial investment cost is lower, start-up time is reduced, and local access is greater.

Licensing

Domestic licensing is a means of extending the value of a product developer's brand without having to provide the expertise to produce the new product. There are many opportunities for licensing. Major brands such as Jones New York and Ralph Lauren have achieved name recognition that crosses many market demographics. Licensing provides them with a way to capitalize on their brand recognition by granting the rights to use their label to companies whose core competencies complement their own but who make different products. In return, they receive a royalty consisting of a percentage of the sale price of all items sold under their name. Sports teams and sports stars, characters from cartoons, movies, and television, and celebrities often represent similar value in the marketplace (Figure 13.5). Licensing agreements specify decision-making responsibilities for each partner involved. Strict guidelines and product specifications are generally a part of licensing agreements.

International licensing is an alternative to exporting that provides a means for well-known brands to establish a presence in global markets without establishing a manufacturing or distribution presence offshore. By contracting with a business partner the rights to use a brand name that has value, the licensee (the producer) assumes responsibility for tailoring the product to the new market and distribution structure. The licensor (the brand owner) protects its brand in that market while not having to learn the ropes of customizing its products to offshore markets.

The Role of Sourcing in Product Development

Any time a design is modified throughout the design process, the sourcing team must be in the loop to assess how the change may affect scheduling or price. The sourcing team may also be present during editing of the line to

Figure 13.5. *Children's licensed apparel under the Sesame Street logo.*

point out styles that are risky in terms of quality, timing, or price. The sourcing team tracks costs from initial estimates through changes in development to final production, and it negotiates or calculates the price for the landed garments. Contractor prices are generally quoted as **free on board (FOB)**, which means ownership is transferred to the importer when the goods are loaded on a transporting vehicle. The importer is responsible for shipping costs. **Landed price** includes the total product costs plus shipping costs and duty charges. Members of the sourcing team are invaluable in helping to price garments. They also work with factories when there are quality issues to try to correct problems and assess responsibility.

Sourcing Strategies

The prevalence of offshore sourcing as an affordable option for the production of apparel products has been a major stimulus for the *deverticalization* of apparel manufacturing in the United States. As domestic apparel product developers seek to shape their businesses around their core competencies, they concentrate more heavily on product development, brand building, and marketing, and increasingly they are outsourcing production. In turn, offshore contractors in developing countries and newly industrialized countries are attempting to become more vertical in their organization by offering an increasing array of services ranging from textile manufacturing and finishing to testing and color matching services, to patternmaking and grading, to apparel manufacturing. As these functions are increasingly outsourced, members of the product development team have had to become more aware of the impact of sourcing decisions on the products they design. They must develop a system of checks and balances to ensure that work is done according to specifications, and they must understand how design decisions affect the production calendar. Personnel responsible for sourcing become an integral part of the product development team for virtual apparel manufacturers. Their knowledge is indispensable in getting the right product to market at the right time.

A company's sourcing strategy is determined by its strategic plan and marketing strategy. Although sourcing shifts the responsibility of manufacturing to contractors and provides production flexibility both in capacity and product scope, it sacrifices a degree of control and brings a new set of risks to the table. It demands pinpoint accuracy in forecasting and increasingly relies on state-of-the-art information technology so that information can be shared throughout the pipeline. Sourcing requires cross-functional expertise in production, management, and law to overcome barriers of distance, varied resources, cultural differences, and a complex system of international trade laws (AAMA 1998).

Sourcing decisions are complex, with implications that affect product characteristics, quality, pricing, and timing. Companies must determine what functions to source and where to source them in order to maximize their marketing

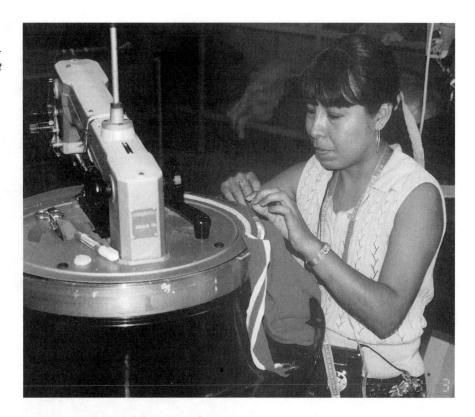

Figure 13.6. *Peru is known for high-quality knitwear manufacturing; its factories use state-of-the-art equipment.*

strategy. Knowledge of the various sourcing options helps product developers to understand the advantages and risks inherent in the sourcing mix they develop.

Evaluating Core Competencies

A company's sourcing requirements depend on the core competencies of its product development team. Branded product development teams may include employees who have experience with companies that at one time manufactured apparel domestically. Experience in sourcing fabrics, patternmaking, grading and marker making, or managing quality allows them to be more involved in those processes. Store brand and private label product developers may be more merchandise-driven, bringing their extensive retail experience to the process. They may look to contract out certain aspects of design, fabric sourcing, patternmaking, grading, or quality assessment functions if these tasks are not among their strengths. Sourcing agreements run the gamut between these two extremes, depending on the experience of the staff assembled and the strategic objectives of the company (Figure 13.6). Companies may operate their own plants, contract out production only, or contract out a full range of services.

Sourcing Levels

Once a company has evaluated its core competencies, it can make a decision as to the level of sourcing it requires.

Figure 13.7. *This full package contractor in Peru offers design, patternmaking, cutting, and manufacturing services.*

Cut, Make, and Trim

Cut, make, and trim (CMT) encompasses agreements that utilize domestic or offshore contractors for cutting, manufacturing, and finishing of garments for which the product developer provides the designs, patterns, and fabrics. Cut, make, and trim agreements appeal to product developers who have well-developed design and patternmaking competencies but who seek the value of offshore production. These product developers seek more control over the design and fabrication of their product. Cut, make, and trim agreements require the product developer to take ownership of the fabric. The contractor charges only for its material components beyond fabrics, labor, and overhead. Small contractors typically start as CMT operations because doing so requires relatively little up-front financing. Product developers may prefer CMT arrangements because they offer more flexibility; by controlling the fabrication decisions, they can make styling and quantity adjustments more readily.

Contracting the manufacture of garments eliminates product developers' financial investment in factories and production labor. Their investment is limited to the fabric, transportation, the costs of quotas and tariffs, and the costs involved with managing sourcing and quality assurance decisions. This arrangement provides more control over the creative processes of design and fabrication and may reduce the risk of products being copied. The typical

CMT operation requires the product developer to supervise the contractor's production more closely. The product developer should be sure that the country's infrastructure and communication system are reliable so that company personnel can readily access the factory for supervision.

Full-Package Suppliers

Another sourcing option is to partner with *full-package suppliers.* This category includes contractors, trading companies, or agents who source materials and provide design, pattern making, cutting, sewing, quality assurance, packaging, and shipping services.

Full-package contracting places the major burden of financing on the contractor. The product developer files a **letter of credit** authorizing its bank to pay the exporting contractor once the contracted goods are loaded on a vessel. The contractor must finance the full cost of fabric, trims, and cost of production until the goods are ready to ship (Figure 13.7).

Agents may facilitate the delivery of full-package contracting by assembling a team of offshore contractors who can provide the services necessary for full-package production. Agents may coordinate the sourcing of fabrics, fabric and product testing, color matching, garment manufacturing, and finishing, using several service providers in partnership, to meet the needs of a product developer seeking full-package sourcing. Full-package suppliers or agents are a good option for product developers with little experience in manufacturing. They can also assist those who lack experience with sourcing in a particular region by navigating cultural differences and quota and customs requirements.

Agents are particularly valuable partners when a company ventures into a new product category in which the product developer lacks experience or when volume is too small to demand company-owned sourcing capacity. An agent can frequently provide for the full range of a product developer's sourcing needs by relying on service providers in several countries within a region. For example, an agent in Hong Kong may facilitate the sourcing of fabrics from Japan, India, or China depending on the fabric needed, with fabric testing in Hong Kong, and production sourcing in China, Sri Lanka, or Bangladesh. Agents provide much of the day-to-day management of the supply chain in these arrangements. They are able to source fabric and design, make patterns, coordinate trims, locate factories, and oversee packaging and shipping. Their knowledge of the language and local laws governing contracts and trade make it easier for product developers to work in multiple countries. Working with an agent greatly reduces the lead time needed to become operational in a country.

Whether full-package contracting is provided through a fully vertical contractor or facilitated through an agent, the markup will be higher for full-package contracting than for CMT. Longer lead times are generally required, and the product developer sacrifices some control over manufacturing processes, safety, and working conditions.

International Trade Policy

The production of textiles and apparel is considered critical to the economies of developed, developing, and less developed countries. The labor-intense nature of these industries makes them an ideal opportunity for providing employment and contributing to their overall economies.. Developed countries seek to maintain a portion of this employment base while recognizing that textile and apparel production may be the only industry through which developing nations can participate in international trade.

A Brief History of International Trade Policy

Historically, the international sourcing of textiles and apparel has been regulated by a system that relied on tariffs and quotas to level the playing field between developed and developing countries. A **tariff** is a tax on imported goods that is assessed by the country of import. A **quota** is an annual limit on the volume of a product, designated by category, that may be shipped from an exporting country to an importing country. An **embargo** is the prohibition from importing products from an exporting nation. This system of tariffs and quotas was put in place in order to manage the impact of global trade. Importing countries use tariffs and quotas to protect their domestic industry and enable it to compete with low-cost import competition. Countries began negotiating **bilateral agreements**, or agreements between two countries, to set quota levels.

After World War II, the United States played a leading role in promoting a multilateral approach to regulating trade. The **General Agreement on Tariffs and Trade (GATT)** was signed in 1947. Its goal was to liberalize trade and create a more global market. GATT was set up as a temporary organization. Although the easing of restraints worked in general, developed countries became very nervous about the impact of textile and apparel imports from developing countries. Developed countries began to pass and enforce a series of discriminatory policies aimed at restricting trade from developing countries.

In order to stem this tide of unilateral controls, the United States negotiated, under the auspices of GATT, the Short-Term Arrangement Regarding International Trade in Cotton Textiles (STA). This multilateral agreement went into effect in October 1961 and authorized one-year restrictions on the trade of 64 categories of cotton textiles to avoid market disruption until a more permanent solution could be negotiated. In 1962 the Long-Term Arrangement Regarding Trade in Cotton Textiles (LTA) became part of GATT policy, extending the restrictive policies of the STA. In 1974, the LTA was expanded to include wool and synthetic fibers and became known as the Multi-Fiber Arrangement (MFA). The STA, LTA, and MFA all allowed for bilateral agreements (and unilateral controls under certain conditions) to control the flow of textile products. These policies were a direct contradiction to GATT's guiding principles, which were to control trade multilaterally, without discrimination, through the elimination of quotas (Dickerson 1999, 51–94, 336–387).

As a result of the Uruguay Round of trade talks, which began in 1986 and ended in 1993, the **World Trade Organization (WTO)** replaced GATT as a permanent organization in 1995. China and Taiwan became members of the WTO in 2001 and thereby committed to abiding by all WTO trade rules. As of January 2007, when Vietnam was admitted, 150 nations were members of the WTO (www.wto.org).

The WTO immediately began a process to align the rules regarding the trade of textiles and apparel to those governing trade of other products. The **Agreement on Textiles and Clothing (ATC)** replaced the MFA and a process was begun for eliminating all quotas governing textiles and apparel over a ten-year period to be completed by January 1, 2005. During 2005 and 2006, the steep rise in Chinese exports into other nations such as the United States and the EU precipitated the re- institution of protective quotas on specific Chinese categories of products for two years, with WTO approval, based on the premise that excessive influx of those products had caused disruption of trade. In other words, the products flooded the markets in the importing nations and caused the domestic industry great hardship. The WTO has cited the United States for its persistent application of high tariffs. While 38 percent of all tariff-eligible items entered the United States duty-free in 2004, the applied tariffs for other textile and apparel products averaged 9 percent, with some as high as 37.7 percent (Zarocostas 2006).

Regional Trade Blocs

In anticipation of the changes brought about by the phaseout of the MFA quota system, countries around the world began to shape regional trade agreements among neighboring countries in advance of the multilateral timelines being imposed for compliance with new WTO rules. These agreements seek to develop loyal trading partnerships in a free trade climate within a region that shares strategic concerns. The purposes of many of these regional agreements were to prevent a flood of increased imports from lower-wage countries, to protect manufacturing business in the region, and to encourage further development of regional trading activity when quota restrictions were eliminated in 2005.

The Americas

The **North American Free Trade Agreement (NAFTA)** is an example of a regional trade agreement. It originated as the Canada–U. S. Free Trade Agreement (CFTA), which became effective on January 1, 1989, and eliminated all

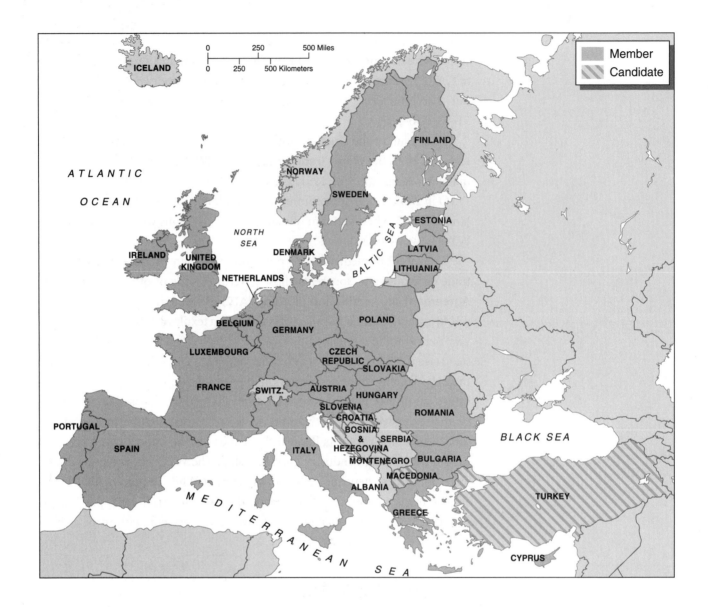

Figure 13.8. *Regional trade blocs such as the European Union (EU) promote trade among countries with shared strategic goals by granting quota and tariff reductions to members.*

tariffs and quotas over a ten-year time period. The agreement was extended to include Mexico with the signing of NAFTA, which went into effect on January 1, 1994. This agreement provides for the elimination of tariffs and quotas on trade among the three countries over a 15-year period. There was talk of creating a Free Trade Area of the Americas (FTAA), which would encompass the entire Western Hemisphere, before 2005. However, those talks have been put on the back burner in light of the present "War on Terrorism" and increased tensions in the Middle East.

Two different regional trade blocs currently exist in South America. The Andean Pact includes Bolivia, Colombia, Ecuador, Peru, and Venezuela. The exports from these countries to the United States increased between 1995 and 1999, but have been reduced somewhat since the lifting of quotas. The Mercosur trading bloc countries include Argentina, Brazil, Chile, Paraguay, and Uruguay. The Mercosur common market signed a free trade agreement with the European Union in 1995; however, exports to the United States have remained relatively modest. Talks have gone on to integrate these two groups into a South American Free Trade Area (SAFTA) that would provide for the elimination of tariffs for internal trade and the negotiation of trade policy as a single, stronger unit.

Europe

With the addition of Romania and Bulgaria in 2007, the **European Union (EU)** became a group of 27 European countries that act as a single internal market while retaining their political autonomy (Figure 13.8). Their economic integration includes the harmonization of trade policy and negotiations; and the adoption of a common currency, the Euro. The exception to the adoption of the Euro is Britain, which chose to retain the pound as its national currency. This union allows for free trade among member nations and has negotiated additional trade agreements with other trade blocs to facilitate expanded free trade zones or outward processing arrangements, especially with nations in the Middle East, Africa, and South Asia.

Additional European nations are seeking membership in the EU or are not economically advanced enough at this time to qualify for full membership. These nations, many of whom were members of the former Soviet bloc, are now functioning as production sourcing sites for more advanced economies within the region.

Asia

The Association of Southeast Asian Nations (ASEAN) membership includes Brunei, Myanmar, Cambodia, Indonesia, Laos, Malaysia, Philippines, Singapore, Thailand, and Vietnam. Organized in 1977, this association was formed to encourage economic, political, social, and cultural cooperation. In 1992, these countries formed their own regional common market, called the ASEAN Free Trade Area (AFTA), and agreed to eliminate tariffs among themselves by 2003.

In 1989, the ASEAN nations joined Japan, South Korea, China, Hong Kong, Taiwan, Australia, New Zealand, the United States, and Canada to form the Asian Pacific Economic Cooperation (APEC). Since 1989, Chile, Mexico, Papua New Guinea, Russia, and Peru have joined. Although APEC cannot be considered a true regional trade bloc because the group includes members outside Asia, its goal is to encourage freer trade and to build the region into a major exporting force.

Current Status of U.S. Trade Policy

As a full member of the WTO, the United States abides by the trade rules of the ATC. However, it has achieved temporary extensions of bilateral quotas on some categories of Chinese apparel products. These quota limits can prevent product developers from sourcing additional products in the affected categories

Figure 13.9. *Finishing processes, such as the stonewashing of jeans, may disqualify apparel products from special duty benefits, if these processes are done offshore.*

when the quota limits are reached. Therefore, it is critical that firms attempting to import from China remain aware of the current status of U.S. quota limits before placing orders that may not be passed through customs if they arrive after the quota level has been reached for the year.

Recent U.S. trade strategy has been to pursue multiple market-opening initiatives in the form of bilateral trade agreements with individual nations. To this end, the United States now has agreements with numerous nations intended to encourage trade with these nations and to decrease or eliminate tariffs on products imported from them. These activities are carried out by the U.S. Trade Representative and the Committee on the Implementation of Textile Agreements (CITA), in concert with representatives of the Department of State and the U.S. Customs and Border Protection agency (under the Department of Homeland Security). Some of the bilateral Free Trade Agreements (FTAs) that have been approved by Congress include Australia, Bahrain, Chile, Israel, Jordan, Malaysia, Morocco, Oman, Panama, and Singapore (Office of the U.S. Trade Representative) Others are in the planning stages, such as with Vietnam. There are also Trade Promotion Agreements (TPAs) with other nations, including Colombia and Peru.

In addition to bilateral agreements, the United States has a multilateral agreement with 37 Sub-Saharan African nations. The **African Growth and Opportunity Act (AGOA)** provides for reductions in tariffs on textile and apparel products and other economic incentives for participating nations (Office of the U.S. Trade Representative, www.ustr). Unfortunately, African nations have not been able to compete as favorably in the global market since the phaseout of quotas. These difficulties are largely due to less well-trained production workers, higher wages, and weaker infrastructure than are available in Asia.

Other U.S.-multilateral trade agreement of interest in textiles and apparel are NAFTA, discussed earlier, and the Central America–Dominican Republic–United States Free Trade Agreement (CAFTA–DR). CAFTA–DR membership provides Costa Rica, Dominican Republic, El Salvador, Guatamala, Honduras, and Nicaraqua freedom from tariffs on many apparel products imported into the United States. Although it has been assumed by many that since the U.S. government has ratified this agreement it is in effect, not all of the participating countries have completed the approval process to put it into full effect for their nations.

It is critical that firms remain aware of any changes in agreements that may affect the tariff structure applied before commiting to sourcing contracts with firms in another nation (Figure 13.9). In addition to the few remaining quota limitations and the tariff structures imposed on products from many nations, there are additional regional agreements involving the United States which contain restrictions. For example, NAFTA and CAFTA-DR require that apparel must be constructed of U.S.-made fabric and thread in order to qualify for tariff reductions when it is imported from member nations (Figure 13.10).

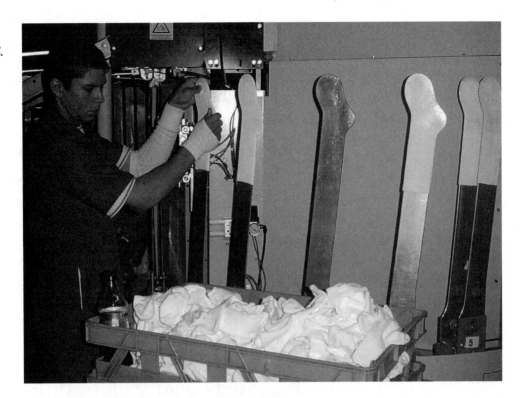

Figure 13.10. *Socks being made in Costa Rica of U.S. yarn, to be shipped to the United States for sale.*

Duty rates are identified in the Harmonized Tariff System (HTS) for virtually every item that exists. The U.S. International Trade Commission maintains a tariff database that will enable product developers to get an approximate idea of the duty rate for a particular product, but the final decision on the actual duty charged for a specific product will be established by **Customs and Border Protection (CBP)**. The CBP will collect the assessed duty on a shipment as it comes through a U.S. port of entry.

Evaluating Sourcing Options

Before contracting any operation, a company must take stock of its strategic position and evaluate how sourcing decisions will affect that position. Each operation, whether it is already being outsourced or is handled in-house, must be analyzed in terms of its effectiveness relative to the company's core products and channels of distribution. Included in this analysis is evaluating the best geographical placement for each operation in relation to the placement of other functions. When determining a sourcing mix, a company must consider a number of factors that go beyond international and regional trade agreements:

- Proposed country's political stability and economic climate
- Proposed country's infrastructure
- Costs
- Quality standards for the product

• Production capabilities
• Ability of sourcing partners to deliver the correct goods on time
• Working conditions of the sources' factories
• Channels of communication

Political Stability and Economic Climate

One of the first things that product developers evaluate when considering a sourcing partner is the political stability and economic climate of the partner's country. Politically, it is advantageous to work in a country with a government that is stable and welcomes foreign investment. It is to be hoped that the government supports the product developer's efforts to adhere to fair labor and wage practices. It is also important that the currency is stable so that agreed-upon prices do not change with currency fluctuations. The possibility of drawing offshore sourcing has had a stabilizing influence on many developing countries around the globe.

Proposed Country's Infrastructure

A country's infrastructure includes its transportation and communications systems; telephone, electricity, and water utilities; and resources for both labor and management. Finding a country with the right balance of resources can be tricky. For example, labor is abundant in all parts of Mexico, but competition can become severe for apparel producers located in major metropolitan areas, creating high employee turnover rates. On the other hand, it may be difficult to lure the best college-educated management candidates to a remote locale. One must also consider the quality of life for foreign executives if it is necessary to send representatives to this location regularly. Quality-of-life considerations include crime and safety issues, cost of living, comfort of accommodations, and safety of food and water supplies.

The transportation infrastructure is important in terms of the ability to get supplies to the plant and finished product out of the country as well as workers' ability to get to work on time. Some countries, including those in Latin America and Sub-Saharan Africa, ration electricity, making auxiliary electrical generators a must. If electricity to residences is rationed during the day in order for businesses to run, the electrical infrastructure for computers is bound to be unreliable. If a country is subject to an annual season of typhoons or hurricanes, this is bound to affect deliveries on a seasonal basis. For example, only 5.5 percent of Bolivia's roads are paved, compared with 90 percent in Uruguay. In Costa Rica, 97 percent of the population has access to sanitation, but in the Dominican Republic that figure drops to 78 percent, and in Haiti it is only 24 percent.

The decision about whether to source to two otherwise equal contractors may be made based on infrastructure and the potential for improvements.

The door is always open for incoming businesses to build and improve the infrastructure, and construct an environment suitable to their needs (Speer, 2000, 1–6).

Sourcing Costs

Gone are the days when sourcing decisions were based solely on the country with the lowest wages. Companies are now seeking to identify sourcing partners for the long term. Today's apparel environment requires sophisticated electronic networking and ongoing investment in technology and training. Once these complex networks are established, every effort is made to protect this investment. Today, for companies that buy complete packages, labor is combined with material and other component costs, giving the product developer little control over or knowledge of the breakdown of costs (AAMA 1997). In addition, product developers recognize the value of timely delivery, the ability to meet specifications, and the aptitude to work with time-saving technology. In the future, pricing at all levels of the supply chain will become more dynamic as the ability of vendors to bid for work through agents and over the Internet increases.

When comparing the costs of manufacturing a product offshore or domestically, product developers must include all the hidden costs of added processes and steps that go hand in hand with offshore production. When using U.S. fabric, cut goods must be bundled and transported by air, truck, ship, or rail. The cut goods must be wrapped to protect them from damage, which adds to materials and labor. The movement of fabric and garments between suppliers in full-package agreements to the port of embarkation, and the associated costs of ocean freight, must be factored into the estimate. If there are any glitches in production scheduling, air freight will need to be used instead of ocean freight. Insurance, customs duties and clearance, agent fees, banking or factor fees, and additional warehousing costs should be included in cost projections. Any finished goods that are received in damaged condition must be repaired, if they are repairable, in a U.S. facility. The percentage of seconds from offshore plants is typically greater than it is from U.S. plants. Shortages are also common. Travel for certification and quality assurance personnel must be factored in (Figure 13.11). These are just a few of the costs that inexperienced sourcers may forget to include. Table 13.2 shows how the costs of making a shirt can vary. Considering all these issues, it is no wonder that some of the biggest offshore sourcing providers are not necessarily the lowest-wage countries.

Related to costing concerns is the ability of a contractor to finance materials and reserve quotas in the instances where they are still used. With full-package sourcing agreements, it is the contractor's or agent's responsibility to take ownership of the fabrics and trims specified and to make sure quota is

Figure 13.11. *Product developers may send quality assurance specialists to inspect garments on-site when using offshore contractors.*

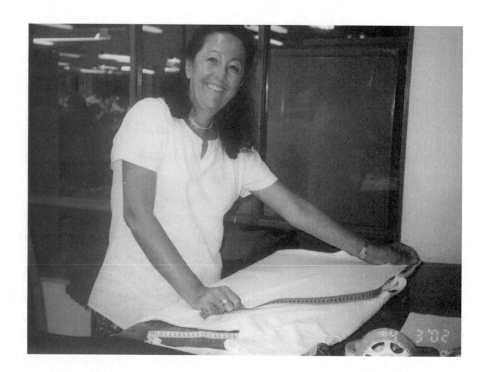

reserved where needed. Knowing that partnerships are sound eliminates risk. Numerous horror stories are told about contractors who accept jobs but do not have the financing capability to order materials. Meanwhile, the product developer assumes that the work is in process when, in reality, the fabric was never ordered or a lower-cost substitution was made. The ability of a sourcing partner to finance the resources needed is critical to successful associations.

Quality Standards

The ability of sourcing partners to produce quality goods consistently depends on a number of factors. Certainly, the skill of the workforce and workers' flexibility to work within a range of apparel categories and fabrics is important. Regions of the world vary as to the skill of their workforce. In general, Asia has a highly skilled workforce adept at working with a variety of difficult fabrics. Latin American workers have more experience with commodity products; companies there are striving to develop the skills to compete for goods at higher price points.

In addition to workers' skills, the caliber of management personnel affects the quality of the product. Management is responsible for providing appropriate machinery and training, creating a sanitary and safe work environment, and scheduling goods through the factory. Mistakes in any of these areas can greatly affect quality.

The third factor in the equation is the accuracy of written communications and instructions received from the product developer. Contractors require well-written specifications and accurate samples in order to interpret quality levels. Product developers from the United States frequently forget that quality

Table 13.2 COMPARING SHIRT-MAKING COSTS

This chart shows how the costs of making a shirt vary, depending on whether it is made in the United States, Mexico, India, Thailand, or in Mexico of U.S. fabric.

EXPENSES	UNITED STATES	MEXICO	INDIA	THAILAND	U.S./MEXICO
Fabric manufacturing	$ 2.37	$ 2.21	$ 2.09	$ 2.13	$ 2.37
Fabric sales and G&A	0.17	0.15	0.15	0.15	0.17
Fabric profit	0.25	0.24	0.22	0.23	0.25
Total fabric cost	2.79	2.60	2.46	2.51	2.79
Garment manufacturing	4.73	2.26	1.80	2.13	2.16
Garment sales and G&A	0.25	0.19	0.21	0.23	0.25
Garment profit	0.78	0.50	0.45	0.49	0.52
Total F.O. B. cost	8.55	5.44	4.91	5.36	5.72
Importing costs	0	1.22	2.18	2.21	0.47
Costs to retailer	8.55	6.66	7.09	7.57	6.19
Ratio	100	78	83	89	72
Price paid by consumer	$15.00	$15.00	$15.00	$15.00	$15.00
Retailer new gross margin %	43%	56%	53%	50%	59%
Cost of goods sold%	57%	44%	47%	50%	41%
Cost of goods sold $	$8.55	$6.66	$7.09	$7.57	$6.19
Retailer net gross margin $	6.45	8.34	7.90	7.43	8.82
Sales per $ of capital employed	$2.50	$2.00	$2.00	$2.00	$2.00
Inventories as % of capital employed	20%	40%	40%	40%	40%
Capital employed/$ per shirt	$6.00	$7.50	$7.50	$7.50	$7.50
Retailer Gross Margin % **Per $ Capital Employed**	108%	111%	105%	99%	118%

standards in other countries may be different from their own. It is essential that contractors communicate clearly what is expected and what is unacceptable. This requires an intricate system of checks and balances achieved through factory visits and regular sampling of garments. For example, significant difficulties can appear when measurements are not understood due to miscommunicated metric/English system measurement conversions. Since we are the only country today not using metric, this can be a substantial issue.

A common quality problem occurs when a sourcer does not know or respect a contractor's capacity limits. Typically, the contractor will take the overload and subcontract the work. The work that is delivered may not meet standards agreed upon between the sourcer and the original contractor, which can result in broken contracts or relationships. It is difficult to assess blame in these situations, but the fault may lie with the sourcer, who should be familiar with the contractor's capacity limits. Many retail product developers have learned this lesson the hard way. They now assess a sourcing partner's capacity limitations and potential for growth before assigning work, and they clearly state in the contract that the work is not to be sourced with a subcontractor.

Production Capabilities

The labor force in each part of the world has its own expertise, and the skills needed to construct a fashionable garment require varying technical capabilities from season to season. Thus, it is advantageous for companies to include sourcing partners from various parts of the world in their sourcing mix. Sourcing offshore often makes hand processes affordable that would be out of reach if sourced domestically (Figure 13.12).

Figure 13.12. *Printed fabrics put out to dry in India. Hand processes add value to products that could not be made domestically.*

Asia

Asia offers textile innovation, workable minimum yardage requirements, and a labor force with excellent sewing skills; countries in this region are highly coveted for production of high-quality goods requiring complex operations and detailed work. South Korea, Hong Kong, and Taiwan became known as the "Big Three" Asian apparel producers in the 1970s and 1980s. As their economies developed—wages now average $3 to $5 per hour—the manufacturing focus in Taiwan shifted to electronics and computers and in South Korea to automobile and electronics products (Chan 1998, 33–38). No longer competitive for assembly work in the discount and moderate sectors of the apparel industry, those still in the business have redirected their skills and experience to working as agents to develop extensive sourcing networks, moving production to developing countries to offer their management expertise to start-up contractors, and to the advanced technology required to produce man-made textiles. Today, Asia is valued for its abilities in full-package sourcing, with excellent resources for fabrics, trims, and high-quality construction.

Hong Kong officially became part of China in 1997, but the region is being treated separately in terms of customs regulations, quotas, and record keeping. Hong Kong had been particularly successful in subcontracting production to China's factories. What began as outward-processing arrangements eventually turned into a relocation of much of Hong Kong's apparel industry to lower-wage countries, with many manufacturers moving to China to set up businesses that utilize its vast employment pool. Hong Kong–based TAL Group is one of the largest apparel producers in the world, with customers including Jos. A. Bank, Ralph Lauren, Talbots, Nordstrom, DKNY, and Eddie Bauer (Speer 2006, 6, 9).

Serving as a regional sourcing hub, Hong Kong now handles apparel orders from around the world, allocating production to offshore manufacturing bases as far away as Sri Lanka, Latin America, and the Middle East, according to cost, level of sophistication, and quality required. Hong Kong is also experienced in providing product development, material sourcing, quality control, and trade financing and logistics services. South Korea and Taiwan have modeled similar services after Hong Kong's example.

China currently plays the most important role in Asian sourcing, ranking as the largest individual national exporter of apparel in the world, with a highly skilled workforce, low hourly wage rates, and significant overall production capacity (Figure 13.13). One risk of sourcing with companies in China is the lack of respect for intellectual property protection there. It is common for Chinese companies to knock off goods they are contracted to produce. Prices of apparel from China showed a drop right after quotas were eliminated on many product categories, but it would be wise for firms to carefully monitor international currency markets for the value of the yuan. The Chinese economy has been growing so significantly in the last decade that if the Chinese government should allow the yuan to float with the global currency

Figure 13.13. *Chinese workers sew dresses at a factory in Anhui province. China is now the largest supplier of apparel products to the United States.*

market, as other national currencies do, it could mean that costs of apparel from China could inflate.

Latin America

Latin America offers close proximity to the United States, permitting quick response times, as well as competitive labor costs and the benefits of recent free trade agreements liberalizing quotas and tariffs. Its proximity to the U.S. market allows product developers to more closely manage the process and results in lower shipping and transportation costs. It is also easier to do business in similar time zones. In general, the Latin American labor force is not as skilled as the Asian labor force. As noted earlier, the bulk of workers' experience is in the production of commodity goods, but that is changing. There are pockets of highly sophisticated manufacturing, such as Peru's sweater manufacturing sector.

In addition, Latin America lacks a high-caliber management pool, a void being seized by entrepreneurial Asian contractors. The region also has not developed the capacity for full-package sourcing and the financing of piece goods because outward processing rules such as 807, 807A, 809, and 9802 encourage a reliance on U.S. fabric and cutting. Because of this reliance on American fabrics, Latin American patternmaking and cutting capacity have never been fully developed. Today, in order to compete with the Far East, fabric sourcing and pattern making skills are increasingly in demand.

Flexible Sourcing

As we have noted before, one of the main advantages of sourcing is flexibility. If fine-gauge sweaters are in fashion one season, a company might tap expertise available in the Far East. If the next season's trends bring a preference for bulky-gauge knits, production options expand to include Latin America. The flexibility of being able to shift production according to the technical capacity needed has always been an advantage of sourcing. But ethically, it is also a drawback. It means that a sourcing relationship developed one season may not be needed the next. In developing countries, this uncertainty from season to season can be a hardship. More and more companies are attempting to narrow their sourcing partnerships in order to guarantee production contracts from season to season. In return, offshore contractors are developing the flexibility to respond to the changing drifts of fashion.

The Gap reportedly had vendors, agents, and buying offices in 100 countries in 2000 (Hickens 2000). Liz Claiborne had a sourcing pool of 32 countries in 1999, basing its decisions on raw material availability, quota constraints, product capability, and logistics. While the company has consolidated its factory roster from well over 500 to 260, it increased total production by over 50 percent (Hickins 2000; Rabon 1999). Initially, the company bought all its own fabric and trims; made all the patterns and markers; and sent everything to contractors along with its own technicians, who worked closely with the contracting factory. Today, this mode of operation has been replaced by strategic sourcing in which buyers and sellers work together to form long-term relationships based on mutual dependencies. The elimination of quota restrictions is causing U.S. firms to focus on fewer locations with superior expertise, production capacity, and the reliability to fill orders, and causing other nations with less developed capabilities to lose significant market share.

Response Time

A key to making sourcing partnerships work is an understanding that orders must be delivered on time. That responsibility is a two-way street. A job cannot be completed on time if all the materials and trims are not delivered on time. This includes spec packages, fabrics, and trims. The delivery of zippers is a good example. There are only a few global suppliers of zippers, with YKK being the largest. Zippers are a somewhat customized trim, which need to be made according to color, length, and weight. If they are not ordered early enough, they may hold up production. However, designers may be hesitant to commit to zipper specs until the line is edited and styling is firm. Although color decisions may be obvious once the fabric story has been approved, length needs may change throughout the product development process. A windbreaker-style jacket that starts out with a length of 26 inches requires a 25-inch zipper. If the jacket is lengthened, the zipper will also need to be lengthened.

Figure 13.14. *H & M's "speed to market" strategies contribute to its great success in the global retail apparel market. This H & M store is in Paris.*

Scheduling all aspects of offshore production is a critical part of planning the merchandise and line calendars. Like a jigsaw puzzle, pulling together materials and assembly processes from many countries is complex, and mistakes can be expensive. Typically, product developers work backward, establishing the required delivery date first. Once the delivery date is established, they calculate the lead time necessary for fabric and trims. This can vary anywhere from weeks to months, depending on the type of fabric and the resources and capacity of the source company. Fabric transit will take anywhere from 10 to 30 days, depending on where it is being shipped for production. Garment construction lead time will vary from 45 to 60 days. Garment transit time will take 20 to 45 days, including time to clear customs. Once these figures are established, product developers can determine when their order must be placed in order to receive the goods on schedule. Schedules should be monitored on a weekly basis to ensure that delivery deadlines will be met. Agents and full-package suppliers are responsible for maintaining their own production schedules. It is their responsibility to inform the product developer if any delays occur.

The success of Zara and H & M has been attributed to their ability to utilize "speed-to-market" strategies, especially management and technology applications, that cut their sourcing time down to 10 to 21 days (Figure 13.14). The traditional sourcing calendar is based on a product development cycle of 120 to 150 days, while replenishment sourcing typically takes 75 to 150 days (Kuthiala 2006).

Working Conditions

Contractor compliance with human rights guidelines is a serious consideration in sourcing decisions. There is considerable sensitivity in the United States to human rights issues. Negative press about human rights issues can negate long-term efforts at brand building. Much of the current attention to human rights has resulted from the efforts of groups such as the National Labor Organization. However, it is important to view human rights standards in relation to the developmental stage of a country, including mandatory schooling and minimum wage and hour laws. If schooling in a given country is mandatory only to age 14, it is unreasonable to expect workers to be 18 or over. The alternative to working in factories is oftentimes a far worse fate. Most certification requirements forbid the use of child labor under the age of 14, or under the age that interferes with compulsory schooling, or under the minimum age established by law, whichever is greater. Serious concerns have been raised about human rights violations in some factories in Asia, especially in Indonesia and Myanmar (Figure 13.15).

Worldwide Responsible Apparel Production (WRAP) is an independent, nonprofit organization dedicated to the certification of lawful, humane, and ethical manufacturing throughout the world. Its basic standards address labor practices, factory conditions, and environmental and customs compliance, as outlined in Table 13.3.

The **International Labor Organization (ILO)** is a UN agency that promotes

Figure 13.15. *Child laborers at a factory in Ho Chi Minh City, Vietnam.*

Table 13.3 WRAP PRINCIPLES

The Worldwide Responsible Apparel Production Principles are core standards for production facilities participating in the Worldwide Responsible Apparel Production Certification Program. The Program's objective is to independently monitor and certify compliance with these socially responsible global standards for manufacturing, and to ensure that sewn products are produced under lawful, humane, and ethical conditions. Participating companies voluntarily agree that their production and that of their contractors will be certified by the WRAP Certification Program as complying with these standards.

IN THE AREA OF	MANUFACTURERS OF SEWN PRODUCTS WILL
Laws and workplace regulations	Comply with laws and regulations in all locations where they conduct business
Prohibition of forced labor	Not use involuntary or forced labor—indentured, bonded, or otherwise
Prohibition of child labor	Not hire any employee under the age of 14, or under the age interfering with compulsory schooling, or under the minimum age established by law, whichever is greater
Prohibition of harassment or abuse	Provide a work environment free of harassment, abuse, or corporeal punishment in any form
Compensation and benefits	Pay at least the minimum total compensation required by local law, including all mandated wages, allowance, and benefits
Hours of work	Assure that hours worked each day, and days worked each week, shall not exceed the legal limitations of the countries in which apparel is produced Provide at least 1 day off in every 7-day period, except as required to meet urgent business needs
Prohibition of discrimination	Employ, pay, promote, and terminate workers on the basis of their ability to do the job, rather than on the basis of personal characteristics or beliefs
Health and safety	Provide a safe and healthy work environment. Where residential housing is provided for workers, provide safe and healthy housing
Freedom of association and collective bargaining	Recognize and respect the right of employees to exercise their lawful rights of free association and collective bargaining
Environment	Comply with environmental rules, regulations, and standards applicable to their operations and observe environmentally conscious practices in all locations where they operate
Customs compliance	Comply with applicable customs law and, in particular, establish and maintain programs to comply with customs laws regarding illegal transshipment of apparel products
Drug interdiction	Cooperate with local, national, and foreign customs and drug enforcement agencies to guard against illegal shipments of drugs

Source: Adapted from WRAP Web site (www.wrapapparel.org)

social justice and internationally recognized human and labor rights. The ILO sets minimum standards for basic labor rights related to collective bargaining and regulating working conditions. It audits factories for compliance to standards and reports results. Product developers should become aware of whether firms they are considering as sourcing partners have been found in violation of ILO standards.

Working with agents in sourcing regions helps to share the risk and responsibility for human rights compliance. Many product developers interviewed in the process of research for this book agreed that human rights violations frequently occur in plants where management is of one nationality or cultural background and workers are of another, setting up a culture clash. When management perceives workers as being less productive than expected—perhaps because of differences in values, climate, or cultural practices—managers may resort to drastic means to meet deadlines and maintain profits.

Product developers are frequently oblivious to abuses because their visits have multiple purposes, among them checking quality, certification, and setting up new programs. Factories may look efficient and well run when product developers visit, but the atmosphere may be much different when the visit is over. Many product developers certify their factories before contracting with them to do work. They believe they are doing everything within their power to ensure that factories producing their apparel follow human rights guidelines. Factories that are found to be noncompliant are given a short time to comply, or their contracts are revoked.

Channels of Communication

Sourcing requires accurate communication of standards and specifications, honest and complete quotes, and efficient dialog regarding the status of lab dips, fabric and garment testing, and prototype and production samples. Electronic information sharing has diminished the problem of physical distance in offshore sourcing. Technology suppliers have developed Web-based software products that have turned the product developer into a hub that manages a combination of buys: the purchase of services, the purchase of components, and the purchase of finished products the company has designed or specified. This software is helping to eliminate the non–value-adding steps in product development. An example is the joint venture between Gerber Technology and Applied Internet Technologies (Ai, formerly Animated Images), which has pooled Gerber's Web PDM and Ai's Web-based sourcing solution, along with data from the American Apparel Producers Network, to create a sourcing database of upward of 5,000 contractors.

Contractors can offer their services on SpecNet; a monthly fee is charged to manufacturers when they select specific contractors with whom they want to network and communicate. ThreadNet is the online textile-buying and tracking function of SpecNet; it features a fabric catalog. Used in conjunction with Gerber's PDM and Style Manager, these services enable the product development team to generate and manage design data, share it in real-time, and reuse data from standards components that are used regularly. The efficiencies of specifying and costing with these tools is expected to reduce the number of samples per style from an average of 4.2 to 2. Karat has a similar interactive Web product that is programmed to distribute input from the product development team to partners anywhere in the world, including sourcing managers, agents, vendors, and quality assurance personnel. Other supply chain management software companies include Lectra, i2 Technologies, Manugistics, RockPort, and Celarix, to name only a few (Conrad 2000, 27).

Summary

The increased use of sourcing has dramatically changed the way products are developed, produced, and distributed. The resulting changes have made the industry more efficient in terms of cycle times, costs, and ability to respond to customer needs. Companies face many decisions when developing a sourcing strategy.

Product developers must decide what functions they want to source. They may to choose cut, make, and trim (CMT) sourcing domestically or offshore, contracting out only the cutting and manufacturing processes and doing the design and patternmaking in-house. They may opt to use full-package sourcing either here or abroad, giving their sourcing partners responsibility for sourcing fabrics and patternmaking, as well as CMT operations. Or they may take advantage of outward processing rules that require they use domestic fabric in order to receive liberalized tariff and duty benefits. Agents may be used to facilitate these arrangements. Their services may include the coordination of logistics between the various fabric and findings suppliers and the manufacturing contractor, overseeing fabric and garment testing, and responsibility for specified certification and quality requirements.

Offshore sourcing is regulated by a combination of international and domestic trade rules. The World Trade Organization was set up to develop and implement multilateral trade policies governing the trade of all products between its members. Although all quotas on apparel and textile products coming into WTO member countries were scheduled to be eliminated by 2005, the United States and EU are among those that have negotiated continued quota limits on selected product categories.

Historically, tariffs and quotas have been used to level the playing field between developed and developing countries in the production of textile and apparel products. Because these industries are an important source of manufacturing jobs for both developed and developing countries, the use of quotas and tariffs helps to lessen the impact of the low wages paid in developing countries.

In anticipation of a quota-free global marketplace, neighboring countries have been motivated to develop regional trading blocs that simplify trade between member nations. The goal of these regional trade blocs is to develop loyal partnerships with countries that share strategic goals. The United States is part of the North American Free Trade Agreement (NAFTA) and the African Growth Opportunity Agreement (AGOA), and it has additional bilateral agreements with numerous nations that grant liberalized trade benefits, usually in the form of reduced tariffs. The European Union represents 27 European countries that negotiate trade agreements as a bloc and enable free trade internally between member nations. Similar trade blocs exist in Latin America and Asia.

In addition to considering the trade agreements and rules that determine tariff and duty levels, a product developer must evaluate potential sourcing partners in terms of the economic and political stability of the country where they are located, infrastructure, production costs, production quality, production capabilities, ability to respond, working conditions, and channels of communication.

These considerations must be discussed throughout the product development process, as they will determine the success of the sourcing partnership and the ultimate cost of the product. Failure to anticipate all the costs involved in offshore sourcing can cause product developers to underestimate the cost of the garment. If the garment is subsequently priced too low, the result will be lower profits.

Key Terms

African Growth and Opportunity Act (AGOA)

Agreement on Textiles and Clothing (ATC)

bilateral agreements

Customs and Border Protection (CBP)

cut, make, and trim (CMT)

domestic contracting

embargo

European Union (EU)

free on board (FOB)

free trade zone

General Agreement on Tariffs and Trade (GATT)

International Labor Organization (ILO)

joint venture

labor-intense

landed price

letter of credit

manufacture

North American Free Trade Agreement (NAFTA)

quota

sourcing

sourcing mix

tariff

World Trade Organization (WTO)

Worldwide Responsible Apparel Production (WRAP)

Discussion Questions

1. How does offshore sourcing affect the product development process at the design level?

2. Select a design from your sketchbook and identify a fabric for the design. Discuss with the class where this garment might need to be sourced. Consider where the fabric is best sourced, the skill level required to construct it, any special processes required, the volume needed, the price point, and how long it may take to get delivery from selected locations.

Activities

1. Assign each person in class a different type of store to shop and a category of clothing for men, women, or children. Look at a variety of garments and record the brand name, price, and country of origin for each garment. Can you identify any patterns about sourcing preferences related to price and garment category?

2. Examine several novelty garments in class. Can you identify specialty operations or materials required to produce the garment that influenced where the garment was sourced?

3. Select a garment from your wardrobe. Document the full price before any markdowns and the country of origin. Using the Internet, research the average hourly wage in the country of origin and what the duty classification would be using the Harmonized Tariff Schedule of the United States.

References

AAMA. 1997. The dynamics of sourcing. 1997 TAC Report, September.

AAMA. 1998. Sourcing without surprises. 1998 TAC Report, September.

Bobbin Publishing Group. 2001. Insight into U.S. apparel imports. *Bobbin*, November.

Bonacich, E., and R. P. Appelbaum. 2000. *Behind the label: Inequality in the Los Angeles apparel industry.* Los Angeles: University of California Press.

Bureau of Industry and Security, U.S. Department of Commerce. 2003. *United States textile and apparel industries: An industrial base assessment.* www.bis.doc.gov/Defense IndustrialBasePrograms/OSTES/DefMarketResearchRpts/Tex_FinalRpt03.pdf, 27.

Chan, P. 1998. Asia: Down, but not out. *Bobbin*, November.

Conrad, A. 2000. The genesis of the apparel hub. *Apparel Industry Magazine*, May.

Dickerson, K. G. 1999. *Textiles and apparel in the global economy.* 3d ed. Upper Saddle River, NJ: Prentice-Hall.

Gustke, C., and E. Clark. 2006. Shifting apparel landscape. *Women's Wear Daily*, August 3.

Hickins, M. 2000. Liz Claiborne spends big to boost production. *Women's Wear Daily*, June 14.

Kuthiala, R. 2006. Smart sourcing: A tailored path. www.just-style.com (accessed January 18, 2006).

Office of the U.S. Trade Representative. www.ustr.gov/Trade_Agreements/Section_Index.html.

Rabon, L. 1999. Navigating new terrain. *Bobbin,* August.

Speer, J. K. 2000. CBI splashdown. *Bobbin,* November.

Speer, J. K. 2006, February. Lessons from a mega-manufacturer. *Apparel,* February. http://www.apparelmag.com (accessed April 18, 2006).

U.S. International Trade Commission. 2004. *Textiles and apparel: Assessment of the competitiveness of certain foreign suppliers to the U.S. market.* U.S. ITC investigation no. 332-448, Publication 3671. www.otexa.ita.doc.gov/#trade (accessed April 17, 2007).

U.S. Department of Labor. 2006. *Occupational employment and wages, May 2005: 51-6099 textile, apparel, and furnishings workers, all other.* www.bls.gov/oes/current/oes516099.htm.

World Trade Organization. www.wto.org.

Zarocostas, J. 2006. U.S. tariffs cited in WTO trade review. *Women's Wear Daily,* March 27.

Additional Resources

Birnbaum, D. 2005. *Birnbaum's global guide to material sourcing.* New York: Fashiondex, Inc.

Kunz, G. I., and M. B. Garner. 2007. *Going global: The textile and apparel industry.* New York: Fairchild Books.

Rosenau, J., and D. L. Wilson. 2001. *Apparel merchandising.* New York: Fairchild.

CHAPTER 14

PRICING AND COSTING

"Money alone sets the whole world in motion."

—PUBLILIUS SYRUS, 100 B.C.

OBJECTIVES

- To learn the basic vocabulary of financial decision making in a firm

- To understand the role of the product development staff in the financial decisions of a firm

- To recognize the calculation of costs in the design process.

- To learn the basics of precosting styles

- To recognize the complexities of the final costing process for an individual style

- To understand basic pricing decisions

The role of the product developer implies emphasis on the creative and technical design processes. The reality is that product developers must be creative within the constraints of a business environment that is governed by monetary considerations. The costs of producing garment styles frequently dictates whether a design idea becomes a reality because of the relationship between garment costs and the expected retail price. This is where creativity meets the realities of economics. For this reason, all individuals who function in any capacity in product development need at least a rudimentary understanding of the financial concepts that drive a firm's decisions. They need to gain insights into the impact that financial decision making has on their products and their job responsibilities.

The Profit and Loss Statement

The accounting system chosen by a firm provides the basic foundation information needed for an understanding of the financial aspects of the business. It tracks information that results in a profit and loss statement. A **profit and loss statement** is a simplified chart that provides a skeleton outline of the accounting categories, with just the totals, to show the status of the business (Figure 14.1). You will recognize that the case study exploring the strategic plan for the Callie Blake line that first appeared in chapter 8 and decisions regarding the spec sheets that have appeared throughout this text all relate back to this profit and loss financial statement.

The profit and loss statement can be expanded and detailed in numerous ways, depending on the accounting system the business uses. But no matter which costing method is utilized, the profit and loss statement always contains the same basic components. All data on the profit and loss statement may be calculated in either total dollar figures or as a percentage of the whole for a stated time period. The profit and loss statement format provides a way to compare (1) the productivity of one season with another through examination of the dollar monetary values, or (2) one business with another business through examination of the percentages. These figures are used to evaluate the firm's performance for the past season, and they become the basis for preparing the next season's strategic financial plan.

Net Sales

The profit and loss statement begins with an estimate of net sales. **Net sales** represent the revenues taken in by a firm after all returns and other required adjustments, such as discounts and chargebacks, have been subtracted from the gross (total) revenue taken into the business. If dollar amounts are used, they are identified as the amount of revenue taken in during a specific time period. If a percentage is used, net sales are always 100 percent. All other amounts on the profit and loss statement are referenced back to this net sales figure.

Cost of Goods Sold

The second item on the profit and loss statement is the **cost of goods sold**. This figure typically drives a product developer's involvement with financial matters. The cost of goods includes both variable and fixed costs. **Variable costs** are costs that increase or decrease in direct proportion to the number of units produced, including such items as labor, materials, tariffs, and logistics (including freight). Also, in those few cases where quota remain in place, there are fees to reserve quota. **Fixed costs** stay the same no matter how many units of a style are produced. They may include the telephone bill, rent, property

Figure 14.1. *A basic profit and loss statement summarizes one year's financial activities.*

Callie Blake Collection
New York, NY 10012
212-555-7357

Income Statement

Year Ending		December 31, 2001	
Net sales			
(Gross sales minus returns)		$12,400,000	100%
Cost of goods sold	-	7,440,000	60%
Materials			
Direct labor costs			
Overhead			
Indirect labor (e.g. quality control)			
Occupancy (e.g. rent)			
Other (e.g. equipment)			
Gross margin	=	$ 4,960,000	40%
General operating expenses	-	$ 4,340,000	35%
(Administrative overhead			
including: merchandising,			
marketing, accounting, clerical)			
Net profit (or loss)	=	$ 620,000	5%

payments, taxes, benefit expenses for employees, and expenses for personnel other than construction labor. These costs are inversely proportional to the units produced—the greater the number of units made, the smaller the unit cost for fixed expenses because the fixed amount is spread over more units.

The cost of goods sold represents the actual or estimated costs of finished goods and/or the materials needed to produce the product, such as fabrics, findings, and trims. At the wholesale level, it also includes **direct labor**, which includes wages for the cutters and sewers, and production overhead. **Overhead** represents all the expenses in addition to materials and direct labor that are required of a contractor or manufacturer at the factory level to produce and deliver garments to the entity that ordered them. This figure typically includes **indirect labor** (wages of individuals who provide essential support to the production process but do not actually make the product, such as the quality assurance team, maintenance, and security), as well as the cost of owning or renting the factory and the cost of utilities to keep it running.

Costs that may be easily overlooked by product developers are transportation, fees for agents and factors (financial lenders in the apparel business), a

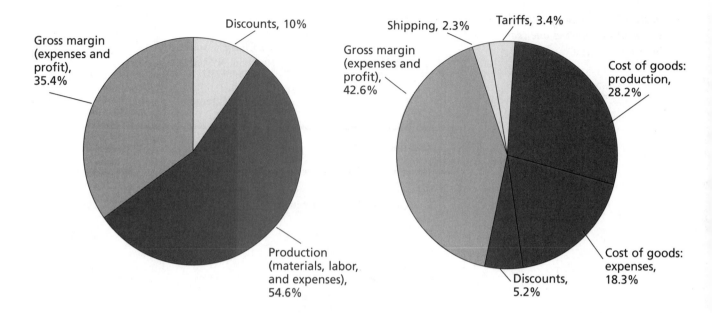

Discounts, 10%

Gross margin (expenses and profit), 35.4%

Production (materials, labor, and expenses), 54.6%

Shipping, 2.3%

Tariffs, 3.4%

Gross margin (expenses and profit), 42.6%

Cost of goods: production, 28.2%

Cost of goods: expenses, 18.3%

Discounts, 5.2%

Figure 14.2a (left). *Basic overview of pricing of a garment as seen by an overseas contractor.*

Figure 14.2b (right). *Basic overview of pricing a garment as seen by a private label developer.*

few remaining quotas, and tariffs (taxes collected on goods that are imported) for the materials used when they contract offshore. We are using the logistics and tariff categories to encompass most of these costs throughout our examples. Profit is typically not listed in this category of a budget for a manufacturer, although a profit for outside contractors will be included in overhead when contractors are involved in the production process.

It is critical that the costs for all these expenses be known and budgeted before manufacturing bids are evaluated and selected for contracts. Many retail businesses estimate the average cost of goods sold at between 40 to 60 percent of total net sales. The typical goal is to keep the average cost of goods for all products as low as possible, preferably less than 50 percent of the wholesale price. For our calculation purposes in this text, we are using a figure of 45 percent. Management will expend considerable effort to control overall cost of goods levels on all products.

If a firm owns its manufacturing or construction facilities, it may elect to put some of their cost of goods expenses into overhead, or it may transfer them to the operational expenses category (found later within the gross margin portion of the profit and loss statement). The approach taken depends on the costing method selected by the firm, but each one of the costs must be included somewhere in the overall cost summary (Figure 14.2a–b).

Gross Margin

The amount left over after cost of goods sold is subtracted from net sales is called the **gross margin**. If 40 to 60 percent of the firm's net sales have been spent on the cost of producing the garments, this leaves a gross margin of 40 to 60 percent. (Remember, net sales are always 100 percent for that firm; 100 percent minus 40 to 60 percent equals 60 to 40 percent.) Gross margin makes it possible to cover operating expenses and profits. **Operating expenses** for producers include sales and marketing costs such as sales personnel, showrooms, and advertising; the cost of discounts and chargebacks; and corporate overhead. Corporate overhead includes the salaries of corporate executives, the product development team (your job), and office personnel. It also includes expenses incurred for corporate real estate and upkeep; insurance and taxes; office equipment and supplies; and computer equipment, technology, and maintenance. If activity-based costing is used in a manufacturing environment, product development costs will appear in overhead under cost of goods, but when offshore sourcing or contractors are used, they stay in corporate overhead. One growing expense within the marketing sector is licensing, which has become a common business practice in recent years, sometimes consuming a considerable portion of the overall expense category for a product.

When firms discuss their business practices and explain the current viability of their businesses, they often refer to their gross margin as an indication of how well they are doing in maintaining their "margins" for the time period (usually a six-month period, or a full fiscal year). Traditionally, a gross margin of around 50 percent reflects a positive business climate, and a gross margin that drops closer to 40 percent is a concern. However, a contractor with no corporate headquarters, showroom costs, or advertising costs may be able to survive on a gross margin as low as 25 percent, while a branded company with a fancy corporate headquarters and a brand portfolio that requires heavy advertising and total use of contractors may need a much higher gross margin in order to be profitable. The costing system selected by the firm may affect the initial gross margin figures. If all costs are moved to the cost of goods category, it tends to leave less in the gross margin pool for distribution to operational expenses and profit, thus putting great pressure on all participants to monitor and contain costs in order to maintain margins close to 50 percent.

In recent years, the Gap has tried to achieve a gross margin of 50 to 55 percent after markdowns, figuring that fabric could sometimes represent 70 percent of **landed cost** of goods. Since it sells private brands almost exclusively, the figures are a window into how specialty retail private label merchants approach their financial planning. *Women's Wear Daily* reports that the industry average gross margin rate for specialty retailers is 39.49 percent, but the highest performers presently are Abercrombie & Fitch Co. at 66.29 percent and Chico's FAS, Inc., at 61.02 (Gustke 2006). This might precipitate queries as to how can there can be so much difference among stores, where do they source, and what accounting methods do they use. For our purposes, we are using 44 percent for the specific Callie Blake example and 47 percent in our estimated retail prices figure to represent the gross margin figure at retail.

It is critical that a firm include every expense and be consistent in costing methods utilized so that effective comparisons can be made between costs of individual styles and the firm's effectiveness from season to season.

Profit

The bottom line of any business statement is the last line of the profit and loss statement. This figure must be a positive number, called a *profit,* if the firm is to remain in business. Profit is dependent on the relationship between net sales and costs as described above. If the final figure is negative, the business is losing money and must make a turnaround to profit, or go out of business. In the apparel business, the average profit is closer to 4 to 8 percent of net sales. For our calculations we have elected to use a figure between 4 and 5 percent.

Pricing Strategies

Starting with the basics, we must differentiate between the concepts of price and cost. Price refers to the monetary value or revenue that is collected from the customer who purchases the product. The customer of a manufacturer may be a retailer, whereas the customer of a retailer is the consumer. **Cost** refers to the monetary value expended to produce—or acquire—a garment style. This includes everything from the materials and labor used to make the style to the overhead expenses of the firm. We must also understand from the outset that in order to stay in business the price must exceed the cost by enough for the firm to make a **profit** or the firm cannot continue without reorganization that could easily mean your job.

Skillful setting of prices is a requirement to generate adequate net sales to cover expenses and generate profits. Companies and their product developers need to consider the strategies to use for establishing prices of their products whether it is to sell at wholesale or retail. Basing the price solely on the cost of goods and adding a set markup such as keystone, which is simply doubling the cost of goods to achieve a price, does not produce a realistic market view. A **demand-based pricing** method considers the value customers place on a manufacturer's or retailer's reputation and its products. There are three demand-based pricing methods:

- *Status/prestige pricing.* The price is set well over merchandise costs based on the theory that customers value the styling and prestige of the brand. This pricing strategy is; most effective in fashion and designer sectors where fashion, quality, and emotional value are factored into how much customers are willing to pay. Designer lines may rely on status or **prestige pricing**, based on the assumption that customers are willing to pay a higher price for products that are perceived to be special in terms of aesthetics, name recognition, quality, value, or service. A prestige pricing strategy relies heavily on image advertising that generally requires a higher gross margin for the manufacturer in order to cover those marketing expenses.

- *Market penetration pricing.* Prices are set as close to costs as feasible

Figure 14.3a. *Merchandise presentation at J. C. Penney reflects a mass merchant.*

Figure 14.3b. *An upper-price point specialty store or designer boutique is reflected in this merchandise presentation.*

to maximize volume of sales by taking sales away from firms already established in a market. Economies of scale have to be employed because profit depends on volume of sales. This method is used to gain market share; prices tend to rise after the firm is established.

• *Market pricing.* Products are priced to match competitors for the same target customers. Companies may have to employ brand names, advertising, and related cost strategies to compete for market share (Glock and Kunz 2005).

These differences in pricing strategies become very visible when considering the environments provided by retailers. One only has to walk into a store to establish the emotional response and expectations of prices on products. Compare the visual impact of presentation of a retailer that focuses on mass appeal and value pricing to that of a retailer that focuses on bridge to higher-priced products that feature status or prestige priced products. The consumers' response is to anticipate the price levels they will encounter (Figure 14.3a–b).

Retail Pricing

The price of a product is the revenue collected from the customer in exchange for ownership of the product. Cost is the amount paid to acquire the product.

Markup represents the amount added to cost of goods to arrive at a final price. Manufacturers add markup to merchandise cost to arrive at a **wholesale price**, and retailers adds markup to the wholesale price to arrive at the **ticketed price** for the consumer.

Retail prices are included in semiannual merchandise plans considering the needs and wants of the target customers, along with types and quantities of merchandise to acquire. Retail merchandisers purchase products at wholesale prices that will allow adequate markup to cover temporary markdowns for product promotion and permanent markdowns for clearance as well as contribute to gross margin.

Wholesale Pricing

Although the cost of the garment itself is the major concern in setting a wholesale price, the product developer must put that dollar amount into a broader perspective. The other three components of the pricing decision are

1. the markup needed to sustain profitability

2. thorough knowledge of the target customer

3. knowledge of the prices and practices of the competition

Designers seeking to increase market share are entering into contracts with retailers for licensing and actually designing exclusive lines for firms that target a different customer than their primary lines. This arrangement enhances the income of the designer, as well as providing cachet that enables the manufacturer or retailer to increase their prices for the product. Some brand producers are entering this environment of being exclusive to specific retailers by developing lines just for those retailers, promising them via legal contract agreements that those products will not be sold elsewhere. In general, these contracts are motivated by financial advantages.

Private label product developers benefit from potential savings in several areas, including marketing costs for the label. These savings enable them to set a lower selling price on a product that is essentially the same as a branded product. This pricing strategy makes private label merchandise look very desirable in comparison with branded merchandise carried by the store. However, private label product developers also have to prepare for the possibility that their garments may not compete well with prestige label goods and that they must set a gross margin that can absorb heavy markdowns once their products hit the selling floor.

Wholesale brand merchandise is generally priced at what merchandisers perceive the market will bear. This strategy is sometimes known as **target market pricing**, which is really a version of market pricing. Two jackets may be similar, but because of subtleties in fabric, trim, or construction, one might cost $50 to make and the other might cost $60. If a 50 percent markup was applied to each style, the $50 jacket would have a wholesale price of $100 and the $60 jacket would wholesale at $120. Although the two styles provide needed variety within the line, the customer may not perceive a significant enough difference between the two to pay more for the $60 jacket. Using target market pricing, the product developer may price both at $110, which equals a 45 percent gross margin on the jacket that cost $60 to produce and a 55 percent gross margin on the jacket that cost $50 to produce. If the jackets sell in equal quantities, the average markup is 50 percent for the manufacturer. Retail merchandisers will then apply their own markup to the wholesale price to achieve an appropriate retail price for the consumer.

Strategies used today to establish the original garment target price are varied. In general, prices are set to reflect an understanding of the target customer and the consumers' expectations for price and value. Familiarity with the marketplace is the greatest tool in understanding the value or worth of a particular garment style. If it is in high demand, the price charged may be higher; but if the style is plentiful, the price needs to be low enough to compete.

The largest trend in mass retailing is the creation of private labels or exclusive labels based on partnerships, especially partnerships with brands or designers who are already successful. Some of these partnerships include I*saac Mizrahi' Mossimo,* and *Liz Lange* with Target. These private label developments give the retailer greater control than working with manufacturers and provide an element of exclusivity for consumers. This practice is further blurring the lines between manufacturers, wholesalers, and retailers; it is providing a more competitive marketplace, but it is also precipitating the squeezing of cost of goods in a valiant attempt to maintain gross margins.

Discounts and Allowances

List price is the manufacturer's suggested retail price or the amount that has been determined by a product developer to come closest to the value of that product to the ultimate consumer. **Discounts and allowances** are reductions in the list price that are granted by manufacturers to their retail customers. From a manufacturer's perspective, a **trade discount** is the percentage subtracted from the list price to establish the *wholesale price* that a retailer actually pays the manufacturer for a product (Figure 14.4).

The traditional trade discount taken off of the list price is about 50 percent, but it varies significantly in today's competitive business climate, particularly between purchasing from manufacturers versus offshore contractors. Other types of allowances are factored or negotiated into the purchase price and are considered contract terms. These terms typically total about 5 percent of the list price. They are identified on a purchase order from a retailer and a manufacturer to confirm the final wholesale price. Examples include quantity discounts, seasonal discounts, shipping terms, and payment terms. An example of a payment term would be a cash discount that is awarded for paying invoices on time.

Manufacturer's Pricing[1]		Callie Blake Skirt[3]	Retailer's Pricing[2]	
Suggested Retail Price	$127		Premium Price	$133
- Quantity/Seasonal discounts	-5 %		+ Additional markup from 1st price	+ 10%
List Price	$121		First Price	$121
- Trade discount	-50 %		- Planned Average Markdown	- 20%
			Planned Average Selling Price	$ 96.80
			- Initial Markup	-50 %
Wholesale Price	$ 60.50		Planned Cost	$ 60.50
- Advertising/Discounts	-10 %		- Advertising/Markdown discounts	- 10 %
Billed Cost	$54.45		Billed Cost	$ 54.45
- Production Costs	-$35.20			
$ Gross Margin	$19.25		$ Gross Margin	$ 42.35
% Gross Margin	35.4 %		% Gross Margin	43.75%
- Cash discount on billed cost	-8 %		- Cash discount on billed cost	- 8%
Reduced billed cost	$ 50.09		Reduced billed cost	$ 50.09
+ Reimbursed shipping	+ $ 2.20		+ Shipping	+ $ 2.20
Amount received	$ 52.29		Amount remitted	$ 52.29
- Other expenses	- $ 2.20		+ Other expenses	+ $ 3.30
- Production cost	- $ 35.20		Net cost of goods	$ 55.59
$ Adjusted Gross Margin	$ 14.89		$ Adjusted Gross Margin	$ 46.21
% Adjusted Gross Margin	28.5 %		% Adjusted Gross Margin	42.6%

Regular Price: $133
Bargain Price: 20% Off $ 96.80

[1] All manufacturers prices based on Wholesale Price.
[2] All retail figures based on Retail First Price.
[3] Consumer's see the retailer's Premium Price as the Regular price on a price tag.

Source: Adapted from Kunz 2005, 174.

Figure 14.4. *Detailed costs of a Callie Blake skirt with a list or first price of $121.*

Retailers may take the wholesale price, add any applicable logistics and tariffs charges if the goods are from offshore contractors, and call this their total cost of goods. Retailers then add their markup to establish the ticketed retail price they will present to consumers.

Chargebacks

One practice of retailers that has been confounding garment producers in recent years is the practice of chargebacks. **Chargebacks** are fees assessed to a vendor by a retailer, after the retailer takes delivery of the goods, which relate to customer returns, advertising fees, mislabeled products, and incomplete orders to the vendor. To be more specific, chargebacks are fees requested by a retailer for items not covered in discounts and allowances in a purchase contract with a vendor. Over the past decade, chargebacks have become a very serious issue. Retailers say chargebacks are critical to running their businesses, as they are a way to maintain the gross margins they must achieve to stay in business. Some vendors consider them just a burden of doing business with big retailers, but some of them are starting to fight back because they feel the application of chargebacks has become abusive.

There are numerous lawsuits currently in the legal system accusing retailers of using unwarranted practices related to chargebacks. Vendors claim that they place undue burden on the producers of apparel when retailers bill them for contract variances that were related to conditions not covered in current purchase contracts. The controversy over this issue reflects the grave importance of correctly interpreting the terms of purchase contracts and the need to be on firm ground when negotiating contract prices among retailers, vendors, and contractors.

Pricing Laws

Laws regarding unfair trade practice and price discrimination sometimes limit pricing contract terms. Those responsible for pricing within a business must be knowledgeable about all current applicable laws. For example, a manufacturer cannot tell a retailer what to charge for a product; the manufacturer can only suggest or recommend a retail price. For a manufacturer to demand that a retailer charge a set price for a style as a condition of purchase is considered price fixing and is illegal.

Another legal issue concerns discounts. If a discount is offered to one customer because the customer purchases a large quantity of a particular style, the manufacturer must be able to prove to another customer, who purchases only a few garments of that style, that the larger order creates a saving for the manufacturer. If this cannot be proved, the government requires the same discount price be offered to both customers.

Product Costing

These simple concepts can become inordinately complicated when basic accounting principles meet the vagaries of fashion change, fickle consumers, and a complex global marketplace. With an understanding of the basic concept of *Sales* minus *Costs* equals *Profit*, it is possible to explore how the business world sorts financial data into basic categories of information, to understand how some of the calculations are done, and to recognize how the resulting cost and price figures affect the day-to-day decisions made by a product development staff.

The impact of these financial concepts is felt everywhere in the product developer's job, from the broader decisions of what brand and category lines to produce to the narrower decisions of how many of selected styles to produce. The decision as to whether or not a misses' suit line should be expanded into a petite or large size line has numerous financial implications. Likewise, the sweep of a flared skirt relates to fabric width and cutting room efficiencies. Individual styles may be altered from the designer's original concept to economize on fabric, or the size range of a style may be limited because fabric requirements are too high in larger sizes. Every apparel design situation is laden with monetary decisions.

Two perspectives—the manufacturer's and the retailer's—on cost/price relationships for a single garment are provided within Figure 14.4. This figure identifies all the major costing components that go into the price of each imported garment. Please note that since 90 percent of apparel sold in the United States is now imported, our perspective must expand to encompass a more global mindset related to costing goods. The example reflects industry averages of percentage of overall retail price. Since each style is different, the calculations will vary significantly from these averages from one garment to the next. Also, there are differences in vocabulary and definitions found among firms for some of these cost category names, depending on accounting methods of the firms involved. No matter how costs are categorized, all the component areas must be included in the bottom line price.

Basic Costing Systems

The costing process requires a system for tracking all expenses and income in order to account for quarterly or annual profits or losses. According to Glock and Kunz, the three most common costing systems are:

1. **Direct costing**, which considers only materials, construction labor, and sales commission as product costs. All other expenses for the firm are placed in a general "expense" category. This system may work for vertically structured manufacturing firms, where all operations occur in one place, but it can be a problem for firms that use outside contractors. This method can be helpful when deciding whether to make or buy a product.

2. **Absorption costing**, which assigns some business costs to product cost and others to operating expenses. This system places a predetermined percentage of all overhead costs (other than for labor and materials) into the labor costs. There are some risks involved with this method, as it can distort overall labor costs.

3. **Activity-based costing (ABC)**, which treats all costs as elements of product costs. This method is considered the most comprehensive and realistic for long-range decisions because all costs, both direct and indirect, are budgeted into product costs. This method is sometimes referred to as a cost management tool because it seems to make it easier to keep track of all expenses, product costs versus support activities, when they consistently appear in one place (Glock and Kunz 2005, 229–233).

Phases of Costing

To fully comprehend the overall process of product costing, we now must divorce ourselves from thinking in terms of retail prices to examine just the components of the costs of production from a product developer's perspective. Studying the cost diagrams and tables in this chapter should help you begin to sort out these concepts.

The cost sheet is a budget or projection of what a product developer thinks it will cost to make an item. The costing process—from the time a new style is an idea to the time it is manufactured, bought, and shipped—determines whether or not the item is profitable. Accurate costing requires continuous estimation and reevaluation of production costs. Any one or a combination of people within an apparel firm may handle the costing responsibilities. Official cost estimators may be hired for that express purpose, or the responsibility may be handled by the designer, merchandiser, product developer, production manager, or industrial engineer who is trained in the fine points of estimating large-quantity production runs. When products are sourced offshore, sourcing managers are integral to the costing process because they are the ones who request and evaluate bids. It is possible that one or more of these people would be responsible for one phase of the process and someone else for another phase.

The costing process occurs in three phases:

- Preliminary, or precosting, for a sample garment

- Production costing, or final cost estimate, for planning quantity production

- Actual costs determined during production

Precosting

The first stage of this process is **precosting** or the **preliminary cost estimate**. Figure 14.5 shows a computerized version of this step. You may want to refer back to the Preliminary Cost Sheet spec form in chapter 9 (Figure 9.6), where this topic was first introduced. Precosting begins with an estimate of the cost of materials, usually 35 to 45 percent of the garment's costs. This estimate is then added to labor costs and the producer's gross margin, covering overhead expenses and the contractor's profit, to make up the other 55 to 65 percent of a contractor's price. This establishes a subtotal representing 100 percent of FOB cost of goods sold. To this you need to add an average 8.4 percent of cost of goods for logistics, as we established previously, and an average tariff cost of 9.0 percent of the basic cost of goods. This figure provides a total cost of goods estimate.

If the contractor is producing for a vendor or manufacturer in the United States who acted as the product developer, the vendor or manufacturer now adds his gross margin to the overall contractor's cost of goods to establish the

Figure 14.5. *A preliminary cost sheet can be created using Freeborders computer software.*

Costing Page - 1: 1 - Blouse

freeborders

Design # 2003_001232_Spring	Group Active	Season Spring	Status Costing
Division Casual	Office/Agency Chamonix Internation	Year 2003	Create Date Aug-13-2002
Department Womens	Prod Desc Floral Top		Revise Date Aug-14-2002
Fabrication			In Store Date

Style Information | **Costing Details**

Target Retail Price	Est. Retail Price	Target Mark Up	Est. Mark Up		Costing Type Internal	Quote Requested Aug-13-2002
28.00	28.00	% 35.00%	% 66.88%		Quote Request	Quote Received Aug-13-2002
Garment Qty. UoM	Minimum Qty. UoM	Color Min. UoM	Patteren Min. UoM		Quote Number 1	Quote Status Others
500.00 Each	100.00 Each	50.00 Each	50.00 Each		Prod Set Comp Blouse	
Comments	Assuming a quantity of 500 with a minimum of 100				Comments Preliminary costing	

Quote Information | **Costing Worksheet   Original Cost**

		Price	Usage	UoM
Quote Variation	Material	3.75	1.50	Yards
Construction Var. 1 Basic	Material	1.50	0.50	Yards
BOM Variation 1 Basic		Target Cost	Estimated Cost	Est. Country
Size Category MIS Missy (001 XS-4XL)		Original: USD - Estimated :Not Defined		Not Defined
BOL Variation		@1		@1
Request. Ship Date Actual Ship Date 01-15-2003	Fabric Cost	6.38	1.91	0.00
Needed for mid January	Trim Cost	4.00	5.50	0.00
Comments	Label Cost	0.55	0.55	0.00
	Packaging Cost	1.00	0.75	0.00
Vendor & Factory Information	Labor cost	1.55	0.00	0.00
Office/Agent Excellent Clothing Lt Commission % 6.00%	Finishes	1.16	0.00	0.00
Contact Robert	Costing	1.00	0.00	0.00
Vendor Accessories International	Free Spot 7	0.00	0.00	0.00
Contact Jay	FOB	15.64	8.71	0.00
Facility	Duty %	0.07	0.04	0.00
Contact	Ship (Load)	1.11	0.00	0.00
FOB Point USA	Commissions	0.94	0.52	0.00
Origin of Goods USA	Quota Fees	0.45	0.00	0.00
HTS 100.1938.47657 (g/f) Duty % 0.45%	Free Spot 8	0.00	0.00	0.00
Duty Category Duty 1	Free Spot 9	0.00	0.00	0.00
Transportation Information	Landed Cost	18.20	9.27	0.00
Air/Ocean/Land Land	Mark Up %	35.00%	66.88%	0.00%
Cost 1.25 per UoM Ounces Ounces	Retail Price	28.00	28.00	0.00
Weight of garment 18.00 UoM Ounces Ounces	Out of Balance	0.00		
Company				
Contact				

Produced by Freeborders CPM Design, ©Freeborders 2002   Page 1 of 1

wholesale price to the retailer. In cases where the garments were contracted by a retail product developer directly to a contractor, savings occur due to cutting out the middleman step for establishing the wholesale price of the brand or manufacturer. In this scenario you go directly from the total cost of goods estimate and provide a larger gross margin for the retailer who is doing this type of private label development.

These cost figures begin with the rough estimates made for an individual style during the line development phase of product development and represent the costs for producing a single unit of merchandise or a sample. The focus here is to establish the identity of the style with a sketch of the garment and informed estimates for the costs.

Estimated construction costs are based on the firm's records of previously produced products and standard construction data. It is left to the contractor to determine whether the garment can be produced for the projected amount. If the manufacturing is to be done in-house, construction costs must reflect far more specific specs and costing of expenses. What expenses are finally included depend heavily on which of the costing methods described earlier in the chapter is used by the firm.

When precosting is complete and the style concept and estimated cost have been approved, a sample of the style will be made in-house or a request will be made for contractors to produce a sample and develop a bid package. If the precost estimate is too high, an unacceptable style will either be adjusted from its original design to meet the desired cost level or simply rejected as too costly to produce.

There are now several software applications available to assist in the process of establishing the preliminary cost estimate for samples and the more detailed production costing that follows. One of these is Sourcing Simulator, which is particularly useful at the product development level for calculating costs, margins, and evaluation of sourcing strategies for a style.

Production Costing

The second phase of costing is typically called **production costing** or the **final cost estimate** (Figure 14.6). This is a cost estimate based on figures derived from approved style samples and from the requirements included in the specification package. It is much more detailed than the preliminary cost estimate because it incorporates information acquired during the sampling phase. At this stage, all costs are estimates for constructing one garment of the style, but in relation to production run quantities. The estimates are made for the entire order, which can range from a few dozen to many thousands of garments, depending on numbers from sales orders or merchandisers' requests. Then the total cost estimates for construction of the entire order are divided to establish the cost of one garment. Companies such as the Gap and Kohl's have indicated they sometimes order close to a million of a particular style. As you can imagine, being even slightly off in your calculations can bring disastrous results when working with this volume of product.

Production costing sheets begin as the precosting sheet did, with a sketch and identifying data for the style that were established when the style was designed. Typically, they also contain proposed size range, colors, and selling

Figure 14.6. *A cost sheet developed using Freeborders computer software calculates the landed cost for one style and the suggested retail price.*

Costing Page - 1: Blouse

Design #	2003_001232_Spring	Group: Active / Season: Spring / Status: Costing
Division	Casual	Office/Agency: Chamonix Internation / Year: 2003 / Create Date: Aug-13-2002
Department	Womens	Prod Desc: Floral Top / Revise Date: Aug-14-2002
Fabrication		In Store Date:

Style Information

Target Retail Price	Est. Retail Price	Target Mark Up	Est. Mark Up
28.00	28.00	% : 35.00%	% : 33.92%

Garment Qty.	UoM	Minimum Qty.	UoM	Color Min.	UoM	Pattern Min.	UoM
500.00		150.00	Each	100.00	Each	0.00	Each

Comments: Costs for each item is needed.

Costing Details

Costing Type	Import / Quote Requested: Aug-14-2002
Quote Request	QR4000058 / Quote Received: Aug-14-2002
Quote Number	/ Quote Status: Others
Prod Set Comp	Blouse

Comments: Final costing

Quote Information

Quote Variation	1 [Q2] - Final
Construction Var.	1 [Q2] - Basic
BOM Variation	1 [Q2] - Basic
Size Category	[Q2] - MIS Missy (001 XS-4XL)
BOL Variation	
Request. Ship Date	12-18-2002 / Actual Ship Date

Comments: Needed for mid December

Vendor & Factory Information

Office/Agent	Excellent Clothing Lt / Commission %: 11.00%
Contact	Robert
Vendor	Knits & Wovens 4 U
Contact	Jonnie
Facility	
Contact	
FOB Point	USA
Origin of Goods	USA
HTS	100.1938.47657 Igjf / Duty %: 0.45%
Duty Category	Duty 1

Transportation Information

Air/Ocean/Land	Air
Cost	0.25 / per UoM: Ounces Ounces
Weight of garment	14.00 / UoM: Ounces Ounces
Company	
Contact	

Costing Worksheet Original Cost

	Price	Usage	UoM
Material	3.75	1.50	Yards
Material	1.50	0.50	Yards

	Target Cost	Estimated Cost	Est. Country
	Original: USD - Estimated :Not Defined		Canada , CAN
	@ 1		@ 1.35
Fabric Cost	6.38	1.91	2.58
Trim Cost	4.00	5.50	7.43
Label Cost	0.55	0.55	0.74
Packaging Cost	1.00	0.75	1.01
Labor cost	1.55	2.00	2.70
Finishes	1.16	0.75	1.01
Costing	1.00	0.55	0.74
Free Spot 7	1.11	1.00	1.35
FOB	16.75	13.01	17.57
Duty %	0.08	0.06	0.08
Ship (Load)	0.94	3.50	4.73
Commissions	1.84	1.43	1.93
Quota Fees	0.45	0.50	0.68
Free Spot 8	0.00	0.00	0.00
Free Spot 9	0.00	0.00	0.00
Landed Cost	18.20	18.50	24.98
Mark Up %	35.00%	33.92%	33.92%
Retail Price	28.00	28.00	37.80
Out of Balance	-1.85		

Produced by Freeborders CPM Design, ©Freeborders 2002

Page 2 of 3

Table 14.1 IMPORT COSTS PER UNIT:
3,000 WOOL JACKETS WEIGHING 32 OZ. EACH FROM HONG KONG

ITEM	CALCULATION	TOTAL PER UNIT
FOB (free on board) (raw bid price of contractor)	Fabric + trim + direct labor + overhead + profit + freight + loading	$38.00
Agent's commission	7.5% FOB	$2.85
Freight (truck and ship)	$0.13 per ounce X 32 ounces	$4.16
Insurance	0.25% of 110% FOB	$0.10
Total offshore costs	FOB + agent's commission + freight + insurance	**$45.11**
Customs duty	$0.463 per kilo + 20% FOB	$8.02
Customs clearance	4 shipments = total $800; ($800/3000 units)	$0.27
TLC (total landed cost)	Total offshore cost + customs duty + customs clearance	**$53.40**
Overland freight to door	$0.50 per unit	$0.50
Other budgeted expenses	10% FOB	$3.80
TOTAL IMPORT COST OF GOODS	TLC + overland freight + other expenses	**$57.70**

Sources: Birnbaum 2005; Kunz 2005b

season. The five main components of this costing estimate are fabrics, findings, labor, overhead expenses of the contractor, and any other gross margin expenses for the contractor or vendor, including profit. Also, more specific logistics and tariffs costs will be entered, rather than the generalized estimates used in precosting. This process has become more complicated in recent years because of rapid fashion changes, greater competition in the global marketplace, and technological advances in production methods. Costing accuracy has become critical, and costs are now commonly figured to the nearest $.01 per dozen (Brown and Rice 2001, 86). The responsibility for the final cost estimate may fall to someone within a firm, if the company does its own production; or it may be completed by a contractor as a formal bid to do the construction of the garments for a specified price. It is not unusual for contractors, especially those who have a computer aided design (CAD) system, to develop a sample marker (layout of pattern pieces) of a mix of sizes to provide accurate estimates of actual fabric usage, thus minimizing **fallout** (fabric waste) costs when completing their bid packages.

Production cost estimates can be misleading if the individuals responsible for evaluating estimates or contractor bids on a style run do not understand all the components involved in the overall cost package. Consider the following example: A garment is to be constructed offshore and bids are submitted from potential contractors with similar materials charges. One of the bids is from a Chinese contractor and has much lower overall labor costs than a bid from a Mexican contractor. The first reaction might be to take the bid with the lower labor costs. However, the expenses involved in shipping garments from China to the United States will be much higher than for those shipped from Mexico. There are quota restrictions and tariffs on products from China, while products from Mexico have lower logistics costs, faster speed to market, and no tariffs because Mexico is a NAFTA member. It is even possible that the quota from China has been exceeded for the time period and the garments will be held up for weeks in customs until quota becomes available. While many quota dilemmas disappeared in 2005, quotas are still a reality of conducting business on some product categories from China.

When all these factors are taken into consideration, the lowest original bid may not end up being the least expensive for the firm. The critical point in comparing bids from contractors, especially from offshore partners, is to be sure that the costs being compared are **landed costs**; that is, they represent the total cost of finished garments entering the United States and include domestic transportation to distribution centers or retail stores—in others words, a final cost of goods. There are many such complications involved, and each of them must be carefully weighed before production contracts are agreed to. Study Table 14.1, as it is an overview of all of the components that go into the costs of an imported garment. Remember that all these items become part of the cost of goods for a retailer before the retailer adds its own markup, or gross margin, to establish the retail price of a garment.

Actual Costs

The final stage of the costing process for a product developer is determining the **actual costs**. Expenses must be monitored during production of the style run. If a contractor bids and successfully acquires a contract to produce a style to written quality specifications for a specific cost, the contractor bears the responsibility of meeting that cost by the delivery date on the contract. If the style is to be produced in-house, the product development staff must monitor the construction and assist members of the production staff in bringing the product to the retail floor at or below the estimated cost. If costs escalate during production because of some unpredicted factor, such as increased fabric costs, new labor rates, or increased insurance costs, the profit margin on the style run will suffer and new projects under development by the firm may have to be curtailed. These figures are compiled from all styles and become a part of the firm's profit and loss statement to determine the status of the business at the wholesale level and to use for projection of the next merchandise plan.

Product Development Costs

Product development costs for individual styles vary a great deal, even in firms with established costing formulas. Product development costs typically include pattern development; refining the style and fit; grading the patterns to the size range to be produced; selecting and sourcing materials; and determining assembly methods to be used, including the equipment to be employed and the stitches and seams to be used. In general, new styles take more time to develop and incur greater overall costs because all information on the garment has to be gathered and evaluated before it can be approved for production. Styles that have been produced before and are only being modified for reuse require far less effort in these areas; hence, the overhead costs for those styles are lower.

Bill of Materials

A detailed materials list is developed for each style before it is made into a sample or put out for bids. Called a **bill of materials**, this detailed list identifies all actual materials to be used to construct one sample garment. It also contains an estimate of the amount each of these materials will cost when produced in quantities. An example of a bill of materials spec sheet may be found in chapter 9 (Figure 9.7).

Fabric

Fabric may be the largest single cost of an apparel product. The type and quality of fabrics selected can significantly affect the overall cost of a garment style. Costs of fabrics are also influenced by delivery charges from the textile mill to the garment producer, duties or tariffs on imported textiles, testing requirements, and inspection costs. The amount of fabric required to construct a single garment, stated by number of linear yards or linear meters (depending on fabric width, how it is packaged, and where it is sourced), is listed along with the price of that exact amount of fabric. Amounts of fabrics are the hardest to estimate because of the **fallout** or waste that can occur when cutting pattern pieces from the yardage. This is especially true when a single sample garment is cut. When projecting for larger production runs, the smaller sizes take less fabric while larger sizes take more. Therefore, it is important to consider the range of anticipated sizes. Factors such as the width in which the fabric is available, minimum purchase orders required for the selected fabrics and flaws or color shadings that are found in the purchased yardage must all be figured into the cost equation. Some estimates include from 2 to 7 percent extra fabric allowance in their orders to ensure they get enough first quality product to complete their order.

Trims and Findings

Trims and findings must be identified and priced. Cost sheets commonly list findings such as thread, trims such as lace and ribbon, closures such as buttons and zippers, labels and other items such as elastic. Costs for findings and trims can vary widely from a few cents for thread to much more for a piece of exquisite lace trim. They are listed on the bill of materials by unit price, although they come packaged and the cost is broken down to the exact unit price for an individual garment. For example, buttons may be sold and priced by the gross (12 dozen); the price of each button must be extrapolated from that figure and then multiplied by the number of buttons needed for the individual garment. When ordering thread, especially when it is dyed specifically for that product, an allowance of 25 percent extra may be suggested to cover any construction errors and operator differences in usage. Hangers, plastic bags, shirt boards, and labels are also included in material costs.

Overall, materials generally account for 35 to 50 percent of the cost of goods for domestically made apparel. For garments made offshore, fabric alone may account for up to 70 percent of the landed cost of a garment (total after adding shipping and tariffs). In today's global sourcing environment, it becomes even more critical to be precise in ordering all of the materials for garments to be sure the quantities of first-quality products are available for retail delivery.

Labor Costs

Labor cost estimates done in the early pre-costing process were just that—estimates. The need for detailed labor costs depends significantly on whether the product developer's firm is a producer or contractor, or a retail product developer. They work differently.

When a product developer works with an offshore producer, the contractor or vendor generally does not provide a detailed breakdown of the direct labor costs; just a summary figure of overall production costs is provided as a final bid. However, vendors will base their overall bids for garment production on the cost of materials, labor, overhead, transportation, and a built-in profit for themselves. Offshore production estimates are often quoted as **free on board (FOB)**, or as FOB origin or FOB factory. This means that the exporter or offshore contractor has included in the price of goods the transportation to port, the handling and loading aboard the vessel, and any cost of reserving quota and export duty charges incurred in country of origin. The ownership transfers when it is loaded on board. If the quote is FOB destination, costs include basic FOB charges as well as transportation costs to the ultimate port or distribution center and import tariffs; ownership transfers when it reaches its destination. No matter which way they are collected, the overall process must include all of these costs.

When contractors are used, product developers calculate basic estimates

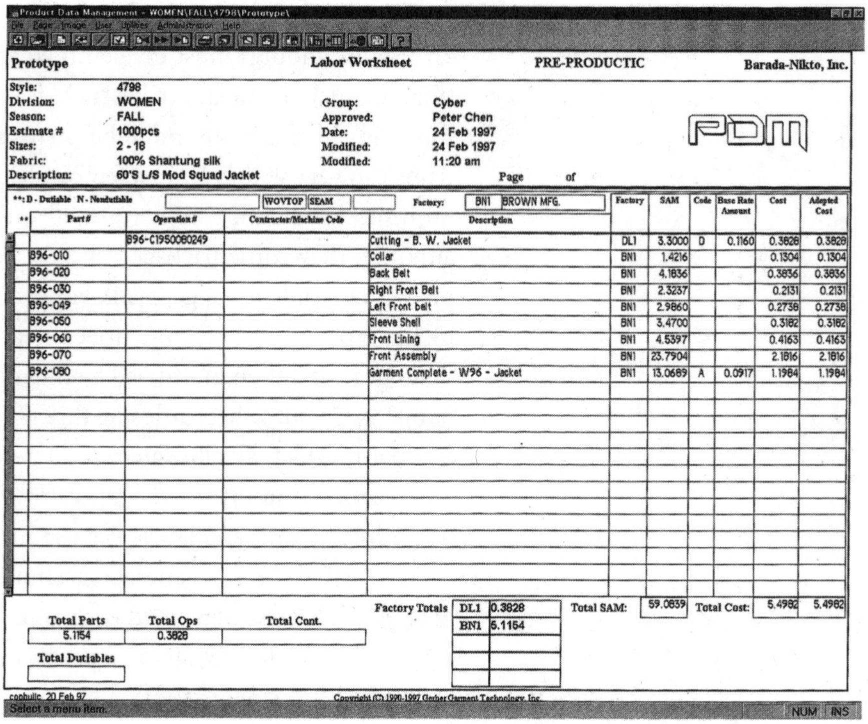

Figure 14.7. *A preproduction work sheet developed using Gerber PDM software reflects labor charges for each production operation.*

Product Data Management - WOMEN\FALL\4798\Prototype

File Layer Image User Utilities Administration Help

| Prototype | | Labor Worksheet | | PRE-PRODUCTIC | | Barada-Nikto, Inc. |

Style: 4798
Division: WOMEN
Season: FALL
Estimate #: 1000pcs
Sizes: 2 - 18
Fabric: 100% Shantung silk
Description: 60'S L/S Mod Squad Jacket

Group: Cyber
Approved: Peter Chen
Date: 24 Feb 1997
Modified: 24 Feb 1997
Modified: 11:20 am

Page   of

**: D - Dutiable N - Nondutiable   [WOVTOP][SEAM]   Factory: [BN1] BROWN MFG.

**	Part #	Operation #	Contractor/Machine Code	Description	Factory	SAM	Code	Base Rate Amount	Cost	Adopted Cost
		B96-C1950080249		Cutting - B. W. Jacket	DL1	3.3000	D	0.1160	0.3828	0.3828
	B96-010			Collar	BN1	1.4216			0.1304	0.1304
	B96-020			Back Belt	BN1	4.1836			0.3836	0.3836
	B96-030			Right Front Belt	BN1	2.3237			0.2131	0.2131
	B96-049			Left Front belt	BN1	2.9860			0.2736	0.2736
	B96-050			Sleeve Shell	BN1	3.4700			0.3182	0.3182
	B96-060			Front Lining	BN1	4.5397			0.4163	0.4163
	B96-070			Front Assembly	BN1	23.7904			2.1816	2.1816
	B96-080			Garment Complete - W96 - Jacket	BN1	13.0689	A	0.0917	1.1984	1.1984

| Total Parts | Total Ops | Total Cont. | Factory Totals | DL1 | 0.3828 | Total SAM: | 59.0639 | Total Cost: | 5.4982 | 5.4982 |
| 5.1154 | 0.3828 | | | BN1 | 5.1154 | | | | | |

Total Dutiables

conbullz 20 Feb 97
Select a menu item.

Copyright (C) 1990-1997 Gerber Garment Technology, Inc.

NUM   INS

and then send out a request, along with the overall specification package, to production firms for bids. If a vendor is awarded the contract, it is responsible for meeting the contracted costs, but it may renegotiate the contract if the product developer makes changes that were not specified in the original bid. Great care must be taken to understand the exact terms of the contract so that everyone understands what is and isn't covered as part of a bid.

When garments are produced in an inside shop (within the firm) or by a domestic contractor, a detailed labor costing process is followed. It is based on identifying the sequence of operations required to produce the garment. These construction operations lists are developed from the specification sheets. Once each process has been identified, the **standard allowed minutes (SAMs)** figures, units of measure used as basis of establishing the cost of each sewing operation, are incorporated into the total labor cost estimates. Those SAM costs figures come from previously developed data charts. The projections can be made from computer systems designed to estimate labor components or from a manufacturer's own records of what specific operations cost (Figure 14.7).

If costs are to be contained, they now must be carefully projected. Labor costs include everything from spreading, cutting, and actual sewing operations to pressing and finishing. They may also include designing, sample making, patternmaking and grading, and marker making. If floor-ready products are specified, estimates may also include application of hangtags and price tickets and placement of garments on hangers in prepack groups containing an array of sizes. Labor costs in the United States can account for a large portion of costs. Imported goods from lower-wage countries typically require lower overall labor costs, but they carry additional costs for quotas, tariffs, and shipping as well as longer production schedules.

Another area of consideration under labor costs is the cost of quality. People are not machines, and they make occasional construction mistakes. When developing production costs, an allowance for seconds or irregulars (mistakes) should be factored into the overall cost. Although the optimum goal would be to move this figure as close to zero as possible, the more realistic figure can easily approach 6 percent of overall production. Allowances for this aspect of costing must be dealt with early in the cost equation or the entire anticipated profit margin for the run could evaporate when errors are encountered.

In general, the more units produced, the more time it takes and the more it costs to produce them. However, production costs are most efficient per unit when garments are produced in quantity (large runs). This is possible when many garments are made of one style. Basic shirts and pants are produced in large, cost-efficient runs. As the number of garments produced in a style decreases, the cost per unit tends to increase. Short runs (few garments of one style) require operators to change their handling methods to accommodate new operations and different fabrics. These changes slow down the operation, which makes the cost per item go up. Women's fashion goods fall into this short-run dilemma.

Tariffs

Tariffs are taxes paid to a government for importing specific goods. We speak of tariffs and tariff rates; but when these tariffs are collected, we are paying **duty**. Some nations charge tariffs and collect duty on their exports in addition to the tariffs charged and duties collected when garments are imported into the United States. When more than one nation is involved, such as fabric coming from one country and garments constructed in another, the complexity of calculating duty costs becomes very convoluted.

Tariff rates for all products coming into the United States are established by Congress, but duties are collected by the U.S. Customs and Border Protection (CBP) service and deposited into the U.S. Treasury. As might be expected, doing business with a government agency is not a simple exercise. In general, individual duty rates are posted online as part of the Harmonized Tariff Schedule (HTS). However, they are very detailed; a caution is given with these posted rates warning people that final duties charged will be established by the U.S. Customs service and billed to the importing firm. When their calculations differ from your calculations, they are right.

For apparel products, tariffs are calculated by establishing the square meter equivalents (SME) of the specific product involved, the fiber content, the country of origin, and the duty rate for each potential fiber combination,

Table 14.2 COMPARISON OF GEOGRAPHIC CONSIDERATIONS OF BIDS FROM CONTRACTORS IN ASIA AND THE CARIBBEAN

PROCESSES	ASIA/CHINA	CARIBBEAN
Ship fabric from mill to factory	Vertical operation; N/A	7 days (ship from U.S.)
Cut and sew	21 days	21 days
Transit to port	7 days	1 day
Sailing time	14 to 21 days (depends on stops of carrier)	3 days
Port and customs clearance plus transport to distribution center	12 to 14 days	4 days
TOTAL TIME:		
Days	54 to 63 days (58.5 average)	36 days
Weeks	8 weeks	5 weeks
WTO estimates each day in shipping adds 0.5% to cost of item	Adds: 27% to 31.5% to cost of goods for transportation	Adds: 18% to cost of goods for transportation

Source: Zarocostas 2004

fabric type, quantity, and nation involved. Even though most importers are dealing with finished garments, the HTS bases its duty on tables of estimated SME for every conceivable garment type. The overall average of tariffs costs on apparel products at the present time is about 9 percent of cost of goods, although some products can range significantly higher, and of course there is no duty charged on many products coming from nations with which the United States. has free trade agreements.

There is no legal requirement for a firm to hire a customs broker to facilitate the movement of its imported goods through the clearance process, but many importers opt to do so for convenience. Even though additional costs are incurred in doing so, it takes the burden of the paperwork and obtaining a CBP bond to cover anticipated duty charges off the importer's hands. The importation of textile items for re-sale at retail is especially cumbersome because of quota or other special requirements such as banned materials. Hiring a broker can help to prevent costly mistakes.

Logistics

The movement of goods between locations has also become more complex with the growing dependence on imported goods. The costs involved in transporting goods go far beyond paying a carrier such as a shipping company to move the goods to the United States. It now involves consolidation of orders for shipping and redistribution at the docks, dock clearance fees, and a myriad of additional factors.

The overall average for shipping costs for a garment will run about 8.4 percent of total cost of goods, but will vary significantly depending upon where the goods are made. Overall costs from China and Hong Kong will be much higher than from the Caribbean area (Table 14.2), and those coming from Sri Lanka, Bangladesh, and India could be the highest, but must be weighed against significantly lower labor costs. Importing is a complex task requiring coordination of many detailed decisions.

According to a WTO study, "Freight costs have greater influence on trade patterns than tariffs" (Zarocostas 2004). Differences among countries in their transport costs and availability of modes of transport are definitely a source of comparative advantage in international trade. Quality of transport infrastructure also affects trade, as poor facilities increase costs. The WTO study also compared shipping costs and found that freight costs in poor, developing countries average 70 percent more than in developed nations. As a point of interest, in 2002 a standard-size 20-foot container shipped from Asia to the United States cost an average of $1,502 (Zarocostas 2004). When you see one of these containers on a truck on one of our highways, consider how many garments may be packed into just one of them and what that garment has gone through to get to that location on its travels to your favorite store.

Summary

The financial context of a business heavily affects the decisions made by product developers. An understanding of the basics of business accounting provides a foundation for those who enter the product development field. Examination of the components of the profit and loss statement is followed by an overview of costing systems.

The phases of the overall costing process include the preliminary cost estimates of samples, the production or final cost estimates for approved production runs, and the areas for monitoring actual costs of production runs. Our exploration of costing concepts concludes with a discussion of the components of the process used to arrive at the list price and wholesale price, and in the case of private label retailer involvement, the final retail price for a garment. Pricing strategies are introduced with information to aid in making fully informed decisions for pricing, such as cost of the garment, markup practices to sustain profitability, knowledge of the target customer, and knowledge of the pricing practices of the competition.

Detailed costs in selected areas of garment production are costs of materials, costs of direct labor, and overhead. In addition, there are costs related to importing goods, specifically logistics and tariffs.

Key Terms

absorption costing	list price
activity-based costing	markup
actual costs	net sales
bill of materials	operating expenses
chargebacks	overhead
cost	precosting
cost of goods sold	preliminary cost estimate
demand-based pricing	prestige pricing
direct costing	price
direct labor	production costing
discounts and allowances	profit
duty	profit and loss statement
fallout	standard allowed minutes (SAMs)
final cost estimate	target market pricing
fixed costs	tariff
free on board (FOB)	ticketed price
gross margin	trade discount
indirect labor	variable costs
landed costs	wholesale price

Discussion Questions

1. How does pricing compare with costing?

2. What factors other than actual expenses affect the establishment of a garment's price?

3. What expenses, other than costs of materials and labor, must be considered by a product developer?

4. Identify retailers that use the various pricing strategies defined on pages 460–461. How does their pricing strategy impact the gross margin they build into their prices?

5. In small groups, estimate the breakdown of costs of three specific apparel products found in retail stores today. Which components need to be included in the price of each of these garments? Use this information to estimate costs for each garment.

Activities

1. Develop your own bill of materials using the materials spec sheet in chapter 9 (Figure 9.7) as your model. List all the costs of producing the sample garment you designed in chapter 8.

2. Project all the costs you listed in the bill of materials for one garment to establish total costs for producing 5,000 items of that garment.

References

Birnbaum, D. 2005. *Global guide to winning the great garment war.* New York: Fashiondex, Inc.

Brown, P., and J. Rice. 2001. *Ready-to-wear apparel analysis.* 3d ed. Upper Saddle River, NJ: Prentice-Hall.

Glock, R. E., and G. I. Kunz. 2005. *Apparel manufacturing: Sewn product analysis.* 4th ed. Upper Saddle River, NJ: Prentice-Hall.

Gustke, C. 2006. The WWD list high profit makers. *Women's Wear Daily,* September 21.

Kunz, G. I. 2005a. *Merchandising: Theory, principles, and practice.* 2d ed. New York: Fairchild.

Kunz, G. I. 2005b. Personal correspondence with Myrna Garner, October.

Zarocostas, J. 2004. Study: Shipping costs key. *Women's Wear Daily,* September 21.

Additional Resources

Barbee, G. 1993. The abc's of costing. *Bobbin,* August.

Lee, G. 2000. Is fashion's biggest headache getting worse? *Women's Wear Daily,* February 9.

CHAPTER 15

SALES, PRODUCTION, AND DISTRIBUTION

"As a fashion designer, I was always aware that I was not an artist, because I was creating something that was made to be sold, marketed, used, and ultimately discarded."

—Tom Ford

OBJECTIVES

- To understand the role of wholesale sales in the product development and production process

- To understand the stages of apparel production

- To explore the components of apparel distribution, focusing on logistics

- To identify the forms of apparel retailing, including store and non-store venues

---

Creative and technical design functions culminate in the sale, production, and distribution of apparel products to the retail marketplace. Members of the product development staff must be attentive to the remaining stages of the marketing chain to fully appreciate and evaluate the value of their contributions to the overall process and to make informed decisions regarding their job-specific activities. The final stages of the apparel product development cycle are wholesale sales, production and distribution including logistics, and the retail marketplace where products finally reach the ultimate consumer.

The retail marketplace is in a state of flux, with some long-standing icons of the business disappearing and direct marketing by computer and television increasing their market share. The impact of technology is being felt throughout the entire product development, marketing, and distribution cycle.

The Role of Sales

In today's apparel environment, a majority of textile products and apparel styles are not produced in quantity until it is known which of these products are wanted by buyers for presentation to consumers in the marketplace and in what volume they are to be produced. In the case of private label merchandise, retail merchandising staff, working with product development staff, determine which products from the styles presented by the designers have the greatest sales potential. They then narrow the offerings to a selection, called their line or unit merchandise plan, that fits the firm's overall plan for the coming season. They determine the size range, colors, and quantity of each style to be offered for sale in their stores.

For branded goods and in more traditional manufacturing settings, an additional step must be taken before garment samples are put into full production. That step is selling the designs to customers, in this case, usually retail buyers. At this point, only samples have been produced to aid in selection of contractors and for sales representatives to use for their sales responsibilities. Sales representatives take original production samples to sell to buyers at major market centers, in wholesale showrooms, and occasionally on the road (Figures 15.1a–c). As orders are taken and processed, styles that sell well enough to be deemed profitable are put into full production. Those styles that are not selling well are typically pulled from the line before any more production capacity is devoted to them.

Trade shows are the foundation of the textile and apparel sales calendar. Referred to in the business as simply a **market** or **market weeks**, they are held in major cities throughout the world at carefully scheduled times throughout the year. They are often set up for specific categories of merchandise such as men's, bridal, children's, or the most visible category, women's fashions. For decades New York City has been the U.S. venue of choice for major fashion markets, especially in women's wear. Eagerly anticipated and reported heavily in the media, the most visible of these is Olympus Fashion Week, held in February and September. Another New York venue is Fashion Avenue Market Expo (FAME), launched to create a new fashion event in New York City for the industry. It is held in January, May, and August.

In recent years, one U.S. trade show venue has evolved into the biggest trade show in the United States. This is MAGIC, held in Las Vegas, Nevada. The show began as the Men's Apparel Guild in California, which set up trade fairs to feature men's sportswear produced in California. The organization's acronym became the name of this market event, the MAGIC Show. The growth of the industry on the West Coast precipitated the addition of many other categories of merchandise and finally a change of location from California to Las Vegas. Now MAGIC consists of four individual markets:

- MAGIC—for men's categories

- WWDMAGIC—for women's categories

- MAGIC kids—for children's categories

- Sourcing at MAGIC—for private developers and brands to find contractors (MAGIConline)

Figure 15.1a. *The California Market Center show in Los Angeles has a new "lifestyle approach."*

Figure 15.1b. *Retail buyers make their selections at WWDMAGIC trade show in Las Vegas, Nevada.*

Figure 15.1c. *Garments are marketed at trade fairs such as the February edition of Nouveau Collective in New York.*

Many other regional markets are held throughout the country, in cities such as Chicago, Atlanta, and Dallas. As the industry has globalized, trade shows have proliferated throughout the world. For example, major textile trade shows include Premiere Vision for textiles, in France; the Pitti Filati for yarns, in Florence, Italy; and Interstoff Asia for fabrics, in Hong Kong. Apparel market weeks are held all over the globe and vary from more traditional prêt-à-porter designer offerings in Paris and Milan, to the expansive market centers in Istanbul, Quangzhou, and Hong Kong. Tokyo has also significantly increased its presence with fashion markets in recent years.

In those instances in which manufacturers have their own signature retail stores or outlets, production quantities will include garments to sell in the firm's stores in addition to the sales orders secured from other retail buyers by the sales staff at market weeks and in their regional sales offices. These additional garments make it possible for manufacturers to have efficient production runs, take full advantage of any overrun production by using up all materials that may have been prepurchased, and take advantage of quantity price breaks or minimums on materials that are required by the firm's suppliers. The signature stores also provide an avenue to try out new styling concepts. A less-well-known practice is that firms that source offshore may order extra goods to ensure having adequate stock in the event of re-orders from retailers. Offshore contractors often are not able to provide additional stock at a later time if there is very high sell-through at retail, so some firms will purchase more than their original orders as a precaution. If no re-orders are forthcoming, they send the overruns to their own signature stores.

Production

Product developers continue their contributions to the process once it is confirmed which styles are targeted for production. They have determined final sizing and fit specifications and have had trial garments made to verify the final production patterns and assembly instructions. Any final adjustments in the pattern size or fit, or construction methods, must be made at this time. Every detail must be finalized now, and all the necessary materials must be contracted to factories based on the quantities requested by the merchandising staff in the case of retailers or the orders received from the sales representatives for brands and traditional manufactures.

Selection of Production Sites

Selection of contractors and actual production scheduling depends heavily on the time required to produce finished garment orders and to meet targeted delivery dates. The most critical dates in the product development calendar are the delivery dates established during contract negotiations with buyers and production contractors. The turnaround time needed to produce and deliver the garments will heavily influence decisions about whether to produce garments internally or to source out the production.

According to Glock and Kunz, three basic considerations strongly affect the selection of contract sites to produce garment orders. These criteria are used to measure the ability of a production facility to actually process the required number of garments. The first consideration is **throughput volume**, or the amount of work that can be accomplished in a given time, which is used to measure a plant's production capacity. The second criterion is **throughput time**, or the time required to produce a single unit from beginning to shipment. Throughput time is used to plan work schedules, determine delivery dates, and establish costs of production. The third criterion is **work in process**, or the number of garments under construction at a given time. This is used to ascertain a firm's flexibility and responsiveness, for a contractor may be doing well on the orders already in process, but become overburdered if it commits to take your order in addition to the previously committed production (Glock and Kunz 2005, 332). Each of these three factors is critical in its own way to making the final decision about awarding a production contract. Production planning requires coordinating the need for finished goods with all of the available resources, including the materials, the production capacity, and the ability to meet delivery schedules.

Today, the ability of manufacturers to incorporate new concepts, such as mass customization and computer communication technology, into mass production must also be considered as part of any long-term partnering or sourcing decisions. Having up-to-date production equipment and quick response capabilities are factoring into the decision with more and more frequency.

Scheduling decisions are also based on an individual contractor's or manufacturer's ability to produce quality garments in a timely manner, products that can meet contracted quality standards and specs without noticable defects. Also consider whether the contractor can maintain enough flexibility to accommodate changes in construction methods if orders are modified or reordered. Consideration is also given to a contractor's ability to accommodate changes in the availability of materials.

In addition, the basic conflict between seeking lower labor costs offshore or seeking speed of production and delivery domestically must be resolved. Remember that garments from Asia will take significantly longer to get to the United States than those produced in Central America or Mexico. The actual shipping time tends to be obvious due to distance traveled, but there is also time needed to get the fabrics required to make the garments in quantity after orders have been confirmed and time required to get finished goods to the dock, loaded, unloaded, and trucked to either the store or a distribution center before being sent to the store. These factors all add to the overall time and can be heavily affected by sourcing in areas where a nation's infrastructure is weak. Poor roads, electrical outages, and political unrest in the country all are potential blocks to meeting a delivery timetable.

If production is to be completed offshore, manufacturers must consult with the U.S. Customs Service to find out tariff or duty charges and regulations regarding quotas from the proposed country of origin. It is critical to know this information to ensure the ultimate entry of the company's product into the United States. Overlooking this step can be very costly to a business, especially if the product is denied entry into the United States because of lack of available quota at the time of the shipment. A company may hire a licensed customs broker to help with these matters. The potential tariffs and the availability of quota can be an essential consideration in selection of offshore

Figure 15.2. *Employees of Cooperative Maquiladora Mujeres in Nicaragua are cutting stacks of fabric plies to begin the process of filling a garment order.*

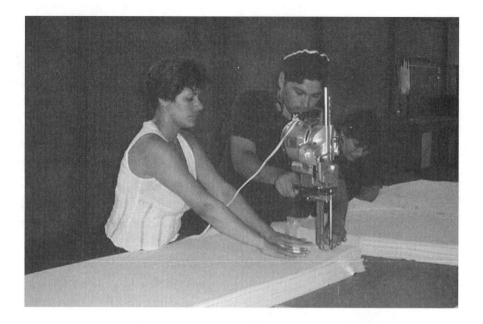

contractors. The import regulations are extremely complex and are in a constant state of flux.

A final area of consideration in the selection of a contractor is the issue of human rights. Awareness of working conditions in a factory where your garments are to be produced may influence your decision even when the costs, timing, and product quality are adequate. Consumers in the United States have become aware of working conditions in other parts of the world and expect firms to monitor the conditions in the factories where the garments they purchase are produced.

For the majority of cases, bid packages containing all the specifications and conditions required of a producer are sent out to contractors who are deemed to be satisfactory sourcing partners. Among those producers who return bids, a final selection is made for the award of the production contract.

Spreading and Cutting

The style fit has been established and a final production pattern prepared. This pattern is graded to increase and decrease the dimensions for the sizes planned for the garment. Cut order planning identifying the styles, sizes, and quantities that are to be cut from a particular fabric is now done to give instructions to the production department. These cut orders will establish the number of garments that are cut, sewn, shipped, and sent through customs. **Markers** are made indicating the layout of all the pattern blocks required for production of the ordered sizes. The goal is to lay out the pattern blocks in the most efficient manner to keep fallout, or wasted fabric, to a minimum.

Actual garment production begins with **spreading** the fabrics (laying them out flat on long tables) and using the paper marker as a template to establish the cutting lines for the pattern blocks. Spreading of the fabric varies greatly, depending on the type of fabrics used and the design of the fabrics (whether they are patterned or plain). The quantity of garments to be produced and the quality level to be achieved in the finished product are also factors affecting the spreading process. Accuracy of placement is most critical when spreading fabrics that are plaid or contain nap or large motifs. Some leniency in placement of grain lines may need to be tolerated at the lower price points if this action produces significant savings in overall fabric use.

Spreading is accomplished by laying multiple **plies** of fabric on a table by hand or by mechanical spreaders to be cut in one pass of the cutter. Companies usually cut many plies, or layers, at one time to reduce costs. For short runs, few plies are laid, but for large orders the layers may be stacked to depths of several inches and contain hundreds of plies of fabric to be cut at one time.

Cutting may be accomplished by a variety of methods, including hand-guided, vibrating electric straight knife tools, electric rotary cutters with circular blades, or computer-driven laser cutters (Figure 15.2). Lasers cut only one or a few plies at a time, so they are not practical for large runs, but they provide accuracy and quick flexibility for short runs. Accuracy in cutting is a basic requirement to ensure consistent assembly of the cut pieces. Some of the smaller pieces, such as cuffs and facings, are stamped out to ensure conformance to the original pattern shape.

Assembly

The cut pieces are typically marked with identification numbers and placed into bundles for the machine operators. Bundles of like pieces are usually tied together for movement to the production line. The temporary marks on the pieces enable the operators to determine which pieces go together; achieve accurate placement of details, such as darts; and ensure consistent construction techniques.

Three major production assembly methods or systems are employed in apparel manufacturing plants. These methods are the progressive bundle system, the unit production system, and the modular manufacturing method.

Progressive Bundle System

The **progressive bundle system** utilizes traditional assembly line concepts (Figure 15.3). Assembly proceeds in a consistent order: Parts (smaller pieces such as collars and cuffs) are completed first; then, parts are attached to major components (e.g., cuffs are attached to sleeves); the final assembly of body parts is accomplished (e.g., sleeves are attached to body); followed by adding the finishing touches such as buttons and trims. The operators in a bundle system are paid piecework rates based on standard allowed minutes (SAMs) established for the specific tasks they perform. This system encourages the operators to complete their tasks quickly and to produce in quantity, but sometimes speed is achieved at the expense of quality. Many people, doing a

Figure 15.3. *Progressive bundle system of garment assembly is utilized in this garment factory in Panjin in China's Llaoning province.*

variety of tasks or operations, handle each garment. A T-shirt may require as few as eight operations, whereas a complex garment such as a man's tailored jacket may exceed 100 separate operations. Labor costs for the individual garments are established by calculating the total number of SAMs required to complete all the individual tasks involved in producing the garment.

Unit Production System

In the **unit production system**, garments are introduced to each operator's station via an overhead transporter. (Figure 15.4) The transporter moves the developing garments from station to station, and the operator attaches the newest component or performs the appropriate tasks on each garment as it reaches the station. Operators are often cross-trained in this system so they can step in to help with an operation that is behind schedule and slowing down the overall completion rate. Pay for the operators in this system is based on number of garments completed rather than on individual tasks. In these cases, garments that do not meet quality standards may be removed from the total number of completed garments when the amount of pay for the production workers is determined.

Modular Manufacturing Method

Modular manufacturing methods group the operators into teams or modules, and each team focuses on efficient completion of each garment moving through its module by passing it off to the next station in the module as the tasks for that station are completed (Figure 15.5). This newer production method focuses on team efforts and utilizes in-process quality assessment, whereby corrections are made as errors occur rather than at the end of the production line, when some errors cannot be repaired. Operator pay in the modular system is based on the number of accurately finished garments produced by the entire team.

This is a relatively new method for garment assembly and has proved to be very effective in reducing the number of seconds produced. It is still uncommon to find this method used in offshore facilities, where the majority of current production is still completed by the traditional bundle system.

Wet Processing

Some products require an additional wet processing stage to add a chemical or physical finish to the assembled garment. **Wet processing** may be used to soften the fabric, to preshrink the garment, or to change the final appearance of a garment via color removal, color addition, or application of a chemical finish to provide wrinkle or soil resistance. These finishes may provide the consumer with the added benefit of a preshrunk product that will fit much the same after being washed as it did when purchased. Buttons, labels, and snaps are added after wet processing has been performed in order to prevent damage to the materials during this step.

Figure 15.4. *Overhead conveyor system of garment assembly is used in this denim jean production line.*

Figure 15.5. *A modular manufacturing team is shown in action as they assemble khaki pants for men.*

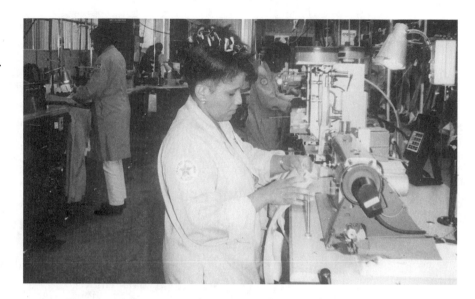

Finishing

The last steps of apparel production are referred to as finishing. The **finishing** process includes trimming threads, final inspection, repairing defects, pressing, folding, and packing. Most garments require finish pressing (Figure 15.6). This is done in addition to any in-process pressing that might have been required to achieve desired effects within the construction process. Some garments, such as T-shirts, require very little pressing; others, such as pants and jackets, require extensive final pressing.

The fold and pack operation includes the addition of accessory items such as belts and hangtags. Garments are then folded or hung on hangers as outlined in the original specifications. The individual garments may be placed in plastic bags for protection, or they may be grouped before being placed in a protective covering to prevent soiling during transportation (Figure 15.7). Finally, the garments are placed into cartons or placed on hanging racks for shipment.

Logistics

Now that 90 percent of the apparel sold in the United States is imported, the movement of products through the development process to their final destination has become a far more complex undertaking. The coordination of all the processes and people involved in distribution of raw materials and finished products has evolved into the science of **logistics**. The complexity of tracking and moving goods on a global basis has precipitated development of computerized systems to handle the process. Participants include not only ships themselves, but consolidators who gather orders from the producers and put full containers together; carriers such as trucks or trains at both the factory and delivery portions of the process; dock capacity and workers to load and unload the containers; and government participants such as customs officials,

Figure 15.6. *End-process pressing is completed by employees in a Chinese factory.*

Figure 15.7. *Garments are bagged and folded before being packed for shipment in this Villatex factory in Honduras. This factory makes intimate apparel for Vanity Fair and Victoria's Secret.*

who collect tariffs and look for illegal shipments. There may also be warehouse capacity and workers to consider during consolidation at the factory end and at distribution centers here.

Orders are packed and scheduled for delivery according to the completion date or contracted delivery date. The delivery date is critical to the manufacturer or contractor because missing a delivery date may be viewed as a breach of contract, and financial penalties may be incurred. Products are shipped via a number of different methods or carrier types. The **carrier** is the mode of

Figure 15.8. *Downloading containers of products arriving from China from a docked ship to a truck for delivery.*

transportation used to move the garments. Air freight is the most expensive carrier method and is typically not used unless garment production is behind schedule or the products are very high cost or fashion-forward. Vessel (ship) is the most common carrier method for offshore shipments. These vessel carriers are contracted with considerable care because some of them follow direct routes, while others make numerous stops in their travels before reaching the ultimate destination. Within the United States, rail may be used as the carrier, but truck is the more common method for domestic delivery. Garments entering the United States from overseas require a combination of carriers to reach inland destinations.

Garment orders are frequently sent to a company distribution center to be checked for quality and sorted for either storage or forwarding to retail destinations (Figure 15.8). Sometimes garments are drop-shipped directly from the contractor to a retail store in order to save time. However, care must be taken to ensure that quality standards are met at the factory, because once orders reach the retail store any recourse for quality errors can become a problem. This is especially true with offshore suppliers.

The majority of finished garments are delivered to retail store locations. In recent years, however, a growing number of apparel products bypass the store and are sent directly to the consumer from a distribution center to complete individual catalog or e-commerce transactions (See Figure 15. 9).

Retail Environment

The final stage of the apparel marketing chain before garments reach the ultimate consumer is the retail sales floor. Retail is the second largest industry in the United States after agriculture. Wal-Mart is the world's largest company and the largest retailer in the United States.

The face of retail selling has changed a great deal in recent years, and the classic definitions and recognized classifications of these businesses and their product lines have become blurred. The traditional brick-and-mortar store sector of the retail environment has grown by leaps and bounds in recent decades, to the point that experts believe we are now "over-stored," or confronted with more retail establishments than can possibly be supported by the consumer market. In addition, the stores are being severely challenged by many non-store or direct marketing merchants, including catalog sales and e-commerce or "e-tailing" on the Internet. However, the basic structure of the retail phase of the apparel marketing chain is still valid. The two basic styles of retail business are store and non-store.

Retail Stores

The major categories of retail stores of the traditional brick-and-mortar model are specialty stores, department stores, and mass merchandisers. There have been a number of buyouts and acquisitions in recent years that have

Figure 15.9. *Merchandise moves through J. C. Penney's regional distribution center near Fort Worth, Texas. State-of-the-art robotics are utilized at this center to facilitate speed to market.*

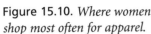

Figure 15.10. *Where women shop most often for apparel.*

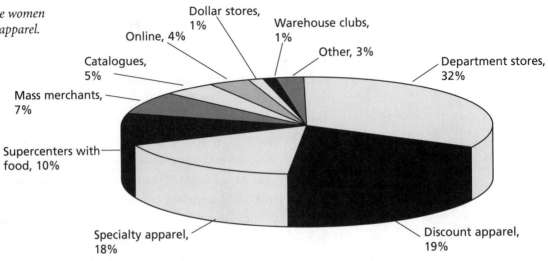

Dollar stores, 1%

Warehouse clubs, 1%

Online, 4%

Other, 3%

Catalogues, 5%

Department stores, 32%

Mass merchants, 7%

Supercenters with food, 10%

Specialty apparel, 18%

Discount apparel, 19%

Sources: WSL Strategic Retail 2006; Sackler 2006.

changed the retail landscape significantly and shifted the power between these forms of operation. Figure 15.10 shows where American women shop for fashion.

Specialty Stores

Specialty stores focus on a few types of merchandise to the exclusion of other products. The most common types of apparel-focused specialty stores today are those that target a specific customer or carry a specific product line. For example, within the moderate price range found in many malls across America, we find Express stores focusing on young women's fashion-forward products, Victoria's Secret stores focusing on lingerie for women (Figure 15.11a), and Claire's stores focusing on accessories for preteen girls. An example of a higher-priced specialty store is Prada, a boutique store that provides upper-priced fashion apparel for women. Two relatively new players in this segment of the business are Chico's and Coldwater Creek. Every product in each of these stores is directed at the perceived desires of its target customer.

There are many variations of the specialty store concept, including single product line stores such as shoe stores and maternity wear shops. Some broader-based specialty stores are meeting with success at the upper to middle price range category, including Saks Fifth Avenue and Nordstrom. These firms offer a wider selection of merchandise than their more narrowly focused counterparts, but they continue to focus their main business activity on apparel and accessories.

Ownership groups in the specialty store category are currently riding the road to success by placing stores in regional malls and city storefronts across the country. An example of this is Gap, Inc., with its Gap, Banana Republic,

Table 15.1 FIFTEEN HIGHEST-VOLUME PUBLICLY OWNED APPAREL SPECIALTY RETAILERS

RANK	RETAILER	DESCRIPTION
1	Gap, Inc.	Its Gap brand has experienced somewhat of a slump in last year.
2	Limited Brands, Inc.	Victoria's Secret and Bath & Body Works have excelled while Express and the Limited have struggled of late.
3	Abercrombie & Fitch Co.	Profits climbed significantly in 2005. Opening in London next year.
4	Charming Shoppes, Inc.	Plus-size retailer spiked significantly in 2005 with Lane Bryant, Fashion Bug, and Catherines brands.
5	American Eagle Outfitters, Inc.	Targets 15- to 25-year-olds. Launching Martin + Osa active lifestyle brand courting 15- to 40-year-old men and women.
6	Ann Taylor Stores Corp.	Considered in a positive turnaround after a slump in 2004.
7	Talbots, Inc.	Known for classic apparel. Purchased J. Jill in 2006.
8	The Children's Place	Also owns Disney Stores; designs and manufactures clothes for kids to age 10.
9	Chico's FAS, Inc.	Started as a Mexican folk art and sweater store, morphed into private label women's retailer.
10	Pacific Sunwear of California, Inc.	Once a little surf shop in California, PacSan has over 1,100 stores.
11	Claire's	Focuses on accessories. Now also in Europe.
12	Aeropostale, Inc.	Mall-based teen retailer.
13	New York & Co., Inc.	Founded in 1918. Target customer: Women 25 to 45.
14	Urban Outfitters, Inc.	Namesake stores, plus Anthropologie and Free People stores.
15	The Dress Barn, Inc.	Targets mid-size cities. Purchased Maurices' to reach small towns.

Source: Gustke 2006

and Old Navy clothing stores. Each of its stores targets a specific consumer profile with a narrow merchandise mix (Gap Inc.). The Gap has become one of the more successful specialty store groups by developing its own private label program to guarantee that it has the type of merchandise it wishes to offer. Currently, the Gap carries its own private label merchandise to the exclusion of almost all other products, and the Gap brand has become one of the largest apparel brands produced. Table 15.1 ranks the fifteen highest-volume specialty retailers.

The merger and acquisition fever that has been sweeping the entire retail

Figure 15.11a. *Victoria's Secret is an apparel specialty store group that focuses on lingerie products.*

Figure 15.11b. *Loehmann's is an off-price retailer.*

Figure 15.11c. *Macy's department stores are owned by Federated. As a result of mergers in recent years, many stores had their nameplates changed to Macy's as they became part of this nationwide department store group.*

Figure 15.11d. *Target is a mass retailer that is becoming more fashion-forward in its quest to increase market share.*

environment has affected the specialty market of late. One example of this is the acquisition of J. Jill by Talbots.

Another form of specialty store is the manufacturer's outlet. These stores provide manufacturers a way to dispose of overruns and irregulars. Consumers find prices in outlets are typically below regular retail prices

A newer, price-oriented specialty store variation is the off-price retailer. **Off-price retailers** such as T. J. Maxx and Marshall's are now common in the apparel business. The merchandise mix in these stores contains broken lots (incomplete size range of a garment), distress goods (inventory from stores that have gone out of business), end-of-season goods, and overruns from manufacturers that the off-price retailer buys at lower than regular wholesale prices. It is then able to pass some of that savings on to the customer and still make a tidy profit (Figure 15.11b).

Department Stores

Department stores have traditionally focused on attracting the woman shopper as she shops for herself and her family. They provide a variety of product lines, including apparel for men, women, and children; soft goods such as sheets and towels for the home; and home furnishings such as furniture and kitchenware. They provide products in a range of prices near the middle to upper price point. The changing demographics of the U.S. population and the growing strength of other forms of retail selling have encroached heavily on their traditional customer base. Women are no longer the only shoppers for their families, as they were in the past. Their shopping time has been somewhat curtailed at the same time that many newer shopping options have been introduced to compete for their attention.

In spite of these drawbacks, some of these stores, such as the Federated Department Store group, owners of Macy's and Bloomingdale stores, are maintaining their hold on a good portion of apparel retail sales. Federated is the largest department store group in the United States since it bought out May department stores in 2005. It changed the nameplates of many established stores during 2006 in order to put the focus on the Macy's nameplate. It has focused on the development of successful private label programs such as *INC International Concepts* for its Macy's stores to complement their branded offerings, and on the exploration and significant growth of their non-store activities, including catalog sales and e-commerce (Figure 15.11c). In addition, Federated has been exploring the concept of exclusive lines from branded manufacturers as a means of increasing its market share. Unlike the Federated group, which is a publicly owned company, Dillards remains a privately owned department store group, with its stores scattered throughout the southern states, focused mainly in the southeast.

Mass Merchandisers

Mass merchandisers, retailers that specialize in selling great quantities of merchandise at lower prices, have grown to such magnitude that the annual list of top-performing retailers routinely includes several of these companies. Wal-Mart is the nation's largest retailer, but another major face on this playing field is Target. These mass merchandisers have honed in on the retail market by establishing their own apparel product development teams with significant private label programs. The *George* label is now synonymous with Wal-Mart, and the company is expanding into a more fashion-oriented area with the new *Metro7* brand. Target has developed many of its own labels, and features exclusive designer lines from Liz Lange, Mossimo, and Isaac Mizrahi (Figure 15.11d).

Two highly recognizable firms, namely Sears and J. C. Penney, cross the line between department store and mass merchant. Sears Holding Corporation came into being when Kmart bought out Sears and consolidated the firms; it now operates both Kmart and Sears stores. J. C. Penney is also hard to classify, although it considers itself a department store, operates 1,021 stores in the United States and Puerto Rico, and is the nation's largest catalog merchant (J. C. Penney). Because of their immense size and focus on moderately priced merchandise, these two firms certainly qualify for our definition of mass merchant.

Direct Marketing

The **direct marketing** category of the apparel business, sometimes referred to as **non-store retailing**, has shown significant growth in recent years. One reason has been the time limitations of adult shoppers, especially working women. Another is the convenience and availability of the Internet.

Catalogs

Shopping from catalogs has become routine for many households as consumers select their merchandise directly from printed catalog offerings and order by mail or phone or online. Some businesses, such as Coldwater Creek, Lands' End, and L. L. Bean, developed almost entirely through their catalog operations. Some of these have expanded into e-commerce and operate their own stores.

Catalog shopping has been a vital segment of the business for over 100 years, but there has been a dramatic shift in the style of catalog. Throughout most of the twentieth century, large multicategory catalogs were the norm. Companies such as Sears and J. C. Penney had "big book" catalogs that contained a multitude of product lines which they released twice a year. That style of catalog is almost a thing of the past, with the exception of Spiegel, which still puts out a big book catalog. The majority of catalogs today tend to be targeted to specific market segments and are more specialized in their offerings.

Many of the newer entries into the catalog field are additions to traditional brick-and-mortar activities of established apparel store retailers such as Bloomingdale's. They have met with catalog success by offering products that are also readily available in their stores and branded products their customers recognize and trust from previous in-store experiences (Figure 15.12).

Television Shopping Networks

Television shopping networks, such as QVC and the Home Shopping Network, depend heavily on impulse purchases. They usually depend on the telephone to complete the purchase transaction. The products are shipped to the consumer from the network's distribution centers. Apparel offerings appear on these channels with regularity, usually shown on live models. Product offerings change with great rapidity.

E-Commerce

E-commerce, also called **e-tailing**, is another form of non-store retailing. The more successful e-commerce activities appear to be the entries from the brick-and-mortar retail community which have developed Internet capabilities and e-mail ordering systems. Almost every major retailer in the United States now operates an Internet site with on-line shopping services (Figure 15.13).

In addition, many apparel catalog businesses also operate successful Internet shopping sites. Lands' End has become a leader in the exploration of interactive experiences online via inclusion of **avatars**, or computerized virtual

Figure 15.12. *Catalog sales contribute heavily to the apparel marketplace.*

models, to aid consumers with their product selection. Internet shopping has become a way of life for some individuals, but there are still issues.

One of the issues of Internet shopping is security. Web sites claim to be secure when consumers provide credit card information to complete a sale, but computer hackers are a problem, and some consumers remain skeptical about divulging personal information online. Many consumers use these sites to gather product and pricing information; then they go to the store to complete their sales transactions. One tool that shows great promise for easing security risks in Internet sales is the introduction of **digital signatures** (Vigoroso 2001a).

Although a portion of the consumer market still does not subscribe to any Internet service or even use a personal computer, there are new entries

Figure 15.13. *Many retailers are increasing their market share by expanding into online marketing on the Internet.*

into e-tailing almost daily, and the continued growth of e-commerce is assured. It appears that as the e-commerce concept becomes a more comfortable environment for consumers, we may anticipate the participation of many entrepreneurial start-ups. The best chance for success for the small retailer in the online environment will come from building brand awareness and offering goods that consumers are unable to find elsewhere (Enos 2001).

Those who regularly work with e-commerce emphasize some requirements for staying power. One of these is the use of a dynamic pricing strategy, where management constantly analyzes data and changes prices in response to fluctuating supply and demand of products. The best example of a dynamic pricing strategy online today is ebay.com. Operated by eBay, Inc., it is primarily an online auction site where individuals and small firms may offer merchandise for sale to the highest bidder; but they also offer same-day, firm-priced sales of a myriad of products. At this time, eBay operates in 29 nations in Asia, Europe, and North America. It is still surprising to some that eBay is so international in its scope.

Financial transactions on Internet sites are done by credit card, sometimes from individual stores, but usually with major bank cards. PayPal is an Internet payment service, owned by eBay, Inc., that handles individual online shopping transactions for a variety of online retail sites, including eBay, and focuses on speed and the security of payments.

The biggest challenge facing e-commerce, and all other forms of non-store retailing, is finding a way to establish garment fit. Estimating garment fit when real garments are not present and a fitting room is not available can be a very real problem. Even though considerable effort is being expended to develop the technology for a **virtual fitting room** via the computer screen, the concept remains elusive. For all forms of non-store retailing, the sizing and fit dilemma—with its attendant problem of customer returns—remains one of the most significant costs of doing business.

Current Conditions

The current environment of the apparel business exhibits noticeable tensions. For example, the wealth of marketing data gathered on individual consumers is significant and should provide product developers with an open field of opportunities for providing diverse and clearly appropriate products for a variety of well-defined consumer markets. There are, however, some issues that may affect the future success of the business.

Sameness in Fashion Products

At the time when a wealth of information for customizing product has become available, fashion offerings in the marketplace have become more similar rather than individualized. This dichotomy is difficult to explain because it appears that many firms are trying to home in on the same market segments to the exclusion of the others, leaving some segments of the consumer market dissatisfied. The sameness of product lines is startling; producers seem to clone one another as their products come off the production lines. The puzzle is why sameness of product occurs at the same time that the potential for individualizing products and matching products to definable market segments has reached a zenith. The sameness of product begs the questions of "Why?" and "How many T-shirts can the population absorb?" There is no simple answer to this duplication problem unless it is explained in the classic tension that exists between the financially oriented business world and the mindset of the creative community.

The tension that remains unresolved between business, with its desire for maintaining the status quo in styling as long as it sells, and the creative people, who argue that new and different styling is the goal, has prevailed at the epicenter of the fashion business for decades. Insistence on providing more and more of the same products may work with cereal or hardware, but it will ultimately not prevail in the apparel business. The makers of Izod polo shirts discovered this the hard way when the fashion life cycle for its prime product ran out and it had not foreseen the inevitable change as consumer interest shifted to the Ralph Lauren polo shirt. Ralph Lauren did not put all his efforts into one product, but accepted the fickle nature of the fashion market and prepared alternatives for the inevitable changes in consumer wants. Yet some apparel companies are staying their course too long, not seeking new concepts in time to weather the inevitability of change.

Consumer Lifestyle Changes

Adjustments in business methods and design direction must be made to accommodate the lifestyle changes of target consumers. Today's consumers are better educated and more aware than at any time in history, and they will make their presence known to those retailers who are unwilling or unable to accept the challenge of providing products that satisfy their needs. Consumers continue to vote the marketplace daily through their purchases, sometimes to the dismay of retailers who have lost the battle by resisting change. One of the long-time retail players unable to read and adjust to changing consumer tastes was Montgomery Ward; this company is no longer in business. Its demise should be a wake-up call to other businesses that have been lax in adjusting to customer preferences when making their business decisions.

From the psychological and social perspective, people still enjoy the shopping experience, and clothing remains the focal point of many shopping expeditions. But there are changes in the behavior of consumers. Some retailers have discovered that consumers are not as brand loyal as they were in past decades; they will accept private label merchandise if it looks good and provides good value. Some consumers will still pay for the emotional value of an appealing shopping experience, as witnessed by the success of companies such as Nordstrom and Von Maur, which stress customer service. On the other side of this coin, consumers will turn their backs if they have a bad experience with a product or a store. Once they have defected, they will often completely avoid taking another risk with that store or brand. There are too many other options available today for any business to take the risk of ignoring its customers' wants and needs.

One of the more successful recent endeavors in the design field has been the advent of lifestyle retailing. **Lifestyle retailing** is built on the concept of providing a well-defined target consumer with a range of compatible products designed to bring continuity to the style of the consumer's home as well as wardrobe. Because these products are designed to complement one another, they ease the stress of repeated decision making for the consumer. Ralph Lauren and Tommy Hilfiger have been quite successful in developing this concept, and other designers such as Vera Wang and Michael Kors are introducing their own entries into the field of coordinated lifestyle offerings.

Trends

A very noticeable trend in the overall apparel business is the shrinking of the haute couture market. European fashion designers who have been the backbone of the fashion business at the highest price levels have been retiring, and their businesses are continuing under the design direction of others. The trend within these businesses has been to significantly decrease custom market offerings and to focus more on the ready-to-wear market. January 2002 brought the announcement of the retirement of Yves Saint Laurent, one of the last remaining icons of the haute couture business.

Another trend is in the retail sector, where we currently have far more stores than are needed, and where there will most likely be considerable fall-out in the coming years. Those that cannot identify and provide for their target customer needs will disappear from the market. The field will be pared down to firms that are able to deliver a complete, but flexible, product package to their carefully defined consumer markets. Some firms will simply disappear, while others will be absorbed into more financially secure operations.

It is anticipated that Wal-Mart, as the largest retailer in the world, will maintain or even grow its market share as it continues its extension into high-population areas in California and the northeastern states. With this goal in mind, Wal-Mart has already initiated a higher-profile fashion presence and is beginning to merchandise stores more to local markets, be they higher price profile or ethnically diverse.

Changes in the Global Market

The phaseout of much of the complex quota system caused some significant ripples in the textile and apparel market early in 2005. However, the extension of quotas on many categories of product from China into the European Union and United States, based on a disruption clause offered by the WTO, slowed the anticipated upheaval in the apparel supply chain. China has significantly increased its share of the apparel market in recent years, but the United States is watching the overall economic conditions with particular attention to the valuation of the Chinese currency, the yuan. Any significant changes in tariffs on Chinese goods or in the currency market could significantly impact the pricing of apparel in the United States.

The slow acceptance of CAFTA–DR is creating considerable interest. New Free Trade Agreements between the United States and other nations are in process and could eliminate tariffs between participating nations. Apparel construction contractors in the Middle Eastern free trade zones, such as the Israeli and Jordanian QIZ areas, have free access to the U.S. market and are moving ahead very rapidly.

Technological Advances

Another major shift in the traditional supply chain is being brought about by technological change, as advances toward creating a virtual world are conceived and developed. Great strides toward this ultimate goal are now being realized. Many technical advances in communication already exist in the apparel supply chain. Internet communications, computerized specification packages, computer aided design (CAD) applications in product development, data management for sourcing, and point-of-sale data mining are all becoming necessary, not novel, tools for maintaining viability in the global marketplace.

Businesses all over the world are incorporating computer patternmaking and grading applications, calculating production capacity and costing analysis problems, and maintaining real-time inventory records with computer applications. Stock reorders are now monitored and triggered by point-of-sale computer inventory management tools. Real-time orders that eliminate delays between the distribution center and the sales floor are becoming routine. One of the most promising areas is the development of product lifecycle management (PLM) software systems. Lectra and Fashionware Solutions, Inc., have released programs combining many CAD and data management functions so that "[d]esign, sourcing, sample making, shipping and even overseas factories can view the same electronic files and see the status of any garment and its compenents at a moment's notice" (Corcoran 2006).

Partnership relationships is an area which is challenging past business practices throughout the product development chain. Proprietary information (confidential information that is owned or used within a firm) must now be more fully shared in order to conduct the business activities of partnering firms in the product development chain. With sharing comes an increasing need for building trust, while still managing to prevent opportunistic behavior between the companies involved (Vigoroso 2001b).

The potential for advancement in the area of fit and sizing is perhaps the most desired and sought-after technical application. With the development of a body scanner that can gather accurate body measurements, it is now possible to create customized apparel.

One of the eagerly anticipated steps in this slowly evolving process is the capability of designing more realistic virtual garments. This step will enable people to visualize how designs will appear on the body without having to construct actual samples of each new style design. The ultimate goal is to develop a method of translating scanned measurement data into a computer avatar model so realistic that consumers may see themselves on the computer screen, depicted in three dimensions, trying on the styles that interest them—the true virtual fitting room. The systems that are on the market remain somewhat idiosyncratic and difficult to move beyond two-dimensional representations of sketched croquis, flat technical drawings of the front and back of garments, and cartoons of fabric designs.

Three-dimensional body forms (avatars) and the ability to design in 3D and flatten the design into 2D patterns are in development. Portraying fabrics that are draped on a form has proved to be a particularly elusive task, especially when movement is desired. These eagerly awaited virtual-world CAD concepts will provide a means of skipping the design sample stage of the product development process to see how a proposed garment will look. The concept of virtual products is palpable, but the tools must undergo further development for the concepts to become truly operational.

The apparel business is truly a vital and changing field. New styles will continue to be the central responsibility of apparel product developers. Those product developers who can move beyond design to fully understand the synergy of all components of the product development process will play a greater role in the apparel industry in years to come.

Summary

The product development cycle and the apparel marketing chain completes itself in the final stages: sales, production, and distribution. Sales at wholesale drive production. The steps of apparel production include scheduling, spreading and cutting, assembly, wet processing, finishing, and distribution to retail venues. Some of the legal aspects of working with offshore contractors involve keeping current on tariffs and quotas.

The retail segment of the apparel business is expanding from primarily brick-and-mortar retailing to embrace a variety of direct marketing avenues, notably catalog, television, and the Internet. Recent trends in the apparel supply chain include the sameness of product line and the growing importance of computer applications throughout the industry. Future directions in technology for apparel product development include the quest for updated sizing standards and a viable virtual fitting room.

Key Terms

avatars

carrier

department stores

digital signatures

direct marketing

e-commerce or e-tailing

finishing

lifestyle retailing

logistics

markers

market or market week

mass merchandisers

modular manufacturing method

non-store retailing

off-price retailer

plies

progressive bundle system

specialty stores

spreading

throughput time

throughput volume

unit production system

virtual fitting room

wet processing

work in process

Discussion Questions

1. What are the final steps of the product development process, beginning with the selection of designs for production?

2. What are the major types or styles of brick-and-mortar apparel retailing?

3. What is the future direction of computer applications in the apparel field?

References

Corcoran, C. T. 2006. PLM grows up with updates from Lectra, others. *Women's Wear Daily*, September 6.

Enos, L. 2001. Making room for niche stores in cyberspace. *E-Commerce Times*, July 31. www.ecommercetimes.com.

Gap Inc. www.gapinc.com/public/OurBrands/brands_ft.shtml/.

Glock, R. E., and G. I. Kunz. 2005. *Apparel manufacturing: Sewn product analysis.* 4th ed. Upper Saddle River, NJ: Prentice-Hall.

Gustke, C. 2006. The WWD list: High-volume specialists. *Women's Wear Daily.* July 20.

J. C. Penney. www.jcpenney.net/company/overview/ overview.htm.

MAGIConline. www.magiconline.com.

Seckler, V. 2006. The great shopping divide. *Women's Wear Daily*, April 16.

Vigoroso, M. W. 2001a. Test shows digital signatures reduce risk for sellers. *E-Commerce Times*, July 31. www.ecommercetimes.com.

Vigoroso, M. W. 2001b. Study: Winning at e-commerce requires evolved management style. *E-Commerce Times*, July 31. www.ecommercetimes.com.

WSL Strategic Retail. 2006. How America shops. www.wslstrategicretail.com/has/everyday.html [subscription service]

Additional Resources

Abend, J. 2001. Tapping into a virtual world. *Bobbin,* February.

Abernathy, F. H., J. H. Hammond, J. T. Dunlop, and D. Weil. 1999. *A stitch in time: Lean retailing and the transformation of manufacturing.* London: Oxford University Press.

Diamond, J., and E. Diamond. 2002. *The world of fashion.* 3d ed. New York: Fairchild.

Diamond, J., and G. Pintel. 2001. *Retail buying.* 6th ed. Upper Saddle River, NJ: Prentice-Hall.

Kunz, G. I. 2005. *Merchandising: Theory, principles, and practice.* 2d ed. New York: Fairchild

Kunz, G., and M. Garner. 2007. *Going global: The textile and apparel industry.* New York: Fairchild Books.

Lewis, R. 2000. Down for count? *Women's Wear Daily,* December 18.

Textiles and Clothing Technology Center [TC2][2], 211 Gregson Drive, Cary, NC 27511. www.tc2/com.

Underhill, P. 1999. *Why we buy: The science of shopping.* New York: Touchstone.

Young, K. 2001. Mall boom is ending as saturation, slump arrest development. *Women's Wear Daily,* June 4.

APPENDIX:
Transition to the Job Market

Your degree is not an automatic ticket to success. You must have a plan and make choices in your education that will give you the skills you need to reach your career goal. If you aspire to travel the world, either as a designer or in sourcing, you should consider learning a language—French or Italian may be helpful in design; Spanish, Cantonese, or Mandarin for a career in sourcing. Know the computer skills required in your career path. Don't ignore the basics: communication skills, both verbal and written, are a universal requirement. Get used to multitasking and deadlines—most postings include phrases such as *high energy, ability to multitask, highly organized,* and *able to handle many projects in a fast-paced environment.*

Specialty companies seek individuals who understand that specific specialty market. Harley-Davidson MotorClothes Division will want someone who has the creative and technical skills as well as experience on a bike. Hot Topic looks for someone who knows music and its influence on fashion and trends. TravelSmith Outfitters seeks someone who understands the functionality required of travel clothes. St. John Knits looks for candidates who understand knit design and technology as well as the designer market. The denim market requires knowledge of jeans assembly and laundry processes.

Experience working with large mass merchants such as Target, J. C. Penney, Wal-Mart. or Kohl's is highly valued. Product developers who work with these mega-retailers must understand their merchandising, pricing, timing, and floor-ready requirements.

Before applying for a job, think through the responsibilities involved in designing for the company to which you are applying. Decisions for men's shirts will revolve around color and pattern selection; active sportswear requires an understanding of cutting-edge fabric developments; and fashion-oriented companies require a keen fashion sense, construction knowledge to understand unique detailing, knowledge of the nuances of fashion fabrics, and superior fit and tailoring experience. Most companies will also require skills on specific computer programs. Experience on a similar type of program is generally readily transferable.

Sometimes you will know the company you're applying to and sometimes the ad will not identify the company until your application is screened and you move to the next level of the interview process. You must know how to respond to both kinds of ads.

If the ad you are responding to identifies the company with the opening, identify whether it is a wholesale, private label, or store direct brand. Become familiar with the range of product it produces, the retail venues where the products are sold, their price point, and their geographic range. To what extent does the company have a presence on the Web? Shop the brand to know the trend level for the current season; identify competitors. Be familiar with the company's brand portfolio.

If you are responding to a blind ad where the name of the company is not disclosed, your task is a bit more challenging. For these jobs you must respond to the skills and competencies identified in the ad. Describe your experience in the terms used in the ad.

Do not limit yourself in your job search. Experience in a niche category such as leather, lingerie, or accessories early on in your career can catapult you up the career ladder, because there is less competition for jobs that require very specialized experience.

Once you have experience working for someone else, freelance work may be an option for designers who need to work out of home. But freelance work is not for everyone. You must be a self-starter, able to balance your workload and personal commitments; cover your own benefits (insurance, retirement); and be able to handle income ups and downs from month to month.

It is informative to track ads in *Women's Wear Daily* or study online position listings on individual company Web sites to identify job titles, salary levels, and the years of experience typically required to attain specific career levels. Some jobs are not advertised but instead are listed with job search firms. Typically these headhunters are paid by the employer who has an opening; they can be a great partner in identifying openings, especially once you have some experience. They are adept at maintaining your anonymity when changing jobs, often provide some great coaching, and can help negotiate salary range. In the early stages of your career, it can be helpful to keep in touch with the faculty of the institution from which you graduated. They often get leads on jobs that require more experience than an entry level job and are happy to recommend alumni, if they know you are looking.

When the job market is depressed, a post-grad internship can be a good foot-in-the-door. Many large companies offer formal internships in a variety of career areas. Some companies offer these internships year-round. Summer positions draw the most applicants; positions in the area of your choice may be more readily available during the first or second semester time frame. In general, design internships draw the biggest pool of applicants and are therefore very competitive; internships for technical designers, fit specialists, and color specialists may not draw as many applicants. These formal internships are highly regarded on any résumé.

Don't get discouraged! In high school you may have been offered nearly every job for which you applied. Now you are seeking jobs at a different level—many of the applicants applying will have similar qualifications to your own, yet only one will get the job. One wise headhunter advised a recent graduate, "Remember, every 'no' is one step closer to a yes." Job hunting is a process that you must go through to reach the final goal. You can learn as much from a rejection as you can from a job offer. Remember, companies are seeking candidates that they identify as a good fit.

Keep a journal or log of your job-seeking process. Keep a copy of the job ad and a note how you learned of the job. Personalize your cover letter and if necessary your résumé to fit the job for which you are applying and make a copy of what you sent. Follow up with a phone call to make sure that they received your letter and inquire as to when they will begin the interview process. Document your phone conversations in your log. If you are asked for an interview, be sure to prepare. Many Web sites and books have lists of interview questions. Thinking through answers for these hypothetical questions will help you to be more articulate during the interview process. Recruiters are looking for candidates who are truly engaged during the interview—they are interested in your answers as well as your questions. Send a handwritten thank-you after your interview. If you don't hear back from them, it is appropriate to call and ask if they have made a decision. If you developed a rapport during the interview, you might ask for some feedback as to why you were not offered the position.

Certain character traits are almost universal requirements; be sure to speak to these traits in your résumé, cover letter, and interview. Universal career traits in apparel product development include:

- Excellent verbal and written communication skills
- High level of motivation
- Excellent organizational skills
- Creative problem-solving skills
- Hands-on approach
- Detail-oriented
- Enthusiastic
- Success-oriented
- Excellent at follow-through
- Able to multitask
- Eager to learn
- Self-starter, able to work independently
- High level of taste
- Team player

JOB CLASSIFICATIONS

The following list describes job classifications common to apparel product development. The information was gathered from on-line position announcements and advertisements in trade papers. Where information was available, each job category goes beyond a job description to include required experience and specific responsibilities, skills, and abilities.

ACCOUNT MANAGER / ACCOUNT EXECUTIVE

Cultivates and manages retail accounts and coordinates production scheduling to meet the needs of those accounts.

Experience and Career Track

- 5 to 10 years' experience in wholesale sales
- Leads to Regional Sales Manager and National Sale Manager positions

Responsibilities

- Cultivate new accounts and maintain existing accounts
- Strategically execute sales plan and achieve account profitability goals
- Review, analyze, and report sales trends
- Conduct day-to-day client communication
- Provide support to wholesale buyers and manage sales support activities and events
- Oversee operational aspects for wholesale accounts with emphasis on EDI, order compliance, and shipping/routing standards
- Act as liaison with production planning to ensure that production is scheduled to arrive on time and according to order specifications
- Communicate customer requirements to product development team

Skills and Abilities

- Strong product background
- Strong customer service and follow-up skills
- Negotiation and problem-solving skills
- Limited travel required

ANALYST

Member of planning group responsible for the use of analytical and system tools to provide selling analysis, monitor retail performance, and follow trends.

Experience and Career Track

- 1 to 3 years of retail or wholesale fashion experience
- Leads to assistant buyer and buyer positions

Responsibilities

- Create reports for buying team
- Analyze sales trends by account, store, and/or geographic region
- Analyze sales by style, color, and size
- Conduct margin analysis

Skills and Abilities

- Proficient in Excel
- Good analytical and communication skills

ASSISTANT MERCHANDISER / MERCHANDISER

Identifies emerging trends for a particular market and interprets those trends from design development through sell-through.

Experience and Career Track

- Assistant Merchandiser, 2 years' experience
- Merchandiser, minimum 5 years' experience

Responsibilities

- Identify emerging trends, forecast future trends, and give direction to design team
- Conduct retail market research
- Collaborate with design on trends, fabrications, colors, shapes, and seasonal products
- Act as liaison between design team and buyers
- Identify new opportunities within category to enhance brand image
- Develop and maintain merchandise and assortment plans in order to maximize sales, profit, and turn goals
- Manage assortments and assortment flow and transition to maximize sales and profits
- Work closely with accounts and production teams to communicate product or delivery changes
- Attend sales meetings for seasonal markets; work closely with team to ensure correct product placement and brand growth
- Follow up on product from sample to production

Skills and Abilities

- Intimate knowledge of customer
- Knowledge of merchandising techniques and financial measurements
- Ability to travel

CAD ARTIST / CAD DESIGNER / GRAPHIC ARTIST

Works with designers and merchandisers to create artwork for product development, presentation, and packaging.

Experience and Career Track

- Entry-level position is CAD Assistant
- 2 to 3 years' experience for CAD Artist position
- Fine art and graphic art experience desirable

Responsibilities

- Research print and pattern trends using current and historic sources
- Translate seasonal concepts and ideas to pattern, print, and trim designs
- Design prints, yarn dyes, and knits
- Modify purchased artwork and develop new artwork
- Approve strike-offs
- Create production-ready artwork including repeats and colorways
- Design trim motifs and repeats

Skills and Abilities

- Strong CAD skills (Adobe Illustrator and Photoshop a must; textile design programs will be specific to product developer, but knowledge of any program shortens the learning curve for others)
- Experienced in technical sketching
- Excellent color sense
- Excellent knowledge of fabrics, weaves, and printing methods
- Knowledge of knit stitches, patterns, and gauges
- Must take direction from designers and merchandisers

CHARGEBACK ANALYST / CHARGEBACK MANAGER

Controls, monitors, and negotiates all chargeback claims.

Experience and Career Track

- 5 years' experience for manager

Responsibilities

- Maintain clear records of order specifications, deliveries, and invoice processing
- Negotiate adjustments
- Communicate with account managers and report to senior management to resolve all errors and disputes with customers

Skills and Abilities

- Clear understanding of contractual terms, various types of vendor allowances, and accounting procedures
- Experience in reconciling valid and nonvalid claims

COLOR SPECIALIST

Manages color decisions throughout the product development process.

Experience and Career Track

- 2 to 3 years' experience

Responsibilities

- Distribute color specifications to vendors
- Oversee physical and digital color approvals for wovens, knits, and trims

Skills and Abilities

- Excellent visual color perception
- Ability to color match different color combinations and understand different fabrications

COMPUTER GRADER AND MARKER MAKER

Interprets brand grade rules for each pattern and develops multisize markers to meet cutting orders.

Experience and Career Track

- 1 to 3 years' experience

Responsibilities

- Ensure that current brand grade rules are correctly entered into software
- Prepare markers for production

Skills and Abilities

- Knowledge of patternmaking, cutting, and garment construction
- Understanding of grade rules and movements
- Knowledge of marker making and yardage consumption

COSTING ASSOCIATE

Tracks costs and determines garment pricing.

Experience and Career Track

- 1 to 3 years' experience in costing and production

Responsibilities

- Interface with design and production to understand all details of the product
- Prepare cost sheets
- Transmit and coordinate cost sheets to overseas offices to secure price quotes
- Complete orders with finalized prices

Skills and Abilities

- Working knowledge of manufacturing and costing in domestic and import manufacturing

DESIGN / PRODUCT DEVELOPMENT ASSISTANT / DESIGN ASSOCIATE / DESIGNER / SENIOR DESIGNER

Responsible for developing seasonal design concepts and designing silhouettes for either item or group lines by delivery. Specific experience in a category or price point may be expected (e.g., leather, children's, lingerie, knits, bags, jewelry, moderate, better, bridge, designer).

Experience and Career Track

- Assistant Designer is entry-level position
- 3 to 5 years' experience for designer positions

Responsibilities

- Identify, forecast, and translate trends for a specific target market
- Research fabric and trims to define seasonal concepts
- Design seasonal lines with an understanding of garment construction, fit, and production calendar constraints; attention to detail
- Interface with sales force, retail accounts, and/or in-house buyers
- Consult with technical designers in preparing spec packages
- Approve sample garments for design aesthetics and fit
- Create presentation boards and give compelling visual presentations

Skills and Abilities

- Strong taste level and color sense; innovative and creative
- Market awareness
- Ability to communicate seasonal direction and develop themes with the entire product development team; an articulate team player
- Extensive working knowledge of materials, trims, and construction
- Knowledge of illustration, flat sketching, presentation boards, specs, and patterns
- Ability to meet deadlines and work under pressure
- Some travel required

DIGITIZER

Responsible for computer functions related to patternmaking.

Experience and Career Track

Entry level

Responsibilities

- Digitize patterns into the computer system
- Prep computer models for further manipulation during fitting, grading, and marker making
- Enter all required information into the computer model
- Prep orders for graders and marker makers

Skills and Abilities

- Computer literate
- Knowledge of industry specific software for digitizing, such as Gerber AccuMark
- Understand digitizing techniques for a variety of different fabrics

DIRECTOR OF LICENSING

Manages existing licensee relationships and further develops the corporate licensing strategy. Responsible for research/analysis; developing/marketing quality products that reflect brand property standards and guidelines.

Experience and Career Track

- 5 to 7-plus years of brand management, merchandising, or licensing experience

Responsibilities

- Collaborate with licensees to develop the business marketing and product plans and conduct monthly business reviews with key licensees
- Interface with licensee management teams, corporate marketing, and divisional design director
- Ensure adherence to contract obligations for sales, advertising, and marketing expenditures
- Direct and oversee the execution of brand imaging throughout licensed categories relating to merchandising, retail sales, marketing, and sales efforts
- Monitor retail sales and strategic planning

Skills and Abilities

- Financial acumen
- Excel skills
- Knowledge of key licensing companies and demonstrated history of successful relationships and launches with them

E-COMMERCE CONTENT ASSOCIATE

Assists the Director of Marketing and E-Commerce with all product photography, digital retouching, and database maintenance.

Experience and Career Track

Not available

Responsibilities

- Prepare fashion information for publishing on a Web site
- Maintain Web site and monitor for troubleshooting

Skills and Abilities

- Knowledgeable in Photoshop and/or other recognized graphic arts software
- Knowledgeable in general photography
- Skill in Web management software
- Computer skills related to database maintenance
- Knowledge of language of apparel if describing or doing graphics for garments

FABRIC COORDINATOR / FABRIC MANAGER / MATERIALS PURCHASING MANAGER

Oversees fabric development and maintains fabric library.

Experience and Career Track

- Fabric Assistant is entry-level position
- 3 to 5 years' experience working with fabric mills in Europe and Asia
- A textile-related degree

Responsibilities

- Make and distribute fabric swatch cards
- Work with designers in fabric/color/print development
- Research new fabric developments and analyze fabrics to determine appropriate construction and quality limitations in relation to availability
- Initiate new fabric development with global suppliers
- Manage and maintain fabric library of current fabric resources
- Oversee lab dips and print approvals
- Manage the sourcing of fabrics/trims used in the sampling and production of finished goods; resolve production-related issues
- Lead sourcing efforts in woven and knit fabrics and trim development
- Order, track, and approve fabric and trim purchases, ensuring that cost, lead-time, aesthetic, and technical goals are met
- Manage ongoing communication, scheduling, and price negotiation with global resources

Skills and Abilities

- Computer-literate
- Strong fabric background; knowledge of fabric standards and testing procedures
- Experience working with fabric mills in Europe and Asia

IMPORT COORDINATOR / SOURCING MANAGER

Develops and manages supplier matrix for all product lines by visiting domestic and foreign locations, negotiating landed price and on-time delivery of merchandise, and assuring quality standards.

Experience and Career Track

- Import Coordinator requires 2-plus years' experience
- Minimum 5 to 10 years' experience with knowledge of South American and Asian markets

Responsibilities

- Track import shipments and allocate orders for branded product
- Negotiate prices and delivery schedules
- Develop product with design and merchandise staff

Skills and Abilities

- Frequent travel, including overseas travel, for sourcing new factories and agents
- Bilingual Spanish or Cantonese a plus
- Exceptional technical knowledge of fabrics and garment construction
- Knowledge of quality control standards, vendor compliance, and auditing procedures

ASSISTANT KNITWEAR DESIGNER / KNITWEAR DESIGNER

Designer with background in knitwear development and sourcing.

Experience and Career Track

- Assistant position is entry level
- 4-plus years' knitwear experience for designer position

Responsibilities

- Research yarns and interpret style trends
- Work with merchandising and sales team
- Approve prototype garments and production samples

Skills and Abilities

- Travel overseas to implement the product development process
- Knowledge of full fashion and cut and sew knits
- Knowledge of yarns, stitches, gauges, patterns, and machinery
- Understanding of knitwear specs
- Good eye for color, fit, and detail
- Computer proficiency required; PrimaVision a plus

MEDIA PLANNER

Coordinates advertising and promotional activities related to marketing of products.

Experience and Career Track

- 3 to 5 years' media experience

Responsibilities

- Issue and monitor contracts and rates
- Plan and schedule media
- Place ads
- Work within budget
- Coordinate artwork

Skills and Abilities

- Ongoing interaction with account executives and clients
- Strong computer skills

PATTERN MAKER

Interprets designs through the development of production patterns, which will be used to cut the fabric. Most firms require computer patternmaking skills in order to work efficiently with offshore contractors.

Experience and Career Track

- 7 years' experience for a patternmaking position with a designer company
- Companies typically seek patternmakers experienced in a particular garment category or size range

Responsibilities

- Develop prototype pattern from designer's sketch, tear sheet, or rub-off of a purchased sample
- Develop production patterns
- Balance and check patterns

Skills and Abilities

- Fitting experience in all types of garments
- Good knowledge of sewing, and ability to instruct sewers in the making of the first sample
- Experience with tech packs
- Computer grading experience
- Understanding of domestic and/or offshore production procedures
- Understanding of fabric testing/shrinkage

PLANNER / MERCHANDISE PLANNER

Plans manufacturer and customer inventories; develops sales forecasts and sales plans to determine production and purchasing requirements.

Experience and Career Track

- Entry-level position might be an analyst
- 4 to 8 years' experience

Responsibilities

- Assist in developing sales forecasts
- Create and maintain unit sales/inventory plans by style and by product category
- Generate and present weekly/monthly sales/inventory reports
- Create seasonal and yearly financial plans and forecasts
- Work with merchandisers and product development team to develop and execute merchandise and assortment plans
- Work with production team to ensure a smooth flow of product to support sales
- Coordinate price quotes and delivery dates with vendors
- Work with the distribution team to ensure on-time shipment of product
- Customize store assortments to maximize sell-through; develop location plans which support the demographic needs and business opportunities of each market; ensure new stores are planned and supported to maximize business
- Monitor and maintain margins necessary to meet profit goals
- Facilitate and promote timely communication and cooperation between stores, merchandising functions, and resources

Skills and Abilities

- Merchandise flow and product delivery knowledge
- Strong Excel skills
- Strong follow-through skills
- Ability to adapt quickly to changing priorities
- Ability to present analytical reports to management and to buyers
- Ability to travel domestically and internationally

QUALITY CONTROL SUPERVISOR

Develops, implements, and maintains systems to ensure compliance with quality standards and regulations.

Experience and Career Track

- 2 to 5 years' experience in a manufacturing environment
- Experience inspecting and measuring garments and/or fabrics for a product developer

Responsibilities

- Maintain systems to ensure compliance with customer quality standards and regulations
- Track prototype, fit, and top of production samples
- Manage social accountability, code of conduct, and quality system assessment programs

Skills and Abilities

- Ability to interface with other departments
- Bilingual Spanish or Cantonese a plus

SPEC TECH / TECHNICAL DESIGNER

Develops specifications for all the materials and processes required to produce the garments, establishes garment fit.

Experience and Career Track

- Spec tech is entry-level position
- 3 to 7 years' experience for technical designer
- Experience on Product Development Management (PDM) programs

Responsibilities

- Prepare all prototypes for fittings, conduct fittings, and enter all fit corrections and revised and graded specs including technical sketches and digital photos into spec packs
- Investigate and assist in troubleshooting line production problems related to patterns, construction, trim, and markers
- Work closely with pattern room and sample room on development samples, spec development, grading, pattern corrections, and sample approvals
- Create technical sketches, including front and back view, according to original design, maintaining silhouette and proportion
- Create spec package from prototype; update with any new or expanded information and follow through on approval process to completed bulk specs
- Conduct sample review sessions making appropriate recommendations for fit, specification, and construction issues
- Communicate corrections regarding construction, quality, and fit to contractors
- Review outgoing samples and tech packages to ensure accurate information is relayed to global factories
- Maintain calendar deadlines
- Interface with design, sales, sourcing, quality control, buyers, and vendors
- Establish and implement standards for function, construction, and specifications

Skills and Abilities

- Experience in measuring, fitting, and grading garments
- In-depth knowledge of patternmaking, garment construction, and grading
- Ability to evaluate fit on a form and live models

GLOSSARY

absorption costing. Accounting system that assigns some business costs to product cost and other costs to operating expenses.

achromatic colors. The neutral shades of black, white, and gray, which have no hue.

activity-based costing (ABC). Accounting system that treats all costs related to acquisition of goods as elements of product costs.

actual costs. Expenses established during the production of the style run, rather than an estimate or cost of a sample.

additive color mixing system. Explains how colored light is mixed, using red, green, and blue or blue-violet as primaries and resulting in yellow, magenta, and cyan as secondaries. When all three of the additive primaries are mixed, we see white.

agents. Firms or individuals that assume responsibility for linking product developers with offshore textile suppliers and apparel producers and managing the interface necessary among all partners.

agile manufacturing environment. A comprehensive response to the business challenges of profiting from rapidly changing, continually fragmenting global markets for high-quality, high-performance, customer-configured goods and services.

Agreement on Textiles and Clothing (ATC). A trade agreement that replaced the Multi-Fiber Arrangement (MFA) and provided for the elimination of most quotas on textiles and apparel products by January 1, 2005.

analogous. A color story based on colors positioned next to each other on the color wheel.

apparel product development. All of the processes that are needed to take a garment from inception to delivery to the customer.

apparel supply chain. The network of fiber, textile, and findings (trim, thread, labels) suppliers, apparel

product developers, manufacturers and contractors, and all the channels of apparel distribution that work together to bring apparel products to the ultimate user.

appliqué. Surface decoration formed by thread, fabric, or materials such as grommets, sequins, and beads.

arrangement. An aspect of layout referring to how motifs are positioned to form a pattern, i.e., random, geometric, along the border, or engineered to fit the shape of the garment that will be cut from it.

assortment plan. A detailed outline of the line plan that addresses customer preferences: what product, how much of it, what colors, what sizes, and for what delivery.

automatic replenishment. Computer programs that assist buyers by applying a predetermined inventory level that triggers an automatic reorder of stock.

auxiliary businesses. Businesses that provide expertise to improve the efficiency of the core apparel supply chain. Includes software providers, trend services, design bureaus, patternmaking services, sourcing agents, factors (credit agents), testing labs, consultants, and advertising agencies.

avatars. Computerized virtual models of people.

balance. Refers to whether a garment is symmetrical or asymmetrical when a silhouette is divided vertically down the middle. In a balanced garment, the right and left sides of the body appear to be even.

bar coding. Technology that allows all products to be preticketed (ticketed before shipping) with a 13-digit code that carry carries vendor, style, color, and size information and that can be easily read by scanning devices to check in shipments and keep track of inventories.

basic goods. Marketable fabrics that form the core fabrications of a group.

belt. A strip of fabric or other material used to hold a garment in place at the waist and to provide a decorative finish to some garment styles. May be tied, buckled, or held together by another form of closure.

bias. A diagonal line that is 45 degrees from the perpendicular lengthwise and crosswise threads.

bilateral agreements. Trade agreements between two countries.

bill of materials. A detailed list identifying all materials to be used to construct one sample garment.

blocks. Original pattern pieces that are kept intact and copied and manipulated to produce patterns for new garment styles. Blocks contain fitting ease, but no seam allowances.

bodies. Recurring silhouettes in a company's line for which perfected patterns have already been fitted and graded.

body. A previously perfected final pattern for a specific style.

boning. Thin strips of plastic that are inserted into garments, usually bodices, to help them retain their shape.

booked seam. Seam formed by stacking fabric layers on top of one another before sewing.

border prints. Patterns arranged along one selvage of either a solid or a print fabric.

bottom-weight fabrics. Textiles weighing 4.0 to 7.0 ounces or more per square yard that are suitable for skirts, pants, and jackets.

bound seam (BS). Seam made by encasing the raw edges of the seam with fabric strips.

boys'. Sizes designed for boys approximately 7 to 17 years old with developing bodies.

bra cups. Component used to provide shape and support to the bustline of such garments as swimsuits and strapless evening gowns.

braid. A trim made by twining sets of threads into a pattern to form narrow strips of trim that are heavier than ribbon.

brand. A distinctive name or logo used to identify products or services.

brand equity. A corporate asset for the owners of a brand or label that reflects the consumer's image of that brand.

brand extensions. Refers to the practice of expanding a brand's reach into the consumer market.

brand image. A consumer's set of assumptions and feelings about products and/or services provided under a brand name.

branding. The process of planning the direction, inspiration, and energy that a brand represents.

brand portfolio. Collection of multiple brands managed by a single company.

breakline. The line on which the lapels turn back.

break point. The point along the front edge of the garment at which the lapel begins to roll back.

budget. Written plan for anticipated monetary income and expenditures of the firm.

busted or **butterflied.** Refers to a seam that is pressed open on the inside of the garment.

buttons. Form of closures commonly made of either molded plastic (nylon) or stamped out of a sheet of plastic (polyester). Functional when used with buttonholes, decorative when used without buttonholes.

callout. A drawing that magnifies complex details of a portion of a technical drawing.

cardigans. Sweaters that have a front opening.

Care Labeling Rule. Government rule supervised by FTC that requires apparel to carry a permanently affixed label with instructions on regular upkeep or care.

certification of suppliers. An arrangement in which the supplier does the testing and the product development company accepts the supplier's results and does not conduct the tests itself.

chain-stitch machine. Sewing machine that interlocks threads supplied from cones, eliminating the need for small bobbins.

chargebacks. Fees requested by a retailer for everything not covered in discounts and allowances in a purchase contract with a vendor.

children's. Unisex sizes 2 to 6 or 7, for young children who do not wear diapers. Categorized by height and weight, not age.

chroma. A color's saturation, or degree of departure from the neutral of the same value. Chroma is determined by the amount of pigment in a color. Hues at 100 percent intensity are fully saturated with pigment; when there is no pigment present, a gray of equal value to the pure color is left.

chromatic colors. Colors that have a hue.

classics. Enduring styles that never go completely out of fashion.

closed specs. Information provided in specifications that is very detailed and can almost guarantee the use of an exact material, predetermine the exact supplier, and ensure the consistency of final products.

closures. Fastenings that may contribute aesthetic appeal to a garment in addition to the functional use of adjusting the garment to the body.

coat-weight fabrics. Textiles weighing over 7.0 ounces per square yard and that are used for coats and heavy-weight jackets.

co-branded products. An exclusive collection of products designed by a branded product developer or designer for a particular retailer, reflecting a partnership between them for a specified length of time.

cohort group. Members of a generation who are linked through shared life experiences of their formative years. Their common experience with pop culture, economic conditions, world events, natural disasters, celebrities, politics, and technology creates a bond that causes them to develop and retain similar values and life skills as they pass through life.

collar fall. The part of the collar that turns over the stand or garment.

collar roll line. The line where the collar fall turns over the stand.

collars. Component parts that surround the neck and are attached permanently or temporarily to the neckline of the garment.

collar stand. The part of the collar that fits close to the neck.

collar stays. Thin strips of plastic that are inserted into garment collars to help them retain their shape.

collar style line. The shape of the outer edge of the collar.

color. The visual perception of certain wavelengths of light by the retina of the eye.

color constancy. A characteristic of colors that are perceived to be the same regardless of the light source.

color inconstancy or **flair.** The phenomenon of a single color sample reading as a slightly different color under different light sources.

color management. A way of communicating color from the product developer through the manufacturing processes to the marketplace.

color standards. Color samples by which fabrications and notions can be matched to ensure color consistency.

color temperature. A term used to describe a color's apparent warmth or coolness in relation to another color. Yellow, orange, and red are traditionally known as warm colors, whereas green, blue, and violet are considered cool colors.

complementary. A color story based on colors opposite one another on the color wheel.

complex subtractive color mixing system. Explains how thick pigments are mixed. When thick pigments or inks are used, a cool and a warm set of red, yellow, and blue result in the broadest gamut of color.

component parts. Elements of a garment that are not part of its basic structure but that add aesthetic interest or provide functionality, including but not limited to collars, cuffs, pockets, and belts.

component spec sheet or **material specifications.** A form listing all of the fabrics, findings, and trims needed to complete construction of the garment.

computer-aided design (CAD). System with digital design and patternmaking functionality allowing for the compression of the product development calendar.

concept boards. A collection of images, sketches, and swatches that express the design direction being explored for a particular group.

consumer intimacy. A benefit to a company that uses all of the tools at its disposal to get to know and respond to its customers.

consumer price index (CPI). A measure of the monthly and yearly changes in the prices of selected consumer items in different product categories.

coordinated group line. Apparel items that are organized around fabric groups and intended to be purchased and worn together.

copyright. The set of exclusive legal rights granted to authors or owners of published or unpublished literary, scientific, and artistic works that are fixed in a tangible form. Includes the right to reproduce, distribute, perform, or display the work, and the right to create derivative works.

copyright law. Legal protection for authors of non-useful original compositions, including literary, dramatic, artistic, and musical works.

cord. Trim made by twining sets of threads into thick strings of trim that are heavier than yarn.

cording. A strip of self-fabric or contrasting fabric enclosing a heavy thread or cord and sewn in a seam.

core competencies. The business functions that a company is best equipped to execute.

corespun thread. Thread with a spun nylon or polyester core that is wrapped with cotton or another staple fiber.

cost. The monetary value expended to produce a garment style.

cost of goods sold. Expense category that includes both variable and fixed costs. This figure typically drives a product developer's involvement with financial matters.

creative planning. Tracking and interpreting trends for the company's target market and developing styles to be produced.

croquis sketches. Quick, working sketches that help a designer to remember or interpret a design idea.

cut and sew construction. Garment construction in which pieces are cut from yardage rather than knit to shape. Ribbings, when used, are sewn on with a seam rather than linked on.

cut, make, and trim (CMT). Includes the processes of actually manufacturing the product; literally, it is cutting the fabric, sewing the garment together, and applying the trims.

data mining. Using data stored in databases to identify, segregate, categorize, and make decisions about individuals known to be decision makers.

data profiling. Gathering, assembling, and collating data about individuals in databases.

decorative edgings and seams. Linear trims used on the surface or edges of a garment.

decorative effects. Embellishments that are added to the fabric of a garment, such as smocking, quilting, tucking, and embroidery.

demand-based pricing. Pricing method that takes into account the value that customers place on the manufacturer's reputation and its product.

demographics. Statistics about a given population with respect to age, gender, marital status, family size, income, spending habits, occupation, education, religion, ethnicity, and region.

department stores. Retail establishments that provide a variety of product lines, including apparel for men, women, and children; soft goods such as sheets and towels for the home; and home furnishings such as furniture and kitchenware. Prices range from near the middle to the upper price point.

design bureaus and patternmaking services. Specialists that work in tandem with a brand's own product development team to ensure that design concepts are correctly interpreted throughout the supply chain.

design ease. The amount added to the combined body and functional ease measurements to make the garment look as planned.

design elements. The building blocks of design that are intrinsic to every apparel product, especially line, color, texture, pattern, silhouette, and shape.

design specs. Specifications based on the line plan summary and initial prototype garments for each new style. Design specs include graphic description, listing of materials, and preliminary cost estimates for making the first sample. Also referred to as prototype specs, preliminary specs, or preadoption specs.

deverticalization. A strategy for eliminating business divisions that are considered nonessential or not part of a firm's core competencies, and outsourcing these tasks to companies that can perform them more efficiently.

differential advantage. A competitive edge that comes from lower price, superior quality, speed to market, or unique product features.

digital printing. Applying patterns on fabric using computer printer technology. Patterns created and stored in the computer can be selected, scaled, and printed directly onto fabric.

digital signatures. Customer's signature is digitally stored in a computer. Used for security purposes.

direct costing. Accounting system that considers materials, construction labor, and sales commission as product costs but places all other expenses for the firm in a general expense category.

direct labor. Costs for wages for the cutters and sewers and for production overhead.

direct marketing. Retailing that goes directly to consumer and skips over the retail store; sometimes referred to as non-store retailing.

direct printing. Printing a pattern directly onto a white cloth or a previously dyed fabric.

discharge printing. A variation of direct printing in which a chemical is applied to a dyed piece of fabric to remove the color in certain areas, thus leaving a lighter color.

discounts and allowances. Reductions in the list price that manufacturers grant to their customers.

diversification. A growth strategy in which a firm expands its product mix in order to capitalize on brand recognition, increase sales, and thus enhance efficiencies for greater profit.

domestic contracting. The use of manufacturing facilities located in the same country as the product developer, but not owned by the product developer.

double welt pocket. A pocket that consists of two welts, one sewn to the top edge of the slash and the other sewn to the bottom edge of the slash.

drape. A term that describes how a fabric hangs (falls, clings, flows) and bends (pleats or gathers).

draping. A patternmaking method in which a fabric is draped or shaped around a body form to create a three-dimensional garment prototype.

dresses. One- or two-piece garments for women or girls that fall from the shoulder or high bust and continue to surround the torso of the body, ending anywhere from the mid-thigh to the floor.

dress forms. Partial body shapes placed on a stand to use in patternmaking and fitting activities.

drop. The difference in the circumference between the chest and waist measurements. A drop of 7 to 10 inches is common.

ease. Difference between the body measurements of the intended wearer and the measurements of the finished garment.

e-broidery. Using yarns and threads with electrical properties to "quilt" electronic circuitry into a garment.

e-commerce or **e-tailing.** A form of non-store retailing utilizing the capabilities of the Internet.

edge finishes (EF). Stitching that completes the edge of a garment to prevent woven fabrics from raveling and knits from curling. May be a turned edge, a hem, or a facing.

edgestitching. Rows of stitching done on the outside edge of a garment that are ornamental in purpose.

elastic. Category of fabric that is characterized by an ability to repeatedly be stretched and then return to its original size.

electronic data interchange (EDI). Electronic transmission of transactional information such as forecasts of requirements, purchase orders, shipping notices, and invoices.

embargo. The prohibition against importing products from an exporting nation.

embroidery. Trim formed by making thread patterns on the surface of the garment.

emphasis or **focal point.** The first place on the garment to which the eye is drawn. It may be created through a convergence of lines, a combination of colors, or a detail.

enclosed seam. A seam that is hidden on the inside of the garment by folding the edges between other plies of fabric.

engineered prints. Patterns designed with a particular end use in mind so that the length of each pattern repeat relates to the shape that will be cut from it. Knit polo shirts or silk scarves are good examples of engineered patterns.

environmental scanning. The ongoing process of surveying a variety of resources for economic, political, social, technological, and cultural conditions for insights into the future.

eyes. Holes in a button that provide access for thread to attach the button to a garment.

fabrication. The process of selecting fabrics for a seasonal line, groups within a line, and each style within a group.

fabric story. Related fabrics chosen for a particular season or group.

facings. Form of edge finish. May be an extension of the main style block, a separate shaped piece, or a bias strip.

factors. Financial middlemen that finance suppliers and manufacturers, and assume responsibility for billing and accounts receivable between various members of the supply chain.

fads. Innovations that are popular for short spurts.

fagoting. Decorative stitching made by connecting two folded edges of shell fabric together via decorative stitching. Appears similar to hemstitching at first glance.

fallout. Waste that can occur when cutting pattern blocks (pieces) from the yardage.

fashion. A reflection of our times and a mirror of the prevailing ideas in our society. The concept of fashion applies not only to apparel, but also to literature, automobiles, home furnishings, architecture, and food, to name a few categories.

finance. Operations area that keeps track of all the accounting activities of the firm.

findings. All materials, except the shell fabric, needed to produce a garment. Includes trims, linings, and interlinings. Referred to as *notions* in home sewing.

finishing. Final garment production processes, including trimming threads, final inspection, repairing defects, pressing, folding, and packing.

fit. Implies the conformance of the garments to the shape and size of the individuals who wear them.

fit models. Individuals selected to represent the age and build of the target customer because they conform to the measurements of the master size of the firm.

fixed costs. Expenses that stay the same no matter how many units of a style are produced.

Flammable Fabrics Act. Government rule supervised by the CPSC requiring the use of fabric finishes to retard or prevent the spread of flames. Affects mostly infant and children's sleepwear in sizes 0 to 6X and 7 to 14.

flap pocket. A pocket that features a flap that is sewn to the top edge of the slash and that falls over the pocket opening. The pocket flap must be lifted to provide access to the pocket.

flat label. Label made of a strip of narrow fabric.

flat-pattern. Making styling changes to basic two-dimensional pattern pieces to produce a new style.

flats. Mechanical drawings without bodies that clearly illustrate all construction details.

flat seams (FS). Seams that join fabric plies by butting the raw edges together and securing them with a 600-class cover stitch or a zigzag stitch.

flounces. Similar to ruffles, but constructed from circular cuts of fabric rather than strips.

folded label. A flat label that is folded in half before being attached.

folded loop label. A longer flat label with ends folded diagonally to the underside to leave create extensions that can be sewn into the seam at the neckline.

free on board (FOB) or **FOB origin** or **FOB factory.** The exporter or offshore contractor includes in the price of goods the transportation to port, the handling and loading aboard the vessel, and cost of quota and export duty charges incurred in country of origin. Ownership transfers when the goods are loaded on board.

free on board (FOB) destination. A costing method that includes basic FOB charges but adds transportation to the ultimate port or distribution center and any import tariffs to the bill. Ownership transfers when the shipment reaches its destination. The vendor bears freight charges.

free trade zones. Areas that allow for the duty-free movement of equipment and supplies.

frogs. Decorative coiled cording closures used instead of traditional buttons and buttonholes.

front hip pocket. A pocket typically found on the front of jeans and pants, featuring a style line that is cut into the garment front at the hip and faced to form the opening.

full-package manufacturing. Services in which the manufacturer supplies both the fabric and the garment production for a product developer, either domestically or offshore.

full-service contractor. A firm that constructs garments and assumes all of the responsibility for patternmaking.

functional ease or **wearing ease.** The amount added to body measurements to compensate for body movement.

garment standards. Diagnostic tools to measure the quality of a product. Includes defect guides to be used throughout the production process.

General Agreement on Tariffs and Trade (GATT). Agreement signed in 1947 that formed a temporary, rather than permanent, organization whose goal was to liberalize trade and create a more global market.

generational marketing. The study of the values, motivations, and life experiences that drive generational cohorts, influencing how they spend and save their money.

geometric layouts. Printed designs that imitate yarn-dyed stripes, plaids, and weaves.

girls'. Sizes designed to fit girls approximately 7 to 11 years of age. Categorized by height and weight, not age.

gorge line. The line where the collar and the lapel are joined.

grade. The difference from one size to the next in a range.

graded. A seam treatment in which the seam is layered or blended by trimming out the excess seam allowances to different lengths.

grade rules. Amounts that are added (or subtracted) from each measurement to mark changes from one size to the next.

grade rule tables. Sets of measurements reflecting the increments between sizes.

grading. Process of scaling the sample size of a garment to other sizes in the range to be produced.

grain. Reflects the direction of the threads in the fabric used in a garment.

gross. Measure consisting of 12 dozen, or 144 individual pieces.

gross margin. The amount of markup left after cost of goods sold is subtracted from net sales, or when the bills are paid.

ground. The background on which motifs are placed.

growth industries. Industries that make products that have not yet saturated the marketplace. Growth products utilize emerging technology that commands a relatively high price, placing them out of reach for some consumers.

hand. The tactile qualities of a fabric as they are affected by fiber content, yarn, fabric construction, and finishing.

harmony. Refers to the way in which all of the design elements in a garment work together to produce a pleasing aesthetic appearance and to give a feeling of unity to the design.

haute couture. Small group of high fashion designers in Paris, France, who meet formal criteria set by the Chambre syndicale de la haute couture.

heat-transfer printing or **thermal transfer printing.** A technique in which disperse dyes are printed on special transfer paper; the paper is then placed on the fabric and passed through a heat-transfer printing machine at about 400 degrees Fahrenheit.

hems. Most common form of edge finish in which the edge of a garment is turned up to conceal the raw edge.

hemstitching. Decorative stitching done by removing parallel threads in the shell fabric and securing groups of the remaining threads together to form a decorative ladder.

hook-and-eye. Garment closure consisting of two parts: a type of curved hook and a receptacle for the hook.

hook and loop tape. Fastener consisting of two separate tapes that stick when pressed together. Best known by the brand name Velcro hook and loop tape, consisting of two separate tapes that stick when pressed together.

horizontal integration. A strategy that prioritizes the acquisition of companies that make similar products in order to expand market penetration and reduce competition.

hue. The attribute of a color that distinguishes one color family from another.

implied warrantee. Expectation that products will do what they are designed to do.

indirect labor. Wages of individuals who provide essential support to the production process but do not actually make the product, such as the quality assurance team, maintenance, and security. Considered part of overhead expenses.

infants'. Apparel styled for babies from birth to approximately 18 months of age, or whenever the child begins to walk. Categorized by height and weight, not age.

in-house patternmaking. Patternmaking department within a firm.

inseam. Pants measurement taken on the inside of the leg from the crotch seam to the bottom of the hem.

in-seam pocket. Pocket designed with access from an existing seam of the garment.

inside pocket. Pocket in which the pouch falls inside the garment and only the pocket opening is visible from the outside.

interlining or **interfacing.** An extra layer of supporting fabric used in almost all structured garments.

International Labor Organization (ILO). A UN agency that promotes social justice and internationally recognized human and labor rights. The ILO sets minimum standards for basic labor rights related to collective bargaining and regulating working conditions.

International Organization for Standardization (ISO). An organization that has developed voluntary standards that, if met and followed, enable certification of a business. When a firm is certified, products coming from its factories are recognized as acceptable or as having met specific requirements regarding management of deliveries, labeling of products, and sizing standards.

intimate wear. Nightwear, lingerie, and other similar product categories for women.

item-driven. Describes a line created around goods that are designed to be sold singly rather than as coordinated ensembles.

jabot. A ruffle or flounce forming a cascade of fabric down the front of a blouse.

jacket. A short coat worn by men or women for indoor wear, often associated with professional dress.

joint venture. The shared ownership of a facility with a business based in another country.

junior. Sizes designed for a woman of about 5 feet 6 inches with a shorter torso, longer limbs, and less mature body development than the misses category.

just-in-time (JIT) inventory. An approach that prioritizes getting fabrics, notions, and finished goods to their destination as they are needed, eliminating the non–value-added cost of warehousing. Suppliers are required to meet all quality specifications through thorough inspection before shipping.

knockoffs. Garment designs that are copied, adapted, or modified versions of products designed by other firms. Ideas are acquired from pictures of products or by copying an actual product purchased off the rack. Rub-offs are adaptations of other company's styles.

lab dips. Samples of a specified fabric dyed to match a color standard.

labels. Printed or woven attachments to garments that provide written information for the consumer.

labor-intense. Describes an industry that requires many workers to complete each product.

lace. An openwork trim or fabric that is made into intricate designs by the intertwining of many threads.

landed costs. The total cost of importing products, including costs of transportation to the United States, tariffs imposed by customs, and cost of transporting them to domestic distribution centers or retail stores.

landed price. The total product cost including shipping costs and duty charges.

lapels. Part of the garment front designed to attach to the collar and turn back over the garment.

lapped seams (LS). Seam formed by overlapping the seam allowances of two or more plies of fabric and sewing them together.

letter of credit. Document authorizing a firm's bank to pay the exporting contractor once the contracted goods are loaded on a vessel.

licensing agreements. An arrangement that grants a business partner exclusive rights to produce or sell products under a proprietary brand name. May be used to expand a brand's product mix, expand distribution into a global market, capitalize on the popularity of a proprietary character, or revive a label's market value.

lifestyle brands. Brands that go beyond the initial apparel product line to include other product categories.

lifestyle retailing. Retailing to provide a well-defined target consumer with a range of compatible products, designed to bring continuity to style of the consumer's home as well as wardrobe.

lignes. Measurement used to determine the size of buttons, equal to 1/40 of an inch or 40 lignes per inch of diameter.

line. Design element that determines the silhouette of the garment and the shapes formed within the garment.

line concept. The mood, theme, and key elements that contribute to the identity of the line.

line development. Translating trend information into sketches of styles.

line plan or **range plan.** A plan that sets sales and margin goals for groups or lines within a division. Includes evaluating the merchandise mix, forecasting merchandise offerings to meet merchandise budgets, and planning merchandise assortments.

line presentation. Showing the proposed line of products to sourcing managers and technical design staff for selection of styles to include in the season's product line.

lining. Lightweight fabric sewn into a garment to give the interior a finished appearance.

list price. The product developer's suggested retail price.

lockstitch machine. Sewing machine that requires both a needle thread and a bobbin thread.

logistics. The science of coordination of all processes and people involved in the efficient distribution of raw materials and finished products from point of origin to point of consumption; focus on moving goods from place to place.

long-term forecasting. A process for analyzing and evaluating trends that are identified by continuous scanning of a variety of sources for information.

loops. Tubes of fabric or thread used instead of buttonholes.

MAGIC. Biggest apparel trade show in the United States. Held in Las Vegas, Nevada.

manufacture. To make or produce.

markers. Large paper sheets indicating the layout of all the pattern blocks required for production of the ordered sizes for a style.

market or **market weeks.** Trade shows held in major cities throughout the world at carefully scheduled events and times throughout the year.

marketing. Area that sets advertising and promotional objectives, recommends sales goals, creates advertising and promotional programs and tools, sells products, and gathers data relative to target customers.

market segmentation or **micromarketing.** The trend in apparel marketing to break down markets into increasingly smaller, well-defined groups to identify niche markets.

markup. Amount retailers add to their cost of goods, or the wholesale price, to achieve the retail price they charge consumers. Markup sets the price.

mass customization. Using technology and mass-production techniques to create a custom-configured garment for one consumer.

mass merchandisers. Retailers that specialize in selling great quantities of merchandise at lower prices.

maternity. Sizes designed for the pregnant woman. A new size grouping.

mature industries. Industries that produce products that are characterized by relatively stable sales from year to year and by a high level of competition.

men's. Size range designed for the average male.

men's furnishings. Product category including shirts, ties, underwear, sleepwear, and accessories for men.

merchandise calendar. Schedule of events required to deliver products to the customer at the right time.

merchandise plan or **budget.** A plan that identifies the resources needed to meet company profit, sales, and margin objectives for a specific season by company division, thereby linking strategic planning to creative planning, technical planning, production planning, and sales and marketing.

merchandising. The process of planning, developing, and presenting product lines for identified target markets with regard to pricing, assorting, styling, and timing.

metamerism. The change in color difference between a pair of samples that are considered a match under one light source and not a match under another.

micro encapsulation. A process that applies or embeds particles filled with an active ingredient, such as moisturizers, vitamins, medicines, therapeutic smells, or insect repellant, to a fabric or garment. Body movement activates the particles, producing a slow release of the ingredient.

minimums. Specifications that require exact levels for acceptance, such as the number of buttons on a shirt, or the lowest acceptable amount, such as amount of yardage.

misses. Size range designed to fit adult females of average build, generally recognized as 5 feet 5 inches to 5 feet 6 inches.

modular manufacturing method. Manufacturing method in which operators work in teams or modules and focus on efficient completion of each garment moving through the module by passing it off to the next station in the module as the tasks for that station are completed.

monochromatic. A color story based on several colors of the same hue.

monofilament thread. A single strand of fiber that is strong, inexpensive, and transparent in color but stiff and scratchy when used in apparel.

motifs. Design elements that create patterns when used in repetition.

Multi-Fiber Arrangement (MFA). A series of discriminatory trade policies that established bilateral agreements (and unilateral controls under certain conditions) to control the flow of textile products, most often in the form of quota allotments.

multifilament thread. Fiber made of several filaments twisted together, and frequently texturized on the surface to prevent slippage. Useful in sewing knits.

nanometer. Unit of measurement used to measure light waves. A nanometer is one millionth of a millimeter.

nanotechnology. The manipulation of atoms and molecules with hyperfine technology that alters the properties of a given material. A nano is equivalent to the width of three or four atoms.

narrow fabric trims. Broad category of linear trims that includes ribbons, passementerie, and laces.

net sales. Represents revenues taken in by a firm after all returns and other required adjustments, such as discounts and chargebacks, have been subtracted from the gross (total) revenue taken into the business.

niche market. A narrowly focused target customer.

North American Industry Classification System (NAICS). Method of classifying firms by the type of product they produce. Introduced in 1997 and revised in 2003 to reflect current industry activities.

notch. The triangular shape between the lapel and the collar, formed where the gorge line ends.

novelty goods. Unusual prints, patterns, wovens, or knits that make a group unique.

off-grain. Describes condition in which lengthwise and crosswise threads in a fabric do not meet at 90 degrees, causing the garment to twist or hang crooked.

off-price retailer. Retail establishment that purchases distress merchandise at lower than wholesale prices and then passes on some of that savings to the customer.

on-grain. Describes condition in which lengthwise and

crosswise threads in a fabric meet at exactly 90 degrees.

open specs. Specifications that are somewhat generic and contain only the very basic necessary facts, allowing flexibility on the part of the producer or contractor.

operating expenses. Producer costs, especially costs for sales and marketing, including sales personnel, showrooms, and advertising; costs of discounts and chargebacks, including refunds on returned goods; and corporate overhead.

operations. Area that oversees the upkeep of equipment used by employees, building facilities, and distribution activities required for securing materials and shipping finished products.

operations list. Form that identifies each step of construction that will be performed during production of the garment.

ornamental stitching (OS). Stitches that serve the purpose of decoration, including embroidery.

overhead. All expenses in addition to materials and direct labor that are required of a contractor or manufacturer at the factory level to produce and deliver garments to the entity that ordered them.

overlap. Extension beyond the edge of the top layer of a garment that provides additional space for a buttonhole without affecting finished size of a garment.

pants. Bifurcated garments worn by men, women, and children.

paper labels. Inexpensive labels of nonwoven fabric that are printed. Frequently used on casual and lower-priced clothing.

passementerie. Umbrella term that includes a broad range of braids and cords in straight, curved, fringe, and tassel forms.

patch pocket or **outside pocket.** Pocket in which the pouch or bag of the pocket is visible from the outside of the garment.

pattern chart. Spec form listing of all of the pattern pieces that make up the set needed to make the style.

pattern drafting. Patternmaking process that begins from scratch for each garment style, starting with body measurements and then adding style lines and ease.

patternmaking. The interpretation of a garment concept, from either a sketch or another existing product, into a paper representation or model for use in production of a finished garment style.

petites. Sizes designed for shorter women, 5 feet 4 inches and under, and of average build.

phase change materials (PCMs). Substances that store, release, or absorb heat as they oscillate between solid and liquid form.

pigment. The substance that imparts color to another substance. Color is perceived when light strikes a surface that contains pigment. The pigments in objects cause some wavelengths to be absorbed and others to be reflected, thus giving the surface its color.

pilling. Formation of fiber balls on the surface of a fabric.

piping. A folded strip of self-fabric or contrasting fabric that is inserted into the seam; does not require cording to plump up the edge.

pocket. Extra fabric attached to the inside or outside of a garment to form a pouch with a top or side opening.

poms. Small bundles of yarn or embroidery floss used by color forecasters to communicate shades of color.

preliminary cost sheet. A form that includes the costs of materials to produce the first sample and estimates of labor and other costs incurred in production and distribution. Helps to establish the wholesale price.

prestige pricing. Pricing method based on the assumption that customers are willing to pay a higher price for products that are perceived to be special in terms of aesthetics, name recognition, quality, value, or service.

prêt-à-porter. Designer ready-to-wear.

price. The monetary value or revenue collected from the customer who purchases the product.

primary colors. The minimum number of hues that can be mixed to make the greatest number of other colors.

printing. The application of a repeated design or pattern on fabric, using dyes or pigments applied in limited areas.

private label. Describes products that are developed and merchandised with labels that are owned by a retailer, for exclusive distribution by that retailer to compete with branded products also carried by the retailer.

product development. The strategic, creative, technical, production, and distribution planning of goods that have a perceived value for a well-defined user group and designed to reach the marketplace when that group is ready to buy.

production costing or **final cost estimate.** Cost estimate based on figures derived from approved style samples and written specification sheet requirements. It is much more detailed than the preliminary cost estimate.

production planning. Function that links merchandising decisions with design and technical decisions in order to plan the activities related to making the product.

production sample. Garment that reflects the exact product expected to come off of a production line. The final stage before the product goes into full production.

production specs or **engineering specs.** Instructions for producing quantities of a product in the manufacturing environment, rather than an individual prototype garment.

production yardage. The amount of fabric needed to fulfill orders.

profit. The amount by which sales exceed cost. Net sales minus costs equals profit.

profit and loss statement. A simplified chart that outlines basic accounting categories and totals to show the current status of a business.

progressive bundle system. Traditional assembly line method where assembly proceeds in a consistent order. Operators in this system are paid piecework rates.

proportion. The relationship or scale of all of the parts of a garment or ensemble to each other and to the body as a whole.

prototype. The first garment made from a pattern.

psychographics. The study of the social and psychological factors that constitute consumers' lifestyles, including reference groups, life stage, activities, personality, attitudes, level of class consciousness, and motivation.

pullovers. Sweaters that are pulled on over the head.

put-up. Type of spool or cone that the thread is on. Spools are used for small quantities and cones are used for larger quantities.

qualitative research. A subjective form of research that relies on methodology such as observation and case studies in which experiences are recorded as a narrative to describe observed behaviors within the context of environmental factors.

quality assurance. Commitment to quality that permeates the entire business and requires a proactive, participatory management style. Every employee is involved in trying to achieve error prevention.

quantitative research. Objective methodology whereby data about a sample population are collected and analyzed to generalize behavioral patterns.

Quick Response (QR). A strategy for getting the right product to the right place at the right time and at the right price.

quota. An annual limit on the volume of a product, designated by category, that may be shipped from an exporting country to an importing country.

random layouts. Pattern arrangements that appear to be scattered haphazardly.

raw material standards. Standards for fabrics and findings that are used to communicate with suppliers during the planning stages of product development.

real-time. Computer systems record each operation within the written specifications as it occurs, providing instant access to information on every project within the system to everyone involved.

registration. The precise alignment of colors in a multicolor pattern.

repeat. The process of adapting a pattern to the printing tools of the industry so it will print continuously along the length and width of the fabric.

resist printing. A two-step procedure in which a pattern is printed on a white or dyed fabric with a chemical or wax that will prevent the dyes from penetrating the fabric.

reverse engineering. A patternmaking process in which the measurements of a garment are transferred to paper or an existing garment is taken apart and each piece is traced or digitized to make new pattern pieces. Used for making knockoffs.

rhythm. Organized movement of the eye through the related elements of a garment.

ribbon. Narrow woven fabric with finished edges.

roller printing. A printing process that utilizes a steel cylinder with an outer layer of copper, into which a design is etched. Each color in the print requires a separate engraved copper roller.

ruching. Pleated ribbon.

ruffles. Strips of self-fabric or contrasting fabrics that are gathered to add fullness and attached to the garment.

sample size. Body measurements from which the full size range is developed.

sample yardage. Fabric purchased for design exploration.

screen printing. A process in which dye is applied through a mesh screen that has some areas blocked off, thus creating a pattern.

seam allowance. Extension between the row of stitching forming a seam and the edges of the fabric.

seams. Stitching that holds together pieces of fabric.

seam tapes. Narrow (less than 1 inch) woven strips of fabric, similar to ribbon.

season. Time of year when products will be worn or used.

seasonal line. A division or firm's overall collection of garments that will be offered for sale at a given time.

secondary (intermediate) colors. Colors that result when two primary colors are mixed together.

seconds or **irregulars.** Products that do not fit within the tolerances designated in the specifications.

separates. Sportswear garments designed as single items rather than as elements in coordinated groups.

set. Smooth fit of a garment with no unwanted wrinkles.

set layouts. Pattern arrangements with motifs organized in an invisible geometric grid. Set layouts are often described by the amount of drop in the repeat of the pattern. A half-drop pattern describes a layout in which the first row of the print is followed by a second row placed at alternate intervals and positioned half a repeat below the first. Computer programs have built-in functions that allow the designer to explore full-, half-, and quarter-drop repeats.

shade. A color that has been mixed with black to decrease the value and darken the hue.

shade sorting. Grouping shades together for distribution to specific customers or regions. Shade sorting of finished goods is a function of quality management.

shank. Loop extension on the back of a button or a thread post. Used to attach the button to the garment and act as spacer to prevent puckering of layers when closed.

shaping devices. Seams, darts, gathers, and pleats that help to shape the garment around the curves of the body.

short-term forecasting. Process of analyzing current events and pop culture to identify new trends that can be communicated to the customer through seasonal color, fabric, and silhouette stories to give fashion a fresh look each season.

shoulder pads. Shaping devices made of molded foam or layers of fiber wadding. Used in the shoulder area of garments to achieve a desired appearance.

signature stores. Stores that are owned and managed by a wholesale product developer. Used to build brand image, test new styles, and learn more about their customers' preferences.

silhouette. Outline or shape of a garment.

simple subtractive color mixing system. Explains how thin films such as printing inks, watercolor paints, and color photography films are mixed.

size chart. Table containing garment measurement specs for all of the sizes that are planned for that style.

size migration. A situation in which one woman typically fits into a range of three or more sizes, depending on the manufacturer and cut of the garment.

SizeUSA. An anthropometric research study developed by [TC]^2, industry participants, and the Department of Commerce to gather actual body measurement data on U.S. consumers using a 3D measurement system, a body scanner.

sizing. The assignment of individuals of a particular body type into categories that reflect the body measurements of those in that size group.

skirt. A garment that hangs from the body at or near the waist and covers the hips and upper legs but is not bifurcated to go around each leg separately as do pants.

slash pocket. A category of pockets frequently used on tailored garments that includes double welt or bound pockets, welt pockets, and flap pockets.

sleeve headers. Narrow strips of wadding sewn into the sleeve cap of tailored coats and jackets to create a soft roll in the cap of the sleeve.

sloper. A five-piece pattern of previously developed and perfected basic body blocks created in a cut and fit that have proven successful with the company's target market .

smart textiles. Textiles that interact with electrical current, light energy, or thermal energy; change physical properties through an external signal from the user or an internal or environmental stimulus; or change properties through the use of elements embedded into the textile or applied as a coating to the textile.

smocking. A trim constructed by pulling a section of fabrics into a smaller area by making many tiny parallel tucks and securing them in place with decorative embroidery.

snap. Fastener or closure made up of two parts, a ball and a socket, that lock when pressed together.

snap tape. A strip of fabric, often twill tape, with mechanically attached snaps; used to apply a series of snaps.

sneakerization. The process of transforming an inexpensive commodity product into a high-tech, cutting-edge specialty product.

sourcing. The practice of procuring materials and production elsewhere.

sourcing mix. The combination of resources a firm uses to produce its products.

specialty stores. Retail establishments that focus on a few types of merchandise to the exclusion of other products.

specification libraries. Collection of a firm's previously developed style, pattern, and measurement specifications that can be recalled and reused within specification packages for new styles.

specification ordering. To define quality by setting product standards and specifications for every order placed. In the case of fabric, for example, width, length, shade variance tolerances, and acceptable levels of flaws must be identified.

specification package. Series of forms that define a garment, including a design sheet with a flat of the garment, a measurement sheet, a piece reference sheet, and an assembly sheet.

specifications (specs). Graphic representations and written descriptions of styling, materials, dimensions, production procedures, and finishing instructions for a garment style. Used as a basis for evaluation to determine whether the final product meets the firm's standards.

spreading. Laying fabrics out flat on long tables.

spun thread. Thread made of staple fibers that are twisted together to form the thread.

standard allowed minutes (SAMs). Unit of measure used as basis of establishing the cost of sewing operations in the construction of a garment.

standards. Characteristics used as the basis of judgments made about products. Standards provide parameters for quality requirements and materials expectations that are required of all products produced by the business.

stitch class. Nomenclature that divides commercial stitches into six classes or groups based on their complexity, configuration, and the type of machine that is required to form the stitching.

stitches. Configurations of thread that form stitching and seams.

stock keeping unit (SKU). Term used to account for each style and the assortment of sizes and colors in which it is offered.

stockout. Occurs when a particular stock keeping unit is not available when a customer wants it.

store brands. A complete assortment of privately developed products under the store's own label(s) for exclusive distribution in its own stores, catalogs, or both.

strategic plan. A plan that defines the structure of the business and outlines the mix of types of merchandise involved, the amounts of finished product, the price lines, the overall budget, and the calendar of activities.

strategic planning. Top-level planning that focuses on a company's business strategy in the marketplace as well as an overall financial strategy.

strike-through. Condition when adhesives on interfacings show through to the surface of the garment during pressing.

style summary sheet. A specification sheet containing a drawing of the front and back of the style and brief description of the product.

stylists. Those who adapt the ideas of others rather than create original garments.

subtractive color mixing system. Describes how pigments are mixed. Paints, inks, dyes, and other color media all absorb certain wavelengths of light, which enable an object to absorb some light waves and reflect back others.

superimposed seams (SS). Seam formed by stacking plies of fabric on top of one another and stitching them together near the edge.

support materials. Garment components other than shell fabrics, including interfacings, interlinings, linings, and other support devices.

talls. Sizes designed for women who are of average girth but who are above average in height, up to 6 feet 1 inch.

target market. A well-defined customer group to which a business wants to sell.

target market pricing. Pricing merchandise according to what merchandisers perceive the market will bear, often averaging the actual costs of several products to achieve a common price for similar products.

tariff. A tax on imported goods that is assessed by the country of import. Money collected as tariffs is called duty.

technical flats. Drawings that define the proportions, details, and construction methods required for production purposes.

technical planning. Process to further define a style by developing fit standards and materials and construction specifications.

technical specs or **style specifications** or **design spec package.** Specification sheets that reflect detailed information on materials needed for construction of a style. Includes identification of quality requirements; fit standards and tolerances; and identification of preferred construction methods needed for development of first production patterns and sales samples.

testing labs. Testing labs are contracted to test fabrics, findings, and finished apparel products, making sure they meet quality standards and specifications.

Textile Fiber Products Identification Act (TFPIA). Government act under FTC requiring garment labels to disclose the fiber content, the identification of the manufacturer or importer, and the country of origin.

texture. The term used to describe the surface or hand of a fabric. Can apply to a combination of the fabric's characteristics: fiber, yarn, construction, weight, and finish.

thread. A strong, slender form of yarn used for stitching garments.

throughput time. Time required to produce a single unit from beginning to shipment. Used to plan work schedules, determine delivery dates, and establish costs of production.

throughput volume. The amount of work that can be accomplished in a given time. Used to measure a plant's production capacity.

tint. A color that has been mixed with white to increase the value and lighten the hue.

toddlers'. Apparel styled and sized for children who are walking but not yet toilet-trained.

toggle. A pair of cord loops secured by a rod that replaces the more traditional buttonhole and button.

tolerance. Difference between the allowable minimum and maximum on a process or finished measurement.

tops. Casual garments worn on the torso of the body.

topstitching. Rows of stitching done on the outside of the garment and ornamental in purpose.

top-weight fabrics. Textiles weighing less than 4.0 ounces per square yard that are used for blouses and dresses. Sometimes referred to as *dressweight* fabrics.

trade discount. A percentage subtracted from the suggested retail price or list price that is given to retailers to arrive at the tentative purchase price or wholesale price charged to a retailer by the manufacturer.

trade dress. A broader term than *trademark* that covers the totality of elements in which a product or service is packaged and presented.

trademark. Any word, name, symbol, device, or combination thereof that is adopted and used by a manufacturer or merchant to identify his goods and distinguish them from those manufactured and sold by others.

trend. A preference for a particular set of product characteristics within a consumer group. Trends may refer to innovation in fiber or fabric or the popularity of a particular color, silhouette, or detail.

trend services. A professional service that sorts through fashion trends in color, fabric, and silhouette to determine which trends are right for their brand's customer.

trims. Decorative materials, surface treatments, or details such as buttons, braids, and lace that are used to embellish a garment.

turnaround time. The lead time required for making, dyeing, and finishing the fabric in order to meet the delivery date determined by the production schedule.

underlap. Extension beyond the edge of the bottom layer of a garment that provides additional space for a button without affecting finished size of a garment.

underlining. Lining variation in which the outer shell fabric and the lining are layered together before the garment is constructed. Used to stabilize shell fabrics or make the shell fabric opaque.

uneven grading or **nonlinear grading.** Grading used when the target customer is shaped somewhat differently than the traditional standards in sizing charts. Allows for uneven amounts to be added from size to size in the grade rule table.

unit production system. Manufacturing system that uses an overhead transporter to introduce garments to each operator's station. Pay in this system is based on number of garments completed rather than on individual tasks.

UNITE HERE! Acronym for the combined Union of Needletrades, Industrial, and Textile Employees and the Hotel Employees and Restaurant Employees International Union.

value. Quality by which we distinguish light colors from dark colors.

vanity sizing. Placing a smaller size label on a larger size garment.

variable costs. Expenses that increase or decrease in direct proportion to the number of units produced, including labor, materials, tariffs, and logistics (including freight).

vertical integration. A strategy that seeks to consolidate a supply chain by acquiring a company at another stage in the supply chain.

virtual fitting room. A computer avatar model so realistic that consumers may see themselves on the computer screen, depicted in three dimensions, trying on the styles that interest them.

virtual supply chain. An interactive network of manufacturing specialists that integrate complementary resources to support a particular product effort for as long as it is economically justifiable to do so.

welt pocket. A pocket with a single welt, typically 1 inch to 1½ inches wide, that is attached to the bottom edge of the slash and flips up over the pocket to cover the opening.

wet processing. Adding a chemical or physical finish to an assembled garment.

wholesale brands. Brands created under a proprietary label and sold at wholesale for distribution to retailers that also carry other wholesale brands.

wholesale price. Amount charged by a contractor or manufacturer when the garment is sold to a retailer or distributor. The list price of a garment minus all discounts and allowances.

wicking. The ability of a fabric to transfer moisture away from the surface of the body.

women's petites. Sizes designed for a shorter figure of larger girth, generally with a fuller torso, and shorter sleeves and hemlines, in comparison to the misses category.

women's plus. Sizes designed for the adult woman of average to above-average height who is fuller and more mature, especially in torso girth, than the misses category figure.

work in process. The number of garments under construction at a given time.

World Trade Organization (WTO). Replaced GATT as a permanent organization in 1995.

Worldwide Responsible Apparel Production (WRAP). An independent, nonprofit organization dedicated to the certification of lawful, humane, and ethical manufacturing throughout the world.

written warrantee. A claim that appears on a label or hangtag regarding a product characteristic. This written claim is legally binding.

yarn-dyed fabrics. Textiles that utilize yarns that have been dyed previous to weaving.

young men's. Sizes designed for younger men whose builds have not reached full maturity.

zippers. Continuous closures used in garments.

INDEX

FIGURE CREDITS